el pods as
er S.2 built
ansferred

The Illustrated Encyclopedia of the World's

MODERN MILITARY AIRCRAFT

Saab AJ37 Viggen

Launch of a Lockheed S-3A Viking from the foredeck catapult of the nuclear carrier USS *Enterprise* (see page 146).

The Illustrated Encyclopedia of the World's
MODERN MILITARY AIRCRAFT

Bill Gunston

a Salamander book

Published by Salamander Books Limited
LONDON

A Salamander Book

This edition published 1977 by
Salamander Books Ltd
Salamander House
27 Old Gloucester Street
London WC1N 3AF
United Kingdom

ISBN 0 86101 010 8

Second impression 1978

© Salamander Books Ltd 1977

Distributed in Australia/New Zealand
by Summit Books, a division of
Paul Hamlyn Pty Ltd., Sidney, Australia.

Credits

Editor: Ray Bonds

Designer: Chris Steer

Colour drawings: © Pilot Press Ltd.;
Gordon Davies (© Salamander Books Ltd.)
and Keith Fretwell (© Salamander Books Ltd.)
Cutaway drawings: © Pilot Press Ltd.
Filmset by SX Composing Ltd., England
Colour reproduction by Metric Reproductions
Ltd. and Kent Litho Ltd., England
Printed in Belgium by Henri Proost et Cie.
Turnhout

Author's Acknowledgements

I am grateful to Salamander for the
opportunity to do this book. There
are many books—as there have been
since about 1920—with titles similar
to this; but I believe this is the first to
have colour photography from
beginning to end. This is partly the
luck of timing, in that such pictures
now exist. An equally important
factor is the publisher's unrivalled
expertise in managing to put together
a package which is truly a Rolls-
Royce, but at the price of a Mini.

As the author I would like to play
down my own part. There is no great
kudos in writing a book of this kind,
though the grey stuff that goes round
the illustrations certainly merits the
space it occupies. The real effort lies
in collecting the pictures. Editor Ray
Bonds and his team have worked in a
way that has never been surpassed in
book production, and their success
can be judged by simply looking at the
book. I am sad that in a very few
cases incessant bombardment by
letter, Telex and telephone still failed
to prise loose the pictures that had
been promised months earlier.

It will be obvious that we have
tended to choose dramatic pictures
showing aircraft blasting off in fire
and smoke. Such choices must always
be a matter for subjective judgement.
Some readers might prefer a pin-
sharp picture of the aircraft on the
ground, while a few would prefer a
set of engineering drawings. Our
objective is to entertain, and give
readers a feel for the subject, so that
they can almost hear the thunder of
afterburners and feel the g in a turn.
And for those unfamiliar with g there
is a glossary at the back.

Obviously there are several ways of
arranging *Modern Military Aircraft*. The
contents could be in rigorous
alphabetical order, or arranged by
country of origin. We have chosen to
divide the contents into 'chapters' by
function. The names of these duties—
such as 'Fighter' or 'Attack/close
support'—are not puzzling, but
several aircraft were hard to fit into
rigid slots. The Il-28, an old bomber,
is today used chiefly as a trainer,
while the main role of many A-3
Skywarriors is electronic warfare.
Each basic type appears once only, so
that all Canberras and B-57s appear
together, as do the Intruders and
Prowler. The main exception is the
Boeing KC-135/707, whose complex
descendent the E-3A AWACS insisted
on separate treatment. For
unavoidable reasons, dictated by the
space needed for each entry, the
alphabetical order within 'chapters'
is not absolutely rigid.

Bill Gunston

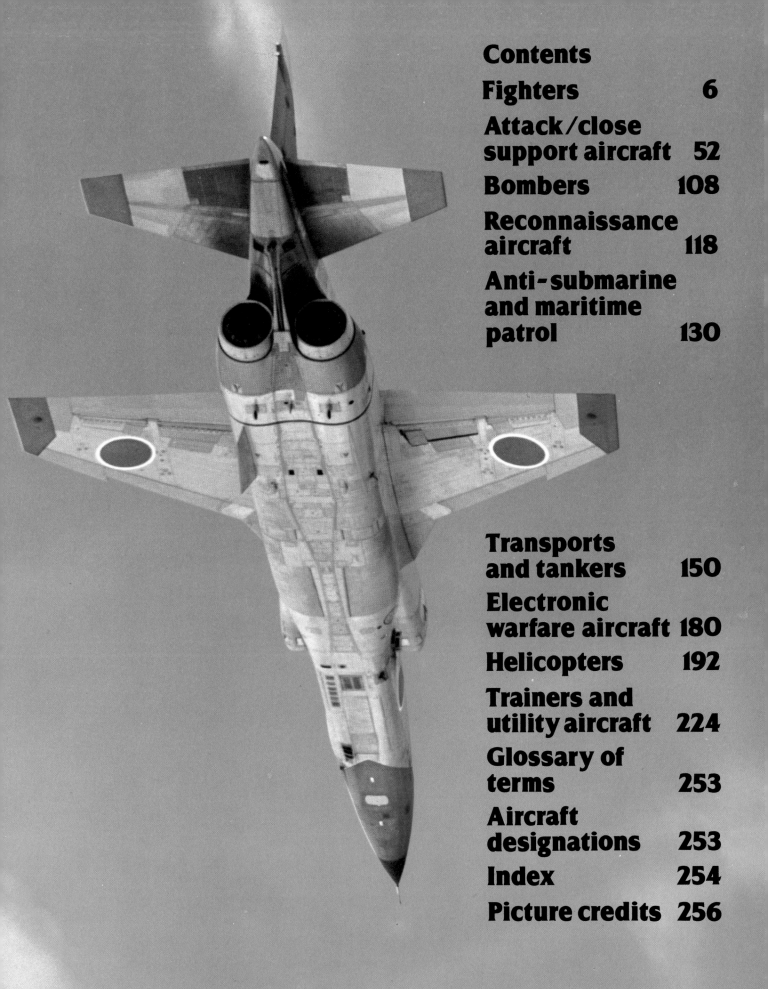

Contents

A Japanese camera records a nice left turn
by two Mitsubishi T-2 supersonic trainers
(see page 87).

Fighters

Before World War I aeroplanes had flown carrying manually aimed machine guns and even large-calibre automatic cannon, but the task of destroying hostile aircraft was soon almost universally assigned to fixed guns firing directly ahead, aimed by aiming the whole fighter at the enemy. From 1916 until 30 years later development was merely of degree, with guns increasing in calibre and lethality, sight systems improving fantastically, and aircraft performance and protection reflecting the fast progress in engines and structures. The only completely new factor was airborne radar, which enabled interceptions to be made in the dark or in bad weather, and temporarily introduced a special class of fighter characterized by larger size and extra crew-members. Jet propulsion gradually opened up the boundaries of flight performance and completely changed the shape of fighters, while the US Air Force led the world in developing advanced interception systems in 1948–52 which almost relegated the pilot to the role of passive machine-minder who just went along for the ride. Some suggested a fighter could have higher performance if the pilot stayed on the ground. Exasperated pilots in Korea, shaken by a totally uncomplicated fighter called a MiG-15, called for smaller and simpler fighters that would stay serviceable, climb above the enemy, fly faster and turn tighter, and thus put them back on top. The technological marvels were derided; instead of the A-1CM radar-ranged gunsight, seasoned fighter "jocks" called for a new invention called a gumsight: a piece of chewing gum fixed exactly in their forward line of sight on the windscreen. In April 1957 Britain went even further: its official view was that all fighters were obsolete.

Fighter development thus progressed in massive leaps, mistaken lurches and steps to the side or backwards. The result of the Korean experience was the F-104 Starfighter, which Lockheed called "the missile with a man in it". The Europeans went even beyond this with a flock of "light fighters" which crashed, faded entirely or were turned into light attack aircraft. The Starfighter likewise turned into an attack/reconnaissance aircraft —though the last

version of all was a fighter (F-104S), but not the kind envisaged when the F-104 was designed. By 1960, partly because of the tremendous all-round capability of the F-4 Phantom II, the wheel had turned full circle and, in contrast to light and simple fighters, the cry was for bigger and more complicated ones. The Phantom did not appeal to poorer or younger air forces, which queued up to buy Dassault's much cheaper Mirage, which looked good and went almost as fast. The Mirage also sold to some air forces that had a real job to do, notably to Israel, where the skies were blue and there was no need for long range, or for long-range weapons. Those that looked to the United States bought equally large numbers of F-5 "Freedom Fighters" for the same reasons. But the United States itself

had no interest in such aircraft; after the "TFX" (F-111) had demonstrated that, despite its unfortunate designation, this 50-ton monster was not a fighter at all, the standard fighter became the Phantom, which poured off the assembly line at St Louis in ever-increasing numbers. Then came Vietnam, where no American pilot was permitted to fire at another aircraft until he had "positive visual identification". This meant the big Phantom had to be brought within Sparrow missile range, within Sidewinder missile range, and right close to the streaking enemy. A dogfight might ensue, but the Phantom was not designed for dogfighting, and tended to stall and spin; and it had no gun. Eventually the Phantom grew a slatted wing and an internal gun, but by this time a new generation of jocks had grown up that longed for the same old things: more climb, more altitude, more speed, tighter turns. This time the un-interceptable "enemy" was the MiG-25.

This time these needs were not confused by a wish to do away with technology, because the modern technology was reliable. But a deadly enemy, cost-inflation, was making it almost impossible to do anything. One of the new fighters was the subject of a dispute between its builder and its first customer because the builder said he could not go on supplying at the price of $16,500,000 per aircraft, and had already lost $135 million on the first four batches (and that was a fighter developed before inflation really began to bite). This profoundly affected all Western defence, and one of its results was yet another American lurch in the direction of small and cheap fighters, leading to today's F-16. This at least appears to combine the qualities needed in a modern fighter: large SEP (specific excess power, a measure of surplus energy available for climb or manoeuvre), high T/W (thrust/weight ratio of considerably better than unity), low W/S (wing loading) obtained by reducing weight and increasing the size of the wing, and achieving the best possible flight-control system by a complex interaction of aerodynamics, system engineering, electronics and various interfaces with other systems in the aircraft and the human pilot. The F-16 has a gun, though quite an old one, and carries medium-range and short-range missiles (again old, but improved over the years).

Both the big F-15 Eagle and the smaller F-16 were planned as uncompromised fighters, to intercept and destroy hostile aircraft. Both eventually sprouted varied burdens of ordnance to fly attack missions. This role-change is hard to accomplish successfully. Two European aircraft, the Viggen and Tornado, were planned primarily for attack missions and are making the reverse transformation into fighters. The Tornado has the benefit of a swing-wing, like the multi-role F-14 Tomcat. Another swing-winger is the MiG-23, but in this case there are quite dissimilar attack and fighter versions. Designing fighters is quite difficult enough, without continuous pressure from the Soviet Union.

The pilot of a J35A Draken of the Flygvapen's F13 wing at Norrköping watches as his mate breaks away, showing the dramatic plan-shape and four Rb 324 missiles. The Draken, of which over 600 were built, was a programme of conspicuous success.

BAC Lightning

Lightning F.1 to 6 and export versions (data for F.6)

Origin: English Electric Aviation (now British Aerospace), UK.
Type: Single-seat all-weather interceptor.
Engines: Two 15,680lb (7112kg) thrust Rolls-Royce Avon 302 augmented turbojets.
Dimensions: span 34ft 10in (10·6m); length 53ft 3in (16·25m); height 19ft 7in (5·95m).
Weights: Empty about 28,000lb (12,700kg); loaded 50,000lb (22,680kg).
Performance: Maximum speed 1,500mph (2415km/h) at 40,000ft (12,200m); initial climb 50,000ft (15,240m)/min; service ceiling over 60,000ft (18,290m); range without overwing tanks 800 miles (1290km).
Armament: Interchangeable packs for two all-attitude Red Top or stern-chase Firestreak guided missiles; option of two 30mm Aden cannon in forward part of belly tank; export versions up to 6,000lb (2722kg) bombs or other offensive stores above and below wings.
History: First flight (P.1B) 4 April 1957; (first production F.1) 30 October 1959; (first F.6) 17 April 1964.
Users: Kuwait, Saudi Arabia, UK.

Development: As he had been with the Canberra, "Teddy" Petter was again moving spirit behind the award, in 1947, of a study contract for a supersonic research aircraft. Later this was built and flown as the P.1 of August 1954, exceeding Mach 1 on two crude unaugmented Sapphire engines mounted one above and behind the other and fed by a plain nose inlet. In mid-1949 specification F.23/49 was issued for a supersonic fighter, and after complete redesign the P.1B was produced and flown in 1957. This had a new fuselage with a two-shock intake, the central cone being intended to house Ferranti Airpass radar. The Avon engines were fitted with primitive afterburning, allowing a speed of Mach 2 to be attained on 25 November 1958. Helped by 20 pre-production aircraft, the Lightning F.1 was cleared for service in 1960. Though relatively complicated, so that the flying rate and maintenance burden were terrible in comparison with more modern aircraft, these supersonic all-weather interceptors at last gave the RAF a modern fighter with radar, guided missiles (heat-homing Firestreaks) and supersonic performance. Production was held back by the belief that all manned fighters

were obsolete (as clearly set forth in the Defence White Paper of April 1957), but the Treasury were persuaded to allow the improved F.2 to be built in 1961 with fully variable afterburner and all-weather navigation. Eventually, as the error of the 1957 doctrine became apparent, the Mk 3 was allowed in 1964, with more powerful engines, more fuel, bigger fin, collision-course fire-control and allattitude Red Top missiles; but it was decided to fit no guns, earlier marks having had two 30mm Aden cannon. Finally, in 1965, the belated decision was taken to follow the advice of BAC and almost double the fuel capacity and also fit the kinked and cambered wing (first flown in 1956) to improve operation at much increased weights. The T.4 and T.5 are dual conversion trainers equivalent to the F.2 and F.3. For Saudi Arabia and Kuwait, BAC paid for development of the Lightning as a multi-role fighter and attack aircraft, adding 57 to the production total to bring it up to 338.

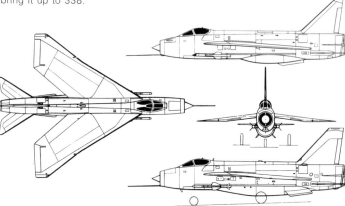

Above: Lightning F.6, with upper side elevation showing F.1.

Right and below: The Lightning F.2A is a rebuild of the early Mk 2 almost up to F.6 standard. Both the 92 Sqn aircraft (right) and the 19 Sqn example (below, at Warton) are shown in the colour-scheme of early 1977, when both squadrons were disbanded.

Left: Lightning F.6 as originally in service with No 5 Sqn, RAF, showing unpainted finish and Firestreak missiles. The flight-refuelling probe can be seen attached beneath the left wing. It does not impair the Lightning's dogfighting capability.

Dassault Breguet Mirage 2000

Mirage 2000 (single- and two-seat versions)

Origin: Avions Marcel Dassault/Breguet Aviation, France.
Type: Originally intended to be interceptor and air-superiority fighter.
Engine: One SNECMA M53 single-shaft afterburning turbofan modified in unspecified ways to achieve maximum thrust of at least 20,500lb (9300kg) dry and 25,000lb (11,340kg) with afterburner.
Dimensions: Not available.
Weights: Not available, but in view of manufacturer's statements loaded weight must be 24,000lb (10,886kg) or less.
Performance: Maximum speed at height 1,780mph (2870km/h, Mach 2·7); time to reach 40,000ft (12,200m) from brakes-release 1min 15sec; service ceiling 65,600ft (20,000m); radius or ferry range, not available.
Armament: Not disclosed, but will include further developments of the Matra Super 530 medium-range and Matra 550 Magic short-range air-to-air missiles.
History: Announcement of study project December 1975; first flight (prototype) 1978; available production aircraft "the beginning of the 1980s".
User: France (Armée de l'Air).

Development: In December 1975 the French government cancelled the Dassault-Breguet Super Mirage, which had been publicised as the Avion de Combat Futur and mainstay of the Armée de l'Air in the 1980s. In its place it announced a decision to award a study contract with Marcel Dassault for a smaller and simpler single-engined delta fighter outwardly looking very much like the Mirage III of 20 years earlier. In fact the Mirage 2000 — sometimes called the Delta 2000 — will differ significantly from the old Mirage, in aerodynamics, propulsion, structure and equipment. Aerodynamically it will be designed to incorporate American discoveries in CCV (control-configured vehicle) technology, in which aircraft are deliberately made unstable — for example, by positioning the centre of gravity much further back than usual — and using high-authority fail-safe flight-control systems to keep them under control. The result is either a smaller wing or, as in the Mirage 2000, dramatically higher manoeuvrability. Unlike the earlier Mirage deltas the 2000 will have leading-edge devices, either hinged droops or some form of slats, which will work in conjunction with the trailing-edge elevons to counteract the unstable pitching moment, or, in a tight turn, relax their effort or even help the aircraft to pitch nose-up. In the landing configuration the leading-edge devices (the French call it a "variable-camber" wing) will allow the elevons to be deflected down, adding to lift, whereas in earlier tailless deltas they have to be deflected up, effectively adding to weight just at the worst time.

Already the Mirage 2000 is being publicised as "being able to outclass combat aircraft presently being developed and produced in the Western world". It will have: "fly-by-wire" multi-channel electrically signalled flight controls; composite materials, carbon fibre being mentioned; large-radius Karman fairings (a reference to area ruling of the fuselage for minimum transonic drag); an elaborate weapon system with "g.p." (general-purpose?) computer and inertial unit; and long-range digital radar. Ratio of thrust to weight is to exceed unity. Such features are what one would expect of such an aircraft, but the problems are clearly enormous, especially in a time of severe inflation and economic pressures. France has since 1975 made attempts to acquire the base of technology, especially in digital avionics, necessary to build the Mirage 2000, but has little capability as yet. Only a single French aircraft, a two-seat Mirage IIIB with Sfena system, has flown with a primitive fly-by-wire system. Thomson-CSF estimate it will take "seven to eight years" to develop a 170-km-range digital radar needed to match the developed Super 530 missile. France has little experience of advanced composite structures, and that only in small test pieces and heli-

copters. SNECMA has not announced how the M53 engine, with very limited flight-time and no other application, is going to be increased in thrust by 35 per cent. If the aircraft to fly in 1978 is truly a prototype, and not the first off a production line, it will need everything to go right to meet an in-service date of 1982 with a developed aircraft. Not least, the proposed price of Fr40 to 50 million (£4·5 to 5·5 million) will be extremely difficult to hold, even in December 1975 Francs, because the magnitude of the system-development problems to France appear to have been grossly under-estimated.

In the original announcement the Mirage 2000 was described as "limited to high-speed and high-level interception and reconnaissance. . . . Attack and penetration at low levels will be undertaken by a different type." (The cancelled Super Mirage had been intended to fulfil all tactical roles.) But in December 1976 the Chief of Staff of the Armée de l'Air said he personally considered it would be necessary to build an interdictor and reconnaissance (he implied at low level) version of the Mirage 2000. It became known at this time that the new delta will apparently have nine weapon stations, which is diametrically opposed to the uncompromised high-altitude dog-fight concept announced in December 1975; and low-level use is diametrically opposed to a large-area delta. The Armée de l'Air has from the start hoped to buy 200 Mirage 2000s, twice the number it judged it could afford of the Super Mirage. But future progress of the programme, helped by US industry strictly on an inter-company rather than a government basis, will be instructive to watch.

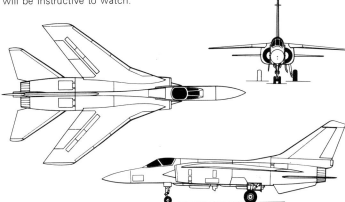

Three-view of the original Super Mirage, abandoned in 1976.

Dassault-Breguet Delta Super Mirage

Type: Long-range multi-role combat aircraft.
Engines: Two SNECMA M53 turbofans each presumably to be rated at about 25,000lb (11,340kg) thrust.
In January 1976 Marcel Dassault announced that, as a private venture, he was launching the Delta Super Mirage as a long-range multi-role aircraft for export. One hesitates to doubt the credibility of either the man or the company, but to fund such a programme would need many times the net worth of the company, and no consortium of overseas buyers (South Africans? Arabs? Black Africans?) appears to be conceivable. It would not be impossible for the company to finish the defunct tailed Super Mirage prototype, which was to have flown in July 1976, as an empty shell to show possible customers what the proposed Delta Super Mirage would look like. To develop it as an operational aircraft does not by any stretch of the imagination appear possible. One is left to conclude that M Dassault either expects the French government to find the money, which is extremely unlikely, or he hopes to organise a programme involving a large number of nations prepared to share the costs and risks.

Below: Artist's impression of the Mirage 2000 in Armée de l'Air service. It will have a blended fuselage and wing, the latter having full-span elevons and leading-edge droops.

Dassault Breguet Mirage F1

Mirage F1.C

Origin: Avions Marcel Dassault/Breguet Aviation, France, in partnership with Aérospatiale, with Fairey and SABCA, Belgium, and CASA, Spain; licence production in S Africa managed by Armaments Development and Production Corporation.

Type: Single-seat multimission fighter.

Engine: (F1.C) 15,873lb (7200kg) thrust (maximum afterburner) SNECMA Atar 9K-50 single-shaft augmented turbojet; (F1.E) 18,740lb (8500kg) thrust (maximum afterburner) SNECMA M53-02 single-shaft augmented by-pass turbojet.

Dimensions: Span 27ft 6¾in (8·4m); length (F1.C) 49ft 2½in (15m); (F1.E) 50ft 11in (15.53m); height (F1.C) 14ft 9in (4·5m); (F1.E) 14ft 10½in (4.56m).

Weights: Empty (F1.C) 16,314lb (7400kg); (F1.E) 17,857lb (8100kg); loaded (clean) (F1.C) 24,030lb (10,900kg); (F1.E) 25,450lb (11,540kg); (maximum) (F1.C) 32,850lb (14,900kg); (F1.E) 33,510lb (15,200kg).

Performance: Maximum speed (clean, both versions) 915mph (1472km/h) (Mach 1·2) at sea level, 1,450mph (2335km/h) (Mach 2·2) at altitude (with modification to cockpit transparency and airframe leading edges F1.E capable of 2·5); rate of climb (sustained to Mach 2 at 33,000ft) (F1.C) 41,930–47,835ft (12,780–14,580m)/min; (F1.E) above 59,000ft (18,000m)/min; service ceiling (F1.C) 65,600ft (20,000m); (F1.E) 69,750ft (21,250m); range with maximum weapons (hi-lo-hi) (F1.C) 560 miles (900km); (F1.E) 621 miles (1000km); ferry range (F1.C) 2,050 miles (3300km); (F1.E) 2,340 miles (3765km).

Armament: (Both versions), two 30mm DEFA 5-53 cannon, each with 135 rounds; five Alkan universal stores pylons, rated at 4,500lb (2000kg) on centreline, 2,800lb (1350kg) inners and 1,100lb (500kg) outers; launch rails on tips rated at 280lb (120kg) for air-to-air missiles; total weapon load 8,820lb (4000kg). Typical air combat weapons, two Matra 550 Magic or Sidewinder on tips for close combat, one/two Matra 530 with infrared or radar homing, and one/two Matra Super 530 for long-range homing with large changes in height. Wide range of weapons for surface attack, plus optional reconnaissance pod containing cameras, SAT Cyclope infrared linescan and EMI side-looking radar.

History: First flight (F1-01) 23 December 1966; (pre-production F1-02) 20 March 1969; (production F1.C) 15 February 1973; (F1-M53, prototype for proposed F1.E) 22 December 1974; (F1.B trainer) 26 May 1976; service delivery (F1.C) 14 March 1973.

Users: Egypt/Saudi Arabia (?), France, Greece, Iraq (?), Kuwait, Libya, Morocco (?), S Africa, Spain. (?) = no firm contract announced at time of writing.

continued on page 12▶

Three-view of the F1.C with Matra R 530s and Sidewinders.

Below: Cutaway drawing of the F1.C showing a representative selection of air-to-air missiles, six of which can be carried simultaneously.

1 Dielectric tip
1 Dielectric tip antenna housings
2 Rear navigation light
3 IFF aerial
4 VHF 1 aerial
5 VOR/LOC aerial
6 Rudder upper hinge
7 Fin structure
8 UHF aerial
9 Main fin spar (machined)
10 Rudder control linkage
11 Rudder central hinge fairing
12 Rudder
13 Fin rear spar
14 VHF 2 aerial
15 Parachute release mechanism
16 Braking parachute
17 Variable nozzle
18 Cooling annulus
19 Pneumatic nozzle actuators
20 Jet pipe mounting link
21 Fuselage aft support frame (tailplane trunnion/fin rear spar)
22 Tailplane trunnion
23 Trunnion frame
24 Honeycomb-stabilized structure
25 Multi-spar box structure
26 Ventral fin (port and starboard)
27 Control input linkage
28 Tailplane power unit
29 Hydraulic lines
30 Fin rear spar attachment
31 Rudder trim actuator
32 Rudder power unit
33 Fin leading-edge structure
34 Port tailplane
35 main spar lower section
36 Spring rod
37 Servo control quadrant
38 Rudder pulley bellcranks and cables
39 Fin main spar
39 Fin main spar attachment
40 Fin root fittings
41 Sealed-sheath hydraulic line
42 Afterburner
43 Engine mounting rail
44 Chem-milled tank inner skin
45 Wing root fairing
46 Rear lateral fuselage fuel tanks
47 Engine mounting access panel
48 Control run access panel
49 Filler/cross-feed system (rear/forward lateral tanks)
50 Aileron linkage
51 Compressor bleed-air pre-cooler
52 Main wing/fuselage mounting frame
53 Machined wing skins
54 Inboard flap composite-honeycomb structure
55 Flap tracks
56 Perforated spoilers
57 Spoiler actuator
58 Wing tank fuel lines
59 Aileron trimjack
60 Aileron servo control
61 Aileron operating rod
62 Aileron inboard hinge
63 Port aileron
64 Aileron outboard hinge
65 Missile attachment points
66 Missile ignition box
67 Matra 550 Magic air-to-air missile
68 Missile adapter shoe
69 Hinged, powered leading-edge
70 Leading-edge actuation system
71 Pylon mount (outboard)
72 Pylon mount (inboard)
73 Port inboard weapon pylon

74 Matra 530 air-to-air missile (infra-red homing)
75 Inboard leading-edge actuator
76 Forged high-tensile steel root fitting
77 IFF aerial
78 Engine duct ventilation
79 Central fuselage fuel tank
80 Aileron control rod
81 Avionics bay
82 Electrical/hydraulic leads
83 Inverted-flight accumulator
84 Amplifier
85 Main radio/electronics bay
86 Water separator and air-conditioning turbo-compressor
87 Canopy hinge
88 Canopy actuating jack
89 Martin-Baker Mk 4 ejection seat
90 Clamshell jettisonable canopy
91 Gunsight
92 One-piece cast windshield frame
93 Instrument panel
94 Control column
95 Instrument panel shroud/gunsight mounting
96 Heated, bird-strike proof windshield
97 Pitot heads

98 Radar attachment points
99 Thomson-CSF Cyrano IV fire-control radar
100 Radar scanner
101 Glass-reinforced plastic radome
102 Tacan aerial
103 Front pressure bulkhead
104 Rudder pedals

105 Aileron control bellcrank
106 Control column base
107 Elevator control bellcrank
108 Retraction jack fairing
109 Nosewheel retraction jack
110 Oleo-pneumatic shock-absorber
111 Twin nosewheels
112 Nose gear forging
113 Guide link
114 Steering/centering jack
115 Nose gear door
116 Pilot's seat
117 Nose gear actuation
118 Elevator linkage
119 Angled rear pressure bulkhead
120 Battery (24 volt)
121 Gun trough
122 Air intake shock-cone
123 Heat exchanger
124 Shock-cone electric motor

125 Boundary-layer bleed
126 Shock-cone guide track
127 Screw jack
128 Starboard air intake
129 DEFA cannon barrel
130 Auxiliary air intake door
131 Starboard airbrake
132 Starboard DEFA 30mm cannon
133 Forward fuselage integral fuel tank
134 Wing root fillet
135 Fuel pipes
136 Machined frame
137 Wing forward attachment point

138 Landing gear door actuator/linkage
139 Ammunition magazine (125 rounds)
140 Pre-closing landing gear door (lower)
141 Main landing gear well (starboard)
142 Main wing/fuselage

mounting frame
143 SNECMA Atar 9K50 turbojet (15,870lb/7,200 kg with afterburner)
144 Main wing attachment
145 Machined frame
146 Wing rear attachment
147 Engine mounting trunnion
148 Inboard flap track

149 Flap actuator and linkage
150 Honeycomb trailing-edge structure
151 Double-slotted flaps
152 Perforated spoilers
153 Spoiler leading-edge piano hinge
154 Multi-spar integral tank structure

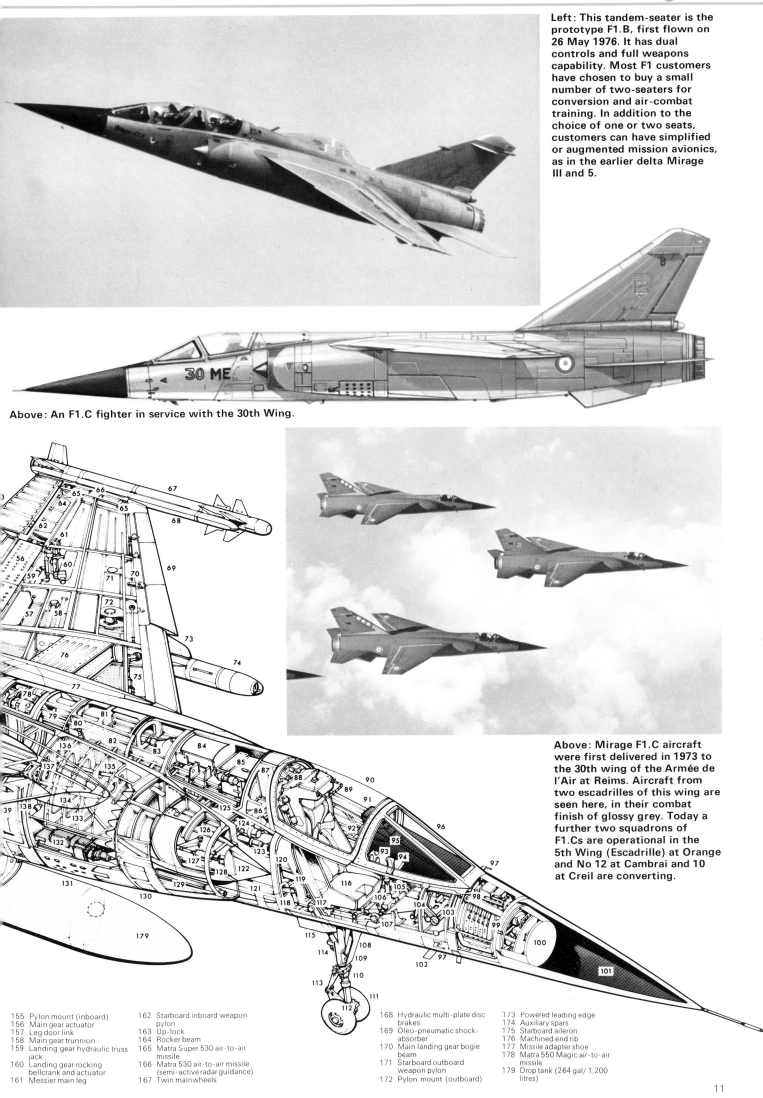

Left: This tandem-seater is the prototype F1.B, first flown on 26 May 1976. It has dual controls and full weapons capability. Most F1 customers have chosen to buy a small number of two-seaters for conversion and air-combat training. In addition to the choice of one or two seats, customers can have simplified or augmented mission avionics, as in the earlier delta Mirage III and 5.

Above: An F1.C fighter in service with the 30th Wing.

Above: Mirage F1.C aircraft were first delivered in 1973 to the 30th wing of the Armée de l'Air at Reims. Aircraft from two escadrilles of this wing are seen here, in their combat finish of glossy grey. Today a further two squadrons of F1.Cs are operational in the 5th Wing (Escadrille) at Orange and No 12 at Cambrai and 10 at Creil are converting.

155 Pylon mount (inboard)	162 Starboard inboard weapon pylon	168 Hydraulic multi-plate disc brakes	173 Powered leading edge
156 Main gear actuator	163 Up-lock	169 Oleo-pneumatic shock-absorber	174 Auxiliary spars
157 Leg door link	164 Rocker beam		175 Starboard aileron
158 Main gear trunnion	165 Matra Super 530 air-to-air missile	170 Main landing gear bogie beam	176 Machined end rib
159 Landing gear hydraulic truss jack	166 Matra 530 air-to-air missile (semi-active radar guidance)	171 Starboard outboard weapon pylon	177 Missile adapter shoe
160 Landing gear rocking bellcrank and actuator	167 Twin mainwheels	172 Pylon mount (outboard)	178 Matra 550 Magic air-to-air missile
161 Messier main leg			179 Drop tank (264 gal/1,200 litres)

►**Development:** Recognising that the Mirage III family would eventually have to be replaced, the French government awarded Dassault a development contract for a successor in February 1964. This aircraft was the large Mirage F2, in the 20 ton (clean) class and powered by a TF306 turbofan engine. It broke away from the classic Mirage form in having a high-mounted conventional swept wing with efficient high-lift slats and flaps, used in conjunction with a slab tailplane. It flew on 12 June 1966. Dassault, however, had privately financed a smaller version of the F2, called F1, sized to be powered by a single Atar engine. This became increasingly attractive and effort was progressively transferred to it from the F2. It went supersonic on its fourth flight and, though it later crashed, the Armée de l'Air decided to buy 100 as replacements for the original Mirage IIIC interceptor and Vautour IIN. Thus was launched an aircraft which in most ways marks a tremendous advance on the tailless delta.

Thanks to the far higher efficiency of the new wing the field lengths and take-off and landing speeds are lower than for the delta Mirages, even though the weights are greater and the wing area much less. Increased thrust comes from the latest Atar engine and among the many less obvious advances are the Cyrano IV multi-mode radar and integral tankage for 45 per cent more fuel (trebling patrol endurance and doubling ground-attack mission radii). Combat manoeuvrability in many situations was increased by as much as 80 per cent and the all-round performance of the new fighter was outstanding. Sales to Israel were prohibited, but orders were soon placed by South Africa and Spain, the former also buying a manufacturing licence. More recently the F1 was chosen by several Middle East countries and many more sales seem certain.

In 1967 the French engine company, SNECMA, began the design of a completely new engine for the Super Mirage. To test the engine the F1 was an obvious choice, and the combination could not fail to be of interest in its own right. The M53 engine confers benefits in acceleration, climb, manoeuvrability and range and, to make up a more modern package, Dassault-Breguet proposed the fully modular Cyrano IV-100 radar and the SAGEM-Kearfott SKN 2603 inertial navigation system, as well as the SFENA 505 digital autopilot of the F1.C. The result is the F1.E, which from early 1974 was strongly, but unsuccessfully, pressed on overseas customers, particularly Belgium, the Netherlands, Denmark and Norway (which agreed a common objective in replacing their F-104Gs). The Armée de l'Air did not want the F1.E, but had agreed to buy a limited quantity had it been chosen by the four NATO nations. Two M53-powered prototypes were flown, but the M53-engined version was shelved in 1975. Today four versions are in production: (C) the basic aircraft, so far chosen by all customers; (E) the C with more advanced avionics (no longer offered with the M53 engine), chosen by Libya; (A) simplified avionics for low-level attack, for Libya and South Africa; (B) two-seater, for Kuwait and Libya.

Top: The Ejercito del Aire (Spanish Air Force) calls the Mirage F1.C the C-14. The Spanish CASA company shares in some Dassault-Breguet manufacturing programmes.
Above: Another F1.C customer is the Hellenic (Greek) Air Force.

Dassault Breguet Mirage III and 5

Mirage III and 5

Origin: Avions Marcel Dassault/Breguet Aviation, France (actual manufacture dispersed through European industry and certain models assembled in Belgium, Switzerland and Australia).
Type: Single-seat or two-seat interceptor, tactical strike, trainer or reconnaissance aircraft (depending on sub-type).
Engine: (IIIC) 13,225lb (6000kg) thrust (maximum afterburner) SNECMA Atar 9B single-shaft turbojet; (most other III and some 5) 13,670lb (6200kg) Atar 9C; (recent III and some 5) 15,873lb (7200kg) Atar 9K-50; (Kfir, see separate entry).
Dimensions: Span 27ft (8·22m); length (IIIC) 50ft 10¼in (15·5m); (IIIB) 50ft 6¼in (15·4m), (5) 51ft (15·55m); height 13ft 11½in (4·25m).
Weights: Empty (IIIC) 13,570lb (6156kg); (IIIE) 15,540lb (7050kg); (IIIR) 14,550lb (6600kg); (IIIB) 13,820lb (6270kg); (5) 14,550lb (6600kg); loaded (IIIC) 19,700lb (8936kg); (IIIE, IIIR, 5) 29,760lb (13,500kg), (IIIB) 26,455lb (12,000kg).
Performance: Maximum speed (all models, clean) 863mph (1390km/h) (Mach 1·14) at sea level, 1,460mph (2350km/h) (Mach 2·2) at altitude; initial climb, over 16,400ft (5000m)/min (time to 36,090ft 11,000m, 3 min); service ceiling (Mach 1·8) 55,775ft (17,000m); range (clean) at altitude about 1,000 miles (1610km); combat radius in attack mission with bombs and tanks (mix not specified) 745 miles (1200km); ferry range with three external tanks 2,485 miles (4000km).
Armament: Two 30mm DEFA 5-52 cannon, each with 125 rounds (normally fitted to all versions except when IIIC carries rocket-boost pack); three 1,000lb (454kg) external pylons for bombs, missiles or tanks (Mirage 5, seven external pylons with maximum capacity of 9,260lb, 4200kg).
History: First flight (MD.550 Mirage I) 25 June 1955; (prototype Mirage III-001) 17 November 1956; (pre-production Mirage IIIA) 12 May 1958; (production IIIC) 9 October 1960; (IIIE) 5 April 1961; (IIIR) 31 October 1961; (IIIB) 19 July 1962; (Australian-assembled IIIO) 16 November 1963; (Swiss-assembled IIIS) 28 October 1965; (prototype 5) 19 May 1967; (Belgian-assembled 5BA) May 1970.
Users: (III) Abu Dhabi, Argentina, Australia, Brazil, Egypt, France, Israel, Lebanon, Libya, Pakistan, S Africa, Spain, Switzerland, Venezuela; (5) Abu Dhabi, Belgium, Colombia, Egypt, France, Gabon, Libya, Pakistan, Peru, Saudi Arabia, Venezuela, Zaïre.

Development: The Mirage, which has come to symbolise modern aerial combat and to bring additional trade to France and incalculable prestige, especially in defence hardware, began in a most uncertain fashion. It was conceived in parallel with the Etendard II to meet the same Armée de l'Air light interceptor specification of 1952 and was likewise to be powered by two small turbojets (but, in this case, boosted by a liquid-propellant rocket engine in addition). As the small French engines were not ready, Dassault fitted the Mirage I with two British Viper turbojets and before the rocket was fitted this small delta was dived to Mach 1·15. With the rocket it reached Mach 1·3 in level flight. But Dassault had no faith in the concept of such low-power aircraft and after some work on the twin-Gabizo Mirage II took the plunge and produced a bigger and heavier Mirage III, powered by the 8,820lb thrust Atar 101G. From this stemmed the pre-production IIIA, with larger but thinner wing and completely redesigned fuselage housing the new Atar 9 engine. On 24 October 1958 Mirage IIIA-01 became the first West European aircraft to attain Mach 2 in level flight.

This clinched the decision of the Armée de l'Air to buy 100 of a slightly developed interceptor called Mirage IIIC, fitted either with guns or with a boost rocket for faster climb and better combat performance at heights up to 82,000ft. Normally the SEP 844 rocket was fitted to the IIIC, the sole armament being air-to-air missiles, such as Sidewinders and the big Matra R.530 used in conjunction with the CSF Cyrano radar, fitted to permit the new fighter to operate in all weather. Altogether 244 C models were delivered, large batches also going to South Africa and Israel (a nation which did much to develop and promote both the III and the 5). From the IIIC emerged the dual-control IIIB trainer, the longer and heavier IIIE for ground attack (with Marconi doppler radar for blind low-level navigation, new fire-control and navigation computer, and increased internal fuel) and the IIIR family of camera-equipped reconnaissance aircraft. By 1977 about 1,200 of the Mirage III family had been sold, including a fairly standard version made in Australia and an extremely non-standard version made in Switzerland after painful development problems which inflated the price and reduced the numbers bought.

In 1965 Israel suggested that Dassault should produce a special VFR (clear weather) version for ground attack in the Middle East, with the radar and fire control avionics removed and replaced by an extra 110 gallons of fuel and more bombs. The result was the Mirage 5 and Israel bought 50 of the first production batch of 60. It can be distinguished by its longer and much more pointed nose, devoid of radar unless the small Aida II is fitted. For political reasons the French refused to deliver the paid-for Mirages to Israel but more than 500 have been sold to many other countries and 106 were assembled, and partly constructed, in Belgium. Largely as a result of the French action, Israel developed its own improved version of the Mirage (see IAI Kfir, separate entry).

In addition to production aircraft there have been many experimental or unsold variants. One of the latter was the Spey-powered Mirage IIIW jointly proposed by Dassault and Boeing as a rival to the F-5 as a standard simple fighter for America's allies. Another non-starter was the Milan (Kite), fitted with retractable "moustache" foreplanes for shorter field-length and better manoeuvrability (this excellent idea is available on the Mirage 5). By far the biggest development programme concerned the enlarged and more powerful Mirage IIIV V/STOL fighter with a 19,840lb thrust SNECMA TF306 augmented turbofan for propulsion and eight 5,500lb thrust Rolls-Royce RB.162-31 lift jets. The IIIT was a non-VTOL of the same size and the equally large F2 led to the smaller (Atar-size) F1.

Above: Not a Mirage delta with a tail but a pair of IIIO ground-attack fighters of the RAAF off the Australian coast.

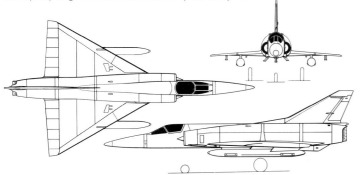

Above: Three-view of Mirage 5, showing multi-sensor pods.

Above: Mirage IIICJ of Heyl Ha'Avir, Israel.

Above: Mirage IIIEP of No 5 Sqn, Pakistan Air Force.

Below: Most Mirage customers have bought dual-control trainer versions for pilot conversion to the speedy delta — with "back of the drag curve" characteristics — and weapon training. This is a Mirage 5-DV of Venezuela.

General Dynamics F-16

Model 401, YF-16, F-16A, F-16B

Origin: General Dynamics/Fort Worth, USA, with widespread sub-contract manufacture in Europe and European assembly of aircraft for European customers (see text).

Type: Single-seat fighter bomber; (B) operational trainer.

Engine: One 24,000lb (10,885kg) thrust Pratt & Whitney F100-PW-100 two-shaft afterburning turbofan.

Dimensions: Span (no Sidewinders) 31ft 0in (9·45m), (with Sidewinders) 32ft 10in (10·01m); length (excl probe) (YF-16) 46ft 6in, (F-16A) 47ft 7·7in (14·52m); height (F-16) 16ft 5·2in (5·01m).

Weights: Empty (YF) about 12,000lb (5443kg); (F) about 14,800lb (6733kg); maximum gross (YF) 27,000lb (12,245kg); (F) 33,000lb (14,969kg).

Performance: Maximum speed, Mach 1·95, equivalent to about 1,300mph (2090km/h); initial climb (YF) 40,000ft (12,200m)/min; service ceiling about 60,000ft (18,300m); range on internal fuel in interception mission, about 1,300 miles (2100km); attack radius at low level with maximum weapon load, 120 miles (193km); attack radius with six Mk 82 bombs, 339 miles (546km).

Armament: One 20mm M61 multi-barrel cannon on left side of fuselage; nine pylons for total external load of up to 15,200lb (6895kg) (YF, seven pylons for total of 11,500lb, 5217kg).

History: First flight (YF) 20 January 1974; service delivery, scheduled for mid-1978.

Users: Belgium, Denmark, Iran, the Netherlands, Norway, Turkey (planned, see text); US Air Force.

Development: One of the most important combat aircraft of the rest of the century was started merely as a technology demonstrator to see to what degree it would be possible to build a useful fighter that was significantly smaller and cheaper than the F-15. The US Air Force Lightweight Fighter (LWF) programme was not intended to lead to a production aircraft but merely to establish what was possible, at what cost. Contracts for two prototypes of each of the two best submissions were awarded in April 1972, the aircraft being the General Dynamics 401 and a simplified Northrop P.530. As the YF-16 and YF-17 these aircraft completed a programme of competitive evaluation, as planned, in 1974. By this time the wish of four European members of NATO – Belgium, Holland, Denmark and Norway – to replace their F-104Gs with an aircraft in this class had spurred a total revision of the LWF programme. In April 1974 it was changed into the Air Combat Fighter (ACF) programme and the Defense Secretary, James Schlesinger, announced that 650 of the winning design would be bought for the USAF, with a vast support depot in Europe. In December 1974 the YF-16 was chosen as the future ACF (announced the following month) and in June 1975, after protracted and tortuous discussions, it was chosen by the four European countries. As an aircraft the F-16 is exciting. It has a flashing performance on the power of the single fully developed engine (the same as the F-15) fed by a simple fixed-geometry inlet. Structure and systems are modern, with control-configured vehicle (CCV) flight dynamics, quad-redundant electrically signalled controls (fly-by-wire), graphite-epoxy structures and a flared wing/body shape. Pilot view is outstanding and he lies back in a reclining Escapac seat and flies the aircraft through a sidestick controller. In the nose is an advanced pulse-doppler radar suitable for attack or interception missions and armament can be carried for both roles, though the basic design was biased strongly in favour of air-to-air missions in good weather at close range. It remains to be seen to what degree the F-16 can be modified to make it a better ground attack, reconnaissance or all-weather interceptor aircraft. Main contractors include

continued on page 16▶

The second YF-16 prototype, pictured whilst undergoing weapon trials in 1976. It has just released 12 bombs each of a nominal 1,000lb. Maximum load, with reduced fuel, is 15,200lb.

1 Air data probe (Rosemount Engineering)
2 SSR-1 radar ranging system (General Electric) (Westinghouse multi-mode radar in F-16)
3 Angle-of-attack transducers (port and starboard)
4 Battery and avionics compartment
5 Central air-data computer (Sperry Flight Systems)
6 Air-data converter
7 Forward pressure bulkhead
8 Rudder pedals
9 Control wiring (fly-by-wire) junction
10 Raised heel-rest line
11 Instrument panel shroud
12 Head-up display unit (Marconi-Elliott Avionic Systems HUDWAS)
13 Side-stick controller
14 Starboard instrument console
15 Lightweight ejection seat (30-deg tilt-back Douglas Escapac IH-8)
16 Arm rest
17 Port instrument console (power lever mounting)
18 Fuselage forebody strakes
19 Cooling louvres
20 Gun gas-suppression nozzle
21 Gun-fairing frames
22 Boundary-layer splitter plate
23 Fixed-geometry air intake
24 Inlet duct
25 Aerial
26 Nosewheel leg (Menasco Manufacturing)
27 Aft-retracting nose gear (Goodyear Tire & Rubber)
28 Shock-absorber scissors
29 Retraction strut
30 Nosewheel door
31 Door hinge
32 Nosewheel well (below duct)
33 General Electric M61 20mm gun
34 Cannon barrels
35 Emergency power-unit pack (Sundstrand Avionics)
36 Canopy hinge
37 Headrest
38 Canopy lock
39 Frameless bubble canopy (Sierracin Corp)
40 Aft glazing
41 Forward fuselage fuel tank
42 Accelerometers (General Electric)
43 Ammunition drum
44 Ammunition feed and link return chutes (General Electric)
45 Forward/centre fuselage joint bulkhead
46 Inlet duct
47 Hydraulic equipment bay
48 Main (forward) fuselage fuel tank
49 Flight-refuelling receptacle
50 Multi-spar wing structure
51 Leading-edge flap hinge-line
52 Leading-edge manoeuvre flap
53 Wing-tip missile adaptor shoe
54 AIM-9 Sidewinder missile
55 Static dischargers
56 Fixed trailing-edge section
57 Starboard flaperon
58 Aerial
59 Forward support link
60 Glass-fibre root fairing
61 Fin/fuselage attachments
62 Aluminium multi-spar fin structure
63 Aluminium-honeycomb leading-edge
64 Steel leading-edge strip
65 Graphite-epoxy skin
66 Identification/navigation light
67 Static dischargers
68 Graphite-epoxy rudder skin
69 Aluminium-honeycomb rudder
70 Empennage flight controls
71 Fully variable articulated nozzle
72 Split trailing-edge airbrake (upper and lower surfaces)
73 Static dischargers
74 Aluminium-honeycomb tailplane
75 Graphite-epoxy skin

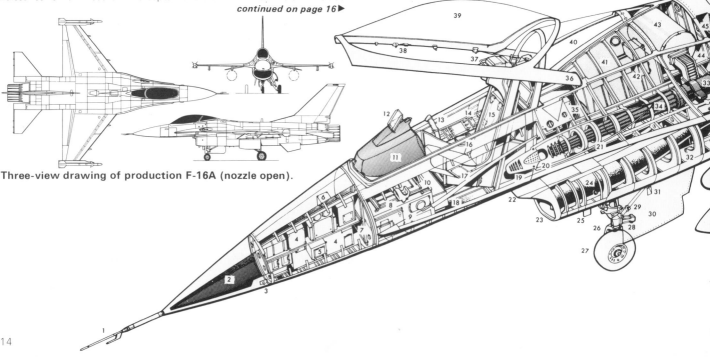

Three-view drawing of production F-16A (nozzle open).

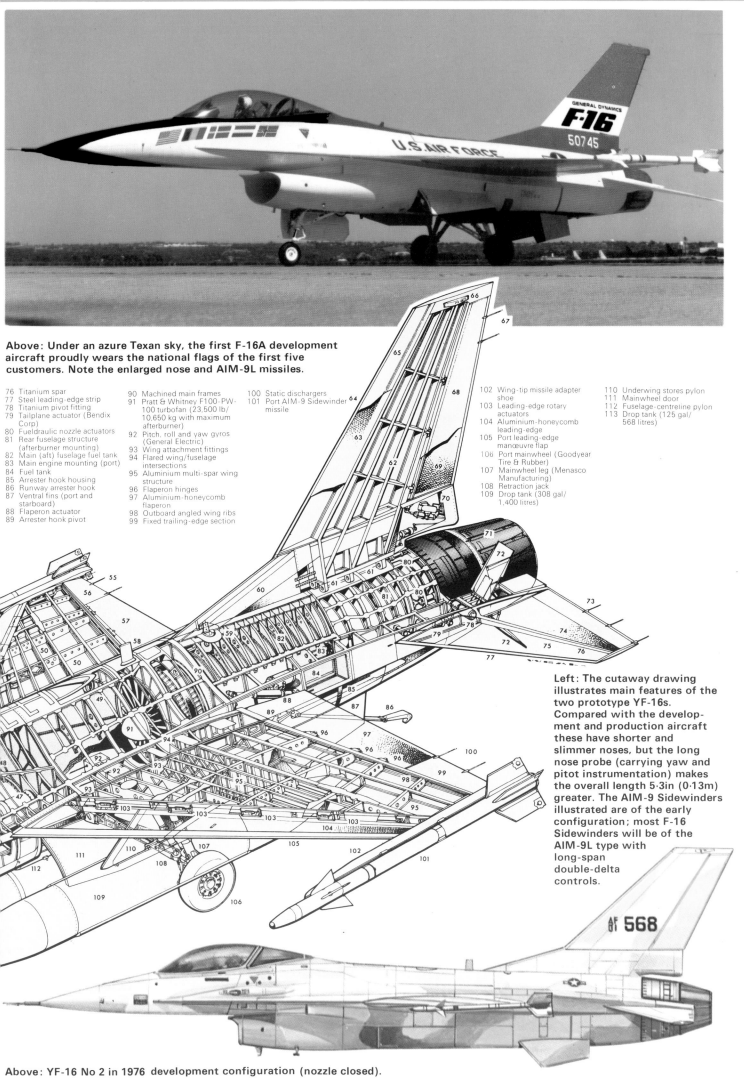

Above: Under an azure Texan sky, the first F-16A development aircraft proudly wears the national flags of the first five customers. Note the enlarged nose and AIM-9L missiles.

76 Titanium spar
77 Steel leading-edge strip
78 Titanium pivot fitting
79 Tailplane actuator (Bendix Corp)
80 Fueldraulic nozzle actuators
81 Rear fuselage structure (afterburner mounting)
82 Main (aft) fuselage fuel tank
83 Main engine mounting (port)
84 Fuel tank
85 Arrester hook housing
86 Runway arrester hook
87 Ventral fins (port and starboard)
88 Flaperon actuator
89 Arrester hook pivot

90 Machined main frames
91 Pratt & Whitney F100-PW-100 turbofan (23,500 lb/ 10,650 kg with maximum afterburner)
92 Pitch, roll and yaw gyros (General Electric)
93 Wing attachment fittings
94 Flared wing/fuselage intersections
95 Aluminium multi-spar wing structure
96 Flaperon hinges
97 Aluminium-honeycomb flaperon
98 Outboard angled wing ribs
99 Fixed trailing-edge section

100 Static dischargers
101 Port AIM-9 Sidewinder missile
102 Wing-tip missile adapter shoe
103 Leading-edge rotary actuators
104 Aluminium-honeycomb leading-edge
105 Port leading-edge manœuvre flap
106 Port mainwheel (Goodyear Tire & Rubber)
107 Mainwheel leg (Menasco Manufacturing)
108 Retraction jack
109 Drop tank (308 gal/ 1,400 litres)

110 Underwing stores pylon
111 Mainwheel door
112 Fuselage-centreline pylon
113 Drop tank (125 gal/ 568 litres)

Left: The cutaway drawing illustrates main features of the two prototype YF-16s. Compared with the development and production aircraft these have shorter and slimmer noses, but the long nose probe (carrying yaw and pitot instrumentation) makes the overall length 5·3in (0·13m) greater. The AIM-9 Sidewinders illustrated are of the early configuration; most F-16 Sidewinders will be of the AIM-9L type with long-span double-delta controls.

Above: YF-16 No 2 in 1976 development configuration (nozzle closed).

Westinghouse (radar), Marconi-Elliott (HUD-sight and portions of flight-control system), Westinghouse and Delco (computers), Kaiser (radar and electro-optical display) and Singer-Kearfott (inertial system). In 1977 the USAF still intends to purchase 650 aircraft, mainly for use in Europe; in 1976 it set up a European System Programme Office to manage the project, and began work on the support depot. Orders are still subject to change, but the planned totals are: Belgium, 90 F-16A and 12 F-16B, with 14 aircraft on option; Denmark 48 (probably 40+8), and 10 on option; the Netherlands, 84, plus 18 on option; Norway, 72 (no options). In July 1976 General Dynamics finally signed co-production contracts with major companies in Belgium and Holland, specifying schedules and output rates of parts for 564 aircraft, a total that would increase with further F-16 sales. Aircraft will be assembled by General Dynamics (USAF), Fairey/SABCA (Belgium and Denmark) and Fokker-VFW (Netherlands and Norway); Kongsberg in Norway has a $163m co-production deal with Pratt & Whitney on more than 400 engines (all engines will be assembled by P & WA). Since early 1976 Turkey has been negotiating to join the European consortium (which has no formal title) and to buy up to 100 aircraft. In September 1976 Congress announced the sale to Iran of 160, costing $3·8 billion; it is doubtful that Iran can participate in manufacture. In December 1976 the first of eight development aircraft flew at Fort Worth, and delivery to the USAF is to begin in August 1978. Up to October 1976 $286 million had paid for basic development and flight test; Fiscal Year 1977 voted $620 million for the first 16 production aircraft, and FY78 is expected to provide $1,128 million. USAF buy in the next four years (1978-81) is planned to be 89, 145, 175 and 180, a total to that date of 605. First flight in Europe is planned to be at Schiphol (Fokker-VFW, Amsterdam) in July 1979.

Prototype YF-16 aircraft have appeared in various colour schemes; this air-to-air picture shows the No 2 machine in low-visibility "two-tone grey".

Below: Grey smoke spews from the Gatling exhaust port of a YF-16 on a low-level firing pass during 1976 weapon trials. Fighters are no longer built without guns.

General Dynamics
F-102 Delta Dagger

F-102A, TF-102A, QF-102A and PQM-102A

Origin: General Dynamics/Convair, USA.

Type: (F) single-seat all-weather interceptor; (TF) trainer; (QF) manned RPV (remotely piloted vehicle); (PQM) drone target.

Engine: One 17,200lb (7802kg) thrust Pratt & Whitney J57-23 two-shaft afterburning turbojet.

Dimensions: Span 38ft 1½in (11·6m); length, (F-102A) 68ft 5in (20·83m); (TF-102A) 63ft 4½in (19·3m); height (F-102A) 21ft 2½in (6·45m); (TF-102A) 20ft 7in (6·27m).

Weights: Empty (F-102A) 19,050lb (8630kg); loaded (F-102A, clean) 27,700lb (12,564kg), (maximum) 31,500lb (14,288kg).

Performance: Maximum speed (F-102A) 825mph (1328km/h, Mach 1·25), (TF-102A) 646mph (1040km/h); initial climb (F-102A) 13,000ft (3962m)/min; service ceiling 54,000ft (16,460m); range 1,350 miles (2172km).

Armament: Air-to-air guided missiles carried in internal bay, typical full load comprising three Hughes AIM-4E Falcon beam-riders with semi-active homing and three AIM-4F with infra-red homing. No armament in TF, QF or PQM.

History: First flight (YF-102) 24 October 1953; (YF-102A) 20 December 1954; (TF) 8 November 1955; (QF) mid-1974; (PQM) early 1975.

Users: Greece, Turkey, USA (F, TF, ANG; PQM, QF, TF, US Air Force).

Development: In 1948 Convair flew the world's first delta-wing aircraft, the XF-92A, which was part of a programme intended to lead to a supersonic fighter. This was terminated, but the US Air Force later issued a specification for an extremely advanced all-weather interceptor to carry the Hughes MX-1179 system which included radar, computer and guided missiles. For the first time the carrier aircraft became subordinate to its avionics, as a mere portion of a weapon system. The whole weapon system represented a major challenge in 1951-52 and it did not help when early flight trials showed that the specified supersonic speed could not be reached. The whole aircraft had to be redesigned to a modified shape complying with the lately discovered Area Rule, making it much longer, and fatter at the back. Once the design had been got right, 875 were delivered in 21 months, together with 63 of the subsonic side-by-side TF version. The Delta Dagger was big and impressive, painted a glossy pale grey, and had a small but comfortable cockpit where the pilot flew with two control columns, that on the left being used to adjust the sweep angle and range gate of the MG-10 radar. In the search mode the pilot flew with one hand on each stick and his eyes pressed into the viewing hood of the radar display screen. In the semi-automatic mode missiles could be extended automatically at the correct moment; as delivered the F-102 also carried FFARs (Folding-Fin Aircraft Rockets) in the missile bay doors. By 1974 surviving F-102s — called "Deuces" — had been assigned to the US Air National Guard and to the air forces of Greece and Turkey. Sperry converted 24 into remotely piloted QF and unmanned PQM versions for use in threat evaluation, F-15 combat and other aerial research.

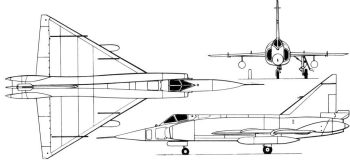

Above: Three-view of F-102A with drop tanks.

Above: A colourful line-up of "Deuces"—so-called because a deuce is a two at cards—pictured in their youth when they were the last word in automatic all-weather interception.

Left: Thirsty Deuce takes on fuel from a KC-135A with high-speed boom modified for probe/drogue refuelling.

Left: One of the final users of the F-102A is the Turkish Air Force. The aircraft retain their original equipment and serial (tail) number, and are compatible with the Nadge air-defence system.

Left: A Deuce in US Air Force or Air National Guard camouflage. They have an excellent service record.

General Dynamics
F-106 Delta Dart

F-106A and F-106B

Origin: General Dynamics/Convair, USA.
Type: (F-106A) single-seat all-weather interceptor; (F-106B) operational trainer.
Engine: One 24,500lb (11,130kg) thrust Pratt & Whitney J75-17 two-shaft afterburning turbojet.
Dimensions: Span 38ft 3½in (11·67m); length (both) 70ft 8¾in (21·55m); height 20ft 3¼in (6·15m).
Weights: (A) empty 23,646lb (10,725kg); maximum loaded 38,250lb (17,350kg).
Performance: (Both) maximum speed 1,525mph (2455km/h, Mach 2·31); initial climb about 30,000ft (9144m)/min; service ceiling 57,000ft (17,375m); range with drop tanks (A) 1,700 miles (2735km); combat radius, about 600 miles (966km).
Armament: One internal 20mm M-61 multi-barrel cannon; internal weapon bay for air-to-air guided missiles, with typical load comprising one AIR-2A and one AIR-2G Genie rockets and two each of AIM-4E, -4F or 4G Falcons.
History: First flight (aerodynamic prototype) 26 December 1956; (F-106B) 9 April 1958, production delivery July 1959 to July 1960.
User: USA (ANG, USAF).

Development: Originally designated F-102B, the 106 was a natural development of the F-102A with new engine and avionics. By redesigning from scratch to the supersonic Area Rule the fuselage was made much neater and more efficient than that of the earlier aircraft and the more powerful engine resulted in a peak speed approximately twice as fast. The Hughes MA-1 fire control, though no bulkier or heavier than that of the 102, was far more capable and integrated with the SAGE (Semi-Automatic Ground Environment) defence system covering the continental United States in an automatic manner, the pilot acting as a supervisory manager. Though bought in modest numbers, the 106 has had an exceptionally long lifespan in the USAF Aerospace Defense Command front-line inventory. At several times the Improved Manned Interceptor program (IMI) has pointed the need for a replacement with longer-range look-down radar and long-range missiles, and much research has been done with the Lockheed YF-12 (described later). At present no replacement, other than the multi-role F-15, is in sight and the F-106 and tandem-seat F-106B force (respectively numbering originally 277 and 63) will continue until at least 1980. They have been repeatedly updated, with improved avionics, infra-red sensors, drop tanks, flight refuelling and a Gatling gun.

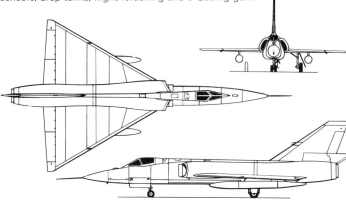

Above: Three-view of F-106A with drop tanks.

Below: An F-106A Delta Dart single-seat interceptor of the 194th FIS, 144th FIG, California ANG at Tyndall AFB, Florida. Foot of page: A tandem-seat dual-control F-106B of the same Aerospace Defense Command unit (no longer active) as the single-seater shown in the drawing.

Above: F-106A of USAF ADC.

Grumman F-14 Tomcat

F-14A, B and C

Origin: Grumman Aerospace, USA.

Type: Two-seat carrier-based multi-role fighter.

Engines: (F-14A) two 20,900lb (9480kg) thrust Pratt & Whitney TF30-412A two-shaft afterburning turbofans; (B and C) two 28,090lb (12,741kg) thrust Pratt & Whitney F401-400 two-shaft afterburning turbofans.

Dimensions: Span (68° sweep) 38ft 2in (11·63m), (20° sweep) 64ft 1½in (19·54m); length 61ft 2in (18·89m); height 16ft (4·88m).

Weights: Empty 37,500lb (17,010kg); loaded (fighter mission) 55,000lb (24,948kg), (maximum) 72,000lb (32,658kg).

Performance: Maximum speed, 1,564mph (2517km/h, Mach 2·34) at height, 910mph (1470km/h, Mach 1·2) at sea level; initial climb at normal gross weight, over 30,000ft (9144m)/min; service ceiling over 56,000ft (17,070m); range (fighter with external fuel) about 2,000 miles (3200km).

Armament: One 20mm M61-A1 multi-barrel cannon in fuselage; four AIM-7 Sparrow and four or eight AIM-9 Sidewinder air-to-air missiles, or up to six AIM-54 Phoenix and two AIM-9; maximum external weapon load in surface attack role 14,500lb (6577kg).

History: First flight 21 December 1970; initial deployment with US Navy carriers October 1972; first flight of F-14B 12 September 1973.

Users: Iran (IIAF), USA (Navy, Marine Corps).

Development: When Congress finally halted development of the compromised F-111B version of the TFX in mid-1968 Grumman was already well advanced with the project design of a replacement. After a competition for the VFX requirement Grumman was awarded a contract for the F-14 in *continued on page 20* ▶

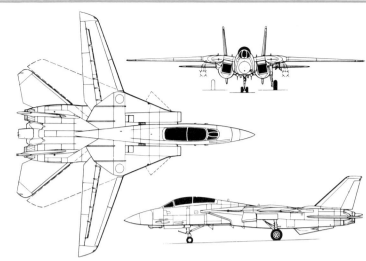

Above: Three-view of an F-14A showing (broken lines) range of wing and glove movement.

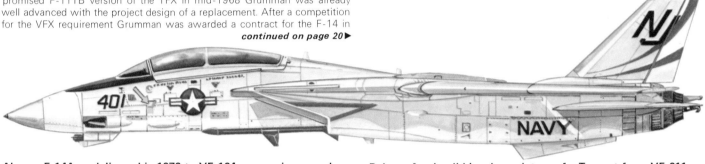

Above: F-14A as delivered in 1972 to VF-124 conversion squadron.

Below: A splendid head-on picture of a Tomcat from VF-211, armed with two AIM-54A Phoenix, two AIM-7F Sparrow and two AIM-9G Sidewinders. At this range the gun would be better.

▶January 1969. The company had to produce a detailed mock-up by May and build 12 development aircraft. Despite sudden loss of the first aircraft on its second flight, due to total hydraulic failure, the programme has been a complete technical success and produced one of the world's outstanding combat aircraft. Basic features include use of a variable-sweep wing, to match the aircraft to the conflicting needs of carrier compatability, dogfighting and attack on surface targets at low level; pilot and naval flight officer (observer) in tandem; an extremely advanced airframe, with tailplane skins of boron-epoxy composite and similar novel construction methods, and one canted vertical tail above each engine; and the extremely powerful Hughes AWG-9 radar which, used in conjunction with the Phoenix missile (carried by no other combat aircraft), can pick out and destroy a chosen aircraft from a formation at a distance of 100 miles. For close-in fighting the gun is used in conjunction with snap-shoot missiles, with the tremendous advantage that, as a launch platform, the Tomcat is unsurpassed (Grumman claim it to be unrivalled, and to be able – by automatic variation of wing sweep – to out-manoeuvre all previous combat aircraft). Introduction to the US Navy has been smooth and enthusiastic, with VF-1 and -2 serving aboard *Enterprise* in 1974. The export appeal of the F-14 is obvious and Iran is introducing 80 from 1976. But costs have run well beyond prediction, Grumman refusing at one time to continue the programme and claiming its existing contracts would result in a loss of $105 million. For the same reason the re-engined F-14B has been confined to two re-engined A-models, and the F-14C with new avionics and weapons remains a paper project. In 1975 production agreements were worked out and by 1977 total deliveries amounted to 243 aircraft, including about 12 for Iran. The US Navy (which includes the aircraft for the Marines) has funds for 306 F-14As and plans to buy 403 by 1981, but the requirement for an eventual total of over 500 is likely to be cut back as the F-18 comes into production. In 1976 severe trouble hit the F-14, affecting engines, fuselage structure, computer/weapon system and accidents attributed to pilot error. Efforts are being made to improve the operational-readiness rate and, if possible, increase installed engine thrust.

Above: Despite various transient problems, the Tomcat is a truly great fighter. This one comes from VF-14, embarked aboard *John F. Kennedy*.

Right: The moment of motor ignition of a Phoenix, the world's longest-ranged (126+ miles) air/air missile.

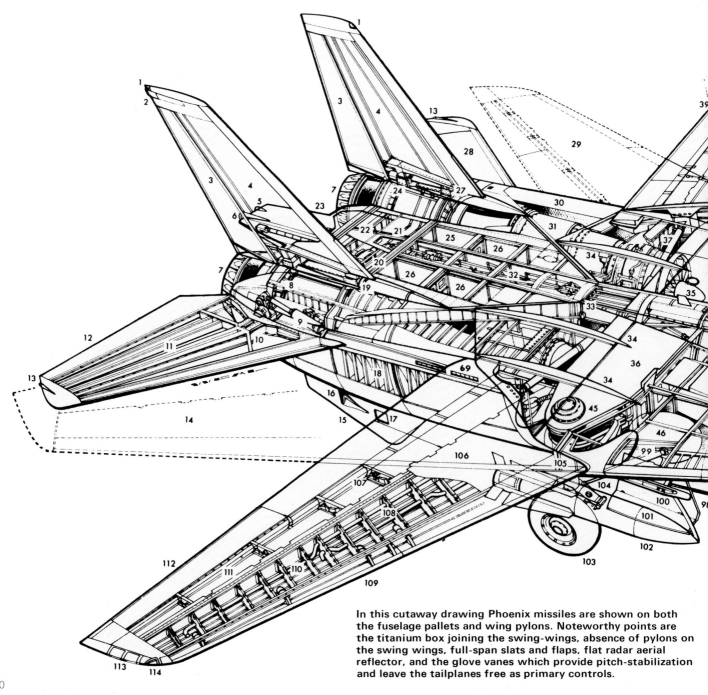

In this cutaway drawing Phoenix missiles are shown on both the fuselage pallets and wing pylons. Noteworthy points are the titanium box joining the swing-wings, absence of pylons on the swing wings, full-span slats and flaps, flat radar aerial reflector, and the glove vanes which provide pitch-stabilization and leave the tailplanes free as primary controls.

1 Anti-collision beacons
2 Countermeasures aerial
3 Honeycomb rudders
4 Honeycomb-sandwich fin skin
5 Rear navigation light
6 Fuel dump line
7 Variable nozzles
8 Engine rear mount/tailplane mounting spectacle beam
9 Tailplane actuator
10 Tailplane pivot mounting
11 Boron-epoxy tailplane
12 Honeycomb trailing edge
13 APR-25 receiving aerial
14 Wing position (fully swept)
15 Ventral fin
16 Engine oil-cooler air intake
17 UHF-band blade aerial
18 Aft fuselage structure
19 Multi-bolt fin attachments
20 Arrester-hook damper
21 Tailplane control linkage
22 Airbrake (upper surface)
23 Revised (reduced) aft fuselage planform (aircraft No 87 onwards)
24 Fin spigot mounting
25 Vent tank
26 Aft fuselage integral tanks

27 Fin root fairing
28 Port tailplane
29 Wing position (fully swept)
30 Inflatable seal (wing fully forward)
31 Port Pratt & Whitney TF30-P-412 turbofan (20,600 lb/9,344 kg thrust with afterburner)
32 Control runs
33 Aft fuselage attachment link
34 Carapace stiffeners (4)
35 VHF aerials
36 Wing spar box pivot support structure (titanium)
37 Wing-fold screw-jack
38 Flap drive shaft
39 Flaps
40 Wingtip formation lights (low intensity)
41 Port navigation light
42 Leading-edge slats
43 Wing integral tank
44 Slat drive shaft
45 Wing pivot
46 Mainwheel wells
47 Inlet bleed air doors
48 ECS (environmental control system) heat exchanger outlets

49 Navigation light (above and below glove vane)
50 Glove vane (open position)
51 Hinged canopy
52 Single-piece canopy frame (forged aluminium)
53 Rear-view mirrors (pilot 3. NFO 1)
54 Detail data display
55 Pilot's ejection seat (Martin-Baker GRU-7A zero-zero)
56 Vertical display indicator group
57 Windscreen (armoured glass)
58 Windscreen rain-removal ducting
59 UHF/ADF aerial
60 Flight refuelling probe (retracted)
61 Windscreen temperature controller
62 AWG-9 planar-array radar scanner
63 IFF array
64 Upward-hinged radome
65 Radar tuning horn
66 Infra-red seeker/TV optical unit
78 Anti-collision beacon
68 Electronics compartment

69 Low-intensity formation lights
70 Ground refuelling point
71 Flight refuelling probe door
72 Rudder pedals
73 Nosewheel doors
74 Catapult tow bar
75 Twin nosewheels
76 Nosewheel leg
77 Retraction jack
78 Lox (liquid-oxygen containers)
79 M61-A1 rotary 20mm cannon below cockpit (port side)
80 ECM receiver/transmitter
81 NFO's ejection seat
82 Aft pressure bulkhead
83 Canopy actuator
84 Transformer rectifiers
85 Air-data computer
86 Machined fuselage frames
87 Forward fuselage integral tanks
88 Main fuselage longerons (titanium)
89 Intake ramp doors (three)
90 Navigation light (above and below glove vane)
91 Glove-vane actuator

92 Pneumatic inlet actuator
93 Wing glove machined spars
94 Glove-vane pivot
95 Inlet upper surface
96 Four Phoenix AAMs in semi-recessed belly installation
97 Intake
98 Mainwheel door
99 Mainwheel drag strut
100 Sidewinder AAM launch-shoe
101 Wing glove stores pylon (cranked)
102 Phoenix AAM
103 Starboard mainwheel
104 Torque links
105 Mainwheel leg
106 Wing skinning
107 Manœuvre-flap actuating linkage
108 Fuel vent and scavenge lines
109 Leading-edge slats
110 Integral wing tank
111 Spoilers
112 Flaps
113 Wingtip formation lights (low intensity)
114 Starboard navigation light

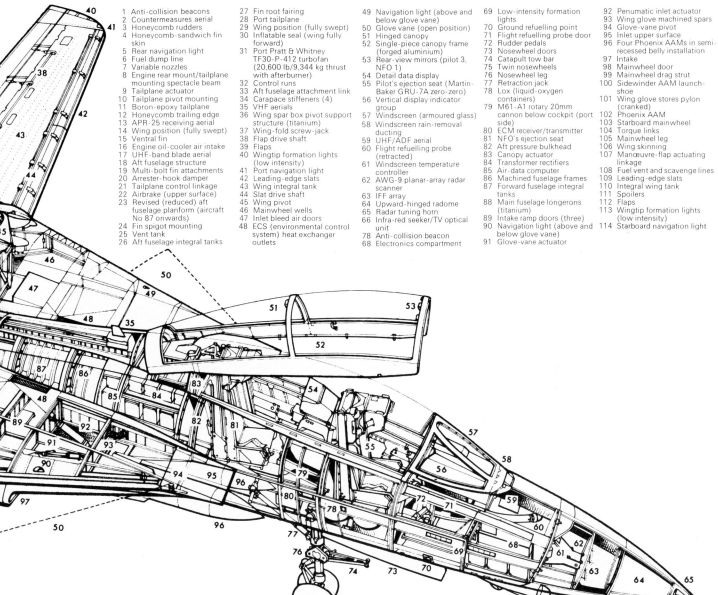

Hawker Siddeley Gnat/HAL Ajeet

Fo 141 Gnat F.1, HAL Gnat and Ajeet, Hawker Siddeley Gnat T.1

Origin: Folland Aircraft (now British Aerospace), UK; Ajeet, Hindustan Aerospace Ltd, India.

Type: (Gnat 1 and Ajeet) single-seat fighter; (Gnat T.1) advanced trainer.

Engine: (Gnat 1) 4,520lb (2050kg) thrust Rolls-Royce (previously Bristol, then Bristol Siddeley) Orpheus 701 single-shaft turbojet; (Gnat II/Ajeet) 4,670lb (2118kg) HAL-built Orpheus 701E; Gnat T.1, 4,230lb (1920kg) Orpheus 101.

Dimensions: Span (1) 22ft 2in (6·75m); (Ajeet) 22ft 1in (6·73m), (T.1) 24ft (7·32m); length (1) 29ft 9in (9·06m), (Ajeet) 29ft 8in (9·04m), (T.1) 31ft 9in (9·65m); height (1, Ajeet) 8ft 10in (2·69m), (T.1) 10ft 6in (3·2m).

Weights: Empty, (1, Ajeet) typically 4,850lb (2200kg); (T.1) 5,613lb (2546kg); loaded (1, Ajeet, clean) 6,650lb (3016kg); (1, Ajeet, with external stores) 8,885lb (4030kg); (T.1, clean) 8,250lb (3742kg); (T.1, maximum) 9,350lb (4240kg).

Performance: Maximum speed, (F.1) 714mph (1150km/h); (T.1) 636mph (1026km/h); initial climb, (F.1) 20,000ft (6096m)/min; (T.1) 9,850ft (3000m)/min; service ceiling, (F.1) over 50,000ft (15,250m); (T.1) 48,000ft (14,600m); range, all versions, maximum fuel, 1,180 miles (1900km).

Armament: (F.1, Ajeet) two 30mm Aden cannon, each with 115 rounds; four underwing hardpoints for 1,100lb (454kg) total load. (T.1) no guns, but same underwing load.

History: First flight (Fo 139 Midge) 11 August 1954; (Fo 141 Gnat) 18 July 1955; (T.1) 31 August 1959; (HAL Gnat) 18 November 1959; final delivery (HAL) early 1973; Ajeet, continuing.

Users: Finland (not operational), India, UK (T.1).

Development: British designer Teddy Petter planned the Gnat to reverse the trend towards larger and more complex combat aircraft, considering a simple lightweight fighter would offer equal performance at much lower cost. Folland Aircraft built the low-powered (1,640lb Viper) Midge as a private venture and eventually gained an order for a development batch of six, the first of which flew in May 1956. India signed a licence agreement in September 1956 and by early 1973 had built 213 at Hindustan Aerospace (HAL) at Bangalore, as well as receiving 25 Mk 1 Gnats and 25 sets of parts from Folland. HAL also built the Orpheus engine. Finland bought 12, three having a three-camera nose for FR duties, and two were supplied to Jugoslavia. The Gnat was modified into a trainer for the RAF, with tandem cockpits, later wing and many other changes and 105 were supplied by Hawker Siddeley (into which Folland was absorbed) in 1962-65. Smoke-

Above: HAL Gnat (one of the last built before the Ajeet programme) photographed in company with an HJT-16 Kiran Mk1.

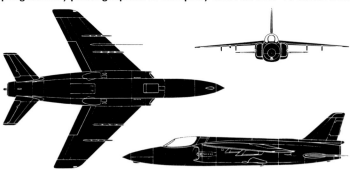

Above: Three-view of the Ajeet, showing four stores pylons.

making Gnat T.1s equip the Red Arrows aerobatic team. In 1969 HAL began to study an improved Gnat which was finally agreed in 1974. Named Gnat II or Ajeet (Unconquerable), it has integral-tank wings housing the same quantity of fuel as was formerly carried in underwing tanks, thus allowing full weapon load to be carried for undiminished range; it also has improved avionics and many minor changes. HAL Gnats are progressively being brought up to this standard. In prolonged combat duty the HAL Gnats have acquitted themselves well and proved most effective in close combat.

Above: This British-built Gnat was a Finnish photo-reconnaissance fighter.

Below: Close-up of a polished HAL Gnat of the Indian Air Force. To achieve a useful combat radius the Gnat has to carry underwing drop tanks, but the Ajeet now in production accommodates the same fuel load in integral wing tanks. Thus the Ajeet combines the same radius as a drop-tanked Gnat with external weapons

Hindustan HF-24 Marut

HAL HF-24 Mk I, IT and II

Origin: Hindustan Aeronautics, India.
Type: Single-seat fighter and ground attack (IT, two-seat trainer).
Engines: Two 4,850lb (2200kg) thrust Rolls-Royce (originally Bristol, then Bristol Siddeley) Orpheus 703 single-shaft turbojets, licence-made by HAL.
Dimensions: Span 26ft 6¼in (9m); length 52ft 0¾in (15·87m); height 11ft 9¾in (3·6m).
Weights: (Mk I) empty 13,658lb (6195kg); loaded (clean) 19,734lb (8951kg); loaded (maximum) 24,085lb (10,925kg).
Performance: Maximum speed, 691mph (1112km/h, Mach 0·91) at sea level, about 675mph (1086km/h, Mach 1·02) at altitude; time to climb to 40,000ft (12,200m) 9min 20sec; range on internal fuel about 620 miles (1000km).
Armament: Four 30mm Aden Mk 2 cannon each with 120 rounds, retractable Matra pack of 50 SNEB 68mm rockets, and four wing pylons each rated at 1,000lb (454kg).
History: First flight 17 June 1961; (pre-production) March 1963; (series production) 15 November 1967; (Mk IT) 30 April 1970.
User: India.

Development: After 1950 the Indian government decided to authorise development of an Indian combat aircraft, and the services of Dipl-Ing Kurt Tank, the renowned Focke-Wulf designer, were secured to lead a new team formed by Hindustan Aircraft at Banglore. Detail design began in 1956, the objective being to create a multi-role aircraft potentially capable of reaching Mach 2 with minimal technical risk. The prototype, powered by two of the same engines already being produced for the Gnat, proved generally successful, and two of the 18 pre-production Maruts ("Wind Spirit") were officially handed over (though as a token delivery) to the IAF in May 1964, the year the company reorganised and expanded into its present form as Hindustan Aeronautics. By the end of 1976 about 100 production Mk Is had been delivered, many of them being used (without loss) in the December 1971 war against Pakistan. The Mk IT has a second Martin-Baker seat in place of the rocket pack and has since 1974 also been produced in small numbers as a dual conversion and weapon trainer. In 1967 the German staff left and an Indian design team has since continued the 20-year search for a more powerful engine. HAL has tested afterburning engines and flew the Marut IBX with one Orpheus replaced by an Egyptian Brandner E-300, but the most likely solution will be the HSS-73 (Marut III) with two Turbo-Union RB.199 engines in a considerably improved airframe. Despite obvious handicaps HAL has already created a useful multi-role platform which could carry radar, cameras or other equipment and has reached a satisfactory state of operational development. The Mk III could continue the same basic design to the end of the century.

Above: Flight-line preparation of Marut Mk I ground-attack fighters. These are early models, built in the late 1960s.

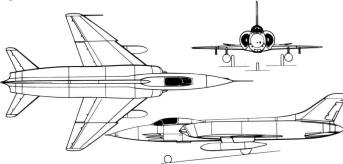

Above: Three-view of HF-24 Marut Mk 1 with drop tanks.

Below: A recent Marut Mk I, with different dielectric (electronic aerial) areas from the examples above. This particular aircraft has metal fairings riveted over the two upper cannon ports. Many Mk IT trainers also have only two guns (four is usual).

Above: Typical production Marut Mk 1.

IAI Kfir

Kfir and Kfir-C2

Origin: Israel Aircraft Industries, Israel.
Type: Single-seat fighter bomber.
Engine: One 17,900lb (8120kg) thrust General Electric J79-17 single-shaft turbojet with afterburner.
Dimensions: Span 26ft 11½in (8·22m); length approximately 54ft (16·5m); height 13ft 11½in (4·25m).
Weights: Empty 14,960lb (6785kg); loaded (fighter mission, half internal fuel, two Shafrir) 20,470lb (9305kg); maximum loaded 32,120lb (14,600kg).
Performance: (Fighter configuration): maximum speed 850mph (1370km/h, Mach 1·12) at sea level, 1,550mph (2495km/h, Mach 2·35) at altitude; initial climb 40,000ft (12,200m)/min; service ceiling, 55,000ft (16,765m); range on internal fuel 700 miles (1125km).
Armament: Two 30mm DEFA 553 cannon, each with 150 rounds; external weapon load up to 8,500lb (3855kg), normally including one ECM pod and two Shafrir air/air missiles.
History: First flight, prior to 1974; service delivery, prior to 1975.
User: Israel.

Development: In the 1950s the beleaguered state of Israel looked principally to France for its combat aircraft and it was mainly with Israeli partnership that Dassault was able to develop the original Mirage IIIC as a combat type. In the fantastic Six-Day War of 5-10 June 1967 the Israeli Mirage IIICJ starred as the most brilliantly flown combat aircraft of modern times; but Dassault was angrily told by Gen de Gaulle not to deliver the improved Mirage 5 attack aircraft which had been developed for Israel and already paid for. With this history it was a foregone conclusion that Israel Aircraft Industries (IAI) at Lod Airport should be directed to apply their great technical expertise to making Israel more self-sufficient in combat aircraft and, in particular, to devising an improved IAI development of the Mirage which could be built in Israel. By 1971 there were reports of a Mirage powered by the J79 engine, supposedly named Barak (Lightning), and such aircraft were even said to have participated in quantity in the 1973 Yom Kippur war. On 14 April 1975 the truth (some of it) escaped when tight Israeli security relented briefly at the public unveiling of the Kfir (Lion Cub). Described as one of the cheapest modern combat aircraft, the Kfir is not a remanufactured IIICJ – though the prototypes were – but a new multi-role fighter bomber making a significant advance over previous delta Mirages. The engine is considerably more powerful and necessitated redesign of the fuselage and addition of a ram-cooling inlet ahead of the fin. The shorter engine results in a shorter rear fuselage, but the nose is much lengthened and equipped with

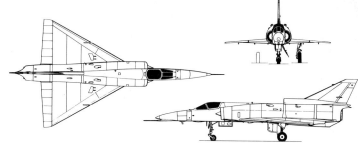

Above: Three-view of IAI Kfir before conversion to C2 standard.

comprehensive avionics. The entire flight-control and weapon delivery system is by IAI companies and a generation later than that even of the Mirage F1. Though the Kfir did not mature in time to participate in the 1973 war, IAI did clear a number of locally built Atar-powered machines called Neshers which took part in that conflict. The Kfir has continued to develop considerably since entering service in early 1975, and by mid-1976 – when about one-third of the planned force of over 100 were in service – details were released of the Kfir-C2. This incorporates a sharply swept fixed foreplane above the wing-root leading edge, dogtooth extensions to the outer wings and small fences on each side of the nose. The C2 has improved takeoff and landing and considerably better flight manoeuvrability. All Kfirs are believed to have one autopilot channel with electric "fly by wire" signalling. Production rate is about four per month, and in 1976 IAI announced that it would welcome export orders, at a unit price (without support or spares) of only about $4·5 million. Discussions were then in progress with Austria and certain S. American countries.

Nesher (Eagle)

When General De Gaulle instructed Dassault not to deliver the Mirage 5 aircraft ordered and paid for by Israel, and developed by Dassault specifically for the Israeli Air Force, IAI was assigned the task of making Israel independent of French help. The ultimate result was the Kfir (see above).but as an interim measure IAI produced a copy of the Mirage 5 with Atar 9C engine. The prototype is reported to have flown in October 1969. Deliveries began in 1972, and about 40 Neshers are said to have participated in the October 1973 war.

Below: A fine picture of an IAI Kfir-C2 pulling round in a tight turn to demonstrate its enhanced manoeuvrability.

McDonnell Douglas
F-101 Voodoo

F-101A, B and C and RF-101A to H

Origin: McDonnell Aircraft Co (division of McDonnell Douglas Corp), USA.
Type: (A, C) day fighter-bomber; (B) all-weather interceptor; (RF) all-weather reconnaissance.
Engines: Two Pratt & Whitney J57 two-shaft turbojets with afterburner; (F-101B) 14,990lb (6800kg) J57-53 or -55 (others) 14,880lb (6750kg) J57-13.
Dimensions: Span 39ft 8in (12·09m); length 67ft 4¾in (20·55m); (RF) 69ft 3in; height 18ft (5·49m).
Weights: Empty (typical of all) 28,000lb (12,700kg); maximum loaded (B) 46,700lb (21,180kg); (all versions, overload 51,000lb, 23,133kg).
Performance: Maximum speed (B) 1,220mph (1963km/h, Mach 1·85); (others, typical) 1,100mph; initial climb (B) 17,000ft (5180m)/min; service ceiling 52,000ft (15,850m); range on internal fuel (B) 1,550 miles (2500km); (others) 1,700 miles (2736km).
Armament: (B) three Falcon (usually AIM-4D) air-to-air missiles semi-submerged in underside, sometimes supplemented by two AIR-2A Genie nuclear rockets on fuselage pylons; (C) three 20mm M-39 cannon (provision for four, with Tacan removed) in fuselage; (RF) none. As built, all A and C and derivatives fitted with centreline crutch for 1 MT tactical nuclear store and wing pylons for two 2,000lb (907kg) bombs, four 680lb (310kg) mines or other ordnance.
History: First flight 29 September 1954; service delivery (A) May 1957; final delivery (B) March 1961.
Users: Canada, Taiwan, USA (ANG).

Development: By far the most powerful fighter of its day, the Voodoo was based on the XF-88 Voodoo prototype flown on 20 October 1948.

Above: RF-101C with (bottom) side view of RF-101G.

Above: RF-101H reconnaissance fighter (G similar).

Originally a long-range escort for Strategic Air Command, the F-101A became a tactical attack machine; 50 were followed by 47 improved C models, all of which set records for accident-free operation and were converted to unarmed RF-101G and H for the Air National Guard, augmenting 35 RF-101A and 166 RF-101C built earlier and used intensively at all levels in Vietnam. The B interceptor sacrificed fuel for a radar operator to work the MG-13 radar fire-control; 478 were built and converted to F-101F or dual-control TF-101F for Air Defense Command (now Air National Guard).

In 1961 66 ex-ADC aircraft were transferred to the RCAF as CF-101s; in 1970 the CAF exchanged the 58 survivors for 66 improved F and TF and there still serve as the only CAF all-weather fighters.

Below: In 1954 the Voodoo, then the world's most powerful fighter, was rejected by the Canadian Air Staff. Today the CAF flies arduous missions with second-hand Voodoos—and they still do a respectable job.

McDonnell Douglas F-4 Phantom II

F-4A to F-4S, RF-4, QF-4, EF-4

Origin: McDonnell Aircraft, division of McDonnell Douglas Corp, St Louis, USA; licence production by Mitsubishi, Japan (F-4EJ) and substantial subcontracting by W German industry.

Type: Originally carrier-based all-weather interceptor; now all-weather multi-role fighter for ship or land operation; (RF) all-weather multisensor reconnaissance; (QF) RPV; (EF) defence-suppression aircraft.

Engines: (B, G) two 17,000lb (7711kg) thrust General Electric J79-8 single-shaft turbojets with afterburner; (C, D) 17,000lb J79-15; (E, EJ, F) 17,900lb (8120kg) J79-17; (J, N, S) 17,900lb J79-10; (K, M) 20,515lb (9305kg) Rolls-Royce Spey 202/203 two-shaft augmented turbofans.

Dimensions: Span 38ft 5in (11·7m); length (B, C, D, G, J, N, S) 58ft 3in (17·76m); (E, EJ, F and all RF versions) 62ft 11in or 63ft (19·2m); (K, M) 57ft 7in (17·55m); height (all) 16ft 3in (4·96m).

Weights: Empty (B, C, D, G, J, N) 28,000lb (12,700kg); (E, EJ, F and RF) 29,000lb (13,150kg); (K, M) 31,000lb (14,060kg); maximum loaded (B) 54,600lb; (C, D, G, J, K, M, N, RF) 58,000lb (26,308kg); (E, EJ, F) 60,630lb (27,502kg).

Performance: Maximum speed with Sparrow missiles only (low) 910mph (1464km/h, Mach 1·19) with J79 engines, 920mph with Spey; (high) 1,500mph (2414km/h, Mach 2·27) with J79 engines, 1,386mph with Spey; initial climb, typically 28,000ft (8534m)/min with J79 engines, 32,000ft/min with Spey; service ceiling, over 60,000ft (19,685m) with J79 engines, 60,000ft with Spey; range on internal fuel (no weapons) about 1,750 miles (2817km); ferry range with external fuel, typically 2,300 miles (3700km) (E and variants, 2,600 miles, 4184km).

Armament: (All versions except EF, RF, QF which have no armament) four AIM-7 Sparrow air-to-air missiles recessed under fuselage; inner wing pylons can carry two more AIM-7 or four AIM-9 Sidewinder missiles; in addition all E versions except RF have internal 20mm M-61 multi-barrel gun, and virtually all versions can carry the same gun in external centreline pod; all except RF, QF have centreline and four wing pylons for tanks, bombs or other stores to total weight of 16,000lb (7257kg).

History: First flight (XF4H-1) 27 May 1958; service delivery (F-4A) February 1960 (carrier trials), February 1961 (inventory); first flight (Air Force F-4C) 27 May 1963; (YF-4K) 27 June 1966; (F-4E) 30 June 1967; (EF-4E) 1976.

Users: W Germany, Greece, Iran, Israel, Japan, Saudi Arabia, Singapore (no contract announced), S Korea, Spain, Turkey, UK (RAF, Royal Navy), USA (Air Force, ANG, Navy, Marine Corps).

continued on page 28 ▶

1 Hinged radome
2 Radar antenna
3 Antenna mounting
4 Radome lock bolts
5 Emergency landing gear system air bottles
6 Radar package (AWG-10)
7 Windscreen rain removal nozzle
8 Emergency brake air bottle
9 Windscreen
10 Optical display unit
11 Forward control stick
12 Manual ejection seat separation handle
13 Instrument panel shroud
14 Push rod
15 Control stick base
16 Rudder pedals
17 Nosewheel drag brace assembly
18 Temperature control assembly
19 Refrigeration unit
20 Nosewheel trunnion
21 Nosewheel command potentiometer
22 Ram air inlet duct
23 Approach/taxi lights
24 Nosewheel leg fairing
25 Torque arm assembly
26 Twin rearward-retracting nosewheels
27 Nosewheel steering power unit
28 Shock strut
29 Retractable steps
30 Entry hand/footholds
31 Seat pan
32 Pilot's ejection seat
33 Pilot's starboard control console
34 Remote rocket initiator
35 Canopy actuating cylinder
36 Face screen handles
37 Variable inlet duct ramp
38 Starboard intake
39 Inflight refuelling probe nozzle
40 Inflight refuelling probe (extended)
41 Support arm
42 Bleed air louvres
43 Aft cockpit canopy
44 Canopy actuating cylinder
45 Aft cockpit starboard console (inertial nav/attack system)
46 Inter-cockpit fixed section window
47 Aft ejection seat

48 Aft control stick
49 Electrical equipment rack
50 Bellcrank
51 Fixed ramp
52 Perforated ramp
53 Boundary air bleed vent
54 Intake
55 Ramp actuator
56 LOX converter
57 Aft solid ramp
58 Flight director computer
59 Bleed air louvre assembly (lower)
60 Air data computer
61 Intake duct
62 Bleed air louvre assembly (upper)
63 Hydraulic reservoir
64 Air bottles (canopy/emergency flap)
65 Stabilator control cable linkage
66 Radio receiver/lead computing gyro and amplifier
67 IFF antenna
68 Wing forward structure (integral fuel)
69 Boundary layer control system
70 Starboard external fuel tank
71 Wing rib assembly (main landing gear support)
72 Front spar
73 Outboard pylon hardpoint
74 Main spar
75 Wing-fold hinge
76 Access doors
77 Outboard leading-edge flap
78 Outer wing section
79 Starboard navigation light
80 Join-up light
81 Starboard droop aileron
82 Wing spoilers
83 Outboard rear spar assembly

84 Starboard trailing-edge flap
85 Inboard rear spar assembly
86 Main landing gear trunnion
87 Mainwheel well
88 Fuel filler access
89 Fuel lines
90 Fuselage No 1 fuel tank
91 Fuselage No 2 fuel tank
92 Bleed air
93 Fuselage structure
94 Fuselage No 3 fuel tank
95 Tacan antenna
96 Ram air turbine (extended)
97 Emergency generator
98 Fuselage No 4 fuel tank
99 Fuselage No 5 fuel tank
100 Arresting gear actuator
101 Overheat detection sensing element
102 Stabilator bellows assembly
103 Fuselage No 6 fuel tank
104 Fuselage No 7 fuel tank
105 Ram air inlet
106 Variable capacitors
107 Starboard stabilator (tailplane)
108 Anti-collision light
109 Pressure pick-up probe and heater
110 Fin front spar
111 Fin structure
112 HF communications antenna
113 Pitot mast
114 Passive warning RF heads

115 Upper UHF communications antenna
116 Rudder upper hinge
117 ILS localiser/glide path aerial
118 Rudder
119 Fuel vent mast
120 Rear navigation light
121 Drag chute door (tail cone)
122 Stabilator
123 Drag chute housing
124 Stabilator hinge
125 Rudder control cylinder
126 Stabilator power control cylinder
127 Arresting hook uplatch mechanism
128 Cooling duct
129 Force link bellcrank
130 Stabilator feel trim system actuator
131 Trim actuator relay panel
132 Undersurface heat-resistant skinning
133 Variable area exhaust nozzle
134 Exhaust collector actuating sleeve
135 Auxiliary air door
136 Turbine cooling leakage air/Rolls-Royce Spey 202 turbofan
137 Engine thermocouple harness
138 Engine front outboard suspension joint
139 Low pressure compressor case
140 Air inlet guide vanes
141 Engine accessories (AC generator/constant speed drive)
142 Oil tank
143 Hydraulic reservoir
144 Landing gear inboard door actuator

145 Port mainwheel well
146 Lateral series servo actuator
147 Flow divider
148 Trailing-edge flap actuating cylinder
149 Access doors
150 Trailing edge flap
151 Droop aileron
152 Aileron viscous damper
153 Aileron power cylinder
154 Dual servo spoiler valve
155 Droop aileron actuating cylinder
156 Hydraulic line (to wing-fold system)
157 Inboard spoiler cylinder
158 Outboard spoiler cylinder
159 Wing-fold actuating cylinder
160 Wing-fold line
161 Wing outer section
162 Join-up light
163 Port navigation light
164 Compass transmitter
165 Outboard leading-edge flap actuating cylinder
166 Outboard leading-edge flap
167 Boundary layer control system
168 Wing-fold hinge
169 Torque links
170 Centre leading-edge flap actuating cylinder
171 Main landing gear shock strut

172 Side brace actuator
173 Main spar
174 Uplock sequence valve
175 Wing fuel tank

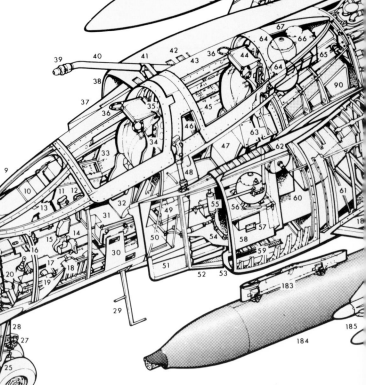

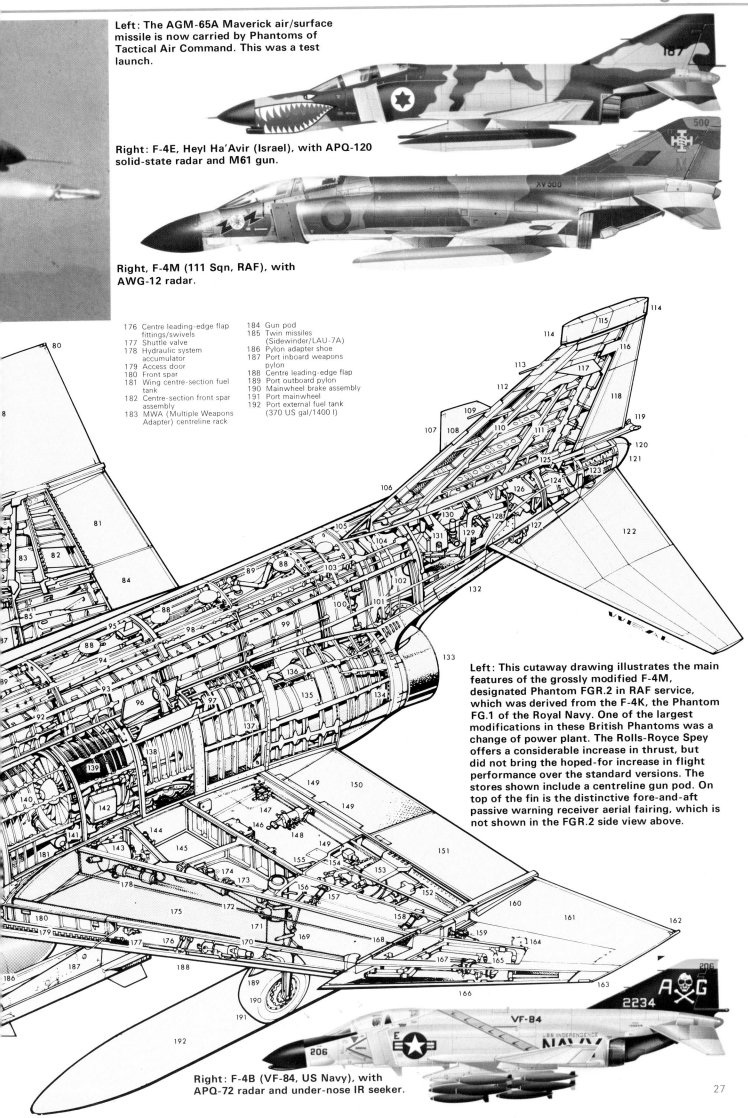

Left: The AGM-65A Maverick air/surface missile is now carried by Phantoms of Tactical Air Command. This was a test launch.

Right: F-4E, Heyl Ha'Avir (Israel), with APQ-120 solid-state radar and M61 gun.

Right, F-4M (111 Sqn, RAF), with AWG-12 radar.

176 Centre leading-edge flap fittings/swivels
177 Shuttle valve
178 Hydraulic system accumulator
179 Access door
180 Front spar
181 Wing centre-section fuel tank
182 Centre-section front spar assembly
183 MWA (Multiple Weapons Adapter) centreline rack

184 Gun pod
185 Twin missiles (Sidewinder/LAU-7A)
186 Pylon adapter shoe
187 Port inboard weapons pylon
188 Centre leading-edge flap
189 Port outboard pylon
190 Mainwheel brake assembly
191 Port mainwheel
192 Port external fuel tank (370 US gal/1400 l)

Left: This cutaway drawing illustrates the main features of the grossly modified F-4M, designated Phantom FGR.2 in RAF service, which was derived from the F-4K, the Phantom FG.1 of the Royal Navy. One of the largest modifications in these British Phantoms was a change of power plant. The Rolls-Royce Spey offers a considerable increase in thrust, but did not bring the hoped-for increase in flight performance over the standard versions. The stores shown include a centreline gun pod. On top of the fin is the distinctive fore-and-aft passive warning receiver aerial fairing, which is not shown in the FGR.2 side view above.

Right: F-4B (VF-84, US Navy), with APQ-72 radar and under-nose IR seeker.

▶**Development:** McDonnell designed the greatest fighter of the postwar era as a company venture to meet anticipated future needs. Planned as an attack aircraft with four 20mm guns, it was changed into a very advanced gunless all-weather interceptor with advanced radar and missile armament. In this form it entered service as the F-4A, soon followed by the F-4B used in large numbers (635) by the US Navy and Marine Corps, with Westinghouse APQ-72 radar, IR detector in a small fairing under the nose, and many weapon options. Pilot and radar intercept officer sit in tandem and the aircraft has blown flaps and extremely comprehensive combat equipment. A level Mach number of 2·6 was achieved and many world records were set for speed, altitude and rate of climb. Not replaced by the abandoned F-111B, the carrier-based Phantom continued in production for 19 years through the F-4G with digital communications, F-4J with AWG-10 pulse-doppler radar, drooping ailerons, slatted tail and increased power, and the N (rebuilt B). In 1961 the F-4B was formally compared with all US Air Force fighters and found to outperform all by a wide margin, especially in weapon load and radar performance. As a result it was ordered in modified form as the F-110, soon redesignated F-4C, for 16 of the 23 Tactical Air Command Wings. The camera/radar/IR linescan RF-4C followed in 1965. In 1964 the Royal Navy adopted the Anglicised F-4K, with wider fuselage housing Spey fan engines and, of 48 delivered to Britain as Phantom FG.1, 28 served with the Royal Navy. The other 20 went to RAF Strike Command, which has also received 120 F-4M (UK designation Phantom FGR.2) which combine the British features with those of the F-4C plus the option of a multi-sensor centreline reconnaissance pod whilst retaining full weapons capability. In the US Air Force the C was followed by the much-improved D with APQ-100 radar replaced by APQ-109, inertial navigation added and many added or improved equipment items. This in turn was followed by the dramatically improved F-4E with slatted wing, internal gun and increased power, the EJ being the version built in Japan and the F being a Luftwaffe version. The Luftwaffe also operate the multi-sensor RF-4E. Australia leased F-4Es from the US government pending delivery of the F-111C. In 1977 deliveries

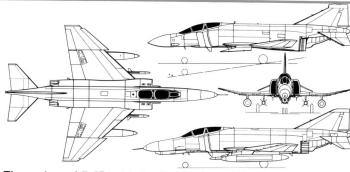

Three-view of F-4E, with (top) side view of F-4M.

of new aircraft, all assembled at St Louis except for the EJ, amounted to just on 5,000, and several batches remained to be built. Most were for export, but a few were outstanding for US services, and very large rebuild programmes were in hand including rebuilding 300 F-4J into F-4S with long-life slatted airframes, rebuilding Marine Corps RF-4Bs with new structure and sensors, rebuilding or refitting over 600 Air Force machines (for example with Pave Tack FLIR/laser pods or Pave Spike TV/laser pods) and complete rebuild of 116 F-4D or E Phantoms into the EF-4E Wild Weasel defence-suppression platform with weapons replaced by special electronics (especially the APR-38 system, with large pod on the fin) to detect, locate and classify hostile electromagnetic emissions, and assist other aircraft to destroy them. Some EF aircraft may do their own killing, with Standard ARM, Shrike and Harm missiles.

Above: F-4D Phantom of Imperial Iranian Air Force.

Above: The only Phantoms not assembled at St Louis are the F-4EJ series built (with major sections shipped in) by Mitsubishi.

Below: Among the most colourful Phantoms are the remotely-piloted QF-4Bs of the US Navy, here with human pilot.

Above: F-4K Phantom FG.1 of 892 Sqn, Royal Navy.

McDonnell Douglas
F-15 Eagle

F-15A, TF-15A

Origin: McDonnell Aircraft, division of McDonnell Douglas Corp, St Louis, USA.

Type: Single-seat all-weather air-superiority fighter; (TF) dual-control trainer.

Engines: Two Pratt & Whitney F100-100 two-shaft augmented turbofans, each rated at 14,871lb (6744kg) thrust dry and 23,810lb (10,800kg) with maximum augmentation.

Dimensions: Span 42ft 9¾in (13·05m); length 63ft 9¾in (19·45m); height 18ft 7½in (5·68m).

Weights: Empty, about 28,000lb (12,700kg); loaded (F or TF, clean) 39,500lb; (F with four Sparrows) about 40,500lb, (three 600gal drop tanks) 54,000lb, (three tanks and two FAST packs) 66,000lb (29,937kg)

Performance: Maximum speed (low) over 921mph (1482km/h, Mach 1·22), (high) over 1,650mph (2660km/h, Mach 2·5); initial climb, over

continued on page 30 ▶

Launch of an AIM-7F Sparrow during weapon trials with F-15 development aircraft. Maximum Sparrow range is 28 miles.

Below: 'Anything you can do, I can do better'—an Eagle lets go a stick of a dozen 1,000lb bombs in a dive-bombing attack, whilst carrying four Sparrow air-to-air missiles.

▶50,000ft (15,240m)/min; service ceiling, over 70,000ft (21,000m); range on internal fuel, about 1,200 miles (1930km); ferry range with maximum fuel, over 3,700 miles (5955km).

Armament: One 20mm M-61 multi-barrel gun with 960 rounds; four AIM-7 Sparrow air-to-air missiles on corners of fuselage and four AIM-9 Sidewinder air-to-air missiles on lateral rails at upper level of wing pylons; centreline pylon stressed for 4,500lb (2041kg) for 600 gal tank, reconnaissance pod or any tactical weapon; inner wing pylons stressed for 5,100lb (2313kg) for any tanks or weapon; outer wing pylons stressed for 1,000lb (454kg) for ECM pods or equivalent ordnance load. Normal external load limit, with or without FAST packs, 12,000lb (5443kg).

History: First flight 27 July 1972; (TF) 7 July 1973; service delivery March 1974 (Cat. II test), November 1974 (inventory).

Users: Israel, USA (Air Force TAC).

Development: Emergence of the MiG-23 and -25 in 1967 accentuated the belief of the US Air Force that it was falling behind in true fighter aircraft. Studies for an FX (a new air-superiority fighter) were hastened and, after a major competition, McDonnell's team at St Louis was selected to build the new aircraft. The Air Force funded a new engine, won by Pratt & Whitney, and a new 25mm gun using caseless ammunition (abandoned after difficult development). The Eagle has emerged as probably the best fighter in the world, with thrust at low levels considerably greater than clean gross weight, a fixed wing of no less than 530 sq ft area, a single seat and an advanced Hughes X-band pulse-doppler radar. Though planned as an uncompromised machine for interception and air combat the Eagle also has formidable attack capability over intercontinental ranges. Undoubtedly its chief attributes are its combat manoeuvrability (it can outfly almost any other US machine without using afterburner) and the advanced automaticity of its radar, head-up display, weapon selectors and quick-fire capability. Internal fuel capacity of 11,200lb can be almost trebled by adding a FAST (fuel and sensor, tactical) pack on each side, a "conformal pallet" housing 10,000lb of fuel and target designators or weapons. Very extensive electronic systems for attack and defence, far beyond any standard previously seen in a fighter, are carried. A total USAF buy of 729 aircraft is planned, and though this has not changed since early in the programme the benefits of the "learning curve" (which reduces costs as production continues) are being much more than nullified by cost-inflation. The unit price of $7·5 million of 1975 had been more than doubled by late 1976 to over $16·7 million, with a figure in excess of $18 million predicted by Congress. Thus the 729 aircraft will now cost at least $12·2 billion, a figure rising by $500–700m each quarter. Nevertheless the outstanding qualities of this superbly capable fighter commend it to many governments; Israel has bought 21 new Eagles plus four reworked development aircraft, costing with support $600 million, and in mid-1976 the F-15 was chosen by Japan as the FX for the Air Self-Defence Force (though as this book went to press no firm programme had been announced). McDonnell Douglas are selling hard to Australia, Canada, France, W Germany and Saudi Arabia.

In 1976 this TF-15 participated in airshows in many countries in this American Revolution Bicentennial livery. It flew the North Atlantic without air refuelling.

1 Nose radome
2 Planar-array radar scanner
3 Hughes APG-63 multi-mode radar
4 Forward bulkhead
5 Instrument panel shroud
6 Head-up display sight
7 Curved windscreen (polycarbonate with cast acrylic surfaces)
8 Polycarbonate one-piece canopy
9 Pilot's headrest
10 Ejection seat (Douglas Escapac)
11 Port control console
12 Nosewheel door
13 Retraction strut
14 Landing/taxi lights
15 Forward-retracting nose-wheel
16 Nosewheel fairing door
17 Port intake
18 Variable inlet ramps
19 Inlet pivot line
20 Port missile station (Sidewinder, Sparrow or advanced missile)
21 Avionics stowage
22 Wing-intake fairing
23 Flight refuelling receptacle
24 Auxiliary intake (and grille)
25 Canopy hinges
26 Provision for second crew member (TF-15)
27 Starboard inlet
28 General Electric M61 20mm gun
29 Ammunition drum, 1,000 rounds
30 Ammunition feed
31 Dorsal speed-brake (shaded, shown retracted)
32 Centre-section fuel tanks (4)
33 Starboard wing tank
34 Vent tank

35 Aluminium wing skinning
36 Honeycomb outboard leading-edge
37 Starboard wingtip aerials
38 Fuel vent pipe
39 Starboard aileron
40 Aileron actuator
41 Flap actuator
42 Starboard flap

43 Starboard Pratt & Whitney F100-PW-100 turbofan

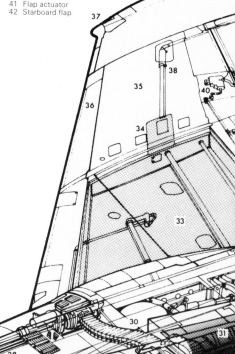

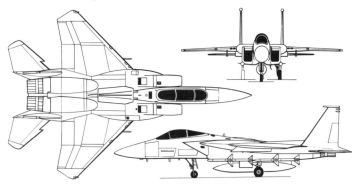

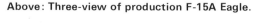

Above: Three-view of production F-15A Eagle.

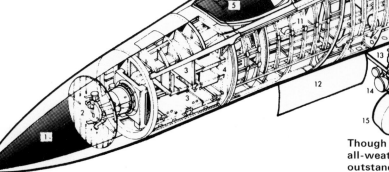

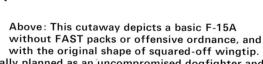

Above: This cutaway depicts a basic F-15A without FAST packs or offensive ordnance, and with the original shape of squared-off wingtip. Though originally planned as an uncompromised dogfighter and all-weather interceptor, the Eagle has been proved to have outstanding capability in certain attack situations demanding very heavy bomb loads delivered at moderate speeds and heights.

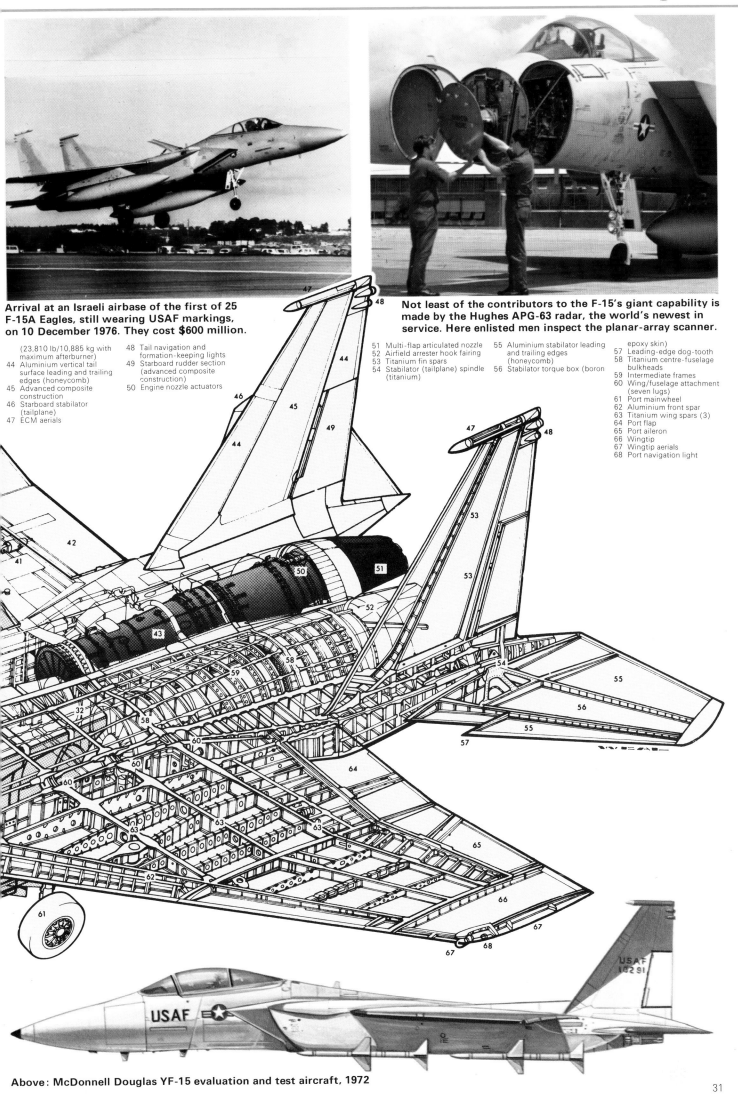

Arrival at an Israeli airbase of the first of 25 F-15A Eagles, still wearing USAF markings, on 10 December 1976. They cost $600 million.

Not least of the contributors to the F-15's giant capability is made by the Hughes APG-63 radar, the world's newest in service. Here enlisted men inspect the planar-array scanner.

(23,810 lb/10,885 kg with maximum afterburner)
44 Aluminium vertical tail surface leading and trailing edges (honeycomb)
45 Advanced composite construction
46 Starboard stabilator (tailplane)
47 ECM aerials
48 Tail navigation and formation-keeping lights
49 Starboard rudder section (advanced composite construction)
50 Engine nozzle actuators

51 Multi-flap articulated nozzle
52 Airfield arrester hook fairing
53 Titanium fin spars
54 Stabilator (tailplane) spindle (titanium)
55 Aluminium stabilator leading and trailing edges (honeycomb)
56 Stabilator torque box (boron epoxy skin)
57 Leading-edge dog-tooth
58 Titanium centre-fuselage bulkheads
59 Intermediate frames
60 Wing/fuselage attachment (seven lugs)
61 Port mainwheel
62 Aluminium front spar
63 Titanium wing spars (3)
64 Port flap
65 Port aileron
66 Wingtip
67 Wingtip aerials
68 Port navigation light

Above: McDonnell Douglas YF-15 evaluation and test aircraft, 1972

McDonnell Douglas/Northrop F-18 Hornet and Cobra

F-18, TF-18 and A-18

Origin: Original basic design, Northrop Corp; prime contractor, McDonnell Douglas Corp, USA, with Northrop building centre and aft fuselage.

Type: (F) single-seat carrier-based multi-role fighter, (TF) dual trainer, (A) single-seat land-based attack fighter.

Engines: Two 16,000lb (7257kg) thrust General Electric F404-400 two-shaft augmented turbofans.

Dimensions: Span (with missiles) 40ft 8½in (12·41m), (without missiles) 37ft 6in (11·42m); length 56ft (17·07m); height 14ft 9½in (4·50m).

Weights: (Provisional) empty 20,583lb (9336kg); loaded (clean) 33,642lb (15,260kg); maximum loaded (catapult limit) 50,064lb (22,710kg).

Performance: Maximum speed (clean, at altitude) 1,190mph (1915km/h, Mach 1·8), (maximum weight, sea level) subsonic; sustained combat manoeuvre ceiling, over 49,000ft (14,935m); absolute ceiling, over 60,000ft (18,290m); combat radius (air-to-air mission, high, no external fuel) 461 miles (741km); ferry range, not less than 2,300 miles (3700km).

Armament: One 20mm M61 Gatling in upper part of forward fuselage; nine external weapon stations for maximum load (catapult launch) of 13,400lb (6080kg), including bombs, sensor pods, ECM, missiles (including Sparrow) and other stores, with tip-mounted Sidewinders.

History: First flight (YF-17) 9 June 1974; (first of 11 test F-18) July 1978; (production F-18) 1980.

User: USA (Navy, Marine Corps).

Above: Takeoff of one of the two Northrop YF-17 development aircraft. These are being used to refine a relaunched Cobra.

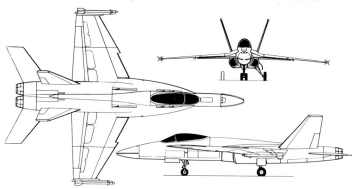

Above: Three-view of F-18 Hornet (A-18 to be similar).

Development: In 1971 the US Navy became concerned at the cost of the F-14 and the resulting reduced rate of procurement and total number that could be afforded. In 1973 it studied low-cost versions and compared them with navalised F-15 versions and improved F-4s. In 1974 the VFX specification emerged for a wholly new and smaller fighter somewhat along the lines of the Air Force Air Combat Fighter. In May 1975 the Navy and Marine Corps announced their choice of the F-18, developed from the existing land-based Northrop F-17 by McDonnell Douglas and Northrop. In fact the F-18 will be almost twice as heavy as the original F-17 proposal but, with more powerful engines, is expected to have adequate dogfight performance through the 1980s. Features include an unswept wing with large dogteeth and forebody strakes at the roots, twin canted vertical tails, simple fixed engine inlets and extensive graphite/epoxy structure. Search radar will be used in the interception and surface-attack roles, and a very wide range of weapons will be carried. In the Navy air-superiority mission the gun will be backed up by two Sparrows and two Sidewinders, and the F-18 is expected to show dramatic improvements over the F-4J in manoeuvrability, reliability and low cost. In Marine attack missions the maximum load can be 14,000lb for airfield operation, and the inertial guidance and weapon-aiming are expected to offer a significant advance over the accuracy of any A-7. The Navy/Marines plan to buy 11 development aircraft plus 800 production machines by the end of 1990 at a unit cost of only $5·924 million in 1975 dollars, without spares. About every ninth aircraft will be a TF mission trainer, with 500lb (272kg) less fuel, rear cockpit (without HUD) and larger canopy.

In late 1976 Northrop — original designer of the YF-17 but a mere sub-contractor on the F-18 — was trying to relaunch the land-based Cobra, but now as a modified F-18. Despite severe competition from the F-16 and other aircraft, Northrop aims to find worldwide sales for the Cobra replacing the F-4, F-104, A-7 and Mirage. It would have less internal fuel than the F-18, and thus even higher performance. Planned export delivery date is 1982, at $8 million in 1975 dollars.

Below: Artist's impression of single-seat Navy F-18 Hornet.

Mikoyan/Gurevich MiG-17

MiG-17, -17P, -17F (Lim-5P and -5M, S-104, F-4), -17PF and -17PFU (NATO name "Fresco")

Origin: The design bureau of Mikoyan and Gurevich, Soviet Union; licence-production as described in the text.
Type: Single-seat fighter; (PF, PFU) limited all-weather interceptor.
Engine: (-17, -17P) one 5,952lb (2700kg) thrust Klimov VK-1 single-shaft centrifugal turbojet; (later versions) one 4,732/7,452lb (3380kg) VK-1F with afterburner.
Dimensions: Span 31ft (9·45m); length (all) 36ft 3in (11·05m); height 11ft (3·35m).
Weights: Empty (all) about 9,040lb (4100kg); loaded (F, clean) 11,773lb (5340kg); maximum (all) 14,770lb (6700kg).
Performance: Maximum speed (F, clean at best height of 9,840ft) 711mph (1145km/h); initial climb 12,795ft (3900m)/min; service ceiling 54,460ft (16,600m); range (high, two drop tanks) 913 miles (1470km).
Armament: (-17) as MiG-15, one 37mm and two 23mm NS-23; (all later versions) three 23mm Nudelmann-Rikter NR-23 cannon, one under right side of nose and two under left; four wing hardpoints for tanks, total of 1,102lb (500kg) of bombs, packs of eight 55mm air-to-air rockets or various air-to-ground missiles.
History: First flight (prototype) January 1950; service delivery, 1952; service delivery (F-4) January 1956; final delivery (Soviet Union) probably 1959.
Users: Afghanistan, Albania, Algeria, Angola, Bulgaria, China, Cuba, Czechoslovakia, Egypt, E Germany, Guinea, Hungary, Indonesia (in storage), Iraq, Kampuchea, N Korea, Mali, Morocco (in storage), Nigeria, Poland, Romania, Somalia, S Yemen, Soviet Union, Sri Lanka, Sudan, Syria, Tanzania, Uganda, Vietnam, Yemen Arab.

Development: Only gradually did Western observers recognise the MiG-17 as not merely a slightly modified MiG-15 but a completely different aircraft. Even then it was generally believed it had been hastily designed to rectify deficiencies shown in the MiG-15's performance in Korea, but in fact the design began in about January 1949, long before the Korean war. This was because from the first the MiG-15 had shown bad behaviour at high speeds, and though the earlier fighter was eventually made completely safe (partly by arranging for the air brakes to open automatically at Mach 0·92) it was still a difficult gun platform due to its tendency to snake and pitch. The MiG-17 — which was probably the last fighter in which Gurevich played a direct personal role — had a new wing with thickness reduced from 11 per cent to about 9 per cent, a different section and planform and no fewer than

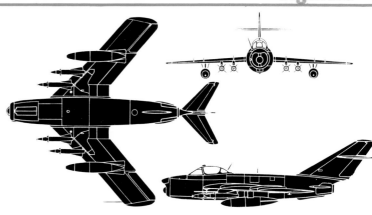

Above: Three-view of typical MiG-17F (NATO name, "Fresco C").

three fences. Without taper and with inboard sweep of 47° this made a big difference to high-Mach behaviour, and in fact there are reasons to believe the MiG-17 can be dived to make a sonic bang. With a new tail on a longer rear fuselage the transformation was completed by considerable revision of systems and equipment, though at first the VK-1 engine was unchanged. In 1958 the first limited all-weather version, the -17P, went into modest production with longer nose housing the same Izumrud ("Scan Odd") AI radar and ranging avionics as was also in production for the MiG-19. With the introduction of an afterburning engine the airbrakes were moved aft of the wing, away from the hot back end, but this was not a good position and they were returned (in enlarged rectangular form) to the tail in the most important sub-type the -17F. This was made in Poland as the Lim-5P (the -5M being a rough-field close-support version with larger tyres and drag chute), in Czechoslovakia as the S-104 and in China as the F-4. The PF was the afterburning all-weather version, and the final model was the PFU with guns removed and wing pylons for four beam-riding "Alkali" air-to-air missiles. Total production for at least 22 air forces must have considerably exceeded 5,000, exports from China alone exceeding 1,000. Many 17F remained in use in the mid-1970s.

Above: MiG-17F of Syrian Air Force (Federation insignia).

Bottom left: Early MiG-17 fighters in service with the AV-MF (Soviet naval air force) Black Sea Fleet, around 1953. At first Western intelligence mistakenly thought the MiG-17 merely a modified -15, the pioneer swept-wing MiG that was such a shock when encountered by Allied pilots over Korea in 1950–51. The MiG-17 did not participate in the Korean war.

Below: A dramatic picture, taken by the combat camera of a USAF F-4 Phantom, showing the last moment of a MiG-17F of the Vietnam People's Air Force. The white shape near the left tailplane is a Sidewinder missile. The MiG is in a tight turn at about 400 knots at low/medium level, typical dogfight conditions.

Above: Chinese-built F-4 of Kampuchea (formerly Cambodia) Air Force.

Mikoyan/Gurevich MiG-19

MiG-19, -19S, -19SF (Lim-7, S-105, F-6), -19PF and -19PM; NATO name "Farmer"

Origin: The design bureau named for Mikoyan and Gurevich, Soviet Union; licence-production as described in the text.

Type: Single-seat fighter (PF, PM, all-weather interceptor).

Engines: (-19, -19S) two 6,700lb (3,040kg) thrust (afterburner rating) Mikulin AM-5 single-shaft afterburning turbojets; (-19SF, PF, PM) two 7,165lb (3250kg) thrust (afterburner) Klimov RD-9B afterburning turbojets.

Dimensions: Span 29ft 6½in (9m); length (S, SF, excluding pitot boom) 42ft 11¼in (13·08m); (-19PF, PM) 44ft 7in; height 13ft 2¼in (4·02m).

Weights: Empty (SF) 12,698lb (5760kg); loaded (SF, clean) 16,755lb (7600kg); (maximum, SF) 19,180lb (8700kg); (PM) 20,944lb (9500kg).

Performance: Maximum speed (typical) 920mph at 20,000ft (1480km/h, Mach 1·3); initial climb (SF) 22,640ft (6900m)/min; service ceiling (SF) 58,725ft (17,900m); maximum range (high, with two drop tanks) 1,367 miles (2200km).

Armament: See text.

History: First flight, September 1953; service delivery early 1955; first flight (F-6) December 1961.

Users: Afghanistan, Albania, Bulgaria, China, Cuba, Czechoslovakia, E Germany (not operational), Hungary, Indonesia (in storage), Iraq, N Korea, Pakistan, Poland, Romania, Soviet Union, Tanzania, Uganda (ex-Iraq), Vietnam.

Development: With the MiG-19 the Mikoyan-Gurevich bureau established itself right in the front rank of the world's fighter design teams. The new fighter was on the drawing board as the I-350 before even the MiG-15 had been encountered in Korea, the five prototypes being ordered on 30 July 1951. Maj. Grigori Sedov flew the first aircraft on 18 September 1953 on the power of two non-afterburning AM-5 engines giving only 4,410lb thrust each. Nevertheless, despite the high wing loading and bold sweep angle of

continued on page 36▶

1 Rear navigation light
2 Amplifier for rear-warning radar
3 Access panels
4 Fin structure
5 Rudder
6 Pen-nib exhaust fairing
7 Slab tailplane
8 Anti-flutter weights
9 Afterburners
10 Tail bumper
11 Afterburner cooling air intakes
12 Fin fillet
13 Braking parachute packing panel
14 Ventral strake
15 Aft fuel tanks
16 Starboard airbrake
17 Fuel filler cap
18 Oil tanks
19 Fuselage break point
20 Fuel dump vents
21 Port auxiliary tank (176 gal/800 litres)
22 Port navigation lamp
23 Port wing fence (full chord)
24 Wing structure
25 Dorsal spine (control rod tunnel)
26 Ram air intake
27 Air conditioning system
28 Klimov RD-9B turbojets 7,165 lb/3,250 kg with afterburner)
29 Main tanks
30 VHF aerial
31 Rear-sliding canopy
32 Ejection seat
33 Optical gunsight
34 Instrument panel
35 Pilot's controls
36 Control column
37 Foot pedals
38 Accumulator
39 Radio altimeter transmitter receiver
40 VHF transmitter
41 VHF receiver
42 Starboard inlet duct
43 Combat camera
44 Bifurcated intake
45 Pitot head (hinged)
46 Nosewheel retraction cylinder
47 Landing light (port side)
48 Forward-retracting nose-wheel
49 Cannon muzzle-brake
50 Taxi-ing light
51 Nosewheel doors
52 30mm NR-30 cannon
53 Case chute
54 Starboard 30mm NR-30 cannon
55 Compressed air bottle
56 Ammunition feed
57 Radio altimeter dipole
58 Perforated ventral airbrake
59 Main undercarriage door
60 Mainwheel retraction cylinder
61 Levered-suspension main landing-gear
62 Starboard mainwheel
63 Auxiliary tank pylon
64 Starboard auxiliary tank (176 gal/800 litres)
65 Starboard navigation lamp

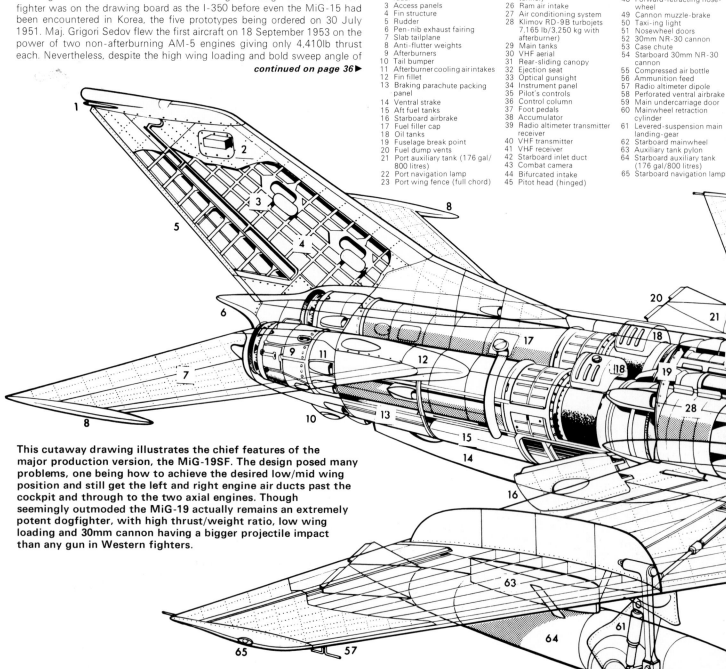

This cutaway drawing illustrates the chief features of the major production version, the MiG-19SF. The design posed many problems, one being how to achieve the desired low/mid wing position and still get the left and right engine air ducts past the cockpit and through to the two axial engines. Though seemingly outmoded the MiG-19 actually remains an extremely potent dogfighter, with high thrust/weight ratio, low wing loading and 30mm cannon having a bigger projectile impact than any gun in Western fighters.

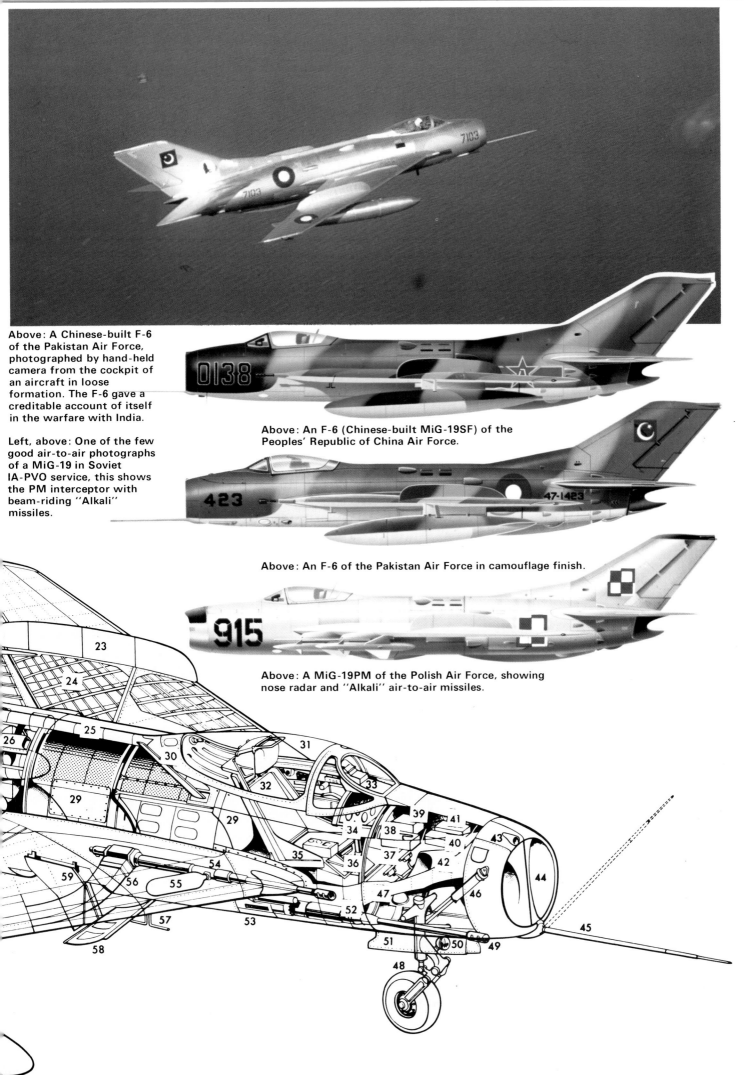

Above: A Chinese-built F-6 of the Pakistan Air Force, photographed by hand-held camera from the cockpit of an aircraft in loose formation. The F-6 gave a creditable account of itself in the warfare with India.

Left, above: One of the few good air-to-air photographs of a MiG-19 in Soviet IA-PVO service, this shows the PM interceptor with beam-riding "Alkali" missiles.

Above: An F-6 (Chinese-built MiG-19SF) of the Peoples' Republic of China Air Force.

Above: An F-6 of the Pakistan Air Force in camouflage finish.

Above: A MiG-19PM of the Polish Air Force, showing nose radar and "Alkali" air-to-air missiles.

▶55° (at 25% chord), the MiG-19 handled well, large fences and Fowler flaps giving satisfactory low-speed control. With afterburning engines the MiG-19 became the first Russian supersonic fighter and it was put into production on a very large scale, rivalling that of the MiG-15 and -17, despite a 100 per cent increase in price. After about 500 had been delivered the MiG-19S (*stabilizator*) supplanted the early model with the fixed tailplane and manual elevators replaced by a fully powered slab. At the same time the old armament (unchanged since MiG-15 and -17) was replaced by three of the new 30mm NR-30 guns, one in each wing root and one under the right side of the nose. A large ventral airbrake was also added. In 1956 the AM-5 engine was replaced by the newer and more powerful RD-9, increasing peak Mach number from 1·1 to 1·3. The new fighter was designated MiG-19SF (*forsirovanni*, increased power), and has been built in very large numbers. Total production possibly exceeds 10,000, including licence-manufacture as the Lim-7 in Poland, S-105 in Czechoslovakia and F-6 in China. The corresponding MiG-19PF (*perekhvatchik*, interceptor) has an Izumrud AI radar (called "Scan Odd" by NATO) in a bullet carried on the inlet duct splitter, with the ranging unit in the upper inlet lip, changing the nose shape and adding 22in to the aircraft length. The final production version was the MiG-19PM (*modifikatsirovanni*), with guns removed and pylons for four early beam-rider air-to-air missiles (called "Alkali" by NATO). All MiG-19s can carry the simple K-13A missile (the copy of Sidewinder, called "Atoll" by NATO) and underwing pylons can carry two 176 gal drop tanks plus two 551lb weapons or dispensers. Perhaps surprisingly, there has been no evidence of a two-seat trainer version of this fine fighter, which in 1960 was judged obsolescent and in 1970 was fast being reappraised as an extremely potent dogfighter. Part of the understanding of the MiG-19's qualities has resulted from its purchase in large numbers by Pakistan as the F-6 from the Chinese factory at Shenyang. The notable features of the F-6 were its superb finish, outstanding dogfight manoeuvrability and tremendous hitting power of the NR-30 guns, each projectile having more than twice the kinetic energy of those of the Aden or DEFA of similar calibre. Though China soon ceased making the MiG-21 the F-6 remains in production, and has even been developed into the F-9.

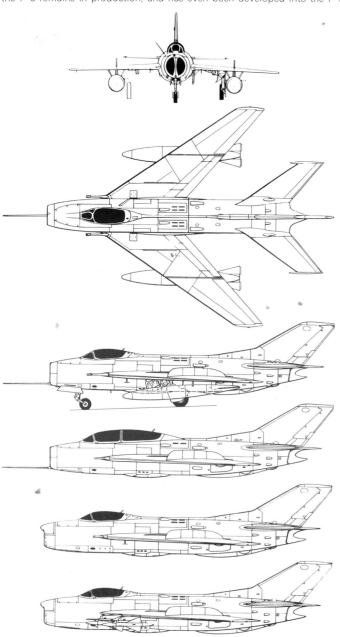

MiG-19 variants: top three views, F-6 (-19SF); then (top to bottom) MiG-19U, -19PF and -19PM with missiles.

Mikoyan/Gurevich MiG-23

MiG-23, -23S and -23U ("Flogger")

Origin: The design bureau named for Mikoyan and Gurevich, Soviet Union; no production outside the Soviet Union yet reported.

Type: (-23S, Flogger B) single-seat all-weather interceptor with Flogger E export variant of unknown designation; (-23U, Flogger C) dual-control trainer and ECM platform.

Engine: One Tumansky afterburning turbofan of unknown type, rated at about 14,500lb (6577kg) dry and 20,500lb (9300kg) with maximum afterburner.

Dimensions: (Estimated) Span (72° sweep) 28ft 7in (8·7m), (16°) 47ft 3in (14·4m); length (export) 53ft (16·15m), (S, U) 55ft 1½in (16·80m); height 13ft (3·96m).

Weights: (Estimated) empty 17,500lb (7940kg); loaded (clean or fighter mission) 30,000lb (13,600kg); maximum permissible 33,000lb (15,000kg).

Performance: Maximum speed, clean, 840mph (1350km/h, Mach 1·1) at sea level; maximum speed, clean, at altitude, 1,520mph (2445km/h, Mach 2·2); maximum Mach number with missiles (MiG-23S) about 2; service ceiling about 55,000ft (16,765m); combat radius (hi-lo-hi) about 400 miles (640km).

Armament: (-23S) one 23mm GSh-23 twin-barrel gun on ventral centreline, plus various mixes of air/air missiles which usually include one or two infra-red or radar-homing AA-7 "Apex" and/or infra-red or radar-homing AA-8 "Aphid", the latter for close combat; (-23U) none reported.

History: First flight, probably 1965; (first production aircraft) believed 1970; service delivery, believed 1971.

Users: E Germany, Iraq, Libya, Poland, Soviet Union, Syria (and almost certainly other countries in 1977).

Development: Revealed at the 1967 Moscow Aviation Day, the prototype swing-wing MiG-23 was at first thought to be a Yakovlev design, though it appeared in company with a jet-lift STOL fighter having an identical rear fuselage and tail and strong MiG-21-like features (though much bigger

than a MiG-21). Over the next four years the Mikoyan bureau greatly developed this aircraft, which originally owed something to the F-111 and Mirage G. By 1971 the radically different production versions, the -23S fighter and -23U trainer, were entering service in quantity, and by 1975 several hundred had been delivered to Warsaw Pact air forces and also to Egypt. Today Egypt is believed no longer to operate the type, but large deliveries have been made to other countries. The MiG-27 attack version is described separately.

There are three main versions. The first to enter service was the MiG-23S all-weather interceptor, with powerful highly-afterburning engine, "High Lark" nose radar (said in 1973 by the then Secretary of the USAF to be "comparable with that of the latest Phantom") and, almost certainly, a laser ranger and doppler navigator. ECM and other EW equipment is markedly superior to anything fitted in previous Soviet aircraft, and apparently as good as comparable installations in Western fighters (other than the F-15).

Several hundred S models are in service with the IA-PVO and Warsaw Pact air forces, and they are replacing the Su-9 and -11 and Yak-28P. Missiles are carried on a centreline pylon (which often carries a drop-tank instead), on pylons under the inlet ducts and under the fixed wing gloves (centre section). For overseas customers a simplified sub-type is in production, with the same high-Mach airframe and systems as the -23S fighter but lacking the latter's radar (NATO calls this model "Flogger E" but the Soviet designation is unknown as this book went to press). The third MiG-23 so far seen is the tandem two-seat -23U, used for conversion training and as an ECM and reconnaissance platform. This again has the fighter's high-speed airframe and systems, but has not been seen with any weapons or delivery systems.

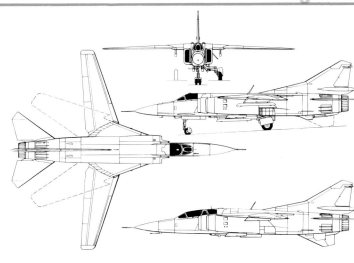

Above: Three-view of MiG-23S, with side view of MiG-23U trainer (lower right).

Below: Called "Flogger E" by NATO, this export version of the MiG-23B is fitted with a radar of lower power, with a smaller radome. This one belongs to the Libyan Air Force, which also has the MiG-23U trainer.

Above: A MiG-23S all-weather fighter of the Soviet IA-PVO.

Mikoyan/Gurevich MiG-21

MiG-21, 21F (S-107), 21FA, 21PF, 21FL, 21PFS, 21PFM, 21PFMA, 21M, 21R, 21MF, 21SMT, 21bis, 21U, 21US and 21UM plus countless special versions. Several versions made in China as F-8

Origin: The design bureau named for Mikoyan and Gurevich; Soviet Union; licence-production as described in the text.

Type: Single-seat fighter; (PFMA and MF) limited all-weather multi-role; (R) reconnaissance; (U) two-seat trainer.

Engine: In all versions, one Tumansky single-shaft turbojet with afterburner; (-21) R-11 rated at 11,240lb (5100kg) with afterburner; (-21F) R-11-F2-300 rated at 13,120lb (5950kg); (-21FL, PFS, PFM and PFMA) R-11-G2S-300 rated at 13,668lb (6200kg); (-21MF and derivatives) R-13-300 rated at 14,500lb (6600kg).

Dimensions: Span 23ft 5½in (7·15m); length (excluding probe) (-21) 46ft 11in; (-21MF) 48ft 0½in (14·6m); height (little variation, but figure for MF) 14ft 9in (4·5m).

Weights: Empty (-21) 11,464lb (5200kg); (-21MF) 12,346lb (5600kg); maximum loaded (-21) 18,740lb (8500kg); (-21MF) 21,605lb (9800kg) (weight with three tanks and two K-13A, 20,725lb).

Performance: Maximum speed (MF, but typical of all) 1,285mph (2070km/h, Mach 2·1); initial climb (MF, clean) 36,090ft (11,000m)/min; service ceiling 59,050ft (18,000m); range (high, internal fuel) 683 miles (1100km); maximum range (MF, high, three tanks) 1,118 miles (1800km).

Armament: See text.

History: First flight (E-5 prototype) late 1955; (production -21F) late 1957; service delivery early 1958.

Users: Afghanistan, Albania, Algeria, Angola, Bangladesh, Bulgaria, China, Cuba, Czechoslovakia, Egypt, Finland, E Germany, India, Indonesia (in storage), Iraq, Nigeria, N Korea, Poland, Romania, Somalia, Soviet Union, Sudan, S Yemen, Syria, Tanzania, Uganda, Vietnam, Yemen Arab, Yugoslavia.

Development: Undoubtedly the most widely used combat aircraft in the world in the 1970s, this trim little delta has destablished a reputation for cost effectiveness and in its later versions it also packs a more adequate multi-role punch. It was designed in the 18 months following the Korean War. While Sukhoi developed large supersonic fighters to rival the American F-100, the Mikoyan-Gurevich bureau, by now led only by Col-Gen Mikoyan (who died in 1970), concentrated on a small day interceptor of the highest possible performance. Prototypes were built with both swept and delta wings, both having powered slab tailplanes, and the delta was chosen for production. At least 30 pre-production aircraft had flown by the time service delivery started and the development effort was obviously considerable. The initial MiG-21 abounded in interesting features including Fowler flaps, fully powered controls, upward ejection seat fixed to the rear of the front-hinged canopy (which incorporated the whole front of the cockpit enclosure except the bullet-proof windshield) to act as a pilot blast-shield, and internal fuel capacity of only 410 gal. Armament was two 30mm NR-30 in long fairings under the fuselage, the left gun usually being replaced by avionics. Part of these avionics serve the two K-13 ("Atoll") missiles carried on wing pylons on the slightly more powerful 21F. This had radar ranging, 515 gal fuel, broader fin, upward-hinged pitot boom attached under the nose (to prevent people walking into it) and two dorsal blade aerials. Czech-built

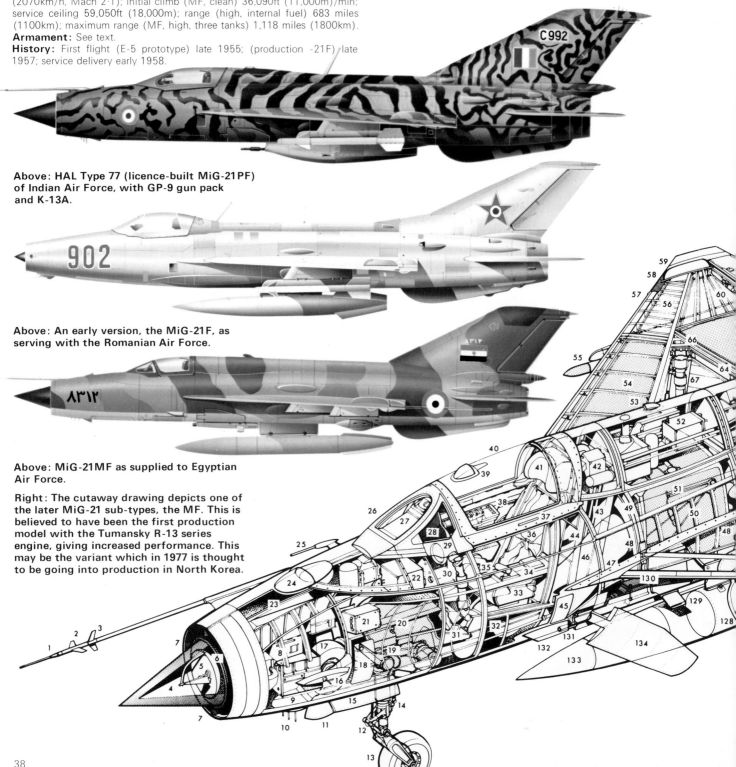

Above: HAL Type 77 (licence-built MiG-21PF) of Indian Air Force, with GP-9 gun pack and K-13A.

Above: An early version, the MiG-21F, as serving with the Romanian Air Force.

Above: MiG-21MF as supplied to Egyptian Air Force.

Right: The cutaway drawing depicts one of the later MiG-21 sub-types, the MF. This is believed to have been the first production model with the Tumansky R-13 series engine, giving increased performance. This may be the variant which in 1977 is thought to be going into production in North Korea.

aircraft (still called 21F) did not have the rear-view windows in the front of the dorsal spine. The F was called "Fishbed C" by NATO and Type 74 by the Indian Air Force; it was also the type supplied to China in 1959 and used as the pattern for the Chinese-built F-8. As the oldest active variant it was also the first exported or seen in the West, the Finnish AF receiving the 21F-12 in April 1963.

At Tushino in 1961 the prototype was displayed of what became the 21PF, with inlet diameter increased from 27in to 36in, completely changing the nose shape and providing room for a large movable centre-body housing

continued on page 40 ▶

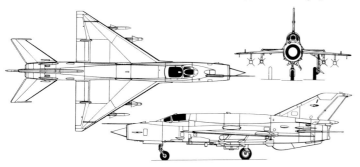

Above: Three-view of MiG-21SMT ("Fishbed K") with four K-13A missiles.

Above: The chief sub-type of the MiG-21 in service with the Soviet IA-PVO is called "Fishbed L" by NATO, its exact Soviet designation being unknown. It is essentially an MF with a Tacan-type navigation/homing system.

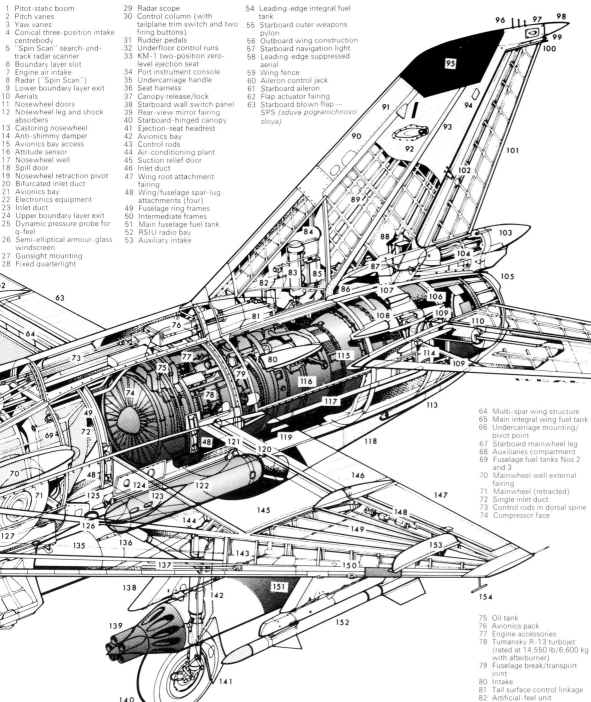

1 Pitot-static boom
2 Pitch vanes
3 Yaw vanes
4 Conical three-position intake centrebody
5 "Spin Scan" search-and-track radar scanner
6 Boundary layer slot
7 Engine air intake
8 Radar ("Spin Scan")
9 Lower boundary layer exit
10 Aerials
11 Nosewheel doors
12 Nosewheel leg and shock absorbers
13 Castoring nosewheel
14 Anti-shimmy damper
15 Avionics bay access
16 Attitude sensor
17 Nosewheel well
18 Spill door
19 Nosewheel retraction pivot
20 Bifurcated inlet duct
21 Avionics bay
22 Electronics equipment
23 Inlet duct
24 Upper boundary layer exit
25 Dynamic pressure probe for q-feel
26 Semi-elliptical armour-glass windscreen
27 Gunsight mounting
28 Fixed quarterlight

29 Radar scope
30 Control column (with tailplane trim switch and two firing buttons)
31 Rudder pedals
32 Underfloor control runs
33 KM-1 two-position zero-level ejection seat
34 Port instrument console
35 Undercarriage handle
36 Seat harness
37 Canopy release/lock
38 Starboard wall switch panel
39 Rear-view mirror fairing
40 Starboard-hinged canopy
41 Ejection-seat headrest
42 Avionics bay
43 Control rods
44 Air-conditioning plant
45 Suction relief door
46 Inlet duct
47 Wing root attachment fairing
48 Wing/fuselage spar-lug attachments (four)
49 Fuselage ring frames
50 Intermediate frames
51 Main fuselage fuel tank
52 RSIU radio bay
53 Auxiliary intake

54 Leading-edge integral fuel tank
55 Starboard outer weapons pylon
56 Outboard wing construction
57 Starboard navigation light
58 Leading-edge suppressed aerial
59 Wing fence
60 Aileron control jack
61 Starboard aileron
62 Flap actuator fairing
63 Starboard blown flap — SPS (sduva pogranichnovo sloya)

64 Multi-spar wing structure
65 Main integral wing fuel tank
66 Undercarriage mounting/pivot point
67 Starboard mainwheel leg
68 Auxiliaries compartment
69 Fuselage fuel tanks Nos 2 and 3
70 Mainwheel well external fairing
71 Mainwheel (retracted)
72 Single inlet duct
73 Control rods in dorsal spine
74 Compressor face
75 Oil tank
76 Avionics pack
77 Engine accessories
78 Tumansky R-13 turbojet (rated at 14,550 lb/6,600 kg with afterburner)
79 Fuselage break/transport joint
80 Intake
81 Tail surface control linkage
82 Artificial-feel unit
83 Tailplane power unit
84 Hydraulic accumulator
85 Tailplane trim motor
86 Fin-spar attachment plate
87 Rudder power unit
88 Rudder control linkage
89 Fin structure

90 Leading-edge panel
91 Radio cable access
92 Magnetic detector
93 Fin mainspar
94 RSIU (radio-stantsiya istrebitelnaya ultrakorotkykh vol'n — very-shortwave fighter radio) aerial plate
95 VHF/UHF aerials
96 IFF aerial
97 Formation light
98 Tail warning radar
99 Rear navigation light
100 Fuel vent
101 Rudder construction
102 Rudder hinge
103 Braking-parachute hinged fairing
104 Braking parachute stowage
105 Tailpipe (variable convergent nozzle)
106 Afterburner installation
107 Afterburner bay cooling intake
108 Tailplane linkage fairing
109 Nozzle actuating cylinders
110 Tailplane torque tube
111 All-moving tailplane
112 Anti-flutter weight
113 Intake
114 Afterburner mounting
115 Fixed tailplane root fairing
116 Longitudinal lap joint
117 External duct (nozzle hydraulics)
118 Ventral fin
119 Engine guide rail
120 JATO rocket canted nozzle

121 JATO rocket thrust plate forks (rear mounting)
122 JATO pack
123 Ventral airbrake (retracted)
124 Trestle point
125 JATO release solenoid (front mounting)
126 Underwing landing light
127 Ventral stores pylon
128 Mainwheel inboard door
129 Splayed link chute
130 Twin 23mm GSh-23 cannon installation
131 Cannon muzzle fairing
132 Debris deflector plate
133 Auxiliary ventral drop tank
134 Port forward air brake (extended)
135 Leading-edge integral fuel tank
136 Undercarriage retraction strut
137 Aileron control rods in leading edge
138 Port inboard weapons pylon
139 UV-16-57 rocket pod
140 Port mainwheel
141 Mainwheel outboard door section
142 Mainwheel leg
143 Aileron control linkage
144 Mainwheel leg pivot point
145 Main integral wing fuel tank
146 Flap actuator fairing
147 Port aileron
148 Aileron control jack
149 Outboard wing construction
150 Port navigation light
151 Port outboard weapons pylon
152 "Advanced Atoll" infrared-guided AAM
153 Wing fence
154 Radio altimeter aerial

▶ the scanner of the R1L (NATO "Spin Scan") AI radar. Other changes include deletion of guns (allowing simpler forward airbrakes), bigger mainwheels (causing large fuselage bulges above the wing), pitot boom moved above the inlet, fatter dorsal spine (partly responsible for fuel capacity of 627gal) and many electronic changes. All PF had an uprated engine, late models had take-off rocket latches and final batches had completely new blown flaps (SPS) which cut landing speed by 25mph and reduced nose-up attitude for better pilot view. The FL was the export PF (L = *lokator*, denoting R2L radar) with even more powerful engine. Like the F models rebuilt in 1963-64, this can carry the GP-9 gunpack housing the excellent GSh-23 23mm twin-barrel gun, has a still further broadened vertical tail and dragchute repositioned above the jetpipe. The PFS was the PF with SPS blown flaps, while the PFM was a definitive improved version with another 19in added to the fin (final fillet eliminated), a conventional seat and side-hinged canopy, and large flush aerials in the fin. One-off versions were built to prove STOL with lift jets and to fly a scaled "analogue" of the wing of the Tu-144 SST. The very important PFMA, made in huge numbers, was the first multi-role version, with straight top line from much deeper spine (housing equipment and not fuel and holding tankage to 572gal), and four pylons for two 1,100lb and two 551lb bombs, four S-24 missiles and/or tanks or K-13A missiles. The 21M has an internal GSh-23 and since 1973 has been built in India as Type 88. The 21R has multi-sensor reconnaissance internally and in pods and wing-tip ECM fairings, as do late models of the 21MF, the first to have the R-13 engine. The RF is the R-13-powered reconnaissance version. One of the few variants still in production is the SMT, with fuel restored to the spine and more comprehensive avionics including tail-warning radar.

Code-named "Mongol" and called Type 66 in India, the U is the tandem trainer, the US has SPS flaps and UM the R-13 engine and four pylons. Many other versions have been used to set world records. About 10,000 of all sub-types have been built, and in 1977 output was continuing at perhaps three per week in the Soviet Union, with a much lower rate in India; in early 1976 N Korea was said to be also in production. Many of the early models of this neat fighter were sweet to handle and quite effective day dogfighters, but the majority of the subtypes in use have many adverse characteristics and severe limitations.

In late 1976 a new version appeared, the MiG-21bis (Fishbed L); this is a cleaned-up and refined MiG-21MF with Tacan-type navigation and other improvements.

Top: This frame from a Soviet motion picture shows a MiG-21, probably a PFM, blasting off with the aid of two large JATO (jet-assisted takeoff) boost rockets, used by many versions.

Above: Hardware counts for more than paint, and the variable (and crude) paintwork on these HAL-built Type 77 (MiG-21FL) does no harm. This was the first model made in India.

Mikoyan/Gurevich MiG-25

Mig-25 ("Foxbat A"), -25R and -25U

Origin: The design bureau named for Mikoyan and Gurevich, Soviet Union.
Type: "Foxbat A" (believed to be MiG-25S), all-weather long-range interceptor; MiG-25R, reconnaissance; MiG-25U, tandem-seat dual trainer with stepped cockpits.
Engines: Two Tumansky R-266 afterburning turbojets each rated at 24,500lb (11,110kg) with full augmentation.
Dimensions: Span 46ft (14·0m); length ("A") 73ft 2in (22·3m), (R) 74ft 6in (22·7m), (U) about 76ft (23·16m); height 18ft 6in (5·63m).
Weights: (Fighter) empty 44,000lb (19,960kg); normal loaded 68,350lb (31,000kg); maximum loaded with external missiles or tanks 77,000lb (34,930kg).
Performance: (Estimated) maximum speed at altitude 2,100mph (3380km/h, Mach 3·2); initial climb, about 50,000ft (15,240m)/min; service ceiling 73,000ft (22,250m); high-altitude combat radius without external fuel, 700 miles (1130km).
Armament: ("-A") four underwing pylons each carrying one AA-6 air-to-air missile (two radar, two infra-red) or other store; no guns; ("-B") none.
History: First flight (E-266 prototype) probably 1964; (production reconnaissance version) before 1969; (production interceptor) probably 1969; service delivery (both) 1970 or earlier.
User: Soviet Union.

Development: This large and powerful aircraft set a totally new level in combat-aircraft performance. The prototypes blazed a trail of world records in 1965-67 including closed-circuit speeds, payload-to-height and rate of climb records. The impact of what NATO quickly christened "Foxbat" was unprecedented. Especially in the Pentagon, Western policymakers recognised that here was a combat aircraft that outclassed everything else, and urgent studies were put in hand for a new US Air Force fighter (F-15 Eagle) to counter it. By 1971 at least two pairs of reconnaissance aircraft were flying with impunity over Israel, too high and fast for Phantoms to catch, while others have made overflights deep into Iran. This version is different in many respects, the nose having cameras instead of a "Fox Fire" radar, and other sensors being carried under the large body. Both versions have twin outward-sloping vertical tails, single mainwheels and a flush canopy shaped for speed rather than pilot view. From the start the main development effort has been applied to the basic MiG-25 (so-called "Foxbat A") interceptor, which has been developed in structure, systems and armament since first entering service with the PVO. In 1975 the original AA-5 missiles were supplemented, and later replaced, by the monster AA-6 "Acrid", which is easily the biggest air/air missile in service in the world. The radar-homing version has a length of about 20ft 2in (6·15m) and effective range of 28 miles (45km); the infra-red missiles have a length of just over 19ft (5·8m) and range of some 12·5 miles (20km). Another major improvement since entering service is flight-refuelling capability, not yet fitted to all MiG-25 versions. The detailed inspection of an interceptor version landed at Hakodate AB, Japan, on 6 September 1976, showed that in service pilots are forbidden to use the limits of the available flight performance, presumably to avoid thermal fatigue of the airframe; it also showed this particular machine to have early "Fox Fire" radar comparable in basic technology with the AWG-10 Phantom radar (as would be expected). Radars in current production are unquestionably solid-state pulse-doppler types able to look down and track low-flying aircraft against ground clutter. Several MiG-25s, most of them MiG-25R models on ELINT missions, have been plotted by Western radars at Mach 2·8. It should be emphasized that at this speed the MiG-25 — and any other aircraft — flies in a straight line. The MiG-25 was not designed for air combat, and if it became involved in a dogfight its speed would — like any other aircraft — soon be subsonic. The MiG-25U trainer carries neither weapons nor sensors, but is needed to convert pilots to what is still, 15 years after design, a very advanced and demanding aircraft.

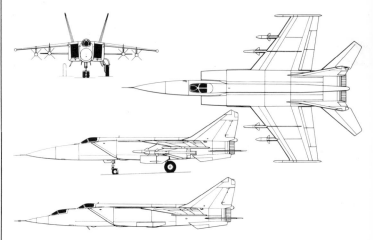

Above: Three-view of MiG-25 ("Foxbat A") with side view (bottom) of -25U.

Top: Though today a 15-year-old design, the MiG-25 is still the world's fastest combat aircraft. This fighter version appears to be streaming fuel from near the outboard leading edges.
Above: In this frame from a Soviet film two MiG-25 fighters are seen carrying two pairs each of radar and IR "Acrid" missiles, the largest air-to-air missiles in the world.

Above: Side elevation of MiG-25 interceptor, with 20ft missiles.

North American F-86 Sabre

F-86A to L, CL-13 (and Orenda-Sabre), CA-26 (and Avon-Sabre)

Origin: North American Aviation Inc, Inglewood, USA; licence-production as described in text.

Type: Basically, single-seat fighter-bomber; certain versions, all-weather interceptor.

Engine: (F-86F) one 5,970lb (2710kg) J47-27 single-shaft turbojet; (F-86H) one 8,920lb (4046kg) GE J73-3E of same layout; (F-86K) one J47-17B rated at 7,500lb (3402kg) with afterburner; (CL-13A Sabre 5) one 6,355lb (2883kg) Orenda 10 single-shaft turbojet; (CL-13B Sabre 6) one 7,275lb (3300kg) Orenda 14; (CA-26 Sabre 32) one 7,500lb (3402kg) CAC-built Rolls-Royce Avon 26 single-shaft turbojet.

Dimensions: Span (most) 37ft 1½in (11·31m); (F-86F-40) and later blocks, F-86H, K, L, CL-13 Sabre 5 (not 6), all 39ft 1in or 39ft 1½in (11·9m); length (most) 37ft 6in (11·43m); (D) 40ft 3¼in, (H) 38ft 10in; (K) 40ft 11in; height (typical) 14ft 8¾in (4·47m).

Weights: Empty (F) 11,125lb (5045kg); (H) 13,836lb; (K) 13,367lb; (Sabre 32) 12,120lb; maximum loaded; (F) 20,611lb (9350kg); (H) 24,296lb; (D) 18,483lb; (K) 20,171lb; (Sabre 32) 18,650lb.

Performance: Maximum speed (F) 678mph (1091km/h); (H, D, K) 692mph; (Sabre 6, 32) both about 705mph (peak Mach of all versions, usually 0·92); initial climb (clean) typically 8,000ft (2440m)/min, with D, H, K and Sabre 6 and 32 at 12,000ft/min; service ceiling (clean) typically 50,000ft (15,240m); range, with external fuel, high, typically 850 miles (1368km).

Armament: (A, E, F, 5, 6) six 0·5in Colt-Browning M-3, usually with 267 rounds per gun, underwing hardpoints for two tanks or two stores of 1,000lb (454kg) each, plus eight rockets or two Sidewinders; (D, L) retractable pack of 24 2·75in folding-fin aircraft rockets; (H) four 20mm M-39 each with 150 rounds plus 1,200lb tac-nuke or 3,000lb of external stores or tanks; (K) four 20mm M-24 cannon each with 132 rounds and two Sidewinders; (Sabre 32) two 30mm Aden with 150 rounds and two Sidewinders.

History: First flight (XJF-1) 27 November 1946; (XP-86) 1 October 1947; service delivery (F-86A) December 1948; first flight (YF-86D) 22 December 1949.

Users: Argentina, Bangladesh, Bolivia, Burma, Ethiopia, Indonesia, Japan, S Korea, Malaysia, Pakistan, Peru, Philippines, Portugal, Saudi Arabia, S Africa, Taiwan, Thailand, Tunisia, Venezuela, Yugoslavia.

Development: Certainly the most famed combat aircraft of its day, if not of the whole period since World War II, the Sabre story began with the award of Army and Navy contracts for jet fighters in 1944. The land-based programme moved fastest, with prototype contracts signed on 18 May 1944; but by 1945 the plans were boldly discarded and replaced by new ones with

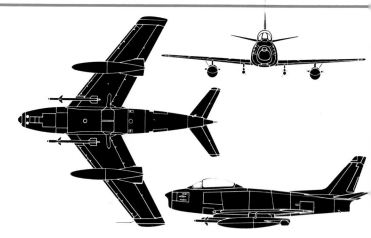

Three-view of North American F-86F with Sidewinder air-to-air missiles.

swept-back wings and tail. The three Navy prototypes, ordered on 1 January 1945, were continued and flown as conventional straight-wing aircraft. The order for 100 Furies was cut to 30, but VF-5A (later VF-51) operated it at sea and this otherwise undistinguished fighter was the first jet to complete an operational tour at sea. The more dramatic XP-86 set a speed of 618mph even with its primitive 3,750lb Chevrolet-built GE TG-180 engine and, with the 5,000lb TG-190 (J47) in 1949, soon broke the world speed record at 671mph (without being in any way modified from the standard fighter). Many hundreds of Sabres were soon on order, and in the Korean war the F-86E, with slatted wing and powered "flying tail", and F-86F, with extended leading edge and small fence, were brilliantly flown against the MiG-15 and established marked superiority, despite inferior climb and altitude performance. The very complex F-86D interceptor introduced the new concept of gunless collision-course interception directed by radar and autopilot; the K was a simpler stern-chase interceptor with guns which was mass-produced by a consortium in Italy and Germany. USAF Sabres were completed by the powerful H model, but Navy counterparts soon appeared, the FJ-2 resembling a cannon-armed F and FJ-3 and 4 (F-1C and E) having much greater power in a new air-frame. The AF-1E was the pinnacle of Sabre development with toss-bombing system, FR probe, extensive new avionics and greatly increased fuel capacity. The CL-13 series built by Canadair began as licensed E and F models (430 being supplied by Mutual Aid funds to the ailing RAF) and continued with the native Orenda engine; Australian CA-27 versions had the Avon and 30mm guns. Total production, including 300 assembled in Japan by Mitsubishi, amounted to 9,502. This handsomely exceeds the total of any other Western military aircraft since 1945, except the "Huey" helicopter.

Above: Canadair Sabre 6 of Pakistan Air Force.

Below: One of the last users of the Sabre is Japan's Air Self-Defence Force, which is phasing out 278 F-86F models after more than 20 years of service. They have been used as fighters and advanced trainers. The JASDF also formerly deployed a unique Sabre variant, the RF-86F converted by Mitsubishi as a fighter reconnaissance machine with a K-17 and two K-22 cameras in a special compartment beneath the cockpit.

Northrop F-5 Freedom Fighter and Tiger II

F-5A, B, E and F, CF-5A and D, NF-5A and B, RF-5A, E and G, and SF-5A and B

Origin: Northrop Aircraft Division, Hawthorne, USA; made or assembled under licence by partnership Canada/Netherlands and by Spain.

Type: (With suffix A, E, and G) single-seat fighter-reconnaissance; (with suffix B, D and F) two-seat dual fighter/trainer.

Engines: (A, B, D, G) two 4,080lb (1850kg) thrust General Electric J85-13 single-shaft afterburning turbojets; (E, F) two 5,000lb (2268kg) J85-21.

Dimensions: Span (A, B, D, G) 25ft 3in (7·7m); (E, F) 26ft 8in (8·13m); length (A, G) 47ft 2in (14·38m); (B, D) 46ft 4in (14·12m); (E) 48ft 3¾in (14·73m); (F) 51ft 9¾in (15·80m); height (A, G) 13ft 2in (4·01m); (B, D) 13ft 1in (3·99m); (E, F) 13ft 4½in (4·08m).

Weights: Empty (A, G) 8,085lb (3667kg); (B, D) 8,361lb (3792kg); (E) 9,588lb (4349kg); (F) 9,700lb (4400kg); maximum loaded (A, G) 20,677lb (9379kg); (B, D) 20,500lb (9298kg); (E, F) 24,080lb (10,922kg).

Performance: Maximum speed at altitude (A, G) 925mph (1489km/h, Mach 1·40); (B, D) 885mph (1424km/h, Mach 1·34); (E) 1,060mph (1705km/h, Mach 1·60); initial climb (A, G) 28,700ft (8760m)/min; (B, D) 30,400ft (9265m)/min; (E) 31,600ft (9630m)/min; service ceiling (A, G) 50,500ft (15,390m); (B, D) 52,000ft (15,850m); (E) 54,000ft (16,460m); range with max fuel, with reserves, tanks retained, (A, G) 1,387 miles (2232km); (B, D) 1,393 miles (2241km); (E) 1,974 miles (3175km).

continued on page 44▶

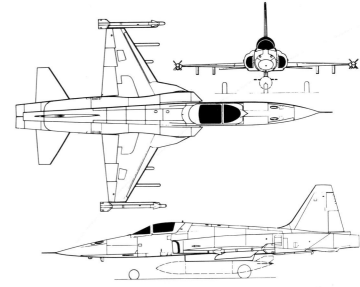

Three-view of F-5E Tiger II; the tandem-seat F-5F is 42in longer.

Above: F-5A of Hellenic (Greek) Air Force.

Above: F-5A of Imperial Iranian Air Force.

Above: Canadair-built CF-5A of Canadian Armed Forces.

Below: Dive-bombing attack by a Northrop F-5A Freedom Fighter, with "Coke-bottle" tip tanks (not carried by F-5E Tiger II). Though lacking sophisticated navigation and weapon-delivery systems, the F-5 has sold in large numbers to at least 28 nations. All versions carry two nose-mounted cannon, and in most there is a lead-computing optical gunsight with roll-stabilized manually depressible reticle for air-to-ground delivery, as here. A few customers, such as Saudi Arabia, have advanced F-5 versions with an inertial navigation system, and most customers have bought a small number of tandem-seat dual-control versions. Here, nominal 2,000lb bombs are being released in sequence by the simple weapon-aiming system. The F-5 cannot be used for blind first-pass attack on ground targets.

▶**Armament:** Two 20mm M-39A2 cannon each with 280 rounds in nose (can be retained in RF versions); five pylons for total external load of about 4,400lb (2000kg) in A, G (total military load for these models, including guns and ammunition, is 5,200lb) or 7,000lb (3175kg) in E; rails on wing-tips for AIM-9 Sidewinder missiles.

History: First flight (XT-38) 10 April 1959, (N-156F) 30 July 1959, (F-5A) 19 May 1964, (F-5E) 11 August 1972, (F-5F) 25 September 1974.

Users: (A, B, D, G) Brazil, Canada, Ethiopia, Greece, Iran, Jordan, S Korea, Libya, Malaysia, Morocco, Netherlands, Norway, Pakistan, Philippines, Saudi Arabia, Spain, Taiwan, Thailand, Turkey, USA (Air Force, not operational); (E, F) Brazil, Chile, Ethiopia (US embargo, supplied by Iran), Iran, Jordan, Kenya, Malaysia, Morocco, Peru, Philippines, Saudi Arabia, Singapore, S Korea, Switzerland, Taiwan, Thailand, Tunisia, USA (Air Force, Navy), Vietnam.

Development: In 1955 Northrop began the project design of a lightweight fighter, known as Tally-Ho, powered by two J85 missile engines slung in pods under a very small unswept wing. It was yet another of the many projects born in the Korean era when pilots were calling for lighter, simpler fighters with higher performance. Gradually Welko Gasich and his team refined the design, putting the engines in the fuselage and increasing the size, partly to meet the needs of the Navy. In June 1956 the Navy had pulled out, while the Air Force ordered the trainer version as the T-38

Talon. Over the next 15 years Northrop delivered 1,200 Talons, all to the USAF or NASA, as the standard supersonic trainer of those services. With this assured programme the company took the unique decision to go ahead and build a demonstration fighter in the absence of any orders — the only time this has ever been done with a supersonic aircraft. By the time it was ready for flight in 1959 the N-156F, dubbed Freedom Fighter had received some US Defense funding, and the prototype carried US serial and stencil markings but no national markings. It was a simple little fighter, carrying about 485 gallons of fuel, two cannon and an old F-86 style sight, and having racks for two little Sidewinder missiles. Today such a prototype would have remained unsold, but in October 1962 the Department of Defense decided to buy the so-called Freedom Fighter in large numbers to

Above: An F-5E Tiger II serving in the ''Aggressor'' role, simulating a hostile aircraft, at the US Navy Fighter Weapons School at NAS Miramar, California. USAF Tigers fly this role at Alconbury, England.

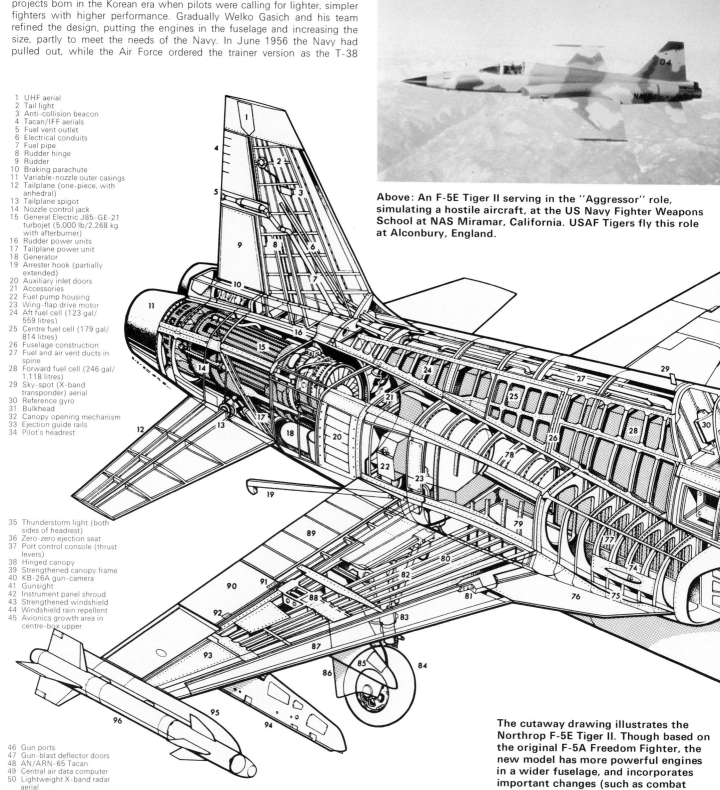

1 UHF aerial
2 Tail light
3 Anti-collision beacon
4 Tacan/IFF aerials
5 Fuel vent outlet
6 Electrical conduits
7 Fuel pipe
8 Rudder hinge
9 Rudder
10 Braking parachute
11 Variable-nozzle outer casings
12 Tailplane (one-piece, with anhedral)
13 Tailplane spigot
14 Nozzle control jack
15 General Electric J85-GE-21 turbojet (5,000 lb/2,268 kg with afterburner)
16 Rudder power units
17 Tailplane power unit
18 Generator
19 Arrester hook (partially extended)
20 Auxiliary inlet doors
21 Accessories
22 Fuel pump housing
23 Wing-flap drive motor
24 Aft fuel cell (123 gal/ 559 litres)
25 Centre fuel cell (179 gal/ 814 litres)
26 Fuselage construction
27 Fuel and air vent ducts in spine
28 Forward fuel cell (246 gal/ 1,118 litres)
29 Sky-spot (X-band transponder) aerial
30 Reference gyro
31 Bulkhead
32 Canopy opening mechanism
33 Ejection guide rails
34 Pilot's headrest

35 Thunderstorm light (both sides of headrest)
36 Zero-zero ejection seat
37 Port control console (thrust levers)
38 Hinged canopy
39 Strengthened canopy frame
40 KB-26A gun-camera
41 Gunsight
42 Instrument panel shroud
43 Strengthened windshield
44 Windshield rain repellent
45 Avionics growth area in centre-box upper

46 Gun ports
47 Gun-blast deflector doors
48 AN/ARN-65 Tacan
49 Central air data computer
50 Lightweight X-band radar aerial
51 Radome
52 Pressure head
53 Search and range track radar
54 UHF/IFF aerial
55 Battery
56 Avionics growth area
57 Transformer rectifier
58 Centre-box nosewheel well

59 Nosewheel door
60 Nosewheel leg
61 Nosewheel
62 Nosewheel door aft
63 Ammunition feed

64 Ammunition box (280 rpg)
65 Starboard 20mm Pontiac M-39 cannon
66 Electrical leads
67 Cartridge ejection chute

68 Forward fuselage/cockpit construction
69 Ventral drop tank (125 gal/ 568 litres)
70 Inlet ramp wall

71 Air-conditioning system
72 Access doors
73 Boundary layer control
74 Position light
75 Airflow fillet cut-out

76 Revised and enlarged wing-root leading-edge fillet
77 Intake framework
78 Intake trunking
79 Mainwheel well

The cutaway drawing illustrates the Northrop F-5E Tiger II. Though based on the original F-5A Freedom Fighter, the new model has more powerful engines in a wider fuselage, and incorporates important changes (such as combat manoeuvring flaps and revised wing roots) to enhance dogfight capability.

give, or sell on advantageous terms, to anti-Communist nations. More than 1,040 of the Freedom Fighter (suffixes A, B, D, G) have been built, all but 178 being exports from Northrop. The Netherlands built the NF-5A and B equipment, heavier mission load, 500lb (227kg) more fuel in the longer fuselage, new inlet ducts, revised body and wing, root extensions and manoeuvring flaps and an X-band radar. Deliveries began in 1972, followed

by the two-seat F in 1975. The US Air Force uses the Tiger II to equip its Tac Ftr Training Aggressor units, simulating hostile aircraft; the US Navy uses it as an Air Combat Trainer for future F-4 or F-14 pilots. Basic price of an E is considerably higher than that of the more powerful Jaguar (a recent sale was 12 for Kenya, priced at $70·6 million), but over 1,000 of the Tiger II type are likely to be supplied on attractive terms to many countries.

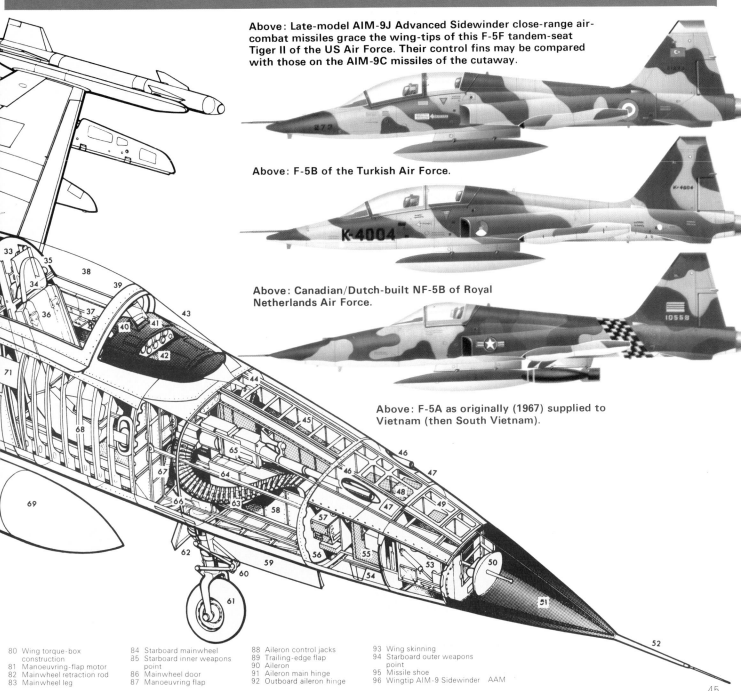

Above: Late-model AIM-9J Advanced Sidewinder close-range air-combat missiles grace the wing-tips of this F-5F tandem-seat Tiger II of the US Air Force. Their control fins may be compared with those on the AIM-9C missiles of the cutaway.

Above: F-5B of the Turkish Air Force.

Above: Canadian/Dutch-built NF-5B of Royal Netherlands Air Force.

Above: F-5A as originally (1967) supplied to Vietnam (then South Vietnam).

80 Wing torque-box construction	84 Starboard mainwheel	88 Aileron control jacks	93 Wing skinning
81 Manoeuvring-flap motor	85 Starboard inner weapons point	89 Trailing-edge flap	94 Starboard outer weapons point
82 Mainwheel retraction rod	86 Mainwheel door	90 Aileron	95 Missile shoe
83 Mainwheel leg	87 Manoeuvring flap	91 Aileron main hinge	96 Wingtip AIM-9 Sidewinder AAM
		92 Outboard aileron hinge	

45

Saab 35 Draken

J35A, B, D and F, Sk35C, S35E and export versions

Origin: Saab-Scania AB, Linköping, Sweden.
Type: (J35) single-seat all-weather fighter-bomber; (Sk35) dual trainer; (S35) single-seat all-weather reconnaissance.
Engine: One Svenska Flygmotor RM6 (licence-built Rolls-Royce Avon with SFA afterburner): (A, B, C) 15,000lb (6804kg) RM6B; (D, E, F and export) 17,110lb (7761kg) RM6C.
Dimensions: Span 30ft 10in (9·4m); length 50ft 4in (15·4m) (S35E, 52ft); height 12ft 9in (3·9m).
Weights: Empty (D) 16,017lb; (F) 18,180lb (8250kg); maximum loaded (A) 18,200lb; (D) 22,663lb; (F) 27,050lb (12,270kg); (F-35) 35,275lb (16,000kg).
Performance: Maximum speed (D onwards, clean) 1,320mph (2125km/h, Mach 2·0), (with two drop tanks and two 1,000lb bombs) 924mph (1487 km/h, Mach 1·4); initial climb (D onwards, clean) 34,450ft (10,500m)/min; service ceiling (D onwards, clean) about 65,000ft (20,000m); range (internal fuel plus external weapons, typical) 800 miles (1300km), (maximum fuel) 2,020 miles (3250km).
Armament: (A) two 30mm Aden M/55 in wings, four Rb 324 (Sidewinder) missiles; (B) as A plus attack ordnance to maximum of 2,200lb (1000kg); (C) none; (D) as B; (E) usually none but provision as A; (F) one 30mm Aden plus two Rb27 Falcon (radar) and two Rb28 Falcon (infra-red) missiles, plus two or four Rb324; (F-35) two 30mm Aden plus nine stores pylons each rated at 1,000lb (454kg) all usable simultaneously, plus four Rb324.
History: First flight 25 October 1955; (production J35A) 15 February 1958; final delivery (35XS) 1975, (Danish TF-35) 1976.
Users: Denmark, Finland, Sweden (RSAF).

Development: Again in advance of any other country in Western Europe, the Saab 35 was designed in 1949–51 as an all-weather supersonic fighter able to use small airfields. Erik Bratt and his team arrived at the unique "double delta" shape after studying different ways of packaging the fuel and equipment, the best arrangement being with items one behind the other

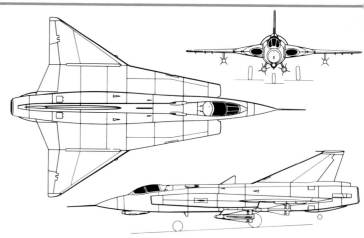

Above: Three-view of the Falcon-armed J35F ("Filip" to the Swedish Air Force).

giving a long aircraft of very small frontal area. In 1960 attack wing F13 found the A (Adam) simple to fly and maintain, sensitive in pitch and yet virtually unbreakable. B (Bertil) was more complex, with S7 collision-course fire control integrated with the Swedish Stril 60 air defence environment. Most Sk35C trainers were converted Adams. D (David) was first to reach Mach 2, despite continual increases in weight mainly due to fuel capacity raised from 493 to 680 gallons. E (Erik) carries French OMERA cameras and in 1973 was updated with external British Vinten night/low-level pods. F (Filip) is an automatic interceptor with Ericsson (Hughes basis) radar of pulse-doppler type. Production was closed at 606 with 40 multi-role F-35/RF-35/TF-35 aircraft for Denmark and 12 XS for Finland assembled by Valmet Oy.

Above: J35A ("Adam" to the Swedish AF).

Below: A pleasing study of one of the six TF-35XD multi-role tandem-seat Drakens of the Royal Danish Air Force. Denmark also uses the most capable of all Draken variants, the single-seat 35XD, and the RF-35 with the Red Baron night reconnaissance pod.

Sukhoi Su-9 and Su-11

Su-9 "Fishpot B", Su-9U "Maiden" and Su-11 "Fishpot C".

Origin: The design bureau named for Pavel O. Sukhoi, Soviet Union.
Type: Single-seat all-weather interceptor (Su-9U, two-seat trainer).
Engine: One Lyulka single-shaft turbojet with afterburner; (Su-9 and -9U) AL-7F rated at 19,840lb (9000kg) thrust with maximum afterburner, (Su-11) AL-7F-1 rated at 22,046lb (10,000kg).
Dimensions: Span 27ft 8in (8·43m); length (-9, -9U) about 54ft (16·5m), (-11) 57ft (17·4m); height 16ft (4·9m).
Weights: (All, estimated) empty 20,000lb (9070kg); loaded (typical mission) 27,000lb (12,250kg), (maximum) 30,000lb (13,610kg).
Performance: (-11, estimated) maximum speed (clean, sea level) 720mph (1160km/h, Mach 0·95), (clean, optimum height) 1,190mph (1910km/h, Mach 1·8), (two missiles and two tanks at optimum height) 790mph (1270km/h, Mach 1·2); initial climb 27,000ft (8230m)/min; service ceiling (clean) 55,700ft (17,000m); range (two missiles, two tanks) about 700 miles (1125km).
Armament: (-9) four AA-1 "Alkali" air-to-air missiles; (-9U) same as -9, or not fitted; (-11) two AA-3 "Anab" air-to-air missiles, one radar and the other IR.
History: First flight (-9) before 1956; (-11) probably 1966; service delivery (-9) probably 1959, (-11) 1967.
User: Soviet Union (IA-PVO).

Development: When first seen, at the 1956 Tushino display, one prototype delta-winged Sukhoi fighter had a small conical radome above the plain nose inlet, while a second had a conical centrebody. The latter arrangement was chosen for production as the Su-9, though development was rather protracted. At first sharing the same engine installation, rear fuselage and tail as the original Su-7, the Su-9 eventually came to have no parts exactly common. No gun was ever seen on an Su-9 by Western intelligence, the primitive missiles being the only armament. At least 2,000 were built, an additional number, probably supplemented by conversions, being tandem-seat dual trainers with a cockpit slightly different from that of the Su-7U. The Su-11 is cleaned up in every part of the airframe, has a longer and less-tapered nose with larger radar centrebody, completely different armament (still without guns) and a fuselage similar to the Su-7B with external duct fairings along the top on each side. Though much larger and more powerful than the MiG-21, these interceptors have an almost identical tailed-delta

configuration. Unlike the MiG-21 they have all-weather capability (interpreted as "night and rain" rather than true all-weather), but are still limited in radius, endurance and armament. In 1976 they were together judged to equip one-quarter of the 2,500-strong interceptor force of the IA-PVO, but were being replaced by the Su-15 and MiG-23S.

Above: Launch of an "AA-3 Alkali" air-to-air missile from No 2 pylon of an Su-9 of the IA-PVO. Though built in very large numbers, few Su-9 interceptors remain in service today.

Below: Another picture of an Su-9, showing the shorter and more tapered nose in comparison with the later Su-11. Like all Sukhoi aircraft of this generation, the Su-9 and -11 have limited internal fuel capacity and a large Lyulka afterburning engine, and endurance without the twin drop tanks is poor. Many Su-9s may have been rebuilt as Su-11s.

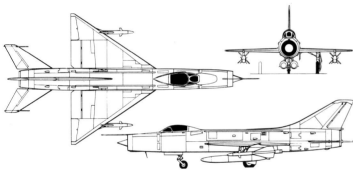

Above: Three-view of Su-11, with "Anab" missiles.

Sukhoi Su-15

Versions known to the West are code-named "Flagon-A to -E"

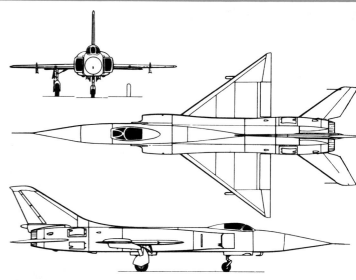

Origin: The design bureau of Pavel O. Sukhoi, Soviet Union.
Type: Most versions, all-weather interceptor.
Engines: Two afterburning engines, believed to be 22,046lb (10,000kg) Lyulka AL-7F single-shaft turbojets.
Dimensions: Span (A) 31ft 3in (9·50m), (D) about 36ft (11·0m); length (all) 70ft 6in (21·50m); height 16ft 6in (5·0m).
Weights: (Estimated) empty (A) 24,000lb (10,900kg), (D) 26,000lb (11,800kg); normal loaded (A) 35,275lb (16,000kg); maximum loaded (D) 46,000lb (21,000kg).
Performance: (Estimated) maximum speed at altitude, with two missiles, 1,520mph (2445km/h, Mach 2·3); initial climb 35,000ft (10,670m)/min; service ceiling 65,000ft (19,800m)· combat radius 450 miles (725km); ferry range about 1,400 miles (2250km).
Armament: Two underwing pylons normally carry one radar "Anab" and one infra-red "Anab"; two fuselage pylons normally carry drop tanks, often with a 23mm GSh-23 two-barrel cannon between them; other missiles such as AA-6 or AA-7 are probably now being carried (but not yet seen by the West).
History: First flight (Su-15 prototype) probably 1964; (production Su-15) probably 1967.
User: Soviet Union (PVO).

Development: Following naturally on from the Su-11, and strongly resembling earlier aircraft in wings and tail, the Su-15 has two engines which not only confer increased performance but also leave the nose free for a large AI radar. The initial "Flagon-A" version entered IA-PVO Strany service in 1969. "Flagon-B" is a STOL rough-field version with three lift jets in the fuselage and a revised "double delta" wing. "Flagon-C" is the Su-15U dual trainer, "-D" is basically a "-B" without lift jets, and "-E" has completely updated electronics and more powerful engines. In 1971 a US official estimated that 400 Su-15 were in service, with production at about 15 monthly. In early 1976 an estimate of PVO establishment gave the number of all Su-15 versions in combat service as 600. Though small numbers have served in Warsaw Pact countries and, in 1973, in Egypt, all Su-15s are at present believed to serve with the IA-PVO. There has been speculation in the West that later models could carry the Fox Fire radar and AA-6 "Acrid" missiles of the MiG-25.

Above: Three-view of "Flagon A" Su-15 without missiles.

Above: "Flagon B" jet-lift STOL prototype.

Below: Three "Flagon A" interceptors of the IA-PVO, with "Anabs".

Bottom: With an extremely highly-loaded wing (quite un-Russian) the Su-15 needs good airfields.

Tupolev Tu-28P

Tu-28 versions of unknown designation; Tupolev bureau, Tu-102

Origin: The design bureau of Andrei N. Tupolev, Soviet Union.
Type: Long-range all-weather interceptor.
Engines: Originally, two large axial turbojets of unknown type, each with afterburning rating of about 27,000lb (12,250kg), probably similar to those of Tu-22; later versions, afterburning turbofans of about 30,000lb (13,610 kg) each, as in later Tu-22.
Dimensions: (Estimated) span 65ft (20m); length 85ft (26m); height 23ft (7m).
Weights: (Estimated) empty 55,000lb (25,000kg); maximum loaded 100,000lb (45,000kg).
Performance: (Estimated) maximum speed (with missiles, at height) 1,150mph (1850km/h, Mach 1·75); initial climb, 25,000ft (7500m)/min; service ceiling (not gross weight) about 60,000ft (18,000m); range on internal fuel (high Patrol) about 1,800 miles (2900km).
Armament: No guns seen in any version; mix of infra-red homing and radar-homing "Ash" air-to-air guided missiles, originally one of each and since 1965 two of each.
History: First flight, believed 1957; service delivery, probably 1961.
User: Soviet Union (PVO).

Development: Largest fighter known to be in service in the world, this formidable machine is essentially conventional yet has the greatest internal fuel capacity of any fighter and the biggest interception radar known to exist. It was one of a number of supersonic types produced by the Tupolev bureau with technology explored with the family of aircraft of the late

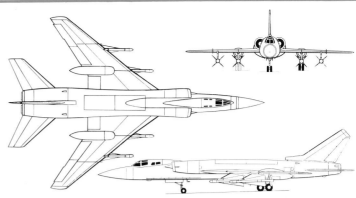

Three-view of the Tu-28P long-range interceptor, with four "Ash" air-to-air missiles.

1950s known to NATO as "Backfin" (another is the Tu-22). Like the others the Tu-28P has a distinctive wing with sharply kinked trailing edge, the outer 45° panels being outboard of large fairings extending behind the trailing edge accommodating the four-wheel bogie landing gears. Two crew sit in tandem under upward-hinged canopies, and all armament is carried on wing pylons. Early versions had twin ventral fins and usually large belly fairings, but these features are absent from aircraft in current service. The Tu-28P would be an ideal strategic patrol fighter to operate in conjunction with the "Moss" AWACS.

Above: A new drawing of the latest Tu-28P, with "Ash" air-to-air missiles.

Below: Dramatic action shot of a Tu-28P "rippling" away all four of its large air-to-air missiles. Though almost 20 years old as a design, the Tu-28P is still an all-weather interceptor of great capability and in most respects remains the world's largest fighter.

Vought F-8 Crusader

Vought F-8A to F-8J, RF-8, DF-8 and QF-8

Origin: Vought Systems Division of LTV, Dallas, USA.

Type: Originally single-seat carrier-based day fighter (see text).

Engine: One Pratt & Whitney J57 two-shaft turbojet with afterburner; (A, B, F, L) 16,200lb (7327kg) J57-12; (C, K) 16,900lb (7665kg) J57-16; others, 18,000lb (8165kg) J57-20A. About 100 F-8J re-engined with P&W TF30-420 afterburning turbofan, rated at 19,600lb (8891kg).

Dimensions: Span 35ft 8in (10·87m); (E, J) 35ft 2in; length 54ft 3in (16·54m); (E, J) 54ft 6in; height 15ft 9in (4·80m).

Weights: Empty (C) about 17,000lb (7710kg); (J) 19,700lb (8935kg); maximum loaded (C) 27,550lb (12,500kg); (J) 34,000lb (15,420kg).

Performance: Maximum speed, clean, at altitude (A, B, L, H) 1,013mph, (RF-8A) 982mph; (RF-8G) 1,002mph; (C, K, J) 1,105mph (1780km/h, Mach 1·68); (E) 1,135mph; (D) 1,230mph; initial climb (typical) 21,000ft (6400m)/min; service ceiling, from 38,400ft for J to 42,900ft (13,100m) for D; combat radius, from 368 miles for C, K to 440 miles (708km) for J and 455 miles (732km) for D.

Armament: (A, B, C) four 20mm Colt Mk 12 cannon each with 84 rounds; one Sidewinder on each side and 32 folding-fin rockets in belly pack; (D) four 20mm plus four Sidewinder; (E, H, J) four 20mm plus four Sidewinder plus 12 Mk 81 bombs, or two Bullpups or eight Zuni rockets; (K, L) as J but 144 rounds per gun; RF versions, none.

History: First flight (XF8U-1) 25 March 1955; (production F-8A) November 1956; service delivery 25 March 1957; final delivery 1965.

Users: France, USA (Navy, Naval Reserve, Marine Corps).

Development: This outstanding carrier-based fighter, notable for its variable-incidence wing, outperformed the F-100 on the same engine, besides having 1,165gal internal fuel! Exceeding Mach 1 on the level on the first flight the F8U (as it then was) was rapidly developed for carrier service, and for 12 years was a popular combat aircraft of the US Navy and Marines.

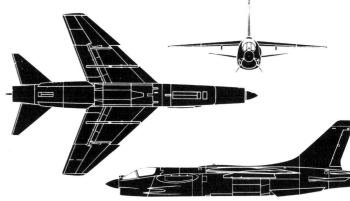

Three-view of F-8J, a remanufactured F-8E now in use with the US Naval Reserve.

Altogether 1,259 were built, plus two prototypes, and in 1966–71 446 were rebuilt to a later standard (B to L, C to K, E to J and D to H). The continual process of improvement added all-weather radar, improved autopilot and weapon-delivery systems, air/ground weapons and, in the 42 F-8E(FN) for the French Navy, slower approach for small carriers. Variants include RF reconnaissance, DF drone RPV and QF RPV-control aircraft; a single dual trainer was also built. Many rebuilt versions remain in combat service, with long life ahead; total Crusader flight time exceeds 3,000,000hr.

Above: F-8L of the US Marine Corps, Squadron VMF-321.

Below: This fine air-to-air portrait of a rebuilt F-8 (probably a J) of VF-201 Sqn, US Navy, pays tribute to one of the most outstanding carrier-based aircraft of all time. It has for 20 years been a saying in the US Navy (and maybe in the Marine Corps) that "when you're out of F-8s, you're out of fighters". This did not imply criticism of the F-4 but reflected the fact that, for air combat, many "jocks" preferred the F-8.

Yakovlev Yak-28P

Yak-28 attack versions, -28P, -28R and -28U

Origin: The design bureau of Alexander S. Yakovlev, Soviet Union.
Type: 28 (unknown designations) two-seat attack; (P) all weather interceptor; (R) multi-sensor reconnaissance; (U) dual-control trainer.
Engines: Two Tumansky RD-11 single-shaft afterburning turbojets each with maximum rating of 13,120lb (5950kg); certain sub-types have RD-11-300 rated at 13,670lb (6200kg).
Dimensions: (Estimated) span 42ft 6in (12·95m) (some versions have span slightly less than standard); length (except late P) 71ft 0½in (21·65m); (late 28P) 74ft (22·56m); height 12ft 11½in (3·95m).
Weights: Empty (estimated, typical) 24,250lb (11,000kg); maximum loaded (U) 30,000lb (13,600kg); (others) 35,300–41,000lb (16,000–18,600kg).
Performance: (Estimated) maximum speed at altitude 735mph (1180km/h, Mach 1·13); initial climb 27,900ft (8500m)/min; service ceiling 55,500ft (16,750m); range (clean, at altitude) 1,200–1,600 miles (1930–2575km).
Armament: (Attack versions) one 30mm NR-30 cannon on both sides of fuselage or on right side only; fuselage weapon bay for internal load of free-fall bombs (estimated maximum, 4,400lb, 2000kg); hard-points or pylons between drop-tank attachments and outrigger gears for light loads (usually pod of 55mm rockets); (28P) two "Anab" air-to-air guided missiles, one radar and the other infra-red; in some aircraft, two additional pylons for two K-13A ("Atoll") missiles, both "Anab" then being radar homers; (R) believed none; (U) retains weapon bay and single gun.
History: First flight, before 1961; (production attack and interceptor versions) before 1961; service delivery not later than mid-1962; final delivery, before 1970.
User: Soviet Union (IA-PVO).

Three-view of the current sub-type of Yak-28P with pointed radome.

Development: Obviously derived from the Yak-25/26/27, the Yak-28 is a completely new aircraft, with high wing of different form, new engines, steerable twin-wheel nose gear and considerably greater weight. Early attack versions had slightly shorter fuselage and shorter nacelles ahead of the wing; many hundreds (possibly thousands) of glazed-nose attack 28s (code name "Brewer") were built, most having been rebuilt as ECM and other specialist tactical machines. The Yak-28P (code name "Firebar") remains a leading interceptor, its "Skip Spin" radar being enclosed in a much longer and more pointed nose from 1967. The 28U trainer (code name "Maestro") has a separate front (pupil) cockpit with canopy hinged to the right. Many 28R versions ("Brewer D"), with cameras and various non-optical sensors, may be converted attack aircraft. Flight refuelling is not fitted.

Above: A long-nose Yak-28P specially drawn for this book.

Below: About to take off, a short-nose Yak-28P lines up on the runway with tailplane at negative incidence to rotate the aircraft about its rear landing-gear truck. This is the ultimate development of the Yak-25 of 1953.

Attack/close support aircraft

In terms of numbers this is the most important category of combat aircraft; yet, if the media are to be believed, the general public have never heard of it, so attack aircraft have to be called either "fighters" or "bombers". Their origin lay in aircraft of 1916–18 called ground strafers or trench fighters which were armoured to survive in close proximity to a land battle whilst doing what they could to harass the enemy land forces. In the 1930s the US Army Air Corps recognized the attack category, as did the Soviet Union, but the RAF and even the Luftwaffe concentrated on traditional fighters and bombers and flew attack missions with such lash-ups as cannon fixed to the Ju 87 or He 177 and rockets fixed to the Typhoon. During the past 30 years air forces have often regarded attack missions as suitable for obsolescent fighters, while the scene has been further confused by concentration in the 1960s on light propeller-driven attack aircraft for use in what were popularly called "brushfire wars" or Co-In (counter-insurgent) operations. To some degree these light attack machines represented a justifiable reaction against the use of totally unsuitable supersonic fighters, which were complex, hard to maintain, costly, inefficient, unable to find their targets or to use short unpaved airstrips.

The one area where attack aircraft were designed for the job was in naval warfare, but here the targets were often easy-to-find ships and the airfields were carriers. This led to excellent aircraft, which in the case of the A-1 Skyraider stayed competitive almost 30 years longer than anyone predicted when it was new. But naval attackers needed changes to fit them for the land battle.

What kind of beast is the attack aircraft? First, it must be survivable. The notion that insurgents carry primitive weapons was predictably discredited by the appearance of shoulder-fired guided weapons with warheads more lethal than an 88mm shell. So we need plenty of armour, and a design philosophy which gives us a spare crew-member, spare engine, spare tail and might even bring back the biplane. We also need powerful ECM and plenty of decoys. There is no point in taking off if we have difficulty finding the target, so we need good navigation systems and sophisticated sensors. To destroy the target we need not just accuracy but blind first-pass accuracy, which means we can come straight across and hit it first time in a snow-blizzard at night. By no means least we need lethal ordnance, which means whopping cannon and smart bombs or guided missiles.

To carry all this demands a large margin between empty and gross weight. To give an idea of what is now possible, the Jaguar, with a wing only three-quarters the span of a Spitfire, can carry a load of fuel and weapons equal to almost *four times the total gross weight* of a Spitfire I. To make life harder, we need a large wing to lift this weight, and especially to give STOL performance; yet high-speed attack at

low level calls for the smallest possible wing, unless the crew are to be shaken to pieces (so some people cheat with swing-wings or vectored thrust). We need long landing gears with squashy soft-field tyres, and possibly drag-chutes and arrester hooks—and all the help we can get from the concealment experts, who are today pushing their luck if they use crude camouflage netting. We also need help from our own troops, who can use laser designators to point out exactly where they want our weapons to hit; the missiles will obediently steer towards the laser light diffused or reflected from the target. Where the attack pilot can see the target he can use a TV-guided missile; to hit armour he can use a gun, especially if he happens to be strapped to an A-10.

The A-10 is the most carefully designed attack platform in history. Like the light Co-In, it offers an alternative to the highly unsuitable ''fighter''. Its designers accepted large size and rather low performance, and did their best to make it survivable. If they have succeeded, the A-10 will be the aircraft enemy ground troops will like least because it is designed to be based closer to the land battle (but not as close as a V/STOL), to carry more weapons, and deliver them more accurately. Nobody could call the A-10 a ''fighter'', so the media have labelled it a ''bomber''. There is no problem in fixing a simple tag to the other class of attack aircraft: they are called helicopters, and are discussed in that section, which begins on page 192.

When the McDonnell Douglas Skyhawk was designed, in 1952, the US Navy doubted it could ever be built, but today it is still in production. This A-4M, called a Camel for obvious reasons, is still an effective attack platform 23½ years after first flight.

Aeritalia G91

G91R, G91T, G91PAN and G91Y

Origin: Fiat SpA (now Aeritalia SpA); see text for multinational production of earlier versions.

Type: G91R and Y, single-seat tactical reconnaissance/fighter; G91T, two-seat weapon trainer; G91PAN, single-seat aerobatic display fighter.

Engines: (G91R, T and PAN) one 5,000lb (2268kg) thrust Rolls-Royce (previously Bristol, then Bristol Siddeley) Orpheus 80302 single-shaft turbojet; (G91Y) two General Electric J85-13A single-shaft augmented turbojets each rated at 4,080lb (1850kg) with full afterburner.

Dimensions: Span (G.91R, T, PAN) 28ft 1in (8·57m); (G91Y) 29ft 6½in (9·01m); length (G91R, PAN) 33ft 9¼in (10·31m); (G91T, Y) 38ft 3½in (11·67m); height (G91R, PAN) 13ft 1½in (4m); (G91T, Y) 14ft 6in (4·43m).

Weights: Empty (G91R) typically 7,275lb (3300kg); (G91Y) 8,598lb (3900kg); maximum loaded (G91R) 12,500lb (5695kg); (G91Y) 19,180lb (8700kg).

Performance: Maximum speed (G91R) 675mph (1086km/h); (G91Y) 690mph (1110km/h); initial climb (G91R) 6,000ft (1829m)/min; (G91Y) 17,000ft (5180m)/min; service ceiling (G91R) 43,000ft (13,106m); (G91Y) 41,000ft (12,500m); combat radius at sea level (G91R) 196 miles (315km); (G91Y) 372 miles (600km); ferry range (G91R) 1,150 miles (1850km); (G91Y) 2,175 miles (3500km).

Armament: (G91R/1) four 0·5in Colt-Browning machine guns, each with 300 rounds and underwing racks for ordnance load up to 500lb (227kg); (G91R/3) two 30mm DEFA 552 cannon, each with 125 rounds, and under wing racks for ordnance up to 1,000lb (454kg); (G91Y) two DEFA 552, underwing load up to 4,000lb (1814kg).

History: First flight 9 August 1956; (G91R) December 1958; (G91Y prototype) 27 December 1966; (production G91Y) June 1971.

Users: (G91Y) Italy; (earlier versions) Angola, W Germany, Italy, Portugal.

Development: In December 1953 the North Atlantic Treaty Organisation (NATO) announced a specification for a light tactical strike fighter. It was to be robust, simple to maintain and capable of operation from rough advanced airstrips, yet had to reach Mach 0·92 and be able to deliver conventional or tactical nuclear weapons. There were three French contenders and the G91 from Italy. On the first flight the test pilot lost control and had to eject, but orders had already been placed by the Italian government and production was put in hand. As the design had been based on that of the F-86, but on a smaller scale, the tail problem of the first prototype was soon rectified; but the French refused to have anything to do with the G91 and the original customers — intended to be all the Continental NATO nations — were only Germany and Italy. Italy took 98 G91R/1, 1A and 1B plus 76 G91T/1, while Germany chose 50 R/3, 44 T/3 and 50 R/4, also building a further 294 R/3 under licence by Messerschmitt (later MBB), Heinkel (later VFW-Fokker) and Dornier. The Orpheus was built by a further European

Above: Three G91R/1 light attack aircraft of the Aeronautica Militare Italiano's 2° Wing, based at Treviso.

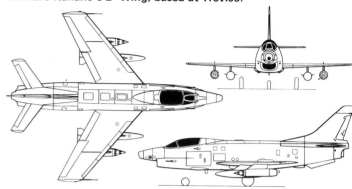

Above: Three-view of the twin-engined Aeritalia G91Y.

consortium. Among many other sub-variants is the PAN version of the Pattuglia Acrobatica Nazionali. The completely redesigned G91Y has much greater thrust, better navigation aids and can fly fighter, attack or reconnaissance missions. Aeritalia, the company formed in 1969 jointly by Fiat and Finmeccanica-IRI, delivered 45 to the Regia Aeronautica in 1971-76.

Above: G91R/3 of LeKG 43 of West German Luftwaffe, based at Oldenburg.

Below: Ear-splitting run at nought metres (slightly higher than nought feet) by a G91Y. Though often called a fighter, the G91Y has no radar and only simple air-to-air weapons (guns and unguided rockets) and is actually a light tactical attack and reconnaissance aircraft. A total of 45 was delivered in 1971-76 to the Aeronautica Militare Italiano's 32° Wing, the original 20 development aircraft having been delivered to 8° Wing at Cervia.

BAC Strikemaster and 145

BAC 145 and Strikemaster

Origin: Hunting/BAC (now British Aerospace), UK.
Type: Two-seat light tactical aircraft and trainer.
Engine: 3,410lb (1547kg) thrust Rolls-Royce Viper 535 turbojet.
Dimensions: Span 36ft 10in (11·23m); length 33ft 8½in (10·27m); height 10ft 11½in (3·34m).
Weights: Empty 6,270lb (2840kg); loaded (clean) 9,200lb (4170kg); maximum 11,500lb (5210kg).
Performance: Maximum speed 481mph (774km/h); maximum speed at sea level 450mph (726km/h); initial climb (max fuel, clean) 5,250ft (1600m)/min; service ceiling 44,000ft (13,410m); ferry range 1,615 miles (2600km); combat radius with 3,300lb weapon load 145 miles (233km).
Armament: Two 7·62mm FN machine guns fixed firing forwards with 550 rounds each; wide range of stores to maximum of 3,000lb (1360kg) on four underwing strongpoints.
History: First flight (Jet Provost) 16 June 1954; (Strikemaster) 26 October 1967; first delivery 1968.
Users: (Jet Provost) Iraq, Kuwait, Rhodesia, S Yemen, Sri Lanka, Sudan, UK, Venezuela; (Strikemaster) Ecuador, Kenya, Kuwait, New Zealand, Oman, Saudi Arabia, Singapore, S Yemen.

Development: The Percival Provost basic trainer flew in February 1950. Hunting then produced a jet version, and flew this in June 1954. Subsequently the Hunting (later BAC) Jet Provost became a successful basic trainer made in great numbers for the RAF and many overseas countries, and more powerful pressurised versions are still one of BAC's current products. From this was developed the BAC.145 multi-role trainer/attack aircraft, which in turn was developed into the highly refined Strikemaster. With a more powerful Viper engine, the Strikemaster proved to be a great world-

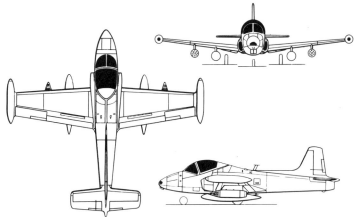

Above: Three-view of basic BAC 167 Strikemaster with rocket pods and tanks.

wide success. It has side-by-side ejection seats, and the ability to operate from the roughest airstrip whilst carrying a combat load three times a typical bomber's load in the 1930s and any desired equipment fit. The Strikemaster has set a world record for the number of repeat orders placed by its export customers. In early 1977 there were no plans to install the most powerful Viper, the Mk 632, because this would reduce time between overhauls and increase cost without meeting any requirement expressed by a customer. In 1973-76 BAC refurbished 177 RAF Jet Provosts, in the course of which VOR, DME and ILS were installed.

Left: Strikemaster Mk 80 of the Royal Saudi Air Force, with typical pylon loads of tanks and 18-round Matra rocket launchers. BAC delivered 25 to this customer in 1968–69, followed by ten Mk 80A. Strikemasters have proved extremely popular among Middle East air forces.

Left: Strikemaster Mk 88 of Royal New Zealand Air Force. The initial batch of ten led to a repeat order for another six used for advanced weapon training.

Left: Strikemaster Mk 87 of Kenya Air Force. Six were delivered and five are currently in use as attack/trainer aircraft. The KAF is soon to have to learn the more costly and complex F-5E.

Left: Strikemaster Mk 82 of the Sultan of Oman's Air Force, taxiing out with 1,000lb bombs and 80mm Sura rockets. The SOAF received 12, followed by eight Mk 82A, and though several have been shot down (some by SA-7 missiles) these tough and simple machines have proved ideal in helping to defeat the Dhofar rebellion, which was officially declared ended in 1976.

BAC Canberra and Martin/GD B-57

Canberra 1 to 24 (data for B(I).12 except where otherwise indicated)

Origin: English Electric Aviation (now British Aerospace), UK; built under licence by Government Aircraft Factories, Australia (B.20) and The Martin Company, USA (see separate entry).

Type: Two-seat interdictor.

Engines: Two 7,500lb (3402kg) thrust Rolls-Royce Avon 109 single-shaft turbojets, (PR.9) two 11,250lb (5100kg) Avon 206.

Dimensions: Span 63ft 11½in (19.5m); (PR.9) 67ft 10in; length 65ft 6in (19·95m); height 15ft 7in (4·72m).

Weights: Empty 23,173–27,950lb (10,400–12,700kg); loaded 43,000lb (19,504kg) maximum permissible 56,250lb (25,515kg).

Performance: Maximum speed 580mph (933km/h) at 30,000ft (9144m) or Mach 0·83; initial climb at maximum weight 3,400ft (1036m)/min; service ceiling 48,000ft (14,630m); range (typical mission at low level) 805 miles (1295km); ferry range 3,630 miles (5,842km).

Armament: Four 20mm Hispano cannon; three 1,000lb (454kg) bombs or sixteen 4·5in flares internally; two AS.30 missiles or two 1,000lb bombs or two packs of 37 rockets externally.

History: First flight (prototype) 13 May 1949; first service delivery October 1950; first flight of B(I) series 23 July 1954.

Users: Argentina, Ecuador, Ethiopia, France (trials), W Germany, India, New Zealand, Peru, Rhodesia, S Africa, Sweden (trials), Venezuela.

Development: When W. E. W. "Teddy" Petter joined English Electric at Preston as chief engineer he already had a scheme for a jet bomber. To meet specification B.3/45 he eventually planned a straightforward unswept aircraft with a broad wing for good behaviour at great heights, with two of the new axial jet engines centred on each wing giving a total of 15,000lb thrust. Like the Mosquito, the A.1 bomber was to be fast enough to escape interception, whilst carrying a 6,000lb bomb load over a radius of 750 nautical miles. It was to have a crew of two and a radar bomb sight for blind attacks in all conditions. The prototype amazed everyone with its low-level manoeuvrability, and the A.1, named Canberra, was a superb flying machine from the start. But the radar bombing system lagged years in development, and a new specification, B.5/47, had to be raised to cover a simpler visual bomber with a transparent nose and crew of three. This entered production without much more trouble and became the first axial-jet aircraft in the RAF. First Canberra B.2s were painted black on sides and under-surfaces, but this changed in 1952 to grey-blue, and the white serial number was

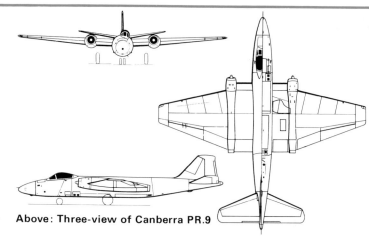

Above: Three-view of Canberra PR.9

painted extra-large to serve as a "buzz number" visible to fighter pilots from a safe distance. In February 1951 a B.2 set a transatlantic record flying out to Baltimore to serve as pattern aircraft for the Martin B-57 programme (see entry). The Korean war caused a sudden jump in orders, and Canberra B.2s were made by EECo and by Handley Page (75), Avro (75) and Short (60). The PR.3 was a reconnaissance version with longer fuselage for more fuel. The T.4 had side-by-side dual controls. The Mk 5 prototype introduced Avon 109 engines and integral wing tanks, and was to be a visual target marker. It led to the B.6, the heavier and more powerful replacement for the B.2. The corresponding reconnaissance version was the PR.7, from which was derived the much more powerful, long-span PR.9 developed and built by Short. Most versatile Canberra was the B(I).8, with offset pilot canopy and nav/bomb position in the nose. With four 20mm cannon (and ammunition for 55 seconds continuous firing) the Mk 8 also carried a wide range of under-wing missiles, bombs, tanks and special pods, and, like earlier versions, proved an export winner, particularly the B(I).12. Until they were ready the B(I).6 served in Germany in the multi-role tasks and also dashed to Kuwait in 1961. Later mark numbers include special trainers, electronic-warfare versions, target tugs, pilotless targets and, as one-off conversions, platforms for testing almost every British postwar engine, missile and airborne device. Total Canberra production was 925 in Britain; Australia made 49 B.20s for the RAAF.

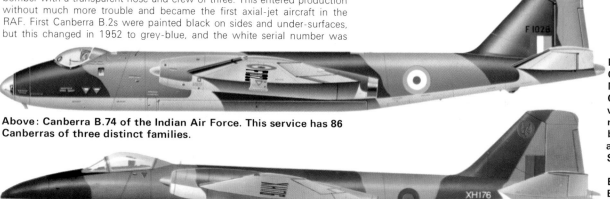

Above: Canberra B.74 of the Indian Air Force. This service has 86 Canberras of three distinct families.

Above: The high-altitude Canberra PR.9 equips 39 Sqn at RAF Wyton. This version was built by Shorts.

Photo below left: Canberra T.17 of No 360 Sqn, RAF Cottesmore. This, with the E.15, is a rebuild of earlier bomber versions, and 360 Sqn is joint-Services-operated.

Below: Canberra B.62 of 1 Escuadron de Bombardeo, Argentine Air Force. This again is a rebuild, but still a tactical bomber.

B-57A to B-57G Night Intruder, RB-57A, D and F

Origin: Design, English Electric Aviation, UK; original US prime contractor, The Martin Co, Baltimore, USA; (RB-57F) GD/Fort Worth.

Type: Two-seat tactical attack and reconnaissance (RB versions, strategic reconnaissance at extreme altitude).

Engines: (A, B, C, E, G) two 7,220lb (3275kg) thrust Wright J65-5 (US Sapphire) single-shaft turbojets; (D) two 11,000lb (4990kg) Pratt & Whitney J57-37A two-shaft turbojets; (F) two 18,000lb (8165kg) Pratt & Whitney TF33-11A two-shaft turbofans and two 3,300lb (1500kg) Pratt & Whitney J60-9 single shaft turbojets.

Dimensions: Span (A, B, C, E, G) 64ft (19·5m); (D) 106ft (32·3m); (F) 122ft 5in (37·32m); length (A, B, C, D, E) 65ft 6in (19·96m); (G) 67ft (20·42m); (F) 69ft (21·03m); height (A, B, C, E, G) 15ft 7in (4·75m); (D) 14ft 10in (4·52m); (F) 19ft (5·79m).

Weights: Empty (A, B, C, E, typical) 26,800lb (12,200kg); (G) about 28,000lb (12,700kg); (D) 33,000lb (14,970kg); (F) about 36,000lb (16,330kg); maximum loaded (A) 51,000lb; (B, C, E, G) 55,000lb (24,950 kg); (D) not disclosed, (F) 63,000lb (28,576kg).

Performance: Maximum speed (A, B, C, E, G) 582mph (937km/h); (D, F) over 500mph (800km/h); initial climb (A, B, C, E, G) 3,500ft (1070m)/min; (D, F) about 4,000ft (1220m)/min; service ceiling (A, B, C, E, D) 48,000ft (14,630m); (D) 65,000ft (19,800m); (F) 75,000ft (22,860m); maximum range with combat load (high altitude) (A, B, C, E, G) 2,100 miles (3380kg); (D) about 3,000 miles (4828km); (F) about 3,700 miles (5955km).

Armament: (A and all RB versions) none; (B, C, E, G) provision for four 20mm or eight 0·5in guns fixed in outer wings (very rarely, other guns fixed in forward fuselage); internal bomb load of 5,000lb (2268kg) on rotary bomb door plus eight rockets, two 500lb bombs or other stores on under-wing pylons (while retaining tip tanks)

History: First flight (Canberra in UK) 13 May 1949; (production B-57A) 20 July 1953; (B) June 1954.

Users: Pakistan, Taiwan, USA (Air Force, ANG), Vietnam.

Development: In October 1949 Martin flew the extremely advanced XB-51 trijet attack bomber, but this proved to be inflexible and operationally unattractive. The much less advanced British Canberra, on the other hand, proved to have precisely the qualities the US Air Force was seeking, with near-perfect operational flexibility, versatility, outstanding manoeuvrability, long range and endurance and a good weapon load. The decision to adopt this foreign combat aircraft — a step unprecedented in the US since 1918 — was swiftly followed by choice of Martin and development of the B-57A as a version built to US standards with many small modifications. The main batch comprised B-57B tandem-seaters, with dual C trainers and multi-role (tactical bomber/recce/trainer/tug) E models. Martin also made 20 grossly redesigned RB-57D reconnaissance aircraft with J57 engines on greatly extended wings. Though incapable of Canberra-style manoeuvres, nor of high speeds at low levels, the D flew many valuable multi-sensor missions over a great deal of Communist territory with the USAF and Nationalist Chinese. There were at least three D sub-types, some having counter-measures and sensing pods on the wing tips and/or tail and one version having large radomes at each end of the fuselage for strategic

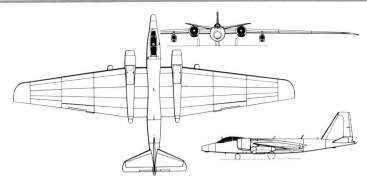

Above: Three-view of General Dynamics RB-57F.

electronic reconnaissance. Another B-57D task was to work with U-2Ds in upper-atmospheric sampling, but all of this type were grounded in 1963 as a result of structural fatigue. It was partly because of the interim nature of the D that, in 1960, General Dynamics was entrusted with the task of designing and building an even more dramatic high-altitude B-57 version, the F. Though the 21 of this type were not new aircraft, little of the old is evident. The wing is entirely new, with more than double the area of the original Canberra wing and a new fatigue-resistant multi-spar structure. Most of the fuselage is new, as is the vertical tail. There are four underwing hard points for pylons, two of which are often occupied by the J60 boost engine pods supplementing the large turbofans. The nose is packed with electronics, and multi-sensor equipment can be seen all over the fuselage. Various F models have operated from the United States, Europe and Middle East, Japan, Alaska, Panama, Argentina and possibly other countries. Meanwhile many of the B, C and E models have been updated by the fitment of modern night and all-weather sensing, target designation and weapon-aiming systems, the rebuilt aircraft being B-57G. Major new items are low-light TV, infra-red detector and laser ranging. About half the 403 B-57s served in the night attack role in Vietnam, the G being developed just too late for the conflict. Though 10 to 15 years old, the B-57 established an outstanding record in accurate weapon delivery under the most difficult conditions.

Above: Reconditioned EB-57B of Kansas Air National Guard.

Above: B-57B of 31 Bomber Wing, Pakistan Air Force.

Below: B-57B of regular USAF unit drops eight 750lb bombs on a target in Vietnam in December 1967.

Cessna A-37 Dragonfly

A-37, -37A and -37B (Model 318E)
(data for -37B)

Origin: Cessna Aircraft Co, USA.
Type: Two-seat light strike aircraft.
Engines: Two 2,850lb (1293kg) thrust General Electric J85-17A single-shaft turbojets.
Dimensions: Span (over tip tanks) 35ft 10½in (10·93m); length (not including refuelling probe) 29ft 3in (8·92m); height 8ft 10½in (2·7m).
Weights: Empty 6,211lb (2817kg); loaded 14,000lb (6350kg).
Performance: Maximum speed 507mph (816km/h) at 16,000ft (4875m); initial climb at gross weight 6,990ft (2130m)/min; service ceiling 41,765ft (12,730m); range (maximum weapons) 460 miles (740km), (maximum fuel) 1,012 miles (1628km).
Armament: One 7·62mm GAU-2B/A six-barrel Minigun in nose; eight wing pylon stations, two inners for up to 870lb (394kg), intermediate for 600lb (272kg) and outers for 500lb (227kg); maximum ordnance load 5,680lb (2576kg).
History: First flight (XT-37) 12 October 1954; (YAT-37D) 22 October 1963; (A-37B) September 1967.
Users: (T-37) Brazil, Burma, Cambodia, Chile, Colombia, W Germany, Greece, Jordan, Pakistan, Peru, Portugal, Thailand, Turkey, US Air Force, Vietnam; (A-37) Brazil, Chile, Ethiopia (delivery embargoed at time of writing), Guatemala, Honduras, Peru, US Air Force and Air National Guard, Vietnam (left by US forces).

Development: The Cessna Model 318 was the first American jet trainer. It entered production for the US Air Force as the T-37A, powered by two 920lb (417kg) thrust Continental J69 (licence-built Turboméca Marboré) engines and with side-by-side ejection seats. All A models were subsequently converted to the standard of the main production type, the T-37B, with J69-25 engines of 1,025lb (465kg) thrust. Export versions were designated T-37C, with provision for underwing armament. Production of the T-37 was completed in 1975 with more than 1,300 delivered to the USAF and 14 other air forces. It was logical to fit the much more powerful J85 engine and restress the airframe to carry greater loads in arduous combat duties. The work began in 1960 at the time of the upsurge of interest in Co-In (counter-insurgency) aircraft to fight "brushfire wars". Deliveries of A-37A aircraft converted from T-37 trainers began in May 1967 and a squadron of 25 had flown 10,000 combat missions in Vietnam in an exten-

Below: A Cessna T-37 trainer rebuilt as one of two YAT-37D development aircraft. Right: Production A-37B in full battle trim, with no national markings (possibly USAF Tactical Air Command).

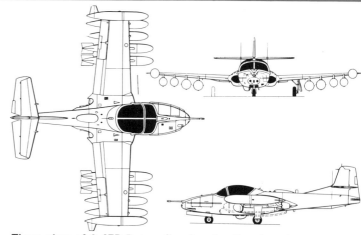

Three-view of A-37B Dragonfly, showing the almost grotesque array of possible stores.

sive evaluation by early 1968. The slightly more powerful A-37B is the definitive production version and by 1977 deliveries had exceeded 600. The A-37B is not pressurised, nor does it have ejection seats, but the dual pilots are protected by layered nylon flak curtains. The wealth of nav/com avionics and possible underwing stores is impressive and nearly all B models have a fixed nose refuelling probe.

Dassault Super Mystère

Super Mystère B2 (SMB.2)

Origin: Avions Marcel Dassault (now Dassault/Breguet), France.
Type: Single-seat fighter bomber.
Engine: 9,920lb (4500kg) thrust (with afterburner) SNECMA Atar 101G single-shaft augmented turbojet.
Dimensions: Span 34ft 5¾in (10·5m); length 46ft 1¼in (14m); height 14ft 10¾in (4·53m).
Weights: Empty 15,400lb (6985kg); loaded 22,046lb (10,000kg).
Performance: Maximum speed 686mph (1104km/h) (Mach 0·9) at sea level, 743mph (1200km/h) (Mach 1·125) at altitude; initial climb 17,500ft (5333m)/min; service ceiling 55,750ft (17,000m); range (clean) at altitude 540 miles (870km).
Armament: Two 30mm DEFA cannon; internal Matra launcher for 35 SNEB 68mm rockets; two wing pylons for tanks or weapons up to total of 2,000lb (907kg).
History: First flight (Mystère IVB) 16 December 1953; (Super Mystère B1) 2 March 1955; (pre-production SMB.2) 15 May 1956; (production SMB.2) 26 February 1957; final delivery October 1959.
Users: France, Israel.

Development: Dassault's policy of progression by logical low-risk steps often makes it difficult to see where one type ends and another begins. The Mystère IVB, flown before 1953 was out, was a major leap ahead, with tapered, milled and chem-milled sheets, integral tanks, flush aerials and a radar gunsight in a new nose. It also introduced the much more powerful and more highly developed Atar 101G with variable afterburner. But it proved to be only a stepping-stone to the bigger, heavier and more formidable·SMB.2, which introduced yet another new wing with 45° sweep and aerodynamics copied from the F-100 (but with outboard ailerons, inboard flaps and a dogtooth leading edge). The flattened nose was also derived from the North American supersonic fighter, but Dassault bravely kept the

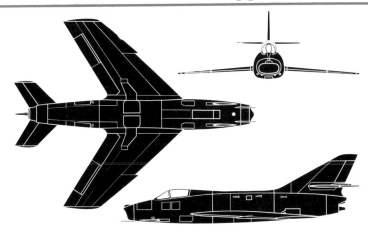

Above: Three-view of Super Mystère B2, without drop tanks.

tailplane well above the fuselage. After successful but prolonged development Dassault made a production run of 180, all powered by the Atar 101G, though the first SMB.2 had flown on an Avon RA.7R and a later Avon had been considered as the production engine. On its fourth flight, SMB.2-01, with Avon, easily exceeded Mach 1 on the level to make this the first supersonic aeroplane to go into production, or in service, in Europe (the first Mystère IVB having gone supersonic on the level on 24 February 1954). Israel purchased 24 SMB.2s and survivors were still in service in early 1977.

Left: Regular colour scheme for the SMB.2 in Armée de l'Air service, the aircraft shown being one of No 12 Wing at Cambrai (now converting to the Mirage F1.C). The SMB.2 was the first supersonic military aircraft produced in Western Europe, and it has a great operational record.

Left: This almost dazzling Super Mystère B2 uses paint not as camouflage but to render the aircraft conspicuous. One of the aircraft formerly flown by EC I/12, it was specially painted for the Tiger Meet at Cambrai on 13–19 June 1972, and proudly remained in its tiger skin for the remainder of its operational life.

Left: Another SMB.2 of No 12 Wing of the Armée de l'Air painted in an unusual camouflage scheme similar to that used by certain Middle East countries. Small numbers of these well-liked tactical aircraft remain in front-line service in 1977, though being replaced by Jaguar and F1.C.

Left: The Heyl Ha'Avir (Israel Defence Force/Air Force) has used several colour schemes for its combat aircraft. This SMB.2 is painted in the most common, designed for use over desert areas.

Left: The most common alternative scheme of camouflage for Heyl Ha'Avir combat aircraft is darker and shows to advantage over water and mountainous areas. Since 1958 Israel has operated this versatile fighter/bomber, but attrition and countless air combats have reduced numbers from the original 24 to about five.

Dassault Etendard

Etendard IVM and IV P

Origin: Avions Marcel Dassault (now Dassault/Breguet), France.
Type: Single-seat carrier strike fighter.
Engine: 9,700lb (4400kg) thrust SNECMA Atar 8B single-shaft turbojet.
Dimensions: Span 31ft 5¾in (9·6m); length 47ft 3in (14·4m); height 14ft (4·26m).
Weights: Empty 12,786lb (5800kg); loaded 22,486lb (10,200kg).
Performance: Maximum speed 683mph (1099km/h) at sea level, 673mph (1083km/h) (Mach 1·02) at altitude; initial climb 19,685ft (6000m)/min; service ceiling 49,215ft (15,000m); range (clean) at altitude 1,056 miles (1700km).
Armament: Two 30mm DEFA cannon each with 150 rounds; four wing pylons carrying variety of stores up to total weight of 3,000lb (1360kg).
History: First flight (Etendard II) 23 July 1956; (Etendard IV-01) 24 July 1956; (Etendard VI) 13 March 1957; (pre-production IVM) 21 May 1958; (production IVM) July 1961; final delivery 1964.
User: France (Aéronavale).

Development: Dassault planned the Etendard (standard, or national flag) to meet a NATO need for a light strike fighter capable of high-subsonic

The Etendard IVP carries five OMERA reconnaissance cameras, three in the nose (no radar) and two in the belly (no cannon).

speed and operation from unpaved forward airstrips. NATO specified that the engine should be the 4,850lb thrust Bristol Orpheus and this aircraft took shape as the Etendard VI. Previously Dassault had been working on a variant, powered by two of the range of very small French turbojets then under development to meet an Armée de l'Air proposal for a light interceptor, and this, though never pressed with enthusiasm, was the first to fly (Etendard II, with two 2,420lb thrust Turboméca Gabizos). Dassault scorned both. He was certain such light and under-powered aircraft would be useless and risked company money to build an Atar-powered Etendard IV. In fact, the Armée de l'Air dropped the light interceptor and the NATO contest was won by the Fiat G91. But Dassault's private-venture IV attracted the attention of the Aéronavale and, after long development, went into production in two forms. The IVM, of which 69 were built, became the standard strike fighter aircraft of the carriers *Foch* and *Clémenceau* (Flotilles 11F and 17F), while the IVP, of which 21 were ordered, is the corresponding reconnaissance aircraft serving with 16F. The IVM has Aida nose radar and a folding refuelling probe, while the camera-equipped IVP has a fixed nose probe.

Above: Three-view of Etendard IVM, with tanks and Matra pods.

Above: Etendard IVM with AS.20 missiles.

Below: Recovery of an Etendard IVM aboard a French carrier (both *Foch* and *Clémenceau* are still in commission). Today the Etendards are usually land-based, Flotille 11F being based at Landivisiau (together with the Etendard IVP reconn-aissance squadron, 16F) and 17F being located in the Riviera at Hyères. The IVM is to be phased out from 1977.

Dassault Breguet Super Etendard

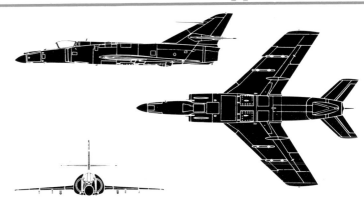

Three-view of the Super Etendard (centreline pylon not shown).

Super Etendard

Origin: Avions Marcel Dassault/Breguet Aviation, France.
Type: Single-seat carrier strike fighter.
Engine: 11,265lb (5110kg) thrust SNECMA Atar 8K-50 single-shaft turbojet.
Dimensions: Span 31ft 5¾in (9·6m); length 46ft 11½in (14·31m); height 12ft 8in (3·85m).
Weights: Empty 13,889lb (6300kg); loaded 25,350lb (11,500kg).
Performance: Maximum speed 745mph (1200km/h) at sea level, Mach 1 at altitude; initial climb 24,600ft (7500m)/min; service ceiling 52,495ft (16,000m); range (clean) at altitude, over 1,243 miles (2000km).
Armament: Two 30mm DEFA cannon; mission load up to 9,921lb (4500kg) carried on five pylons.
History: First flight (converted Etendard) 28 October 1974; first delivery, late 1977.
User: France (Aéronavale).

Development: During the late 1960s it had been expected that the original force of Etendards would be replaced, in about 1971, by a specially developed version of the Jaguar, the M version with single main wheels, full carrier equipment and specially fitted for the naval strike role. A Jaguar M completed flight development and carrier compatability, but for various reasons, mainly concerned with politics and cost, this was rejected by the Aéronavale and a search began for an alternative. After studying the A-4 Skyhawk and A-7 Corsair, the Aéronavale chose Dassault-Breguet's proposal for an improved Etendard. This has a substantially redesigned structure, for operation at higher indicated airspeeds and higher weights; a new and more efficient engine, obtained by removing the afterburner from the Atar 9K-50 of the Mirage F1.C; completely new inertial navigation system, produced mainly by SAGEM with American help; new multi-mode nose radar, produced jointly by Thomson-CSF and Electronique Marcel Dassault, with especially good performance in surface vessel detection and attack; and much greater and more varied mission load. Flight development was completed in 1974-77 with three converted Etendard IVs, the first testing the engine, the second the avionics and weapons, and the third the new wing with slats and double-slotted flaps like the Jaguar. In 1973 the Aéronavale announced it would buy 100, but this has now been cut back to 80, and budget problems have delayed service delivery until late 1977.

Below: Portrait of the first Super Etendard development aircraft, externally almost indistinguishable from the production version. This aircraft was fitted with most of the operational equipment, including the SAGEM (Singer-Kearfott) inertial navigation system and the Thomson-CSF/EMD Agave radar. Though called a "strike fighter", in fact the Super Etendard is a tactical attack machine for low-level use.

Douglas A-1 Skyraider

BT2D, AD, A-1 Skyraider

Origin: Douglas Aircraft Co, El Segundo, USA.
Type: Initially, naval torpedo and dive bomber; later, many roles (see text).
Engine: One 3,020hp Wright R-3350-26W or 3,050hp R-3350-26WB Cyclone 18-cylinder two-row radial.
Dimensions: Span 50ft (A-1J, 50ft 9in) (15·24m); length 38ft 2in to 40ft 1in (A-1J 38ft 10in, 11·84m); height 15ft 5in to 15ft 10in (A-1J, 15ft 8¼in, 4·77m).
Weights: Empty 10,090–12,900lb (A-1J, 12,313lb, 5585kg); maximum loaded 18,030lb–25,000lb (A-1J, 25,000lb, 11,340kg).
Performance: Maximum speed 298–366mph (A-1J) 318mph (512km/h); initial climb (typical) 2,300ft (700m)/min; service ceiling (typical) 32,000ft (9753m); range, from 900 miles with maximum ordnance to 3,000 miles (4828km) with maximum external fuel.
Armament: Varies with sub-type, but attack variants generally four 20mm cannon in outer wings and 15 pylons for total ordnance/fuel load of 8,000lb (3630kg).
History: First flight (XBT2D-1) 18 March 1945; service delivery (AD-1) November 1946; termination of production February 1957.
Users: Chad, Central African Rep.; non-combat, France, Kampuchea, USA, Vietnam.

Development: Like so many of Ed Heinemann's designs the Skyraider simply refused to grow obsolete. Planned in 1944 as the first combined torpedo/dive bomber to be a single-seater, the XBT2D competed against three rival designs and, due to Martin's protracted detailed development of the more powerful AM-1 Mauler, soon became the favoured type. Its obvious versatility led to modifications for additional missions, explored in 1946 with prototypes fitted with various kinds of radar, searchlights and countermeasures. Of 242 AD-1s, 35 were AD-1Q ECM aircraft with a countermeasures operator in the rear fuselage. The AD-2 was strengthened and given greater fuel capacity and several were equipped for drone control and target towing. The AD-3 branched out into anti-submarine detection/strike and, with a vast belly radome, airborne early-warning. The further refined AD-4 was built in the largest number (1,032), of which 40 were supplied to the Royal Navy in 1952. Still in their USN "midnight blue" these AD-4W early-warners equipped 849 Sqn. Much larger numbers were used from land airfields by the Armée de l'Air. In the redesigned AD-5 (later

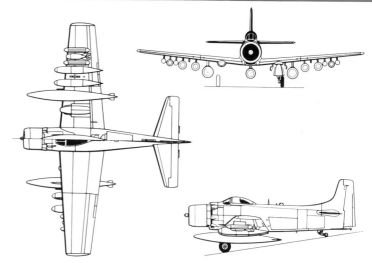

Above: Three-view of the final sub-type, the A-1J (plus assorted store

redesignated A-1E) the wider fuselage allowed some versions to have side-by-side seating, with a rear cabin for 12 seats or four stretchers. None of the A-1E variants were single-seaters, but the A-1H (AD-6) reverted to the single seat and 713 were built for multi-role operations. The final A-1J (AD-7) version had strengthened wings for low-level tactical attack. Altogether 3,180 of this amazingly versatile aircraft were built. Whereas it was almost terminated in 1946, by 1962 the Skyraider was fast becoming one of the most important weapon platforms in the US inventory with the renewed outbreak of warfare in Vietnam. Eventually more than 1,000 Skyraiders were sent to Vietnam, operated not only by the Navy and Marines but also by the US Air Force and the air force of the Republic of Vietnam (ARVN). It proved one of the most effective combat types as it had done earlier in Korea, with huge weight-lifting ability, ten-hour endurance and ability to survive severe flak. Its popularity is shown by its two nicknames: Sandy, and Spad.

Below: A flight of A-1H Skyraiders of the South Vietnam Air Force (VNAF), which no longer exists.

FMA IA58 Pucarà

IA 50 GII, IA 58 and Astafan Trainer

Origin: FMA (Military Aircraft Factory), Argentina.
Type: IA 58, tactical attack and counter-insurgency; IA 50, utility transport and survey; Trainer, trainer and light attack.
Engines: (IA 58) two 1,022ehp Turboméca Astazou XVIG single-shaft turboprops; (IA 50) two 1,000ehp Turboméca Bastan VIC single-shaft turboprops; (Trainer) two 2,710lb (1230kg) thrust Turboméca Astafan geared turbofans.
Dimensions: Span (IA 58 and Trainer) 47ft 6¾in (14·5m); (IA 50) 64ft 3¼in (19·59m); length (IA 50 and Trainer) 46ft 3in (14·1m); (IA 50) 50ft 2½in (15·3m); height (IA 58 and Trainer) 17ft 7in (5·36m); (IA 50) 18ft 5in (5·61m).
Weights: Empty (IA 58) 8,900lb (4037kg); (IA 50) 8,650lb (3924kg); (Trainer) 8,377lb (3800kg); loaded (IA 58) 14,300lb (6486kg); (IA 50) 17.085lb (7750kg); (Trainer) 14,330lb (6500kg).
Performance: Maximum speed (IA 58) 323mph (520km/h); (IA 50) 310mph (500km/h); (Trainer) about 400mph (643km/h); initial climb (IA 58) 3,543ft (1080m)/min; (IA 50) 2,640ft (805m)/min; service ceiling (IA 58) 27,165ft (8280m); (IA 50) 41,000ft (12,500m); range with maximum fuel (IA 58) 1,890 miles (3042km); (IA 50) 1,600 miles (2575km).
Armament: IA 58, and optional for Trainer, two 20mm Hispano cannon and four 7·62mm FN machine guns in forward fuselage; pylons under fuselage and outer wings for up to 3,307lb (1500kg) of stores or tanks.
History: First flight (IA 50) 23 April 1963; (IA 58) 20 August 1969; (service delivery of IA-58) November 1974.
User: Argentina.

Development: The unusual but effective Pucará was derived from the larger IA 50 GII (Guarani II) multi-role transport, noted for its slender unswept wings but sharply swept fin and rudder. The first production batch of GII's comprised 18 to the Argentine Air Force for communications and seating for up to 15 passengers, four as photo survey aircraft with the Military Geographic Institute and one as a VIP transport for the President of Argentina. Many others were ordered later, some having ski gear for use in the Antarctic. The smaller IA 58 seats pilot and observer in tandem Martin-Baker ejection seats and is well equipped for all-weather tactical Co-In operations. Deliveries began in 1975 on the first batch of 30 for the Argentine Air Force, with further batches up to a predicted total of 100 being discussed.

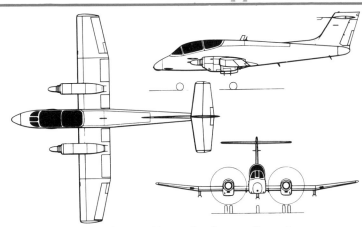

Three-view of IA 58 Pucará in production configuration.

Interest has been expressed by several other nations in this versatile and cost/effective aircraft, which can operate from rough strips down to about 2,000ft in length. The Trainer uses the IA 58 airframe restressed to have two turbofan engines on the sides of the fuselage, the twin-wheel main gears retracting forwards into wing pods in the same locations as the engine nacelles on the IA 58. It was expected that this project would lead to a tactical Co-In version, but development has been delayed by inflation.

Above: First prototype flying with right engine feathered.

Below: Production Pucará of the Fuerza Aeréa Argentina, with bombs and rocket pods. Interest in this Co-In type machine has been expressed by other air forces in S America and Africa.

Fairchild Republic A-10A

A-10A

Origin: Fairchild Republic Co, USA.
Type: Single-seat close-air-support aircraft.
Engines: Two 9,275lb (4207kg) thrust General Electric TF34-100 two-shaft turbofans.
Dimensions: Span 57ft 6in (17·53m); length 53ft 4in (16·26m); height 14ft 5½in (4·4m).
Weights: Empty 21,813lb (9894kg); maximum loaded 47,200lb (21,410 kg).
Performance: Maximum speed (clean) 460mph (740km/h), 380mph (612km/h) at maximum weight; initial climb 1,000ft (328m)/min at maximum weight; take-off distance (at maximum weight) 3,850ft (1173m), (at forward-airstrip weight with six Mk 82 bombs) 1,130ft (344m); steady speed in 45° dive with full airbrake 299mph (481km/h); close-air-support radius with reserves 288 miles (463km); ferry range 2,723 miles (4382km).
Armament: 30mm high-velocity GAU-8/A cannon in forward fuselage; 11 pylons for total external ordnance load of 16,000lb (7257kg) (exceptionally, 18,500lb, 8392kg).
History: First flight 10 May 1972; service delivery for inventory December 1974.
User: US Air Force.

continued on page 66▶

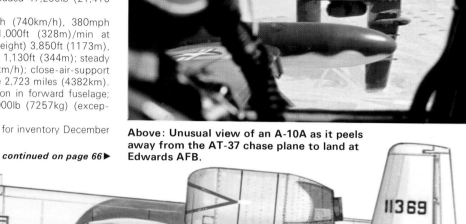

Above: Unusual view of an A-10A as it peels away from the AT-37 chase plane to land at Edwards AFB.

Above: The first YA-10A prototype, in 1972 trim.

1 Flight refuelling probe (removable)
2 Universal aerial refuelling receptacle slipway (UARRSI) for drogue or boom
3 Nosewheel (retracted) position
4 Forward electrical compartment
5 Battery
6 Gun muzzle
7 Nosewheel door
8 Nosewheel leg (offset to starboard)
9 Twin landing/taxying lamps
10 Forward retracting nosewheel
11 Nosewheel linkage
12 General Electric GAU-8A 30mm Gatling-type gun
13 Forward gun support pallet
14 Gun recoil pack
15 Linkless feed chutes
16 Hydraulic pump
17 Pave Penny laser target-seeker pod (offset to starboard)
18 Integral titanium armour (lower cockpit area and vital controls)
19 Rubber pedals
20 Control column
21 Head-up display
22 Bullet-resistant glass windscreen
23 Upward-hinged canopy
24 Headrest
25 Pilot's zero-zero ejection seat
26 Electrical and avionics equipment bays
27 Forward fuselage structure
28 Ammunition drum (1,350 rounds)
29 Ammunition chute interchange
30 Heavy skin panelling area (HE shell triggering)
31 LB warning aerial
32 Fuselage fuel cells forward wall (fire retardant foam filling)
33 Fuselage forward fuel cell
34 Fuselage 'notch' (wing centre-section carry-through)

35 Centre bulkhead
36 Fuselage aft fuel cell
37 Control runs/plumbing/wiring service trough
38 Port wing fuel cell (wing break to fuselage centreline)
39 Front spar
40 Leading edge structure
41 Fuselage port bomb pylon
42 Triple bomb-rack shoe
43 Fuselage starboard triple bomb cluster
44 Fuselage port triple bomb cluster
45 Wing centre-section bomb pylon

46 Mk 82 bomb (nominal 500 lb/227 kg)
47 Mainwheel gear door
48 Landing gear fairing
49 Wing strengthening
50 Wing centre/outer section break
51 Main landing gear (port and starboard identical)
52 Wing outer-section bomb pylons
53 Single Mk 82 bombs
54 Port mainwheel
55 Outboard pylon (extended forward)
56 Front spar (outer section)
57 Centre spar
58 Rear spar
59 Wing structure
60 Drooped wingtip
61 Port navigation light
62 Port aileron
63 Flaps
64 Port engine nacelle
65 X-band beacon
66 Hydraulic reservoirs (2)
67 Auxiliary power unit
68 Environmental control system
69 Aerials
70 APU exhaust
71 VHF Tacan
72 Port nacelle forward attachment
73 Port nacelle aft attachment
74 Control runs
75 Tailplane centre-section
76 IFF aerial (beneath fuselage)
77 Tailplane structure
78 Tailplane/fin bolt attachments
79 Rudder lower hinge
80 Port rudder (same as 91)
81 Port fin (same as 92)
82 Rudder upper hinge
83 Port elevator (same as 88)
84 Elevator hinge fairing
85 Rear navigation light
86 Tail cone
87 Elevator actuation system
88 Starboard elevator
89 Tailplane stringers
90 Starboard tailplane (same as 77)

91 Starboard rudder
92 Starboard fin
93 Upward canted exhaust pipe
94 Nacelle module installation fairing
95 Steel engine bearers
96 General Electric TF34-100 turbofan (9,065 lb/4,112 kg thrust, identical port and starboard)
97 Centrebody
98 Engine intake
99 VHF/AM aerial
100 VHF/FM aerial
101 Starboard wing centre-section
102 VHF Tacan aerial
103 Starboard bomb pylons
104 Single Mk 82 bombs
105 Outboard pylon (extended forward)
106 Flaps
107 Wing skinning
108 Starboard aileron
109 Drooped wingtip
110 Starboard navigation light

Above: Firing the tank-killing GAU-8/A gun, with greater muzzle horsepower than any other aircraft gun in history.

Above: A production A-10A lets go a Mk 82 laser-guided bomb, one of a large family of pinpoint munitions used by the US Air Force since 1968. The A-10A can carry six of the AGM-65A Maverick missiles or 28 unguided Mk 82 bombs each weighing 580lb (nominal 500lb).

The cutaway drawing shows the size of the monster GAU-8/A gun and its drum of 1,350 milk-bottle-sized rounds. What it cannot show is that as far as possible left and right parts of the A-10A are interchangeable (eg, rudders, elevators and main landing gears). More than any previous aircraft, the A-10A is designed to be "survivable" in the face of point-blank AA fire. A two-seat version is planned.

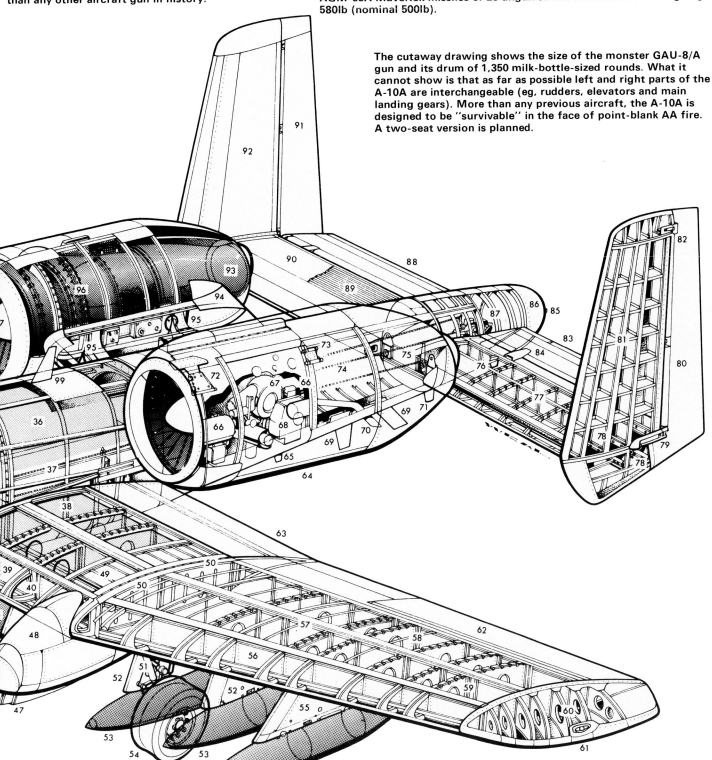

▶**Development:** Despite the more overt attractions of Mach 2 aircraft the US Air Force was forced to consider the CAS (close air support) mission because of the total unsuitability of its existing equipment. In both the wars it had had to fight since World War II — Korea and Vietnam — its aircraft had been worldbeaters but planned for a totally different kind of war. What was needed, it appeared, was something like an up-to-date Skyraider that could carry a heavy load of ordnance, had good endurance and could survive severe damage from ground fire. Between 1963-69 extensive studies gradually refined the AX specification, which had begun by presupposing a twin turbo prop and ended with a larger aircraft powered by two turbofans. After an industrywide competition the Northrop A-9A and Fairchild A-10A were chosen for prototype fly-off evaluation, which took place with two of each type at Edwards in October–December 1972. The A-10A was announced winner and GE the winner of the contest to produce the 30mm tank-busting gun, the most powerful ever fitted to any aircraft, with very high muzzle velocity and rate of fire, and muzzle horsepower 20 times that of the 75mm gun fitted to some B-25s in World War II. Named Avenger, this gun is driven hydraulically at either 2,100 or 4,200rds/min, and is fed by a drum containing 1,350 milk-bottle-size rounds. Empty cases are fed back into the rear of the drum. By 1978 ground-reloading will probably be done by a special powered system. Underwing load can be made up of any stores in the Tactical Air Command inventory, the landing gears (which protrude when retracted for damage-free emergency landing) and all tail surfaces are interchangeable, the cockpit is encased in a "bath" of thick titanium armour, and the engines are hung above the rear fuselage where their infra-red signature is a minimum. Originally Tactical Air Command intended to buy 600 of these grey-painted brutes, but despite unavoidable escalation in cost and degradation in performance the planned number has grown to 735, to be operational by 1982. By mid-1976 orders had been placed for 95, all of which had flown or were on the line, and the 1977 budget included a further 100.

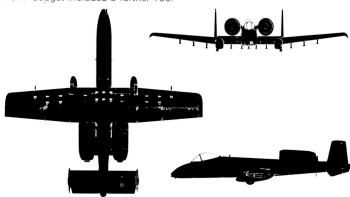

Three-view of standard Fairchild A-10A showing 11 pylons.

Below: Airbrakes open, a production A-10A of USAF Tactical Air Command releases a Hughes AGM-65A Maverick, TAC's main air/surface guided missile. Later Mavericks use TV, IR or laser guidance.

General Dynamics F-111

"TFX", F-111A to F-111F, EF-111A and FB-111A

Origin: General Dynamics/Fort Worth (EF-111A, Grumman Aerospace), USA.

Type: Two-seat all-weather attack bomber; (EF) two-seat electronic warfare; (FB) two-seat strategic bomber.

Engines: Two Pratt & Whitney TF30 two-shaft afterburning turbofans, at following ratings: (F-111A, C) TF30-3 at 18,500lb (8390kg); (D, E) TF30-9 at 19,600lb (8891kg); (F) RF30-100 at 25,100lb (11,385kg); (FB) TF30-7 at 20,350lb (9230kg).

Dimensions: Span, 72·5° sweep (A, D, E, F) 31ft 11½in (9·74m); (C, FB) 33ft 11in (10·34m); span, 16° sweep (A, D, E, F) 63ft (19·2m); (C, FB) 70ft (21·34m); length 73ft 6in (22·4m); height 17ft 1½in (5·22m).

Weights: Empty (A, C) 46,172lb (20,943kg); (D, E, F) about 49,000lb (22,226kg); (FB) about 50,000lb (22,680kg); maximum loaded (A, 3) 91,500lb (41,500kg); (D, E, F) 99,000lb (44,906kg); (FB) 119,000lb (54,000kg).

Performance: Maximum speed (clean), Mach 2·2 at 35,000ft or above, or about 1,450mph (2335km/h); maximum speed at low level (clean) Mach 1·2 or 800mph (1287km/h); maximum speed at maximum weight, subsonic at low level; service ceiling (clean) (A) 51,000ft (15,500m); (F) 60,000ft (18,290m); range on internal fuel (A, C) 3,165 miles (5093km).

continued on page 68 ▶

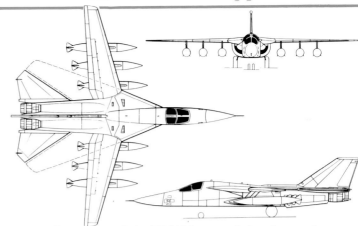

Above: Three-view of the FB-111A strategic bomber version.

Below: Destruction rains down from an F-111A development aircraft during weapon-delivery tests in 1966. Using only the two inboard (swivelling) pylons on each swing-wing, 24 Mk 82 bombs, each of a nominal 500lb mass (actual weight, 580lb), fall in a loose cluster. Maximum bomb load of most F-111 tactical versions is 28,000lb, while the FB-111A can carry 31,500lb (14,288kg).

►**Armament:** Internal bay for two 750lb (341kg) bombs or 20mm M-61 multi-barrel gun; eight underwing pylons for total of 31,500lb (14,290kg) of stores, inner pylons swivelling with wing sweep and outer four being fixed and loaded only with wing at 16°.

History: First flight 21 December 1964; service delivery June 1967; first F-111F with -100 engine, May 1973; EF-111A (Grumman ECM conversion) 1976–7.

Users: Australia, US Air Force.

Development: Developed to meet a bold Department of Defense edict that a common type of "fighter" called TFX should be developed to meet all future tactical needs of all US services, the F-111A proved both a world-beater and a great disappointment. Thrown into the public eye by acrimonious disagreement over which bidder should get the production contract, it then stayed in the news through being grossly overweight, up in drag and suffering from severe problems with propulsion, structure and systems. Eventually almost superhuman efforts cleared the F-111A for service, overcoming part of the range deficiency by a considerable increase in internal fuel. The RAAF bought 24 F-111C with long-span wings and stronger landing gear and took delivery after they had been nine years in storage. The RAF ordered 50 similar to the C but with updated avionics, but this deal was cancelled. Only 141 low-powered A-models were built, the US Navy F-111B fighter was cancelled, and the next batch was 94 of the E type with improved intakes and engines (20th Tac Ftr Wing at Upper Heyford, England). Then came the 96 F-111D with improved avionics (27th TFW in New Mexico) and finally the superb F-111F with redesigned P-100 engine of greatly increased thrust and cheaper avionics (366 TFW, in Idaho). The heavier FB-111A, with the ability to carry six AGM-69A SRAM missiles externally, was bought to replace the B-58 and early B-52 models in Strategic Air Command. Cost-inflation cut the FB order from 210 back to 76. With several RF and ECM conversions the total programme amounted to 539 plus 23 development prototypes. To keep the line open a further 12 were authorised in 1974 to be built at a low rate until 1976. In 1977 the only work on F-111s was structural improvement of aircraft in service and the Grumman programme to convert two A models to EF-111A configuration carrying comprehensive electronic-warfare equipment including ALQ-99 jammers of the type fitted to the Navy's EA-6B. If the EF-111A performs well Grumman may convert a further 40 to equip two USAF squadrons. The EF will not carry weapons, and will direct other aircraft. No aircraft has ever had worse luck or a worse press, and in combat in South East Asia the sudden loss of three of the first six aircraft was eventually found to be due to a faulty weld in the tailplane power unit. In fact all models of the F-111 are valuable machines with great range and endurance, excellent reliability and great ability to hit a point target in a first-pass strike, even in blind conditions. These aircraft are bombers, with much greater power and weight than four-engined bombers of World War II. It was unfortunate they were loosely launched as "fighters".

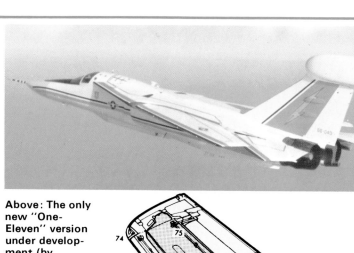

Above: The only new "One-Eleven" version under development (by Grumman), the EF-111A is a most sophisticated tactical electronic-warfare aircraft. Visible modifications include the ALQ-99 canoe (belly) and tail aerials.

Above: An unusual view of an F-111E, a simpler aircraft than the D but fitted with enlarged inlet ducts for the same sub-type of TF30 engine. Since 1970 the E has equipped the 20th TFW in England.

Below: Receptacle open, and carrying four SRAMs, an FB-111A of SAC thrusts gently ahead so that the KC-135 boomer can make contact.

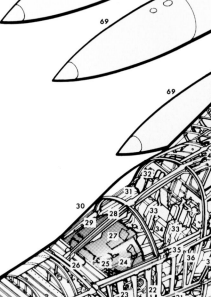

Above: The cutaway drawing illustrates the F-111D, a tactical bomber generally similar to the F-111A but with slightly more powerful engines and greatly enhanced—and much more costly—electronics. The sophisticated "Mk II" electronics of the D were later simplified, with little degradation in capability, to save money in the final sub-type, the F-111F.

An F-111C of the type used by 1 and 6 Sqns, RAAF.

1 Hinged radome
2 General Electric APQ-113 attack radar
3 Texas Instruments APQ-110 terrain-following radar
4 Radome hinges (2)
5 Radar mounting
6 Nose lock
7 Angle-of-sideslip probe
8 Homing aerial (high)
9 Forward warning aerial
10 Homing aerial (low and mid)
11 ALR-41 aerial
12 Flight control computers
13 Feel and trim assembly
14 Forward avionics bay
14 Forward avionics bay Mk II digital computer
15 Angle-of-attack probe
16 UHF Comm/TACAN No 2
17 Module forward bulkhead

and stabilization flaps (2)
18 Twin nosewheels
19 Shock strut
20 Underfloor impact attenuation bag stowage (4)
21 Nosewheel well
22 Lox converter
23 Rudder pedals
24 Control column
25 Lox heat exchanger
26 Auxiliary flotation bag pressure bottle
27 Weapons sight
28 Forward parachute bridle line
29 De-fog nozzle
30 Windscreen
31 Starboard console
32 Emergency oxygen bottles
33 Crew seats
34 Bulkhead console

35 Wing sweep control handle
36 Recovery chute catapult
37 Provision/survival pack
38 Attenuation bags pressure bottle
39 Recovery chute
40 Aft parachute bridle line
41 UHF data link/AG IFF No 1 (see 123)
42 Stabilization-brake chute
43 Self-righting bag
44 UHF recovery
45 ECM aerials (port and starboard)
46 Forward fuselage fuel bay
47 Ground refuelling receptacle
48 Weapons bay
49 Module pitch flaps (port and starboard)
50 Aft flotation bag stowage
51 Flight refuelling receptacle

52 Primary heat-exchanger (air-to-water)
53 Ram air inlet
54 Rate gyros
55 Rotating glove
56 Inlet variable spike
57 Port intake
58 Air brake/undercarriage door
59 Auxiliary inlet blow-in doors
60 Rotating glove pivot point
61 Inlet vortex generators
62 Wing sweep pivot
63 Wing centre-box assembly
64 Wing sweep actuator
65 Wing sweep feedback
66 Control runs
67 Rotating glove drive set
68 Inboard pivot pylons (2)
69 Auxiliary drop tanks (500 gal/ 2,271 litres)
70 Outboard fixed pylon(s);

subsonic/jettisonable
71 Slat drive set
72 Wing fuel tank (325 gal/ 1,473 litres)
73 Leading-edge slat
74 Starboard navigation light
75 Flap drive set
76 Outboard spoiler actuator
77 Starboard spoilers
78 Inboard spoiler actuator
79 Flaps
80 Wing swept position
81 Auxiliary flap
82 Auxiliary flap actuator
83 Nuclear weapons and weapons control equipment package
84 Wing sweep/Hi Lift control box

85 Flap, slat and glove drive mechanism
86 Starboard engine bay
87 Yaw feel spring
88 Roll feel spring
89 Yaw trim actuator
90 Yaw damper servo
91 Roll stick position transducer
92 Pitch trim actuator (manual)
93 Roll damper servo
94 Pitch trim actuator (series)
95 Pitch feel spring
96 Pitch-roll mixer
97 Pitch damper servo
98 Pitch stick position transducer
99 Aft fuselage frames
100 Aft fuselage fuel bays
101 Tailplane (stabilizer) actuator
102 Starboard tailplane
103 Rear-warning radar aerials
104 HF aerials
105 Detector scanner
106 X-band radar
107 Rudder
108 Integral vent tank
109 Fin aft spar
110 Fin structure
111 Fin/fuselage attachment
112 Rudder servo actuator
113 Variable nozzle
114 Tailfeathers
115 ECM aerials
116 ALR-41 aerials
117 Tailplane structure
118 Tailplane pivot point
119 Free floating blow-in doors
120 Afterburner section
121 Tailplane power unit
122 Wing swept position
123 UHF data link/AG IFF No 2
124 Ventral fin
125 Fire detection sensing element loops
126 Cross frame
127 Engine access hatches

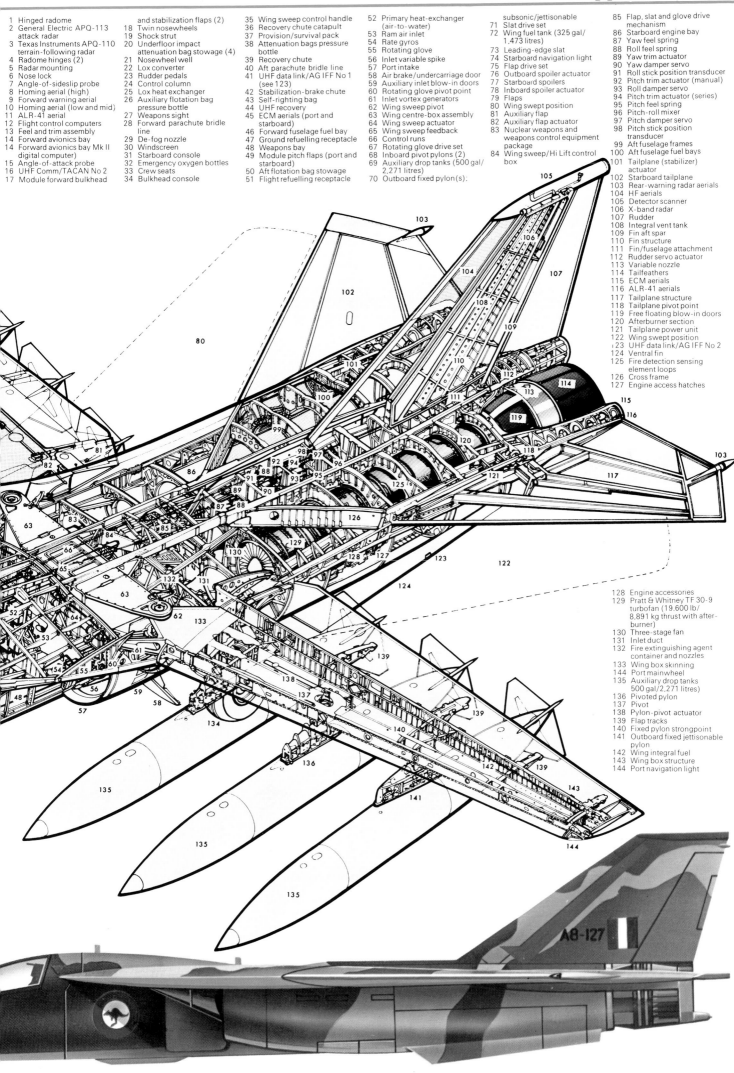

128 Engine accessories
129 Pratt & Whitney TF 30-9 turbofan (19.600 lb/ 8,891 kg thrust with afterburner)
130 Three-stage fan
131 Inlet duct
132 Fire extinguishing agent container and nozzles
133 Wing box skinning
144 Port mainwheel
135 Auxiliary drop tanks 500 gal/2,271 litres)
136 Pivoted pylon
137 Pivot
138 Pylon-pivot actuator
139 Flap tracks
140 Fixed pylon strongpoint
141 Outboard fixed jettisonable pylon
142 Wing integral fuel
143 Wing box structure
144 Port navigation light

Grumman A-6 Intruder and Prowler

Grumman A-6A, B, C, E, EA-6A and B and KA-6D

Origin: Grumman Aerospace, USA.
Type: (A-6A, B, C, E) two-seat carrier-based all-weather attack; (EA-6A) two-seat ECM/attack; (EA-6B) four-seat ECM; (KA-6D) two-seat air-refuelling tanker.
Engines: (Except EA-6B) two 9,300lb (4218kg) thrust Pratt & Whitney J52-8A two-shaft turbojets; (EA-6B) two 11,200lb (5080kg) J52-408.
Dimensions: Span 53ft (16·15m); length (except EA-6B) 54ft 7in (16·64m); (EA-6B) 59ft 5in (18·11m); height (A-6A, A-6C, KA-6D) 15ft 7in (4·75m); (A-6E, EA-6A and B) 16ft 3in (4·95m).
Weights: Empty (A-6A) 25,684lb (11,650kg); (EA-6A) 27,769lb (12,596kg); (EA-6B) 34,581lb (15,686kg); (A-6E) 25,630lb (11,625kg); maximum loaded (A-6A and E) 60,626lb (27,500kg); (EA-6A) 56,500lb (25,628kg); (EA-6B) 58,500lb (26,535kg).
Performance: Maximum speed (clean A-6A) 685mph (1102km/h) at sea level or 625mph (1006km/h, Mach 0·94) at height; (EA-6A) over 630mph; (EA-6B) 599mph at sea level; (A-6E) 648mph (1043km/h) at sea level; initial climb (A-6E, clean) 8,600ft (2621m)/min; service ceiling (A-6A) 41,660ft (12,700m); (A-6E) 44,600ft (13,595m); (EA-6B) 39,000ft (11,582m); range with full combat load (A-6E) 1,077 miles (1733km); ferry range with external fuel (all) about 3,100 miles (4890km).
Armament: All attack versions, including EA-6A, five stores locations each rated at 3,600lb (1633kg) with maximum total load of 15,000lb (6804kg);

1 Radome
2 APQ-92 radar antenna
3 Bulkhead
4 Rain removal nozzle
5 ALQ-126 receiver antenna fairing
6 Refuelling boom (detachable)
7 In-flight refuelling receptacle
8 Two-piece windscreens
9 Senior EWO's panoramic/video display consoles
10 Pilot's instrument panel shroud
11 Control column
12 Rudder pedals
13 Pitot static tubes (port and starboard)
14 Power brake
15 APQ-92 transmitter
16 Anti-collision beacon
17 "L"-band antenna
18 ALQ-92 (IFF) antenna
19 Taxi/landing light
20 Nosewheel leg fairing
21 Nosewheel leg
22 Tow link (landing position)
23 Tow link (launch position)
24 Dual nosewheel assembly
25 Nosewheel retraction jack
26 Nosewheel well door
27 Approach lights
28 Shock-absorber link
29 APQ-92 high and low voltage
30 APQ-92 modulator
31 Cockpit floor level
32 Anti-skid control
33 Fuselage forward frames
34 Pilot's ejection seat
35 Senior Electronic Warfare Officer's (ALQ-99 tactical jamming) ejection seat
36 Upward-hinged forward cockpit canopy
37 Canopy mechanism
38 Aft cockpit port EWO's console
39 Handgrips
40 Security equipment
41 Splitter plate
42 Port engine intake
43 Intake frames
44 Aft cockpit entry ladder
45 Electric hydraulic pump
46 Manual selector valves
47 Cockpit aft bulkhead
48 Third Electronic Warfare Officer's (ALQ-92 comms jamming) ejection seat
49 Second Electronic Warfare Officer's (ALQ-99 tactical jamming) ejection seat
50 Canopy mechanism
51 Upward-hinged aft cockpit canopy
52 Starboard outer ECM pod
53 Intake
54 Pod turbine power-source
55 ALQ-41/ALQ-100 starboard spear antenna
56 Leading-edge slats (deployed)
57 Starboard inner integral wing fuel cell
58 Starboard inner wing fence
59 Wing-fold cylinders
60 Hinge assembly
61 Wing-fold line
62 Starboard outer integral wing fuel cell
63 Fuel probe
64 Wing structure
65 Starboard outer wing fence
66 Starboard navigation light
67 Starboard formation light
68 Wingtip speed-brakes (open)

69 Speed-brake actuating cylinder fairing
70 Fence
71 Wingtip fuel dump outlet
72 Starboard single-slotted flap (outer section)
73 Starboard flaperons
74 Flaperon mechanism
75 Starboard single-slotted flap (inner section)
76 UHF/TACAN antenna
77 Directional control
78 Dorsal fairing frame
79 Computer power trim
80 Fuel lines
81 Control runs
82 Dorsal anti-collision beacon
83 Relay assembly group
84 Control linkage (bulkhead rear face)
85 Fuselage forward fuel cell
86 ALQ-126 receiver/transmitter
87 Hydraulic reservoir
88 Wingroot section front spar
89 Wingroot leading-edge spoiler
90 Engine bay frames
91 Port J52-P-408 turbojet
92 Mainwheel door mechanism
93 Engine accessories
94 Mainwheel well door
95 Port mainwheel well
96 Transducer/accelerometer
97 Power distribution/transfer panels
98 Fuselage mid fuel cell
99 Roll trim actuator
100 Lateral actuator control
101 ARA-48 antenna
102 Vent lines
103 Fuselage aft fuel cell
104 Longitudinal control
105 Air-conditioning scoop
106 Fuel vent scoop
107 TACAN receiver
108 ALQ-92 air scoop
109 LOX (3)
110 Heat exchanger
111 Gyroscope assembly
112 Fuel control relay box
113 Adaptor-compensator compass
114 Arresting hook lift
115 Analogue to digital converter
116 Relay box/blanking unit

117 Control runs
118 Frequency and direction encoder
119 Fuel vent
120 Dorsal fillet
121 Starboard horizontal stabilizer (tailplane)
122 Multi-spar vertical stabilizer (fin) structure
123 Horizontal stabilizer actuator
124 Transmitter remote compass
125 Power divider
126 System Integration Receiver (SIR) antennae/receiver fairing
127 SIR antennae (Bands 4 and 7/8)
128 SIR receivers (Bands 4-9)
129 SIR antennae (Bands 4 and 5/6)
130 ALQ-41 transmit antennae
131 Attenuator
132 RF divider
133 Rudder upper hinge
134 Rudder (honeycomb structure)
135 Antenna (Band 1)
136 Antenna (Band 2)
137 Rudder lower hinge
138 Rear navigation light
139 ALQ-126 transmit antenna
140 Fuel vent
141 Receiver antenna
142 Rudder actuator
143 Port horizontal stabilizer structure
144 Horizontal stabilizer pivot
145 Aft power supply
146 ALQ-41 transmitter
147 ALQ-41 receiver/transmitter
148 ALQ-100 receiver/transmitter
149 Chaff dispensers
150 UHF "L"-band antenna

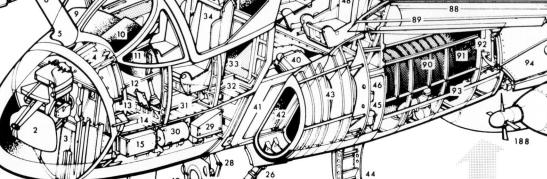

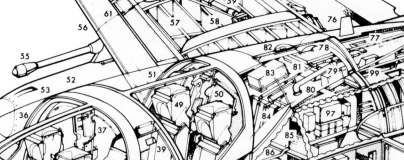

typical load thirty 500lb (227kg) bombs; (EA-6B, KA-6D) none.

History: First flight (YA2F-1) 19 April 1960; service acceptance of A-6A 1 February 1963; first flight (EA-6A) 1963; (KA-6D) 23 May 1966; (EA-6B) 25 May 1968; (A-6E) 27 February 1970; final delivery 1975.

User: USA (Navy, Marine Corps).

Development: Selected from 11 competing designs in December 1957, the Intruder was specifically planned for first-pass blind attack on point surface targets at night or in any weather. Though area ruled, the aircraft (originally designated A2F) was designed to be subsonic and is powered by two straight turbojets which in the original design were arranged with tilting jetpipes to help give lift for STOL (short takeoff and landing). Despite its considerable gross weight — much more than twice the empty weight and heavier than most of the heavy World War II four-engine bombers — the Intruder has excellent slow-flying qualities with full span slats and flaps. The crew sit side-by-side under a broad sliding canopy giving a marvellous view in all directions, the navigator having control of the extremely comprehensive navigation, radar and attack systems which are integrated into

continued on page 72▶

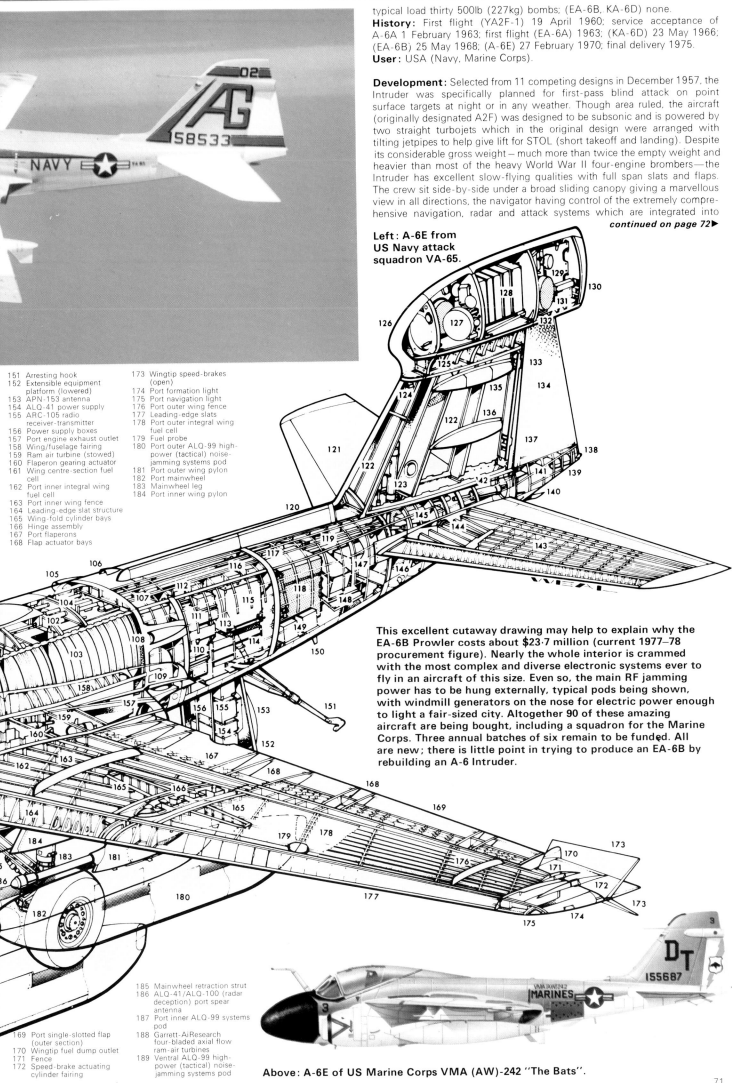

Left: A-6E from US Navy attack squadron VA-65.

151 Arresting hook
152 Extensible equipment platform (lowered)
153 APN-153 antenna
154 ALQ-41 power supply
155 ARC-105 radio receiver-transmitter
156 Power supply boxes
157 Port engine exhaust outlet
158 Wing/fuselage fairing
159 Ram air turbine (stowed)
160 Flaperon gearing actuator
161 Wing centre-section fuel cell
162 Port inner integral wing fuel cell
163 Port inner wing fence
164 Leading-edge slat structure
165 Wing-fold cylinder bays
166 Hinge assembly
167 Port flaperons
168 Flap actuator bays

173 Wingtip speed-brakes (open)
174 Port formation light
175 Port navigation light
176 Port outer wing fence
177 Leading-edge slats
178 Port outer integral wing fuel cell
179 Fuel probe
180 Port outer ALQ-99 high-power (tactical) noise-jamming systems pod
181 Port outer wing pylon
182 Port mainwheel
183 Mainwheel leg
184 Port inner wing pylon

This excellent cutaway drawing may help to explain why the EA-6B Prowler costs about $23·7 million (current 1977–78 procurement figure). Nearly the whole interior is crammed with the most complex and diverse electronic systems ever to fly in an aircraft of this size. Even so, the main RF jamming power has to be hung externally, typical pods being shown, with windmill generators on the nose for electric power enough to light a fair-sized city. Altogether 90 of these amazing aircraft are being bought, including a squadron for the Marine Corps. Three annual batches of six remain to be funded. All are new; there is little point in trying to produce an EA-6B by rebuilding an A-6 Intruder.

169 Port single-slotted flap (outer section)
170 Wingtip fuel dump outlet
171 Fence
172 Speed-brake actuating cylinder fairing

185 Mainwheel retraction strut
186 ALQ-41/ALQ-100 (radar deception) port spear antenna
187 Port inner ALQ-99 systems pod
188 Garrett-AiResearch four-bladed axial flow ram-air turbines
189 Ventral ALQ-99 high-power (tactical) noise-jamming systems pod

Above: A-6E of US Marine Corps VMA (AW)-242 "The Bats".

►DIANE (Digital Integrated Attack Navigation Equipment). In Vietnam the A-6A worked round the clock making pinpoint attacks on targets which could not be accurately bombed by any other aircraft until the arrival of the F-111. The A-6E introduced a new multi-mode radar and computer and supplanted earlier versions in Navy and Marine Corps squadrons. The EA-6A introduced a valuable group of ECM (electronic countermeasures), while retaining partial attack capability, but the extraordinary EA-6B is a totally redesigned four-seat aircraft where the entire payload comprises the most advanced and comprehensive ECM equipment ever fitted to a tactical aircraft, part of it being carried in four external pods with windmill generators to supply electric power. The latest addition to attack versions was TRAM (Target Recognition Attack Multisensor), a turreted electro-optical/infra-red system matched with laser-guided weapons. In 1977 Grumman was building new Prowlers and the last A-6Es, and converting A-6A models to the latest E standard. In the course of 1977 the first Intruders were to be modified to fire the Harpoon active-seeker missile.

Above: As project pilot Peter Timillo climbs down the ladder, navigator Jim Johnson inspects the TRAM (Target-Recognition Attack Multisensor) under the nose of their special test A-6E.

Above: Three-view of A-6E, with side views of EA-6A (centre) and EA-6B (bottom).

Below: Cadillac among combat aircraft, an EA-6B Prowler of US Navy VAQ-129 shows off its ALQ-99 high-power jamming pods with windmill generators—and staircase to get aboard.

Above: Hectic launch of an A-6A strike during the involvement in Vietnam. Intruders of VA-165 aboard *Constellation*.

Left: Two Rockwell AGM-53B Condor long-range homing air/surface missiles adorn the wings of this A-6A trials aircraft of the Naval Ordnance Test Station at China Lake, California.

Hawker Siddeley Buccaneer

Buccaneer S.1, 2, 2A, 2B, 2C, 2D and 50

Origin: Hawker Siddeley Aviation (formerly Blackburn Aircraft, now British Aerospace), UK.

Type: Two-seat attack and reconnaissance.

Engines: (S.1) two 7,100lb (3220kg) thrust Bristol Siddeley (previously de Havilland) Gyron Junior 101 single-shaft turbojets; (all later marks) two 11,030lb (5003kg) Rolls-Royce Spey 101 two-shaft turbofans.

Dimensions: Span (1) 42ft 4in (12·9m); (2 and subsequent) 44ft (13·41m); length 63ft 5in (19·33m); height 16ft 3in (4·95m).

Weights: Empty (1) 26,000lb (2) about 30,000lb (13,610kg); maximum loaded (1) 46,000lb (20,865kg); (2) 62,000lb (28,123kg).

Performance: Maximum speed (all) 645mph (1038km/h, Mach 0·85) at sea level; initial climb (2, at 46,000lb) 7,000ft (2134m)/min; service ceiling not disclosed but over 40,000ft (9144m); range on typical hi-lo-hi strike mission with weapon load (2) 2,300 miles (3700km).

Armament: Rotating bomb door carries four 1,000lb (454kg) bombs or multi-sensor reconnaissance pack or 440gal tank; (S.2 and later) four wing pylons each stressed to 3,000lb (1361kg), compatible with very wide range of guided and/or free-fall missiles. Total internal and external stores load 16,000lb (7257kg).

History: First flight (NA.39) 30 April 1958; (production S.1) 23 January 1962; (prototype S.2) 17 May 1963; (production S.2) 5 June 1964; final delivery late 1975.

Users: S Africa, UK (RAF, Royal Navy).

continued on page 74 ▶

Above: Spin-stabilized 68mm rockets ripple from the 18-tube launchers of a Buccaneer of the RAF.

Below: Buccaneer S.2 of 809 Sqn, Royal Navy, with flight-refuelling "Buddy" Mk 20B hose-reel pod on inner right pylon.

Foot of page: Low-level run by a Buccaneer S.2A of 12 Sqn, RAF. Over the years the Buccaneer has been equipped with ever-better ECM and other defensive avionics, some of which show externally. Most aircraft carry wing drop tanks and a fixed FR probe.

▶**Development:** After the notorious "Defence White Paper" of April 1957, which proclaimed manned combat aircraft obsolete, the Blackburn B.103, built to meet the naval attack specification NA.39, was the only new British military aircraft that was not cancelled. Development was grudgingly permitted, and this modest-sized subsonic machine was gradually recognised as a world-beater. Designed for carrier operation, its wing and tail were dramatically reduced in size as a result of very powerful tip-to-tip supercirculation (BLC, boundary-layer control) achieved by blasting hot compressed air bled from the engines from narrow slits. The S.1 (strike Mk 1) was marginal on power, but the greatly improved S.2 was a reliable and formidable aircraft. The first 84 were ordered by the Royal Navy and most of these have been transferred to RAF Strike Command, designated S.2B when converted to 'launch Martel missiles. Those remaining with the Navy are S.2Ds (2C if they are not Martel-compatible). In January 1963 the South African Air Force bought 16 S.50s with BS.605 boost rocket built into a retractable pack in the rear fuselage to facilitate use from hot and high airstrips. Finally — perhaps rather surprisingly, considering the scorn vented on Buccaneer during the TSR.2 era — the RAF signed in 1968 for 43 new S.2Bs with adequate equipment, including a refuelling probe which is never used in front-line service in Germany. Within the limits of crippling budgets the RAF Buccaneers have been updated by improved avionics and ECM, and all models have the advantage of an unbreakable long-life airframe and the ability to carry weapons internally. In 1977 they were getting Pave Spike laser-guided bomb systems. Altogether the Mk 2 Buccaneer is one of the most cost/effective aircraft ever designed for tactical use.

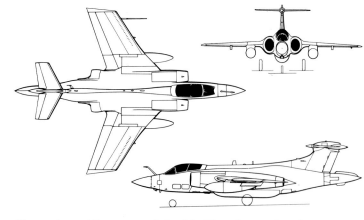

Three-view of Buccaneer S.2 with FR probe and bomb-door tank.

Right: One of the missions of the Buccaneer is the LABS "over the shoulder" toss of nuclear weapons. Here, in vertical attitude, is an S.2A of 237 OCU.

Far right: Heading into the sunset, this S.2B of 15 Sqn, RAF Laarbruch, has bulged weapon-door fuel tank and rocket pods.

Buccaneer S.2B of 16 Sqn, Laarbruch.

1 In-flight refuelling probe
2 Radar scanner
3 Multi-mode search and fire-control radar
4 Weapon recorder
5 Radome (folded)
6 Radome hinge
7 Weapon release computer
8 Windscreen rain dispersal duct
9 Windscreen wiper
10 Birdproof windscreen
11 Pilot's head-up display
12 Instrument panel shroud
13 Rudder pedals
14 Nosewheel leg hinge point
15 Landing and taxi lamp
16 Shock absorber strut
17 Nosewheel forks
18 Aft retracting nosewheel
19 Avionics equipment
20 Engine throttles
21 Canopy side rail
22 Pilot's ejector seat
23 Seat firing handle
24 Aft sliding canopy
25 Observer's blast shield
26 Observer's instrument display
27 Starboard engine air intake
28 Observer's ejection seat
29 Cockpit floor structure
30 Head-up display symbol generator
31 Port engine air intake
32 Anti-icing air line
33 Air intake duct
34 Cockpit aft pressure bulkhead
35 Forward main fuselage fuel tank
36 Canopy motor
37 Canopy top rail
38 Rolls-Royce RB.168-1A Spey Mk 101 turbofan
39 Bleed air ducting
40 Detachable bottom cowling
41 Engine front mounting
42 Firewall frame
43 Engine aft mounting
44 Forward fuselage structure
45 Bleed air cross-over duct
46 Canopy hand winding shuttle
47 Detachable engine top cowling

48 Starboard slipper tank
49 Data link acquisition pod
50 Data link inboard pylon
51 Martel air-to-surface missile
52 Wing fold hinge line
53 Leading edge blowing air duct
54 UHF antenna
55 Dorsal spine structure
56 Anti-collision light
57 Wing-fold actuator
58 Wing-fold operating link
59 Starboard outer pylon
60 ARI 18218 aerial housing
61 Blown leading edge
62 Starboard navigation light
63 Formation light
64 Starboard blown aileron
65 Aileron actuator
66 Starboard wingtip (folded)
67 Aileron and flap blowing ducts
68 Starboard blown flap
69 Port wing tip (folded)
70 Centre fuselage fuel tank
71 Machined spar ring frames
72 Ring frame bolted attachment
73 Aft fuselage fuel tank
74 Electrical cable ducting in dorsal spine
75 Avionics equipment bay
76 Air data computer
77 HF notch aerial
78 Equipment bay cooling air intake
79 Fin spar attachment
80 Fin structure
81 Tailplane actuator
82 Tailplane operating rod
83 Tailplane blowing air duct
84 Bullet fairing
85 Forward passive warning system antenna
86 Blown tailplane leading edge
87 All-moving tailplane structure

88 Tailplane flap
89 Tailplane flap actuator
90 Hinge attachment point
91 Top fairing
92 Rear navigation light
93 Formation light
94 Aft passive warning system antenna
95 Port tailplane flap
96 Rudder structure
97 Rudder operating link
98 Rudder actuator
99 Airbrake jack
100 Drag-link hinge attachment
101 Airbrake operating slide
102 Split tailcone airbrake
103 Top strake
104 Honeycomb reinforcing panel
105 Bottom strake
106 Airbrake (open)
107 Hinge arm
108 Aft fuselage structure
109 Vent pipe
110 Arresting hook
111 Jet efflux fairing
112 Engine jet pipe
113 Bomb bay door actuator
114 Bomb door aft hinge
115 Port blown flap structure
116 Flap actuator
117 Port blown aileron
118 Blowing air duct
119 Wing spar bolted attachment
120 Wing fold actuator
121 Top of main undercarriage leg
122 Mainwheel well

123 Main undercarriage jack
124 Inboard blown leading edge
125 Inboard pylon fitting
126 430 Imp gal (1956 l) slipper tank
127 Wing fold main-spar hinge
128 Rear spar hinge
129 Main undercarriage levered suspension
130 Inboard retracting mainwheel
131 Mainwheel door
132 Outboard pylon fitting
133 Aileron operating rod
134 Port aileron actuator
135 Outer wing structure
136 Machined skin panels

137 Port wingtip
138 Formation light
139 Crash trip switches
140 Wing lifting lug
141 Port navigation light
142 Blown outboard leading edge
143 Pitot head
144 Port ARI 18218 aerial housing
145 Outboard pylon
146 Port Martel air-to-surface missile
147 Thirty-six tube rocket pod
148 Rotary bomb bay door
149 Bomb door locks
150 1,000lb bomb (four internal)

151 Forward hinge point
152 425 Imp gal (1932 l) bomb door auxiliary tank

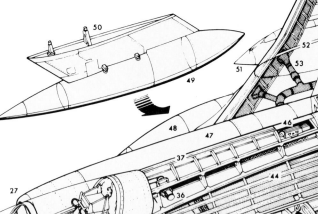

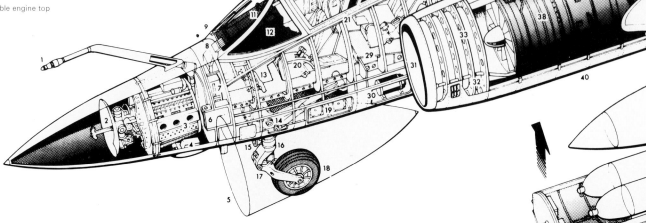

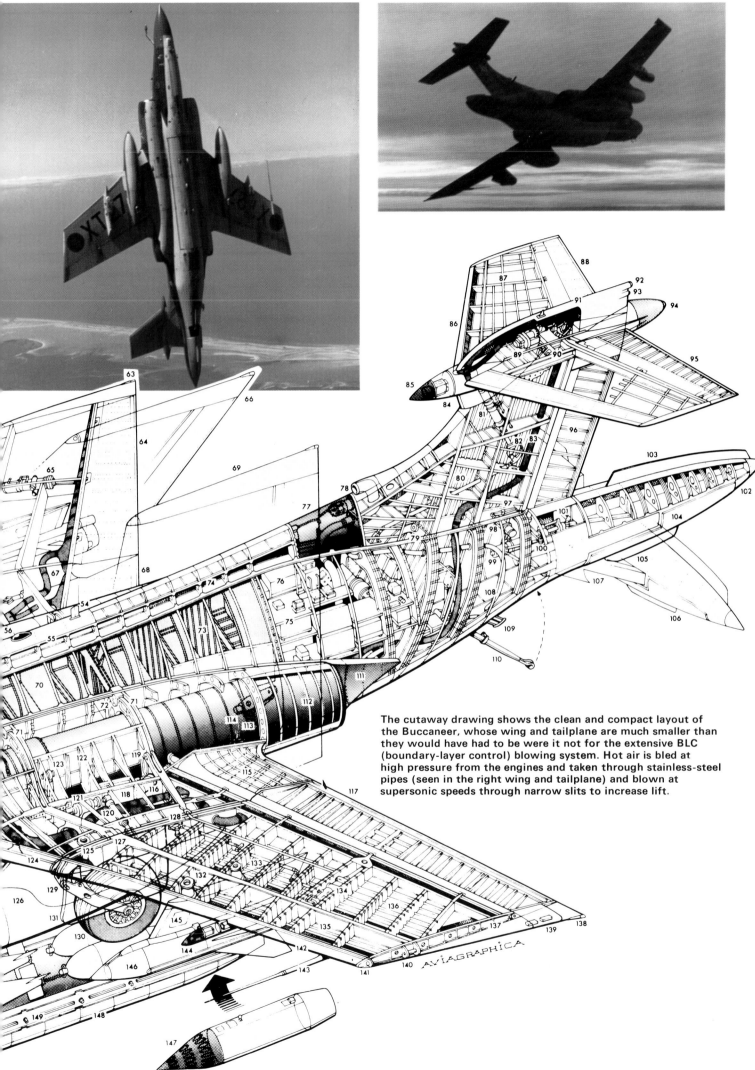

The cutaway drawing shows the clean and compact layout of the Buccaneer, whose wing and tailplane are much smaller than they would have had to be were it not for the extensive BLC (boundary-layer control) blowing system. Hot air is bled at high pressure from the engines and taken through stainless-steel pipes (seen in the right wing and tailplane) and blown at supersonic speeds through narrow slits to increase lift.

Hawker Siddeley Harrier and Sea Harrier

Harrier GR.3 and T.4, AV-8A, TAV-8A and Sea Harrier FRS.1

Origin: Hawker Siddeley Aviation (now British Aerospace), UK.
Type: Single-seat tactical attack and reconnaissance; (T.4, TAV) dual trainer or special missions; (Sea Harrier) single-seat ship-based multi-role.
Engine: One 21,500lb (9752kg) thrust Rolls-Royce Pegasus 103 two-shaft vectored-thrust turbofan (US designation F402); (Sea H, Pegasus 104).
Dimensions: Span 25ft 3in (7·7m), (with bolt-on tips, 29ft 8in); length 45ft 6in (13·87m), (laser nose, 47ft 2in; two-seat trainers, 55ft 9½in; Sea Harrier, 48ft); height 11ft 3in (3·43m) (two-seat, 13ft 8in).
Weights: Empty (GR.1) 12,200lb (5533kg); (Sea H) 13,000lb (5897kg); (T) 13,600lb (6168kg); maximum (non-VTOL) 26,000lb (11,793kg).

continued on page 78▶

Above: Harrier GR.3 in hovering mode, modulating the airbrake to come to rest at the exact desired location. Flying the Harrier is basically simple, but is nevertheless a new technique.

Right: A sunny pair of AV-8As of US Marine Corps VMA-231 at Cherry Point, North Carolina. This is a more basic aircraft than the RAF GR.3, with no inertial system and armed with bombs and Sidewinders.

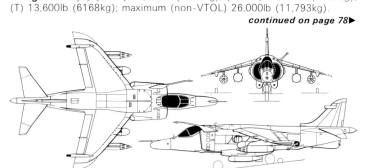

Above: Three-view drawing of Harrier GR.3 with FR probe, laser nose and (dotted) ferry tips.

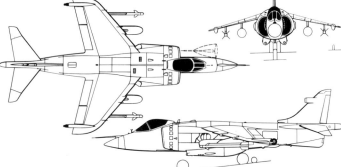

Above: Three-view drawing of Sea Harrier FRS.1.

1 Starboard navigation light
2 Detachable wingtip
3 Outrigger wheel fairing
4 Hydraulic retraction jack
5 Leg fairing (upper section)
6 Starboard outrigger wheel
7 Leg fairing (lower section)
8 Telescopic oleo strut
9 Roll reaction valve
10 Roll reaction outlet
11 Aileron hinge fairing
12 Bonded aluminium honeycomb structure
13 Fuel jettison pipe
14 Aileron hinge
15 Tandem aileron jack and autostabilizer
16 Pylon spigot
17 Starboard outer pylon
18 Leading-edge duct to roll-reaction valve
19 Leading-edge wing fences
20 Riveted rolled stringers
21 Fuel/air valves

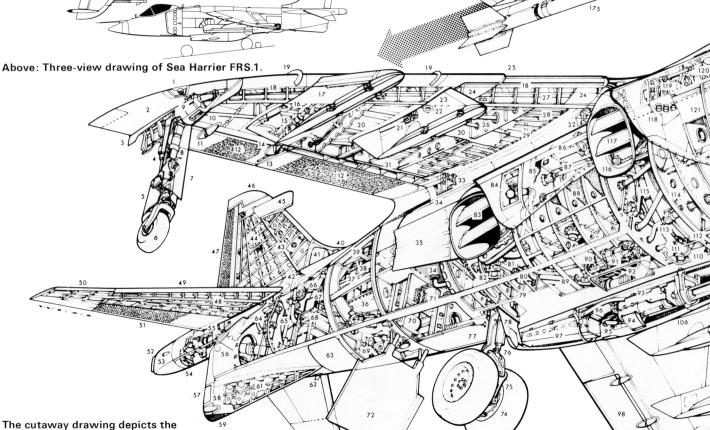

The cutaway drawing depicts the Harrier GR.3 with laser ranger in an extended nose. Three generations later than the P.1127 of 1960, this aircraft is a refined and useful tactical attack and reconnaissance platform. It can be based closer to friendly front-line troops than any other fixed-wing aircraft, and has often been in action within 90 seconds of a scramble call. In the British Sea Harrier and US Marine Corps AV-8B the basic concept is being taken further

22 Pylon spigot
23 Starboard inner pylon
24 Wing fuel tank
25 Wing leading-edge dog-tooth
26 Tank pressurizing air
27 Aileron control rod
28 Front spar web
29 Machined skin plank
30 Centre spar web

31 Rear spar web
32 Main wing attachment point
33 Rear spar/fuselage attachment point
34 Fuselage rear fuel tank
35 Rear nozzle heat shield
36 Vibration-isolating equipment rack
37 IFF-SSR transponder
38 TACAN trans-receiver

39 Ram-air turbine
40 HF tuner
41 HF notch aerial
42 Tailfin attachment bracket
43 Tailfin structure
44 Total temperature sensor
45 ECM pod
46 VHF aerial
47 Rudder
48 Tailplane front spar

61 Ventral fin structure
62 UHF stand-by aerial
63 Rear fuselage access hatch
64 Hydraulic filter No 2 (tailplane)
65 Tandem tailplane jack
66 Rudder cable tensioner
67 UHF stand-by
68 Batteries shelf
69 Airbrake jack

86 Reservoir No 2 system
87 Rear nozzle bearings
88 Starboard centre fuel tank

115 Intermediate chain
116 Chain and sprocket nozzle actuation
117 Fan air nozzle
118 Ground servicing points No 2 system: hydraulics, fuel and air supply external connections
119 GTS/APU
120 Venting air
121 Titanium heat shield (internal)
122 Rolls-Royce Bristol Pegasus 103 engine (buried)
123 Starboard front fuel tank
124 Machined nose-gear/keel beams
125 Nose-gear fairing
126 Nosewheel steering motor
127 Shock absorber strut
128 Nosewheel
129 Nosewheel fork
130 Landing lamp
131 Port front fuel tank
132 Supplementary air doors (free-floating)
133 Port intake
134 Pre-closing nose-gear door
135 Bleed-air duct
136 Nosewheel steering hydraulics accumulator
137 Nosewheel input mechanism
138 Control cables
139 Intake centre-body
140 First-stage fan
141 Supplementary air doors (free-floating)
142 Boundary air bleed doors (suction-operated)
143 Cabin air-conditioning and pressurization plant
144 Entry hand/footholds
145 Seat mounting frame
146 Nozzle actuation cable tension regulator
147 TACAN aerial
148 Bulkhead labyrinth seal
149 Pitch reaction valve ducting
150 Rudder quadrant
151 Starboard instrument console (TACAN and IFF control panels)
152 Top longeron
153 Canopy MDC (miniature detonating cord)
154 Martin-Baker Type 9A rocket-assisted ejection seat
155 Canopy
156 Machined windscreen frame and arch
157 Birdstrike-proof windscreen
158 Rear-view mirror
159 Head-up display
160 Instrument panel
161 Rudder pedals
162 Front pressure bulkhead
163 Pitch reaction valve
164 Nose cone attachment spigots
165 IFF aerial
166 Port-facing camera
167 Circular camera port
168 Nose cone
169 Ferranti Laser Ranger and Marked Target Seeker array
170 Laser mirror
171 Pitot boom
172 Outer weapons pylons
173 Adaptor shoe
174 Missile launch-rail
175 Sidewinder air-to-air missiles (USMC a/c)

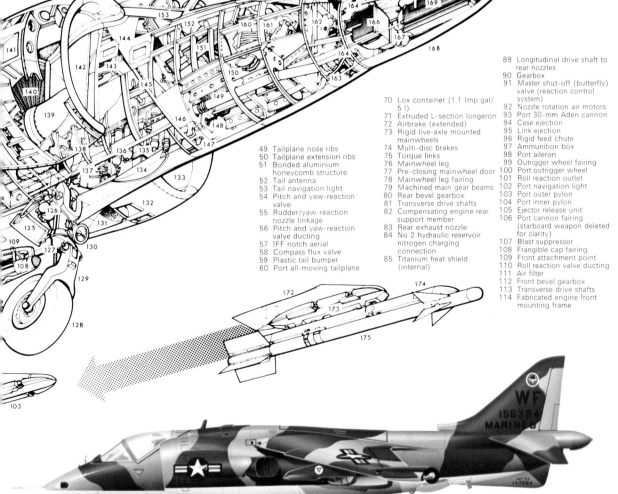

49 Tailplane nose ribs
50 Tailplane extension ribs
51 Bonded aluminium honeycomb structure
52 Tail antenna
53 Tail navigation light
54 Pitch and yaw-reaction valve
55 Rudder/yaw-reaction nozzle linkage
56 Pitch and yaw-reaction valve ducting
57 IFF notch aerial
58 Compass flux valve
59 Plastic tail bumper
60 Port all-moving tailplane

70 Lox container (1.1 Imp gal/5 l)
71 Extruded L-section longeron
72 Airbrake (extended)
73 Rigid live-axle mounted mainwheels
74 Multi-disc brakes
75 Torque links
76 Mainwheel leg
77 Pre-closing mainwheel door
78 Mainwheel leg fairing
79 Machined main gear beams
80 Rear bevel gearbox
81 Transverse drive shafts
82 Compensating engine rear support member
83 Rear exhaust nozzle
84 No 2 hydraulic reservoir nitrogen charging connection
85 Titanium heat shield (internal)

89 Longitudinal drive shaft to rear nozzles
90 Gearbox
91 Master shut-off (butterfly) valve (reaction control system)
92 Nozzle rotation air motors
93 Port 30-mm Aden cannon
94 Case ejection
95 Link ejection
96 Rigid feed chute
97 Ammunition box
98 Port aileron
99 Outrigger wheel fairing
100 Port outrigger wheel
101 Roll reaction outlet
102 Port navigation light
103 Port outer pylon
104 Port inner pylon
105 Ejector release unit
106 Port cannon fairing (starboard weapon deleted for clarity)
107 Blast suppressor
108 Frangible cap fairing
109 Front attachment point
110 Roll reaction valve ducting
111 Air filter
112 Front bevel gearbox
113 Transverse drive shafts
114 Fabricated engine front mounting frame

Hawker Siddeley AV-8A of US Marine Corps VMA-513, Beaufort, South Carolina.

77

Performance: Maximum speed 737mph (1186km/h, Mach 0·972) at low level; maximum dive Mach number, 1·3; initial climb (VTQL weight) 50,000ft (15,240m)/min; service ceiling, over 50,000ft (15,240m); tactical radius on strike mission without drop tanks (hi-lo-hi) 260 miles (418km); ferry range 2,070 miles (3330km).

Armament: All external, with many options. Under-fuselage strakes both replaceable by pod containing one 30mm Aden or similar gun, with 150 rounds. Five or seven stores pylons, centre and two inboard each rated at 2,000lb (907kg), outers at 650lb (295kg) and tips (if used) at 220lb (100kg) for Sidewinder or similar. Normal load 5,300lb (2400kg), but 8,000lb (3630kg) has been flown.

History: First hover (P.1127) 21 October 1960; first flight (P.1127) 13 March 1961; first flight (Kestrel) 13 February 1964; (development Harrier) 31 August 1966; (Harrier GR.1) 28 December 1967; (T.2) 24 April 1969; squadron service (GR.1) 1 April 1969.

Users: Spain (Navy, AV-8A), UK (RAF, Royal Navy), USA (Marine Corps).

Development: In the 1950s the realisation that the thrust/weight ratio of the gas turbine made possible a new class of high-speed jets having VTOL (vertical takeoff and landing) capability led to a rash of unconventional prototypes and research machines. Only one has led to a useful combat aircraft. It was the P.1127, designed by Camm's team in 1957-59 around a unique engine, planned at Bristol by Stanley Hooker, in which the fan and core flows are discharged through four nozzles which, by means of chain drives from a single pneumatic motor, can be swivelled to point downwards, to lift the aircraft, or point to the rear, for propulsion. Gradually the P.1127 was transformed into the Kestrel, which equipped a UK/USA/German evaluation squadron in 1965. This was further developed into the Harrier (the much bigger, Mach 2, P.1154 for the RAF and RN having been cancelled in 1965). Powered by a Pegasus 101 rated at 19,000lb, the GR.1 was capable of flying useful combinations of fuel and stores out of any hastily prepared site and did more than any other aircraft to explore the advantages and problems of operational deployment of combat aircraft well away from any airfield. Numerous flights were made from a wide variety of naval vessels and record flights were made from the centre of London to the centre of New York and vice versa. The GR.1A had the 20,000lb Mk 102 engine and at this thrust the Harrier was adopted as the AV-8A by the US Marine Corps in both beach assault and defensive roles. All RAF and USMC aircraft have been re-engined with the Pegasus 103, giving a payload/range performance adequate for a wide spectrum of missions, many of which cannot be flown by any other aircraft. Using VIFF (vectoring in forward flight) the Harrier can fly "impossible" manoeuvres and has proved itself an extremely tricky customer in a dogfight. This is not its main mission, however, and the RAF Harrier GR.3 (92 built) is primarily a tactical attack platform with Ferranti INAS (inertial nav/attack system) and laser ranger. The USMC AV-8A (112, plus six for Spain named Matador) does not have either of these equipments but carries Sidewinder air/air missiles. Including two-seaters, production by 1977 amounted to 231. In Britain the main effort is completing development of the redesigned Sea Harrier, which should fly in 1977. The Royal Navy will deploy 24 from throughdeck cruisers and possibly other ships, and several other navies are discussing possible orders. The Sea Harrier has a completely new nose, with raised cockpit, Blue Fox radar, much enhanced systems and equipment and weapons for surface attack, reconnaissance, anti-submarine warfare and air combat. Since 1975 talks have been held with China, which is interested in buying a large number of Harriers. The next-generation AV-8B is discussed under McDonnell Douglas.

Above: Harrier GR.3 carrying four Matra 155 launchers lets go the 19 SNEB 68mm rockets from No 3. Such missiles are of value chiefly in the air/surface role.

Hawker Siddeley Hunter

Hunter 1 to 79

Origin: Hawker Aircraft, UK (now British Aerospace); licence-production in Belgium/Netherlands.

Type: Single-seat fighter, fighter-bomber and fighter-reconnaissance; two-seat dual trainer.

Engine: One Rolls-Royce Avon single-shaft turbojet (see text).

Dimensions: Span 33ft 8in (10·26m); length (single-seat, typical) 45ft 10½in (13·98m), (two-seat) 48ft 10½in (14·9m); height 13ft 2in (4·26m).

Weights: Empty (1) 12,128lb (5501kg); (9) 13,270lb (6020kg); loaded (1) 16,200lb (7347kg); (9, clean) 17,750lb (8051kg); (9, maximum) 24,000lb (10,885kg).

Performance: Maximum speed (typical of all) 710mph (1144km/h) at sea level, 620mph (978km/h, Mach 0·94) at height; initial climb (Avon 100-series) about 5,500ft (1676m)/min; (Avon 200-series) 8,000ft (2438m)/min; service ceiling 50,000ft (15,240m); range on internal fuel 490 miles (689km), with maximum fuel 1,840 miles (2965km).

Armament: Four (two-seaters, usually one, sometimes two) 30mm Aden cannon beneath cockpit floor, each with 150 rounds; single-seaters normally have underwing pylons for two 1,000lb (454kg) bombs and 24 3in rockets, later or refurbished aircraft carrying two 230 Imp gal drop tanks in addition.

History: First flight (P.1067) 20 June 1951; (production F.1) 16 May 1953; (two-seater) 8 July 1955; final delivery from new, 1966.

Users: Abu Dhabi, Chile, India, Iraq, Kenya, Kuwait, Lebanon, Oman, Peru, Qater, Rhodesia, Singapore, Switzerland, UK (RAF, Royal Navy).

Development: Undoubtedly the most successful British post-war fighter, the Hunter epitomised the grace of a thoroughbred and has always delighted its pilots. The prototype, with 6,500lb thrust Avon 100, was built to Specification F.3/48. It was easily supersonic in a shallow dive and packed the devastating four Aden cannon in a quick-release pack winched up as a unit. After being fitted with bulged cartridge boxes and a stuck-on airbrake under the rear fuselage it became a standard fighter, with Armstrong Whit-

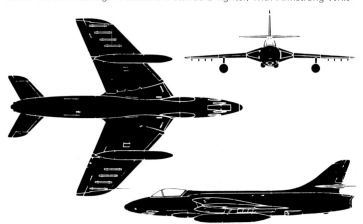

Three-view of Hunter FGA.9, typical of most single-seaters today.

Hawker Siddeley Sea Hawk

Hawker P.1040, Armstrong Whitworth Sea Hawk 1-6, 50 and 100-1

Origin: See text.

Type: Single-seat carrier-based fighter bomber (F.1, 2, fighter).

Engine: One Rolls-Royce Nene single-shaft centrifugal turbojet; (Mks 1–4) 5,000lb (2268kg) Nene 101; (Mk 5 onwards) 5,400lb (2450kg) Nene 103.

Dimensions: Span 39ft (11·89m); length 39ft 8in (12·08m); height 8ft 8in (2·79m); (Mks 100–1) 9ft 9½in (3m).

Weights: Empty 9,200–9,720lb (4173–4410kg); loaded (clean) 13,220lb (6000kg), maximum 16,200lb (7355kg).

Performance: Maximum speed 599mph (958km/h) at sea level, 587mph (939km/h, Mach 0·83) at height; initial climb 5,700ft (1737m)/min; service ceiling 44,500ft (13,560m); range on internal fuel 740 miles (1191km), with drop tanks 1,400 miles (2253km).

Armament: Four 20mm Hispano cannon each with 200 rounds beneath cockpit floor; (Mks 3, 5) underwing racks for two 500lb (227kg) bombs; (Mks 4, 6 and later) racks for four 500lb bombs or equivalent.

History: First flight (P.1040) 2 September 1947; (N.7/46) 3 September 1948; (production F.1) 14 November 1951; squadron service, March 1953; final delivery, (Mk 101) December 1956, (India) 1961.

User: India (Navy).

Development: Sir Sydney Camm's first jet fighter was conventional in having a Nene engine with wing-root inlets and unswept wings and tail, but most unusual (possibly unique) in that the jet pipe was split to serve two propelling nozzles, one on each side at the trailing edge. This gave the P.1040 a neat and graceful appearance, compared with the closely similar

worth building the F.2 with 8,000lb Sapphire 101, which, unlike the early Avon, stayed going when the guns were fired. The one-off Mk 3 gained a world speed record at 727·6mph, the F.4 had fuel capacity raised from 334 to 414 gal and carried underwing stores, and the F.5 was a Sapphire-engined 4. The F.6 introduced the 10,000lb Avon 203 and extended-chord dog-tooth wing. The T.7 had the 8,000lb Avon 122 and side-by-side dual controls, the T.8 was a naval trainer, and the most important mark of all was the FGA.9 with 10,150lb Avon 207 and heavier underwing load. The FR.10 was a camera-equipped fighter and the GA.11 was a ground-attack naval trainer. Total Hunter production was 1,985, including 445 made in Belgium and Holland. While 429 were exported as new aircraft, well over

700 additional Hunters have been refurbished or completely remanufactured for more than 17 air forces, with mark numbers up to 79. A superb all-round combat aircraft, it is gradually being recognised that, had a further 1,000 been constructed (or fewer scrapped in Britain) all would have found ready buyers today.

Above: Hunter F.51 used by 724 Sqn, Royal Danish Air Force 1956–63.

Above: Hunter FGA.9 of 45 Sqn, RAF (see photograph below)

Above: Hunter F.56 of the Indian Air Force, which bought 112 new.

Below, left: A pair of Hunter F.74B fighters of the Singapore Air Defence Command wing their way out on an offshore patrol. Singapore has 38 single-seat Hunters (F.74B, FGA.74 and FR.74) and nine dual-control T.75 trainers. It is one of many younger or smaller air forces to have found the Hunter ideal in offering high potency and reliability at a low price.

Below: A scene to set the pulse racing—the start of a training sortie in FGA.9s, on an autumn afternoon. The Avon-207-powered Mk 9 incorporated all the experience gained with earlier marks, and is tougher and carries a heavier weapon load in the ground-attack mission. All were converted for the RAF from earlier sub-types, but large numbers of generally similar aircraft were built new for overseas customers. Most remanufactured Hunters have likewise begun life as Mk 4 or 6 fighters (often ex-Belgium or Netherlands).

Grumman F9F, and also enabled a substantial fuel tank to be accommodated in the rear fuselage. RAF interest waned but naval specification N.7/46 was used for a second aircraft with carrier equipment and the span increased by 2ft 6in. The Royal Navy ordered 151, but Hawker Aircraft built only 35 F.1s, all subsequent design and production being handled by Armstrong Whitworth. The Coventry firm built a further 60 F.1s before delivering 40 F.2 with powered ailerons and 116 FB.3 with racks for two bombs. There followed 90 FGA.4, with four pylons, and then 86 FGA.6 with more powerful engine. Many FB.3 were converted to FB.5s by changing to the Nene 103, and many FGA.4 were brought up to Mk 6 standard. The 22 Mk 50s were Mk 6s supplied to the Royal Netherlands Navy in 1956-57 for the carrier *Karel Doorman*. The final batches comprised 34 Mk 100 similar to the FGA.6 for the West German Marineflieger and 34 Mk 101 night fighters with Ekco 34 radar in a pod on the right wing. Three years after production had ceased the Indian Navy ordered 24, half new and half ex-RN; eventually the Indians bought 74, serving aboard *Vikrant* and ashore until 1977.

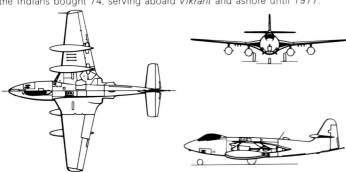

Above: Three-view of Sea Hawk 100 with revised fin and rudder.

Above: One of a row of trim Sea Hawk Mk 6 advanced fighter trainers of 300 Sqn, Indian Navy, aboard INS *Vikrant*. For several years the Harrier has been studied as a possible replacement.

Lockheed F-104 Starfighter

F-104A to G, J and S, CF-104, QF-104, RF and RTF-104, TF-104 (data for F-104G)

Origin: Lockheed-California Co, USA; see text for multinational manufacturing programme.

Type: (A, C) single-seat day interceptor; (G) multimission strike fighter; (CF) strike-reconnaissance; (TF) dual trainer; (QF) drone RPV; (F-104S) all-weather interceptor; (RF and RTF) reconnaissance.

Engine: One General Electric J79 single-shaft turbojet with afterburner; (A) 14,800lb (6713kg) J79-3B; (C, D, F, J) 15,800lb (7165kg) J79-7A; (G, RF/RFT, CF) 15,800lb (7165kg) J79-11A; (S) 17,900lb (8120kg) J79-19 or J1Q.

Dimensions: Span (without tip tanks) 21ft 11in (6·68m); length 54ft 9in (16·69m); height 13ft 6in (4·11m).

Weights: Empty 14,082lb (6387kg); maximum loaded 28,779lb (13,054kg).

Performance: Maximum speed 1,450mph (2330km/h, Mach 2·2); initial climb 50,000ft (15,250m)/min; service ceiling 58,000ft (17,680m) (zoom ceiling over 90,000ft, 27,400m); range with maximum weapons, about 300 miles (483km); range with four drop tanks (high altitude, subsonic) 1,380 miles (2220km).

Armament: In most versions, centreline rack rated at 2,000lb (907kg) and two underwing pylons each rated at 1,000lb (454kg); additional racks for small missiles (eg Sidewinder) on fuselage, under wings or on tips; certain versions have reduced fuel and one 20mm M61 Vulcan multi-barrel gun in fuselage; (S) M61 gun, two Sparrow and two Sidewinder.

History: First flight (XF-104) 7 February 1954; (F-104A) 17 February 1956; (F-104G) 5 October 1960; (F-104S) 30 December 1968; final delivery from United States 1964; final delivery from Aeritalia (F-104S) 1975.

Users: Belgium, Canada, Denmark, W Germany, Greece, Italy, Japan, Jordan, Netherlands, Norway, Pakistan, Spain, Taiwan, Turkey, USA (ANG).

Development: Clarence L. ("Kelly") Johnson planned the Model 83 after talking with fighter pilots in Korea in 1951. The apparent need was for superior flight performance, even at the expense of reduced equipment and other penalties. When the XF-104 flew, powered by a 10,500lb J65 Sapphire with afterburner, it appeared to have hardly any wing; another odd feature was the downward-ejecting seat. The production F-104A had a more powerful engine and blown flaps and after lengthy development entered limited service with Air Defense Command in 1958. Only 153 were built and after a spell with the Air National Guard, survivors again saw ADC service with the powerful GE-19 engine. Three were modified as Astronaut trainers with rocket boost, one gaining a world height record at nearly 119,000ft in 1963. The B was a dual tandem trainer, the C a fighter-bomber for Tactical Air Command with refuelling probe, the D a trainer version of the C and the DJ and F respectively Japanese and German versions of the D. The G was a complete redesign to meet the needs of the Luftwaffe for a tactical nuclear strike and reconnaissance aircraft. Structurally different, it introduced Nasarr multi-mode radar, inertial navigation system, manoeuvring flaps and other new items. Altogether 1,266 were built, including 970 by a NATO European consortium and 110 by Canadair. Canadair also built 200 basically similar CF-104s, while Japan built 207 J models closely resembling the earlier C. The German RF and RTF are multi-role-sensor reconnaissance and trainer versions, while increasing numbers of all versions are being turned into various QF-104 RPVs.

The only type of Starfighter built new since 1967 has been the Italian F-104S. Developed jointly by Lockheed and Fiat (Aeritalia), the S is an air-superiority fighter armed with two Sparrow air/air missiles (hence the suffix-letter S). Built under Lockheed licence, the S has a more powerful J79 engine, updated Autonetics R21G radar (with MTI, ECCM and improved reliability) and several detail changes to improve air/air role performance. The secondary ground-attack capability is retained, and in recent months the Regia Aeronautica force of 205 F-104S have begun to carry the Orpheus multi-sensor reconnaissance pod carried on the centre-line. Turkey has bought 40, but has not yet taken up an option for a further 18.

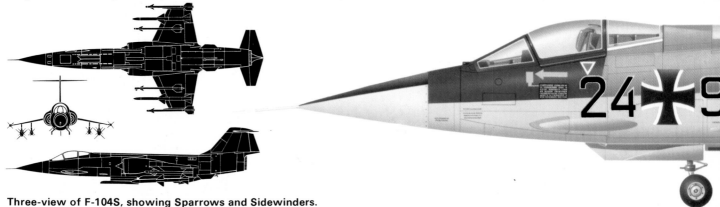

Three-view of F-104S, showing Sparrows and Sidewinders.

Above: The Ejercito del Aire (Spanish Air Force) was one of the recipients of the F-104G from Canadian production. The EdA squadron of 24 is no longer operational.

Far left: The Aeritalia F-104S is the only Starfighter model still in production. These examples belong to 53° Stormo of the Aeronautica Militare Italiano, based at Cameri, used in the interceptor role.

Near left: Rockets ripple away from a CF-104 of No 1 Air Group, of Canadian Forces Europe.

RF-104G with internal camera compartment, serving with Luftwaffe AG 52.

Jurom VTI/CIAR-93 Orao

VTI-CIAR 93 Orao

Origin: Joint programme by Centrala Industriala Aeronautica Romana, Bucharest, Romania, and Vazduhoplovno-Techniki Institut, Zarkovo, Yugoslavia.
Type: Single-seat tactical attack.
Engines: Two 4,000lb (1814kg) thrust Rolls-Royce/Fiat Viper 632 single-shaft turbojets.
Dimensions: (Estimated) span 24ft 10in (7·56m); length 42ft 4in (12·9m); height 12ft 5in (3·78m).
Weights: (Estimated) empty 9,480lb (4300kg); loaded (fighter mission) 15,875lb (7200kg); maximum loaded 19,850lb (9000kg).
Performance: (Estimated) maximum speed, equivalent to about Mach 0·95 over wide height band (thus, about 700–720mph, 1150km/h, clean at sea level); maximum speed with weapons, about 550mph (885km/h) at sea level; initial climb (clean) at least 15,000ft (4600m)/min; range on internal fuel (clean, high altitude) about 900 miles (1450km).
Armament: Two Nudelmann-Richter NR-30 30mm cannon, each with 125 rounds; centreline and underwing hardpoints, each reported to be rated to 500kg (maximum total external load, 4,840lb, 2200kg) for wide range of Yugoslav cluster bombs, frag bombs, h.e. and napalm (some retarded), rocket pods (12×57mm) or photoflashes.
History: Start of design 1971; first flight believed August 1974; official demonstration 15 April 1975; service delivery, probably December 1976.
Users: Romania, Yugoslavia.

Development: In 1971 the governments of Romania and Yugoslavia agreed to attempt to meet a common requirement of their air forces for a new tactical combat aircraft by building their own. The decision was specifically aimed to help the two countries become more independent of what had previously been a unique source of military equipment. It is significant that the necessary technical help to carry out what was a most challenging project for the two countries came from the West, especially from the UK (which provides engines and most of the airborne system-hardware, and has probably also assisted with the design and development phases). As no bilateral management organization has been announced observers call the project the "Jurom" (Jugoslavia/Romania), but its correct designation is given above (Orao means eagle).

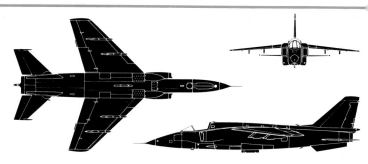

Above: Three-view of Orao prototype as at first showing in 1975.

The aircraft is intended to fulfil several important roles, especially tactical interdiction, close-air support (with laser ranger) and multi-sensor reconnaissance. A two-seat version is among the development batch of 11 aircraft, and several of these roles are judged to need a second crew-member (despite the payload/range limitation with aircraft of modest power). The two-seater will also fulfil the need for a trainer more advanced than the Soko Galeb. Later it is hoped to produce a fighter version, with afterburning engines and a lightweight multimode radar. From the start the Orao has been planned to operate from unpaved and relatively short airstrips, though the early pre-production machines did not have the expected slats and double-slotted flaps (but they did have a braking chute and soft-field tyres). By 1977 it was reported that all 11 development aircraft had flown (apparently some assembled in each country, but all bearing the joint VTI-CIAR designation) and that production deliveries were about to begin. If the partners achieve their objective of export sales it may enable work to go ahead on a modern air-combat fighter version with a restressed airframe, and possibly canards, twin vertical tails and double-shock variable inlets. There appears to be the potential in this joint effort for long-term competition for both East and West.

Below: Prototype Orao landing after making public demonstration at Batajnica airbase near Belgrade on 15 April 1975. Engines are Anglo-Italian, landing gear by Messier-Hispano of France, and many other parts and equipments come from Western Europe or Sweden. Soko of Yugoslavia has project leadership under the VTI, and will assemble about 200; Romania needs about 80.

McDonnell Douglas/Hawker AV-8B

AV-8B and proposed variants

Origin: McDonnell Douglas Corporation (MCAIR, St Louis), USA; principal associate, British Aerospace (Hawker Aircraft, Kingston), UK.
Type: V/STOL light attack; proposed versions include sea-based air defence, reconnaissance and dual trainer/multi-role.
Engine: One Rolls-Royce Pegasus 103. (Pratt & Whitney F402) vectored-thrust turbofan rated at 21,500lb (9752kg).
Dimensions: Span 30ft 3½in (9·20m); length 42ft 11in (13·1m); height 11ft 3½in (3·4m).
Weights: Empty 12,400lb (5625kg); design, 22,750lb (10,320kg); loaded (close-support seven Mk 82 bombs) 25,994lb (11,790kg); maximum over 29,000lb (13,150kg).
Performance: Maximum speed, clean, over Mach 1; operational radius (VTO, 7,800lb/3538kg weapons) 115 miles (185km), (STO, 12 Mk 82 Snakeye, internal fuel) 172 miles (278km), (STO, seven Mk 82, external fuel) 748 miles (1204km); ferry range over 3,000 miles 4830km).
Armament: Two 20mm Mk 12 cannon in single belly pods, six underwing pylons and centreline hardpoint for weapon/ECM/fuel load of 8,000lb (3630kg) for VTO or 9,000lb (4080kg) for STO.
History: First flight (YAV-8B) late 1978; preliminary evaluation mid-1979; initial operational capability fourth quarter 1982.
Users: US Marine Corps, US Navy.

Development: Following proposals in 1973 by Hawker Siddeley and McDonnell Douglas for an advanced development of the Harrier the then UK Defence Minister, Roy Mason, said there was "not enough common ground" for a joint programme. This caused a delay of many months, but the US government eventually studied an improved aircraft designated AV-16A with a new wing and the uprated Pegasus 15 engine, before deciding to try to achieve as much as possible of the same advantages in payload/range and weapon load with the existing engine. Rolls-Royce and Pratt & Whitney have studied the Pegasus 11D (800lb extra thrust) and 11+ (1,000lb more) but these remained mere proposals as this book went to press, despite the fact Rolls-Royce ran a Pegasus at over 25,000lb thrust

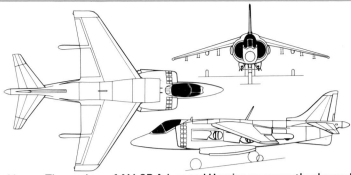

Above: Three-view of AV-8B Advanced Harrier as currently planned.

in May 1972. Under the present programme all changes are confined to the airframe, the main improvement being a completely new wing, with greater span and area, less sweep, a supercritical section and graphite-epoxy construction throughout the main wing box and large single-slotted flaps and drooping ailerons. Strakes and a large hinged belly flap will increase air pressure under the fuselage in VTO, while other changes include inlets matched to the engine (they are too small on previous production Harriers) and front nozzles cut off square with the efflux.

Overall improvement in payload/range, compared with an AV-8A, is about 100 per cent. There is still a chance that further gains may result from improvement to the F402 engine, and production AV-8Bs may have the raised cockpit of the British Sea Harrier. The US Marine Corps requirement is for 336, and a variant might possibly be purchased by the US Navy for its own use. Present plans envisage the AV-8B having the Angle-Rate Bombing System, with dual-mode TV and laser spot coupled via IBM computer to the Marconi-Elliott HUD. Fixed or retractable probe refuelling is likely, but radar will not be fitted. Two AV-8As are being rebuilt by McDonnell Douglas as YAV-8Bs, and production aircraft will be built 50/50 US/UK with assembly at St Louis in 1983–91. Engine production is not yet decided.

Below: Two views of the full-scale AV-8B engineering model in the 40ft × 80ft tunnel at NASA Ames Laboratory. The supercritical wing is quite unlike that of the Harrier, while the right picture shows the hollow box formed by the keel-straked cannon pods and the large flap joining the pods at the front.

McDonnell Douglas A-4 Skyhawk

A-4A to A-4S and TA-4 series

Origin: Douglas Aircraft Co, El Segundo (now division of McDonnell Douglas, Long Beach), USA.

Type: Single-seat attack bomber; TA, dual-control trainer.

Engine: (B, C. L, P, Q, S) one 7,700lb (3493kg) thrust Wright J65-16A single-shaft turbojet (US Sapphire); (E, J) 8,500lb (3856kg) Pratt & Whitney J52-6 two-shaft turbojet; (F, G, H, K) 9,300lb (4218kg) J52-8A; (M, N) 11,200lb (5080kg) J52-408A.

Dimensions: Span 27ft 6in (8·38m); length (A) 39ft 1in; (B) 39ft 6in (42ft 10¾in over FR probe); (E, F, G, H, K, L, P, Q, S) 40ft 1½in (12·22m); (M, N) 40ft 3¼in (12·27m); (TA series, excluding probe) 42ft 7¼in (12·98m); height 15ft (4·57m); (early single-seaters 15ft 2in, TA series 15ft 3in).

Weights: Empty (A) 7,700lb; (E) 9,284lb; (typical modern single-seat, eg M) 10,465lb (4747kg); (TA-4F) 10,602 (4809kg); maximum loaded (A) 17,000lb; (B) 22,000lb; (all others, shipboard) 24,500lb (11,113kg); (land-based) 27,420lb (12,437kg).

Performance: Maximum speed (clean) (B) 676mph; (E) 685mph; (M) 670mph (1078km/h); (TA-4F) 675mph; maximum speed (4,000lb, 1814kg bomb load) (F) 593mph; (M) 645mph; initial climb (F) 5,620ft (1713m)/min; (M) 8,440ft (2572m)/min; service ceiling (all, clean) about 49,000ft (14,935m); range (clean, or with 4,000lb weapons and max fuel, all late versions) about 920 miles (1480km); maximum range (M) 2,055 miles (3307km).

Armament: Standard on most versions, two 20mm Mk 12 cannon, each with 200 rounds; (H, N, and optional on other export versions) two 30mm DEFA 553, each with 150 rounds. Pylons under fuselage and wings for total ordnance load of (A, B, C) 5,000lb (2268kg); (E, F, G, H, K, L, P, Q, S) 8,200lb (3720kg); (M, N) 9,155lb (4153kg).

History: First flight (XA4D-1) 22 June 1954; (A-4A) 14 August 1954; squadron delivery October 1956; (A-4C) August 1959; (A-4E) July 1961; (A-4F) August 1966; (A-4M) April 1970; (A-4N) June 1972; first of TA series (TA-4E) June 1965.

Users: Argentina, Australia, Israel, Kuwait, New Zealand, Singapore, USA (Air Force in SE Asia, Navy, Marine Corps).

Development: Most expert opinion in the US Navy refused to believe the claim of Ed Heinemann, chief engineer of what was then Douglas El Segundo, that he could build a jet attack bomber weighing half the 30,000lb specified by the Navy. The first Skyhawk, nicknamed "Heinemann's Hot Rod", not only flew but gained a world record by flying a 500km circuit at over 695mph. Today, more than 23 years later, greatly developed versions are still in production, setting an unrivalled record for sustained manufacture. These late versions do weigh close to 30,000lb, but only because the basic design has been improved with more powerful engines, increased fuel capacity and much heavier weapon load. The wing was made in a single unit, forming an integral fuel tank and so small it did not need to fold. Hundreds of Skyhawks have served aboard carriers, but in the US involvement in SE Asia "The Scooter" (as it was affectionately known) flew many kinds of mission from land bases. In early versions the emphasis was on improving range and load and the addition of all-weather avionics. The F

model introduced the dorsal hump containing additional avionics, and the M, the so-called Skyhawk II, marked a major increase in mission effectiveness. Most of the TA-4 trainers closely resembled the corresponding single-seater, but the TA-4J and certain other models have simplified avionics and the TA-4S (Singapore) is a rebuild by Lockheed Aircraft Service with two separate humped cockpits and an integral-tank fuselage. Production of the M for the US Marine Corps may continue until the AV-8B becomes available in 1983-84, 30 years after first flight. Deliveries in 1977 neared 3,000.

Above: Brace of A-4s (A-4B rebuilt by LAS) of Singapore, which has 40. Some Singapore A-4s have two cockpit canopies.

1 Fixed flight refuelling probe
2 Dielectric nose
3 APG-53A radar scanner
4 Pitot head
5 Electronics pack
6 Avionics pack
7 Cockpit forward bulkhead
8 Control column
9 Rudder pedal
10 Internal armour plate
11 Single nosewheel door
12 Oleo leg
13 Steering cylinder
14 Nosewheel
15 Shortening link
16 Retraction jack
17 Integral armour area
18 Port instrument console
19 Throttle control lever
20 Instrument panel shroud
21 Fixed or lead-computing gunsight
22 Bullet-resistant rectangular windscreen
23 Cockpit canopy
24 Headrest
25 Zero-zero ejection seat
26 Leading-edge slat (open position)
27 Starboard flow fences
28 Leading-edge slat
29 Starboard navigation lamp
30 Aerials
31 Vortex generators
32 Aerodynamically-balanced aileron
33 Wing inspection panels
34 Split flap
35 Aerial
36 Dorsal avionics pack
37 Self-sealing fuel cell (200 gal/909 litres)
38 Engine intake
39 Intake trunk
40 11,200 lb (5,443 kg) thrust Pratt & Whitney J52-408 two-shaft turbojet
41 Inspection panel
42 Power-supply amplifier
43 Compass adapter
44 Engine firewall

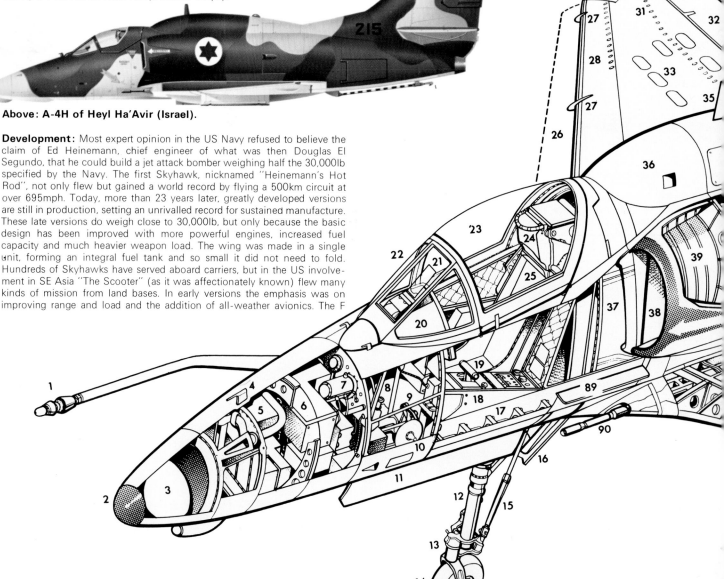

Above: A-4H of Heyl Ha'Avir (Israel).

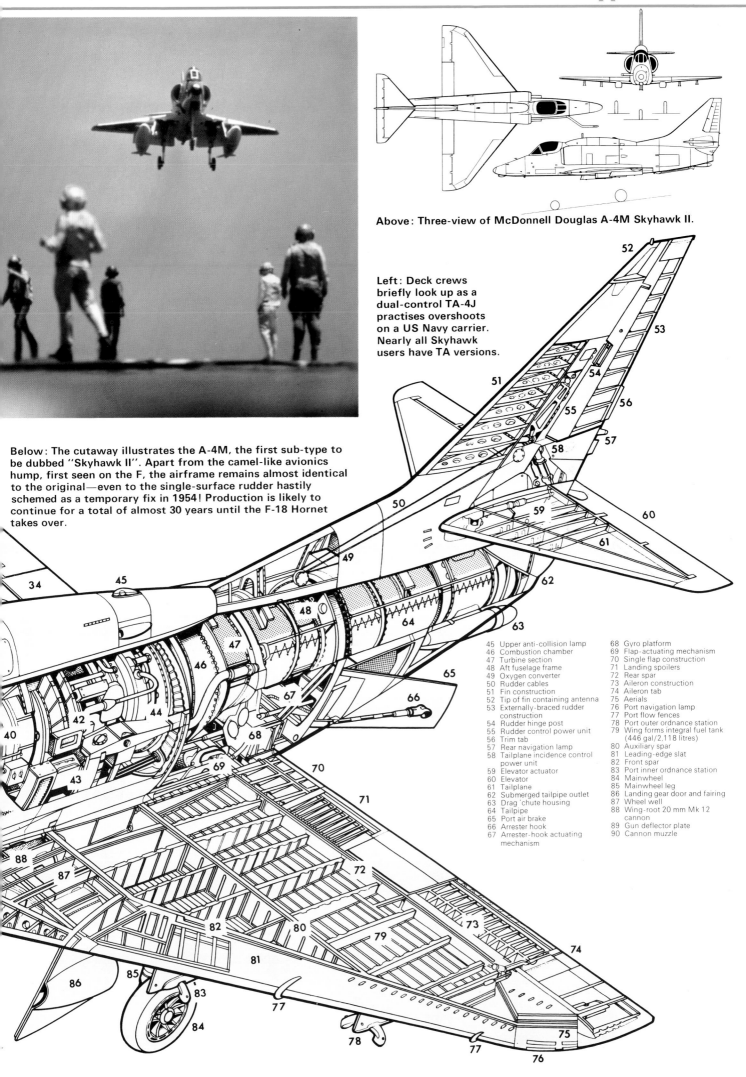

Above: Three-view of McDonnell Douglas A-4M Skyhawk II.

Left: Deck crews briefly look up as a dual-control TA-4J practises overshoots on a US Navy carrier. Nearly all Skyhawk users have TA versions.

Below: The cutaway illustrates the A-4M, the first sub-type to be dubbed "Skyhawk II". Apart from the camel-like avionics hump, first seen on the F, the airframe remains almost identical to the original—even to the single-surface rudder hastily schemed as a temporary fix in 1954! Production is likely to continue for a total of almost 30 years until the F-18 Hornet takes over.

45 Upper anti-collision lamp
46 Combustion chamber
47 Turbine section
48 Aft fuselage frame
49 Oxygen converter
50 Rudder cables
51 Fin construction
52 Tip of fin containing antenna
53 Externally-braced rudder construction
54 Rudder hinge post
55 Rudder control power unit
56 Trim tab
57 Rear navigation lamp
58 Tailplane incidence control power unit
59 Elevator actuator
60 Elevator
61 Tailplane
62 Submerged tailpipe outlet
63 Drag 'chute housing
64 Tailpipe
65 Port air brake
66 Arrester hook
67 Arrester-hook actuating mechanism

68 Gyro platform
69 Flap-actuating mechanism
70 Single flap construction
71 Landing spoilers
72 Rear spar
73 Aileron construction
74 Aileron tab
75 Aerials
76 Port navigation lamp
77 Port flow fences
78 Port outer ordnance station
79 Wing forms integral fuel tank (446 gal/2,118 litres)
80 Auxiliary spar
81 Leading-edge slat
82 Front spar
83 Port inner ordnance station
84 Mainwheel
85 Mainwheel leg
86 Landing gear door and fairing
87 Wheel well
88 Wing-root 20 mm Mk 12 cannon
89 Gun deflector plate
90 Cannon muzzle

Mikoyan/Gurevich MiG-27

MiG-27 "Flogger D" and "Flogger F"

Origin: The design bureau named for Mikoyan and Gurevich, Soviet Union; no production outside the Soviet Union yet reported.
Type: Single-seat tactical attack, probably with reconnaissance capability.
Engine: One afterburning turbofan of unknown type (probably Tumansky, related to that of MiG-23) rated at about 13,500lb (6125kg) dry and 24,250lb (11,000kg) with maximum afterburner.
Dimensions: Similar to MiG-23 except fuselage nose is longer but pitot head shorter giving fractionally shorter overall length; height about 15ft (4.6m).
Weights (estimated): Empty 17,300lb (7850kg); maximum loaded 39,130lb (17,750kg).
Performance: Maximum speed at low level (clean) about Mach 1.2, (maximum weight) subsonic; maximum speed at high altitude (clean) about 1,055mph (1700km/h, Mach 1.6); take-off to 50ft (15m) at 34,600lb (15,700kg) 2,625ft (800m); service ceiling (clean) about 50,000ft (15,250m); combat radius with bombs and one tank (hi-lo-hi) 600 miles (960km); ferry range (wings spread with three tanks) over 2,000 miles (3200km).
Armament: One 23mm six-barrel Gatling-type gun in belly fairing; seven external pylons (centreline, fuselage flanks under inlet ducts, fixed wing gloves and swing-wings) for wide range of ordnance including guided missiles (AS-7 "Kerry") and tactical nuclear weapons to total weight of 4,200lb (1900kg). All ECM are internal and all pylons are thus usable by weapons or tanks. Those on the outer wings are not always fitted; they are piped for drop tanks, but do not pivot and thus may be loaded only when the wings remain unswept.
History: First flight, possibly about 1970; service delivery, before 1974.
Users: E Germany, Poland, Soviet Union (FA) and Syria (and almost certainly other countries in 1977).

Development: Derived from the same variable-geometry prototype flown by the MiG bureau at the 1967 Aviation Day, this aircraft was at first called "MiG-23B" in the West but is now known to have a different Soviet service designation that is almost certainly MiG-27. Bureau numbers are generally unknown for the MiG series; Mikoyan himself died in December 1970 and Gurevich in November 1976, and recent designs are known only by their service numbers. Compared with the MiG-23 this attack version carries heavier loads and is simpler and optimised for low-level operation. The airframe differs in having a shallower nose with a flat pointed profile housing mapping/terrain-following radar, laser ranger, doppler radar and radio altimeter, with good pilot view ahead and downward. The cockpit is heavily armoured. The engine is more powerful than that of the MiG-23 but is fed by fixed inlets and has a shorter and simpler nozzle. Main wheels are fitted with

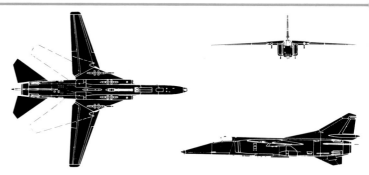

Above: Three-view of MiG-27 without swing-wing pylons.

Above: An extremely revealing photograph showing one of the latest MiG-27 sub-types festooned with mission equipment.

large low-pressure tyres, and special provision is made for rough-field operation. Internal ECM equipment is extensive, and pods on the wing-glove leading edges appear to contain an opto-electronic seeker (left) and passive radar receiver (right). Internal fuel capacity is estimated at 1,183 Imp gallons (5380lit) including fuel in the fin; no provision for flight refuelling has been noted. The "Flogger F" has the engine installation and gun of the MiG-23, with variable inlets, and lack the comprehensive MiG-27 avionics. These are thought to be development aircraft or an export version. Possible problems with the basic aircraft are suggested by reports that in a few months the Syrian AF has written off 13 out of 50 supplied.

Below: The MiG variable-geometry attack aircraft—almost certainly MiG-27 in FA service—is an extremely refined and cost/effective aircraft, probably being built at a higher rate than any other combat aircraft in the world.

Mitsubishi F-1 and T-2

F-1 and T-2A

Origin: Mitsubishi Heavy Industries Ltd, Japan.

Type: (T-2A) two-seat supersonic trainer; (F-1) single-seat close-support fighter-bomber.

Engines: Two Ishikawajima-Harima TF40-801A (licence-built Rolls-Royce/Turboméca Adour 102) two-shaft augmented turbofans with maximum rating of 7,140lb (3238kg); (F-1) may later have more powerful version.

Dimensions: Span 25ft 10in (7·87m); length 58ft 7in (17·86m); height (T-2) 14ft 7in (4·445m), (F-1) 14ft 9in.

Weights: Empty (T-2) 13,668lb (6200kg); (F-1) 14,330lb (6500kg); loaded (T-2, clean) 21,274lb (9650kg); (T-2 maximum) 24,750lb (11,200 kg); (F-1 maximum) 30,200lb (13,700kg).

Performance: Maximum speed (at clean gross weight) 1,056mph (1700km/h, Mach 1·6); initial climb 19,680ft (6000m)/min; service ceiling 50,025ft (15,250m); range (T-2 with external tanks) 1,785 miles

(2870km); (F-1 with eight 500lb bombs) 700 miles (1126km).

Armament: One 20mm M-61 multi-barrel gun under left side of cockpit floor; pylon hardpoints under centreline and inboard and outboard on wings, with light stores attachments at tips. Total weapon load (T-2) normally 2,000lb (907kg); (F-1) 6,000lb (2722kg) comprising 12,500lb bombs, eight 500lb plus two tanks of 183gal, or two 1,300lb (590kg) ASM-1 anti-ship missiles, and four Sidewinders.

History: First flight (XT-2) 20 July 1971; (T-2A) January 1975; (FST-2) June 1975; service delivery (T-2A) March 1975; (F-1) 1977.

User: Japanese Air Self-Defence Force.

Development: Japan's first post-war military aircraft was the Fuji T-1 tandem-seat intermediate trainer, looking like an F-86 Sabre and powered

continued on page 88▶

Below: Are Japanese air-to-air pictures especially beautiful? Certainly this unusual view of Mitsubishi T-2 tandem-seat supersonic trainers captures all the freedom and grace of jet flight.

▶by a licence-built Bristol Orpheus. First flown in 1958, 42 were delivered as the T-1A, followed by 22 T-1B with the Japanese J3 engine. To replace the T-1 and other trainers such as the T-33 a design team led by Dr Kenji Ikeda designed the T-2, Japan's first supersonic aircraft, using the Anglo-French Jaguar as a basis. After flight trials had shown the validity of the design a single-seat version, the FST-2-Kai, was ordered to replace the F-86 as a close-support fighter. By mid-1975 orders had been placed for 46 T-2A trainers and the first 4th Air Wing unit had formed at Matsushima Air Base. The T-2A has proved efficient and popular in service, and is incidentally the first properly supersonic aircraft to be designed in Asia. Though a trainer, it carries Mitsubishi Electric radar, with air search, mapping, lock-on and ranging modes, as well as a J/AWG-11 (Thomson-CSF) HUD. Production is at the rate of two per month; by the start of 1977 orders stood at the planned level of 59, to be completed in 1980, and deliveries at 37. The first 18 FST-2 fighters (since redesignated F-1) had also been bought, with four flown in 1975. Total F-1 procurement is to be 68, all delivered by the end of 1979. The F-1 has a Ferranti inertial nav/attack system and Mitsubishi Electric weapon-aiming computer, radar altimeter and radar homing and warning system, most of the added boxes being installed in the bay occupied by the rear cockpit in the T-2A. Production began in 1977, with the letter of intent for a force of 68, all to be delivered by March 1980. Planned total is 110.

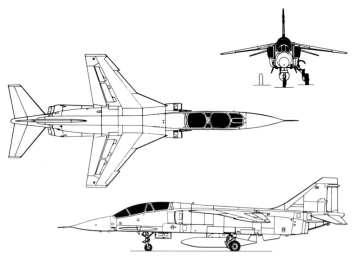

Three-view of Mitsubishi T-2A without wing pylons.

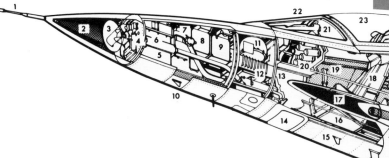

1 Pitot probe
2 Nose cone
3 Radar dish scanner
4 Mounting frame/bulkhead
5 Radar
6 Attitude/heading reference system
7 Toyo Communication J/APX-100 SIF/IFF
8 Nippon Electric J/ARN-53 TACAN
9 Mitsubishi Electric J/ARC-51 UHF
10 TACAN aerial
11 Liquid-oxygen converter
12 Cooling louvres
13 Rudder pedals
14 UHF/DF aerial
15 SIF/IFF aerial
16 Seat mounting frame
17 Gun trough
18 Weber ES-7J zero-zero ejection seat
19 Control column
20 Instrument panel
21 Optical sight
22 Windscreen
23 Rearward-hinged jettisonable forward canopy
24 Canopy actuating mechanism
25 Mid-section glazing
26 Instrument panel
27 Control column
28 Gun forward support
29 UHF aerial
30 Nosewheel doors
31 Door actuating member
32 Nosewheel leg
33 Torsion links
34 Nosewheel
35 Single-fork axle
36 Shock absorber
37 Retraction strut
38 Nosewheel bay
39 Pre-closing nosewheel door
40 Cooling louvres
41 M-61A-1 Vulcan multi-barrel 20mm cannon (combat training version only)
42 No 1 fuselage tank
43 Ammunition feed
44 Control quadrant
45 Weber ES-7J zero-zero ejection seat
46 Canopy release lever
47 Rearward-hinged jettisonable rear canopy
48 Ammunition drum (750 rounds)
49 Intake splitter plate
50 Fixed-geometry intake
51 Supplementary blow-in intake doors
52 Fuselage frame
53 No 2 fuselage tank
54 No 3 fuselage tank
55 Wing root fillet
56 Leading-edge flap actuator
57 Honeycomb-structure leading-edge inboard flap (electrically actuated)
58 Leading-edge dog-tooth
59 Port wingtip (AAM attachment)
60 Honeycomb trailing-edge structure
61 Electrically-actuated flap
62 Stores pylons
63 Practice rocket pods (19 x 2·75in)
64 Wing/fuselage pick-up points
65 Wing multi-spar torsion box
66 No 4 fuselage tank
67 Port mainwheel door
68 No 5 fuselage tank
69 Auxiliary intake
70 No 6 fuselage tank
71 7,070 lb (3,206 kg) thrust Ishikawajima-Harima TF40-IHI-801A (Adour) turbofans
72 No 7 fuselage tank
73 Fuel valve
74 Fin structure
75 Formation light
76 Fuel vent pipe
77 UHF aerial
78 Rear navigation light
79 Vent outlet
80 Hydraulically-operated rudder
81 Rudder actuator
82 Control runs
83 Rolling (differential) tailplane actuator
84 Tailplane pivot
85 Port tailplane
86 Upward-hinged tailcone
87 Braking parachute housing
88 Starboard tailplane
89 Arrester hook
90 Heat shield
91 Variable nozzle
92 Nozzle actuators
93 Afterburner
94 Engine starter
95 Accessories
96 Ventral fins
97 Air brakes (extended)
98 Port mainwheel
99 Shock absorbers (oleo-pneumatic)
100 Axle forks
101 Main undercarriage leg
102 Landing lights
103 Retraction struts
104 Mainwheel bay (pre-closing doors)
105 Centreline pylon
106 Weapons (reconnaissance pod
107 Stores pylons
108 Practice rocket pods (19 x 2·75in)
109 Starboard mainwheel
110 Starboard wing structure

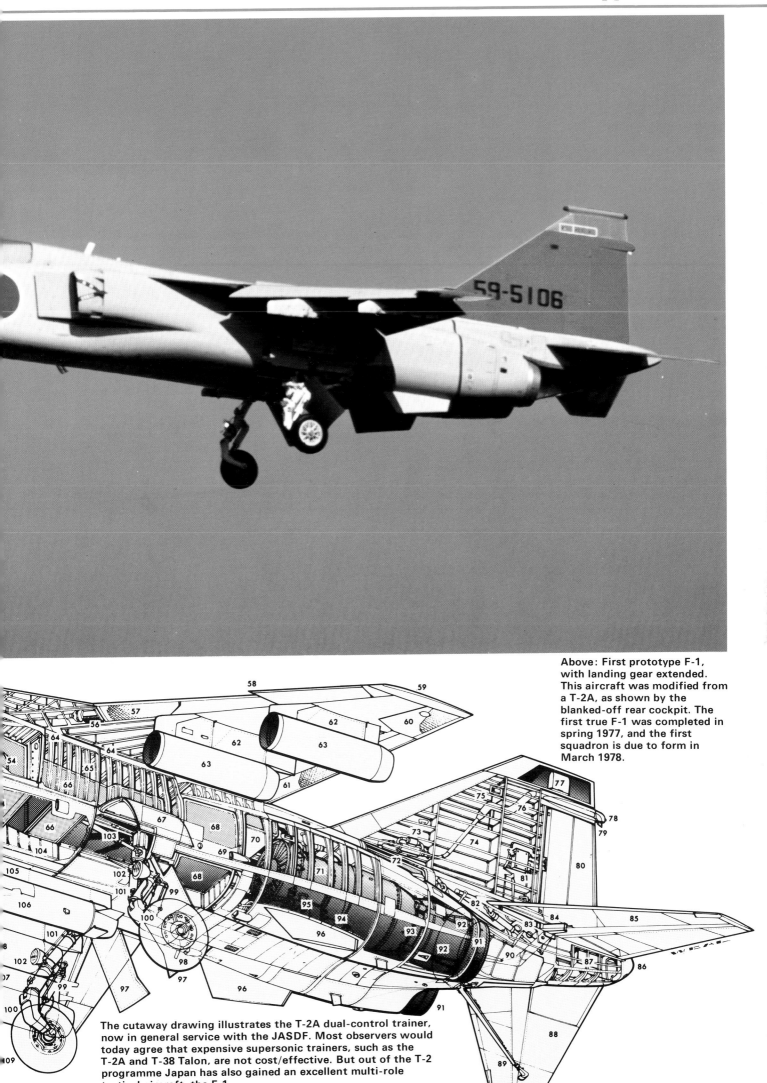

Above: First prototype F-1, with landing gear extended. This aircraft was modified from a T-2A, as shown by the blanked-off rear cockpit. The first true F-1 was completed in spring 1977, and the first squadron is due to form in March 1978.

The cutaway drawing illustrates the T-2A dual-control trainer, now in general service with the JASDF. Most observers would today agree that expensive supersonic trainers, such as the T-2A and T-38 Talon, are not cost/effective. But out of the T-2 programme Japan has also gained an excellent multi-role tactical aircraft, the F-1.

North American (Rockwell) F-100 Super Sabre

F-100A to F-100F and DF-100F

Origin: North American Aviation Inc, Inglewood, USA.

Type: Single-seat fighter-bomber; (F-100F) two-seat operational trainer; (DF) missile or RPV director aircraft.

Engine: One Pratt & Whitney J57 two-shaft turbojet with afterburner, (most blocks of A) 14,500lb (6576kg) J57-7; (late A, all C) 16,000lb (7257kg) J57-29; (D, F) 16,950lb (7690kg) J57-21A (all ratings with afterburner).

Dimensions: Span (original A) 36ft 7in; (remainder) 38ft 9½in (11·81m); length (except F, excluding pitot boom) 49ft 6in (15·09m), (fuselage, 47ft exactly); (F) 52ft 6in (16·0m), (boom adds about 6ft to all models); height (original A) 13ft 4in; (remainder) 16ft 2¾in (4·96m).

Weights: Empty (original A) 19,700lb; (C) 20,450lb; (D) 21,000lb (9525kg); (F) 22,300lb (10,115kg); maximum loaded (original A) 28,935lb; (C, D) 34,832lb (15,800kg); (F, two tanks but no weapons) 30,700lb (13,925kg).

Performance: Maximum speed (typical of all) 864mph at height (1390 km/h, Mach 1·31); initial climb (clean) 16,000ft (4900m)/min; service ceiling (typical) 45,000ft (13,720m); range (high, two 375gal tanks) 1,500 miles (2415km).

Armament: Usually four (F, only two) 20mm M-39E cannon each with 200 rounds; (A) pylons for two 375gal supersonic tanks and four additional hardpoints (seldom used) for 4,000lb ordnance; (C, D) two tanks and six pylons for 7,500lb (3402kg) ordnance; (F) two tanks and maximum of 6,000lb (2722kg) ordnance.

History: First flight (YF-100) 25 May 1953; production (A) 29 October 1953; final delivery October 1959.

Users: Denmark, France (until 1977), Taiwan, Turkey, USA (ANG).

Development: The success of the Sabre made it natural to attempt a successor, and in February 1949 this was planned as a larger and much more powerful machine able to exceed the speed of sound in level flight (had it been started two years later it might have been smaller, in view of the Korean pressure for simple fighters with the highest possible climb and performance at extreme altitudes). Unusual features were the 6 per cent wing with 45° sweep, no flaps, inboard ailerons, full-span slats and a slab tailplane mounted as low as possible. Level supersonic speed was achieved, for the first time with a combat aircraft, but after very rapid development, with the first (479th) wing fully equipped, the F-100A was grounded in November 1954. Trouble due to inertia coupling between the roll and yaw axes necessitated urgent modification, the wings and fin being lengthened. Subsequently the career of the "Hun" was wholly successful, the 203 A fighters being followed by the stronger C fighter-bomber, the D with flaps and autopilot and the tandem-seat F. Total production was lower than

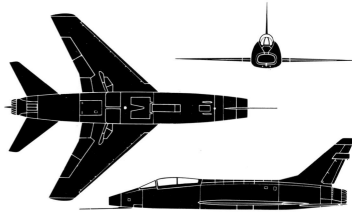

Three-view of tandem-seat F-100F in clean configuration.

expected at 2,294, many being built by NAA's newly occupied factory at Columbus, Ohio. In their early years the later versions pioneered global deployment of tactical aircraft by means of probe/drogue refuelling, and in Vietnam they proved outstandingly good at both low attack and top cover, flying more missions than over 15,000 Mustangs flew in World War II. In 1977 the survivors of what two decades earlier had been among the world's élite warplanes were in their final months of combat duty after countless inspection, repair and modification programmes.

Above: Despite its venerable age the F-100 was one of the hardest-worked warplanes in the SE Asia conflict, flying both top cover and low-level attack. This well-used F-100D is burdened by four bombs and two supersonic tanks; and the cannon have obviously worked hard.

Below: Pop goes the drag chute as an F-100C of the Turkish Air Force recovers after a training sortie.

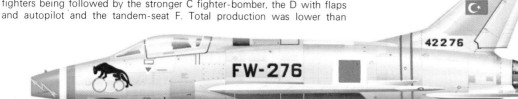

Above: F-100D-15 of Turkish Air Force, assigned to 1st TAF.

Panavia Tornado

Model 200 MRCA (S), (AD) and (T)

Origin: Panavia Aircraft GmbH, international company formed by British Aerospace, MBB of W Germany and Aeritalia.
Type: Two-seat multi-role combat aircraft, (S) optimised for strike, (AD) for air defence, (T) dual trainer.
Engines: Two 14,500lb (6577kg) thrust Turbo-Union RB.199-34R three-shaft augmented turbofans.
Dimensions: Span (25°) 45ft 7¼in (13·90m), (65°) 28ft 2½in (8·60m); length 54ft 9½in (16·70m); height 18ft 8½in (5·70m).
Weights: Empty, about 24,000lb (10,890kg); loaded (clean) about 35,000lb (15,880kg); maximum loaded, about 50,000lb (22,680kg).
Performance: Maximum speed (clean), at sea level, about 910mph (1465km/h, Mach 1·2), at height, over 1,320mph (2135km/h, Mach 2); service ceiling over 50,000ft (15,240m); range, about 1,000 miles (1610km) on internal fuel (high, wings spread), or over 3,000 miles (4830km) in ferry mode with maximum fuel.
Armament: Two 27mm Mauser cannon in lower forward fuselage; seven pylons, three on the body and four on the swinging wings, for external load of up to "more than 18,000lb" (8165kg). Tornado ADV, main armament comprises two Mauser guns plus four HSD Skyflash and two Sidewinder air/air missiles recessed into fuselage.
History: First flight 14 August 1974; planned service delivery 1977.
Users: W Germany (Luftwaffe, Marineflieger), Italy, UK (RAF).

Development: No combat aircraft in history has ever been planned with such care by so many possible customers. Studies began in 1967, after the French had abandoned the AFVG aircraft in the same class and decided not to participate in collaborative aircraft of this type. Panavia Aircraft was registered on 26 March 1969 in Munich as a three-nation company to manage the MRCA (multi-role combat aircraft) programme, with shares held in the ratio BAC 42½ per cent, MBB 42½ per cent and Aeritalia 15 per cent. In September 1969, after intense competition with the United States, the RB.199 was selected as the engine and a month later Turbo-Union was formed as the engine-management company with shares held in the ratio Rolls-Royce 40 per cent, MTU 40 per cent and Fiat 20 per cent. Thanks to the careful planning the MRCA programme has since demonstrated that it is possible for several nations to work together to create a modern military aircraft which promises to exceed all possible rivals in mission effectiveness, versatility and low cost, having already demonstrated better mission capability than the latest competing types designed specifically for that mission. Its design missions are: close air support/battlefield interdiction; long-range interdiction/strike; naval strike; air superiority; air defence/interception; reconnaissance; training. At one time it was planned that the three nations should develop slightly different versions with either one or two seats and dry or wet wings, but all basic aircraft now in production are identical, with two seats and sealed integral-tank wings. From stem to stern the MRCA is totally modern — a fact which its many competitors

have sought to counter by claiming it to be "complicated" or "expensive". In fact it is not possible to fly the required missions without carrying the equipment, and the fly-away price of £3·9 million (in September 1974 sterling) is by a very wide margin cheaper than any comparable aircraft. The only aircraft that bears comparison with MRCA is the larger F-14, which cannot meet the MRCA requirements in the attack and reconnaissance roles, and is officially doubted as having the capability — in the European environment — to fly the interception missions of the Tornado ADV. Other combat aircraft with a single seat and non-swinging wing are grossly deficient in all roles except close-range air combat, a specialised mission for which the common version of Tornado is not intended (though its performance in this role is considerably better than a Mirage III, F-5 or F-4).

The basic MRCA has outstandingly efficient and compact engines of extremely advanced design, with automatically scheduled inlets and nozzles. Flight control is by large tailerons, augmented at low sweep angles by wing spoilers; the system is fully digital and signalled by quad fly-by-wire via an automatic command and stability augmentation system. For high lift at low speeds the wings have full-span slats and double-slotted flaps. Other equipment includes a mapping radar, terrain-following radar and computer, and laser target ranger for extreme accuracy. ECM and other penetration aids are exceptional. Planned production for the three original partners comprises 809 aircraft, of which 385 will be for the RAF, 202 for the Luftwaffe (replacing the F-104G and G91R), 122 for the Marineflieger

continued on page 92 ▶

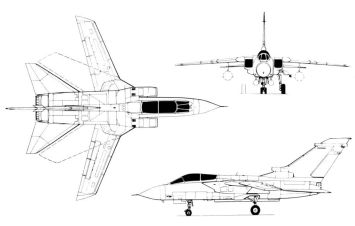

Three-view of Tornado IDS (interdictor/strike) variant.

Above: 02 Tornado development prototype with "tri-national" markings.

Below: Shock diamonds glow in the jets thrusting aloft the first Italian-assembled Tornado, prototype 05. This first flew at Turin Caselle in December 1975, but subsequently spent a long period being repaired after a heavy landing.

▶(replacing the F-104G) and 100 for the Regia Aeronautica (replacing the F-104G and G91Y) in all roles. The variety of external stores to be carried by MRCA exceeds that for any other aircraft in history, embracing almost every airborne store of three major nations in virtually all combat roles. A proportion of aircraft for the first three customers will be dual trainers (the first flew on 5 August 1975) which retain all the fuel capacity and weapons of single-pilot versions.

Above: Four 1,000lb (454kg) low-drag bombs fall from the fuselage pylons of Tornado 02 during the first weapon trials in 1975.

Of the RAF total of 385, about 220 will be of the common IDS (interdiction strike) variant; the other 165 will be of the ADV (air-defence variant) type, planned to replace the Phantom in the air defence of the UK. Commonality with the common airframe will be very high, to give overall commonality estimated at 80 per cent. Differences lie in systems and weapons, notably in the Marconi-Elliott/Ferranti radar, obviously of the "look down" pulse-doppler type but with a mapping mode for the ADV's secondary attack role. The ADV will have slightly more powerful engines, and its missiles will be carried recessed as in the Phantom; it will have a modified computer with totally different program, and other changes will be made to increase flight performance and effectiveness in the interception role. Unit cost was put at £6·492 million in August 1976 (compared with £5·29 million for the IDS version in 1976–77). There is a strong likelihood that the other Panavia nations, and other countries, will also adopt this extremely cost/effective fighter version.

In 1977 the nine prototypes of the IDS and trainer versions were all flying, and in July of 1976 the first production order was placed covering 20 aircraft for assembly in the UK, 16 in Germany and four in Italy. Panavia is, at the time of writing, being restructured to bring in Turbo-Union and IKWA-Mauser so that NAMMA (the buying agency for the three customers) can do all negotiating with one "seller". A second batch of 40 was to be ordered in early 1977. Deliveries will begin later in 1977 with the six pre-series aircraft now coming off the line. These will go to RAF Cottesmore, where the OCU (Operational Conversion Unit) is being set up for all customers. A tri-national weapons training unit will be at Decimomannu, Sardinia.

1 Pitot head
2 Radome (AEG-Telefunken)
3 Ground mapping/attack radar scanner (Texas Instruments)
4 Terrain following radar scanner (Texas Instruments)
5 Yaw vane
6 Radar processing unit
7 IFF aerial
8 Windscreen rain repelling air duct
9 Avionics bay
10 Angle of attack probe
11 Canopy release handle
12 Port cannon port
13 Laser ranger and marked target seeker (Ferranti)
14 Windscreen (Lucas-Rotax)
15 Instrument panel shroud
16 Cockpit bulkhead
17 Rudder pedals
18 Avionics bay
19 Cannon barrel
20 Nosewheel door
21 Flight refuelling probe, extended
22 Pilot's head-up display (Smiths)
23 Instrument panel
24 Control column
25 Engine throttles
26 Wing sweep control
27 Command and Stability Augmentation System (CSAS) controller (Marconi-Elliott)
28 Autopilot panel (Elliott)
29 Pilot's ejection seat (Martin-Baker Mk 10)
30 Port 27-mm cannon (Mauser)
31 One piece canopy, open (Kopperschmidt)

32 Rear-view mirrors
33 Canopy jettison charge
34 Navigator's instrument console
35 Port two-dimensional air intake
36 Ammunition feed to starboard cannon
37 Ammunition tank
38 Oxygen bottle
39 Nose undercarriage leg (Dowty Rotol)
40 Twin nosewheels (Dunlop)
41 Cold air inlet
42 Navigator's rear-view mirrors
43 Navigator's instrument display
44 Starboard air intake
45 Navigator's ejection seat (Martin-Baker Mk 10)
46 Canopy jack
47 Air-intake ramp jacks (Liebherr Aerotechnik)
48 Formation light
49 Intake variable-area ramp doors
50 Bleed air louvres
51 Supplementary intake doors

52 Air conditioning plant (Normalair-Garrett)
53 Intake control system (Nord-Micro)
54 Intake trunking
55 Wing-root glove fairing
56 Krüger flap, extended
57 Wing pivot sealing fairing
58 Front fuselage bag fuel tank (Uniroyal)
59 Wing sweep actuator (Microtecnica)

60 Wing sweep hydraulic motor
61 Slat and flap combined motor (Microtecnica)
62 Communications aerials
63 Anti-collision light
64 Starboard wing sweep actuator
65 Wing pivot titanium box carry-through structure
66 Starboard wing pivot
67 Upper surface wing seal
68 Inboard pylon pivot point
69 Wing torque box
70 Integral fuel tank

71 Full-span leading-edge slats
72 Outboard pylon pivot point
73 Matra rocket launcher pod
74 Starboard navigation light
75 Wing tip antenna
76 Spoilers
77 Spoiler jacks
78 Full-span double-slotted flaps
79 Starboard external fuel tank
80 Wing root pneumatic seal
81 Pressurising air inlet
82 Fin root fairing
83 Tailplane mechanical emergency linkage
84 Air-conditioning supply
85 Pre-cooler
86 Air outlet
87 Two-spar fin construction

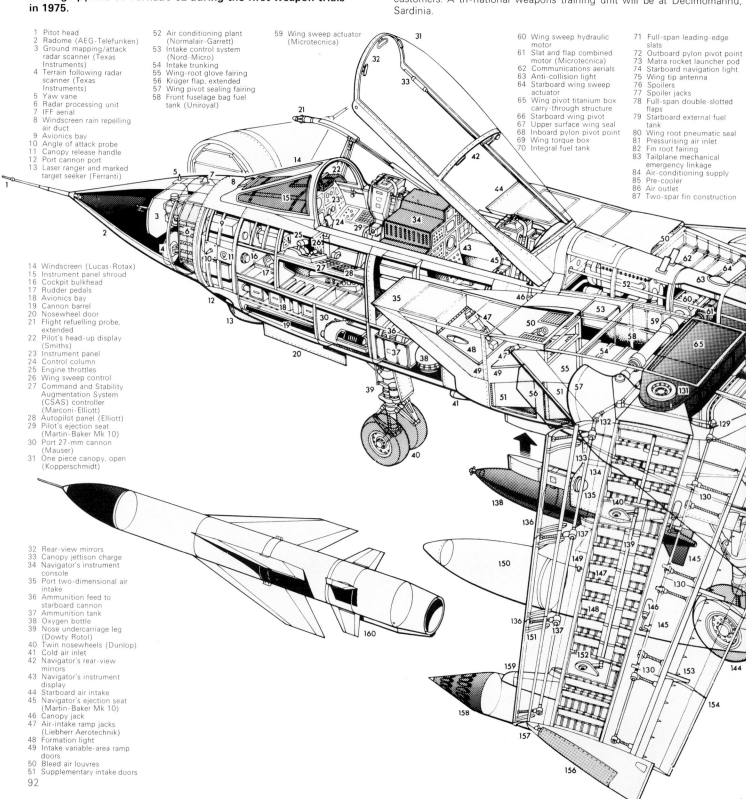

Above: The second (04) and third (07) German-assembled Tornadoes flying from Manching with MBB crews. The second is carrying a large store on the right-hand body pylon.

Above: Prototype 06, flown by BAC at Warton in December 1975, was the first Tornado to carry the internal armament of two 27mm IKWA-Mauser cannon. Here it has supersonic drop tanks.

88 Communications antenna
89 Passive ECM housing
90 Electronic tuning controls
91 Fin tip antenna
92 Tail warning radar (Elettronica)
93 Tail navigation light
94 Rudder
95 Starboard taileron surface
96 Thrust-reverser bucket-doors, open
97 Starboard fully-variable exhaust nozzle
98 Rear spine end fairing
99 Port fully variable exhaust nozzle
100 Thrust-reverser bucket-door, closed
101 Bucket-door actuator
102 Nozzle actuator
103 Rear spine

104 Port taileron construction
105 Taileron tip fairing
106 Runway arrester hook (Nardi)
107 Taileron actuating link
108 Taileron pivot
109 Port taileron actuator (Fairey Hydraulics)
110 Turbo-Union RB. 199-34R-2 engine
111 Airbrake jack
112 Port airbrake, extended
113 Vortex generators
114 Rudder actuator (Fairey Hydraulics)

115 Airbrake hinge point
116 Fly-by-wire tailplane control unit
117 Engine access doors
118 Intake frame
119 APU (KHD) in starboard gearbox bay
120 Rear fuselage bag fuel tank (Uniroyal)
121 Intake ducting

122 Hydraulic reservoir
123 Hydraulic system accumulator (Dowty)
124 Engine drive auxiliary gearbox (KHD)
125 Wing-housing cross frame
126 Wing-root pneumatic seal
127 Undercarriage frame
128 Main undercarriage retraction jack
129 Flap control shaft

130 Flap screw jacks
131 Port wing pivot bearing
132 Drive shaft gearbox
133 Leading-edge slat drive shaft
134 Main undercarriage door
135 Landing lamp
136 Full-span leading-edge slats, extended
137 Slat control units
138 1,000lb bomb (454kg)
139 Pylon pivot control rod
140 Inboard pylon pivot point
141 Main undercarriage leg (Dowty Rotol)
142 Fuselage bomb rack

143 Wing swept position
144 Port mainwheel (Dunlop)
145 Spoilers
146 Spoiler jack (Fairey Hydraulics)
147 Wing box construction
148 Integral fuel tank
149 Port inboard pylon
150 Port external fuel tank
151 Leading-edge slat rails
152 Outboard pylon pivot point
153 Flap track rail
154 Full-span double-slotted flaps, extended
155 Line of wing sweep
156 Wing tip antenna
157 Port navigation light
158 Matra rocket launcher
159 Port outboard pylon
160 MBB Jumbo air-to-surface missile (cancelled)

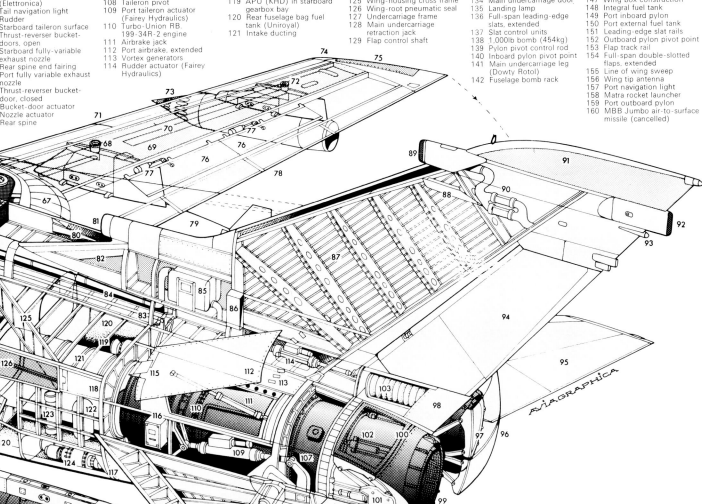

The cutaway drawing is remarkably complete, bearing in mind the fact that most of the equipment and system details of even the IDS Tornado are subject to security restrictions. The MBB Jumbo missile is, in fact, unlikely to be developed, but Tornado still has to be cleared to carry a wider range of stores and equipment than any other combat aircraft in history. By the spring of 1977 nearly all weapon trials had been completed except for the extreme upper end of the flight envelope which had been held back by unavailability of full-thrust engines—a problem now overcome.

Republic (Fairchild) F-105 Thunderchief

F-105B, D, F and G

Origin: Republic Aviation Corp (now Fairchild Republic Co), USA.

Type: Single-seat all-weather fighter-bomber; (F-105F) two-seat operational trainer; (G) two-seat ECM.

Engine: One Pratt & Whitney J75 two-shaft afterburning turbojet; (B) 23,500lb (10,660kg) J75-5; (D, F, G) 24,500lb (11,113kg) J75-19W.

Dimensions: Span 34ft 11¼in (10·65m); length (B, D) 64ft 3in (19·58m); (F, G) 69ft 7½in (21·21m); height (B, D) 19ft 8in (5·99m); (F, G) 20ft 2in (6·15m).

Weights: Empty (D) 27,500lb (12,474kg); (F, G) 28,393lb (12,879kg); maximum loaded (B) 40,000lb (18,144kg); (D) 52,546lb (23,834kg); (F, G) 54,000lb (24,495kg).

Performance: Maximum speed (B) 1,254mph; (D, F, G) 1,480mph (2382km/h, Mach 2·25); initial climb (B, D, typical) 34,500ft (10,500m)/min; (F, G) 32,000ft (9750m)/min; service ceiling (typical) 52,000ft (15,850m); tactical radius with 16 750lb bombs (D) 230 miles (370km); ferry range with maximum fuel (typical) 2,390 miles (3846km).

Armament: One 20mm M-61 gun with 1,029 rounds in left side of fuselage; internal bay for ordnance load of up to 8,000lb (3629kg), and five external pylons for additional load of 6,000lb (2722kg).

History: First flight (YF-105A) 22 October 1955; (production B) 26 May 1956; (D) 9 June 1959; (F) 11 June 1963; final delivery 1965.

User: USA (Air Force Reserve, ANG).

Development: The AP-63 project was a private venture by Republic Aviation to follow the F-84. Its primary mission was delivery of nuclear or conventional weapons in all-weathers, with very high speed and long range. Though it had only the stop-gap J57 engine the first Thunderchief exceeded the speed of sound on its first flight, and the B model was soon in production for Tactical Air Command of the USAF. Apart from being the biggest single-seat, single-engine combat aircraft in history, the 105 was notable for its large bomb bay and unique swept-forward engine inlets in the wing roots. Only 75 B were delivered but 600 of the advanced D were built, with Nasarr monopulse radar and doppler navigation. Production was completed with 143 tandem-seat F with full operational equipment and dual controls. Known as "the Thud" the greatest of single-engined combat jets bore a huge burden throughout the Vietnam war. About 350 D were rebuilt during that conflict with the Thunderstick (T-stick) all-weather blind attack system — a few also being updated to T-stick II — with a large saddleback fairing from cockpit to fin. About 30 F were converted to ECM (electronic countermeasures) attackers, with pilot and observer and Wild Weasel and other radar homing, warning and jamming systems. Westinghouse jammers and Goodyear chaff pods were carried externally.

Above: Two-seat F-105G Wild Weasel of 561st TFS, 35th TFW, George AFB, California.

Three-view of typical F-105D before T-stick rebuild.

Below: A tandem-seat F-105F shows its versatility by making a level bombing run whilst carrying AGM-45A Shrike anti-radiation missiles (white-painted). Shrikes were normally carried only by the "Wild Weasel" F-105G ECM aircraft.

Rockwell International XFV-12

XFV-12A prototype, constructor's designation NR-356

Origin: Rockwell International, Columbus, USA.
Type: Fighter/attack technology prototype.
Engine: One modified Pratt & Whitney F401-400 two-shaft afterburning turbofan rated at 16,400lb (7438kg) dry and 28,090lb (12,741kg) with maximum afterburner.
Dimensions: Span (wing) 28ft 6¼in (8·69m), (canard) 12ft 1¼in (3·69m); length 43ft 11in (13·39m); height 10ft 4in (3·15m).
Weights: (Empty, fully equipped) 13,800lb (6259kg), (max VTOL) 19,500lb (8845kg), (max STOL) 24,250lb (11,000kg).
Performance: Maximum speed at maximum STOL weight, supersonic at low level, and in excess of Mach 2 (1,320mph, 2125km/h) at optimum height; take-off run at maximum STOL weight 300ft (91m).
Armament: Space for internal M61 gun in lower fuselage; provision for carrying air-to-surface or air-to-air weapons, with fuselage recesses for two Sparrow missiles.
History: Contract award November 1972; roll-out December 1976; first flight 1977.
User: US Navy.

Development: In 1965–74 the US Navy studied the Sea Control Ship, an attractive form of small aircraft carrier with neither catapults nor arrester gear but equipped on a highly automated basis for use as a base for V/STOL aircraft. Though the Soviet Union is producing ships of this type, much bigger than the projected SCS, the US Navy had to abandon the proposal through lack of money. Work continued, however, on this extremely interesting technology-demonstrator aircraft, which to save money has

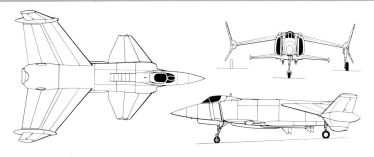

Three-view of XFV-12A showing Sparrow missiles.

been designed by Rockwell's Columbus Aircraft Division in Ohio to incorporate the main wing box and parts of the inlet ducts of an F-4 Phantom, and the nose, cockpit and forward fuselage, and nose and main landing gears, of an A-4 Skyhawk. Pratt & Witney developed the large electro-hydraulic diverter valve which, for V/STOL, shuts off the engine nozzle and diverts the entire efflux through large high-temperature ducts. One duct feeds the canard's augmentor (ejector) flaps, while the larger duct feeds the similar flaps along the wings. Each surface has front and rear flaps across the full span, with endplates, and the ejector slits not only give direct lift and thrust but entrain an airflow 7½ times as great to give enough lift for VTOL or higher-weight STOL. All flap sections are of titanium honeycomb, fully powered to serve as control surfaces in forward flight, when the wing and canard are closed for forward speeds up to Mach 2. The fins carry small rudders above the wing but there are no leading-edge movable surfaces. There is no suggestion of producing an FV-12A in quantity, but the technology is expected to be valuable in refining the requirements for supersonic V/STOL fighter and attack aircraft for shipboard use in the late 1980s.

Below: Artist's impression of XFV-12A fighter/attack research aircraft in jet-lift V/STOL mode.

Saab 37 Viggen

AJ37, JA37, SF37, SH37 and Sk37

Origin: Saab-Scania AB, Linköping, Sweden.

Type: (AJ) single-seat all-weather attack; (JA) all-weather fighter; (SF) armed photo-reconnaissance; (SH) armed sea surveillance; (SK) dual trainer.

Engine: One Svenska Flygmotor RM8 (licence-built Pratt & Whitney JT8D two-shaft turbofan redesigned in Sweden for Mach 2 and fitted with SFA afterburner); (AJ, SF, SH and Sk) 25,970lb (11,790kg) RM8A; (JA) 28,086lb (12,750kg) RM8B.

Dimensions: Span of main wing 34ft 9¼in (10·6m); length (AJ) 53ft 5¾in (16·3m); (JA37 with probe) 53ft 11in; height 18ft 4½in (5·6m).

Weights: Not disclosed, except AJ37 "normal armament" gross weight of 35,275lb (16,000kg).

Performance: Maximum speed (clean) about 1,320mph (2135km/h, Mach 2), or Mach 1·1 at sea level; initial climb, about 40,000ft (12,200m)/min (time from start of take-off run to 32,800ft—10,000m = 100sec); service ceiling, over 60,000ft (18,300m); tactical radius with external stores (not drop tanks), hi-lo-hi profile, over 620 miles (1000km).

Armament: Seven pylons (option: nine) for aggregate external load of 13,200lb (6000kg), including Rb04E or Rb05A missiles for attack, and Rb27, Rb28 and Rb324 missiles for defence. In addition the JA37 has a 30mm Oerlikon KCA gun and will carry "new long- and short-range missiles for air-to-air interception"; Skyflash is being evaluated.

History: First flight 8 February 1967; (production AJ) 23 February 1971; service delivery (AJ) June 1971.

User: Sweden (RSAF).

Development: Yet again blazing a trail ahead of other nations, the Royal Swedish Air Board planned System 37 in 1958–61 as a standardized weapon system to be integrated with the Stril 60 air-defence environment of radars, computers and displays. Included in the system is a standard platform (in this case a supersonic manned aircraft) produced in five versions each tailored to a specific task. Thanks to a unique configuration with a 400 sq ft wing preceded by a canard foreplane with trailing-edge flaps, the Viggen (Thunderbolt) has outstanding STOL (short take-off and landing) performance and excellent turn radius at all speeds. Efficient and prolonged operations are possible from narrow strips 500m (1,640ft) in length, such as stretches of highway. Equipment in all versions includes headup display, autothrottle/speed control on approach, no-flare landing autopilot and thrust reverser. The AJ operates camouflaged in attack wings F7, F15 and F6, with production continuing in 1977 on a mix of AJ, SF, SH and Sk models. At the beginning of the year about 145 had been delivered of the total orders for 180 of these versions. During 1976 Viggens in RSAF service were grounded until the cause of inflight structural (wing) failures

continued on page 98 ▶

Three-view of JA37, with side view (centre) of SK37 trainer.

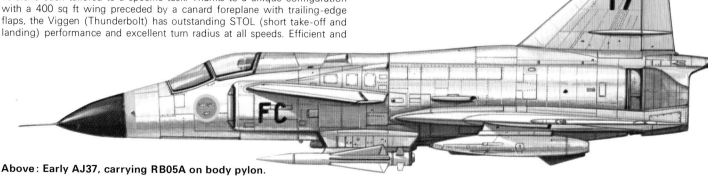

Above: Early AJ37, carrying RB05A on body pylon.

1 Dielectric radome
2 Planar-array scanner
3 Ericsson PS-Ø1 pulse-doppler radar
4 Avionics bay
5 Radar/avionics cooling air
6 Nosewheel doors
7 Twin nosewheels (forward retracting)
8 Nosewheel leg
9 Control runs
10 Nosewheel leg pivot point
11 Rudder pedal
12 Canopy frame (with wind-shield de-icing)
13 Control column
14 Head-up display shroud
15 Starboard console (weapons, avionics)
16 Weapons/gunsight
17 Windshield
18 Canopy
19 Starboard intake
20 Headrest
21 Ejection seat
22 Port engine intake
23 Inlet duct
24 Forward (canard) wing/fuselage attachment points
25 Main fuselage fuel tank
26 Canopy hinges
27 Starboard forward (canard) wing
28 Canard flaps
29 Intakes
30 Radio equipment bay
31 Engine oil coolers (centre and starboard tanks)
32 Electric generator drive

cooler (port tank)
33 Centre fuselage avionics pack
34 Port avionics bay
35 Hydraulics tank
36 Forward (canard) wing structure
37 Honeycomb flap construction
38 Ram-air turbine
39 Aircraft gearbox
40 Starter
41 Oxygen cylinder
42 Central computer and avionics
43 Engine intake
44 Fuselage saddle fuel tank (forward wall) (see 52)
45 Cabin air outlet
46 Cooling package
47 Engine forward attachment point
48 Fuel lines
49 Volvo Flygmotor RM 8 turbofan (25,970 lb/11,790 kg with afterburner)

50 Aircraft gearbox cooler
51 Main wing attachment point
52 Fuselage saddle fuel tank (rear wall) (see 44)
53 Air brake
54 Engine aft attachment point
55 Control runs
56 Fin front spar/fuselage attachment point
57 Starboard integral fuel tank
58 Starboard ECM bullet
59 Starboard outer elevon actuator
60 Starboard elevon (outer section)
61 Fin structure
62 VHF aerial
63 Rudder honeycomb construction

64 Rudder
65 Rudder actuator fairing
66 Actuator support
67 Fin rear spar/fuselage attachment point
68 Control linkage
69 Afterburner
70 Reverser clamshells
71 Rear navigation light
72 Tail fairing
73 Primary nozzle
74 Port elevon (inner section)
75 Elevon actuator (inner)

76 Rear spar
77 Elevon actuator (centre)
78 Port elevon (outer section)
79 Honeycomb construction
80 Elevon actuator (outer)
81 Outer leading-edge structure
82 Port ECM bullet
83 Port integral fuel tank
84 Main spar

85 Undercarriage door (inner)
86 Wheel well
87 Mainwheel leg pivot point
88 Inner leading-edge structure
89 Mainwheel leg (Motala)
90 Mainwheel leg door (outer)
91 Mainwheel scissors
92 Tandem mainwheels

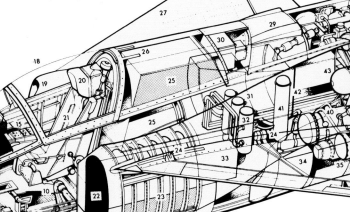

Above: Though departure of an AJ37 is marked by extreme noise and fuel consumption, this unique tandem-delta aircraft offers great advantages. It is especially outstanding in radar and weapon-delivery systems, turn radius with heavy ordnance load, and short no-flare landing with thrust-reverser.

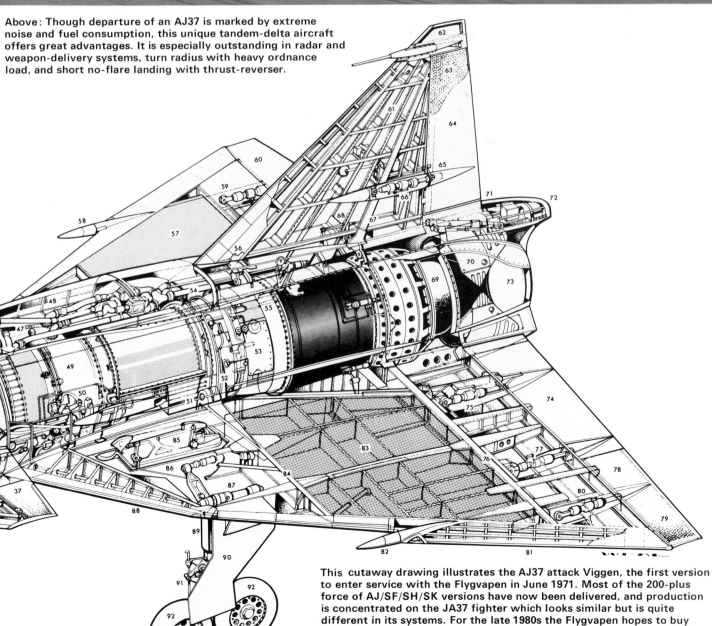

This cutaway drawing illustrates the AJ37 attack Viggen, the first version to enter service with the Flygvapen in June 1971. Most of the 200-plus force of AJ/SF/SH/SK versions have now been delivered, and production is concentrated on the JA37 fighter which looks similar but is quite different in its systems. For the late 1980s the Flygvapen hopes to buy a new multi-role aircraft, at present called Attack System 85 (and also referred to as A20), derived from the JA37.

▶had been fully explained and aircraft rectified. Apart from this the Viggen has proved as outstanding as it looked on paper in the 1960s, and even today no other Western European aircraft can rival it for radar performance, flight performance and short field length in all weathers. The latest Viggen variant, the JA37, is considerably different, with a new engine, very powerful gun, UAP 1023 pulse-doppler radar, digital automatic flight control system and extremely advanced inertial measurement and central computer systems. The development effort for the JA37 rivals that for the complete original aircraft, but with the help of a fleet of special-purpose test aircraft (some new and most rebuilds of early AJ and other models) the JA was cleared for production in 1976. By the start of 1977 most of the initial batch of 30 were on the line, and service delivery is due in 1978. Eventually 200 are to equip eight squadrons.

Right: A tandem-seat SK37 of F15 wing at Soderhamm taxies out for a training sortie. This replaces the fuselage fuel tank and electronics by a rear cockpit, with Saab-Scania rocket-assisted seat, bulged canopy and twin periscopes. To counter the extra side area the fin has increased height and area. This dual-control version can fly attack missions with any AJ37 weapons.

Below: An AJ37 with some of the more common external stores. The largest is the centreline fuel tank. In the front row are low-drag bombs with stand-off fuzes. In the second row are (from the outside) RB28 Falcon air/air missile; RB05A air/surface missile (now being supplemented by RB05B with long TV seeker nose); two types of store apparently carrying multi-sensor reconnaissance equipment; two types of launcher for Bofors 135mm rockets; and RB324 Sidewinder air/air missiles. Under the wings are large RB04E anti-ship missiles.

SEPECAT Jaguar

Jaguar GR.1 and T.2, Jaguar A and E, and Jaguar International

Origin: SEPECAT, consortium formed by British Aerospace (BAC) and Dassault-Breguet, France.

Type: (GR.1, A and International (I.)) single-seat all-weather attack; (T.2 and E) dual operational trainer.

Engines: Two Rolls-Royce/Turboméca Adour two-shaft augmented turbofans: (except I.) 7,305lb (3313kg) Adour 102; (I.) 8,000lb (3630kg) Adour 804.

Dimensions: Span 28ft 6in (8·69m); length (except T.2, E) 50ft 11in (15·52m); (T.2, E) 53ft 11in (16·42m); height 16ft 1½in (4·92m).

Weights: Empty, classified but about 15,000lb (6800kg); "normal take-off" (ie, internal fuel and some external ordnance) 23,000lb (10,430kg); maximum loaded 34,000lb (15,500kg).

Performance: Maximum speed (lo, some external stores) 820mph (1320km/h, Mach 1·1), (hi, some external stores) 1,055mph (1700km/h, Mach 1·6); climb and ceiling, classified; attack radius, no external fuel, hi-lo-hi with bombs, 507 miles (815km); ferry range 2,614 miles (4210km).

Armament: (A, E) two 30mm DEFA 553 each with 150 rounds; five pylons for total external load of 10,000lb (4536kg); (GR.1) as above but guns two 30mm Aden; (T.2) as above but single Aden. (International) wide range of options including increased external loads.

History: First flight (E) 8 September 1968; (production E) 2 November 1971; (production GR.1) 11 October 1972; squadron delivery (E, A) May 1972, (GR, T) June 1973.

Users: Ecuador, France, Oman, UK (RAF).

Development: Developed jointly by BAC in Britain and Dassault-Breguet in France, to meet a joint requirement of the Armée de l'Air and RAF, the Jaguar is a far more powerful and effective aircraft than originally planned and has already demonstrated unmatched capabilities in service. The

continued on page 100 ▶

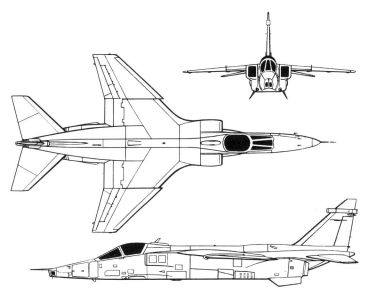

Above: Three-view of Jaguar GR.1 without stores.

Above: Takeoff of a prototype E-type trainer in France in 1969, with "dual-nationality" markings. All 40 of this simple training version have now been delivered to the Armée de l'Air, the main units being the 7th wing at St Dizier and 11th at Toul.

Above: Close formation fly-past by Jaguar A-type attack aircraft and E-type trainers of the 7e wing. The Armée de l'Air deliberately bought simpler Jaguars than the RAF, though they are now being updated by optional laser and/or radar equipment.

Below: A dramatic firing picture of a Matra 550 Magic air-to-air dogfight missile being loosed from an overwing pylon. The aircraft was a BAC-modified Jaguar International, with uprated Adour 804 engines, trials with which were very successfully completed in 1976.

▶original idea was a light trainer and close-support machine, with 1,300lb weapon load, but with British pressure this was upgraded to today's outstanding aircraft whose only marketing problem is the fact that the French partner prefers aircraft which appear to be all-French (yet, in fact, Dassault makes only the same proportion of the Mirage F1 as it does of the Jaguar, namely, about 50 per cent). Despite this unhappy political scene the sheer merit of the Jaguar, and the enthusiastic missionary work done by its operating units in the Armée de l'Air and RAF, is gradually winning valuable orders, beginning with Ecuador and Oman in 1974. Further sales are likely with the more powerful International version now flying. The two basic single-seat versions share a common airframe but are totally different in equipment. The French A model has a simple twin-gyro platform, doppler, and a basic navigation computer; in 1977 an Atlis laser pod was being added. The RAF GR.1 has inertial navigation, head-up display, projected map display, radar height, integrated nav/attack system and laser ranger, as well as comprehensive ECM and option of a multi-sensor reconnaissance pod. All versions can have nose radar, refuelling probe and the option of overwing pylons for light dogflght missiles (Jaguar development aircraft have flown with Matra Magics in these positions). Thanks to a dynamic programme of engine development Jaguar users have the option of various increased-thrust Adours, including the Mk 804 (Adour 26) fitted to the basic Jaguar International, and the even more powerful Adour 56 and 58 (in the 10,000lb, 4500kg class) which will be available from 1980. It is the intention of the RAF to select one of the uprated engines and convert all Jaguar engines to this standard, to gain even better field length and flight performance with large mission loads. By 1977 some 300 aircraft had been delivered, and several new customers were engaged in contract negotiation.

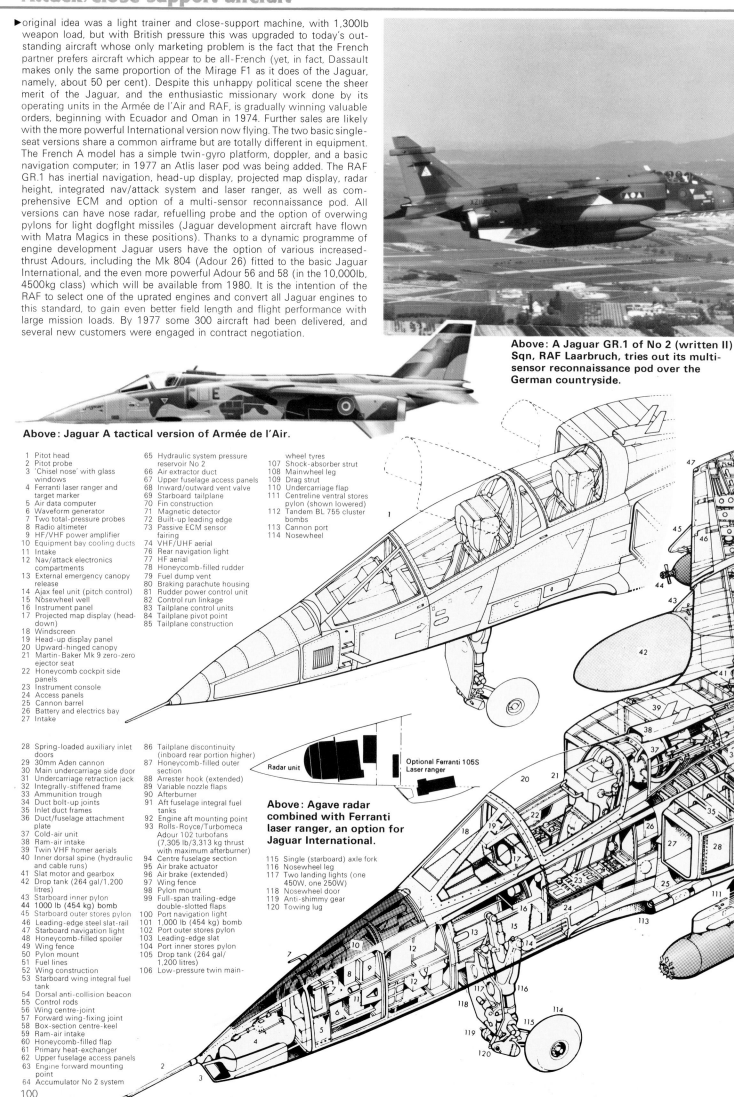

Above: A Jaguar GR.1 of No 2 (written II) Sqn, RAF Laarbruch, tries out its multi-sensor reconnaissance pod over the German countryside.

Above: Jaguar A tactical version of Armée de l'Air.

1 Pitot head
2 Pitot probe
3 'Chisel nose' with glass windows
4 Ferranti laser ranger and target marker
5 Air data computer
6 Waveform generator
7 Two total-pressure probes
8 Radio altimeter
9 HF/VHF power amplifier
10 Equipment bay cooling ducts
11 Intake
12 Nav/attack electronics compartments
13 External emergency canopy release
14 Ajax feel unit (pitch control)
15 Nosewheel well
16 Instrument panel
17 Projected map display (head-down)
18 Windscreen
19 Head-up display panel
20 Upward-hinged canopy
21 Martin-Baker Mk 9 zero-zero ejector seat
22 Honeycomb cockpit side panels
23 Instrument console
24 Access panels
25 Cannon barrel
26 Battery and electrics bay
27 Intake
28 Spring-loaded auxiliary inlet doors
29 30mm Aden cannon
30 Main undercarriage side door
31 Undercarriage retraction jack
32 Integrally-stiffened frame
33 Ammunition trough
34 Duct bolt-up joints
35 Inlet duct frames
36 Duct/fuselage attachment plate
37 Cold-air unit
38 Ram-air intake
39 Twin VHF homer aerials
40 Inner dorsal spine (hydraulic and cable runs)
41 Slat motor and gearbox
42 Drop tank (264 gal/1,200 litres)
43 Starboard inner pylon
44 1000 lb (454 kg) bomb
45 Starboard outer stores pylon
46 Leading-edge steel slat-rail
47 Starboard navigation light
48 Honeycomb-filled spoiler
49 Wing fence
50 Pylon mount
51 Fuel lines
52 Wing construction
53 Starboard wing integral fuel tank
54 Dorsal anti-collision beacon
55 Control rods
56 Wing centre-joint
57 Forward wing-fixing joint
58 Box-section centre-keel
59 Ram-air intake
60 Honeycomb-filled flap
61 Primary heat-exchanger
62 Upper fuselage access panels
63 Engine forward mounting point
64 Accumulator No 2 system

65 Hydraulic system pressure reservoir No 2
66 Air extractor duct
67 Upper fuselage access panels
68 Inward/outward vent valve
69 Starboard tailplane
70 Fin construction
71 Magnetic detector
72 Built-up leading edge
73 Passive ECM sensor fairing
74 VHF/UHF aerial
76 Rear navigation light
77 HF aerial
78 Honeycomb-filled rudder
79 Fuel dump vent
80 Braking parachute housing
81 Rudder power control unit
82 Control run linkage
83 Tailplane control units
84 Tailplane pivot point
85 Tailplane construction
86 Tailplane discontinuity (inboard rear portion higher)
87 Honeycomb-filled outer section
88 Arrester hook (extended)
89 Variable nozzle flaps
90 Afterburner
91 Aft fuselage integral fuel tanks
92 Engine aft mounting point
93 Rolls-Royce/Turbomeca Adour 102 turbofans (7,305 lb/3,313 kg thrust with maximum afterburner)
94 Centre fuselage section
95 Air brake actuator
96 Air brake (extended)
97 Wing fence
98 Pylon mount
99 Full-span trailing-edge double-slotted flaps
100 Port navigation light
101 1,000 lb (454 kg) bomb
102 Port outer stores pylon
103 Leading-edge slat
104 Port inner stores pylon
105 Drop tank (264 gal/1,200 litres)
106 Low-pressure twin main-

wheel tyres
107 Shock-absorber strut
108 Mainwheel leg
109 Drag strut
110 Undercarriage flap
111 Centreline ventral stores pylon (shown lowered)
112 Tandem BL 755 cluster bombs
113 Cannon port
114 Nosewheel

Radar unit

Optional Ferranti 105S Laser ranger

Above: Agave radar combined with Ferranti laser ranger, an option for Jaguar International.

115 Single (starboard) axle fork
116 Nosewheel leg
117 Two landing lights (one 450W, one 250W)
118 Nosewheel door
119 Anti-shimmy gear
120 Towing lug

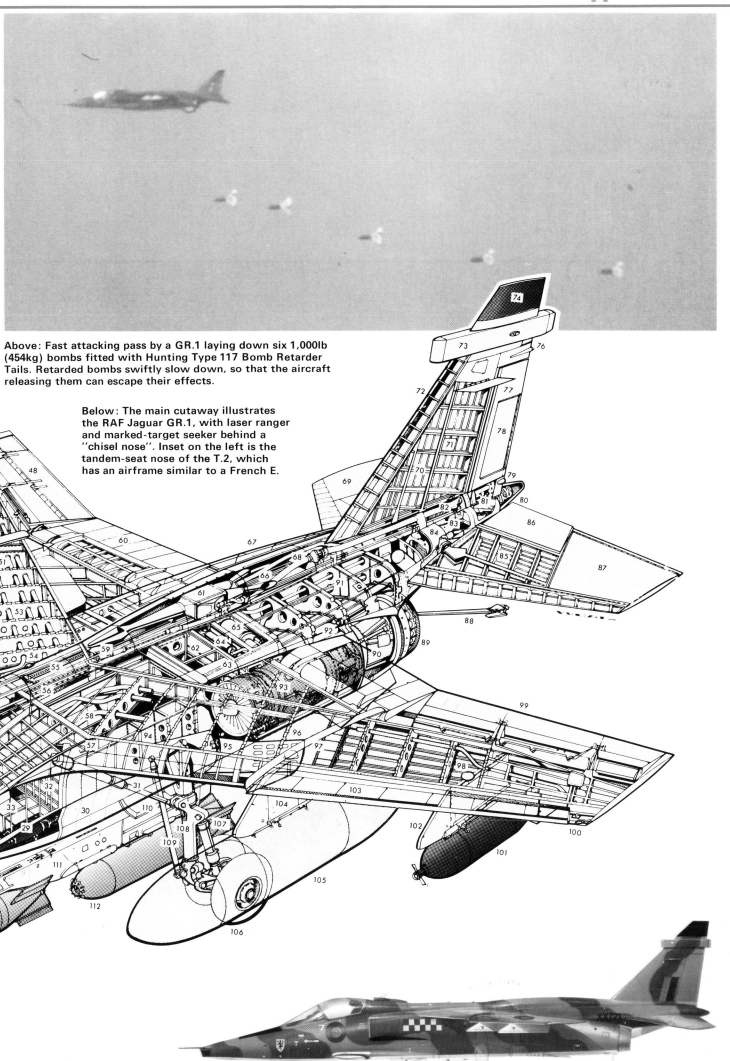

Above: Fast attacking pass by a GR.1 laying down six 1,000lb (454kg) bombs fitted with Hunting Type 117 Bomb Retarder Tails. Retarded bombs swiftly slow down, so that the aircraft releasing them can escape their effects.

Below: The main cutaway illustrates the RAF Jaguar GR.1, with laser ranger and marked-target seeker behind a "chisel nose". Inset on the left is the tandem-seat nose of the T.2, which has an airframe similar to a French E.

Above: Jaguar GR.1 of 54 Sqn, RAF Coltishall.

Shenyang F-9

F-9 (NATO code name "Fantan A")

Origin: State Aircraft Factory, Shenyang, People's Republic of China.
Type: All-weather fighter, attack and reconnaissance aircraft.
Engines: Two axial turbojets with afterburners (see text).
Dimensions (estimated): Span 33ft 5in (10·2m); length 50ft (15·25m); height 11ft (3·35m).
Weights: (estimated) Empty 13,670lb (6200kg); loaded (clean) 20,285lb (9200kg), (maximum) 23,600lb (10,700kg).
Performance (estimated): Maximum speed, clean (sea level) about 760mph (1225km/h, Mach 1), (high altitude) about 1,190mph (1910km/h, Mach 1·8); combat radius (hi-lo-hi, two bombs, two tanks) 500 miles (800km).
Armament: Not known, but almost certainly includes internal guns, external stores pylons for tanks and ordnance and comprehensive ECM equipment.
History: First flight, possibly 1968; service delivery, probably early 1970s.
Users: People's Republic of China (AF, Navy).

Development: Obviously derived from the F-6, the Chinese-built MiG-19SF, the F-9 represents the first (enforced) attempt by the Shenyang-based home industry to produce combat aircraft independently. Despite extreme difficulties caused by a lack of industrial backing and skilled labour, the production of nationally developed aircraft was forced on the PRC (People's Republic of China) by its isolation from technically advanced nations and imminence of the Soviet threat. The excellent qualities of the MiG-19 basic design eventually led to the F-6 being chosen for development in preference to the F-8, the illegally manufactured MiG-21PF. During the 1960s the Shenyang F-9 took shape as an enlarged F-6 with lateral inlet ducts feeding direct to the two engines (a Chinese illustration suggests that the mid-wing has been retained, with ducts above and below), leaving the nose free for a large search radar of unknown type. The sketch referred to showed no wing cannon, but the two 30mm NR-30s of the F-6 have probably been retained in view of the great length of inlet duct ahead of the wing, interfering with pilot view. The inlets are apparently simple and non-variable, efficient at low level but limiting high-altitude Mach number.

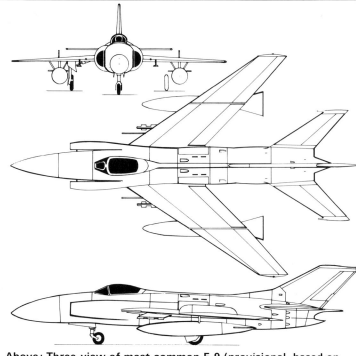

Above: **Three-view of most common F-9 (provisional, based on Chinese pictures).**

The radar could be a derivative of the "Spin Scan B" as used in later North Vietnamese MiG-21PF fighters sent via China, but in the author's opinion is more likely to be a copy of the much more powerful AWG-10 or APQ-109 fitted to Phantoms of the late 1960s. Whether the PRC has also copied Sparrow and/or Sidewinder is problematical.

In his Fiscal Year 1977 report the US SecDef (then Donald Rumsfeld) described the "Fantan-A" as a principal tactical aircraft of the PRC Navy;

Sukhoi Su-7

Su-7B, -7BM, -7BMK and -7U; NATO name "Fitter"

Origin: The design bureau of Pavel A. Sukhoi, Soviet Union.
Type: Single-seat close-support and interdiction; (-7U) dual-control trainer.
Engine: One Lyulka AL-7F turbojet rated at 15,430lb (7000kg) dry or 22,046lb (10,000kg) with maximum afterburner.
Dimensions: Span 29ft 3½in (8·93m), length (all, incl probe) 57ft (17·37m); height (all) 15ft 5in (4·70m).
Weights: Empty (typical -7) 19,000lb (8620kg), maximum loaded (typical -7) 30,000lb (13,610kg).
Performance: Maximum speed, clean, at altitude, (all) 1,055mph (1700km/h, Mach 1·6), initial climb (-7BM) 29,000ft (9120m)/min; service ceiling (-7BM) 49,700ft (15,150m); range with twin drop tanks (all) 900 miles (1450km).
Armament: (-7) two 30mm NR-30 cannon, each with 70 rounds, in wing roots; four wing pylons, inners rated at 1,653lb (750kg) and outers at 1,102lb (500kg), but when two tanks are carried on fuselage pylons total external weapon load is reduced to 2,205lb (1000kg).
History: First flight (-7 prototype) not later than 1955; service delivery (-7B) 1959.
Users: (-7) Afghanistan, Algeria, Czechoslovakia, Egypt, Hungary, India, Iraq, N Korea, Poland, Romania, Soviet Union, Syria, Vietnam.

Development: Two of the wealth of previously unknown Soviet aircraft revealed at the 1956 Aviation Day at Tushino were large Sukhoi fighters, one with a swept wing (called "Fitter" by NATO) and the other a tailed delta (called "Fishpot"). Both were refined into operational types, losing some of their commonality in the process. The delta entered service as the Su-9 and -11, described separately. The highly-swept Su-7 was likewise built in very large numbers, optimised not for air superiority but for ground attack. As such it has found a worldwide market, and despite severe short-comings has been exported in numbers which exceed 700. All Sukhoi combat aircraft have been made within the Soviet Union. The good points of the Su-7 family are robust structure, reasonable reliability and low cost; drawbacks are vulnerability to small-calibre fire and the impossibility of getting adequate field length, weapon load and radius of action all together. There are many variants. The original -7B was quickly superseded by the more powerful -7BM, with twin ribbon tail chutes. The most common export model is the -7BMK with low-pressure tyres and other changes to improve behaviour from short unpaved strips. The -7U is the tandem dual trainer. Since 1964 many BMK have been seen with take-off rockets and four wing pylons.

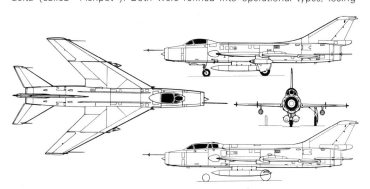

Above: **Three-view of Su-7BMK, with side view (bottom) of -7U "Moujik".**

Above: **Flame envelops the leading edge as an Su-7B fires its cannon.**

earlier it was known to be in service with the PRCAF. Compared with the F-6 it should be a considerably more effective machine, provided engine power has risen at least in proportion to the weight. Some Western reports suggest that the engines are the Tumansky RD-9B-811, of 8,270lb (3750kg) maximum thrust; in the author's view an equally plausible possibility is that the bigger and more powerful R-11 engine of the F-8 (13,120lb, 5950kg) could have been chosen. Indeed use of this engine in the F-9 might in some degree explain the early termination of Chinese production of the F-8. As this book went to press little is known of the F-9, and it could even

Above: Artist's impression of an F-9 in operational service. There is abundant evidence that Chinese arms output has increased to levels probably greater than that of any other nation.

be subject to severe problems and limitations. It should in any case not be confused with the entirely different combat aircraft (believed to be a twin-engined delta) which will be powered by the Chinese-assembled Rolls-Royce Spey.

Above: Four Su-7BM tactical aircraft of the Egyptian Air Force. About 120 are in service, plus some Su-7U trainers.

Above, right: This section of Su-7Bs are carrying the twin drop tanks needed by this aircraft to supplement its limited internal capacity.

The -7BM has a number of detail differences, and in late sub-types has a low-pressure nosewheel tyre for soft fields, needing bulged doors.

Above: Well-worn Su-7B of Indian Air Force.

Above: Su-7BM of Egyptian AF.

Above: Su-7B (early sub-type) of Czech Air Force.

Sukhoi Su-17 and Su-20

Su-17 "Fitter C", Su-20 and Su-22

Origin: The design bureau named for Pavel O. Sukhoi, Soviet Union.
Type: Single-seat attack and close-support aircraft.
Engine: (-17) one Lyulka AL-21F-3 single-shaft turbojet with afterburner rated at 17,200lb (7800kg) dry and 25,000lb (11,340kg) with maximum afterburner, (-20, -22) believed to be AL-7F-1 rated at 22,046lb (10,000kg).
Dimensions (all): Span (28°) 45ft 11¼in (14·00m), (62°) 34ft 9½in (10·60m); length (incl probe) 61ft 6¼in (18·75m); height 15ft 7in (4·75m).
Weights: (-17 estimated, -20 and -22 slightly less) empty 22,046lb (10,000kg); loaded (clean) 30,865lb (14,000kg), (maximum) 41,887lb (19,000kg).
Performance: (-17, clean) maximum speed at sea level 798mph (1284 km/h, Mach 1·05), maximum speed at optimum height 1,432mph (2305 km/h, Mach 2·17); initial climb 45,275ft (13,800m)/min; service ceiling 59,050ft (18,000m); combat radius with 4,410lb (2000kg) external stores (hi-lo-hi) 391 miles (630km).
Armament: Two 30mm NR-30 cannon, each with 70 rounds, in wing roots; eight pylons under fuselage, fixed gloves and swing-wings for maximum external load of 11,023lb (5000kg) including the AS-7 "Kerry" air-to-surface missile (-20, -22, six pylons).
History: First public display at Domodedovo 1967; service delivery, possibly 1970 (-17) and 1972-3 (-20).
Users: Egypt (-20), Peru (-22), Poland (-20), Soviet Union (FA, -17).

Development: A ogical direct modification of the somewhat limited Su-7B, the Su-17 has variable-geometry "swing-wings" pivoted far outboard, hinged to a slightly modified -7B centre section with strengthened landing gear. At maximum sweep the trailing edge of the centre section aligns with the outer section, and it carries two shallow fences on each side. At the pivots are large square-fronted fences combined with pylons which

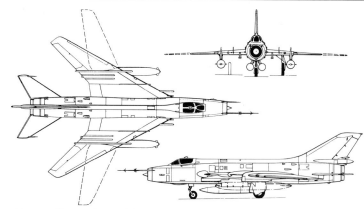

Above: Three-view of Su-20, showing range of wing sweep.

are stressed to carry 2,200lb (1000kg) stores which in the Polish Su-20 are invariably drop tanks with nose fins. The swing-wings carry full-span slats, slotted ailerons and flaps which retract inside the centre section. Compared with the Su-7B the result is the ability to lift twice the external load from airstrips little more than half as long, and climb and level speed at all heights are much increased, even in the lower-powered Su-20 and export Su-22. Equipment in the -17 includes SRD-5M "High Fix" radar, an ASP-5ND fire-control system and comprehensive communications and IFF. Landing performance is so much better than the -7B that a braking chute is not fitted; in its place is the aft-facing aerial for a Sirena 3 radar homing and warning system at the rear of the prominent dorsal spine. Peru's 36 aircraft were to be delivered in 1977.

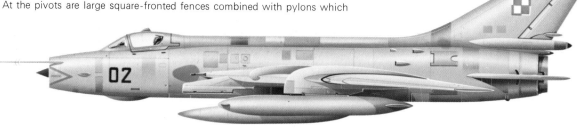

Below: On 6 October 1976 the Egyptian Air Force sprang a surprise on foreign observers by including this group of Su-20 variable-sweep attack aircraft in its parade commemorating the October war three years earlier.

Above: Su-20 in service with Polish Air Force (wings swept).

Sukhoi Su-19

Su-19 versions known to NATO as "Fencer"

Origin: The design bureau of Pavel O. Sukhoi, Soviet Union.
Type: Two-seat multi-role combat aircraft.
Engines: Two afterburning turbofan or turbojet engines, probably two 24,500lb (11,113kg) Lyulka AL-21F3.
Dimensions: (Estimated) span (spread, about 22°) 56ft 3in (17·5m), swept (about 72°) 31ft 3in (9·53m); length 69ft 10in (21·29m); height 21ft (6·4m).
Weights: (Estimated) empty 35,000lb (15,875kg); maximum loaded 70,000lb (31,750kg).
Performance: (Estimated) maximum speed, clean, 950mph (1530km/h, Mach 1·25) at sea level, about 1,650mph (2655km/h, Mach 2·5) at altitude; initial climb, over 40,000ft (12,200m)/min; service ceiling, about 60,000ft (18,290m), combat radius with maximum weapons, about 500 miles (805km); ferry range, over 2,500 miles (4025km).
Armament: One 23mm GSh-23 twin-barrel cannon in lower centreline; at least six pylons on fuselage, fixed and swinging wings, for wide range of stores including guided and unguided air-to-ground or air-to-air missiles.
History: First flight, probably about 1970; service delivery, 1974 or earlier.
User: Soviet Union (mainly FA).

Development: First identified publicly in the West by the Chairman of the US Joint Chiefs of Staff, who described the Su-19 as "the first modern Soviet fighter to be developed specifically as a fighter-bomber for the ground-attack mission", this aircraft will probably be the chief tactical attack aircraft of the Soviet V-VS in 1980. Like the rival but much smaller MiG-27, the Su-19 is an extremely clean machine strongly reminiscent of the F-111 and Mirage G, having side-by-side seats and wing and tailplane

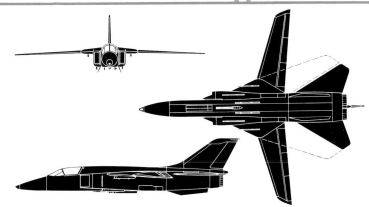

Three-view of Su-19, showing range of sweep (provisional).

at the same level, as in the US machine, yet following the French aircraft in general layout. In general capability the nearest Western equivalent is the F-14 Tomcat, which shows just how formidable this aircraft is. Whereas "Foxbat" was on many Western lips in the 1960s, so is "Fencer" a big scare-word in the 1970s. Features of the first service version include a typical Sukhoi tail, but with ventral fins; double-shock side inlets; full-span slats and double-slotted flaps; and very extensive avionics (thought to include a multi-mode attack radar, doppler, laser ranger and very comprehensive EW/ECM installations).

Left: A side view of an Su-19 in service with the Soviet FA. Like the three-view this is provisional. There is some evidence that the rear fuselage and tail resembles that of the Su-15 interceptor, and the engines may be the same.

Vought A-7 Corsair II

Vought A-7A to E and TA-7C

Origin: Vought Systems Division of LTV, Dallas, USA.
Type: Single-seat attack bomber (carrier- or land-based); (TA) dual trainer.
Engine: (A) one 11,350lb (5150kg) thrust Pratt & Whitney TF30-6 two-shaft turbofan; (B, C) 12,200lb (5534kg) TF30-8; (D) 14,250lb (6465kg) Allison TF41-1 (Rolls-Royce Spey derivative) of same layout; (E) 15,000lb (6804kg) TF41-2.
Dimensions: Span 38ft 9in (11·80m); length 46ft 1½in (14·06m); (TA) 48ft 2in (14·68m); height 16ft 0¾in (4·90m); (TA) 16ft 5in (5m).
Weights: Empty (A) 15,904lb (7214kg); (D) 19,781lb (8972kg); maximum loaded (A) 32,500lb (14,750kg); (D) 42,000lb (19,050kg).

Performance: Maximum speed (all single-seat versions, clean) 698mph (1123km/h) at low level; climb and ceiling, not reported (seldom relevant); tactical radius with weapon load, typically 715 miles (1150km); ferry range with four external tanks, typically 4,100 miles (6600km).
Armament: (A, B) two 20mm Colt Mk 12 in nose; six wing and two fuselage pylons for weapon load of 15,000lb (6804kg). (D, E) one 20mm M61 Vulcan cannon on left side of fuselage with 1,000-round drum; external load up to theoretical 20,000lb (9072kg).
History: First flight 27 September 1965; service delivery October 1966; first flight of D, 26 September 1968.
Users: Greece, Pakistan, USA (Air Force, Navy).

continued on page 106 ▶

Below: A Hughes AGM-65A (TV version of Maverick) blasts away from a Vought A-7D during weapon development tests at the USAF Armament Development and Test Center at Eglin AFB, Florida. Now, all TAC A-7 squadrons have Mavericks.

▶**Development:** Though derived from the Crusader, the Corsair II is a totally different aircraft. By restricting performance to high subsonic speed, structure weight was reduced, range dramatically increased and weapon load multiplied by about 4. Development was outstandingly quick, as was production. Vought built 199 A-7A, used in action in the Gulf of Tonkin on 3 December 1967, followed by 196 B models. The C designation was used for the first 67 E models which retained the TF30 engine. In 1966 the Corsair II was adopted by the US Air Force, the A-7D having the superior TF41 engine, Gatling gun and more complete avionics for blind or automatic weapon delivery under all conditions, with head-up display and inertial/doppler navigation. By late 1976 over 480 had been delivered, with reduced production continuing. The Navy adopted the same model, with an even more powerful TF41, and by late 1976 about 540 E models had been built, bringing output to well over 1,400 within a decade. Vought funded development of a tandem-seat YA-7H, and is converting 81 B and C into the dual TA-7C. Greece is receiving 60 A-7H, similar to the D but without the on-board starter or flight-refuelling receptacle, at a price of $259·2 million. Pakistan accepted sale of 110, on condition (it was reported) it did not buy a nuclear reactor offered by France!

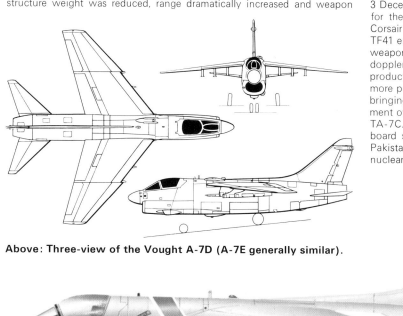

Above: Three-view of the Vought A-7D (A-7E generally similar).

Above: Vought A-7A Corsair II of VA-195, US Navy (USS *Kitty Hawk*).

Below: Four colourful A-7E attack aircraft of the US Navy look like fighters yet have more offensive punch (even discounting nuclear weapons) than twice as many four-engined bombers of World War II. The red-tailed machine comes from a unit embarked aboard USS *Coral Sea*, while the others are from the nuclear-powered super-carrier *Enterprise*.

Yakovlev Yak-36

Yak-36 "Forger A" and -36U (?) "Forger B"

Origin: The design bureau of Aleksander S. Yakovlev, Soviet Union.
Type: Single-seat VTOL naval attack (and possibly reconnaissance) aircraft; ("Forger B") two-seat dual trainer.
Engines: One lift/cruise turbojet or turbofan of unknown type with estimated maximum thrust of 17,000lb (7710kg); two lift jets of unknown type with estimated thrust of 5,600lb (2540kg) each.
Dimensions (estimated): Span 25ft (7·6m); length (A) 49ft 3in (15·0m), (B) 58ft (17·7m); height 13ft 3in (4·0m); width with wings folded 14ft 10in (4·51m).
Weights (estimated): Empty 12,000lb (5450kg) (B slightly heavier); maximum loaded 22,050lb (10,000kg).
Performance (estimated): Maximum speed at sea level 722mph (1160 km/h, Mach 0·95); maximum level speed at optimum height 860mph (1380km/h, Mach 1·3); service ceiling about 50,000ft (15,250m); radius on hi-lo-hi attack mission without external fuel, not greater than 200 miles (320km).
Armament: Contrary to early reports there appears to be no internal gun; four pylons under the non-folding wing centre section carry gun pods, reconnaissance pods, ECM payloads, bombs, missiles (said to include AA-2 "Atoll" AAM and AS-7 "Kerry" ASM) and tanks. Maximum external load, about 4,000lb (1814kg). (B two-seater) none seen.
History: First flight probably about 1971; service delivery possibly 1975.
User: Soviet Union (AV-MF).

Development: At the 1967 show at Domodedovo a single V/STOL jet-lift research aircraft gave a convincing display of hovering and transitions. Called "Freehand" by NATO, it was at first thought to be the Yak-36, but this is now believed to be the service designation of the combat aircraft carried above *Kiev*, the first of the large Soviet carriers (officially classed as anti-submarine cruisers) which also carry ASW helicopters and an unprecedented array of shipboard weapons. The "Freehand", of which fewer than ten are thought to have been built, conducted trials from a specially built platform on the carrier *Moskva*. It provided information to assist the

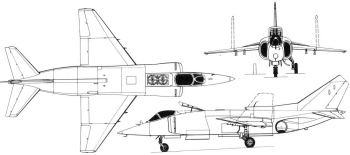

Above: Three-view of single-seat "Forger A" (note wing fold).

design of the Yak-36, which probably has the same large lift turbofan engine plus aft-angled lift jets behind the cockpit. To take off, the three engines must be used together and a vertical ascent made, the main nozzles being rotated to about 100° to balance the rearward thrust of the lift jets. STOL takeoffs are not thought to be possible, neither is Viffing (vectoring in forward flight) to increase combat manoeuvrability. The design is simple, though one wonders why the wing was mounted in the mid-position instead of the much lighter solution of putting it above the main engine. The latter has plain inlets with a row of auxiliary doors as on the Harrier, but supersonic speed at height is judged possible in the clean condition. Other features include Fowler flaps, large ailerons on the folding outer wings, wingtip and tail control nozzles, a ram inlet duct in the dorsal spine, rear airbrakes, a large vertical tail with dielectric tip, and a dielectric nosecap probably covering a small ranging radar. The "Forger" B has a completely different tandem-seat nose angled downwards and a lengthened rear fuselage to preserve directional stability. The development squadron aboard *Kiev* on her shakedown cruise from the Nikolayev yard to Murmansk flew intensively, and observers especially noted the repeated precision of take-offs and landings, indicating ship guidance. Even this aircraft is almost certainly an interim type.

Below: Single-seater making one of its characteristically precise recoveries aboard *Kiev*. A later V/STOL combat type is awaited. Foot of page: Tandem-seat (dual-control?) "Forger B".

Bombers

The bomber was the first type of military aircraft, though in November 1911 the bombs were carried in the cockpit and dropped by hand over the side. Since that time the bomber has come a very long way indeed, but it still does what is basically a trucking job, it still has to deliver accurately on target and it still has to penetrate hostile airspace. Unlike the attack aircraft it can use good paved airfields, but as its mission is over long distances against enemy heartlands it is likely to run the gauntlet of formidable defence systems. The fact that both the defence system and the means by which the bomber penetrates it are electronic was firmly established by 1943, but since then there have been major upheavals. Just on the score of basic aircraft performance, the products of one manufacturer show the extent of the change: in 1944 a typical B-24 would bomb from 28,000ft at 220mph; in 1950 a B-36D might bomb from 42,000ft at 405mph; in 1959 a B-58 could bomb from 64,000ft at 1,385mph; and the last B-58 went to the "boneyard" long ago.

While jet propulsion lifted the bomber to new heights and speeds, nuclear bombs enabled single aircraft to flatten the largest cities. Early thermonuclear bombs had a diameter of nine feet and length of 20ft, so the strategic bomber automatically became a large aircraft capable of carrying a considerable load of conventional bombs. Predictably the technology of nuclear weapons moved at breakneck speed during the 1950s, so that by 1957 fission warheads fitted 28cm artillery shells and into small bombs carried by such aircraft as the A-4 Skyhawk, considerably smaller than contemporary fighters. Today even devastating thermonuclear devices weigh only a few hundred pounds. They can be packaged into MIRVs—multiple independently targeted re-entry vehicles—carried in the tips of ICBMs and submarine-launched missiles. Perfection of the intercontinental missile led some observers to jump to the wholly erroneous conclusion that the bomber was "an anachronism in the missile age". The full wealth of tasks a modern bomber can accomplish are breathtaking, but unfortunately classified. But a few are obvious. Its targets need not be fixed in precisely known locations. It can be retargeted instantly. It can be recalled, and so can be launched, to the safety of the sky, upon mere warning of an enemy attack. A nation with missiles but no bombers dare not fire its missiles upon a mere warning; it must wait until the enemy attack has struck home, possibly destroying all its missiles, before daring to retaliate (and then it is too late).

Today's bombers are a select bunch. The Il-28 is not included because, though several air forces still use it in that role, modern airspace would not take it seriously. The B-52, the next oldest type, and

the Vulcan, inevitably find life hard. They have radar cross-sections like a barn door, and their big airframes do not take kindly to full-throttle operation at extremely low altitudes in dense air, trying to keep under the defending radar coverage. It is a measure of progress in aeronautical technology that the replacement for the Vulcan is the Tornado, which looks like a fighter (in fact in one version it is a fighter). Can the Tornado really carry the loads of a Vulcan and fly the missions of a Vulcan? The answer should be self-evident, though to be fair Britain's geographical posture is not quite what it was. Switching from the Vulcan to the Tornado does not imply one iota of degradation in mission capability—quite the reverse, though one sympathises with the redundant crew-members — and capabilities of

bombers are again being dramatically improved by the ALCM (air-launched cruise missile) which combines the small size and hard hitting power of the SRAM (short-range attack missile) with ranges of around 2,000 miles.

Such weapons take just a little of the pressure off the carrier vehicle. Shortsightedly the US Administration has used this to justify termination of the B-1 production programme. This appears to be a decision of far-reaching and potentially catastrophic consequences because the Soviet Union is supplementing its terrifying and rapidly growing superiority in ballistic missiles with an extremely versatile strategic bomber, which we so far know only as Backfire. The more one-sided strategic arms become, the greater the danger to peace.

A beautiful study of the first USAF B-1, turning gently with wings in the swept position. In a halcyon world, Americans find the need for the B-1 less obvious than its cost. Meanwhile its opposite number in the USSR rolls off the assembly lines.

Boeing B-52 Stratofortress

B-52 to B-52H

Origin: The Boeing Company, USA.
Type: Strategic bomber and ECM platform with crew of six.
Engines: (B-52F, G) eight 13,750lb (6238kg) thrust (water-injection rating) Pratt & Whitney J57-43W two-shaft turbojets; (B-52H) eight 17,000lb (7711kg) thrust Pratt & Whitney TF33-3 two-shaft turbofans.
Dimensions: Span 185ft (56·4m); length 157ft 7in (48m); height 48ft 3in (14·75m); (B-52G, H) 40ft 8in (12·4m).
Weights: Empty 171,000–193,000lb (77,200–87,100kg); loaded 450,000lb (204,120kg) (B-52G, 488,000lb, 221,500kg; B-52H, 505,000lb, 229,000kg).
Performance: Maximum speed about 630mph (1014km/h) at over 24,000ft (7315m); service ceiling 45,000–55,000ft (13,720–16,765m); range on internal fuel with maximum weapon load (C, D, E, F) 6,200 miles (9978km); (G) 8,500 miles (13,680km); (H) 12,500 miles (20,150km).
Armament: Remotely directed tail mounting for four 0·50in (B-52H, 20mm six-barrel ASG-21 cannon). Normal internal bomb capacity 27,000lb (12,247kg) including all SAC special weapons; (B-52D) internal and external provision for up to 70,000lb (31,750kg) conventional bombs; (B-52G and H) external pylons for two AGM-28B Hound Dog missiles or 12 AGM-69A SRAM missiles, with optional rotary dispenser for eight SRAM internally.
History: First flight (YB-52) 15 April 1952; (B-52A) 5 August 1954; combat service with 93rd BW, 29 June 1955; final delivery (H) June 1962.
User: US Air Force (Strategic Air Command).

Development: Still the heaviest and most powerful bomber ever to be built, the mighty B-52 was planned in 1946 as a straight-winged turboprop.

Below: Boeing B-52G showing current anti-flash colour scheme and EVS blisters.

Top: First launch of powered AGM-86 (ALCM) from NB-52G in May 1976.

Above: Launch of AGM-69A SRAM from B-52H.

Below: Nose of B-52H showing ASQ-151 EVS blisters.

At that time no jet engine existed capable of propelling an intercontinental bomber, because fuel consumption was too high. It was Pratt & Whitney's development of a more efficient turbojet, the two-shaft J57, that tipped the scales and led to the new bomber being urgently redesigned in October 1948 as a swept-wing jet. In some ways it resembled a scaled-up B-47, but in fact the wing was made quite different in section and in construction and it housed most of the fuel, which in the B-47 had been in the fuselage. Although the J57, with an expected rating of 10,000lb (4536kg), was the most powerful engine available, an unprecedented four double pods were needed. The two prototypes had pilots in tandem, as in the B-47, but the production B-52A had side-by-side pilots with an airline-type flight deck. The crew of six included a rear gunner in the extreme tail to look after his four radar-directed 0·5in guns. The B-52B had provision for 833 Imp gal (3800 litre) underwing tanks and could carry a two-crew camera or countermeasures capsule in the bomb bay. As the first true service version it encountered many problems, especially with the accessory power systems driven by high-speed air turbines using hot air bled from the engines. The four two-wheel landing gear trucks swivelled for cross-wind landings, the lofty fin could fold to enter hangars, and normal bomb load was 10,000lb (4536kg) carried for 8,000 miles (12,875km). The B-52C had much more fuel, the D was similar but used for bombing only (not reconnaissance) and the E and F introduced completely new nav/bombing systems. The G had an integral tank "wet wing" housing far more fuel, more powerful engines driving the accessories directly, as on the F, and many other changes including shorter fin, Quail countermeasures vehicles and a pair of Hound Dog stand-off missiles. Final model was the B-52H, the 102 of which brought the total to 744. Powered by TF33 fan engines the H got rid of engine water injection, greatly extended range and performance, had a new tail stinger (a 20mm "Gatling" with operator up front as in the G) and many other improvements. In Vietnam D to F models carried up to 70,000lb (31,750kg) of "iron bombs", most of which were rained down without precision aiming (because targets were seldom seen), while the G and H remained in SAC service as multi-role low-level strategic systems pending the introduction of the Rockwell B-1.

Since 1961 new equipment installations and structural reinforcement and reconstruction of the airframes have cost several times the original price. In 1977 the main striking force of SAC comprised 13 Wings equipped with about 165 G and 90 H models. These have been completely rebuilt and later refurbished with SRAM capability, ALE-25 diversionary rocket pods under the wings, and the ASQ-151 electro-optical viewing system (which includes two steerable chin turrets under the nose, the left housing a Westinghouse low-light TV and the right a Hughes forward-looking infra-red). Another new device is the GBU-15 glide bomb, of the Pave Strike family, first tested from a B-52 in July 1976. Later, in 1979, the Boeing AGM-86A ALCM (air-launched cruise missile) may be available; a B-52G or H carry 12 externally and eight on the internal SRAM dispenser. The remaining long-range SAC force comprises 80 structurally rebuilt Ds devoid of the ASQ-151 and equipped only for free-fall bombs, but with updated defensive avionics. A training wing, detached to Okinawa, is equipped with 22 Fs.

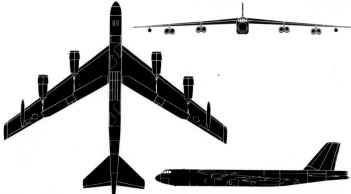

Above: Three-view of B-52H (without SRAMs or EVS).

Above: A black B-52D BUFF (Big Ugly Fat Fella) thunders aloft from the switchback runway at Guam for distant North Vietnam.

Below: A B-52F, a version no longer in service, rains down 750lb bombs under Loran guidance—perhaps on empty forest.

Dassault Breguet Mirage IVA

Mirage IVA

Origin: Avions Marcel Dassault/Breguet Aviation, France.
Type: Limited-range strategic bomber with crew of two.
Engines: Two 15,432lb (7000kg) thrust (maximum afterburner) SNECMA Atar 9K single-shaft augmented turbojets.
Dimensions: Span 38ft 10½in (11·85m); length 77ft 1in (23·5m); height 17ft 8½in (5·4m).
Weights: Empty 31,967lb (14,500kg); loaded 73,800lb (33,475kg).
Performance: Maximum speed (dash) 1,454mph (2340km/h) (Mach 2·2) at 40,000ft (13,125m), (sustained) 1,222mph (1966km/h) (Mach 1·7) at 60,000ft (19,685m); time to climb to 36,090ft (11,000m), 4min 15sec; service ceiling 65,620ft (20,000m); tactical radius (dash to target, hi-subsonic return) 770 miles (1240km); ferry range 2,485 miles (4000km).
Armament: No defensive armament other than ECM; one 60 kiloton freefall bomb recessed in underside of fuselage; alternatively, up to 16,000lb (7257kg) of weapons on hard points under wings and fuselage.
History: First flight (Mirage IV-001) 17 June 1959; (production IVA) 7 December 1963; first delivery 1964; final delivery March 1968.
User: France (Armée de l'Air CFAS).

Development: When the French government decided in 1954 to create a national nuclear deterrent force the most obvious problem was to choose a delivery system for the bombs. The likely enemy appeared to be the Soviet Union and this involved a long mission flown at high speed. After studying developments of the Vautour — a type used to form the nucleus of the *Force de Frappe* — Dassault began work on a bomber derived from a 1956 project for a twin-engined night fighter. After a year the design had to be scaled up to be powered by two Pratt & Whitney J75B engines, to meet more severe demands on speed, load and the range sufficient to reach de-sirable targets and then fly to places outside the Soviet Union. The final choice was to adopt extensive flight refuelling, which allowed the design to shrink again to an intermediate level. As a result the force of 62 bombers that was eventually created relies totally upon Boeing KC-135F tankers,

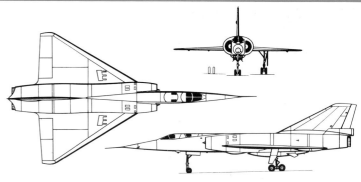

Above: Three-view of Mirage IVA showing bomb but not drop tanks.

with booms fitted for probe/drogue refuelling, and also upon the "buddy technique" whereby aircraft would fly a mission in pairs, one carrying a bomb and the other spare fuel and a refuelling hose-reel for transfer to its partner. Even so, the initial planning of the Commandement des Forces Aériennes Stratégique presupposed that most missions would be one-way (or at least would not return to France). Dispersal has been maximised, with the force divided into three Escadres (91 at Mont de Marsan, 93 at Istres and 94 at Avord), which in turn are subdivided into three four-aircraft groups, two of which are always dispersed away from Escadrille HQ. Despite being a heavy and "hot" aircraft, the IVA has also been rocket-blasted out of short unpaved strips hardened by quick-setting chemicals sprayed on the soil. Of the original total of 62 about 51 remain operational, 36 being at readiness as noted above and the remainder in reserve. They will be used only for reconnaissance after 1985.

Above: Mirage IVA with tanks; some are now camouflaged.

Below: Practice takeoff by a Mirage IVA of 93e Escadre using ATO rockets. This technique is used to allow the bombers to be dispersed to otherwise unusable short airfields.

Hawker Siddeley Vulcan

Vulcan B.1, 1A, 2 and SR.2

Origin: A. V. Roe Ltd (now British Aerospace).
Type: Five-seat bomber (SR.2, strategic reconnaissance).
Engines: Four Rolls-Royce (originally Bristol, then Bristol Siddeley) Olympus two-shaft turbojets; for details see text.
Dimensions: Span (1) 99ft (30·18m); (2) 111ft (33·83m); length (1) 97ft 1in (29·6m); (2) 105ft 6in (32·15m) (99ft 11in with probe removed); height; (1) 26ft 1in (7·94m); (2) 27ft 2in (8·26m).
Weights: Not disclosed: loaded weights probably about 170,000lb for B.1A and 250,000lb for B.2 and SR.2.
Performance: Maximum speed (1) about 620mph; (2) about 640mph (1030km/h) at height (Mach 0·97); service ceiling (1) about 55,000ft; (2) about 65,000ft (19,810m); range with bomb load (1) about 3,000 miles; (2) about 4,600 miles (7400km).
Armament: Internal weapon bay for conventional (21 1,000lb bombs) or nuclear bombs; (SR.2) none.
History: First flight (Avro 698) 30 August 1952; (production B.1) 4 February 1955; (prototype B.2) 31 August 1957; (production B.2) 30 August 1958; final delivery 14 January 1965.
User: UK.

Development: Few aircraft have ever created such an impression as did the prototype Avro 698. This almost perfect triangle, painted white, demonstrated fighter-like manoeuvrability at very low levels within ten hours of first flight, despite its great size and low-powered engines (6,500lb Avons). In 1953 the second prototype was repeatedly rolled at low level. From the start the Vulcan was a winner and with a modified wing with kinked and cambered leading edge the B.1 went into service with the RAF in February 1957, powered by the 11,000lb Olympus 101. Altogether 45 Mk 1s and 1As were built, re-engined by the 12,000lb Olympus 102 and 13,500lb Olympus 104 and, in the 1A, having an extended and bulged rear fuselage full of countermeasures. Some B.1As carried refuelling probes fixed above the

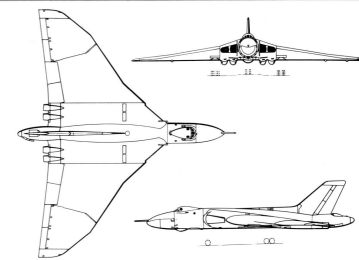

Above: Three-view of Vulcan B.2 (SR.2 is similar outwardly).

huge bombing radar in the nose; all were painted in anti-radiation white. The B.2 was designed to have much better performance at great heights and matched the 17,000lb Olympus 201 with a new thinner wing of greater span and area with elevon controls. Most were equipped to carry the Blue Steel stand-off missile, but by 1966 the force of about 50 had been painted in green/grey camouflage, re-engined with the 20,000lb Olympus 301 and deployed in the tactical low-level role using gravity bombs, with terrain-following radar. No 27 Sqn is equipped with the SR.2 multi-sensor strategic reconnaissance conversion.

Below: A Vulcan B.2 of 617 "Dam Busters" squadron deploys to Cyprus high above the cloud layer. In an operational mission this aircraft would penetrate hostile territory right "down on the deck". The Vulcan remains a fully competitive aircraft, as does its equally venerable partner the B-52.

Above: Vulcan B.2 of 101 Sqn, RAF Coningsby (original three-colour markings).

Tupolev Tu-26 "Backfire"

Two main versions with NATO code names "Backfire-A" and "-B"

Origin: The design bureau named for Andrei N. Tupolev, Soviet Union.
Type: Reconnaissance bomber and missile platform with probable crew of four.
Engines: Two afterburning turbofans, probably Kuznetsov NK-144 two-shaft engines each with maximum rating of 48,500lb (22,000kg).
Dimensions: Span (15°) 113ft (34·44m), (56°) 86ft (26·2m); length (excluding probe) 132ft (40·23m); height 33ft (10·1m).
Weights: (Estimated) 99,250lb (45,000kg); maximum loaded 231,500lb (105,000kg).
Performance: (Estimated, "Backfire B") maximum speed at altitude 1,520mph (2445km/h, Mach 2·3); speed at sea level, over Mach 1; service ceiling over 60,000ft (18,290m); maximum combat radius on internal fuel 2,110 miles (3400km); ferry range, about 5,900 miles (9500km).
Armament: Internal weapon bay(s) for free-fall bombs up to largest thermonuclear sizes, with provision for carrying two AS-6 stand-off missiles (often only one) on external wing racks; nominal weapon load 17,500lb (7935kg).
History: First flight ("Backfire-A" prototype) not later than 1969; ("Backfire-B") probably 1973; entry to service, probably 1974.
User: Soviet Union (ADD, possibly AV-MF).

Development: Owing to the obvious inability of the Tu-22 to fly strategic missions the Tupolev bureau designed this far more formidable aircraft, larger in size and fitted with a swing-wing. "Backfire-A" was apparently not a very successful design, with multi-wheel main gears folding into large fairings projecting in typical Tupolev fashion behind the only moderately swept wing. About half the gross wing area was fixed, just the outer portions swinging through a modest arc. Today's "Backfire-B", which is believed to have the service designation of Tu-26, has no landing-gear boxes and is improved in other ways, though the details are still largely a matter for conjecture. The large engines are fed through wide inlet ducts which probably pass above the wing; a flight refuelling probe is fitted above the nose, but even without this "Backfire-B" has an endurance of some ten hours. The Chairman of the US Joint Chiefs of Staff said in 1974: "It is expected to replace some of both the current medium and heavy bombers and, when deployed with a compatible tanker force, constitutes a potential

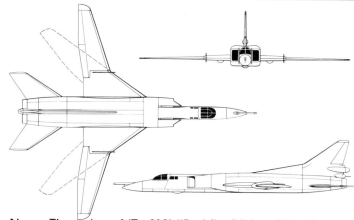

Above: Three-view of (Tu-26?) "Backfire B" (provisional).

threat to the continental United States." The speed of development is also disquieting to the West, because these aircraft were being encountered on long oversea missions in early 1975. Even in 1977 details of the aircraft were sparse, not even its correct Soviet bureau or service designations having surfaced publicly. It is believed to have a crew of three, a very large radar and extremely sophisticated ECM/EW fits. The internal bomb load has been estimated at the low level of 17,500lb (B-1 carries 6·5 times as much), and the Russian insistence on having a radar-directed tail cannon is believed to have prevailed over those who think such installations a waste of cost and payload. Unusual features include the double-taper outer wings pivoted no less than 19ft from the centreline; another puzzle is where the landing gears are in the main production (B) version. Production rate is estimated at five per month, with 95 in service by the end of 1976 out of a planned total (ADD and AV-MF combined) of possibly 450.

Below: Specially drawn for this book. "Backfire B" carrying AS-6, a missile with pinpoint accuracy (often only one is carried).

Below: This long-range telephoto shows a B-model climbing to altitude. Some observers calculate that much of the fuselage must be empty (for c.g. reasons), leading to lower weights and ranges.

Rockwell International B-1

B-1

Origin: Rockwell International Corp, USA.
Type: Four-seat strategic bomber and missile platform.
Engines: Four 30,000lb (13,610kg) class General Electric F101-100 two-shaft augmented turbofans.
Dimensions: Span (15°) 136ft 8½in (41·7m); (67½°) 78ft 2½in (23·8m); length 150ft 2½in (45·8m); height 33ft 7in (10·24m).
Weights: Empty, about 140,000lb (63,500kg); maximum loaded 395,000lb (179,170kg), (gross weight likely to settle at about 400,000lb).
Performance: Maximum speed at sea level (std day) about 646mph (1040km/h, Mach 0·85); maximum speed at high altitude (prototypes) 1,320mph (2135km/h, Mach 2·0); service ceiling over 60,000ft (18,300m); range with maximum weapon load, 6,100 miles (9820km).
Armament: 24 Improved SRAM (AGM-69B thermonuclear missiles) internally, with provision for eight more externally; alternatively the same number of AGM-86A ALCM (air-launched cruise missiles) carried on the same mounts; 75,000lb (34,020kg) of free-fall bombs internally with provision for 40,000lb (18,144kg) externally.
History: First flight 23 December 1974; cancelled 30 June 1977.
User: Not at present funded for service.

Development: By far the most expensive combat aircraft in history, the B-1 has also had by far the longest, most minutely studied and most costly gestation period. When the B-52 was bought for Strategic Air Command in 1951 it was just another aircraft — albeit a large and costly one, with a unit price of around $6 million — but in the late-1970s cost-inflation has put the much-needed B-1 almost out of reach. There are many, including Congressmen who vote on defence procurement, who cannot understand how a large manned vehicle can penetrate hostile airspace without getting shot down. This book is not the place to spell out the several compelling reasons for retaining a manned bomber in SAC's inventory, but the fact must be emphasised that the B-1 has been planned with unbelievable care and had to be professionally developed with inadequate funds in an environment of extreme parsimony. Only a single prototype was carrying the entire flight test programme for considerably more than a year, posing a frightening risk of severe delay should that aircraft have been lost. The technology of the B-1 is of immense breadth and depth, extending to every branch of aerodynamics, structures, propulsion and weapons. Much smaller than the B-52, it uses extremely advanced and efficient engines and a high-lift variable-sweep wing to carry twice the weapon load for a much greater distance at much

continued on page 116▶

Below: Transit of the California badlands at medium altitude by the first B-1, which flew in 1974. Two more have flown (three by late 1978) and flight development is proceeding successfully despite President Carter's cancellation of the programme.

▶higher speed and with many times greater penetrative capability. Almost all B-1 missions would be flown at about tree-top height; Mach 2·0 at high altitude would be used extremely rarely. Seen from the front a B-1's radar signature is approximately one-thirtieth as great as that of a B-52, and its defensive avionics (managed by associate contractor Boeing) are the most powerful and comprehensive ever fitted into a combat aircraft. These systems guard the B-1 against defensive radars by jamming, confusing and spoofing, in ways at present highly classified. Another design feature is the ability to scramble quickly from an airfield under nuclear attack and to survive the effects of enemy thermonuclear explosions in fairly close proximity. All systems can be automatically checked and held at immediate readiness for long periods, so that on an alert being sounded the first man to reach the aircraft has only to hit a button behind the nose landing gear to energise all engines and systems for immediate take-off even before the crew are completely strapped in. Yet another design feature is low-altitude ride

control (LARC) effected by gust sensors and operated by small canard surfaces on each side of the nose and the lowest section of rudder, to guide the speeding monster through turbulent air without the crew compartment suffering significant undulation. So vital is the need for the B-1 that even an economy-minded Congress, in the midst of a Presidential election, voted to commit funds for production in November 1976, but President Carter terminated production plans in 1977. The USAF had hoped to buy at least a small B-1 force, to form the third leg of the strategic deterrent Triad. The SAC requirement is for 241 aircraft, at an estimated unit price of $77 million (allowing for R&D and inflation), amounting to a total investment of $18,600,000,000.

Above: The third B-1 prototype flies with its T-38 chase-plane over the flat primeval lake beds near Palmdale. This aircraft has been flying since April 1976 and is also pictured opposite.

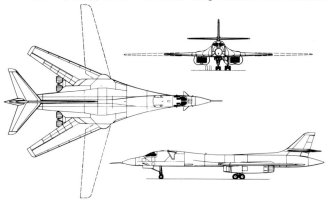

Above: Three-view of B-1 prototypes (with crew-escape pod) showing range of wing sweep.

Above: B-1 first prototype in first-flight configuration.

1 Radome
2 General Electric APQ-144 forward-looking radar
3 Flight refuelling receptacle
4 Forward avionics bay
5 Nosewheel well
6 Structural mode control actuator (LARC)
7 Noseplane, LARC (low-altitude ride control) system
8 Nosewheel door
9 Drag brace links
10 Twin landing/taxi lights
11 Shock absorber strut (Menasco Manufacturing)
12 Twin nosewheels
13 Torque arms
14 Steering and damping unit
15 Nosewheel leg door
16 Nosewheel leg
17 Gear hydraulic actuators
18 Spoiler housing, crew escape module (prototype only)
19 Forward flotation bladder stowage, crew escape module
20 Instrument panel shroud
21 Control columns
22 Wing-sweep control handles
23 Pilot's seat (Aircraft Mechanics)
24 Co-pilot's seat
25 Supernumerary seat
26 Overhead panel (escape system manual operation)
27 Offensive systems officer's station
28 Systems operator instructor's fold-down seat
29 Defensive systems officer's station
30 Underfloor impact attenuator bladders, crew escape module (Goodyear Aerospace)
31 Toilet
32 Rocketdyne solid-fuel rocket motor (gimballed) escape module

33 Rocketdyne solid-fuel rocket motor (fixed booster) escape module
34 Entry ladder
35 Stabilizing fin (stowed), crew escape module
36 Pilot 'chute, escape module
37 Ring-sail main parachutes (3) escape module (Pioneer Parachute)
38 Mortar-deployed drogue chute
39 Main-chute risers
40 VHF aerial
41 Central avionics bays (port and starboard)
42 Forward fuel cells
43 Forward weapons bay
44 Aluminium forward fuselage structure
45 Electrics
46 Middle weapons bay
47 Fuselage skinning
48 Fuselage side fairing bay (penetration aids systems)
49 Wing sweep actuator
50 Wing sweep power drive unit
51 Flap/slat power drive unit
52 Fuselage centre line
52 Fuselage centreline longeron
53 Titanium (diffusion bonded) wing carry-through assembly
54 Control lines
55 Starboard twin inlet
56 Starboard wing pivot pin
57 Double titanium plates
58 Leading-edge slats
59 Outer wing box (integral fuel)
60 Starboard navigation light
61 Starboard flap box
62 Wing (fully swept) position
63 Starboard outer engine bay
64 Nacelle structure
65 Upper longeron (reinforced boron epoxy)

66 Mainwheel well equipment bay (environmental control systems)
67 Mainwheel well
68 Environmental control systems
69 Grille
70 Aft fuel cells
71 Rear weapons bay
72 Control rods
73 Aft SCAS (stability control augmentation system) pitch and roll mixer bay
74 Rear fuel bay
75 Hydraulic lines
76 Flight controls (yaw)
77 Tailplane actuators
78 Tailplane spigot
79 Fin root rib
80 Leading-edge structure
81 Starboard tailplane (Martin Marietta)
82 Lower trailing-edge skin
83 Fin assembly
84 Rear navigation light
85 Upper rudder
86 Rudder controls
87 Intermediate rudder
88 SCAS yaw servos and actuators
89 Lower rudder panel actuators (4)
90 Lower rudder
91 Trailing-edge construction
92 Tailplane assembly
93 Tailcone radar
94 Aft avionics bay
95 Lower fuselage longerons
96 Titanium wing-root fairing
97 Exhaust nozzles
98 Ram-air overboard dump
99 Nacelle bearer
100 Engine shroud
101 General Electric F101 turbofans (over 30,000 lb/ 13,610 kg thrust)
102 Pre-cooler

103 Engine installation firewall/ frame
104 Supplementary intake
105 Fire extinguishers
106 APU
107 Gearbox
108 Electrical generator
109 Air induction control system
110 Fixed-geometry intake
111 Idler panels
112 External ramp
113 Flexible cowl
114 Four-wheel bogie assembly (Cleveland Pneumatic Tool)
115 Goodyear mainwheel brakes and tyres
116 Leading-edge slat actuators
117 Wing skinning
118 Flight controls
119 Wing structure (integral fuel)
120 Single-slotted main flaps
121 Port navigation light
122 AGM-69A SRAMs

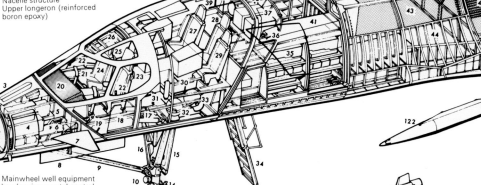

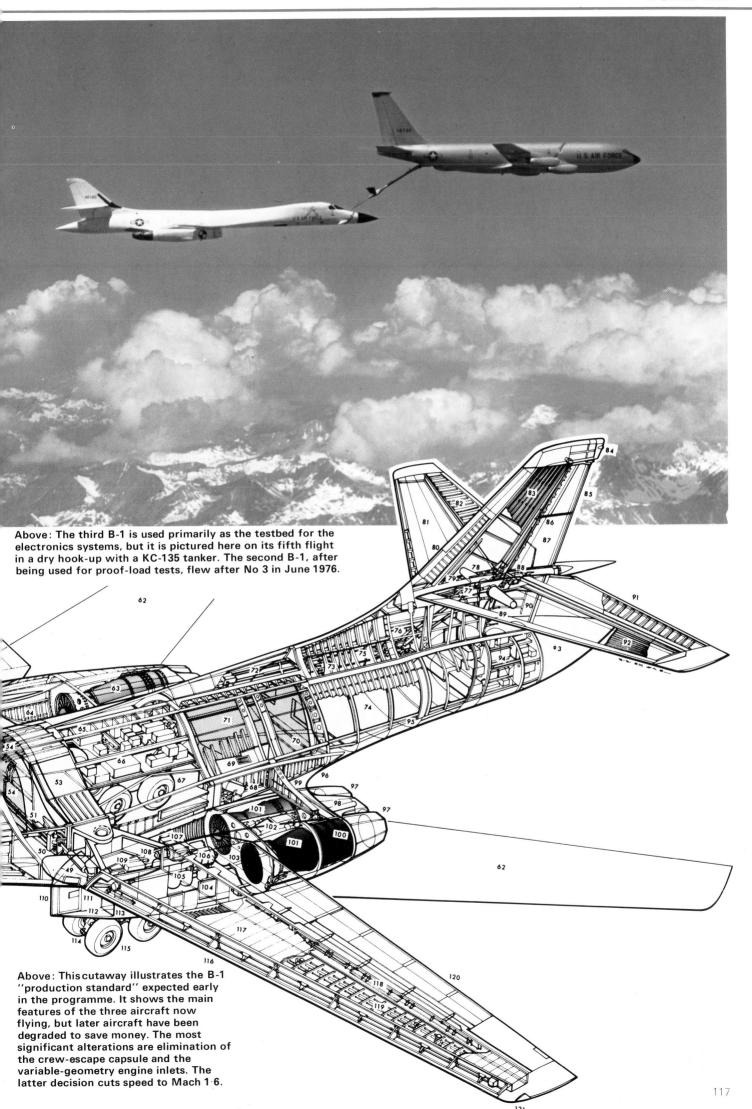

Above: The third B-1 is used primarily as the testbed for the electronics systems, but it is pictured here on its fifth flight in a dry hook-up with a KC-135 tanker. The second B-1, after being used for proof-load tests, flew after No 3 in June 1976.

Above: This cutaway illustrates the B-1 "production standard" expected early in the programme. It shows the main features of the three aircraft now flying, but later aircraft have been degraded to save money. The most significant alterations are elimination of the crew-escape capsule and the variable-geometry engine inlets. The latter decision cuts speed to Mach 1·6.

Reconnaissance aircraft

Reconnaissance was the only task which senior officers of armies and navies before World War I thought aeroplanes might be able to perform. When pioneer military aviators set about doing it they found the task difficult. With no opposition, and working in broad daylight, they mistook wet patches on roads for enemy transport columns, shadows of trees for marching men, and farm workers for troops advancing across fields. Even when there was no error the message had to be written on a piece of paper and dropped accurately over the right headquarters, where someone had to retrieve and correctly read it. Aerial photography had been experimented with as early as 1912, but it was not until 1916 that the art made much progress. But in World War II, thanks to the spur of one civilian—Leslie Irvin, who flew his camera-equipped Lockheed over the German fleet to show what could be done—the art and science of photo-reconnaissance made giant strides. Cameras grew larger aperture lenses and longer focal lengths, film emulsions grew faster and, in particular, much finer-grained (to stand enormous enlargement without completely losing definition), and oblique cameras were fitted to low-level fighters which could take pin-sharp pictures whilst racing across sensitive targets at full throttle.

Today we still fit batteries of even more impressive optical cameras into large bombers and into specially designed noses of fighters; but mostly it is done differently. More important still, optical photography is just one of the tools of the reconnaissance trade. Another is infra-red (IR). Linescan IR sensors can take a "picture" on which cooler areas look dark and warmer areas look light, with fine definition almost comparable with optical film. The resulting pictures show a camouflaged truck as a camouflaged truck, and they can show buried pipelines, hidden troops and countless other things, such as which aircraft on an airfield is running its engines. If a truck was parked near a wood, and driven under cover as the aircraft approached, the IR film will show the slightly warmed patch where it was parked. But IR is still just another wavelength of the electromagnetic spectrum. Some of the most important wavelengths are much longer, in radio frequencies. One of the biggest reconnaissance tasks is ESM (electronic surveillance measures),

which means detecting, measuring and analysing all radio signals and emissions in hostile territory, or emanating from ships or aircraft. The first ESM mission was courageously flown by a Wellington of the RAF in 1943, which deliberately lured a radar-equipped Ju 88 night fighter near enough for its radar signals to be linked with positive visual identification (shot to ribbons, the Wellington ditched near to Britain, with every member of its crew wounded).

Today ESM seldom leads to shots being fired, because it is all part of the ceaseless snooping war that goes on between East and West, which both sides play to the limit—sometimes, waving to each other, from cockpit, or the bridge of a so-called "trawler", to show there are no hard feelings. Of course, if anyone violates foreign territory they do invite a shot, and not merely a warning one. In 1953–65 a sobering number of American aircraft, most of them "honest" and bearing the markings of the Air Force or Navy, were shot down or just disappeared whilst engaged in ESM and other kinds of reconnaissance in the course of which they accidentally or deliberately violated the Soviet frontier. In parallel, Lockheed built the unique U-2 for "dishonest" missions, flown by civilians with unmarked aircraft, which accomplished much at the price of highly-publicized losses over the Soviet Union, Cuba and China. Since the early 1960s "overflights" have increasingly been the duty of drones (RPVs, remotely piloted vehicles) and satellites.

Tactical reconnaissance, in association with a land campaign and involving relatively short distances, is another matter. The US Army still has a unique aircraft, the OV-1, built specially for this purpose. Lockheed developed an even stranger family of extremely quiet reconnaissance platforms intended to fly low overhead without being heard, though the aeroplane transparent to radar has not yet been invented. Most important of all, modern combat aircraft can clip on multi-sensor reconnaissance pods which can in a few minutes transform them into gatherers of intelligence of a kind and at a rate that would amaze any of the low-level reconnaissance pilots of World War II. If a fighter were to roar overhead as I write this he might well report my make of typewriter—and whether it had any electrical fault.

Almost everything about the USAF's SR-71A "Blackbird" is special. To fly 2,100 mph at 80,000 feet needs special aircrew, special flight suits and a rather fantastic flying machine in which to sit. Just how vulnerable these costly wonders are is arguable.

Grumman OV-1 Mohawk

OV-1A to -1D, EV-1, JOV, RV

Origin: Grumman Aerospace, USA.
Type: (OV) multi-sensor tactical observation and reconnaissance; (EV) electronic warfare; (JOV) armed reconnaissance; (RV) electronic reconnaissance;.
Engines: Two 1,005shp Lycoming T53-7 or -15 free-turbine turboprops; (OV-1D) two 1,160shp T53-701.
Dimensions: Span (-1A, -C) 42ft (12·8m); (-1B, -D) 48ft (14·63m); length 41ft (12·5m); (-1D with SLAR, 44ft 11in); height 12ft 8in (3·86m).
Weights: Empty (-1A) 9,937lb (4507kg); (-1B) 11,067lb (5020kg); (-1C) 10,400lb (4717kg); (-1D) 12,054lb (5467kg); maximum loaded (-1A) 15,031lb (6818kg); (-1B, C) 19,230lb (8722kg); (-1D) 18,109lb (8214kg).
Performance: Maximum speed (all) 297–310mph (480–500km/h); initial climb (-1A) 2,950ft (900m)/min; (-1B) 2,250ft (716m)/min; (-1C) 2,670ft (814m)/min; (-1D) 3,618ft (1103m)/min; service ceiling (all) 28,800–31,000ft (8534–9449m); range with external fuel (-1A) 1,410 miles (2270km); (-1B) 1,230 miles (1980km); (-1C) 1,330 miles (2140km); (-1D) 1,011 miles (1627km).
Armament: Not normally fitted, but in South East Asia the 1A, -1B and -1C all operated with a wide variety of air-to-ground weapons including grenade launchers, Minigun pods and small guided missiles.
History: First flight (YOV-1A) 14 April 1959; service delivery, February 1961; final delivery December 1970.
Users: Israel (EV), US Army.

Development: Representing a unique class of military aircraft, the OV-1 Mohawk is a specially designed battlefield surveillance machine with characteristics roughly midway between lightplanes and jet fighters. One of its requirements was to operate from rough forward airstrips and it has exceptional STOL (short takeoff and landing) qualities and good low-speed control with full-span slats and triple fins and rudders. Pilot and observer sit in side-by-side Martin Baker J5 seats and all versions have extremely good all-round view and very comprehensive navigation and communications equipment. All versions carry cameras and upward-firing flares for night photography. Most variants carry UAS-4 infra-red surveillance equipment and the -1B carries APS-94 SLAR (side-looking airborne radar) in a long pod under the right side of the fuselage, with automatic film processing giving, within seconds of exposure, a permanent film record of radar image on either side of the flight path. The -1D combined the functions of the two previous versions in being quickly convertible to either IR or SLAR missions. Underwing pylons can carry 150 US gal drop tanks, ECM (electronic countermeasures) pods, flare/chaff dispensers, or, in the JOV-1A such weapons as FFAR pods, 0·50in gun pods or 500lb (227kg) bombs – though a 1965 Department of Defense rule forbids the US Army to arm its fixed-wing aircraft! The EV-1 is the OV-1B converted to electronic surveillance with an ALQ-133 target locator system in centreline and tip

Above: In untypical maritime surroundings, the OV-1D was the final production Mohawk, with the APS-94 side-looking radar in a long external pod.

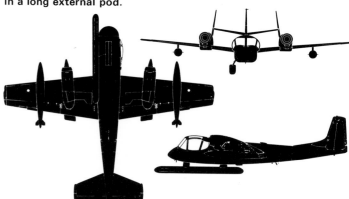

Above: Three-view of OV-1D as originally built.

pods. The RV-1C and -1D are conversions of the OV-1C and -1D for permanent use in the electronic reconnaissance role. Total production of the Mohawk was 375.

Lockheed QT-2/X-26 YO-3

QT-2, X-26B, Q-Star and YO-3A

Origin: Lockheed Missiles and Space Company, San Jose, California, USA.
Type: Quiet reconnaissance.
Engine: (QT-2, X-26B) one 100hp Teledyne Continental O-200A flat-four piston engine; (Q-Star) originally one O-200A, then 185hp Curtiss-Wright Wankel RC2-60 rotating-combustion engine; (YO-3A) one 210hp Teledyne Continental IO-360D flat-six piston engine.
Dimensions: Span 57ft 1in (17·4m); length (QT-2, X-26B) 30ft 10in (9·40m), (Q-Star) 31ft, (YO-3A) 30ft (9·14m); height, not disclosed.
Weights: Empty (QT-2) 1,576lb (715kg), (Q-Star) 1,969lb (894kg), (YO-3A) about 2,200lb (1000kg); gross (QT-2) 2,182lb (989kg), (Q-Star) 2,860lb (1297kg), (YO-3A) 3,200lb (1452kg).
Performance: Operating speed range (all) 50 to 120kt (58–138mph, 93–222km/h); quietest speed, around 71mph (114km/h); endurance (QT-2) 4hr, (Q-Star, YO-3A) 6hr.
Armament: None.
History: First flight (QT-2) July 1967, (Q-Star) June 1968, (YO-3A) May 1969; combat duty (Q-2PC) January 1968, (YO-3A) 1970.
Users: (QT-2PC) US Army, (X-26B) US Navy, (YO-3A) US Army.

Development: It was the impossibility of catching the elusive Viet Cong and North Vietnam forces in the open with noisy conventional aircraft that led the US Department of Defense to discuss with Lockheed the possibility of building reconnaissance aircraft so quiet they could not be heard even in low-level operation. Lockheed assigned the task to its LMSC subsidiary which produced the QT-2 by rebuilding a Schweizer SGS 2-32 sailplane with a heavily muffled piston engine behind the pilot driving a large slow-speed propeller by a 1:5·34 ratio belt. The operational Q-2PC (PC from *Prize Crew*, the project code-name) served in SE Asia and proved to have capabilities impossible with any other aircraft. The X-26B served at the US Navy Test Pilot School. The Q-Star had tailwheel landing gear, more fuel and various engine/propeller combinations with up to six blades. The

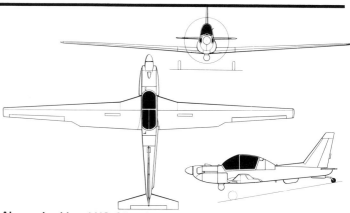

Above: Lockheed YO-3A, with sensors.

Above: The second YO-3 on an early test flight, before it was fitted with sensors for deployment to Vietnam.

production YO-3A was a new design, still based on the SGS 2-32 but with a low wing with extended inner chord, new fuselage with nose engine, very large canopy over two tandem seats and various sensors including radar and infra-red. At a height of 400ft these aircraft are said to make a gentle rustling like leaves in a slight breeze; at 800ft they are almost impossible to detect.

Lockheed U-2

U-2A, C, D, R, CT and EPX, WU-2 and HASP U-2

Origin: Lockheed-California Co, USA.

Type: High-altitude photo reconnaissance, multi-sensor reconnaissance and special reconnaissance; (CT) dual trainer; (EPX) electronics patrol experiment, (WU) weather research; (HASP) high-altitude sampling programme.

Engine: (U-2A) one 11,200lb (5080kg) Pratt & Whitney J57-13A or -37A two-shaft turbojet; (all other models) one 17,000lb (7711kg) Pratt & Whitney J75-13 two-shaft turbojet.

Dimensions: Span (except R) 80ft (24·38m), (U-2R) 103ft (31·39m); length (except R) 49ft 7in (15·1m), (U-2R) 63ft (19·2m); height (except R) 13ft (3·96m), (U-2R) 16ft (4·88m).

Weights: Empty (A) 9,920lb (4500kg), (others, except R) typically 11,700lb (5305kg), (U-2R) 14,990lb (6800kg); loaded (A) 14,800lb (6713kg), (others, except R, clean) 15,850lb (7190kg), (with two 89-gal wing tanks) 17,270lb (7833kg); maximum over 21,000lb (9526kg), (R) 29,000lb (13,154kg).

Performance: Maximum speed (A) 494mph (795km/h); (others) 528mph (850km/h); service ceiling (A) 70,000ft (21,340m); (others) 85,000ft (25,910m); maximum range (A) 2,600 miles (4185km); (others) 4,000 miles (6437km).

Armament: None.

History: First flight 1 August 1955; service delivery, early 1956; final delivery of new aircraft, July 1958.

Users: Taiwan, USA (Air Force, NASA).

Above: A black-painted U-2B of the US Air Force photographed over Edwards Air Force Base in 1968. Most USAF U-2 aircraft have since been rebuilt or modified as different models.

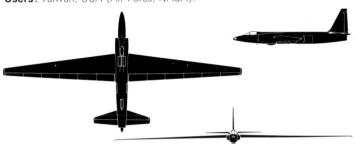

Above: Three-view of original Lockheed U-2A.

Above: This U-2D belongs to the 6512th Test Sqn at the Air Force Flight Test Centre at Edwards AFB.

Development: No aircraft in history has a record resembling the U-2. It was in operational use from Lakenheath (England) and Wiesbaden (Germany) in 1956, attracting the attention of spotters and amateur photographers who commented on its graceful glider-like appearance and on the odd fact that at take-off it jettisoned the small outrigger wheels under the outer wings, returning to land on small centreline wheels and the down-turned wingtips. When interest had reached fever-pitch the government blandly announced that the U-2, as it was called (a Utility designation) was used by the NACA (the National Advisory Committee for Aeronautics) for atmospheric research at heights up to 55,000ft. When one force-landed in Japan the public were frantically kept away at gun-point and it was clear the incident was regarded as serious. In fact the U-2 had been designed for clandestine reconnaissance over the territory of any nation. Aircraft were delivered to Watertown Strip, a remote airfield in Nevada, where CIA pilots converted and prepared for operational missions over Communist territory. Their aircraft bore no markings and operated — immune to interception, and often undetected — at far above the announced 55,000ft. Other U-2s were assigned to the 4080th Strategic Wing and carried USAF markings. Most were of the more powerful U-2B type with much greater height and range. On 1 May 1960 a U-2B flown by a CIA pilot took off from Peshawar (Pakistan) to fly across the Soviet Union to Bodø (Norway), but was shot down over Sverdlovsk, presenting the Russians with unprecedented material for a diplomatic incident. Later U-2s were shot down over China and Cuba, and the survivors were assigned to lawful missions involving many kinds of surveillance and sampling. The C and two-seat D make up the bulk of the fleet used today, numbering about 40 out of the 55 built. All have been extensively rebuilt, none more so than the enlarged U-2R special-reconnaissance platform which carries four times the 3,000lb (1361kg) payload of other models. The D was the original tandem-seat version, needing a second crew-member; the U-2CT dual trainer is a complete rebuild with instructor pilot seated high up behind the pupil (the U-2 needs extreme pilot skill near and on the ground); the C has a long dorsal "doghouse" housing avionics and equipment. The proposed EPX for the Navy carried APS-116 ocean surveillance radar (S-3A type) but never entered service.

Below: One of the trickiest aircraft in the world to taxi, takeoff or land, the U-2CT conversion trainer. This one with trestle supporting the wing, is 56-6692 of 100th SRW, 349th SRS at Davis-Monthan AFB.

Lockheed SR-71

A-11, YF-12A and C, SR-71A, B and C
(data for SR-71A)

Origin: Lockheed-California Co, USA.

Type: YF-12, research interceptor; SR-71, strategic reconnaissance.

Engines: Two 32,500lb (14,740kg) thrust Pratt & Whitney J58 (JT11D-20B) single-shaft by-pass turbojets with afterburner.

Dimensions: Span 55ft 7in (16·95m); length 107ft 5in (32·74m); height 18ft 6in (5·64m).

Weights: Empty (typical) 60,000lb (27,215kg); loaded 170,000lb (77,110kg).

Performance: Maximum speed, in excess of 2,000mph (3220km/h, Mach 3); service ceiling, higher than 80,000ft (24,400m); range at Mach 3 at 78,740ft (24,000m), 2,982 miles (4800km). Performance limit, about 2,200mph and altitude of 86,000ft sustained.

Armament: SR-71 series, none; YF-12, see text.

History: First flight 26 April 1962; (production SR-71A) 22 December 1964; final delivery, about 1968.

User: USA (Air Force, NASA).

Development: Despite their great size and intense noise these amazing aircraft were designed, built, test flown and put into use without a word leaking out into public until disclosed by President Johnson in February 1964. The A-11 was originally designed as a follow-on to the U-2, capable of flying even higher and many times faster in penetrating hostile airspace on clandestine overflights. Early in their career the three A-11s, with serial numbers 60-6934 to 6936, did overfly Communist territories in several parts of the world. Later they were completed as YF-12A research aircraft in the Improved Manned Interceptor programme, carrying Hughes ASG-18 pulse-doppler radar, infra-red sensors and eight Hughes AIM-47A large long-range air-to-air missiles in an internal bay. Made largely of a specially developed alloy of titanium, the YF-12A was the most advanced aircraft of its day and the only one to sustain a speed of Mach 3. One set a world speed record at 2,070mph on 1 May 1965, and another beat this at 2,189mph (3522km/h) in July 1976, in which month a 1,000km circuit was flown at 2,086mph (3356km/h) and an altitude of 86,000ft (26,212m) sustained. Surviving YF-12A variants have been stripped of weapon systems and used in supersonic transport research, flown by NASA. The SR-71 strategic reconnaissance aircraft is longer and heavier, with a fuel capacity of over 80,000lb. Known as "Blackbirds" (though officially their external areas are painted indigo blue), they equip the 9th Strategic Reconnaissance Wing, from which detachments have operated over Vietnam, the Middle East and many other trouble-spots. Total production is at least 30, including SR-71B and C dual trainer versions. In September 1974 a standard A model

Above: The Lockheed YF-12A, the first species of Blackbird, has now been rebuilt for Mach 3 research.

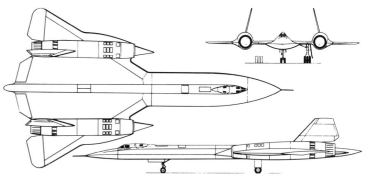

Above: Three-view of the SR-71A in original form.

set a transatlantic record at almost Mach 3 with a time from passing New York to passing London of 1hr 55min. Most SR-71s in the active inventory (some are stored) use special JP-7 high-temperature fuel, air-refuelled by specially equipped KC-135Q tankers.

Below: Compared with the YF-12A the SR-71A is an appreciably longer and heavier aircraft. This SR was photographed in 1976 about 70,000 feet below its normal mission altitude.

Myasishchev M-4

M-4 (three versions, known to West as "Bison A, B and C")

Origin: The design bureau of Vladimir M. Myasishchev, Soviet Union.
Type: (A) heavy bomber; (B) strategic reconnaissance and ECM; (C) multi-role reconnaissance bomber.
Engines: (A) four 19,180lb (8700kg) Mikulin AM-3D single-shaft turbojets; (B and C) four 28,660lb (13,000kg) Soloviev D-15 two-shaft turbojets.
Dimensions: (A) estimated, span 165ft 7½in (50·48m); length 154ft 10in (47·2m); height 46ft (14·1m).
Weights: Estimated, empty (A) 154,000lb (70,000kg); (B, C) 176,400lb (80,000kg); maximum loaded (A) 352,740lb (160,000kg); (B, C) 375,000lb (170,000kg).
Performance: (Estimated) maximum speed (all) 560mph (900km/h); service ceiling (A) 42,650ft (13,000m); (B, C) 49,200ft (15,000m); range (all) 6,835 miles (11,000km) with 9,920lb (4500kg) of bombs or electronic equipment.
Armament: (A) ten 23mm NR-23 cannon in manned turret in tail and four remotely controlled turrets above and below front and rear fuselage (two guns in each turret); internal bomb bays in tandem for at least 22,050lb (10,000kg) stores; (B, C) six 23mm cannon in two forward turrets and tail turret; internal bay for at least 10,000lb (4500kg) stores. In many versions a single 23mm gun is fixed on the right side of the nose, firing ahead.
History: First flight, probably 1953; service delivery, probably 1955; final delivery, probably about 1958.
User: Soviet Union (DDA, AV-MF).

Development: A single example of this large aircraft took part in the 1954 May Day parade fly past over Moscow, its size being gauged from the escorting MiG fighters. It was expected to appear in large numbers, but

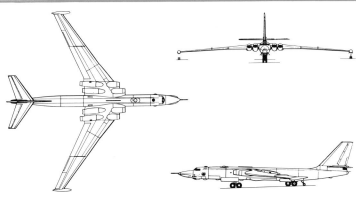

Above: Three-view of M-4 of "Bison C" sub-type.

little was heard of it for years. In fact a useful run of about 150 had been delivered, at first being used as bombers ("Bison A"). In 1959 a re-engined aircraft, called Type 201-M, set up world records by lifting a payload of 10,000kg (22,046lb) to 50,253ft (15,317m) and the formidable weight of 55,220kg (121,480lb) to 2000m (6,561ft). By this time the M-4 bombers were being likewise fitted with more powerful engines, and their role changed from bomber to long-range oversea reconnaissance, ECM and, in some cases, flight-refuelling tanker. All aircraft were given large fixed FR probes, the rear turrets were removed and a vast amount of special reconnaissance equipment fitted, with from five to 17 aerials visible all over the aircraft. In the "Bison C" sub-type a large search radar fills the entire nose, lengthening the nose by about 6ft and changing its shape. Since 1967 these now obsolescent aircraft have been frequently encountered on probing missions far over the Arctic, Atlantic, Pacific and elsewhere, at both high and low levels, the C-model having been seen most frequently.

Left: An M-4 of the sub-type called "Bison B" by NATO, photographed by an RAF Lightning over solid overcast. Most of these aircraft have been in service over 20 years.

Below: A frame from a Soviet film showing the British type of probe/drogue refuelling system used by the Soviet air forces. The receiver is an M-4 of the "Bison C" type.

Rockwell RA-5C Vigilante

A-5A, A-5B and RA-5C

Origin: North American Aviation, now Rockwell International, USA.
Type: (A, B) carrier-based attack; (C) carrier-based reconnaissance, with crew of two.
Engines: Two General Electric J79 single-shaft afterburning turbojets; (A, B) as originally built, 16,150lb J79-2 or -4; (RA-5C, pre-1969), 17,000lb (7710kg) J79-8, (post-1969) 17,860lb (8118kg) J79-10.
Dimensions: Span 53ft (16·15m); length 75ft 10in (23·11m), (folds to 68ft); height 19ft 5in (5·92m).
Weights: Empty (C) about 38,000lb (17,240kg); maximum loaded, 80,000lb (36,285kg).
Performance: Maximum speed at height 1,385mph (2230km/h, Mach 2·1); service ceiling (C) 67,000ft (20,400m); range with external fuel, about 3,200 miles (5150km).
Armament: None (A, see text).
History: First flight (YA3J-1) 31 August 1958; (A-5A) January 1960; (A-5B) 29 April 1962; (RA-5C) 30 June 1962; final delivery of new aircraft 1971.
User: USA (Navy).

Development: No aircraft in history introduced more new technology than the first Vigilante, planned in 1956 as a carrier-based attack aircraft. Among its features were automatically scheduled engine inlets and nozzles, single-surface vertical tail, differential slab tailplanes, linear bomb bay between the engines (with two emptied fuel tanks and a nuclear weapon ejected rear-wards in the form of a long tube) and a comprehensive radar-inertial navigation system. Another feature was flap-blowing, and in the A-5B

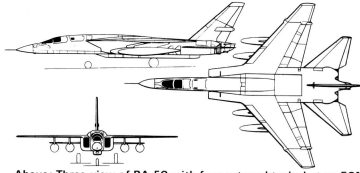

Above: Three-view of RA-5C with four external tanks but no ECM.

full-span leading-edge droop blowing was added to allow a 15,000lb weight increase from saddle tanks in the new hump-backed fuselage. When carriers gave up a strategic nuclear role, the 57 A-5A were followed by the RA-5C, the airborne element of an integrated intelligence system serving the whole fleet and other forces. The RA-5C is extremely com-prehensively equipped with multiple sensors including a side-looking radar under the fuselage. These valuable aircraft have been hard-worked in many theatres; 63 were built in 1962–66, 53 A-5A and the 6 A-5B were converted to RA-5C standard, and in 1969–71 the production line at Columbus was reopened for 46 Phase II with GE-10 engines and improved intakes and wing/body fillets.

Below: Unusual view of an RA-5C Vigilante as it leaves the catapult of the nuclear-powered super-carrier USS *Enterprise*. It belongs to squadron RVAH-3.

Saab 32 Lansen

A32A, J32B, S32C

Origin: Saab-Scania AB, Linköping, Sweden.
Type: (A) two-seat all-weather attack; (B) all-weather and night fighter; (C) reconnaissance.
Engine: One Svenska Flygmotor licence-built Rolls-Royce Avon single-shaft turbojet with afterburner: (A and C) 10,362lb (4700kg) thrust RM5A2; (B) 15,190lb (6890kg) RM6A.
Dimensions: Span 42ft 7¾in (13m); length (A) 49ft 0¾in (14·94m); (B) 47ft 6¾in (C) 48ft 0¾in; height 15ft 3in (4·65m).
Weights: Empty (A) 16,398lb (7438kg); (B) 17,600lb; (C) 16,520lb; maximum loaded (A) 28,660lb (13,600kg); (B) 29,800lb; (C) typically 26,500lb.
Performance: Maximum speed (all) 692mph (1114km/h, Mach 0·91); initial climb (A, C) 11,800ft (3600m)/min; (B) 19,700ft/min; service ceiling (A, C) 49,200ft (15,000m); (B) 52,500ft; range with external fuel (all, typical) 2,000 miles (3220km).
Armament: (A) four 20mm Swedish Hispano Mk V under nose; wing pylons for external load of up to 3,000lb including two Rb04C air-to-surface missiles or two 1,320lb (600kg) bombs; (B) four 30mm Aden M/55 cannon under nose and four Rb324 (Sidewinder) missiles or FFAR pods; (C) none.
History: First flight 3 November 1952; service delivery (A) December 1955; first flight (B) 7 January 1957; (C) 26 March 1957; final delivery (B) 2 May 1960.
User: Sweden (RSAF).

Development: Designed to replace the Saab 18, the Type 32 was a large all-swept machine of outstanding quality, designed and developed ahead of similar aircraft elsewhere in Western Europe. Owing to its size it was

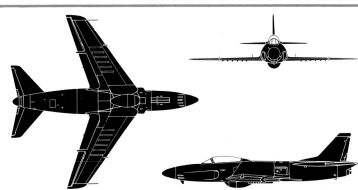

Above: Three-view of the Lansen A32A with wing pylons and ventral radar.

capable of development for three dissimilar missions, proving so valuable that many survive in front-line service well into the 1970s. Supersonic in a shallow dive, the A32A entered service with F17 and soon gained a great reputation for good handling, ease of maintenance and accurate weapon delivery. It equipped all four Swedish attack wings until the Saab AJ37 began to replace it in 1971. The more powerful J32B night fighter was fitted with S6 radar fire control for lead/pursuit interception and equipped seven squadrons in 1958–70. The S32C force was several times updated by fitting advanced new sensors and ECM, and is in 1977 still not fully replaced by the SF37 and SH37. Total Lansen (meaning lance) production was 450.

Below: The S32C is one of the versions of the excellent Lansen still in service in 1977 with the Swedish Flygvapen. The main S32C units are two squadrons of wing F11 at Nyköping. There are still a few A32A attack Lansens in F6 at Karlsborg, and the most powerful sub-type, the J32C (originally a night fighter) is a target tug.

Above: J32B Lansen, formerly with F12 at Kalmar.

Tupolev Tu-16

Sub-types known to West as "Badger A" to "Badger G"; Tupolev bureau, Tu-88

Origin: The design bureau of Andrei N. Tupolev, Soviet Union; built (probably without licence) at Shenyang, China.

Type: Designed as strategic bomber; see text.

Engines: Believed in all versions, two Mikulin AM-3M single-shaft turbojets each rated at about 20,950lb (9500kg).

Dimensions: Span (basic) 110ft (33·5m) (varies with FR system, ECM and other features); length (basic) 120ft (36·5m) (varies with radar or glazed nose); height 35ft 6in (10·8m).

Weights: Empty, typically about 72,750lb (33,000kg) in early versions, about 82,680lb (37,500kg) in maritime/ECM roles; maximum loaded, about 150,000lb (68,000kg).

Performance: Maximum speed, clean at height, 587mph (945km/h); initial climb, clean, about 4,100ft (1250m)/min; service ceiling 42,650ft (13,000m); range with maximum weapon load, no missiles, 3,000 miles (4,800km); extreme reconnaissance range, about 4,500 miles (7250km).

Armament: In most variants, six 23mm NR-23 cannon in radar-directed manned tail turret and remote-aimed upper dorsal and rear ventral barbettes; versions without nose radar usually have seventh NR-23 fixed firing ahead on right side of nose. Internal weapon bay for load of 19,800lb (9000kg), with certain versions equipped to launch missiles (see text).

History: First flight (Tu-88), believed 1952; service delivery 1954; final delivery (USSR) about 1959, (China) after 1975.

Users: China, Egypt, Indonesia (in storage), Iraq, Soviet Union (AV-MF).

Development: Representing a simple and low-risk approach to the strategic jet-bomber requirement, the Tu-88 prototype was generally in the class of the Valiant but incorporated heavy defensive armament. Technology throughout was derived directly from the Boeing B-29, which Tupolev's bureau had in 1945–53 built in large numbers as the Tu-4. The first ("Badger A") version had blind-bombing radar and glazed nose, and a few were supplied to Egypt and Iraq. The B carried two "Kennel" cruise missiles on underwing pylons and served the AV-MF (Navy) and Indonesian AF. C carried the large "Kipper" stand-off missile on the centre-line, with panoramic nose radar for ship search and missile guidance. D is a maritime reconnaissance type, with comprehensive radars and ECM. E is a photo and multi-sensor reconnaissance type, F is an E with major new ECM and ESM installations, and G is an updated B which launched many missiles against Israel in 1973. Total production exceeded 2,000, and production (without Soviet aid) continues in China.

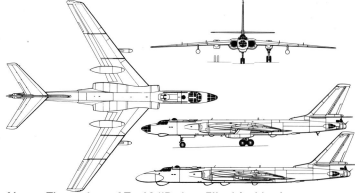

Above: Three-view of Tu-16 "Badger F" with side view (bottom) of "D".

Above: Tu-16 of the AV-MF, photographed on a "Zombie" electronic reconnaissance mission near Britain by a Phantom FG.1 of 892 Sqn, Royal Navy. It is a "Badger D" type.

Above: Tu-16 of "Badger D" type, in service with the AV-MF.

Left: A Tu-16 of the "Badger F" type, photographed by a Nimrod of the RAF as it wheels low over the North Atlantic. This type of Tu-16 is visually distinguished by its two small electronic pods carried on pylons beneath the wings. Frequently Tu-16s engaged in ESM (electronic surveillance measures) missions have worked in pairs, the "Badger D" and "Badger F" apparently being complementary. Several versions have been converted as air refuelling tankers, using an unusual wing-tip/wing-tip hook-up method.

Tupolev Tu-20

Tu-95 (Tupolev bureau designation) in versions known to West as "Bear A" to "Bear F"

Origin: The design bureau of Andrei N. Tupolev, Soviet Union.
Type: Designed as strategic bomber; see text.
Engines: Four 14,795ehp Kuznetsov NK-12M single-shaft turboprops.
Dimensions: Span 159ft (48·5m); length 155ft 10in (47·50m) (certain versions differ by up to 6ft); height 38ft 8in (11·78m).
Weights: Empty, probably about 160,000lb (72,600kg); maximum loaded (estimate) about 340,000lb (154,000kg).
Performance: Maximum speed (typical Bear, clean) 540mph (870km/h); service ceiling, about 44,000ft (13,400m); range with 25,000lb (11,340kg) bomb load, 7,800 miles (12,550km).
Armament: Normally six 23mm NS-23 in radar-directed manned tail turret and remote-aimed dorsal and ventral barbettes (defensive guns often absent from late conversions); internal weapon bay for load of about 25,000lb (11,340kg).
History: First flight (prototype) mid-1954; service delivery, 1956; final delivery, probably about 1962.
User: Soviet Union (ADD, AV-MF).

Development: Making use of identical systems, techniques and even similar airframe structures as the Tu-16, the Tu-95 (service designation, Tu-20) is much larger and has roughly double the range of its turbojet predecessor. The huge swept wing, forming integral tanks, was a major accomplishment in 1952–54, as were the monster turboprop engines and their eight-blade 18ft 4½in (5·6m) contraprops. The basic bomber called "Bear A" had a glazed nose, chin radar and gun-sight blisters on the rear fuselage. First seen in 1961, "Bear B" featured a solid nose with enormous radome, refuelling probe and centreline attachment for a large cruise missile ("Kangaroo"). C appeared in 1964 with a large new blister on each

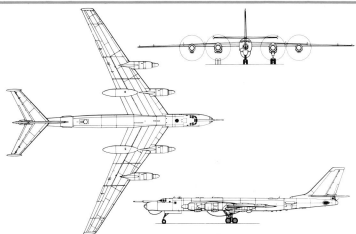

Above: Three-view of Tu-20 (Tu-95) of "Bear D" type.

side of the fuselage (on one side only on B), while D was obviously a major ECM/ESM reconnaissance type with chin radar, very large belly radar, and from 12 to 21 avionic features visible from stem to stern. E is a multi-sensor reconnaissance conversion of A, while F is a recent further conversion with an array of ventral radars and stores bays in place of the ventral guns.

Above: Tu-20 (Tu-95) of the "Bear C" maritime surveillance type.

Above: A monster "AS-3 Kangaroo" air/surface missile drops away from its recess in the belly of a Tu-20 of the "Bear B" sub-type. This is the largest stand-off missile in the world (48ft 11in, 14·9m, long).

Left: A fine picture of a Tu-20 of the "Bear D" sub-type, taken by the pilot of an RAF Lightning north of Scotland. This model helps to guide anti-ship missiles.

Tupolev Tu-22

Tu-22 in versions known to West as "Blinder A" to "Blinder D"; Tupolev bureau, Tu-105

Origin: The design bureau of Andrei N. Tupolev, Soviet Union.
Type: Originally bomber: see text.
Engines: Two afterburning turbojets, of unknown type, each with maximum rating estimated at 27,000lb (12,250kg).
Dimensions: Span 90ft 10½in (27·70m); length (most versions) 132ft 11½in (40·53m); height 35ft 0in (10·67m).
Weights: Empty, about 85,000lb (38,600kg); maximum loaded, about 185,200lb (84,000kg).
Performance: Maximum speed (clean, at height) 920mph (1480km/h, Mach 1·4); initial climb, about 11,500ft (3500m)/min; service ceiling 59,000ft (18,000m); range (high, internal fuel only) 1,400 miles (2250km).
Armament: One 23mm NS-23 in radar-directed barbette in tail; internal weapon bay for at least 20,000lb (9070kg) of free-fall bombs or other stores, or (Blinder B) one "Kitchen" stand-off cruise missile semi-recessed under centreline.
History: First flight, well before public display in 1961; service delivery, probably 1963.
Users: Libya, Soviet Union (ADD, AV-MF).

Development: Having an efficient wing closely related to that of the Tu-28P, this supersonic bomber is a large aircraft with a bigger body and higher gross weight than the USAF B-58 Hustler. Typical crew appears to be a pilot, upward-ejecting, and two more members in tandem at a lower level who eject downwards. "Blinder A" was a reconnaissance bomber, seen in small numbers. B carried the stand-off missile, had a larger nose radar and semi-flush FR probe. C is the main variant, used by Naval Aviation for oversea ECM/ESM surveillance, multi-sensor reconnaissance and with limited weapon capability. D is a dual trainer with stepped cockpits. Recent versions appear to have later engines (probably turbofans) with greater airflow. There have been persistent reports of an interceptor version, but this seems unlikely. The abiding shortcoming of the Tu-22 has been limited range, only partially alleviated by flight refuelling.

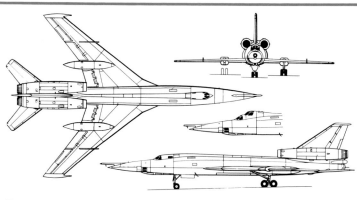

Three-view of Tu-22 "Blinder A" with (inset) nose of "Blinder D".

Above: Tu-22 "Blinder A" ("Blinder C" is similar).

Below: These Tu-22 supersonic aircraft are from a unit of the AV-MF. They are probably of the "Blinder B" type with weapon bays tailored to the 37ft "AS-4 Kitchen" stand-off missile.

Yakovlev Yak-26

Yak-26, -27P and "Mandrake"

Origin: The design bureau of Alexander S. Yakovlev, Soviet Union.
Type: Two-seat reconnaissance (27P, interceptor).
Engines: (26, 27P) Two Tumansky RD-9B or other RD-9 versions rated at from 7,165lb (3250kg) to 8,820lb (4000kg) with maximum afterburner; ("Mandrake") two non-afterburning turbojets, probably RD-9 rated at about 6,000lb.
Dimensions: Span (26 and 27P) 38ft 6in (11·75m); (original 27) 36ft 1in; ("Mandrake") estimated at 71ft (22m); length (26) 62ft (18·90m); (27P) about 55ft (16·75m); ("Mandrake") about 51ft (15·5m); height (26, 27P) 14ft 6in (4·40m); ("Mandrake") about 13ft (4m).
Weights: Empty (all) about 18,000lb (8165kg); maximum loaded (26) about 26,000lb (11,800kg); (27P) about 24,000lb (10,900kg); ("Mandrake") possibly nearly 30,000lb (13,600kg).
Performance: Maximum speed (26, 27P, at altitude) 686mph (1104km/h, Mach 0·95); ("Mandrake") about 470mph (755km/h); initial climb, about 15,000ft (4600m)/min ("Mandrake", less); service ceiling (26, 27P) 49,200ft (15,000m); ("Mandrake") about 62,000ft (19,000m); range at altitude (26) about 1,675 miles (2700km); (27P) 1,000 miles (1600km); ("Mandrake") possibly 2,500 miles (4000km).
Armament: (26) one 30mm NR-30 cannon in fairing low on right side of forward fuselage; (27P) small batches with cannon and rockets, then small batches with two missile pylons; ("Mandrake") none.
History: First flight (26) before mid-1956; (27P) before mid-1956; ("Mandrake") possibly 1957.
User: Soviet Union.

Development: Stemming directly from the Yak-25, these aircraft introduced various changes, of which the most significant was afterburning engines in the Yak-26 and 27P. The leading edge was swept very sharply at the root and the trailing edge extended inboard of the longer nacelles to

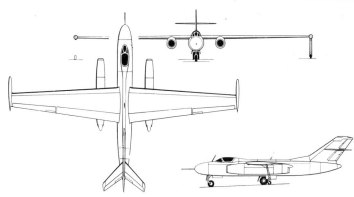

Three-view of Yak-26 "Mandrake" (provisional).

meet the body at 90° and give much greater root chord. The nose was pointed (glazed on the 26 and a radome on the 27P) and in the production aircraft the outer wings were extended beyond the outrigger gear and fitted with drooped extended-chord leading edges. Only the 26 was built in large numbers (NATO name "Mangrove"). The 27P was called "Flashlight C". The high-altitude, unswept "Mandrake", whose proper designation is not known, made overflights in Eastern Asia, the Middle East and along the borders of Communist territory in Europe before being withdrawn from most front-line units. Today a few "sneak" missions are still being made, and it may be that the aircraft making them are remotely piloted (because Mandrake and other Yak twin-jets have been important radio-controlled targets used in Soviet missile tests).

Below: The several Yak-27 sub-types (NATO name "Mangrove") were interim aircraft which led to the Yak-28 "Brewer" family—which look similar but are totally redesigned.
Foot of page: Yak-26 "Mandrake", from Soviet ciné film.

Anti-submarine and maritime patrol aircraft

During World War II the biggest problem in the war against the U-boat was building aircraft with sufficient range to remain on station in mid-Atlantic, and thus close the "aircraft gap" where Admiral Raeder's wolf-packs lurked unmolested from the sky. Today range is no great problem, but it is still a challenge to track down and kill a skilfully handled nuclear submarine, which can speed through the depths without any of the limitations imposed on conventional submarines. And the fact that submarines are today strategic weapons, able to destroy cities thousands of miles away, has added fresh impetus to the overall problem of ASW (anti-submarine warfare).

ASW is usually the main task facing the maritime patrol aircraft. It is also the primary mission of several important helicopters, as explained in that section. The helicopter is bound to be potentially faster and more agile than 10,000 tons of steel deep in the ocean, but unless he is endowed with telepathic reception the helicopter skipper cannot know in advance what his adversary intends to do next, so the chase is not one-sided. In fact, as was the case with U-boats after mid-1943, future submarines may even choose to surface and fight it out, because it is only a matter of time before they carry short-range surface-to-air missiles (such as the Vickers SLAM, submarine-launched airflight missile, which is a pop-up cluster of six Shorts' Blowpipe missiles fired from the top of the submarine fin without any other part of the vessel needing to break surface). Once at close quarters, a duel between aircraft and submarine tends to be violent. In general, the ASW aircraft presents a target that is much easier to see and easier to hit than the submarine, which is another reason why submarines are likely to carry SAMs (surface-to-air missiles).

Finding and tracking submarines is a task calling for several kinds of sensor. A submarine on the surface is almost an unfair situation, for it can be seen miles away on radar. Modern maritime radars are powerful and sensitive, and contain circuitry that automatically eliminates most of the interference called "sea clutter" caused by reflections from the moving waves. Despite the close proximity of the sea-clutter background, such radars are specifically designed to detect such small objects as the tips of submarine fins, radio or radar aerials, schnorkels (snorts) and the other small probes the modern submarine likes to stick up into the atmosphere. A diesel-powered submarine at snort depth can be detected by radar at a range of well over ten miles, but ASW aircraft often carry an "Autolycus" sniffer that can pick them up at greater distances by detecting the concentration of a few parts per billion of diesel exhaust constituents in the atmosphere (snags here are that diesel exhaust travels only downwind, and there are lots of other diesel-powered ships going about their lawful occasions). Many ASW aircraft have a MAD (magnetic anomaly detector) either sticking out at the back or towed on a long wire to get it away from the disturbance of the aircraft itself. The MAD detects the extremely small but characteristic disturbance to the Earth's magnetic field caused by large masses of metal, such as a submerged submarine (or, to name another snag, an uncharted wreck). Probably the most important ASW sensors of all are acoustic. Sono-buoys, either passive or active, are slim cylinders dropped accurately into the sea (helicopters can cheat by "dunking", fishing the buoy out and trying in a different place). Passive buoys listen for the hydrodynamic disturbance, mostly from the screw, and machinery noise of a submerged submarine. Active buoys radiate sharp "pings" of sound and listen for reflections from an otherwise silent submarine hull. Sonics has become a subject almost as rich in measures and countermeasures as radar.

It is almost an anti-climax to report that ASW aircraft carry AS torpedoes, depth bombs, missiles and various other weapons. They also keep an eye on legitimate sea traffic, offer many kinds of assistance, conduct a great deal of reconnaissance, and in many countries help prevent smuggling, illegal immigration, violation of fishing frontiers, and even such misdemeanours as dumping tanker wastes.

With a touch of flap and its MAD boom extended, a US Navy S-3A Viking whispers across a Poseidon-missile submarine. Perhaps the most cleverly packaged aircraft in history, this carrier-based four-seater can fly ASW, ESM, reconnaissance and attack missions.

Beriev M-12 Tchaika

Be-12 Tchaika; NATO code-name "Mail"

Origin: Design bureau of Georgi Mikhailovich Beriev, Taganrog, Soviet Union.

Type: Ocean reconnaissance and utility amphibian.

Engines: Two 4,190ehp Ivchenko AI-20D single-shaft turboprops.

Dimensions: Span 97ft 6in (29·7m); length overall 99ft (30·2m); height on land 22ft 11½in (7m).

Weights: Empty approximately 48,000lb (21,772kg); maximum approximately 66,140lb (30,000kg).

Performance: Maximum speed about 380mph (612km/h); cruising speed 199mph (320km/h); service ceiling 38,000ft (11,582m); range with full equipment 2,485 miles (4000km).

Armament: At least 6,600lb (3000kg) sonobuoys and AS bombs in internal weapon bay; one to three external hard points for stores under each outer wing.

History: First flight 1960 or earlier; combat service probably about 1962; set many world records in 1964, 1968, 1972 and 1973.

User: Soviet Union (possibly also Egypt and/or Syria).

Above: An M-12 Tchaika takes off from an AV-MF base (note the Tu-22 "Blinder C" in the distance).

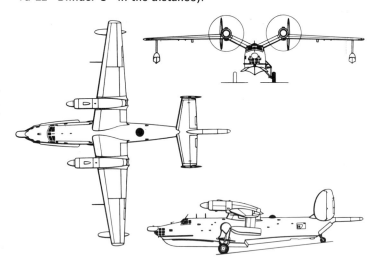

Above: Three-view of M-12 with landing gear extended.

Below: From all accounts the M-12 is a thoroughly good aircraft on land, sea or in the air. The amphibian is a species extinct in the West.

Development: The bureau of Georgi M. Beriev, at Taganrog on the Azov Sea, is the centre for Soviet marine aircraft. The Be-6, powered by two 2,300hp ASh-73TK radial engines and in the class of the Martin PBM or P5M, served as the standard long-range ocean patrol flying boat from 1949 until about 1967. In 1961 Beriev flew a remarkable large flying boat, the Be-10, powered by two Lyulka AL-7PB turbojets, but though this set world records it never entered major operational service. Instead a more pedestrian turboprop aircraft, first seen at the 1961 Moscow Aviation Day at the same time as the swept-wing Be-10, has fast become the Soviet Union's standard large marine aircraft. The Be-12 Tchaika (Seagull) is an amphibian, with retractable tailwheel-type landing gear. Its twin fins are unusual on modern aircraft, and the gull wing, which puts the engines high above the spray, gives an air of gracefulness. The Be-12 is extremely versatile. The search and mapping radar projects far ahead of the glazed nose, and a MAD (magnetic anomaly detector) extends 15ft behind the tail. Much of the hull is filled with equipment and there is a weapon and sonobuoy bay aft of the wing with watertight doors in the bottom aft of the step. Be-12s, known as M-12s in service with the Soviet naval air fleets, have set many class records for speed, height and load-carrying. They are based all around the Soviet shores, mainly with the Northern and Black Sea fleets.

Boeing Model 1041-133-1

Various US Navy study programmes

Origin: Model 1041, Boeing Aerospace Co; other proposals by other manufacturers.

Type: V/STOL ship-based platform for various missions, particularly ASW and AEW.

Engines: (Model 1041) two 8,080shp Allison XT701 single-shaft turbines, arranged as described in the text.

Dimensions: (Model 1041, as proposed) span 41ft 3in (12·6m); length 48ft 1in (14·7m); height 17ft 10in (5·4m).

Weights: Premature to quote, but in the order of 15,000lb (6800kg) empty and 30,000lb (13,600kg) loaded.

Performance: Subsonic (maximum Mach number about 0·8); ceiling over 40,000ft (18,000m); endurance at least 4hr except in continuous low-level operation.

Armament: Suitable for ASW mission; none in AEW.

History: Study 1975–77; possible hardware funding in 1978 for first flight after 1980 and service deployment by 1983–4.

User: Studies funded by US Navy.

Development: This entry has been included purely for interest, though those participating might describe it as premature. The proven advantages of V/STOL capability in a fast jet aeroplane, demonstrated in operation by the Harrier/AV-8A, have led to intensive study of how jet-lift technology might be applied to the full range of seaborne air power. The US Navy is funding studies by several companies to determine the feasibility of a cost/effective ASW and/or AEW aircraft that could be based on ships other than large carriers. The proposal by Boeing, Model 1041-133-1, would have VTOL capability at reduced weights, but would normally operate as a STOL from short decks. The two turboshaft engines would be geared by high-speed shafts to three lift fans. One would be in the nose, normally covered by doors except during jet-supported modes. The other two would be in ducts on each side of the rear fuselage, with either the nozzles or the whole fan/duct units swivelling to give lift or thrust.

There are many other attractive configurations. The McDonnell Douglas 260 could use the swivel-nozzle Pratt & Whitney F402 (RR Pegasus).

In February 1977 Grumman revealed their proposal for what is called the A-mission. This, the Model 698, has a fuselage similar to that of the Lockheed S-3A and two pivoted geared-fan engines with a by-pass ratio of about 15. Vanes in the efflux of the engines control the aircraft in yaw and pitch, while differential fan pitch controls the aircraft in roll. Many Navy and

Above: McDonnell Douglas proposes the Model 260, the sub-type pictured being a Carrier On-board Delivery transport.

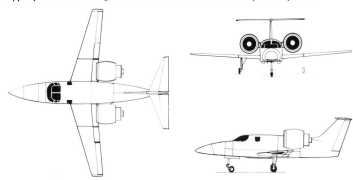

Three-view of Boeing 1041 (engines in forward-flight mode).

FAA (Federal Aviation Agency) visitors have been impressed by a large free-flight model of this proposal. In the even longer term the Navy is interested in the possibility of a V/STOL supersonic aircraft, in which thrust for forward flight would in any case be great enough for VTOL if the correct scheme could be found. The Rockwell XFV-12 is described elsewhere.

Below: Though pictured on a carrier, the point of the Boeing 1041 is that it (and similar proposals) could use small decks.

Breguet Alizé

Br.1050

Origin: Ateliers Louis Breguet (now Dassault-Breguet), France.
Type: Three-seat carrier anti-submarine search and strike.
Engine: 1,975shp Rolls-Royce Dart RDa.21 single-shaft turboprop.
Dimensions: Span 51ft 2in (15·6m); length 45ft 6in (13·86m); height 15ft 7in (4·75m).
Weights: Empty 12,566lb (5700kg); loaded 18,190lb (8250kg).
Performance: Maximum speed 285mph (460km/h) at sea level, about 295mph (475km/h) at altitude; initial climb (gross weight with landing gear down) 1,380ft (420m)/min; service ceiling 20,500ft (6250m); endurance at 144mph (235km/h) patrol speed at low level 5hr 12min; ferry range with auxiliary fuel 1,785 miles (2850km).
Armament: Weapon bay for acoustic torpedo or three 353lb (160kg) depth charges; underwing racks for two Nord SS.11M or AS.12 missiles, or various combinations of rockets, bombs or depth charges.
History: First flight (Br 960) 3 August 1951; (Br 1050 aerodynamic prototype) 26 March 1955; (Br 1050 prototype) 6 October 1956; (Br 1050 production model) 22 June 1957; first delivery 26 March 1959.
Users: France (Aéronavale), India (Navy).

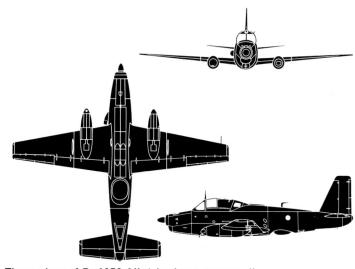

Three-view of Br.1050 Alizé (radome retracted).

Development: In 1948 the Breguet company began work on a design to meet a requirement of the Aéronavale for a carrier-based strike aircraft. The resulting Br.960 Vultur (vulture) looked conventional, but in fact had a speed of 559mph (900km/h) on the thrust of a Rolls-Royce Nene jet at the back and an AS Mamba turboprop in the nose. With the jet shut down it had a long range and endurance. This never went into production, though it was very successful and pleasant to fly. Instead, in 1954, the long task began of turning the Vultur into an anti-submarine aircraft carrying both search radar and weapons. So different did it become that it was renamed Alizé (trade-wind). The retractable radome replaced the turbojet, the main landing gears retracted forwards into nacelles also housing sonobuoys and the cockpit was arranged for the pilot on the left, a radar operator on the right and a second sensor operator behind. Flottiles 4F, 6F and 9F still deploy most of the 75 built for the carriers *Foch* and *Clémenceau*, and a further 12 were supplied for 310 Sqn Indian Navy aboard the carrier *Vikrant*.

Below: It is testimony to a satisfactory weapon system that no Alizé has been withdrawn from front-line service. Both 310 Sqn of the Indian Navy, ashore and embarked in INS *Vikrant*, and the carrier ASW squadrons (Flotille 4F and 6F) of the French Aéronavale, still use the Alizé exclusively, and see no replacement. This one is landing on *Clémenceau*.

Breguet (Dassault Breguet) Atlantic

Br.1150 Atlantic

Origin: Design, Louis Breguet, France; manufacture, SECBAT multi-national consortium.
Type: Maritime patrol and anti-submarine aircraft with normal crew of 12.
Engines: Two 6,106ehp Rolls-Royce Tyne 21 two-shaft turboprops.
Dimensions: Span 119ft 1in (36·3m); length 104ft 2in (31·75m); height 37ft 2in (11·33m).
Weights: Empty 52,900lb (24,000kg); maximum 95,900lb (43,500kg).
Performance: Maximum speed (above 16,400ft/5000m) 409mph (658km/h); patrol speed 199mph (320km/h); initial climb at gross weight 2,450ft (746m)/min; service ceiling 32,800ft (10,000m); patrol endurance 18 hours; maximum range 5,592miles (9000km).
Armament: Unpressurised weapon bay carries all NATO standard bombs, 385lb (175kg) depth charges, four homing torpedoes (or nine acoustic torpedoes) and HVAR rockets. Underwing racks for up to four AS.12, Martel or other missiles with nuclear or conventional warheads.
History: First flight 21 October 1961: (production aircraft) 19 July 1965; service delivery 10 December 1965.
Users: France (Aéronavale), W Germany (Marineflieger), Italy, Netherlands (Navy), Pakistan.

Development: The history of NATO shows the almost continual failure of its members to agree on weapon standardization, especially in aircraft. One of the few real attempts to do better was the 1958 decision to procure a standard aircraft to replace the Lockheed P-2. The French Br.1150 was selected from 25 designs submitted and in December 1959 two prototypes were ordered from NATO funds. Though most NATO members refused to have anything to do with it — often because their own design had not been

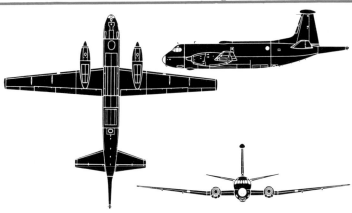

Three-view of Br.1150 Atlantic (radome retracted).

chosen — the programme was launched by France and Germany, which ordered 40 and 20 respectively. Subsequently the Netherlands Navy bought nine and the Italian Navy 18, so that finally the airframe was being built in all four countries, with avionics partly supplied from the USA and Britain. The engines were made by a British/Belgian/German/French/Italian consortium, with assembly by SNECMA of France. The Atlantic proved a most comfortable and efficient machine, with pressurization above the floor of the double-bubble fuselage and a great amount of room. The airframe is skinned mainly in metal honeycomb sandwich. Five of the German Atlantics bristle with special electronic countermeasures, and in 1977 plans were continuing to be studied for a heavier Atlantic II with M45 turbofan pods under the wings to allow operation at weights as high as 110,000lb (50,000kg).

Below: Pleasing study of an Atlantic in its element. It belongs to 30° Stormo, Italian Marinavia, based at Cagliari.

Canadair CP-107 Argus

Argus Mk 1 and 2

Origin: Canadair Ltd, Canada.
Type: Maritime patrol and anti-submarine aircraft with normal crew of 15.
Engines: Four 3,700hp (water-injection rating) Wright R-3350-32W (TC18-EA1) Turbo-Compound 18-cylinder piston engines with exhaust turbines geared to crankshaft.
Dimensions: Span 142ft 3½in (43·37m); length 128ft 3in (39·1m); height 36ft 9in (11·2m).
Weights: Empty 81,500lb (36,967kg); loaded 148,000lb (67,130kg).
Performance: Maximum speed 288mph (463km/h) at sea level, 315mph (507km/h) at 20,000ft (6096m); initial climb 1,700ft (518m)/min; service ceiling 29,000ft (8840m); range at 190mph (306km/h) at low level 5,900 miles (9495km); endurance 30 hours.
Armament: Two 18ft 6in (5·65m) internal bays accommodate all normal large sonics, depth bombs, acoustic torpedoes, homing torpedoes, mines and other stores, to total weight of 8,000lb (3629kg). Additional 7,600lb (3450kg) can be carried on two underwing racks.
History: First flight 29 March 1957; (33rd and last aircraft) 13 July 1960.
User: Canadian Armed Forces.

Development: In the early 1950s the Royal Canadian Air Force examined ways of replacing the Lancaster MR.10 and Catalina as standard ocean patrol aircraft. It needed great endurance and the ability to carry comprehensive ASW (anti-submarine warfare) search and attack equipment. It eventually adopted the solution of Canadair Ltd, which like its US parent, General Dynamics, was anxious to produce developed versions of the British Britannia turboprop airliner. To meet the RCAF need the CL-28 was produced by replacing the Britannia's turboprops by Turbo-Compound engines giving maximum range and endurance at low level, together with a new unpressurised fuselage incorporating weapon bays ahead of and behind the low wing. Comprehensive equipment was installed including APS-20 radar in the nose, desks for seven sensor operators and, in the rear fuselage, batteries of sonobuoys dropped or fired through dispensers. MAD equip-

Three-view of CP-107 Argus Mk 2.

ment resulted in the long tail "stinger". At the 13th aircraft production switched to the Mk 2 with a more advanced British radar with smaller scanner and completely rearranged communication and navigation equipment plus ECM gear requiring two small dorsal aerials. The wing pylons were planned for the defunct Petrel missile and have seldom been used. Arguses have served well for almost 20 years with four squadrons of the Canadian Armed Forces and will eventually be replaced by the far more costly Lockheed CP-140 Aurora.

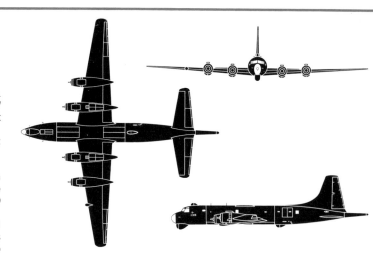

Above: CP-107 Argus Mk 2 (all Mk 1 now converted) of CAF 415 Sqn.

Below: After logging many thousands of hours in harsh environments the very first CP-107 Argus still looks fresh. Here seen crossing the wake of a submarine, it will have to go on filling a vital role until the CP-140 Aurora becomes available in 1980. By then this particular Argus will have been in service almost 23 years.

Grumman S-2 Tracker and derivatives

S-2A to -2E Tracker, DHC CS2F, C-1A Trader and E-1B Tracer

Origin: Grumman Aerospace, USA; licence-built in Canada (see text).

Type. (S-2) carrier ASW aircraft; (C-1) COD transport; (E-1) AEW aircraft.

Engines: Two 1,525hp Wright R-1820-82WA (early versions, -82) Cyclone nine-cylinder radials.

Dimensions: Span (S-2A to -2C, C-1 and E-1) 69ft 8in (21·23m); (S-2D to -2G) 72ft 7in (22·13m); length (S-2A to -2C) 42ft 3in (12·88m); (S-2D to -2G) 43ft 6in (13·26m); height (S-2A to -2C) 16ft 3½in (4·96m); (S-2D to -2G) 16ft 7in (5·06m).

Weights: Empty (S-2A) 17,357lb (7873kg); (S-2E) 18,750lb (8505kg); loaded (S-2A) 26,300lb (11,929kg); (S-2E) 29,150lb (13,222kg); (C-1A, E-1B) 27,000lb (12,247kg).

Performance: Maximum speed (S-2A) 287mph (462km/h); (S-2E) 267mph (430km/h); (C-1A) 290mph (467km/h); initial climb (S-2A) 1,920ft (586m)/min; (S-2E) 1,390ft (425m)/min; service ceiling (S-2A) 23,000ft (7010m); (S-2E) 21,000ft (6400m); range (S-2A) 900 miles (1448km); (S-2E) 1,300 miles (2095km).

Armament: Weapon bay accommodates two electric acoustic-homing torpedoes, two Mk 101 depth bombs (some versions, one) or four 385lb (175kg) depth charges; six underwing pylons for 5in rockets, Zuni rockets or 250lb (113kg) bombs, or for ferrying torpedoes (two on each wing); (S-2E) as above, with provision for Betty nuclear depth charge, AS.12 or other guided missiles and 7·62mm Miniguns; (C-1 and E-1) no armament.

History: First flight (XS2F-1) 4 December 1952; production S2F-1 (S-2A) 30 April 1953; combat service February 1954; final delivery February 1968.

Users: Argentina, Australia, Brazil, Canada, Italy, Japan, Peru, Taiwan, Thailand, Turkey, Uruguay, USA, Venezuela.

Development: This very ordinary-looking piston aircraft entered a world of advanced gas-turbine machines and has outlasted nearly all of them. It stemmed from the belief than an aircraft compatible with carrier operation could be made to combine the two roles of anti-submarine warfare (ASW) search and strike, previously accomplished by one aircraft equipped with sensors and another equipped with weapons. Grumman developed the Tracker extremely rapidly, despite the need to package an extraordinary diversity of equipment into a small space. Its low-speed handling stemmed from the long span, with almost full-span slotted flaps and fixed slots on the outer folding wings. In the nose were seats for pilot, co-pilot/navigator, and two radar plotters. In the S-2A (formerly S2F-1) the radar was the APS-38, in a retractable ventral bin. A magnetic anomaly detector (MAD) boom extended behind the tail, an upper search radar had its scanner above the cockpit, a 70 million candlepower searchlight was hung under the right wing and the engine nacelles were full of sonobuoys ejected through tubes to the rear. The TS-2A was an ASW trainer and the CS2F-1 and -2 were built by de Havilland Canada. The S-2B was equipped with the Julie acoustic (explosive) echo-ranger and associated Jezebel passive acoustic sensor. The S-2C had a bulged asymmetric weapon bay and larger tail, most being converted into US-2C utility or RS-2C photo aircraft. The S-2D, ordered in 1958, was physically larger, with improved accommodation and equipment. The S-2E incorporated further new equipment. The total of these versions was 1,281, including 100 Canadian-built, and several hundred have been modified to the S-2F and G versions for service until late 1977 with many of the 12 countries that have used Trackers. The C-1A

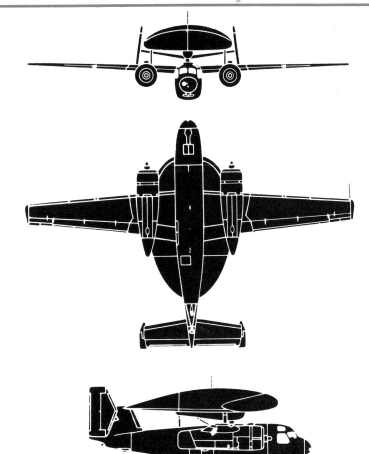

Three-view of the E-1B Tracer. The C-1A has a similar fuselage.

is a nine-passenger carrier on-board delivery transport, and the E-1B is an airborne early warning machine with a huge teardrop-shaped radome above a C-1 size fuselage, with a three-finned tail.

Above: Grumman S-2E Tracker, as formerly used by VS-26 aboard USS *Randolph*.

Below: Canada's CP-121 Trackers were built at Toronto by de Havilland Canada. They remain operational.

Hawker Siddeley Shackleton

Shackleton MR.1 and 1A, MR.2 and AEW.2, MR.3 and 3 series 3, T.4

Origin: A. V. Roe Ltd (now British Aerospace), UK.

Type: (MR) maritime reconnaissance and ASW, with usual crew of ten; (AEW) airborne early warning; (T) crew trainer.

Engines: Four 2,455hp Rolls-Royce Griffon 57A vee-12 liquid-cooled; (MR.3 Series 3), in addition two 2,500lb (1134kg) thrust Rolls-Royce Viper 203 single-shaft turbojets.

Dimensions: Span (1, 2, 4) 120ft (36·58m); (3) 119ft 10in (36·53m); length (1,4) 77ft 6in (23·6m); (2) 87ft 3in (26·59m); (3) 92ft 6in (28·19m); height (1, 2, 4) 16ft 9in (5·1m); (3) 23ft 4in (7·11m).

Weights: Empty (1) about 44,000lb (20,000kg); (3) 57,800lb (26,218kg); maximum loaded (1, 4) 86,000lb (39,000kg); (2) 98,000lb (44,450kg); (3) 100,000lb (45,360kg).

Performance: Maximum speed (2) 272mph (439km/h); (3) 302mph (486km/h); initial climb (typical) 850ft (260m)/min; service ceiling (typical) 20,000ft (6100m); range (typical for MR.3) 4,215 miles (6780km).

Armament: (1) two 20mm Hispano cannon in dorsal turret; at least 10,000lb (450kg) depth charges, torpedoes or other ordnance carried in weapon bay; (2) as MR.1 plus two 20mm cannon in nose, aimed by gunner seated above, with bomb aimer below; (3) as (2) without dorsal turret; (4) none.

History: First flight (Mk 1 prototype) 9 March 1949; service delivery (MR.1) 28 September 1950; (MR.2) October 1952; (MR.3) October 1957; final delivery June 1959.

Users: S Africa (MR.3), UK.

Development: Derived from the Lincoln to Specification R.5/46, the Shackleton MR.1 had contra-rotating propellers, large single-wheel main

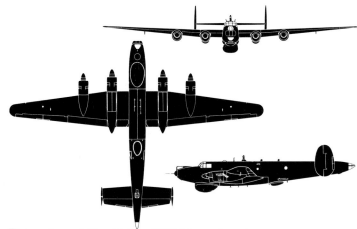

Three-view of Shackleton AEW.2 in cruise trim.

gears and a chin radome. After delivering 77, many of which were converted into T.4 trainers after 1956, Avro delivered 69 MR.2 with redesigned fuselage of better form with semi-retractable rear-ventral radar. In 1962 many were updated as MR.2C with better navaids, and survivors now serve as the UK airborne early-warning aircraft with APS-20 radar (taken from Skyraiders and Gannets) and extra fuel. The 42 MR.3 introduced twin-wheel tricycle landing gear and tip tanks. Eight were supplied to the South African AF. To ease strain on the engines most RAF MR.3 were updated to Series 3 standard with Viper turbojets in the outer nacelles to assist during take-off and initial climb.

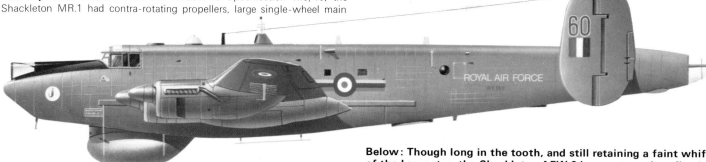

Above: AEW.2 of 8 Sqn, RAF, with Orange Harvest ECM.

Below: Though long in the tooth, and still retaining a faint whiff of the Lancaster, the Shackleton AEW.2 is an extremely refined electronics platform. Its weakest point is the old APS-20F radar.

Hawker Siddeley Nimrod

HS.801 Nimrod MR.1 and 2 and R.1

Origin: Hawker Siddeley Aviation (British Aerospace), UK.
Type: (MR) maritime reconnaissance and anti-submarine aircraft, with operating crew of 12, with several secondary roles; (R) electronic reconnaissance and countermeasures.
Engines: Four 11,995lb (5441kg) thrust Rolls-Royce Spey 250 two-shaft turbofans.
Dimensions: Span 114ft 10in (35m); length 126ft 9in (38·63m); (R.1) 118ft; height 29ft 8½in (9·08m).
Weights: Empty (MR, typical) 92,000lb (41,730kg); loaded 192,000lb (87,090kg).
Performance: Maximum speed 575mph (926km/h), economical transit speed 490mph (787km/h); climb and ceiling, not disclosed; mission endurance 12 hours; ferry range, typically 5,755 miles (9265km).
Armament: 50ft (15m) weapon bay capable of carrying very wide range of stores, including AS torpedoes, mines, depth bombs, nuclear weapons, conventional bombs and fuel tanks; two (optionally four) underwing pylons for air-to-surface missiles such as Martel or AS.12.
History: First flight (aerodynamic prototype) 23 May 1967; (production MR.1) 28 June 1968; service delivery 2 October 1969.
User: UK (RAF).

Development: Though it is derived from the Comet civil transport the Nimrod has proved an outstandingly successful aircraft. The original MR.1 was tailored to an equipment standard which, for budgetary reasons, fell short of the ideal, but still combined very complete ASW (anti-submarine warfare) sensing systems with digital and analog computers, advanced

continued on page 140▶

Above: Few aircraft have been worked harder than the Nimrod MR.1 squadrons of the RAF. This aircraft taking off from Gibraltar is from 206 Sqn, RAF Kinloss, Morayshire (Scotland). It was participating in NATO Exercise Open Gate.

Below: On any number of engines from one upwards, the Nimrod is a splendid aircraft. No other ocean patroller offers such effortless performance, and in 1977-79 the RAF MR.1 force is being updated internally to improve combat effectiveness still further.

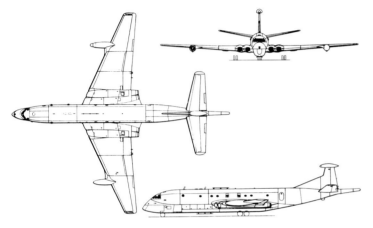

Above: Three-view of Nimrod MR.1 or 2 (R.1 has short tailcone).

▶tactical displays and comprehensive inertial, doppler and three other navigation systems. The best thing about the MR.1 is the aircraft itself, which surpasses all other aircraft in use for ocean patrol in speed, quietness, flight performance, reliability and all-round mission efficiency. In emergency it can be fitted with 45 passenger seats in the rear compartment without significantly disturbing operational equipment. The RAF force of 46, which have operated around the clock in often extremely severe conditions, are being completely modernised at their half-life point in 1977-78, with new Searchwater radar, greatly increased computer capacity and a new acoustic processing system matched with the Barra sonobuoy. The R.1 force of three aircraft are specially equipped for sensing, recording and emitting electromagnetic and other data. Since 1973 a detailed study has been made of a Nimrod AEW (airborne early warning) aircraft as a replacement for the Shackleton. Distinguished by large radomes at nose and tail, this machine would have outstanding capabilities in the European environment. The AEW trials Nimrod was to fly in 1977, and if NATO fails to agree on the E-3A/E-2C purchase could have a bright future as the standard European warning aircraft.

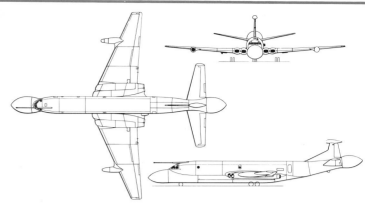

Three-view of proposed Nimrod AEW. If adopted by the RAF, 11 airframes are immediately available for rebuilding to this standard, which in many respects promises to be superior to the Boeing E-3A AWACS.

Above: Nimrod MR.1 of 236 OCU (fin number is last two digits of serial).

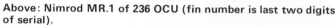

Left: Pilots and (left) flight engineer in a 201 Sqn Nimrod operating out of Kinloss. Bonedomes are not worn, and in endurance flying on two engines the flight deck is virtually devoid of background noise.

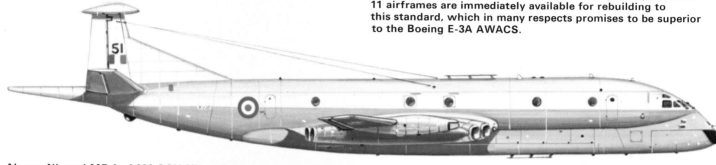

1 Dielectric radome
2 Taxi lamp
3 ASV-21D search and weather radar (MR.2, Searchwater)
4 Radome hoist point
5 Front pressure bulkhead
6 Windscreen for all-weather use
7 Four wipers
8 Instrument panel coaming
9 Co-pilot's seat
10 Eyebrow window
11 Pilot's seat
12 Pitot head
13 Twin nosewheels
14 Sonics homing aerial
15 Doppler bay
16 Forward radio pack
17 Autolycus diesel sniffer
18 Autolycus equipment rack
19 Port D.C. electrics crate
20 Engineer's station
21 Emergency escape hatch
22 Starboard D.C. electrics crate
23 Crew entry door
24 Periscopic sextant
25 Equipment systems crate
26 Toilet
27 Ground supply socket
28 Weapons-pannier door ground control

45 Radio operator
46 Tactical commander
47 Sonics station (2)
48 Sonics operators (2)
49 ASV operator
50 Partition
51 Space provision for extra sensor operator's station
52 Radio trough
53 Sonics cupboard
54 Port AC electrics crate
55 Starboard AC electrics crate
56 Aft radio rack
57 ESM/MAD operator
58 Machined inner-wing skin
59 Undercarriage bay upper panel

77 Flap inner section
78 Inboard airbrake (upper surface only)
79 Blackout curtain
80 Emergency escape panels
81 Fuselage frames
82 Electrics trough
83 Dinette
84 Fixed galley
85 Partition with folding door

29 Weapons-pannier door
30 Door strut
31 Mixed ASW weapons load
32 Tank blow-off
33 'On-top' sight
34 Port beam lookout's seat
35 Domed observation window (hinged, pressure-bearing, with sight linked to computer)
36 Starboard beam lookout's seat
37 Domed observation window (fixed)
38 Analog computer rack
39 Digital computer rack
40 Blackout curtain
41 Map projector station
42 Routine navigator
43 Plot display
44 Tactical navigator

60 Starboard weapons pylon
61 Flow spoiler
62 Searchlight, 70 million candle power
63 External fuel tank
64 Wing bumper
65 Fixed slot
66 Integral fuel tanks
67 Skin butt-joint rib
68 Over-wing filler
69 Starboard navigation light
70 Wingtip fuel vent
71 Starboard aileron
72 Aileron tab
73 Flap outer section
74 Airbrake (upper and lower surfaces)
75 Fuel dump pipes
76 Fuel vent

86 Size A sonobuoy stowage
87 Underfloor bag-type keel tanks
88 Port lookout and stores-loader
89 Starboard lookout and stores-loader
90 Observation ports (port and starboard)
91 Pressurized launchers
92 Rotary launchers
93 Ready-use oxygen stowage
94 Intercom panel
95 Stores control panel
96 Emergency door
97 Hand extinguisher
98 Underfloor parachute stowage
99 First-aid kit
100 Escape rope stowage
101 Camera magazine stowage

102 Retro-launcher (cancels airspeed)
103 F.135 camera hatch
104 Hat-rack
105 ESM amplifier
106 Equipment cooling fans
107 Rear pressure bulkhead
108 Dorsal fin
109 HF aerial
110 Starboard tailplane
111 VOR aerial
112 Dielectric fairing
113 ESM aerial
114 Dummy ESM (test) aerial
115 Rudder
116 Fin structure
117 Dielectric tailcone
118 MAD aerial
119 Elevator tab
120 Port elevator
121 VOR aerial

122 Tailplane structure
123 Tail bumper/fuselage vent
124 Fin/fuselage frame
125 De-icing conduit
126 Rudder and elevator linkage
127 APU
128 APU and aft fuselage access hatch
129 Safe
130 Liquid oxygen pack
131 F.126 camera access hatch
132 Intercom panel
133 Main door
134 Ground-operated doors (rear loading of stores)
135 Tailpipes
136 Dinghy stowage
137 Thrust reverser (outboard only)
138 Rear spar/fuselage attachment point

139 Rolls-Royce Spey 250 turbofan (12,140 lb/ 5,506 kg thrust)
140 Inboard engine bay (engine not shown)
141 Heat exchanger
142 Front spar/fuselage attachment point
143 Landing/taxi light
144 Anti-iced intakes
145 Ram air to heat exchanger
146 Flow spoiler
147 Undercarriage well
148 Weapon pylon (two Aérospatiale AS.12 missiles)
149 External fuel tank
150 Access panels
151 Wing structure
152 Port navigation light
153 Wingtip vent
154 Port aileron

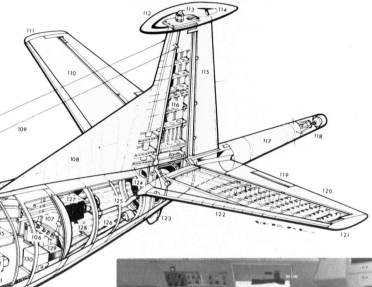

Above: Typical of the daily routine missions of the RAF Nimrod MR force is the finding and shadowing of Soviet surface warships and submarines. This MR.1 is trailing the helicopter cruiser *Leningrad,* a task which calls for the maximum ESM capability as well as considerable computer memory and processing capacity. With withdrawal from Malta the RAF has four squadrons (42, 120, 201 and 206), based at St Mawgan and Kinloss.

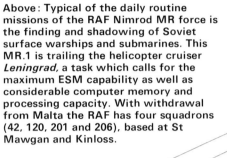

Above. Nerve centre of a Nimrod. The routine navigator (left) gets the aircraft to where the action is—which it can do faster than other ASW aircraft —whereupon the tactical navigator goes to war and builds marvellous pictures on his 24-inch display.

Above: The cutaway drawing shows all salient features of the standard MR.1 or 2 Nimrod, which in practice seldom carry external weapons such as the small wire-guided AS.12. All MR.1 Nimrods are being recycled back through the Woodford factory to emerge in updated MR.2 form, with EMI Searchwater radar with Ferranti FM 1600D computer, a 920C central processor with 256K words, and the new Marconi-Elliott AQS-901 acoustic system (compatible with Barra sonobuoys) with two more 920C computers.

155 Aileron tab
156 Flap outer section
157 Airbrake (upper and lower surfaces)
158 Dump pipes
159 Vent
160 Flap structure

Ilyushin Il-38

Il-38

Origin: Bureau named for Ilyushin, Soviet Union.
Type: Maritime patrol and anti-submarine.
Engines: Four Ivchenko AI-20 single-shaft turboprops, probably rated at about 5,000shp each.
Dimensions: Span 122ft 8½in (37·4m); length 129ft 10in (39·6m); height about 35ft (10·7m).
Weights: Empty, approximately 90,000lb (40,820kg); maximum loaded, approximately 180,000lb (81,650kg).
Performance: Maximum speed, about 450mph (724km/h); maximum cruising speed, about 400mph (644km/h); range with typical mission load, about 4,500 miles (7240km); endurance, about 15hr.
Armament: Internal weapon bay ahead of and behind wing accommodating full range of anti-submarine torpedoes, bombs, mines and other stores; possibly external racks for stores such as guided missiles between weapon-bay doors under wing and beneath outer wings.
History: First flight (Il-18 transport) July 1957; first disclosure of Il-38, 1974, by which time it was well established in operational service.
Users: Egypt (or Soviet detachments in Egypt) until 1976, India, Soviet Union (AV-MF).

Development: Following the example of the US Navy and Lockheed with the Electra/P-3 Orion transformation, the Soviet Naval Air Arm (AV-MF) used the Il-18 transport as the basis for the considerably changed Il-38, known to NATO by the code-name of "May". Compared with the transport it has a wing moved forward and a considerably longer rear fuselage, showing the gross shift in centre of gravity resulting from the changed role. Whereas in the transport the payload is distributed evenly ahead of and behind the wing, the rear fuselage of the Il-38 contains only sensors, sonobuoy launchers of several kinds and a galley, with the main tactical compartment just behind and above the wing, with a probable tactical crew of eight. Most of the heavy stores and consoles are ahead of the wing, together with the search radar. The only added item at the rear is the MAD

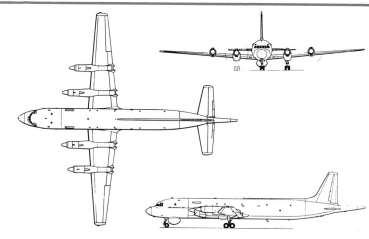

Above: Three-view of Il-38 (NATO name "May").

(magnetic anomaly detector) stinger, not a heavy item. So far little is known of the Il-38 and photographs show few of the items one would expect to see. There is no weapon bay below the wing and pressurized fuselage, as in the Nimrod and P-3, no major sensor outlets and aerials and no apparent external stores pylons. On the other hand the Il-38 is potentially as good as a P-3, though probably not up to the sensor and computer standard of the P-3C.

Above: As used by the Soviet AV-MF the Il-38 is a notably clean aircraft.

Below: One of the best photographs available of an Il-38, this was taken by a Nimrod of 120 Sqn, RAF Kinloss. It shows a drogue-stabilized sonobuoy being dropped from medium altitude by an Il-38 taking part in Atlantic exercises.

Kawasaki P-2J

GK-210, P-2J

Origin: Kawasaki Heavy Industries, Gifu, Japan (airframe built under licence from Lockheed Aircraft).

Type: Maritime patrol and anti-submarine aircraft.

Engines: Two 2,850hp General Electric T64-10 single-shaft turboprops made under licence by Ishikawajima-Harima Heavy Industries; two Ishikawajima-Harima J3-7C single-shaft turbojets each rated at 3,085lb (1400kg) static thrust.

Dimensions: Span over tip tanks 101ft 3½in (30·87m); length 95ft 10¾in (29·32m); height 29ft 3½in (8·93m).

Weights: Empty 42,500lb (19,277kg); maximum loaded 75,000lb (34,019kg).

Performance: Maximum "dash" speed with jets 403mph (649km/h); typical cruising speed 230mph (402km/h); maximum rate of climb 1,800ft (550m)/min; range with maximum fuel 2,765 miles (4450km).

Armament: Internal weapon or sensor load up to 8,000lb (3630kg); underwing attachments for 16 rockets.

History: First flight of original P-2 Neptune 17 May 1945; (P-2J) 21 July 1966; (production P-2J) 8 August 1969; squadron delivery October 1969; final delivery 1977.

User: Japanese Maritime Self-Defence Force.

Development: In 1959–65 Kawasaki licence-built 48 Lockheed P-2H Neptunes for the JMSDF, and it was to replace these that the company developed the GK-210 to meet a JMSDF requirement for a more modern machine. In fact the design is based on the P-2H, but the new turboprops were substituted for Turbo-Compound engines, in new nacelles housing twin-wheel main gears, the fuselage is lengthened, the vertical tail broadened,

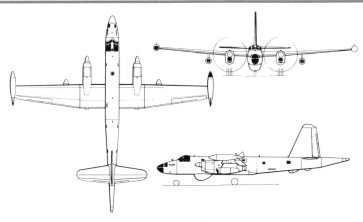

Above: Three-view of Kawasaki P-2J.

a "Varicam" trimming surface incorporated in the horizontal tail and fuel capacity increased. Electronics are greatly updated, though still to a poor standard by modern yardsticks. Altogether 89 P-2J aircraft are being delivered, and the last may have flown before this book appears. In the 4th Defence Buildup Programme their electronics and mission equipment are being updated, though still using old radar, the outdated Jezebel/Julie echo ranging system, and navigation, communications and computer technology of the 1960 era.

Below: Most of the planned force of 89 P-2J aircraft have been delivered; about 75 were in service by March 1977. This one belongs to No 3 Sqn, 4 Wing, of the JMSDF.

Lockheed P-2 Neptune

P-2A to H

Origin: Lockheed-California Co, USA.

Type: Maritime patrol and ASW aircraft.

Engines: (P2V-1) two 2,300hp Wright R-3350-8 Cyclone 18-cylinder two-row radials; (-2) 2,800hp R-3350-24W; (-3) 3,080hp R-3350-26W; (later batches of -4) 3,250hp R-3350-30W Turbo-Compound; (-5F, P-2E) same plus two 3,400lb (1540kg) thrust Westinghouse J34-36 turbojets; (-7, P-2H) same jets but 3,700hp R-3350-32W Turbo-Compound.

Dimensions: Span (early versions) 100ft (30·48m); (H) 103ft 10in (31·65m); length (-1) 75ft 4in; (-2 to -4/D) 77ft 10in (23·7m); (E) 81ft 7in; (H) 91ft 8in (27·94m); height 28ft 1in (8·58m); (H, 29ft 4in, 8·94m).

Weights: Empty (-1) 31,000lb (14,061kg); (-3) 34,875lb (15,833kg); (H) 49,935lb (22,650kg); maximum loaded (-1) 61,153lb (27,740kg); (-3) 64,100lb (29,075kg); (H) 79,895lb (36,240kg).

Performance: Maximum speed (-1) 303mph (489km/h); (H) 356mph (403mph, 648km/h, with jets); initial climb (all) about 1,200ft (366m)/min; (H, 1,800ft/min with jets); service ceiling 25,000–30,000ft depending on sub-type; range (early models, typical) 4,000 miles (6440km); (H) about 2,500 miles (4000km).

Armament: See text.

History: First flight (XP2V-1) 17 May 1945; service delivery (-1) March 1947; (-7, H) 26 April 1954.

Users: Argentina, Brazil, Chile, France, Japan, Netherlands, Portugal, USA (Naval Reserve).

Development: On 1 October 1946 the P2V leapt into prominence. Three days earlier the third production P2V-1 had taken off from Perth, Western Australia, at 85,000lb, with fuel weighing 1½ times its empty weight. By flying non-stop 11,235 miles to Columbus, Ohio, it set a world distance record for piston-engined aircraft that has never been broken. In the course of the next 15 years the Burbank plant delivered over 1,000 of these capable aircraft, 838 for the US Navy and the rest for Allied and friendly

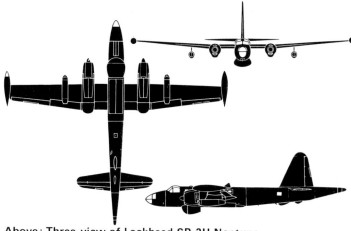

Above: Three-view of Lockheed SP-2H Neptune.

customers. Early versions had up to six 20mm cannon firing ahead, two more in a power tail turret and two 0·5in in the dorsal turret. Gradually defensive or offensive gun armament was removed, later models having instead many tons of extra anti-submarine sensing systems, as well as retaining the 8,000lb (3629kg) weapon bay. The final models, no longer in US Navy first-line use, were the anti-submarine SP-2H and Antarctic ski-equipped LP-2H. Various models are used by the countries listed, and the Japanese P-2J is described separately

Below: Red Kangaroos adorn this SP-2H, which happens to be Royal Australian Air Force number A89-270, of 10 Sqn, at Townsville, Queensland. Like many other P-2 versions around the world, it can still do a useful job, though the deficiencies are becoming daily more apparent. 10 Sqn, RAAF are looking forward to getting their first P-3C Update-Two Orions before the end of 1977.

Above: SP-2H of 320 Sqn, Royal Netherlands Navy.

Lockheed P-3 Orion

P-3A, -3B and -3C with derivatives

Origin: Lockheed-California Co. USA.
Type: Maritime reconnaissance and anti-submarine, normally with flight crew of five and tactical crew of five; variants, see text.
Engines: Four Allison T56 single-shaft turboprops; (P-3A) T56-10W, 4,500ehp with water injection; (remainder) T56-14, 4,910ehp.
Dimensions: Span 99ft 8in (30·37m); length 116ft 10in (35·61m); height 33ft 8½in (10·29m).
Weights: Empty (typical B, C) 61,491lb (27,890kg); maximum loaded 142,000lb (64,410kg).
Performance: Maximum speed 473mph (761km/h); initial climb 1,950ft (594m)/min; service ceiling 28,300ft (8625m); range 4,800 miles (7725km).
Armament: Very varied load in bulged unpressurized weapon bay ahead of wing and on ten wing pylons; maximum internal load 7,252lb (3290kg) can include two depth bombs, four Mk 44 torpedoes, 87 sonobuoys and many other sensing and marking devices; underwing load can include six 2,000lb (907kg) mines or various mixes of torpedoes, bombs, rockets or missiles. Maximum expendable load 20,000lb (9071kg).
History: First flight (aerodynamic prototype) 19 August 1958; (YP-3A) 25 November 1959; (production P-3A) 15 April 1961; (P-3C) 18 September 1968.
Users: Australia, Canada, Iran, New Zealand, Norway, Spain, USA (Navy, Naval Reserve).

Development: In August 1957 the US Navy issued a requirement for an "off the shelf" anti-submarine patrol aircraft derived from an established type, and this was met in April 1958 by Lockheed's proposal for a conversion of the Electra turboprop airliner. The third Electra was quickly modified as an aerodynamic prototype and deliveries of production P-3As began in August 1962. From the 110th aircraft the Deltic system was fitted with more sensitive sensors and improved displays. Four early A models were converted as WP-3A weather reconnaissance aircraft, while others became EP-3A flying special electronic missions. Three As were supplied ex-USN to Spain. The B model introduced more powerful engines without water/alcohol injection and many were sold to Australia, New Zealand and

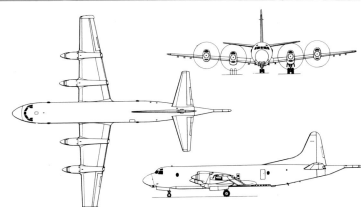

Above: Three-view of Lockheed P-3C Orion.

Norway or modified, as EP-3B electronic reconnaissance and counter-measures, with huge "canoe radars" above and below and a radome under the forward fuselage. The completely different P-3C packages into the same airframe a new and more modern tactical system with sensors and weapons controlled by a digital computer. Derivatives include the P-3F for Iran and a variant for Australia. Other versions include the RP-3D for mapping the Earth's magnetic field and special reconnaissance and transport conversions. Production in 1977 was centred upon the P-3C Update, with computer memory increased from 65,000 to 458,000 words, a new computer language, receiver for the global Omega navigation system, increased acoustic-sensor capability, tactical displays for two of the sensor stations, and other improvements. Canada is buying yet another new version, the CP-140 Aurora, with the ASW systems of the S-3A Viking. Deliveries exceed 450, and output is being increased to deliver to the US Navy 12 in 1977, rising to 16 in 1980 and 24 in 1981.

Below: The P-3C is the current production model of Orion, the favourite maritime-patrol choice of the Western world largely on account of adequate capability and a price below that of the otherwise extremely attractive Nimrod. Despite its propellers the P-3C is a good performer; in 1971 one flown by a US Navy crew set a record at 500·89mph.

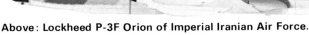

Above: Lockheed P-3F Orion of Imperial Iranian Air Force.

Lockheed S-3A Viking

S-3A Viking, US-3A

Origin: Lockheed-California Co, USA.
Type: (S-3A) four-seat carrier-based anti-submarine aircraft; (US-3A) carrier on-board delivery transport.
Engines: Two 9,275lb (4207kg) General Electric TF34-2 or TF34–400 two-shaft turbofans.
Dimensions: Span 68ft 8in (20·93m); length 53ft 4in (16·26m); height 22ft 9in (6·93m).
Weights: Empty 26,600lb (12,065kg); normal loaded for carrier operation 42,500lb (19,277kg); maximum loaded 47,000lb (21,319kg).
Performance: Maximum speed 506mph (814km/h); initial climb, over 4,200ft (1280m)/min; service ceiling, above 35,000ft (10,670m); combat range, more than 2,303 miles (3705km); ferry range, more than 3,454 miles (5558km).
Armament: Split internal weapon bays can house four Mk 46 torpedoes, four Mk 82 bombs, four various depth bombs or four mines; two wing pylons can carry single or triple ejectors for bombs, rocket pods, missiles, tanks or other stores.
History: First flight 21 January 1972; service delivery October 1973; operational use (VS-41) 20 February 1974; final delivery after 1980.
User: USA (Navy); W Germany negotiating.

Development: Designed to replace the evergreen Grumman S-2, the S-3 is perhaps the most remarkable exercise in packaging in the history of aviation.

continued on page 148▶

Above: Sniffing its way across the Atlantic rollers, this S-3A Viking belongs to US Navy VS-22 (anti-submarine squadron 22). The squadron is embarked aboard USS *Saratoga*, CVA-60.

1 Radome
2 Texas Instruments AN/APS-116 radar scanner
3 Radome hinge line
4 Forward pressure bulkhead
5 Nosewheel well
6 Landing and taxi light
7 Launch bar
8 Nosewheel shock absorber
9 Twin nosewheels
10 Approach lights
11 Nosewheel doors
12 Nosewheel retraction mechanism
13 Forward (port) avionics bay
14 Rudder pedals
15 Control column
16 Instrument panel shroud
17 Windscreen wipers
18 Central console
19 Curved windscreen panels
20 Eyebrow instrument panel
21 Anti-glare roof panels
22 Centre section control housing
23 Co-pilot's side console
24 Co-pilot's seat (Douglas Escapac IE-1 all four seats)
25 Pilot's seat
26 Ryan Doppler ground velocity system
27 Texas Instruments forward-looking infra-red (FLIR) scanner stowage
28 Infra-red scanner (extended)
29 Hot-air exhaust panel (Williams Research APU)
30 Electronics compartment
31 Hartman Systems integrated control system (INCOS) tray sensor
32 Observation window
33 Sensor operator's seat
34 Tactical co-ordinator (TACCO) seat
35 In-flight refuelling probe (stowed)
36 UHF L-Band communications, IFF antenna
37 Preamp VHF antenna
38 Starboard engine pylon
39 Starboard stores pylon
40 Wing hinge line
41 Leading-edge flap actuator
42 Leading-edge flap
43 Electronic support measures (ESM) antennas
44 Wingtip ESM pod (IBM AN/ALR-47 system)
45 Wing skinning
46 Starboard aileron
47 Trailing edge flaps outer section
48 Aileron control system
49 Spoilers/speed brakes
50 Wing fold hydraulic actuator
51 Wing integral fuel system (shaded area)
52 In-flight refuelling point
53 LF-ADF antenna
54 Spoiler servos
55 Roll trim actuator
56 Aileron servo
57 Aft pressure bulkhead
58 Univac 1832 general-purpose digital computer
59 Mission avionics starboard console
60 Centre aisle
61 Starboard keelson
62 Attack stores port bay
63 Bomb bay door
64 Engine intake
65 Engine pylon

66 General Electric TF34-GE-400A turbofan
67 Mainwheel leg
68 Port mainwheel
69 Port external stores pylon
70 Aero 1D auxiliary fuel tank, 300-US gal (1136 l)
71 Leading-edge flaps
72 Wing spar
73 Spoiler actuators
74 Aileron actuator
75 Electronic support measures (ESM) system antennas
76 Port navigation light
77 Wingtip ESM pod
78 Port aileron
79 Aileron tab
80 Flap tracks
81 Trailing-edge flaps (extended)
82 Spoilers/speed brakes
83 Arresting hook
84 Wing hinge point
85 Mainwheel well
86 Sonobuoy chutes
87 Avionics cooling plant
88 UHF L-Band (Collins), TACAN (Hoffman) antenna
89 AiResearch environmental control system (ECS)
90 HF (Collins) antenna coupler
91 ECS intake
92 ECS intake trunking
93 Fuselage/empennage joint
94 Aft (port) avionics bay
95 MAD (Texas Instruments AN/ASQ-81) boom (stowed)
96 Elevator servo
97 Tailplane carry-through
98 ECS outlet
99 Fuel dump line
100 Fuel vent line
101 Heated leading-edge
102 Tailplane construction
103 Elevator mass balance
104 Static discharger

105 Port elevator
106 Elevator tab
107 MAD boom (extended)
108 Fin (hinged for stowage)
109 Rear navigation light
110 Pitch trim actuator
111 Rudder trim actuator

112 Fin hinge line
113 Starboard elevator
114 Fin-fold hydraulic actuator
115 Rudder servo
116 Rudder structure
117 Rudder tab
118 Rudder hinge
119 Sonobuoy ref and RCVR antenna
120 Rudder upper hinge
121 Static dischargers
122 Anti-collision beacon

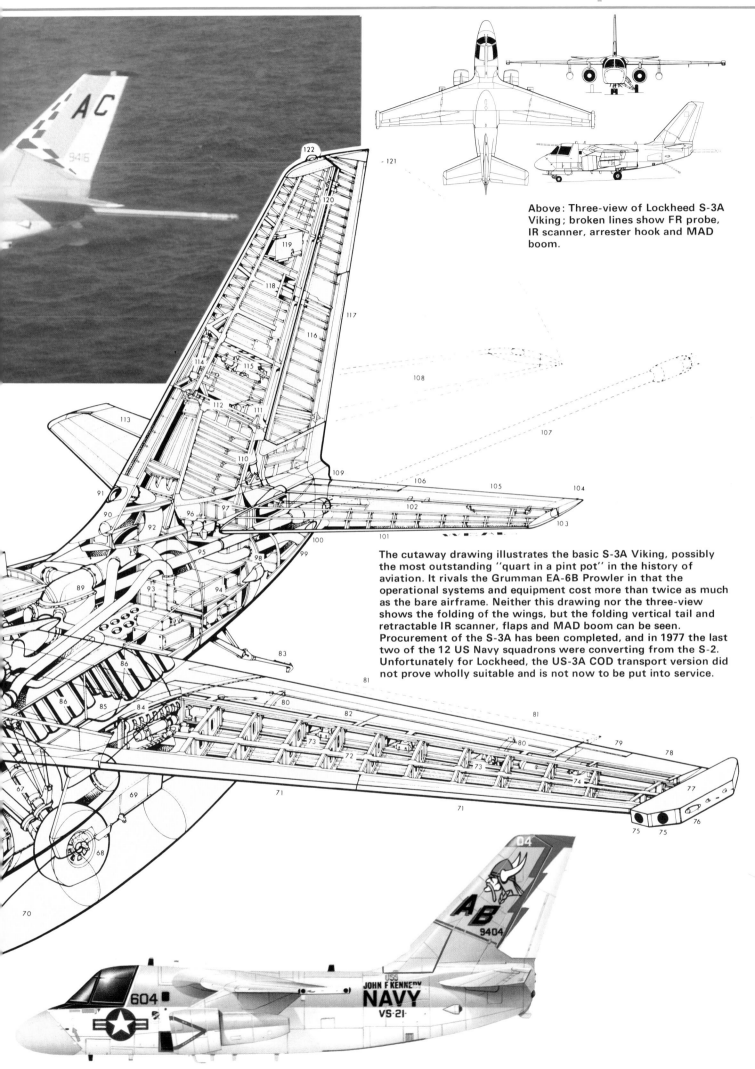

Above: Three-view of Lockheed S-3A Viking; broken lines show FR probe, IR scanner, arrester hook and MAD boom.

The cutaway drawing illustrates the basic S-3A Viking, possibly the most outstanding "quart in a pint pot" in the history of aviation. It rivals the Grumman EA-6B Prowler in that the operational systems and equipment cost more than twice as much as the bare airframe. Neither this drawing nor the three-view shows the folding of the wings, but the folding vertical tail and retractable IR scanner, flaps and MAD boom can be seen. Procurement of the S-3A has been completed, and in 1977 the last two of the 12 US Navy squadrons were converting from the S-2. Unfortunately for Lockheed, the US-3A COD transport version did not prove wholly suitable and is not now to be put into service.

Above: An S-3A Viking of VS-21 (USS *John F. Kennedy*).

▶ It is also an example of an aircraft in which the operational equipment costs considerably more than the aircraft itself. Lockheed-California won the Navy competition in partnership with LTV (Vought) which makes the wing, engine pods, tail and F-8 type landing gear. To increase transit speed the refuelling probe, MAD tail boom, FLIR (forward-looking infra-red) and certain other sensors all retract, while the extremely modern specially designed APS-116 radar is within the nose. Equipment includes CAINS (carrier aircraft inertial navigation system), comprehensive sonobuoy dispensing and control systems, doppler, very extensive radio navaid and altitude systems, radar warning and ECM systems, extensive communications, and a Univac digital processor to manage all tactical and navigation information. By the end of 1975 more than 100 of the first buy of 186 Vikings were in service and foreign orders (beginning with Federal Germany) were being discussed. Procurement of the Navy force of 184 (plus two prototypes) was completed in FY77, but additional production is likely, both for the US Navy and export. The first US-3A COD transport flew in July 1976. It carries a crew of two and six passengers plus 4,600lb (2087kg) cargo, of which 2,000lb can be accommodated in large underwing pods; the all-cargo payload is 7,500lb (3402kg), but production is unlikely.

Above: An S-3A prototype making one of 40 touch-and-go landings on *Forrestal* during trials.

Above: Launch of an S-3A from foredeck catapult of the nuclear carrier USS *Enterprise*, CVA-65.

Above: America's two fixed-wing ASW aircraft are both products of Lockheed-California Company. The Orion is carrying special avionic gear under the fuselage.

Shin Meiwa SS-2

PX-S, SS-2 (PS-1) and SS-2A (PS-1 Kai)

Origin: Shin Meiwa Industry Co, Japan.
Type: (2) anti-submarine flying boat; (2A) air/sea rescue amphibian.
Engines: Four 3,060ehp Ishikawajima-built General Electric T64-IHI-10 single-shaft turboprops (plus one 1,400shp or 1,250shp T58-IHI-10 in hull for blowing flaps, rudder and elevators).
Dimensions: Span 108ft 8¾in (33·14m); length 109ft 11in (33·5m); height (2) 31ft 10½in (9·715m); (2A) 32ft 1in.
Weights: Empty (2) 58,000lb (26,300kg); (2A) 56,218lb (25,500kg); maximum loaded (2) 94,800lb (43,000kg); (2A) 99,200lb (45,000kg).
Performance: Maximum speed (2) 340mph (547km/h); (2A) 299mph (481km/h); initial climb (2) 2,264ft (690m)/min; service ceiling (2) 29,500ft (9000m); range with full weapon load (2) 1,347 miles (2168km).
Armament: (2) weapons compartment on upper deck accommodates four 330lb (150kg) AS bombs (plus much heavier load of sensors); external pylons between engines carry containers each housing two homing torpedoes; launchers on wing tips for triple groups of 5in rockets.
History: First flight (2) 5 October 1967; (production PS-1) 1972; (2A) 1974.
User: Japan (Maritime Self-defence Force).

Development: After seven years of study Shin Meiwa were awarded a contract for the prototype of a novel ASW (anti-submarine warfare) flying boat in January 1966. The resulting PX-S demonstrated the technique of flying not much faster than submerged nuclear submarines, using extensive blowing over flaps and tail, and of tracking its quarry by repeatedly alighting

on the sea (even in a storm) and listening with a large non-expendable sonar. By 1975 the first 14 production SS-2 (Japan Maritime Self-Defence Force designation PS-1) were in service, with nine more on order. The amphibian SS-2A (PS-1 Kai = PS-1 Mod) has a crew of nine and carries 64 passengers and cargo or 12 seated and 12 stretcher (litter) survivors. Deliveries to the JMSDF began in 1975. A projected water-bomber to fight forest fires could carry 12 tons of water.

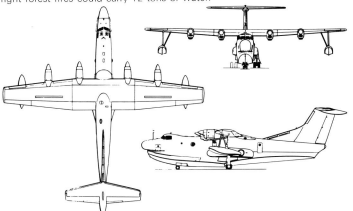

Above: Three-view of US-1 (PS-1 Kai).

Below: Colourful and quiet, the Shin Meiwa US-1 (PS-1 Kai) is the only fixed-wing air/sea rescue aircraft in production. This example is serving with JMSDF No 71 Sqn at NAS Atsugi.

Above: The two prototypes flying in formation off the Japanese coast. In the background is No 5801, the original PS-1 flying boat. No 9071 is the first PS-1 Kai (PS-1 modified) air/sea rescue amphibian, called SS-2A or US-1 by Shin Meiwa. By March 1977 17 PS-1 and three PS-1 Kai were in service.

Transports and tankers

Both these important categories of military aircraft emerged in the years immediately following World War I, in which transport aircraft were conspicuously absent. Possibly the first military transports were the Vernons delivered to the infant RAF in 1922 after Trenchard and his team—fighting a political war of survival against the older services—had demonstrated that lawless parts of the far-flung Empire could be policed at lowest cost by using small numbers of troops backed up by bomber-transport aircraft. In fact the bomber-transports seldom bombed and the last of this species was the Bombay of 1935, though at the very end of the European part of World War II more than 2,500 heavy bombers of the RAF and USAAF served briefly in the transport role flying out food and bringing back prisoners of war. The US Army Air Service also bought its first transport in 1922; this was the T.2 built by enterprising Anthony Fokker, and in May 1923 it flew non-stop from New York to San Diego, taking longer than a day and a night. Three months later another US Army crew completed the first rudimentary trials in flight refuelling.

During World War II the chief transports were merely derived from airliners, but credit is due to the Germans for building the Me 323 and Ar 232, both of which were members of the totally different family that are tailored to the military role. Fairchild built the C-82, but this missed the war. Douglas built the very large civil DC-7, but PanAm eventually turned it down and it became the C-74 Globemaster (much later there was a different DC-7). The C-74 was pressurized, but for the military role more volume was needed, and the result was the C-124 Globemaster II which had a cavernous unpressurized fuselage whose harsh comforts did not go well with 15hr sectors. The truly great advance was the C-130 Hercules of 1954, which combined adequate space and payload with pressurization, full-section rear loading or para-dropping door, and high speed with turboprop propulsion. Today we are so cosseted we even carp at the comfort of a Herky-bird, but thanks to aggressive "product improvement" by Lockheed-Georgia Company this old-stager "keeps acting newer and newer" and King Hussein just said he would buy some more "because they are such good workhorses". Some 41 other air forces think the same. Loads that will not fit a C-130 can go by a C-5A or An-22 Antei, and there is not much that these big birds cannot carry. Where we go from there depends partly on oil prospecting, opening up Siberia and similar quasi-civil tasks, because air forces do not have the money for development of much larger transports. Who knows, they might turn out to be airships?

Compared with large civil jets the military transport tends to have bigger doors (sometimes a full-section door at each end), less wing sweep and more wheels. This is because it carries bulkier loads and may need to drop them by parachute, has to operate from shorter airstrips, need not cruise so fast, and must be able to land and taxi on unpaved surfaces. A glimpse of the future is afforded by the AMST YC-14 and YC-15, which were the last word in military transports and have no sweep at all. On the other hand the most numerous fleet of jet transports is the USAF's force of C-135 variants, and these are mainly KC-135s built as tankers and forming an intermediate stage between Boeing's company-funded prototype and the civil 707. Boeing had previously built 888 piston-engined tanker/transports designated C-97 or KC-97 (K being the prefix for a tanker), and these flew too low and too slow to be compatible with jet bombers. Accordingly a mighty force of 732 KC-135 jet tankers was built, with 35° swept wing and, originally, mostly with turbojet propulsion (today often changed to turbofan). Boeing were thereby enabled to go ahead

A Victor K.2 of 232 OCU, RAF, feeds fuel through No 1 hose to a dual-control Harrier T.4. This method of inflight refuelling is applicable to almost any combat aircraft, and an increasing number of air forces are now studying its cost/effectiveness.

with the civil 707, which is bigger and heavier. Today large numbers of KC-135s are serving in many special roles, while air forces have also bought civil 707s for duty as transports and tankers. In December 1977 a version of the DC-10 was selected as the USAF's Advanced Tanker/Cargo Aircraft to supplement and replace the KC-135 fleet. Initially, 20 are being bought.

Inflation is a good reason for getting more work out of each aircraft by equipping it to fly more kinds of mission. Canada studied the 707 as a long-range ocean patrol aircraft, overland surveillance platform, transport, tanker and anti-submarine warfare aircraft, before deciding to use 707 transport/tankers and ocean patrol Orions. Unlike the Orion, the British Nimrod can do a substantial transport job with minimal interior rearrangement. Iran has even put refuelling pods on military 747s. Except for certain parts of the US Air Force, which uses the Flying Boom method in which a boom operator fires a telescopic pipe into a receptacle on the receiver aircraft, military forces all use the British-developed probe/drogue method of flight refuelling which among other advantages allows one tanker to top-up three receiver aircraft simultaneously. A secondary role for transport-type aircraft is to serve as parent for launching and controlling drones and RPVs (remotely piloted vehicles). There are many other duties; for example, some transports are equipped (or can be equipped in a few hours) as a complete surgical hospital, with helicopter to collect casualties, the whole hospital and staff being able to fly at once to the scene of any large natural disaster.

Aeritalia G222

G222

Origin: Aeritalia SpA, Naples (main factory Turin; new plant at Amendola, Naples, near corporate headquarters), Italy.

Type: Tactical transport.

Engines: Two 3,400shp General Electric T64-P4D single-shaft turboprops made under licence by Fiat; provision for eight Aerojet take-off rockets with total thrust of 7,937lb (3600kg) to be attached to fuselage.

Dimensions: Span 94ft 6in (28·8m); length 74ft 5½in (22·7m); height 32ft 1¾in (9·8m).

Weights: Empty 32,165lb (14,590kg); maximum useful load 19,840lb (9000kg); maximum loaded 58,422lb (26,500kg).

Performance: Maximum speed 336mph (540km/h) at 15,000ft; cruising speed 224mph (360km/h); initial climb 2,034ft (620m)/min; take-off or landing over 50ft (15m) about 2,700ft (825m); service ceiling 29,525ft (9000m); range with 11,025lb (5000kg) load 1,833 miles (2950km); ferry range 3,075 miles (4950km).

Armament: None.

History: First flight 18 July 1970; service delivery December 1975.

Users: Argentina, Dubai, Italian Air Force.

Development: In the early 1960s the NATO NBMR-4 competition had more than a dozen companies in Europe and North America sketching V/STOL transports with lift jets to meet the extremely short field-length requirement. None of these ever came to anything except the Fiat G222, with two Dart turboprops and eight lift jets. Eventually the lift jets were replaced by fuel, the Darts were replaced by T64 engines and despite an increase of two tonnes in empty weight the G222 eventually won an order for 12 aircraft placed in 1974. The Italian AF has a requirement for 44, and this number is expected to be built. Two more were ordered in 1974 by Argentina, with a third on option. This neat but rather limited machine can carry 44 troops, 32 paratroops, 36 stretchers (litters) plus eight attendants or sitting casualties, or various light trucks and artillery. Manufacture is shared by many Italian companies, and in an urgent need to win more orders demonstrations have been made in Egypt and Tunisia.

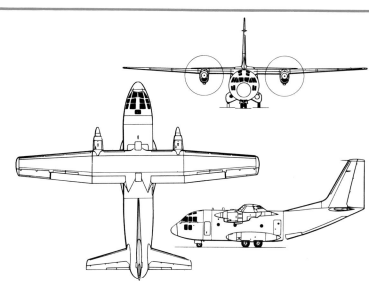

Above: Three-view of G222 production aircraft.

Above: G222 of Aeronautica Militare Italiano.

Below: Italian paratroops leave in a stick from one of the first G222s now joining the Aeronautica Militare Italiano.

Antonov An-12

An-12; NATO code name "Cub"

Origin: Design bureau of Oleg K. Antonov, Kiev, Soviet Union.
Type: Paratroop, passenger and freight transport.
Engines: Four 4,000ehp Ivchenko AI-20K single-shaft turboprops.
Dimensions: Span 124ft 8in (38m); length 121ft 4½in (37m); height 32ft 3in (9·83m).
Weights: Empty 61,730lb (28,000kg); loaded 121,475lb (55,100kg).
Performance: Maximum speed 482mph (777km/h); maximum cruising speed 416mph (670km/h); maximum rate of climb 1,970ft (600m)/min; service ceiling 33,500ft (10,200m); range with full payload 2,236 miles (3600km).
Armament: Powered tail turret with two 23mm NR-23 cannon.
History: First flight (civil An-10) 1957; (An-12) believed 1958.
Users: Algeria, Bangladesh, Egypt, India, Indonesia, Iraq, Poland, Soviet Union, Sudan, Yugoslavia.

Development: In 1958 Antonov flew a large twin-turboprop which owed something to German designs of World War II and the C-130. From this evolved the An-10 airliner and the An-12, which since 1960 has been a standard transport with many air forces. Fully pressurised, the An-12 has an exceptionally high performance yet can operate from unpaved surfaces. At least one was fitted with large skis with shallow V planing surfaces equipped with heating (to prevent sticking to ice or snow) and brakes. Nearly all have the tail turret, and under the transparent nose is a weather and mapping radar, which in most Soviet Air Force An-12s has been changed to a more powerful and larger design. The rear ramp door is made in left and right halves which can be folded upwards inside the fuselage, either for loading heavy freight with the aid of a built-in gantry or for the dispatch of 100 paratroops in less than one minute. Typical freight load is 44,090lb (20,000kg), and the An-12 can carry all Soviet APCs, the ASU-85 SP-gun and such anti-aircraft vehicles as the ZSU-23-4 and SA-6 missile carrier. In manoeuvres of Warsaw Pact forces as many as 30 of these capable aircraft have landed at one airstrip in simulated battle conditions.

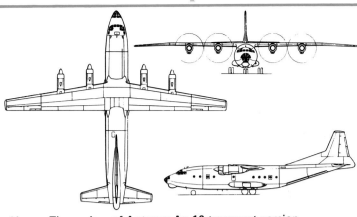

Above: Three-view of Antonov An-12 transport version.

Below: A typical An-12 as used in large numbers by the Soviet VVS and many other air forces. Many An-12s are now serving as Elint (electronic intelligence) platforms.

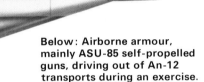

Below: Airborne armour, mainly ASU-85 self-propelled guns, driving out of An-12 transports during an exercise.

Antonov An-22 Antei

An-22 Antei (Antheus) (NATO name "Cock")

Origin: The design bureau of Oleg K. Antonov, Soviet Union.
Type: Heavy logistic transport.
Engines: Four 15,000shp Kuznetsov NK-12MA single-shaft turboprops.
Dimensions: Span 211ft 4in (64·40m); length overall (prototype) 189ft 7in (57·80m); height overall 41ft 1½in (12·53m).
Weights: Empty, equipped 251,325lb (114,000kg); maximum loaded 551,160lb (250,000kg).
Performance: Maximum cruise 422mph (679km/h); range with max payload of 176,350lb (80,000kg) 3,100 miles (5000km), range with max fuel and payload of 99,200lb (45,000kg) 6,800 miles (10,950km).
History: First flight 27 February 1965; final delivery, believed 1974.
User: Soviet Union.

Development: Largest aircraft in the world apart from the 747 and C-5A, the An-22 is the result of a surprisingly late decision to mate the great NK-12M engine/propeller combination with a capacious freight fuselage. As early as July 1967 three Soviet air force Anteis took part in an air display in the assault role, and since then an unknown number have operated with both the civil operator, Aeroflot, and the air force. Anteis carried almost all the war material supplied to the MPLA in Angola, and have made many other long overseas flights besides setting various world records for payload/height and speed/payload, the speeds all being in the region of 370mph (596km/h). The nose does not open but houses two large radars, for navigation, mapping, weather and airdropping, as well as several other avionic aids. There are seats for about 29 passengers aft of the flight deck, while at the lower level is a hold 14ft 5in (4·40m) square in section, with beaver-tail rear doors.

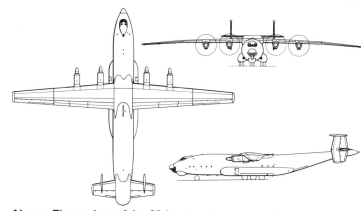

Above: Three-view of An-22 (note wing anhedral).

Above: Civil An-22 of Aeroflot seen on final approach. It is not a STOL aircraft.

Below: An-22 in service with V-TA of Soviet Air Force. Few military Anteis have been seen; those that carried weapons to the MPLA in Angola belonged to Aeroflot.

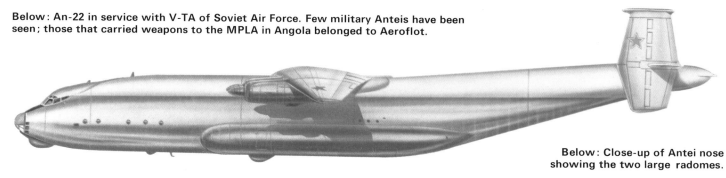

Below: Close-up of Antei nose showing the two large radomes.

Antonov An-26

An-24V, 24RV, 24T, 26 and 30
(NATO names: (24) "Coke", (26) "Curl")

Origin: The design bureau of Oleg K. Antonov, Soviet Union.

Type: (24V and RV) passenger and transport, (24T and 26) freight transport, (30) aerial survey and mapping.

Engines: (24V and T) two Ivchenko AI-24A single-shaft turboprops, shaft power not disclosed but 2,550ehp; (24RV) same, plus one 1,985lb (900kg) RU-19-300 auxiliary turbojet in right nacelle; (26 and 30) two AI-24T each rated at 2,820ehp plus (26) one RU-19-300, or (30) one 1,765lb (800kg) RU-19A-300.

Dimensions: Span 95ft 9½in (29·20m); length overall (24) 77ft 2½in (23·53m), (26) 78ft 1in (23·80m), (30) 79ft 7in (24·26m); height (24, 30) 27ft 3½in (8·32m), (26) 28ft 1½in (8·575m).

Weights: Empty (24V) 29,320lb (13,300kg), (26) 33,113lb (15,020kg); maximum loaded (24V, T) 46,300lb (21,000kg), (24RV) 48,060lb (21,800 kg), (26) 52,911lb (24,000kg), (30) 50,706lb (23,000kg).

Performance: Typical cruising speed 267mph (430km/h); range with max payload of 12,125lb (5500kg), no reserves, (24V) 341 miles (550km), (24T) 397 miles (640km), (26) about 400 miles (645km).

History: First flight (24) April 1960, (26) late 1960s.

Users: (Mainly 24) Bangladesh, Congo, Czechoslovakia, Egypt, E Germany, Hungary, Iraq, Laos, Mongolia, Poland, Romania, Somalia, Soviet Union, Sudan, Vietnam, S Yemen, Yugoslavia.

Development: One of the world's most numerous turboprop transports, the An-24 is primarily civil but small numbers of several versions have been

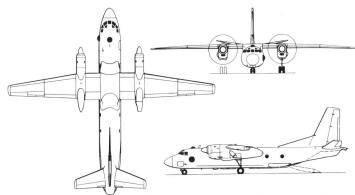

Above: Three-view of An-26; note engine nacelles in plan view.

supplied to the air forces listed above. The more powerful An-26 has a beaver-tail rear door for loading or airdropping bulky loads; it serves with Bangladesh and Poland. The An-30 can carry IR, magnetic and other sensors.

Below: An Antonov An-26 short-haul transport of the Yugoslav Air Force.

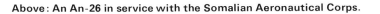

Above: An An-26 in service with the Somalian Aeronautical Corps.

Boeing C-135 family and military 707

C-135 Stratolifter family, KC-135 Stratotanker family (data KC-135A)

Origin: The Boeing Company, USA.

Type: Originally, tanker/transport; now many other roles.

Engines: Four 13,750lb (6238kg) thrust (water injection rating) Pratt & Whitney J57-59W two-shaft turbojets.

Dimensions: Span 130ft 10in (39·7m); length 136ft 3in (41·0m); height 38ft 4in (11·6m).

Weights: Empty 109,000lb (49,442kg); loaded 297,000lb (134,715kg).

Performance: Maximum speed 600mph (966km/h); cruising speed 552mph (890km/h); service ceiling 40,000ft (12,192m); typical range 4,000 miles (6437km).

Armament: None.

History: First flight (civil 367–80) 15 July 1954; (KC-135) 31 August 1956; final delivery (RC-135S) mid-1966.

Users: (C-135/variants) France, US Air Force; (C-137 and other 707–320 variants) Argentina, Canada, Egypt, W Germany, Iran, Israel, Portugal, Saudi Arabia, Taiwan, US Air Force.

Development: Boeing jet transports all stemmed from a company-funded prototype, the 367-80, flown in July 1954. After evaluation of this aircraft the US Air Force decided in October 1954 to buy 29 developed versions to serve in the dual roles of tanker for Strategic Air Command and logistic transport for MATS (later Military Airlift Command). In fact, though all KC-135 Stratotankers can serve as transports, they have seldom had to do so, because production of C-135 Stratolifters has been considerable. The Boeing 717 tanker introduced a new high-speed Boeing Flying Boom refuelling system, mounted under the rear fuselage. This is aimed by aerodynamic controls at the receptacle on the receiver aircraft; then the boom operator "fires" the telescopic boom to make a fuel-tight joint. Total fuel capacity on the KC-135A is about 26,000 Imp gal (118,000 litres), leaving the upper fuselage free for cargo. Between June 1957 and January 1965 no fewer than 732 were delivered to SAC. Another 88 Model 739 aircraft have been supplied as various models of C-135, most having 18,000lb (8165kg) thrust TF33 fan engines. At least 28 species of modifications are in USAF service, including VC-135 VIP aircraft, command posts, and more than 21 types of 135 used for electronic intelligence, countermeasures and special research. Twelve KC-135F tankers were supplied to refuel the nuclear Mirage IVA *force de frappe* of the Armée de l'Air, these having booms modified for probe/drogue refuelling. Though not armed with guns or bombs, the huge and varied fleets of 135s are very much "combat" aircraft in the context of an electronically based form of warfare and will continue to pry, probe and spoof — and feed fuel to thirsty fighters "below bingo" — for many years.

In comparison with C-135 models the 707-320 has a considerably longer and fatter fuselage, bigger wing, greater fuel capacity and much greater weight. All 707-320 versions in military service have the TF33 turbofan engine. The USAF flies various VC-137s, including the two VC-137Cs flown by the 89th Military Airlift Wing and bearing the legend "United States of America" as the personal long-range transports of the President. The Canadian Armed Forces CC-137 fleet includes two aircraft with Beech flight-refuelling hosereel pods on the wingtips, while the Imperial Iranian AF fleet of 12 707-3J9Cs have optional pods on the wingtips and a Flying Boom installation on the rear fuselage.

Above: During the SE Asia involvement, F-4E Phantoms cluster round a nice fat KC-135A like minnows round a whale.

Above: This VC-135B is a special-missions VIP transport but smaller than "Air Force One", the US President's VC-137C.

Above: This CC-137 of the Canadian Armed Forces is the only example pictured here of the larger and heavier 707-320 family.

Above: Three-view of KC-135B with TF33 turbofans.

Above: Selected from numerous special electronic and test versions, this is an EC-135N used for space range instrumentation.

Facing page, upper: One of the 12 KC-135F tanker/transports with boom/drogue systems used by the French Armée de l'Air.

Facing page, lower: The third KC-135, built in 1956, is serving as an EC-135A command post with the 9th Strategic Recce Wing (SR-71) at Beale AFB. Here it lands at Kadena AFB, Japan.

Boeing C-97 Stratofreighter

C-97 to KC-97L (data for -97G)

Type: Air refuelling tanker and logistic transport with crew of six or seven.
Engines: Four 3,500hp Pratt & Whitney R-4360-59B Wasp Major 28-cylinder four-row radials (KC-97L, in addition two 5,200lb, 2359kg thrust GE J47 turbojets).
Dimensions: Span 141ft 3in (43·05m); length 117ft 5in (35·8m); height 38ft 3in (11·7m).
Weights: Empty 85,000lb (38,560kg); loaded 175,000lb (78,980kg).
Performance: Maximum speed 370mph (595km/h); service ceiling 30,000ft (9144m); range at 300mph (482km/h) without using transfer fuel 4,300 miles (6920km).
Armament: Normally, none.
History: First flight (XC-97) 15 November 1944; (production C-97A) 28 January 1949; (KC-97G) 1953; final delivery July 1956.
Users: Israel, United States (Air National Guard).

Development: Big as the B-29 Superfortress was, it was dwarfed by the transport derived by adding on top of the existing fuselage a second fuselage of much greater diameter so that the final whale-like body had a section like a figure 8 (called "double bubble"). The Army Air Force had ordered three of these monster XC-97s in January 1942 when it first bought the B-29, but their development took second place behind the vital bomber programmes. But when the first did fly it soon startled everyone; on 9 January 1945 it flew non-stop from Seattle to Washington in 6hr 4min, at an average of 383mph (616km/h), whilst carrying a payload of ten tons. Only a few years earlier the transcontinental journey had required three days (air by day, rail by night). The YC-97A was even more capable, for it had the Wasp Major engine. Eventually 50 C-97As were built, with nose radar and extra outer-wing tankage, plus 14 aeromedical C-97Cs for casualty evacuation in Korea. But it was Strategic Air Command's need for a refuelling tanker that made the C-97 a giant programme. By July 1956 Boeing had delivered 60 KC-97Es, carrying nearly double the original fuel load, plus 159 KC-97F and no fewer than 592 KC-97G with underwing tanks and the capability of serving as a heavy cargo aircraft without removing the refuelling gear. Many Gs were converted to jet-boosted Ls, and these are

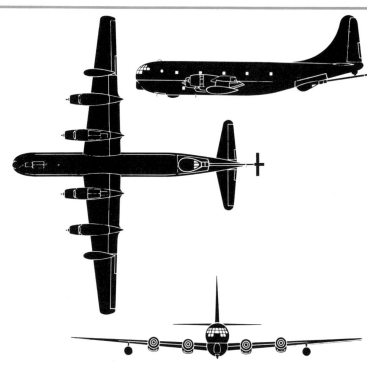

Three-view of the KC-97G differs little from the 1944 prototype.

serving with the Air National Guard. The Israeli Heyl Ha'Avir uses 12 similar aircraft with refuelling pods under the outer wings and extensive ECM equipment.

Below: The jet-assisted KC-97L tanker/transports of the Air National Guard often deploy to overseas bases. This one belongs to Illinois ANG (previously assigned to Minnesota).

Boeing YC-14

YC-14

Origin: The Boeing Company, USA.
Type: Advanced military transport.
Engines: Two 51,000lb (23,133kg) thrust General Electric F103 turbofans.
Dimensions: Span 129ft (39·32m); length 131ft 8in (40·13m); height 48ft 8in (14·83m).
Weights: Empty, about 85,000lb (38,555kg); loaded (STOL) 172,000lb (78,020kg); loaded (long runway) 216,000lb (97,975kg).
Performance: Maximum speed 460mph (740km/h) at 30,000ft (9144m); takeoff and landing to and from 50ft (15m) 2,000ft (610m); range approximately 1,250 miles (2000km) with STOL payload of 27,000lb (12,247kg) or conventional payload of 65,000lb (29,500kg).
Armament: None, though gunship versions may be developed.
History: First flight 9 August 1976; possible initial operational deployment 1979, but terminated by President Carter on 2 February 1978.
User: Not at present funded for service.

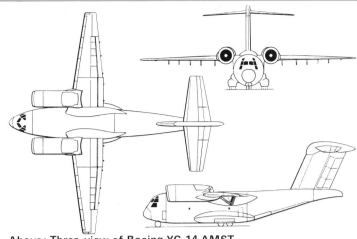

Above: Three-view of Boeing YC-14 AMST.

Development: In early 1972 the USAF requested proposals for an Advanced Medium STOL (short take-off and landing) Transport (AMST), primarily as a replacement for the C-130 but also to gather all the diverse new technology of increasing wing lift at low airspeeds and the possibility of integrating wings and propulsion systems to achieve better short-field performance. The two finalists were the McDonnell Douglas YC-15 and Boeing YC-14. Boeing chose to use a challenging but outstandingly promising method of powered lift called upper-surface blowing (USB). The two large turbofans discharge through a flattened nozzle above the upper surface of the wing. In the high-lift regime the inboard flaps are depressed to 85°, with sliding link-plates forming a smooth and continuous upper surface, while vortex generators emerge above the wing. The engine efflux passes across the wing and curves down over the flaps, giving lift almost equal to the net engine thrust. The outboard flaps are large double-slotted units, and the entire leading edge is a variable-camber slat blown by air bled from the engines. To fly the YC-14 Marconi-Elliott of Britain supplied an extremely advanced electronic flight control system, with fibre-optical data-links between three lanes (each with its own computer) and electrical "fly by wire" signalling to the surface power units. The flight deck is also totally new, with EADI (electronic attitude display indicators) which superimpose flight guidance symbols on a TV picture of the ground ahead. The whole aircraft abounds with other advanced features, whilst having a simple airframe to meet the stringent customer requirement that the 300th aircraft should cost not more than $5 million (1972 dollars, excluding R&D). Obvious advantages of the YC-14 configuration are: the wing is left clear underneath for payloads; ground vehicles cannot hit the engines, which can be left running for quick turnrounds; noise and infra-red signature are minimised; reverse thrust pushes the aircraft downwards, making the wheelbrakes more effective, and flight performance is extremely high (even on one engine), making steep approaches and climb-outs easy. The C-14 was designed to carry 150 troops, have a flight-refuelling receptacle, be able to use 2,000ft (610m) strips and fly at less than 85kt (157km/h).

Below: Even in the cruise mode the YC-14 (first aircraft shown) is clearly out of the ordinary. Boeing's giant gamble with USB has been defeated by budgetary constraints.

CASA C.212 Aviocar

C.212 (T.12)

Origin: CASA, Madrid, Spain; licence-built by Lipnur, Indonesia.
Type: Utility transport.
Engines: Two 776ehp Garrett-AiResearch TPE331-251C single-shaft turboprops.
Dimensions: Span 62ft 4in (19·0m); length 49ft 10½in (15·2m); height 20ft 8in (6·3m).
Weights: Empty 8,157lb (3700kg); maximum useful load 4,410lb (2000kg); maximum loaded 13,889lb (6300kg).
Performance: Maximum speed 230mph (370km/h) at 12,000ft; economical cruising speed at 12,000ft 198mph (315km/h); initial climb at sea level 1,800ft (548m)/min; service ceiling 26,700ft (8140m); take-off or landing over 50ft (15m) 1,500ft (480m); range with maximum cargo 298 miles (480km); range with maximum fuel and 2,303lb (1045kg) load 1,093 miles (1760km).
Armament: None normally fitted.
History: First flight 26 March 1971; pre-production aircraft 17 November 1972; service delivery 1973.
Users: Indonesia, Jordan, Portugal, Spain, Venezuela.

Development: Designed to replace the Ju 52/3m (T.2), DC-3 (T.3) and CASA 207 Azor (T.7) in the Spanish Air Force, the C.212 is designated T.12 in that service and has also been widely sold outside Spain. A simple unpressurized machine, it is intended as a 16-passenger transport, freighter (with full-section rear loading and air-dropping door), ambulance, photographic and survey aircraft and crew trainer. A civil version is also available. Deliveries began to No 461 Sqn at Gando (Las Palmas, Canary Is) and continued with 403 Sqn at Cuatro Vientos which has six photographic Aviocars. The Spanish AF is receiving eight pre-production and 32 production machines. Total orders exceed 100.

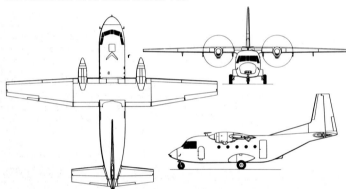

Above: Three-view of C.212 (transport, photo, nav trainer similar).

Above: In service with the Indonesian Air Force, this utility transport version of the Aviocar is designated T.12B; there is also the C.212B photo-survey version, designated TR.12A in service. The Aviocar has also sold well in foreign markets.

DH Canada Caribou

DHC-4 Caribou (C-7A and CC-108)

Origin: De Havilland Aircraft of Canada.
Type: STOL tactical transport.
Engines: Two 1,450hp Pratt & Whitney R-2000-D5-7M2 fourteen-cylinder two-row radials.
Dimensions: span 95ft 7½in (29·15m); length 72ft 7in (22·13m); height 31ft 9in (9·7m).
Weights: Empty, equipped, 18,260lb (8283kg); normal gross 28,500lb (12,928kg); maximum 31,300lb (14,197kg).
Performance: Maximum speed 216mph (347km/h); initial climb 1,355ft (413m)/min; service ceiling 24,800ft (7560m); range, 242 miles (390km) with maximum payload of 8,740lb (3965kg), 1,307 miles (2103km) with maximum fuel; take-off run to 50ft (15m) and landing distance from same height, both 1,200ft (366m).
Armament: Not normally fitted.
History: First flight 30 July 1958; service delivery (evaluation) August 1959; service delivery (inventory) 1961.
Users: Abu Dhabi, Australia, Cameroun, Ghana, India, Kenya, Kuwait, Malaysia, Oman (aircraft for sale), Spain, Tanzania, Uganda, Zaïre, Zambia.

Development: Designed to combine the carrying capacity of a C-47 (DC-3) with the STOL (short take-off and landing) performance of the company's earlier Beaver and Otter, the Caribou was a company venture undertaken in partnership with the Canadian Department of Defense Production. One was ordered by the RCAF (later Canadian Armed Forces), designated CC-108. Five, designated YAC-1, were delivered for evaluation

Above: Personnel of the 1st Brigade, 101st Airborne Division, US Army, jump from a C-7A Caribou at Dong Ba Thien, in what was South Vietnam, in July 1965. This is just one of many duties the Caribou performs with consummate ease.

Above: The Ejercito del Aire (Spanish Air Force) calls the Caribou the T.9. The main operating unit is 372 Sqn at Villanubla, with 12 short-nose (no radar) examples. Until 1972 the EdA still operated the CASA-built Ju 52/3m, which was in many ways surprisingly similar to the T.9.

by the US Army and subsequently 159 of a heavier version were delivered to that service in 1961-65; at first called AC-1, they were redesignated CV-2A and CV-2B. In 1967, when many were serving in SE Asia, this force was transferred to the US Air Force and restyled C-7A. Meanwhile, production continued for 12 other air forces around the world, as well as the United Nations and several civilian organizations. By 1975 over 330 had been built. Carrying up to 32 equipped troops, 22 stretchers (litters) or two small combat vehicles, the Caribou's main attribute is its ability to operate from short rough strips inaccessible to other fixed-wing aircraft. One C-7A, equipped with nine separate communications stations along the fuselage, served in Vietnam as an airborne command post with the 1st (Air) Cavalry Division.

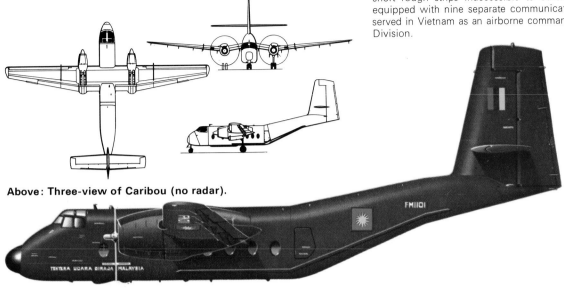

Above: Three-view of Caribou (no radar).

Above: Radar-equipped Caribou of the Royal Malaysian Air Force.

Below: The Indian Air Force, with 20, is the second-largest user of the Caribou (the Royal Australian Air Force originally operated 31). Despite its use of piston engines the Caribou has proved to be well suited to the demanding needs of many air forces, and India has flown over 40,000 hours with Caribous in some of the most extreme ''hot and high'' regions in the world, where even a Caribou has a job to get airborne and most other fixed-wingers would fail to get airborne at all. STOL performance of the Buffalo (overleaf) is even better, but this aircraft costs twice as much.

DH Canada Buffalo

DHC-5 Buffalo (C-8A, CC-115)

Origin: De Havilland Aircraft of Canada.
Type: STOL tactical transport.
Engines: Two 2,850ehp General Electric T64-10 single-shaft turboprops (CC-115) 3,060ehp T64-CT-820; (DHC-5D) T64-820-4 rated at 3,133shp (about 3,300ehp) to 38°C.
Dimensions: Span 96ft (29·26m); length (C-8A) 77ft 4in (23·57m), (CC-115) 79ft (24·1m); height 28ft 8in (8·73m).
Weights: Empty, equipped 23,157lb (10,505kg); loaded 41,000lb (18,598kg) (DHC-5D, 49,000lb, 22,226kg).
Performance: Maximum speed 271mph (435km/h), which is also maximum continuous cruising speed; initial climb 1,890ft (575m)/min; service ceiling 30,000ft (9145m); range, 507 miles (815km) with maximum payload of 13,843lb (6279kg), 2,170 miles (3490km) with maximum fuel and full allowances; take-off and landing distances, in order of 1,100ft (335m). The DHC-5D Improved Buffalo has slightly longer field length and slower climb at gross weight but can airlift an 18,000lb (8165kg) payload 691 miles (1112km).
Armament: Not normally fitted.
History: First flight 9 April 1964; service delivery (evaluation) April 1965; production terminated 1972, then line reopened 1974 to deliver the Improved Buffalo, the DHC-5D.
Users: Brazil, Canada, Ecuador, Kenya, Peru, Togo, Zaïre, Zambia.

Development: Unlike the Caribou, the Buffalo was designed to meet a customer requirement, winning, against 24 other contenders, an order from the US Army for a new STOL transport specified in May 1962. Obviously based on the Caribou, the Buffalo has an even higher maximum lift co-efficient, T-tail, advanced turboprop engines and considerably increased gross weight. Development costs were shared one-third each by DHC, the US Army and the Canadian government. Four aircraft, designated CV-7A, were supplied to the US Army for evaluation, but a change of policy terminated the whole programme. DHC were rescued by an order for 15 CC-115s, with uprated engines and nose radar, for the Canadian Armed Forces. Subsequently the Brazilian Air Force bought 24 and Peru 16 and by 1972 59 were built. One of the US aircraft, redesignated C-8A by the US Air Force, was converted into an experimental augmentor-wing machine powered by blown and deflected Spey turbofans. In 1974 the line re-opened and thanks to the superior DHC-5D aircraft are now authorized to No 102. As an assault transport the Buffalo can carry 41 troops, a 105mm gun or Pershing missile.

Above: Two of the 16 Buffaloes operated by the STOL squadron of Grupo 41 of the Fuerza Aerea del Peru (Peruvian Air Force). Earthquake relief has been a major assignment.

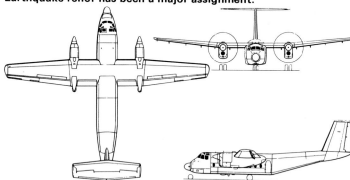

Above: Three-view of typical DHC-5 with radar.

Below: Daylight shows under the wheels as an uprated C-8B (DHC-5D) storms into the air from a dirt strip. At the 1976 SBAC Show at Farnborough a -5D made the shortest fixed-wing take-off.

Fairchild C-119 Packet

C-119 to -119K Boxcar and AC-119 Shadow

Origin: Fairchild Aircraft Division (now Fairchild Industries), USA.
Type: C-119 tactical transport; AC-119 multi-sensor armed interdiction.
Engines: In most variants two 3,350hp Wright R-3350-85WA or 3,700hp R-3350-89B Turbo-Compound 18-cylinder two-row radials (older versions, two 3,250hp Pratt & Whitney R-4360-20WA Wasp Major 28-cylinder four-row radials); (AC-119K) two additional underwing booster pods each containing 2,850lb (1293kg) thrust General Electric J85-17 turbojet; (Indian AF C-119) one dorsal booster pod containing HAL Orpheus of 4,700lb, 2132kg thrust, or Westinghouse J34 of 3,400lb, 1542kg thrust.
Dimensions: Span 109ft 3in (34·3m); length 86ft 6in (26·36m); height 26ft 6in (8·07m).
Weights: Empty (C-119B) 37,691lb (15,981kg); (C-119K) 44,747lb (20,300kg); (AC-119K) 60,955lb (27,649kg); maximum loaded (C-119B) 74,000lb (33,600kg); (C-119K) 77,000lb (34,925kg); (AC-119K) 80,400lb (36,468kg).
Performance: Maximum speed (all versions) 243–250mph (391–402km/h); initial climb (all) 1,100–1,300ft (335–396m)/min; service ceiling, typically 24,000ft (7315m); range with maximum payload 990–1,900 miles (1595–3060km).
Armament: Transport versions, none; (AC-119K) two 20mm and four 7·62mm multi-barrel rapid-fire guns firing laterally, with over 100,000 rounds total ammunition. For sensors, see text.
History: First flight (XC-82) 10 September 1944; (C-119A) November 1947; service delivery (C-119B) December 1949; (AC-119) 1967.
Users: Brazil (not operational), Ethiopia, India, Italy, Kampuchea, Taiwan, USA (AF/Navy, not operational), Vietnam. (Civil conversions) many countries.

Development: Fairchild began the design of a purpose-built cargo and troop transport — the first specialised transport ever designed for the Army Air Corps — in 1941. This flew in 1944 as the XC-82 Packet and 220 C-82s were delivered by 1948. The C-119 introduced a new nose, with the flight deck ahead of the cargo compartment instead of on top. Fuselage width was increased, engine power was greatly increased and the wings were strengthened for operation at higher weights. By 1955, when production of new aircraft ceased, 946 C-119s had been delivered to US forces, plus 141 supplied under the Mutual Defense Assistance Program to Italy, Belgium and India. Subsequently many ex-USAF C-119s were sold to Nationalist China, Brazil, Ethiopia and other countries, while those in India were fitted

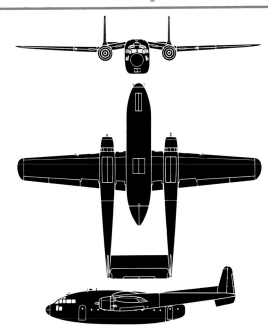

Above: Three-view of C-119G Flying Boxcar.

with jet pods to improve the near-zero engine-out rate of climb from hot-and-high airstrips. Some "dollar-19s" were converted to the C-119J configuration with a rear beaver-tail openable in flight, instead of a hinged rear end that could be opened only on the ground. The AC-119G and jet-boosted AC-119K are extremely heavily armed interdiction aircraft formerly used by night in Southeast Asia. Fitted with batteries of Gatling guns, 26 AC-119Gs were delivered with night illumination systems, image intensifiers, computer fire-control, various gunsights, flare launchers, crew armour and other gear. The 26 AC-119Ks, with underwing jets, added 20mm Gatlings, forward looking infra-red (FLIR), forward and side-looking radar (SLAR) and precision nav/com equipment.

Below: In the twilight of its long career the C-119 suddenly blossomed out as a combat aircraft. The heavily armed, jet-boosted AC-119K Shadow carried enough night sensors to kill pinpoint targets even when they could not be seen visually.

Fairchild C-123 Provider

C-123 B, J, K and variants

Origin: Supported by Fairchild Industries, Germantown, Maryland, USA.
Type: Tactical assault transport, with variants.
Engines: Two 2,500hp Pratt & Whitney R-2800-99W 18-cylinder radial piston engines; (C-123J) plus two 1,000lb (454kg) thrust Fairchild J44-3 turbojets on wing tips; (C-123K) plus two 2,850lb (1293kg) thrust General Electric J85-17 turbojets in underwing pods.
Dimensions: Span 110ft (33·53m); length 76ft 3in (23·92m); height 34ft 1in (10·63m).
Weights: Empty (K) 35,366lb (16,042kg); maximum useful load 15,000lb (6804kg); maximum loaded 60,000lb (27,215kg).
Performance: (K) maximum speed with jets 228mph (367km/h); maximum cruising speed 173mph (278km/h); range with maximum useful load 1,035 miles (1666km).
Armament: Various, see text.
History: First flight (XC-123) 14 October 1949; (Fairchild C-123B) 1 September 1954; (first C-123K conversion) 27 May 1966.
Users: Kampuchea, Saudi Arabia, South Korea, Taiwan, Thailand, United States (Air Force, Air National Guard), Venezuela, Vietnam.

Development: Chase Aircraft flew a USAF cargo glider, the XCG-20, from which was derived the powered XC-123 Avitruc. Tested by the USAF, this proved to be a good assault transport with short field performance and robust structure. Five pre-production machines were ordered, plus 300 to be built by Kaiser-Frazer at the giant Willow Run factory. K-F failed to produce, and the contract was taken over by Fairchild, which refined the C-123B Provider and delivered 302 by 1958. The original designer, Stroukoff, formed his own firm but failed to sell interesting C-123 developments with

Above: Three-view of Fairchild C-123K with jets and drop tanks.

blown flaps and "pantobase" landing gear for land, snow, ice or water. Of the original B-models six went to Saudi Arabia, 18 to Venezuela and an unspecified number to South Vietnam and Thailand. The C-123 was intensively used in SE Asia, with K jet pods; many were armed as AC-123K gunships with multiple cannon and night sensors. The UC-123B defoliated trees, and the NC-123K is a late transport model. The J served with the Alaska ANG until 1976.

Below: Hectic scene in SE Asia in 1970 as Vietnamese troops, civilians and cargo arrive by C-123B (note unpainted B model overhead). Most Providers later had tip or underwing jet pods.

Fokker-VFW F27

F27M Series 400, 500, 600 and Maritime

Origin: Fokker-VFW BV, Schiphol, Netherlands.
Type: Transport, photographic/survey, ambulance, coastal patrol and offshore reconnaissance.
Engines: Two 2,280ehp (2,140shp) Rolls-Royce Dart 532-7R single-shaft turboprops.
Dimensions: Span 95ft 2in (29·0m); length 77ft 3½in (23·56m) (500M 82ft 2½in, 25·06m); height 27ft 11in (8·5m) (500M, Maritime 28ft 7¼in, 8·71m).
Weights: Empty (400M) 23,360lb (10,596kg), (500M, Maritime) about 26,000lb (11,793kg); maximum useful load (typical) 13,550lb (6145kg); maximum loaded (all) 45,000lb (20,410kg).
Performance: Normal cruising speed at 20,000ft (6100m) at 38,000lb (17,237kg) 298mph (480km/h); initial climb at 40,000lb (18,144kg) 1,620ft (494m)/min; field length (sea level, 40,000lb) 2,310ft (704m); range with military reserves, all-cargo, standard fuel 1,375 miles (2213km); maximum endurance, with pylon tanks at 20,000ft (6100m) 12hr 47min.
Armament: Provision on Maritime, see text.
History: First flight (F27) 24 November 1955; (400M) 24 April 1965; (Maritime) 25 March 1976.
Users: (Military F27) Algeria, Argentina, Ghana, Iceland, Indonesia, Iran, Ivory Coast, Netherlands, Nigeria, Pakistan, Peru, Philippines, Uruguay.

Development: Originally a civil passenger and passenger/freight transport, the F27 is today widely used as a multi-role military transport, the main versions for air forces being the Mk 400M (formerly known as the Troopship), 500M with lengthened fuselage, and the Maritime patrol aircraft. Basic aircraft accommodate 45 paratroops (50 in the 500M) or 24 stretchers (30 in the 500M) plus six or seven attendants. All military machines have a large forward freight door, and paratroop rear doors on each side. The 400M Cartographic has a comprehensive camera/mapping installation and inertial navigation. Iranian re-orders have a double underwing Marquardt target-towing installation with 25,000ft (7620m) of wire. The Maritime was intended primarily for 200 n.m. fishery patrol, but is very fully equipped for military ocean surveillance. Litton provide both the LTN-72 inertial system and the APS-503F radar. Armament schemes are being developed as options.

Above: The tactical centre in the prototype Maritime, showing the neat sensor displays and navigational equipment.

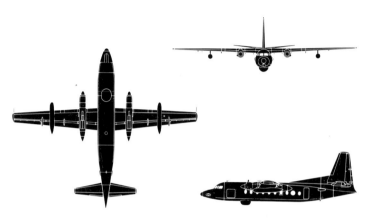

Above: Three-view of Fokker-VFW F27 Maritime with tanks.

Below: An attractive paint scheme does not belie the para-military nature of the F27 Maritime. By 1977 orders had been placed by the Icelandic Coast Guard and Peruvian Navy.

Handley Page Victor

H.P.80 Victor 1, 1A and 2

Origin: Handley Page Ltd, UK; K.2, rebuilt by Hawker Siddeley (now British Aerospace).
Type: (B.1, 1A and 2) five-seat strategic bomber; (K.1A and 2) four-seat air-refuelling tanker; (SR.2) strategic reconnaissance.
Engines: (1, 1A) four 11,000lb (4990kg) thrust Rolls-Royce (previously Armstrong Siddeley and then Bristol Siddeley) Sapphire 202 single-shaft turbojets; (2) four 17,500lb (7938kg) thrust Rolls-Royce Conway 103 two-shaft turbofans; (B.2R, SR.2, K.2) 20,600lb (9344kg) thrust Conway 201.
Dimensions: Span (1) 110ft (33·53m); (2) 120ft (36·58m); length 114ft 11in (35·05m); height (1) 28ft 1½in (8·59m); (2) 30ft 1½in (9·2m).
Weights: Empty (1) 79,000lb (35,834kg); (2) 91,000lb (41,277kg); loaded (1) 180,000lb (81,650kg); (2) 233,000lb (101,150kg).
Performance: Maximum speed (both) about 640 mph (1030km/h, Mach 0·92) above 36,000ft; service ceiling (1) 55,000ft (16,764m); (2) 60,000ft (18,290m); range (1) 2,700 miles (4345km); (2) 4,600 miles (7400km).
Armament: No defensive armament except ECM; internal weapon bay for various nuclear or conventional weapons, including 35 1,000lb (454kg) bombs; (B.2 and 2R) provision for launching one Blue Steel Mk 1 air-to-surface missile carried semi-externally beneath fuselage; (K.2) none.
History: First flight (1) 24 December 1952; (production B.1) 1 February 1956; (2) 20 February 1959; (K.1A conversion) 28 April 1965; (K.2 conversion) 1 March 1972; final delivery of new aircraft 2 May 1963.
User: UK.

Development: Designed to Specification B.35/46, the same as the Vulcan, the Handley Page H.P.80 was expected to fly so fast and high as to be virtually immune to interception. To achieve the highest cruising Mach number the wing was designed to what was called a "crescent" shape, with a sharply swept but thick inner section housing the buried engines and progressively less swept but thinner outer panels, the structure being largely of light-alloy double-skin sandwich with corrugated or honeycomb filling. As a technical achievement the aircraft was superb. Named Victor it was the third and last of the V-bombers to go into service with RAF Bomber Command in 1955-58, but it took so long to develop that, by that time it

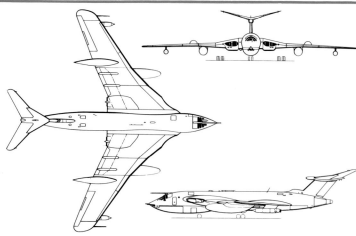

Above: Three-view of Handley Page (Hawker Siddeley) Victor K.2.

entered service, it could be intercepted by fighters or shot down by missiles and the number ordered was so small the cost was high. To offer better protection the B.1 was brought up to B.1A standard with much enhanced ECM and survivors of the 50 built were in 1965-67 converted as K.1A tankers. The much more powerful B.2, with completely redesigned airframe and systems, offered a great increase in all-round performance, but at height was no less vulnerable in penetrating hostile airspace and by 1964 was consigned to the low-level role, carrying the big Blue Steel missile. Several of the 30 built were converted as SR.2 strategic reconnaissance photographic aircraft and in 1973-75 the final 20 were converted as three-point K.2 tankers. This work was done by Hawker Siddeley at Woodford, the old Handley Page firm having gone into liquidation in 1970. Delivery of the K.2 began in May 1974, and by 1977 the last K.1 was withdrawn.

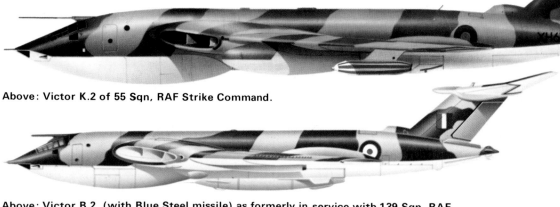

Above: Victor K.2 of 55 Sqn, RAF Strike Command.

Above: Victor B.2 (with Blue Steel missile) as formerly in service with 139 Sqn, RAF.

Below: One of the early Victor K.1A tankers, in service with 57 Sqn, pipes fuel to a thirsty Buccaneer. Though fitted with three hose-reels (some have only two) the K.1A is gradually being phased out as the much superior K.2 Victor comes into service.

Hawker Siddeley Andover, 748 and Coastguarder

HS.748, Andover, Coastguarder

Origin: Hawker Siddeley Aviation, Manchester, UK (also assembled by Hindustan Aeronautics, India).

Type: Multi-role transport; Coastguarder, maritime patrol.

Engines: Two 2,280ehp (2,140shp) Rolls-Royce Dart 534-2 or 535-2 single-shaft turboprops; (Andover C.1, two 3,245ehp Dart 201).

Dimensions: Span 98ft 6in (30·02m) (Andover C.1, 98ft 3in); length 67ft 0in (20·42m) (Andover C.1, 78ft 0in, 23·77m); height 24ft 10in (7·57m) (Andover C.1, 30ft 1in).

Weights: Empty (passenger) 27,000lb (12,247kg), (military freight) 25,516lb (11,574kg), (Coastguarder) about 27,000lb; maximum loaded 46,500lb (21,092kg) (Andover C.1, 50,000lb, 22,680kg; military overload limit 51,000lb, 23,133kg).

Performance: Typical cruise at 38,000lb, 281mph (452km/h); initial climb at 38,000lb, 1,420ft (433m)/min; typical military field length at normal gross weight 3,200ft (1000m); range with 20 per cent reserves at normal weight, 1,105 miles (1778km) with max load, 1,646 miles (2649km) with max fuel; radius of action at normal weight with airdrop of 12 containers of 750lb (340kg) 720 miles (1158km); (Coastguarder has almost doubled range and endurance).

Armament: Normally none, but options available on Coastguarder.

History: First flight 24 June 1960; (production Andover C.1) 9 July 1965; (Coastguarder) early 1977.

Users: (Military only) Australia (AF, Navy), Belgium, Brazil, Brunei, Colombia, Ecuador, Egypt, India, S Korea, Malaysia, Nepal, New Zealand, Thailand, UK (RAF, Royal Flight), Zambia, plus undisclosed AF.

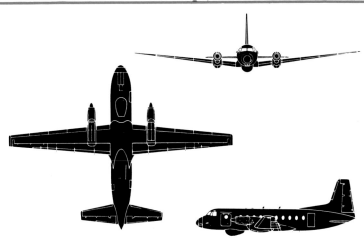

Above: Three-view of the HS.748 Coastguarder.

Development: Of total sales approaching 350, almost half of all versions of this versatile STOL transport have been military. The Andover C.1 was a redesigned aircraft for the RAF, with different wing, more powerful engines driving larger propellers, a different fuselage with rear loading/dropping door, different tail and "kneeling" landing gear. These 31 machines are being sold and 10 bought by the RNZAF may later be equipped for maritime patrol. The latter is the primary duty of the Coastguarder, which has extra fuel, MAREC search radar, Decca Doppler/TANS computer and Omega VLF navigation, chute for flares and rescue dinghies sufficient for an entire 747-load of passengers. All military 748s have the option of a large freight door, strong floor and fittings for many specialized roles.

Left: The HS.748 is one of the mainstays of the Brazilian Air Force. The last six delivered have large freight doors of the kind pictured below.

Below: This Belgian 748 is fitted with a large rear freight door. The Andover, which had more powerful engines and a rear ramp/door for vehicles, was not exported.

IAI-201 Arava

IAI-201 Arava

Origin: Israel Aircraft Industries, Lod, Israel.
Type: Light STOL transport and utility aircraft.
Engines: Two 750shp Pratt & Whitney Canada PT6A-34 turboprops.
Dimensions: Span 68ft 9in (20·96m); length 42ft 9in (13·03m); height 17ft 1in (5·21m).
Weights: Empty (fully equipped, no armament) 8,816lb (3999kg); maximum loaded 15,000lb (6804kg).
Performance: (At max weight) maximum speed 203mph (326km/h) at 10,000ft (3048m); economical cruise 198mph (319km/h); initial climb 1,290ft (393m)/min; service ceiling 25,000ft (7620m); take-off or landing over 50ft (15m) about 1,500ft (465m); range with max fuel (45min reserve) 812 miles (1306km).
Armament: Customer option of 0·5in Browning machine-gun pack on each side of fuselage firing ahead, with Librascope pilot sight, rear manually aimed machine gun, and pylons on lower forward fuselage for rocket pods (seven 68mm) or similar stores.
History: First flight (civil) 27 November 1969, (military 201) 7 March 1972, service delivery 1973.
Users: Bolivia, Ecuadorean Army, Guatemala, Israel, Honduras, Mexico, Nicaragua, Salvador.

Development: Originally produced as a civil prototype, the Arava has been sold chiefly as a multi-role military aircraft. An all-metal unpressurized

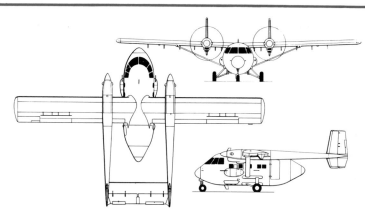

Above: Three-view of IAI-201 Arava (gun packs and stores pylons).

transport, it has a strong freight floor, three doors and a hinged rear fuselage which can be opened or removed on the ground. Maximum freight load is 5,184lb (2351kg) and 24 equipped troops can be carried, 17 paratroops and two dispatchers, or 12 stretcher casualties and two attendants. By 1977 deliveries had reached nearly 60, the majority for export.

Below: The first IAI-201 military Arava, which was command-eered by the Israeli Heyl Ha'Avir and operated under lease during the 1973 Yom Kippur war. Under-fuselage pipes are non-standard.

Ilyushin Il-76

Il-76

Origin: Bureau named for Ilyushin, Soviet Union.
Type: Heavy freight transport.
Engines: Four 26,455lb (12,000kg) thrust Soloviev D-30KP two-shaft turbofans.
Dimensions: Span 165ft 8in (50·5m); length 152ft 10½in (46·59m); height 48ft 5in (14·76m).
Weights: Empty, about 159,000lb (72,000kg); maximum loaded 346,125lb (157,000kg).
Performance: Maximum speed, about 560mph (900km/h); maximum cruising speed 528mph (850km/h); normal long-range cruising height 42,650ft (13,000m); range with maximum payload of 88,185lb (40,000kg) 3,100 miles (5000km).
Armament: Normally none.
History: First flight 25 March 1971; production deliveries 1973.
User: Soviet Union (V-TA).

Development: First seen in the West at the 1971 Paris Salon, the Il-76 created a most favourable impression. Though superficially seeming to be another Ilyushin copy of a Lockheed design, in this case the C-141, in fact the resemblance is coincidental. The design was prepared to meet a basic need in the Soviet Union for a really capable freighter which, while carrying large indivisible loads, with a high cruising speed and intercontinental range, could operate from relatively poor airstrips. The result is a very useful aircraft which, though initially being used by Aeroflot in the 1971-75 and 1976-80 plans for opening up Siberia, the far north and far east of the Soviet Union, is obviously a first-class strategic and tactical transport for military use. It has very powerful engines, all fitted with reversers, a high-lift wing for good STOL performance and a high-flotation landing gear with 20 wheels. The nose is typical of modern Soviet aircraft for "outback" operation, and closely resembles that of the An-22. The big fuselage, usefully larger in cross-section than that of the C-141, is fully pressurized and incorporates a powerful auxiliary power unit and freight handling systems. There seems no reason why the rear clamshell doors should not be opened in flight to permit heavy dropping. In 1977 deliveries appeared to have swung in favour of the military, and a special tanker version was reported to be under development to support the Tupolev "Backfire". NATO code-name of the Il-76 is "Candid".

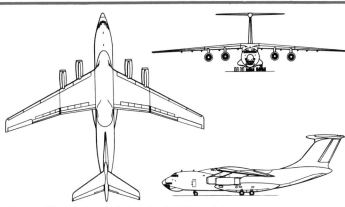

Above: Three-view of standard Il-76 freighter.

Above: This US Navy photograph shows several of the Il-76's good qualities, among them large body cross-section, STOL wing and "high flotation" multi-wheel landing gear. These are assets for military use.

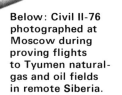

Below: Civil Il-76 photographed at Moscow during proving flights to Tyumen natural-gas and oil fields in remote Siberia.

Above: Il-76 as used by V-TA and AV-MF; tanker may be similar.

Lockheed C-130 Hercules

C-130 variants, see text (data for C-130H)

Origin: Lockheed-Georgia Co, USA.

Type: Basic aircraft, multi-role transport; for variants see text.

Engines: Four Allison T56 single-shaft turboprops; (C-130A) 3,750ehp T56-1A; (B and E families) 4,050ehp T56-7; (F and H families) 4,910ehp T56-15 or -16 flat-rated at 4,508ehp.

Dimensions: Span 132ft 7in (40.41m); length 97ft 9in (29.78m); (HC-130H and AC-130H and certain others are longer, owing to projecting devices); height 38ft 3in (11.66m).

Weights: Empty 65,621lb (34,300kg); maximum loaded 175,000lb (79,380kg) (YC-130, 108,000lb).

Performance: Maximum speed 384mph (618km/h); initial climb 1,900ft (579m)/min; service ceiling 33,000ft (10,060m); range (maximum payload) 2,487 miles (4,002km); (maximum fuel) 5,135 miles (8,264km).

Armament: Normally none; (AC-130H) one 105mm howitzer, one 40mm cannon, two 20mm cannon or T-171 "Gatlings", two 7.62mm "Gatling" Miniguns; optional grenade dispenser, rockets, missiles, bombs and various night or day sensors and target designators.

History: First flight (YC-130) 23 August 1954; (production C-130A)

7 April 1955; service delivery December 1956.

Users: Abu Dhabi, Argentina, Australia, Belgium, Brazil, Canada, Chile, Colombia, Denmark, Egypt, Gabon, Greece, Indonesia, Iran, Iraq, Israel, Italy, Jordan, Kuwait, Libya, Malaysia, Morocco, New Zealand, Nigeria, Norway, Pakistan, Peru, Philippines, Saudi Arabia, Singapore, S. Africa, Spain, Sweden, Syria, Turkey, UK, USA (AF, Marines, Navy), Venezuela, Vietnam, Zaïre.

Development: Though actually conventional and logical and a synthesis of known techniques, the YC-130 appeared radical and bold in 1954. Among its features were a pressurized fuselage with full-section rear doors which could be opened in flight, very neat turboprop engines and rough-field landing gear retracting into bulges outside the pressure hull. Lockheed-

continued on page 172▶

Above: AC-130H night gunship of interdiction squadrons in SE Asia, 1970–75.

1 Radome
2 Sperry AN/APN-59 radar
3 External interphone connection
4 Nose-gear forward door
5 Twin nosewheels
6 Accumulators (port and starboard)
7 Nose landing gear shock strut
8 External electrical power receptacles
9 Battery compartment
10 Pilot s side console
11 Portable oxygen cylinder
12 Pilot's seat
13 Control column
14 Main instrument console
15 Windshields
16 Co-pilot's seat
17 Systems engineer's seat
18 Navigator's seat
19 Navigator's desk
20 Crew bunks (upper and lower)
21 Forward emergency escape hatch
22 Control runs in bulkhead
23 Fire-extinguisher
24 Crew closet
25 Galley
26 Access steps to flight deck
27 Crew entry well
28 Crew entry door
29 Lower longeron
30 Window ports
31 Cargo floor panels
32 Cargo floor support frames
33 Troop seats (stowed)
34 Overhead emergency equipment stowage
35 Fuselage frames
36 Booster hydraulic system reservoir and accumulator
37 Control runs
38 Starboard main landing gear access (sealed)
39 Wingroot frame strengthener
40 Fuselage/centre section join
41 Inboard leading-edge structure
42 Fuel valve inspection access
43 Nacelle panels
44 Starboard auxiliary tanks
45 Tank pylon
46 Fuel filler points
47 Fuel tanks
48 Dry bay
49 Allison T56-A-15 turbo-prop
50 Reduction gear
51 Four-blade reversible pitch Hamilton Standard

propeller
52 Engine starter
53 Engine oil tank
54 Limit of wing walkway
55 Starboard navigation lights
56 Starboard aileron
57 Aileron tab
58 Outer wing flap
59 Centre-section flap
60 Centre-section wing box beam structure
61 Flap drive control
62 Internal corrugation
64 Port main landing gear bay
65 Hydraulic actuator motor
66 Fire-extinguisher bottles
67 Main landing gear shock struts
68 Retraction mechanism
69 Air turbine motor (driven by GTC, item 71, to supply electric and hydraulic power)
70 Utility hydraulic system reservoir and accumulator
71 Gas turbine compressor (air supply for engine starting, ground conditioning and to drive ATM, item 69)
72 Main gear fairing
73 Landing light in outer door forward section
74 Twin tandem mainwheels
75 Main landing gear outer door
76 Inner door section
77 Air deflector door
78 Tank pylon
79 Port auxiliary tank
80 Spinner
81 Chin intake
82 Nacelle structure
83 Engine bearer
84 Exhaust outlet
85 Outboard leading-edge structure
86 Port navigation lights
87 Aileron control bell crank
88 Aileron structure
89 Aileron tab
90 Outer wing box beam structure
91 Flap structure
92 Idler bell crank
93 Auxiliary ground-loading ramp
94 Ramp actuating cylinder
95 Cargo ramp (lowered)
96 Port paratroop door
97 Cargo ramp floor panels
98 Ramp hinge line
99 Ramp actuating mechanism
100 Miscellaneous stores bin
101 Starboard paratroop door

102 Centre emergency escape hatch
103 Wing-root fairing
104 Fuselage frames
105 Toilet
106 Urinal
107 Ramp and auxiliary hydraulic reservoir
108 Troop water bottles
109 Ramp actuator housing
110 Auxiliary hydraulic system reservoir

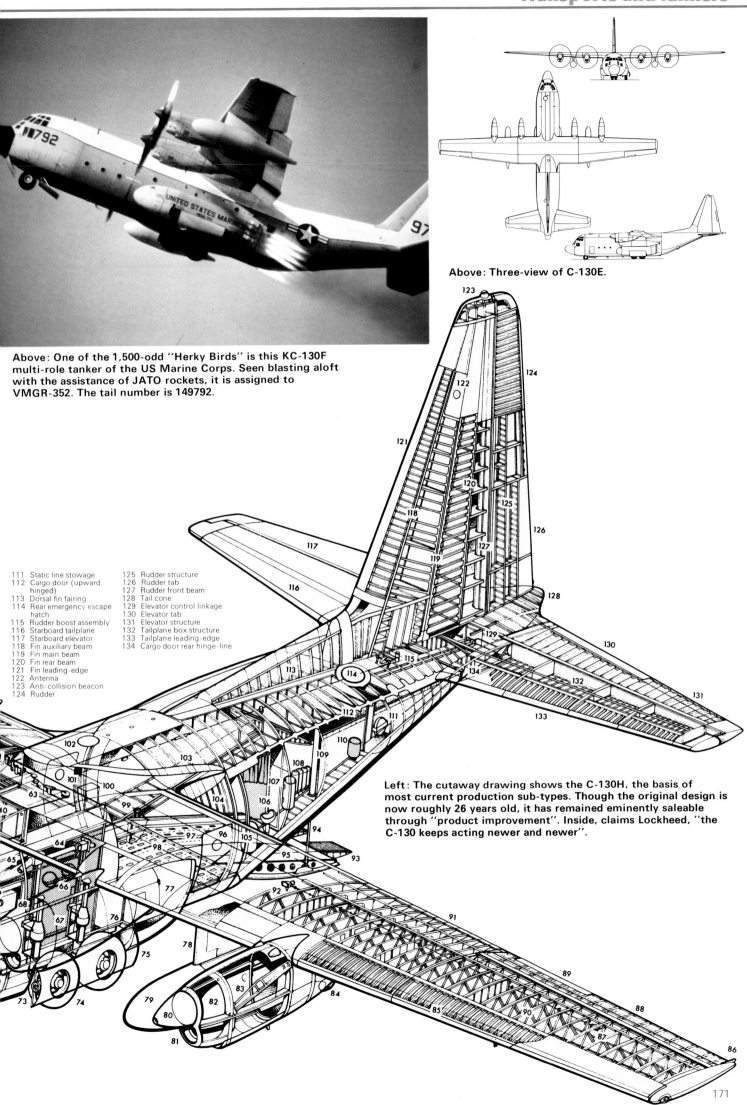

Above: One of the 1,500-odd "Herky Birds" is this KC-130F multi-role tanker of the US Marine Corps. Seen blasting aloft with the assistance of JATO rockets, it is assigned to VMGR-352. The tail number is 149792.

Above: Three-view of C-130E.

111 Static line stowage
112 Cargo door (upward hinged)
113 Dorsal fin fairing
114 Rear emergency escape hatch
115 Rudder boost assembly
116 Starboard tailplane
117 Starboard elevator
118 Fin auxiliary beam
119 Fin main beam
120 Fin rear beam
121 Fin leading-edge
122 Antenna
123 Anti-collision beacon
124 Rudder

125 Rudder structure
126 Rudder tab
127 Rudder front beam
128 Tail cone
129 Elevator control linkage
130 Elevator tab
131 Elevator structure
132 Tailplane box structure
133 Tailplane leading-edge
134 Cargo door rear hinge-line

Left: The cutaway drawing shows the C-130H, the basis of most current production sub-types. Though the original design is now roughly 26 years old, it has remained eminently saleable through "product improvement". Inside, claims Lockheed, "the C-130 keeps acting newer and newer".

171

►Georgia delivered 461 A and more powerful B models, following in 1962 with 503 heavier E series with more internal fuel. The H introduced more powerful engines and gave rise to numerous other sub-types. Special role versions related to the E or H include DC RPV-directors, EC electronics, communications and countermeasures, HC search/rescue, helicopter fueller and spacecraft retrieval, KC assault transport and probe/drogue tanker, LC wheel/ski and WC weather (the RAF uses the W.2 meteorological conversion of the British C-130K). One colour profile shows the AC-130H gunship, with formidable armament for night interdiction and equipped with forward-looking infra-red (FLIR), low-light-level TV (LLLTV), laser target designator and other fire control devices. Known and respected all over the world as the "Herky bird", the C-130 has remained in production for more than 23 years and no end to new orders can yet be seen. Constant product-improvement has steadily improved payload, range, fatigue life and reliability and in the mid-1970s the C-130 remained the standard transport and special-equipment platform for a growing list of users. Though the later fan-engined C-141 and C-5A were completed programmes, demand for the C-130 has actually increased as more and more military and civil customers find it meets their needs. Total sales by 1977 were close to 1,600 (including civil L 100 models) and the list of customer air forces speaks for itself. The C-130, in a vast range of sub-types, will have no difficulty meeting tactical airlift needs of most nations (except the United States) until the winner of the AMST competition becomes available — if it survives cutbacks and inflation — in the 1979-80 period.

Above: Colourful and technically interesting this DC-130E is carrying on its left outer pylon a Teledyne Ryan BQM-34B (supersonic Firebee RPV) which in turn is carrying an AGM-65A Maverick TV-guided missile (white). This three-stage delivery system for air/surface weapons could become operational.

Left: XV291, a Hercules C.1 (C-130K) of RAF Strike Command, lets go a series of supply bundles during Exercise Khama Cascade to relieve famine in Nepal in March 1973. Dropping such packs at safe minimum-control speed is a fine art, especially in such "hot and high" environments.

Left: The C-130B equips No 28 Sqn of the South African Air Force, at Waterkloof, together with the C-160Z Transall.

Left: This C-130H is one delivered to 721 Sqn of the Flyvevaabnet (Royal Danish Air Force) at Vaerlose in 1975. Three Hercules were bought to replace five C-54s and eight C-47s.

Left: This C-130H is one of eight purchased by the Elliniki Aeroporia (Hellenic Air Force) to modernise the transport force of the Greek Air Materiel Command. They are part of the equipment of 355/356 Sqns at Eleusis.

Left: A Hercules C.1 (C-130K) of the RAF's Hercules Wing based at Lyneham, Wiltshire. The wing at present comprises 24, 30, 47 and 70 Sqns, plus 242 OCU, flying 45 aircraft.

Lockheed C-5A Galaxy

C-5A

Origin: Lockheed-Georgia Co, USA.
Type: Strategic transport.
Engines: Four 41,000lb (18,642kg) thrust General Electric TF39-1 two-shaft turbofans.
Dimensions: Span 222ft 8½in (67·88m); length 247ft 10in (75·54m); height 65ft 1½in (19·85m).
Weights: Empty 325,244lb (147,528kg); loaded 769,000lb (348,810kg).
Performance: Maximum speed 571mph (919km/h); initial climb 1,800ft (549m)/min; service ceiling at 615,000lb, 34,000ft (10,360m); range with maximum (220,967lb, 100,228kg) payload 3,749 miles (6033km); ferry range 7,991 miles (12,860km).
Armament: None.
History: First flight 30 June 1968; service delivery 17 December 1969; final delivery May 1973.
User: USA (Air Force, MAC).

Development: On some counts the C-5A is the world's largest aircraft, though it is surpassed in power and weight by late models of B.747. Compared with the civil 747 it has less sweep and is considerably slower, because part of the Military Airlift Command requirement was that it should lift very heavy loads out of rough short airstrips. To this end it has a "high flotation" landing gear with 28 wheels capable of operating at maximum weight from unpaved surfaces. During development extremely difficult aerodynamic and structural problems had to be solved and there were severe difficulties concerned with fatigue and structure weight. As a result of these problems, combined with inflation, the price escalated and eventually the production had to be cut to a total of 81, equipping four squadrons. The original requirement of carrying 125,000lb for 8,000 miles was not met, but in most respects the final production C-5A is substantially above prediction and an outstanding logistic vehicle which has set an impressive record of capability and reliability. The unobstructed interior has a section 19ft wide and 13ft 6in high, not including the upper deck. Freight is normally carried in containers or on 36 standard Type 463L pallets; two M-60 battle tanks can be driven on board and there is room for three packaged CH-47 Chinook heavy helicopters. Equipment includes a refuelling boom receptacle in the roof and a Norden multi-mode radar in the nose. In 1977 the trouble with wing fatigue was finally to be solved by a complete rebuild of the wing centre and inner sections. It will cost about $1,000 million to rebuild the 70 aircraft in the active inventory (seven others will not be rebuilt) in the years 1980-84.

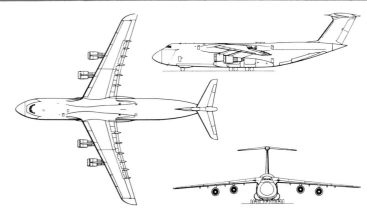

Above: Three-view of C-5A Galaxy as delivered to MAC.

Above: One of the basic requirements of the C-5A was that it should use unpaved airfields, necessitating 28 landing wheels.
Below: Le Bourget's fire engine and ambulance look puny as a USAF Military Airlift Command C-5A blots out the sky during a Paris international air show. Not infrequently a single Galaxy has carried the entire US participation to major overseas events.

Lockheed C-141 StarLifter

C-141A and B

Origin: Lockheed-Georgia Co. USA.
Type: Strategic transport.
Engines: Four 21,000lb (9525kg) thrust Pratt & Whitney TF33-7 two-shaft turbofans.
Dimensions: Span 159ft 11in (48·74m); length 145ft (44·2m); (B) 168ft 4in (51·3m); height 39ft 3in (11·96m).
Weights: Empty 133,773lb (60,678kg); loaded 316,600lb (143,600kg).
Performance: Maximum speed 571mph (919km/h); initial climb 3,100ft (945m)/min; service ceiling 41,600ft (12,680m); range with maximum (70,847lb, 32,136kg) payload 4,080 miles (6565km).
Armament: None.
History: First flight 17 December 1963; service delivery October 1964; final delivery July 1968.
User: USA (Air Force, MAC).

Development: Designed to meet a requirement of USAF Military Airlift Command, the StarLifter has since been the most common of MAC's transports and has a very useful combination of range and payload. Compared with civil jet transports in the same weight category it has a less-swept wing and thus lower cruising speed (typically 495mph, 797km/h), but can lift heavier loads out of shorter airstrips. The body cross-section is the same 10ft by 9ft as the C-130, and this has proved the only real shortcoming in prohibiting carriage of many bulky items (though it is said the C-141 can carry "90 per cent of all air-portable items in the Army or Air Force"). The largest item normally carried is the packaged Minuteman ICBM, for which purpose several StarLifters have had the cargo floor slightly reinforced to bear the box skids of this 86,207lb load. Alternative loads are 154 troops, 123 paratroops or 80 stretchers (litters) and 16 attendants. A C-141 holds the world record for air-dropping, with a load of 70,195lb. Total production was 285 and these aircraft equip 14 MAC squadrons. During the Vietnam war they bore the main burden of airlifting supplies westwards and casualties eastwards. All are fitted with an all-weather landing system. The user has bitterly regretted not specifying a fatter fuselage, but is funding a major rebuild programme which is adding two "plugs" to extend the fuselage 23ft 4in (7·1m) whilst adding a flight refuelling receptacle and a new wing/body fairing to reduce drag. The first rebuild was flown in March 1977; the FY78 budget includes 70 rebuilds, and eventually 274 aircraft (all in the combat inventory) may be rebuilt as C-141Bs at a cost exceeding $700 million.

Above: One of the ubiquitous M-113 armoured vehicles emerges from a MAC C-141A. Three can be carried.

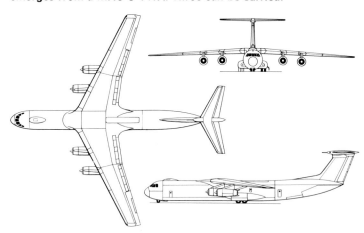

Above: Three-view of YC-141B showing 23ft 4in greater length.

Below: The 274 survivors of the original force of 284 StarLifters have flown several million hours in MAC service all over the world. Kadena AFB, Japan, is a frequent port of call.

Kawasaki C-1A

C-1

Origin: Kawasaki Heavy Industries, Gifu, Japan.
Type: Medium-range transport.
Engines: Two Mitsubishi (Pratt & Whitney licence) JT8D-9 two-shaft turbofans each rated at 14,500lb (6575kg).
Dimensions: Span 100ft 4¾in (30·6m); length 95ft 1⅜in (29·0m); height 32ft 9¼in (9·99m).
Weights: Empty 51,410lb (23,320kg); maximum payload 17,416lb (7900kg); maximum loaded 85,320lb (38,700kg).
Performance: Maximum speed at optimum height at 78,150lb (35,450kg) 501mph (806km/h); economical cruise at same weight at greater height of 35,000ft (10,670m) 408mph (657km/h); initial climb at max weight 3,500ft (1065m)/min; service ceiling 38,000ft (11,580m); typical max-weight take-off and landing over 50ft (15m) 3,000ft (914m); range with max payload 807 miles (1300km).
History: First flight 12 November 1970; handover to Japan Defence Agency for evaluation 24 February 1971; first delivery of production aircraft December 1974.
User: Japan Air Self-Defence Force.

A production C-1A displays its strange angularities above a Japanese cloudscape. Though a competently handled exercise, the short range and small payload of the C-1 limit its value.

Development: Designed from 1966 as a replacement for the C-46 Commando, the C-1 is almost the size of a Transall but has less than half the payload and range. Though the JT8D was an available and reliable engine it is fundamentally not as well suited to STOL military transport propulsion as a turboprop or high by-pass ratio fan engine. Designed by Nihon (NAMC) the C-1 is made by a consortium of Japanese companies, with Kawasaki handling assembly and test. Typical loads include 60 troops, 45 paratroops, or 36 stretcher casualties plus attendants. The wing has quad-slotted flaps, slats, spoilers and small manual ailerons, and the engines have reversers. By 1977 about 20 had been delivered of 24 on order, and further batches were planned.

Below: The modest size of the C-1A can be judged by comparing the first prototype with two Mitsubishi-assembled F-4EJ Phantom fighters. All have Air Proving Wing tail badge.

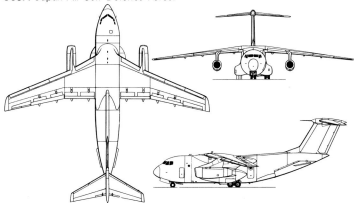

Above: Three-view of Kawasaki C-1A (landing gear extended).

McDonnell Douglas
C-9 Nightingale/Skytrain II

C-9A Nightingale, VC-9C and C-9B Skytrain II

Origin: Douglas Aircraft Company, Long Beach, USA.
Type: (C-9A) aeromedical airlift transport; (VC-9C) special executive transport; (C-9B) passenger/cargo transport.
Engines: Two 14,500lb (6575kg) Pratt & Whitney JT8D-9 two-shaft turbofans.
Dimensions: Span 93ft 5in (28·47m); length 119ft 3½in (36·37m); height overall 27ft 6in (8·38m).
Weights: Empty (VC) about 57,190lb (25,940kg), (C-9A, C-9B in passenger configuration) about 65,283lb (29,612kg); maximum loaded (C-9A, VC-9C) 121,000lb (54,884kg), (C-9B) 110,000lb (49,900kg).
Performance: Maximum cruise 564mph (907km/h); typical long-range cruise 510mph (821km/h); range with full payload and reserves (C-9A, VC) about 1,923 miles (3095km), (C-9B with 10,000lb, 4535kg) 2,923 miles (4704km).
History: First flight (DC-9) 25 February 1965; service delivery (C-9A) 10 August 1968, (C-9B) 8 May 1973, (VC) 1975.
User: United States (AF, Navy, Marine Corps).

Development: In addition to well over 800 civil examples, Douglas has delivered 38 military models. The C-9A Nightingale, of which 21 are serving with Aeromedical Wings of Military Airlift Command of the USAF, carries up to 40 stretcher (litter) patients and/or more than 40 ambulatory patients, with two nurses and three technicians. It has three entrances, two with stairways, and a controlled-atmosphere special-care compartment. The US Navy's order for Skytrain II transports was raised from five to eight and finally 14. These have special Omega and inertial navigation systems and seat 107, or 45 passengers with three freight pallets, and are the longest-ranged DC-9s ever built.

Above: Longest-ranged DC-9s in the world are the C-9B Skytrain IIs of the US Navy. This one serves with VR-30 at NAS Alameda (note Golden Gate bridge) and can reach Hawaii.

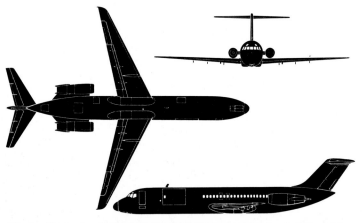

Above: Typical military DC-9-30 (C-9B has windows full length).

Above: A red-crossed C-9A Nightingale of the USAF, Scott AFB.
Below: An immaculate C-9B Skytrain II of the US Marine Corps air transport force.

McDonnell Douglas C-133 Cargomaster

C-133A and 133B

Origin: Douglas Aircraft Co, Long Beach, USA.
Type: Heavy logistic freighter.
Engines: (C-133A) four 7,000ehp Pratt & Whitney T34-7 single-shaft axial turboprops; (C-133B) 7,500ehp T34-9W.
Dimensions: Span 179ft 8in (54·75m); length 157ft 6½in (48·02m); height 48ft 3in (14·7m).
Weights: Empty 120,263lb (54,550kg); maximum loaded 286,000lb (129,727kg).
Performance: Maximum speed 359mph (578km/h); initial climb 1,280ft (389m)/min; service ceiling at gross weight 29,950ft (9140m); range with 44,000lb (19,960kg) payload, 4,300 miles (6920km).
Armament: None.
History: First flight (first production C-133A) 23 April 1956; service delivery 29 August 1957; first flight of C-133B 31 October 1959.
User: USA (USAF MAC, ANG).

Development: Designed to meet a US Air Force requirement for a logistic transport capable of carrying indivisible bulky loads which could not easily be loaded into the C-124, the C-133 was a bold, clean design with four of the powerful single-shaft turboprops developed at Pratt & Whitney since 1944. These engines had powered C-97, R7V-2 (Navy Super Constellation) and YC-124B aircraft and were fully developed in time for the C-133. No prototype was ordered, a contract for 35 being signed in 1954. While these aircraft were being delivered, from the Long Beach plant, changes were made in the shape of the rear fuselage and freight door arrangement and the final three introduced clamshell rear doors. A further 15 more powerful aircraft were then ordered as the C-133B, delivery being com-

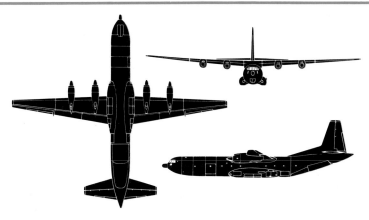

Above: Three-view of McDonnell Douglas C-133B (133A similar).

pleted in 1961. These B-models were specially adapted to the carriage of the Thor, Jupiter, Atlas, Titan and Minuteman ballistic missiles, which they delivered to operational sites throughout the United States and to Europe. An A-model set a world record by lifting a load of 117,900lb and approximately 96 per cent of all US military equipment could be carried by these capable machines. The C-133 will be retired from Military Airlift Command before 1980, after about 20 years of service.

Below: The Golden Gate bridge gets into the act yet again, in a fine portrait of a C-133B Cargomaster in the livery of the Military Air Transport Service (now Military Airlift Command). Three USAF MAC squadrons were equipped with C-133s, but this was reduced to two squadrons as the C-5A force increased, and the Cargomasters are expected to be phased out completely before 1980.

McDonnell Douglas YC-15

YC-15 AMST

Origin: McDonnell Douglas (Douglas Aircraft Co), Long Beach, USA.
Type: Advanced STOL transport.
Engines: Four Pratt & Whitney JT8D-17 two-shaft turbofans each rated at 16,000lb (7257kg); see text for other engines.
Dimensions: Span (original) 110ft 4in (33·63m), (new wing) 132ft 7in (40·41m); length 124ft 3in (37·87m); height 43ft 4in (13·21m).
Weights: Empty (equipped) 105,000lb (47,630kg); weight-limited payload (STOL) 27,000lb (12,247kg), (normal) 62,000lb (28,123kg); maximum loaded (normal) 216,680lb (98,284kg).
Performance: Maximum speed (broad height band) 500mph (805km/h); take-off or landing field length in STOL operation 2,000ft (610m); tactical radius with STOL payload/runway or normal payload/runway 461 miles (742km); ferry range 2,994 miles (4818km).
History: Contract award December 1972; first flight 26 August 1975 (No. 1), 5 December 1975 (No. 2); cancelled 2 February 1978.
User: Not at present funded for service.

Development: The AMST (Advanced Medium STOL Transport) programme was launched to determine how new technology could best be applied to the problem of replacing the C-130 as the standard American tactical transport. While Boeing investigated upper-surface blowing with the YC-14, Douglas engineers chose EBF (externally-blown flaps), in conjunction with well-proven transport engines. The four JT8Ds discharge through multi-lobe mixer nozzles directly under the wing lower surface, so that when the extremely powerful titanium double-slotted flaps are lowered the whole engine efflux is diverted downwards. With a much greater flow of entrained air this gives sufficient lift for STOL and for flight at speeds below 100mph (160km/h). The two prototypes completed their initial programme in 473hr in August 1976, including wet flight refuellings by boom, night operations from "austere" strips and other difficult tasks. The first now has a larger wing and a CFM56 turbofan in the No. 2 position; the second has a refanned JT8D-209 in the same position. Money is the sole reason for terminating the whole AMST programme, despite the long-term implications.

Above: First takeoff in February 1977 of the first YC-15 with the new wing of 22ft greater span, and CFM56 engine.

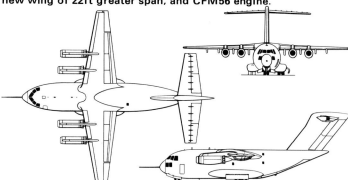

Above: Three-view of YC-15 with original wing and engines.

Below: Takeoff at the McDonnell Douglas plant at Long Beach of the second YC-15, which is camouflaged. After extensive trials this aircraft is now flying with a JT8D-209 engine.

Transall C-160

C-160D, C-160F and C-160Z

Origin: AG Transall, registered in Bremen.
Type: Tactical transport.
Engines: Two 6,100ehp Rolls-Royce Tyne 22 two-shaft turboprops.
Dimensions: Span 131ft 3in (40·00m); length 106ft 3½in (32·40m); height 40ft 6¾in (12·36m).
Weights: Empty (equipped) 63,400lb (28,758kg); maximum payload 35,274lb (16,000kg); maximum loaded 112,435lb (51,000kg).
Performance: Maximum speed at 16,000ft (4875m) 368mph (592km/h); economical cruise at 20,000ft (6096m) 282mph (454km/h); initial climb 1,300ft (396m)/min; service ceiling 25,500ft (7770m); typical take-off and landing distances over 50ft (15m) with no reverse-pitch on landing 2,900ft (884m); range with max payload and allowances 1,056 miles (1700km); ferry range 3,230 miles (5200km).
History: First flight 25 February 1963; service delivery April 1968; last delivery October 1972; start of delivery of additional batch 1979.
Users: France (C-160F and civil 160P for Night Mail Service), W Germany (160D), S Africa (160Z) and Turkey (160D).

Development: Transall is a name coined from Transporter Allianz, a consortium formed in 1959 by what are today Aérospatiale, MBB and VFW-Fokker. The objective was to produce a military transport to replace the Noratlas (which had been built by both countries) and also meet civil and export needs. Provision was made for jet-lift or jet-boosted STOL versions, but in the event all the 179 production aircraft were basic freighters and the only export sale was nine to S Africa. The engines were made by a consortium (Rolls-Royce, SNECMA, MTU and FN) as were the 18ft (5·5m) propellers (HSD, Rateau-Figeac). The airframe is pressurized and has electric wing and tail anti-icing (almost unique). The 110 bought by the Luftwaffe were more than was needed; 20 were later transferred to Turkey and others are in storage. Despite this in 1976 Aérospatiale secured a commitment from the French government to build a further 75, not to meet customer demand but to maintain employment. The Armée de l'Air has agreed to take 25 of the new batch, and 50 export sales are being sought at a price subsidized to make it competitive.

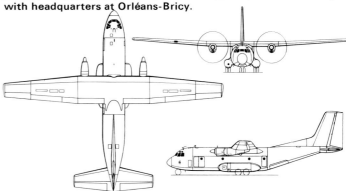

Above: Takeoff of a C-160F of the 61e Escadre, Armée de l'Air, with headquarters at Orléans-Bricy.

Above: Three-view of C-160 (all sub-types similar).

Below: A C-160D of the Luftwaffe, which has 76 Transalls in wings LTG 61 and 62 and 14 in an OCU at Wunstorf. Another 20 are in storage, yet Aérospatiale intends to build more.

Electronic warfare aircraft

The initials EW also stand for "early-warning", and the AEW (airborne early-warning) aircraft is the chief type discussed in this chapter. But it is a specialized type, too costly for all but a few nations—preferably a group acting in collaboration—even to consider acquiring. Far more important in terms of numbers and platforms are the EW (electronic warfare) systems that today must be carried not only by combat aircraft but also by army vehicles and naval

craft. This kind of EW involves detecting, evaluating, precisely locating and then neutralizing or penetrating hostile electronic defences. The EW inventory of a modern air force includes systems for noise and deception jamming against current and future threats, missile-fuze jamming, RF (radio frequency) warning and homing, real-time warning and reconnaissance of enemy RF emitters, physical and dispensed countermeasures (some of which are not ECM—electronic countermeasures—but IR heat sources to decoy infra-red homing missiles), and countermeasure control and display. One aircraft was specially designed for this kind of EW, and it is naturally included in this section. A few other special EW aircraft are modifications of existing combat types, notably the F-105G Wild Weasel Thunderchief, the EF-4E Phantom and the EF-111A. But the majority of EW systems in aerial warfare are carried by regular combat aircraft. Modern aircraft, such as the F-15 and B-1, carry a comprehensive "suite" of EW devices internally, betraying their presence only by small aerials flush with the

skin or projecting in the form of streamlined fairings pointing to the front or rear. Older aircraft, or aircraft which only occasionally have to penetrate hostile electronic defences, carry their EW systems packaged into self-contained standardized payloads, either in the form of a pod carried on an external weapon pylon or as a blister attached to the underside of the fuselage.

Whereas ECM is an active EW function intended to confuse or mislead the enemy's electronic defence systems, ESM (electronic surveillance measures) is a passive function. It normally comprises listening, as far as possible on every possible electronic defence frequency simultaneously, to detect all the enemy's signals. Clever airborne equipment instantly displays each new signal, giving its bearing, frequency and pulse-width, and probably also its pulse-repetition interval and signal level. This is a form of reconnaissance, and as well as being practised by many purpose-designed reconnaissance aircraft is also an important duty of maritime patrol aircraft as they probe potentially

Modern warfare is invariably based on an electronic environment. This Grumman E-2C Hawkeye of USS *Constellation* can protect the ship and its aircraft, double the number of kills made by the carrier's Tomcats and serve as a powerful data-link.

dangerous warships.

But the king of the military sky is an aircraft that carries no armament yet costs more than any other aircraft in history. The AWACS, today's pinnacle of the AEW species, provides the most detailed surveillance of everything in the airspace within a radius of some 245 miles (400km). The chief reason underlying its long and costly development was the fact that, in the 1950s, combat aircraft took to flying very low. Streaking along "the nap of the Earth" they could not be detected because of the line-of-sight limitations of ground radars, and because the radars in AEW aircraft could not detect the low-flier against the massive reflection from the ground. The solution was extremely advanced radars which can discriminate between airborne targets and ground clutter. The Westinghouse radar of the Boeing E-3A is a pulse-doppler type which, by comparing the frequency of transmitted and received pulses, measures the speeds of every target that reflects back its radar energy. Digitally processed signals are sent out in succession from numerous apertures across an aerial face about 24ft (7.5m) long and 5ft (1.52m) deep, rotating six times per minute. One of the features of this radar is that virtually all the energy goes into the main narrow beam; the sidelobes, present in all normal radars, are extremely small, almost eliminating "clutter" from ground reflections. Part of the E-3A's cost of some $100 million is accounted for by computers, handling some 740,000 operations each second, and comprehensive displays for the command and control of an entire theatre of operations. One can expect the Tu-126 ("Moss") to have similar capabilities.

Heaviest of all military aircraft, the Boeing E-4A is the successor to the EC-135 as the carrier of the National Military Command System. Whether one can class these as combat aircraft is problematical, though they are certainly military. They are merely a way of ensuring that, should the US seat of government be destroyed, a complete national military command system will survive in the safety of the sky.

Boeing E-3A (AWACS)

E-3A (AWACS)

Origin: The Boeing Company, USA.
Type: Airborne warning and control system platform, with crew of 17.
Engines: Four 21,000lb (9525kg) thrust Pratt & Whitney TF33-100A turbofans.
Dimensions: Span 145ft 9in (44·42m); length 152ft 11in (46·61m); height 42ft 5in (12·93m).
Weights: Empty 172,000lb (78,020kg); maximum, 325,000lb (147,420kg).
Performance: Maximum speed, about 600mph (966km/h) at high altitude (about 300mph, 483km/h at low levels); normal operating height, over 40,000ft (12,190m); endurance, at least 12hr on station without refuelling.
Armament: None.
History: First flight (EC-137D test aircraft) 9 February 1972; (E-3A) 31 October 1975.

continued on page 184 ▶

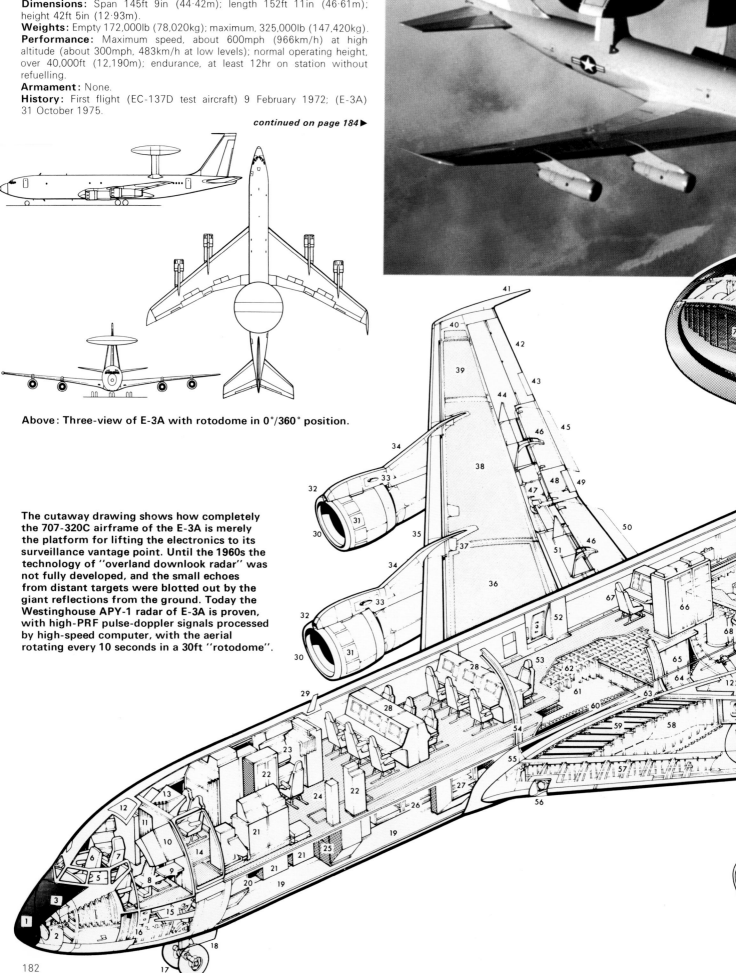

Above: Three-view of E-3A with rotodome in 0°/360° position.

The cutaway drawing shows how completely the 707-320C airframe of the E-3A is merely the platform for lifting the electronics to its surveillance vantage point. Until the 1960s the technology of "overland downlook radar" was not fully developed, and the small echoes from distant targets were blotted out by the giant reflections from the ground. Today the Westinghouse APY-1 radar of E-3A is proven, with high-PRF pulse-doppler signals processed by high-speed computer, with the aerial rotating every 10 seconds in a 30ft "rotodome".

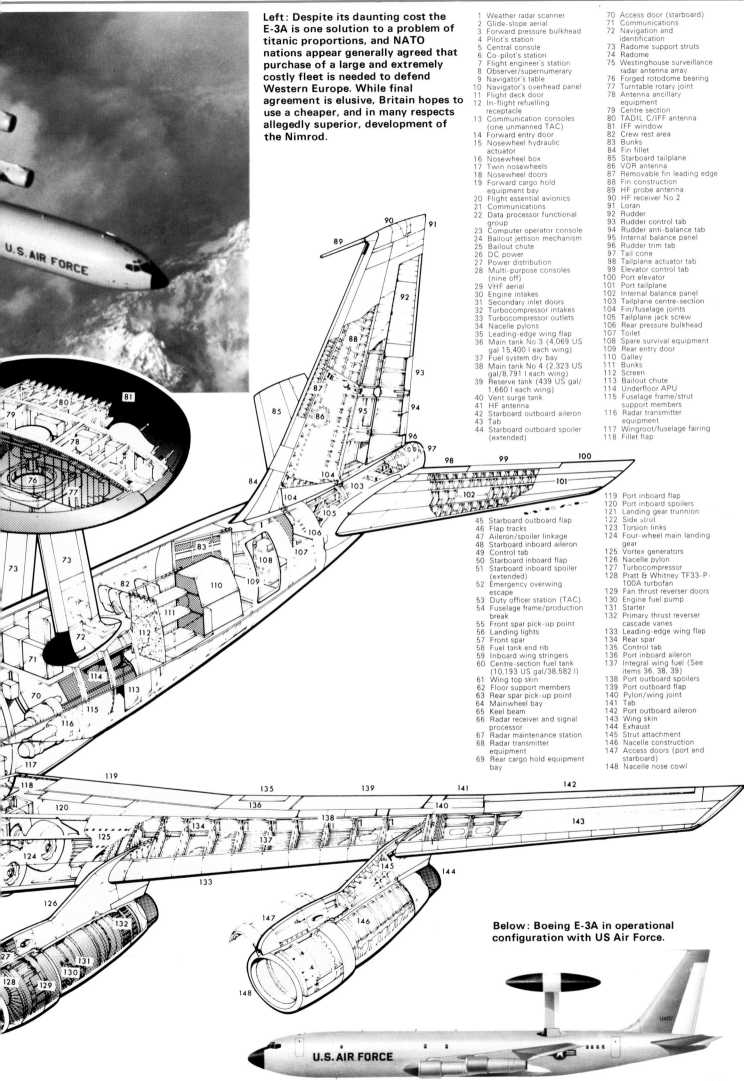

Left: Despite its daunting cost the E-3A is one solution to a problem of titanic proportions, and NATO nations appear generally agreed that purchase of a large and extremely costly fleet is needed to defend Western Europe. While final agreement is elusive, Britain hopes to use a cheaper, and in many respects allegedly superior, development of the Nimrod.

1 Weather radar scanner
2 Glide-slope aerial
3 Forward pressure bulkhead
4 Pilot's station
5 Central console
6 Co-pilot's station
7 Flight engineer's station
8 Observer/supernumerary
9 Navigator's table
10 Navigator's overhead panel
11 Flight deck door
12 In-flight refuelling receptacle
13 Communication consoles (one unmanned TAC)
14 Forward entry door
15 Nosewheel hydraulic actuator
16 Nosewheel box
17 Twin nosewheels
18 Nosewheel doors
19 Forward cargo hold equipment bay
20 Flight essential avionics
21 Communications
22 Data processor functional group
23 Computer operator console
24 Bailout jettison mechanism
25 Bailout chute
26 DC power
27 Power distribution
28 Multi-purpose consoles (nine off)
29 VHF aerial
30 Engine intakes
31 Secondary inlet doors
32 Turbocompressor intakes
33 Turbocompressor outlets
34 Nacelle pylons
35 Leading-edge wing flap
36 Main tank No 3 (4,069 US gal 15,400 l each wing)
37 Fuel system dry bay
38 Main tank No 4 (2,323 US gal/8,791 l each wing)
39 Reserve tank (439 US gal/ 1,660 l each wing)
40 Vent surge tank
41 HF antenna
42 Starboard outboard aileron
43 Tab
44 Starboard outboard spoiler (extended)

45 Starboard outboard flap
46 Flap tracks
47 Aileron/spoiler linkage
48 Starboard inboard aileron
49 Control tab
50 Starboard inboard flap
51 Starboard inboard spoiler (extended)
52 Emergency overwing escape
53 Duty officer station (TAC)
54 Fuselage frame/production break
55 Front spar pick-up point
56 Landing lights
57 Front spar
58 Fuel tank end rib
59 Inboard wing stringers
60 Centre-section fuel tank (10,193 US gal/38,582 l)
61 Wing top skin
62 Floor support members
63 Rear spar pick-up point
64 Mainwheel bay
65 Keel beam
66 Radar receiver and signal processor
67 Radar maintenance station
68 Radar transmitter equipment
69 Rear cargo hold equipment bay

70 Access door (starboard)
71 Communications
72 Navigation and identification
73 Radome support struts
74 Radome
75 Westinghouse surveillance radar antenna array
76 Forged rotodome bearing
77 Turntable rotary joint
78 Antenna ancillary equipment
79 Centre section
80 TADIL C/IFF antenna
81 IFF window
82 Crew rest area
83 Bunks
84 Fin fillet
85 Starboard tailplane
86 VOR antenna
87 Removable fin leading edge
88 Fin construction
89 HF probe antenna
90 HF receiver No 2
91 Loran
92 Rudder
93 Rudder control tab
94 Rudder anti-balance tab
95 Internal balance panel
96 Rudder trim tab
97 Tail cone
98 Tailplane actuator tab
99 Elevator control tab
100 Port elevator
101 Port tailplane
102 Internal balance panel
103 Tailplane centre-section
104 Fin/fuselage joints
105 Tailplane jack screw
106 Rear pressure bulkhead
107 Toilet
108 Spare survival equipment
109 Rear entry door
110 Galley
111 Bunks
112 Screen
113 Bailout chute
114 Underfloor APU
115 Fuselage frame/strut support members
116 Radar transmitter equipment
117 Wingroot/fuselage fairing
118 Fillet flap

119 Port inboard flap
120 Port inboard spoilers
121 Landing gear trunnion
122 Side strut
123 Torsion links
124 Four-wheel main landing gear
125 Vortex generators
126 Nacelle pylon
127 Turbocompressor
128 Pratt & Whitney TF33-P-100A turbofan
129 Fan thrust reverser doors
130 Engine fuel pump
131 Starter
132 Primary thrust reverser cascade vanes
133 Leading-edge wing flap
134 Rear spar
135 Control tab
136 Port inboard aileron
137 Integral wing fuel (See items 36, 38, 39)
138 Port outboard spoilers
139 Port outboard flap
140 Pylon/wing joint
141 Tab
142 Port outboard aileron
143 Wing skin
144 Exhaust
145 Strut attachment
146 Nacelle construction
147 Access doors (port and starboard)
148 Nacelle nose cowl

Below: Boeing E-3A in operational configuration with US Air Force.

►**User:** US Air Force (Aerospace Defense Command and TAC).

Development: Developments in radars and airborne data processing led first to the basic early-warning aircraft, exemplified by the Douglas EA-1 series and Grumman E-1B, and then, around 1965, to the concept of the Airborne Warning And Control System (AWACS). This is a flying surveillance and management station from which the entire air situation of a small nation, or part of a large one, can be controlled. Carrying an extremely powerful surveillance radar, a mass of sensing and data-processing systems and advanced displays both for the crew and for transmission to the ground, an AWACS can maintain perfect watch on every kind of aerial vehicle, hostile and friendly, over a radius exceeding 200 miles (322km). This facilitates the most efficient handling of every situation, right down to air traffic control at a beach-head or the best route for helicopters to rescue a friendly pilot. The first AWACS is the Boeing E-3A. Derived from the 707-320B airliner, it was to have had eight TF34 engines but owing to their fantastic overall cost these aircraft now retain the TF33 and have emerged somewhat less complex than once planned. Trials with rival Hughes and Westinghouse radars were held with EC-137D test aircraft; the Westinghouse was chosen, with aerial rotating at six times a minute in a 30ft (9·14m) dome high above the rear fuselage. Except for the E-4A the E-3A is almost certainly the most expensive aircraft ever to enter military service. Initial operational service in 1977-78 is to be followed by a total of 34 planned aircraft for efficient protection of US airspace. By the time this book appears the European NATO nations may also have decided to buy the E-3A. In late 1976 discussion had centred around 27 European-based aircraft costing $2,273 million.

Above: Multi-Purpose Display Consoles (MPDC) are the operational heart of the AWACS. They provide the mission crew with the enormously comprehensive display and control interfaces to carry out the surveillance, command and weapons-direction tasks. This aft-looking view shows the radar receiver in the background.

Above: Takeoff of one of the EC-137D test aircraft in 1972. These were commercial 707-320 airframes converted to test "brassboard" models of the two competing radars. Westinghouse won.

Boeing E-4A and 747

E-4 (AABNCP)

Origin: The Boeing Company, USA.
Type: Airborne command post, with crew/staff of 28–60.
Engines: (E-4A) four 45,500lb (20,639kg) thrust Pratt & Whitney F105-100 (JT9D) turbofans; (E-4B) four 52,500lb (23,815kg) thrust General Electric F103-100 turbofans.
Dimensions: Span 195ft 8in (59·64m); length 231ft 4in (70·5m); height 63ft 5in (19·33m).
Weights: Empty, probably 380,000lb (172,370kg); loaded 803,000lb (364,230kg).
Performance: Maximum speed 608mph (978km/h) at 30,000ft (9144m); maximum Mach number 0·92; normal operational ceiling 45,000ft (13,715m); normal unrefuelled range about 6,500 miles (10,460km).
Armament: None.
History: First flight (747) 9 February 1969; (E-4) January 1973.
User: US Air Force (see text); basic 747 is used by Iran (see text).

Development: Since the late 1950s the United States has created a growing fleet of various kinds of EC-135 aircraft as airborne command posts. Operated by the National Military Command System and SAC, these are the platforms carrying the national strategic and economic command and decision-taking machinery, with perfect unjammable communications to all government and military organizations and the capacity to survive even a nuclear war. Since 1965 the EC-135 has become restrictive, and to meet

future needs and provide for a larger staff in greater comfort, with the capability of more flexible action and response, the 747B airframe was adopted to carry the Advanced Airborne National Command Post (AABNCP).

The first two were fitted with Pratt & Whitney JT9D engines, but the standard was later adopted as that of the fourth aircraft, bought for $39 million in December 1973 with GE engines and later equipment. Much of the special equipment has been taken from the EC-135A, H, J, K, L and P force. There are three decks, the main deck being a mixture of executive offices and luxurious living quarters and the rest being packed with advanced electronics. The first three (E-4A) aircraft are based at Andrews AFB near Washington; eventually, without cost to the Air Force, they will be retro-fitted with F103 engines and they will also be provided with E-4B equipment. It is planned to base the E-4B and two further E-4B aircraft at Offutt AFB, headquarters of SAC in Nebraska. The Imperial Iranian AF uses a fleet of 747 transports, most of which have boom and pod installations to serve as tankers.

Above: Three-view of typical JT9D-powered 747.

Above: E-4A before conversion to E-4B (same aircraft pictured below as E-4B).

Below: The world's most powerful military aircraft, the E-4B is a much more advanced and comprehensive aircraft than the E-4A. Programme cost for the force of six amounts to more than $850 million. It carries a larger battle staff, and unique SHF/LF/VLF communications radio systems.

Grumman E-2 Hawkeye

E-2A, B and C Hawkeye and C-2A Greyhound

Origin: Grumman Aerospace, USA.
Type: E-2 series, AEW aircraft; C-2, COD transport.
Engines: Two 4,050ehp Allison T56-8/8A single-shaft turboprops.
Dimensions: Span 80ft 7in (24·56m); length 57ft 7in (17·55m); (C-2A) 56ft 8in; height (E-2) 18ft 4in (5·59m); (C-2) 15ft 11in (4·85m).
Weights: Empty (E-2C) 37,616lb (17,062kg); (C-2A) 31,154lb (14,131 kg); loaded (E-2C) 51,569lb (23,391kg); (C-2A) 54,830lb (24,870kg).
Performance: Maximum speed (E-2C) 374mph (602km/h); (C-2A) 352mph (567km/h); initial climb (C-2A) 2,330ft (710m)/min; service ceiling (both) about 28,500ft (8650m); range (both) about 1,700 miles (2736km).
Armament: None.
History: First flight (W2F-1) 21 October 1960; (production E-2A) 19 April 1961; (E-2B) 20 February 1969; (E-2C) 20 January 1971; (C-2A) 18 November 1964; growth E-2C, possibly late 1977.
Users: Israel (E-2C, from December 1977); US Navy.

Development: Originally designated W2F-1, the E-2A Hawkeye was the first aircraft designed from scratch as an airborne early-warning surveillance platform (all previous AEW machines being modifications of existing

continued on page 188▶

Above: Three-view of E-2C Hawkeye.

1 Two-section rudder panels
2 Starboard outboard fin
3 Glassfibre fin construction
4 Passive defence system antenna (PDS)
5 Rudder construction
6 Static discharger
7 Fin construction
8 Leading edge de-icing
9 Wing fold jury-strut lock
10 Wing folded position
11 Rudder jack
12 PDS receivers
13 Starboard inboard rudder sections
14 Starboard inboard glass fibre fin
15 Port elevator construction
16 Port inboard fixed fin
17 Port outboard rudder sections
18 Rudder controls
19 Tailplane construction
20 Fuel jettison pipes
21 Rearward PDS antenna

22 Tailplane fixing
23 Rear fuselage construction
24 Tailskid jack
25 Arresting hook
26 Tailskid
27 Arresting hook jack
28 Lower PDS receiver and antenna
29 Rear pressure dome
30 Toilet
31 Rotodome rear mounting struts

32 Rotating radar scanner housing (Rotodome)
33 Rotodome edge de-icing
34 UHF aerial array, AN/APS-125 set
35 Pivot bearing housing
36 IFF aerial array
37 Rotodome motor
38 Hydraulic lifting jack
39 Front mounting support frame
40 Radar transmission line
41 Fuselage frame construction
42 Toilet compartment doorway
43 Antenna coupler
44 Rear cabin window
45 Air controller's seat
46 Radar and instrument panels

47 Combat information officer's seat
48 Combat information radar panel
49 Radar operator's seat
50 Radar panel and instruments
51 Swivelling seat mountings
52 Wing fold fixing
53 Wing fold break-point
54 Spar locking mechanism
55 Wing fold hinge

56 Wing folding hydraulic jack
57 Starboard outboard flap
58 Flap construction
59 Flap guide rails
60 Flap drive motors and shaft
61 Starboard drooping aileron
62 Flap to drooping aileron connection
63 Aileron jack
64 Aileron construction
65 Aileron hinges
66 Starboard wing tip
67 Navigation light
68 Jury strut locking mechanism
69 Outer wing construction
70 Leading edge construction

71 Leading edge de-icing
72 Lattice rib construction
73 Engine exhaust pipe fairing
74 Front spar locking mechanism
75 Main undercarriage leg
76 Undercarriage leg door
77 Single mainwheel
78 Mainwheel door
79 Engine pylon construction
80 Engine mounting strut
81 Allison T56-A-425 engine
82 Oil cooler
83 Oil cooler intake
84 Engine intake
85 Hamilton Standard four-bladed propeller
86 Gearbox drive shaft
87 Propeller mechanism
88 Cooling air intake
89 Engine-to-propeller gearbox
90 Oil tank, usable capacity

9·25 US gal (35 l) each nacelle
91 Bleed air supply duct
92 Vapour cycle air conditioning plant
93 Wing front fixing
94 Computer bank
95 Wing centre rib joint
96 Inboard wing section fuel tank, capacity 912 US gal (3451 l) each wing
97 Lattice rib construction
98 Port inboard flap
99 Wing fold hinge
100 Wing fold joint line
101 Sloping hinge rib
102 Port outboard flap
103 Aileron jack
104 Port aileron
105 Port outer wing panel
106 Port wing tip

107 Navigation light
108 Leading edge de-icing
109 Aileron control cable mechanism
110 Engine mounting strut attachment
111 Engine-to-propeller gearbox
112 Propeller spinner fairing
113 Hamilton Standard four-bladed propeller
114 Engine intake
115 Gearbox drive shaft
116 Port engine
117 Fuel system piping

Above: Test-flying an E-2C development aircraft. The aircraft itself was familiar, but the new radar, computers and displays meant exhaustive airborne debugging.

Above: The fully proven aircraft, outwardly not greatly dissimilar to the one on the left apart from the unit markings. The TE-2C trainer also looks similar.

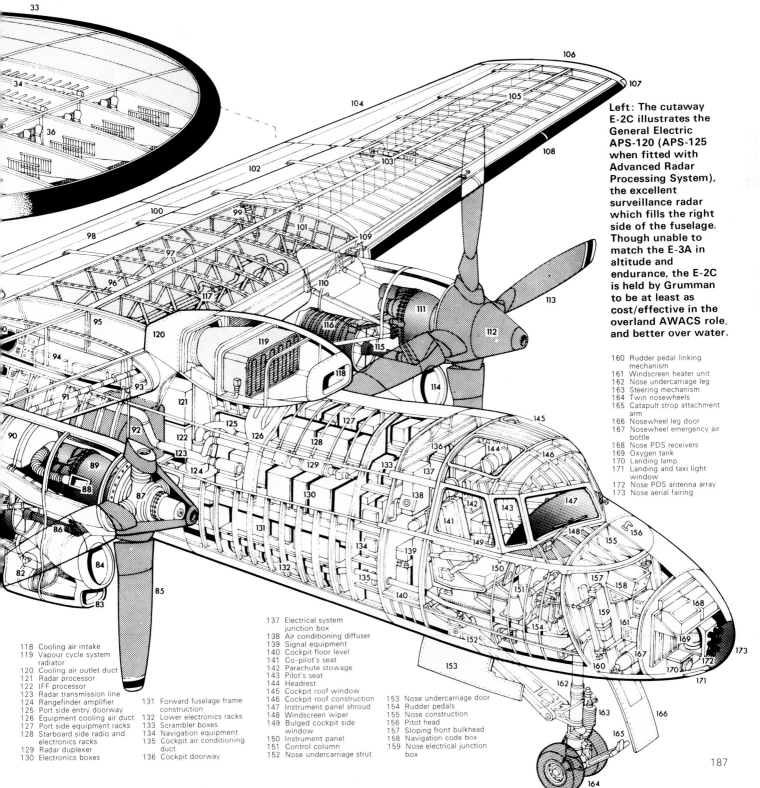

Left: The cutaway E-2C illustrates the General Electric APS-120 (APS-125 when fitted with Advanced Radar Processing System), the excellent surveillance radar which fills the right side of the fuselage. Though unable to match the E-3A in altitude and endurance, the E-2C is held by Grumman to be at least as cost/effective in the overland AWACS role, and better over water.

160 Rudder pedal linking mechanism
161 Windscreen heater unit
162 Nose undercarriage leg
163 Steering mechanism
164 Twin nosewheels
165 Catapult strop attachment arm
166 Nosewheel leg door
167 Nosewheel emergency air bottle
168 Nose PDS receivers
169 Oxygen tank
170 Landing lamp
171 Landing and taxi light window
172 Nose PDS antenna array
173 Nose aerial fairing

118 Cooling air intake
119 Vapour cycle system radiator
120 Cooling air outlet duct
121 Radar processor
122 IFF processor
123 Radar transmission line
124 Rangefinder amplifier
125 Port side entry doorway
126 Equipment cooling air duct
127 Port side equipment racks
128 Starboard side radio and electronics racks
129 Radar duplexer
130 Electronics boxes

131 Forward fuselage frame construction
132 Lower electronics racks
133 Scrambler boxes
134 Navigation equipment
135 Cockpit air conditioning duct
136 Cockpit doorway
137 Electrical system junction box
138 Air conditioning diffuser
139 Signal equipment
140 Cockpit floor level
141 Co-pilot's seat
142 Parachute stowage
143 Pilot's seat
144 Headrest
145 Cockpit roof window
146 Cockpit roof construction
147 Instrument panel shroud
148 Windscreen wiper
149 Bulged cockpit side window
150 Instrument panel
151 Control column
152 Nose undercarriage strut

153 Nose undercarriage door
154 Rudder pedals
155 Nose construction
156 Pitot head
157 Sloping front bulkhead
158 Navigation code box
159 Nose electrical junction box

▶types). Equipped with an APS-96 long-range radar with scanner rotating six times per minute inside a 24ft diameter radome, the E-2A has a flight crew of two and three controllers seated aft in the Airborne Tactical Data System (ATDS) compartment, which is constantly linked with the Naval Tactical Data System (NTDS) in Fleet HQ or the appropriate land base. The E-2A can handle an entire air situation and direct all friendly air operations in attacking or defensive missions. From the E-2A were derived the E-2B, with microelectronic computer, and the C-2A Greyhound COD (carrier on-board delivery) transport, able to make catapult takeoffs and arrested landings with 39 passengers or bulky freight. The final version was the dramatically new E-2C, with APS-120 radar and APA-171 aerial system, with OL-93 radar data processor serving a Combat Information Center (CIC) staff with complete knowledge of all airborne targets even in a land-clutter environment. Though it has an advanced and costly airframe, more than three-quarters of the price of an E-2C is accounted for by electronics. This version entered service with squadron VAW-123 at NAS Norfolk, Virginia, in November 1973. In 1977 Grumman is nearing the completion of E-2C manufacture, and with US government help is making a strong sales effort within NATO and in Middle East countries, emphasising the low price (about $13 million in 1975 US dollars). Four aircraft were bought by Israel, but the NATO nations appear to prefer the Boeing E-3A. Grumman hope to sell the Growth E-2C with up to 50 per cent greater radar range, increased computer capacity and fuel in the outer wings.

Above: Thoroughly popular with the US Navy aircrew who fly it, the Hawkeye is a reliable and relatively forgiving aircraft. Here, one approaches to an arrested landing.

Below: An E-2C Hawkeye of VAW-125 (USS *John F. Kennedy*).

Bottom: An E-2C Hawkeye of VAW-125, embarked aboard USS *Constellation*. This aircraft is one of the early deliveries being retrofitted with the Advanced Radar Processing System.

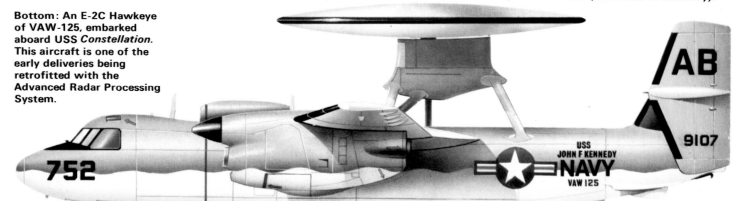

Lockheed EC-121 Warning Star

EC-121C to EC-121T

Origin: Lockheed California Company, Burbank, USA.
Type: Electronic reconnaissance and specialist missions.
Engines: Four 3,250hp Wright R-3350-91 Turbo-Compound 18-cylinder radials.
Dimensions: Span over tip tanks 126ft 2in (38·45m); length (most) 116ft 2in (35·41m); height overall (most) 24ft 8in (7·52m).
Weights: Empty (typical of most) 80,611lb (36,564kg); maximum loaded 145,000lb (65,770kg).
Performance: Maximum speed at altitude 321mph (517km/h); typical cruise 259mph (417km/h); service ceiling 20,600ft (6279m); range 4,600 miles (7400km); endurance limit 20 hours.
History: First flight (Constellation) 9 January 1943, (prototype C-121C) 1952; final delivery of rebuilt EC-121T 1973.
Users: India (Navy), US Air Force and Navy.

Development: After delivery of 135 military versions of the Constellation and "stretched" Super Constellation, Lockheed began in 1953 to deliver special electronic platforms (then designated RC-121C for USAF Air Defense Command, now serving as EC-121C and later versions with Aerospace Defense Command). At least 223 of four main families of electronic Super Constellation were supplied to the US Air Force and Navy, and these have been several times re-equipped or completely rebuilt, with designation EC-121K, P, Q, R, S and T. Most served in SE Asia, their main duties being electronic reconnaissance, early warning, and acting as airborne relay stations in the Igloo White system for detecting and pinpointing hostile road traffic. Crew in these variants ranges from seven to 28. The less-specialised Warning Stars still serve with ADC and the Air Reserve 79th Sqn at Homestead AFB, Florida, operating over the Atlantic, and several highly refined EC models serve with the Navy. These aircraft are all highly sophisticated platforms and the fact their equipment is inside a basically old airframe is irrelevant. The more basic Super Constellations used for reconnaissance by the French Armée de l'Air and Indian AF have been withdrawn.

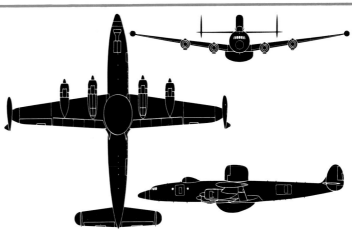

Above: Three-view of EC-121H Warning Star of USAF.

Above: EC-121H photographed at Sioux City, Iowa, as basic AEW-Elint platform with R-3350-93 engines and crew of 17 to 26.

Below: Lockheed NC-121K of US Navy VAQ-33, with Elint collection system, pulse analysers and Litton ALQ-124 ECM installation. Operating crew of 16 to 19.

McDonnell Douglas
EA-3 Skywarrior and EB-66

A-3 Skywarrior and B-66 Destroyer

Origin: Douglas Aircraft Co (see text), USA.
Type: Originally (A3D) carrier-based strategic bomber, (B-66) tactical attack bomber; later, different roles (see text).
Engines: (A-3) two 12,400lb (5625kg) thrust Pratt & Whitney J57-10 two-shaft turbojets; (B-66) two 10,000lb (4536kg) thrust Allison J71-13 single-shaft turbojets.
Dimensions: Span 72ft 6in (22·1m); length, typical (EA-3B) 76ft 4in (23·3m); (EB-66E) 75ft 2in—78ft 9in (22·9–24m); height 23ft 6in (7·16m).
Weights: Empty (A-3B) 39,409lb (17,875kg); (B-66B) 42,369lb (19,218kg); maximum loaded (A-3B) 82,000lb (37,195kg); (B-66B) 83,000lb (37,648kg).
Performance: (Typical) maximum speed 610mph (982km/h); initial climb 3,600ft (1100m)/min; service ceiling 43,000ft (13,110m); range with maximum fuel 2,000 miles (3220km).
Armament: Normally none; as built, most ·bomber A-3s and B-66s had two remotely controlled 20mm cannon in a tail turret and internal provision for 12,000lb (5443kg) bombs (15,000lb. 6804kg in the B-66).
History: First flight (XA3D-1) 28 October 1952; (RB-66A) 28 June 1954, service delivery (A3D-1) December 1954 (first squadron, March 1956); (RB-66B) March 1956; last delivery of new aircraft (A3D-2Q) January 1961. (WB-66D) September 1958.
User: USA (A-3, Navy; B-66, Air Force, not operational).

Development: The Douglas El Segundo design team under Heinemann produced the A3D as the world's first carrier-based strategic bomber, matching the design both to the predicted size and mass of future thermo-nuclear bombs and to the deck length and strength of the super-carriers of the *Forrestal* class in 1948. The bomb bay dictated a high wing, which in turn meant the landing gears had to retract into the fuselage. Outer wings and vertical tail folded hydraulically and the nose was filled with an advanced blind-bombing radar. Unfortunately Westinghouse, supplier of both the engines and the radar, succeeded in delivering only the Aero-21B tail turret. Redesigned with the J57 engine the A3D-1 finally equipped VAH-1 (Heavy Attack Squadron 1) in 1956. Soon the Skywarriors on the catapults of giant carriers of the 6th Fleet in the Mediterranean and the 7th Fleet in the Pacific were playing a central role in the balance of power in the Cold War, and giving a new global dimension to naval air power. Eventually, though only 280 Skywarriors were built (not enough, as it turned out), the changing scene called for numerous completely different versions mainly achieved by rebuilding bombers. Major production was of the A3D-2 bomber, restyled A-38B. From this evolved the A3D-2P (RA-3B) reconnaissance, A3D-2Q (EA-3B) electronic countermeasures and A3D-2T (TA-3B) radar/nav trainer, followed by rebuilds for the KA-3B tanker, EKA-3B ECM/tanker and various special-mission and test versions. The EKA-3B is still standard equipment of tanker/EW detachments aboard attack carriers, and the USNR has two squadrons of KA-3Bs.

The B-66 Destroyer was produced by the Long Beach plant to meet the needs of the US Air Force. What had begun as a minimum modification of the Skywarrior turned into a totally different aircraft. Though it looked similar, hardly a single airframe part or item of equipment was common and the

Above: The rebuilt B-66 bombers pioneered tactical ECM and ESM. This is an EB-66E, with five tons of electronics.

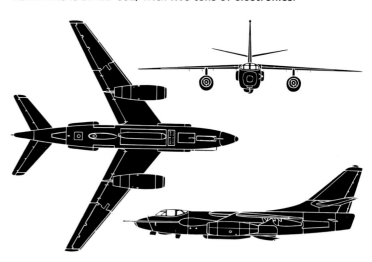

Above: Three-view of EKA-3B Skywarrior.

B-66 proved difficult and expensive. After building five RB-66As for indoctrination, Long Beach and a re-opened wartime plant at Tulsa built 145 RB-66B reconnaissance aircraft as well as 72 B-66B bombers. There followed 36 RB-66C electronic reconnaissance aircraft with four-man crew and 36 WB-66Ds for weather reconnaissance. Modified further over the years for many clandestine special ferreting missions, a number of EB-66E aircraft served throughout the Vietnam war, but were withdrawn from combat duty in 1974.

Below: Like the Hunter, the A-3 Skywarrior has had a long life in rebuilt versions, and twice the number actually built were eventually needed. One of the variants still in use is this TA-3B radar/ESM/nav trainer, with six pupils in a transport-type fuselage, seen landing at Atsugi AB, Japan. Note the refuelling probe, tail bumper, and large airbrakes on the rear fuselage. The other sub-type still in operational use is the EKA-3B (above).

Above: Demilitarized A-3B as flown by the Aerospace Recovery Facility, NAS El Centro, California.

Tupolev Tu-126

Design bureau Tu-126; service designation, possibly Tu-24 (NATO name "Moss")

Origin: The design bureau named for Andrei N. Tupolev, Soviet Union.
Type: Airborne warning and control system.
Engines: Four 14,795ehp Kuznetsov NK-12MV single-shaft turboprops.
Dimensions: Span 167ft 8in (51·10m); length 182ft 6in (55·48m), (with FR probe) 188ft 0in (57·30m); height overall 52ft 8in (16·05m).
Weights: Empty (estimate) 198,400lb (90,000kg); maximum loaded 375,000lb (170,000kg).
Performance: Probable maximum speed 500mph (805km/h); on-station height 40,000ft (12,200m); normal operational endurance 18hr; ferry range at least 6,000 miles 9,650km.
History: First flight probably 1962–64; service delivery not later than 1967.
User: Soviet Union (almost certainly IA-PVO).

Development: Tupolev's family of swept-wing turboprops bigger and faster than any others ever put into service began with the long-range bomber Tu-95 (service designation Tu-20). From this evolved the considerably bigger Tu-114 civil airliner and the same-size Tu-114D special transport. The Tu-114 was never used as the basis for a large military freighter, but it was tailor-made for the Tu-126 AWACS (airborne warning and control system). Even examination of photographs indicates that this is a sophisticated and highly developed aircraft. Though details are sparse in the West, it is unlikely that its surveillance radar can quite equal that of the Boeing E-3A. On the other hand there is an element of wishful thinking in the supposed US belief that it is "of limited effectiveness over water and ineffective over land." At least one Tu-126 was detached with its crew to serve with the Indian Air Force during the 1971 fighting with Pakistan. The

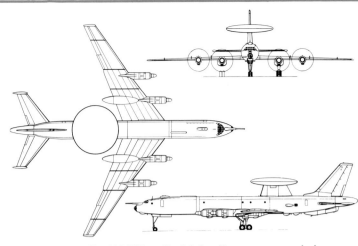

Three-view of Tu-126 "Moss" with landing gear extended.

number in Soviet service in 1976 was put at "at least ten" but ten times that number would be needed to patrol even the main sections of the Soviet frontier.

Above: Drawn for this book, a recent Tu-126.

Below: Enlargement from a Soviet ciné film. The "Moss" force is probably being increased by rebuilding Tu-114 transports.

Helicopters

Though the first two helicopters flew only four years after the Wright Brothers' first powered flight, the problems of rotating-wing VTOL were extremely difficult and held back the development of useful helicopters until after World War II. Today, however, the helicopter is a refined and reliable vehicle whose great versatility and unique command of the air have overcome its inherent high installed power, high initial and operating costs (compared with aeroplanes of similar payload and performance), and inability to match the speed and range of most other combat aircraft. Though there is a place in the world's air forces and navies for the light piston-engined "chopper" almost all the machines in this chapter have turboshaft engines, which have dramatically improved the helicopter's payload, per-

formance, reliability and operating cost-levels. The turboshaft has also brought other advantages to the military helicopter. It has reduced its infra-red signature, especially when this was a basic design objective, making the machine harder to hit by heat-seeking missiles. It has also reduced its noise, again especially when this was deliberate policy, though some quiet-engined helicopters still suffer from "rotor slap" which gives the enemy at least 60 seconds' warning. It has made it possible to slam the throttle(s) open and thereafter forget about the automated power plant and concentrate on the mission. It has made possible the provision of two engines when one would do, giving genuine twin-engine safety. And it has facilitated the uplift of fuel from other Service units, because, though armies

Over terrain affording little cover, a Westland Scout AH.1 of the British Army fires a blue-tipped SS.11 anti-tank missile, with burning specks ejected at the moment of motor ignition. The box projecting above the cabin is the stabilized sight head.

and navies have gasoline, they do not have 100/130-grade suitable for aviation piston engines.

A few helicopters have been equipped to participate in air combat (for example, the US Navy Seasprite with Sparrow missiles), and the predecessor of the very first military helicopter, the Flettner 265, demonstrated that in 20 minutes of determined attacks with camera-guns a Bf 109 and Fw 190 could not score a single hit. Another important helicopter role is to find crashed aircraft—friendly or hostile—no matter whether or not they are in enemy-held territory, and recover them for examination and possible repair and re-use. Of course, the evacuation of casualties, including downed aircrew, was one of the very first tasks assigned to helicopters. Another duty associated with the air battle is radar surveil-

lance; 20 years ago the most powerful type of helicopter then available in the West throbbed aloft carrying a large radar to fly the AEW mission described in the last section of this book. This was a sensible idea only if the local commander had no carrier or airstrip available from which an AEW aeroplane could climb much higher and stay up much longer, and the AEW helicopter is today extinct. Apart from these roles helicopters have not played much part in air battles; most of those described on the following pages spend their life with soldiers or sailors.

Of course, the pure trainer or large transport helicopter explain themselves, and considerable numbers are used by almost every major country. Some helicopters are useful in both roles, and in many others, so it should not be surprising that the

military aircraft built in the largest numbers since World War II is probably the "Huey" family of helicopters (the only type that might exceed it is the MiG-21), and these machines are also used by more air forces than any type other than the DC-3 derivatives. Many of the Hueys are slim two-seaters which were the original production examples of the "gunship", bristling with sensors and weapons and intended to participate directly in the land battle. The Advanced Attack Helicopters of the US Army are the latest of this class, designed to have the best possible chance of survival in proximity to hostile troops who in future may have powerful

anti-aircraft weapons. Gunships cannot, however, carry troops or supplies. The Lynx typifies the versatile multi-role class that can hit enemy troops or armour, whilst trying to stay hidden itself, and can also carry sections of ten men and/or army weapons and supplies. A third battlefield family carry payloads but not weapons.

In the sea war the chief roles of the helicopter are transport for amphibious assault, transport for vertical replenishment (supplying all kinds of ships or beachheads) and ASW (dealt with in a separate section). Most of the early ASW choppers were incapable of carrying both sensors and A/S weapons, and so worked in pairs. Later the US Navy decided the primary controlling task should be performed by surface ships, using helicopters (or even remotely piloted drone helicopters, no longer in service) merely to carry sensors and weapons a few miles distant. The British boldly decided the ASW helicopter could operate as a self-contained search and attack platform, and the Westland Sea King was the first to carry a complete tactical centre as well as sensors and weapons.

Aérospatiale Alouette

SA.313 Alouette II, 315 Lama, 316 Alouette III, 318 Alouette II (Astazou) and 319 Alouette III (Astazou).

Origin: Aérospatiale, Marignane, France; licence-built by Hindustan Aeronautics, India, and previously in Romania, Sweden and Switzerland.
Type: Multi-role utility helicopter.
Engine: One Turboméca turboshaft, (SA 313B) 360shp Artouste II, (318C) 523shp Astazou IIA, (316C, Lama) 870shp Artouste IIID, (319B) 870shp Astazou XIV.
Dimensions: Diameter of main rotor (II) 33ft 5in (10·20m), (III) 36ft 1¾in (11·02m); length of fuselage (II) 31ft 11¾in (9·75m), (III) 32ft 10¾in (10·03m); height (II) 9ft 0in (2·75m), (III) 9ft 10in (3·00m).
Weights: Empty (II, 318C) 1,961lb (890kg), (Lama) 2,235lb (1014kg), (III, 316B) 2,520lb (1143kg); maximum loaded (II, 318C) 3,630lb (1650kg), (Lama) 5,070lb (2300kg), (III, 316B) 4,850lb (2200kg).
Performance: Maximum speed (318C) 127mph (205km/h), (316B) 130mph (210km/h); range with max payload (318C) 62 miles (100km), (316B) 300 miles (480km).
History: First flight (313B) 12 March 1955, (316) 28 February 1959, (Lama) 17 March 1969.
Users: (II, Lama, military) Argentina, Belgium, Cent. Af. Rep., Chile, Colombia, Congo, Dahomey, Ecuador, W Germany, India, Ivory Coast, Kenya, Laos, Lebanon, Liberia, Malagasey Rep., Mexico, Senegal, Sweden, Switzerland, Togo, Tunisia; (III) Abu Dhabi, Austria, Bangladesh, Burma, Cameroun, Congo, Denmark, Dominica, Ecuador, Ethiopia, Gabon, Ghana, Hong Kong, India, Indonesia, Iraq, Ireland, Israel, Ivory Coast, Jordan, Laos, Lebanon, Liberia, Malagasey Rep., Mexico, Netherlands, Pakistan, Peru, Portugal, Rhodesia, Romania, Rwanda, Singapore, S Africa, Spain, Switzerland, Venezuela, Yugoslavia, Zaïre, Zambia.

Development: By far the most successful European helicopter, the Alouette (Lark) owes its customers to the Turboméca company which was first in the world to develop light turbine aero engines. When production of the five-seat Alouette II ended in 1975 1,305 had been built, about 1,000 being 313s. The HAL Lama is a high-altitude weight-lifter with II airframe and III engine and transmission (all III engines are de-rated to give about 570shp under hot/high conditions). It is made by Aérospatiale and HAL, the Indian Army name being Cheetah. By 1977 over 1,450 seven-seat IIIs had been sold, most current models being 319Bs, called Chetak when made in India. Options include various weapons, pontoon floats, rescue hoist and simple radar.

Above: An Aérospatiale SS.11 anti-tank missile accelerates away from an Alouette III of the ALAT, French Army.

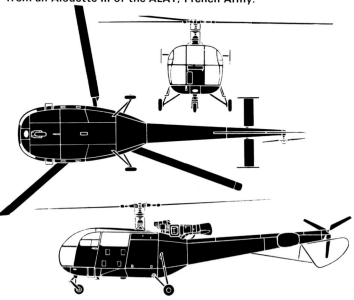

Above: Three-view of SA 316C Alouette III (319 similar).

Below: Representing a large and diverse group of military Alouette III users around the world, this machine of the Royal Danish Navy is more colourful than most. It is one of eight which are maintained by 722 Sqn (Sea King) of the RDAF. It is typical of the basic SA 316C sub-type with seven seats, wheels, and no armament.

Above: Alouette III general-utility model of Royal Malaysian AF.

Aérospatiale Super Frelon

321 G, Ja and L

Origin: Soc. Aérospatiale, France.
Type: (G) Anti-submarine and offshore patrol helicopter; (Ja, L) utility transport.
Engines: Three 1,630hp Turboméca Turmo IIIC turboshafts.
Dimensions: Diameter of main (six-blade) rotor 62ft (18·9m); length (rotors turning) 75ft 7in (23m); height (tail rotor turning) 21ft 10in (6·66m).
Weights: Empty, equipped 14,607lb (6626kg); maximum 28,660lb (13,000kg).
Performance: Maximum speed 171mph (275km/h) (a Super Frelon prototype in racing trim set a record at 212mph in 1963); maximum rate of climb 1,312ft (400m)/min (three engines), 479ft (146m)/min (two engines); service ceiling 10,325ft (3150m); endurance in ASW role 4hr.
Armament: See text.
History: First flight, SA.3210 Super Frelon December 1962; SA 321G November 1965.
Users: China, France (Aéronavale), Iran, Israel, Libya, S. Africa; Syria reported but unconfirmed by Aérospatiale.

Development: The biggest and heaviest helicopter yet produced in quantity to a West European design, the Super Frelon first flew in 1962 at the Marignane (Marseilles) plant of what was then Sud-Aviation. It was derived from the SA.3200 Frelon with the assistance of Sikorsky Aircraft whose technology and experience were used in the lifting and tail rotors and drive systems. Fiat of Italy assisted with the main gearbox and power transmission and continue to make these parts. The Super Frelon has been made in three versions: SA 321F civil airliner; SA 321G anti-submarine and SA 321Ja utility. The 321Ja is the most numerous version and has been sold to several air forces. A sub-variant called SA 321L serves in quantity with the South African Air Force, and Israel used Super Frelons to carry commando raiders to Beirut Airport. The 321G is a specialised ASW aircraft, which equips Flotille 32F of the Aéronavale (French Naval Air Arm). It operates in groups, usually of four, one carrying a Sylphe panoramic radar and dunking sonar to find targets and the others each armed with four homing torpedoes. In the anti-ship role the 321G can carry two of the big Exocet long-range missiles. Another role is towing and mine-sweeping

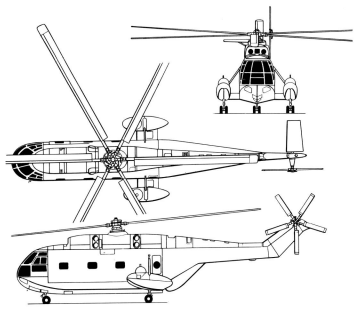

Above: Three-view of SA 321Ja (most non-radar versions similar).

and the three powerful engines provide enough power reserve for a towing pull of 6,600lb (3000kg). All combat Super Frelons can operate from airfields, ships or from water.

Below: Though the primary mission of most of the SA 321G Super Frelon force of the Aéronavale is anti-submarine patrol in support of the French nuclear-missile submarines, this G-model is seen engaged in launch tests for the AM39 Exocet missile. Weighing 1,430lb (650kg), the air-launched version of Exocet is a formidable anti-ship missile, with speed of Mach 0·93 and range (helicopter-launched at 330ft altitude) of just over 32 miles (52km).

Aérospatiale/Westland Gazelle

SA 341 B, C, D, E, F and H and SA 342K

Origin: Aérospatiale, Marignane, France; produced in association with Westland Helicopters, Yeovil, UK; licence-produced by Soko, Yugoslavia.
Type: Multi-role utility helicopter.
Engine: One 592shp Turboméca Astazou turboshaft (IIIA, IIIC or IIIN, depending on customer); (SA 342K) 858shp Astazou XIVH flat-rated at 592shp.
Dimensions: Diameter of three-blade main rotor 34ft 5½in (10·50m); length overall (rotors turning) 39ft 3¼in (11·97m); height 10ft 2½in (3·15m).
Weights: Empty (H) 2,002lb (908kg); maximum loaded (H) 3,970lb (1800kg), (342J) 4,190lb (1900kg).
Performance: Maximum cruise 164mph (264km/h); range with max fuel 416 miles (670km), (with 1,102lb/500kg payload) 223 miles (360km).
Armament: Two pods of 36mm rockets, two forward-firing Miniguns or four AS.11, Hot or TOW missiles or two AS.12, each with appropriate sight system, side-firing Minigun, GPMG or Emerson TAT with sight system.
History: First flight 7 April 1967, (production 341) 6 August 1971.
Users: (Military) include Egypt, France, Kuwait, Qatar, Senegal, UK (Army, RAF, RN), and Yugoslavia.

Development: A natural successor to the Alouette, this trim five-seater has much higher performance, and has been cleared for IFR Cat.I operation. Orders placed under the Anglo-French agreement of February 1967— which made this French design a joint project—included 135 Gazelle AH.1 (341B) for the British Army, and smaller numbers of HT.2 (341C)

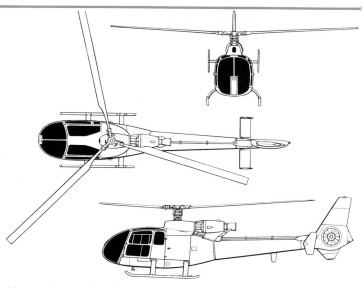

Above: Three-view of typical SA 341 with Astazou IIIA, no wheels.

for the Navy and HT.3 and HCC.4 (D and E) for the RAF. The 341F is the French Army type, the H the export variant and the 342K the first of a heavier and basically more powerful family. By 1977 well over 800 had been ordered.

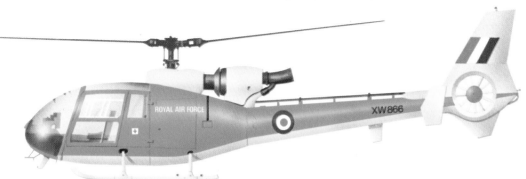

Above: Gazelle HT.3 trainer of RAF CFS, Shawbury.

Below: Today the Alouette is vulnerable over the battlefield, but the much faster and more nimble Gazelle has a fair chance of survival. This Gazelle AH.1 of the British Army is scouting on manoeuvres with armour (the Chieftain Mk 3 battle tank has its turret pointing astern). Note the two blade aerials under the tail boom for Army communications.

Aérospatiale/Westland
Puma and Super Puma

SA 330B, C, E, H and L and SA 331 Super Puma

Origin: Aérospatiale, Marignane, France; produced (except 331) in association with Westland Helicopters, Yeovil, UK.

Type: All-weather transport.

Engines: (330) two Turboméca Turmo turboshaft, (B, C, E) 1,328hp Turmo IIIC4, (H, L) 1,575hp Turmo IVC; (331) two 1,800hp Turboméca Makila.

Dimensions: Diameter of four-blade main rotor 49ft 2½in (15·00m); length overall (rotors turning) 59ft 6½in (18·15m), (331) over 67ft (20m); height 16ft 10½in (5·14m).

Weights: Empty (H) 7,795lb; maximum loaded (H) 15,430lb (7000kg), (L) 16,315lb (7400kg), (331) about 22,050lb (10,000kg).

Performance: Maximum cruise (S/L) 159mph (257km/h); max range with standard fuel (330, typical) 360 miles (580km).

Armament: Many customer options including weapon pylons for gun pods or missiles, and various axial- or side-firing cannon or Minigun installations.

History: First flight 15 April 1965; service delivery (330B) April 1969.

Users: (Military) includes Abu Dhabi, Algeria, Belgium, Cameroun, Chad, Chile, Ecuador, France, Gabon, Ivory Coast, Kuwait, Morocco, Nepal, Nigeria, Pakistan, Portugal, S Africa, Togo, Tunisia, UK (RAF), Zaïre.

Development: Developed for the French Army ALAT (Aviation Léger de l'Armée de Terre), this fast and capable helicopter has surpassed all expecta-

Three-view of SA 330 Puma, without armament.

tions in sales to both military and civil customers. By 1977 sales exceeded 500, most of them outside the Anglo-French partner countries that build the original version. There are large sliding doors on each side and loads include 20 troops or 6,600lb (3000kg) slung. The technically more advanced Super Puma, likely to prove an equally successful machine, is not a collaborative project.

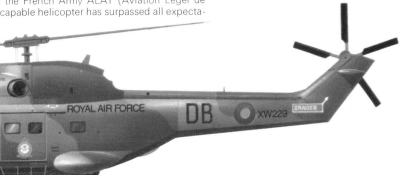

Above: Puma HC.1 of 230 Sqn, RAF Odiham.

Below: Winching down a heavy load of goodies to some very exposed infantry from an even more exposed Puma HC.1 of 33 Sqn, in the RAF tactical helicopter force based at Odiham. Though designed to meet the needs of the ALAT (French Army Aviation), the Puma has proved to be exactly right for military customers (and now offshore oil support operators) all over the world. SA 331 Super Puma promises to be as great a sales success in the 1980s.

Agusta A109 Hirundo

A 109A military and A 129

Origin: C. A. Giovanni Agusta, Gallarate, Italy.
Type: (A 109) multi-role, (129) gunship.
Engines: Two 420shp Allison 250-C20B turboshafts; (129) see text.
Dimensions: Diameter of four-blade main rotor 36ft 1in (11·00m); length overall (rotors turning) 42ft 10in (13·05m); height 10ft 10in (3·30m).
Weights: Empty about 3,120lb (1415kg); maximum loaded over 5,400lb (2450kg).
Performance: maximum cruise 165mph (266km/h); max range at S/L 351 miles (565km).
Armament: (109) one remotely sighted and aimed Minigun or GPMG and either two rocket pods or four TOW or Hot missiles with sight system.
History: First flight 4 August 1971; (production) 1976.
Users: Italian Army (evaluation).

Development: Not yet in production, the military version of the sleek and attractive A 109 is one of the smallest high-performance twin-turbine helicopters with all-weather capability. Five are being tried in simulated battle conditions by the Italian Army, primarily in the anti-tank role but also as electronic-warfare platforms, as troop carriers (seven plus pilot) and as casevac ambulances with two stretchers and two attendants. The projected

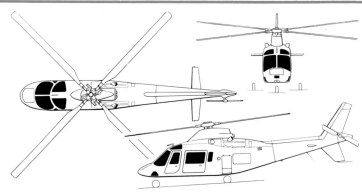

Above: Three-view of A 109A (without TOW missiles).

A 129 would have a slim tandem-seat nose similar to that of the Hughes AH-64, with pilot in the rear, and extensive weapon options; proposed engines are Allison 250-C30 derated to 450hp, with 550hp available from either in emergency.

Below: One of the prettiest helicopters, the Agusta A 109A is being evaluated by the Italian Army. Production could be large.

Bell 47

AB 47, KH-4, H-13 Sioux

Origin: Bell Helicopter Co (now Bell Helicopter Textron), Fort Worth, USA; licence-built by Kawasaki, Japan; Agusta, Italy; Westland, UK.
Type: Three-seat utility and training.
Engine: Flat-six piston engine with crankshaft vertical, usually 178/200hp Franklin (early models), 240hp Lycoming VO-435 or (late) 270hp TVO-435.
Dimensions: (Typical of late models) diameter of two-blade main rotor 37ft 1½in (11·32m); length overall (rotors turning) 43ft 4¾in (13·20m); height overall 9ft 3½in (2·83m).
Weights: (47J-3) empty 1,819lb (825kg); maximum loaded 2,950lb (1340kg).
Performance: (Typical late model) maximum speed 105mph (169km/h); cruising speed 86mph (138km/h); range at low level, no reserve, 210 miles (338km).
Armament: Many equipped with fixed forward-firing gun (LMG, GPMG or Minigun), rocket pods or early anti-tank wire-guided missiles.
History: First flight (prototype) 8 December 1945; service delivery of first YH-13 and HTL-1, 1946.

Users: Argentina, Australia, Austria, Brazil, Burma, Cambodia (not believed operational), Canada, Chile, Dahomey, Ecuador, Greece, Guinea, Honduras, India, Indonesia, Iran, Italy, Jamaica, Japan, Kenya, Libya, Malagasy, Malaysia, Malta, Mexico, Morocco, New Zealand, Pakistan, Paraguay, Peru, Spain, Sri Lanka, Taiwan, Tanzania, Turkey, UK (Army).

Development: Larry Bell flew his first helicopter in mid-1943, and in 1946 the completely redesigned Model 47 became the first helicopter in the world to be certificated for general use. Over 5,000 were built by Bell, Kawasaki (KH-4 variants) and Westland; Agusta still builds at a low rate, with 1,200 delivered since 1954. Most military 47s are liaison and training machines seating the pilot centrally in front and two passengers behind.

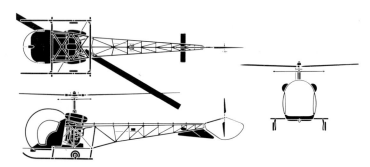

Above: Three-view of typical 47G.

Above: 32 years after first flight thousands of Bell 47 variants still clatter people to and fro. Here, an Agusta-built Sioux AH.1 of British Army passes Schloss Marienburg, south of Hanover.

Bell 209 HueyCobra

AH-1G to -1T HueyCobra (data for -1G)

Origin: Bell Helicopter Textron, USA.
Type: Two-seat combat helicopter.
Engine: 1,100shp Lycoming T53-L-13 turboshaft.
Dimensions: Main-rotor diameter 44ft (13·4m); overall length (rotors turning) 52ft 11½in (16·14m); length of fuselage 44ft 5in (13·54m); height 13ft 5½in (4·1m).
Weights: Empty 6,073lb (2754kg); maximum 9,500lb (4309kg).
Performance: Maximum speed 219mph (352km/h); maximum rate of climb (not vertical) 1,230ft (375m)/min; service ceiling 11,400ft (3475m); hovering ceiling in ground effect 9,900ft (3015m); range at sea level with 8% reserve 357 miles (574km).
Armament: Typically one 7·62mm multi-barrel Minigun, one 40mm grenade launcher, both in remote-control turrets, or 20mm six-barrel or 30mm three-barrel cannon, plus four stores pylons for 76 rockets of 2·75in calibre or Minigun pods or 20mm gun pod, or (TOWCobra) eight TOW missiles in tandem tube launchers on two outer pylons, inners being available for other stores.
History: First flight 7 September 1965; combat service June 1967 (TOW-Cobra January 1973).
Users: Iran, Saudi Arabia, Spain (Navy), US Army, US Marine Corps.

Development: First flown in 1965 after only six months of development, the HueyCobra is a combat development of the UH-1 Iroquois family. It combines the dynamic parts — engine, transmission and rotor system — of the original Huey with a new streamlined fuselage providing for a gunner in the front and pilot above and behind him and for a wide range of fixed and power-aimed armament systems. The first version was the US Army AH-1G, with 1,100hp T53 engine, of which 1,124 were delivered, including eight to the Spanish Navy for anti-ship strike and 38 as trainers to the US Marine Corps. The AH-1Q is an anti-armour version often called TOWCobra because it carries eight TOW missile pods as well as the appropriate sighting system. The AH-1J SeaCobra of the Marine Corps and Iranian Army has twin engines, the 1,800hp UAC Twin Pac having two T400 power sections driving one shaft. Latest versions are the -1Q, -1R, -1S and -1T, with more power and new equipment. All Cobras can have a great variety of armament.

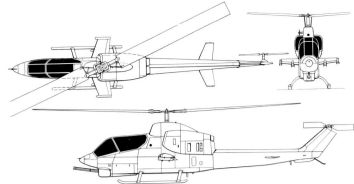

Above: Three-view of AH-1J or similar Twin Pac model.

Above: Bell AH-1J SeaCobra of Imperial Iranian Army Aviation Service, with twin T400 engines. Note XM197 electrically-driven turret with triple 60in (1·52m) barrels.

Above: Original Cobra, the US Army AH-1G.

Below: Probably the most important anti-tank missile in the world (pending a new one from the Soviet Union), TOW gets its name from Tube launched, Optically sighted and Wire guided. It arms the AH-1Q TOW Cobra.

Bell "Huey" family

XH-40, UH-1 Iroquois series (Models 204, 205, 212 and 214), CH-118 and -135, and Isfahan

Origin: Bell Helicopter Textron, Fort Worth, USA; built under licence by Agusta, Italy; Fuji, Japan; and AIDC, Taiwan.

Type: Multi-role utility and transport helicopter.

Engine: Originally, one Lycoming T53 free-turbine turboshaft rated at 600–640shp, later rising in stages to 825, 930, 1,100 and 1,400shp; (some Agusta-built AB 204) Rolls-Royce Gnome, 1,250shp; (212) 1,800shp P&WC PT6T-3 (T400) coupled turboshafts, flat-rated at 1,250shp and with 900shp immediately available from either following failure of the other; (214) 2,930shp Lycoming LTC4B (T55) flat-rated at 2,050shp.

Dimensions: Diameter of twin-blade main rotor (204, UH-1B, C) 44ft 0in (13·41m), (205, 212) 48ft 0in (14·63m) (tracking tips, 48ft 2¼in, 14·69m); (214) 50ft 0in (15·24m); overall length (rotors turning) (early) 53ft 0in (16·15m) (virtually all modern versions) 57ft 3¼in (17·46m); height overall (modern, typical) 14ft 4⅝in (4·39m).

Weights: Empty (XH-40) about 4,000lb (1814kg), (typical 205) 4,667lb (2116kg), (typical 212) 5,549lb (2517kg), (214/214B) about 6,000lb (2722kg); maximum loaded (XH-40) 5,800lb (2631kg), (typical 205) 9,500lb (4309kg), (212/UH-1N) 10,500lb (4762kg), (214B) 16,000lb (7257kg).

Performance: Maximum speed (all) typically 127mph (204km/h); econ cruise speed, usually same; max range with useful payload, typically 248 miles (400km).

Armament: See text.

History: First flight (XH-40) 22 October 1956, (production UH-1) 1958, (205) August 1961, (212) 1969, (214) 1974.

Users: (Bell-built) Argentina, Australia, Austria, Brazil, Brunei, Burma, Canada, Chile, Colombia, Dubai, Ethiopia, W Germany, Ghana, Greece, Guatemala, Indonesia, Iran, Israel, Italy, Jamaica, Japan, Kampuchea, S Korea, Lebanon, Malaysia, Mexico, Morocco, Netherlands, New Zealand, Norway, Oman, Panama, Peru, Philippines, Spain, Taiwan, Thailand, Turkey, Uganda, Uruguay, USA (AF, Navy, Marines, Army, Coast Guard),

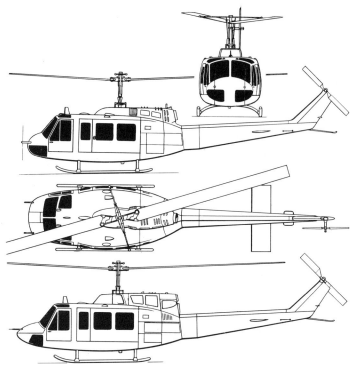

Above: Three-view of Bell UH-1H Iroquois, with additional side view (bottom) of UH-1N.

Venezuela, Yugoslavia, Zambia; (Agusta-built) Austria, Iran, Italy, Kuwait, Lebanon, Morocco, Netherlands, Norway, Oman, Saudi Arabia, Somalia, Spain, Sweden, Turkey, United Arab Emirates, Yemen, Yugoslavia, Zambia; (Fuji-built) Japan; (AIDC-built) Taiwan.

Above: Agusta-Bell AB.204B of Luftstreitkräfte (Austrian Air Force).

Above: Bell 205 of Heyl Ha'Avir (Israel Defence Force/Air Force).

Foot of page, left: Agusta builds unique ASW versions with radar, sonobuoys and (yellow) torpedoes. This is the latest of this family, the twin-engined 212ASW, in production for Italy and Turkey.

Below: a locally developed Bofors Bantam guided missile zips from an Agusta-Bell 204B of the Swedish Army Aviation Department.

Above: Bell UH-1D Iroquois (US Army).

Above: Large numbers of Huey versions served in Vietnam. Here an air gunner blasts away with a 7·62mm M60 from a new UH-1H.

Below: UH-1N twin-engined "Two-Twelve" of the US Navy, with seats for 14 passengers.

Bottom: The kind of mission that Huey pilots took as routine in SE Asia; putting down troops where landing was impossible

Foot of page, left: Test launch of a Sistel Sea Killer Mk 1 missile from AB.204AS of Italian Navy.

Development: Used by more air forces, and built in greater numbers, than any other military aircraft since World War II, the "Huey" family of helicopters grew from a single prototype, the XH-40, for the US Army. Over 20 years the gross weight has been almost multiplied by three, though the size has changed only slightly. Early versions seat eight to ten, carried the occasional machine-gun, and included the TH-1L Seawolf trainer for the US Navy and the Italian-developed Agusta-Bell 204AS with radar and ASW sensors and torpedoes. The Model 205 (UH-1D, -1H &c) have more power and carry up to 15 passengers. Dornier built 352 for the W German Army, and similar versions are still in production at Agusta, Fuji and AIDC. Canada sponsored the twin-engined 212 (UH-1N, Canada CH-135), which again is made in Italy in an ASW version, with a new radar, AQS-13B variable-depth sonar and two torpedoes. Most powerful Huey is the 214 and 214B, first ordered by Iran, in whose service the 214A Isfahan has set several climb and altitude records. The 214 series have a new high-rated transmission system. "Noda-Matic" vibration-damping suspension and broad rotor blades allowing speed to rise to 150mph (241km/h). Many Hueys (called thus from the original "HU" designation, later changed to UH) carry guns, anti-tank missiles and special night-fighting gear, but most are simple casevac and assault transports. Official US military name is Iroquois. The HueyCobra "gunship" models are described on the previous page.

Bell Kiowa and JetRanger

Variants, see text.

Origin: Bell Helicopter Textron, Fort Worth, USA; licence-built by Agusta, Italy (and some by Commonwealth Aircraft, Australia).

Type: Light multi-role helicopter.

Engine: One 317shp Allison T63-700 or 250-C18 turboshaft; (206B models) 420shp Allison 250-C20B or 400shp C20.

Dimensions: Diameter of two-blade main rotor 35ft 4in (10·77m), (206B) 33ft 4in (10·16m), (206L) 37ft 0in (11·28m); length overall (rotors turning) 40ft 11¾in (12·49m), (206B) 38ft 9½in (11·82m); height 9ft 6½in (2·91m).

Weights: Empty 1,464lb (664kg), (206B slightly less), (206L) 1,962lb (890kg); maximum loaded 3,000lb (1361kg), (206B) 3,200lb (1451kg), (206L) 4,000lb (1814kg).

Performance: Economical cruise (Kiowa S/L) 117mph (188km/h), (206B 5,000ft, 1525m) 138mph (222km/h); max range S/L no reserve with max useful load, 305 miles (490km), (206B and L) 345 miles (555km).

Armament: usually none (see text).

History: First flight (OH-4A) 8 December 1962, (206A) 10 January 1966, (206B) 1970.

Users: (Military) U Arab Emirates, Argentina, Australia, Austria, Brazil, Brunei, Canada, Chile, Colombia, Dubai, Iran, Israel, Italy, Jamaica, Japan, Liberia, Malaysia, Malta, Mexico, Morocco, Oman, Saudi Arabia, Spain, Sri Lanka, Sweden, Tanzania, Thailand, Turkey, Uganda, United States, Venezuela.

Development: First flown as the OH-4A, loser in the US Army Light Observation Helicopter contest of 1962, the 206 was marketed as the civil JetRanger, this family growing to encompass the more powerful 206B and more capacious 206L LongRanger. In 1968 the US Army re-opened the LOH competition, naming Bell now winner and buying 2,200 OH-58A Kiowas similar to the 206A but with larger main rotor. US Navy trainers are TH-57A Sea Rangers, Candian designation is CH-136, and Australian-assembled models for Army use are 206B standard. Agusta builds AB 206B JetRanger IIs, many for military use (Sweden uses the HKP 6 with torpedoes) and the big-rotor AB206A-1 and B-1. Sales of all versions exceed 5,500, most being five-seaters (206L, seven) and US Army Kiowas having the XM27 kit with Minigun and various other weapons (probably to be modified to OH-58C standard).

Above: The Canadian Armed Forces have 74 brightly painted CH-136

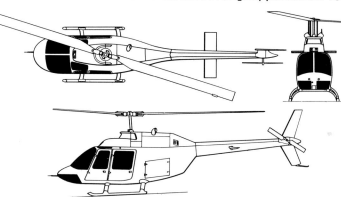

Above: Three-view of typical 206B JetRanger II.

Below: The US Army received 2,200 OH-58A Kiowas, which have flown a seven-figure number of hours. Standard armament includes the XM27 kit based on the 7.62mm multi-barrel Minigun. The force may now be reworked to OH-58C standard.

Boeing-Vertol YUH-61A

YUH-61A (to be named if adopted)

Origin: Boeing Vertol, Philadelphia, USA.
Type: Proposed LAMPS helicopter (see text).
Engines: Two 1,536shp General Electric T700 turboshafts.
Dimensions: Diameter of four-blade main rotor 49ft 0in (14·94m); length overall (rotors turning) 60ft 8½in (18·50m); height over stopped tail rotor 15ft 6in (4·72m).
Weights: Empty 9,750lb (4422kg); maximum loaded 19,700lb (8935kg).
Performance: Cruise at 4,000ft (1220m) 167mph (268km/h); range with max 5,924lb (2687kg) payload and 30min reserve 370 miles (595km).
History: First flight 29 November 1974.
User: Under evaluation for US Navy.
Development: Under a $91 million contract awarded in August 1972 Boeing Vertol designed and delivered three prototypes of this outstanding tactical transport helicopter to compete against the Sikorsky YUH-60A in the UTTAS (Utility Tactical Transport Aircraft System) programme. The YUH-61A is extremely important to Vertol, even though the civil Model 179 is already a firm programme with an order for 28 from one oil company placed in 1975. The company failed to win the UTTAS programme, but it would be premature to eliminate the YUH-61A from this book because a modified version could win the important US Navy LAMPS III competition. The Light Airborne Multi-Purpose System is intended to provide DDG-963 and FFG-7 warships with helicopters to destroy hostile submarines and fire missiles at hostile surface ships.

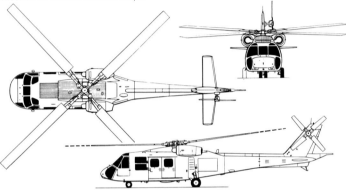

Above: Three-view of YUH-61A (LAMPS III will differ in detail).

Above: Seen in a tight turn near the ground, the YUH-61A was competing for a potentially large US Navy order as this book went to press.

Above: For shipboard use a LAMPS III version would have a redesigned landing gear and totally different mission equipment including radar, sonobuoys, MAD ''bird'' and AS torpedoes.

Boeing-Vertol H-46 family

CH-46 Sea Knight, UH-46, CH-113, KV-107

Origin: Boeing Vertol, Philadelphia, USA; licence-built by Kawasaki, Japan.
Type: Transport, search/rescue, minesweeping.
Engines: Two 1,250–1,870shp General Electric T58 or Rolls-Royce Gnome turboshafts.
Dimensions: Diameter of each three-blade main rotor 50ft 0in (15·24m); fuselage length 44ft 10in (13·66m); height 16ft 8½in (5·09m).
Weights: Empty (KV-107/II-2) 10,732lb (4868kg), (CH-46E) 11,585lb (5240kg); maximum loaded (KV) 19,000lb (8618kg), (E) 21,400lb (9706kg).
Performance: Typical cruise 120mph (193km/h); range with 30min reserve (6,600lb, 3000kg payload) 109 miles (175km), (2,400lb, 1088kg payload) 633 miles (1020km).
History: First flight (107) April 1958, (prototype CH-46A) 27 August 1959.
Users: Canada, Japan, Sweden, USA (Marine Corps, Navy).

Development: The CH-46A Sea Knight was an assault transport carrying up to 25 equipped troops or 4,000lb (1814kg) cargo. Over 600 of these were followed by more powerful CH-46D and F versions, the Navy UH-46A for ship replenishment and the CH-46E and UH-46D with 1,870hp T58-10 engines. Canada uses CH-113 Labradors and 113A Voyageurs, Sweden uses the HKP-7 with Gnome engines, and in Japan Kawasaki has built nearly 100 of various KV-107 versions.

Above: Kawasaki builds several versions of the basic 107, including the KV-107/IIA-3 of the JMSDF (upper) and KV-107/II-5, designated HKP-7 by Swedish Navy (lower).

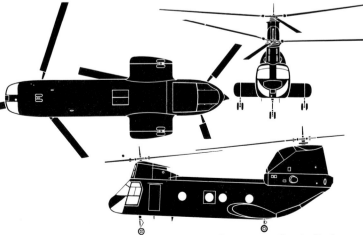

Above: Three-view of CH-46D (other versions generally similar).

Boeing-Vertol CH-47 Chinook

CH-47A, B and C Chinook (data for C)

Origin: Boeing Vertol Company, USA; built under licence by Elicotteri Meridionali and SIAI-Marchetti, Italy.

Type: Medium transport helicopter with normal crew of two/three.

Engines: Two 3,750shp Lycoming T55-L-11A free-turbine turboshafts.

Dimensions: Diameter of main rotors 60ft (18·29m); length, rotors turning, 99ft (30·2m); length of fuselage 51ft (15·54m); height 18ft 7in (5·67m).

Weights: Empty 20,616lb (9351kg); loaded (condition 1) 33,000lb (14,969kg); (overload condition II) 46,000lb (20,865kg).

Performance: Maximum speed (condition I) 189mph (304km/h); (II) 142mph (229km/h); initial climb (I) 2,880ft (878m)/min; (II) 1,320ft (402m)/min; service ceiling (I) 15,000ft (4570m); (II) 8,000ft (2440m); mission radius, cruising speed and payload (I) 115 miles (185km) at 158mph (254km/h) with 7,262lb (3294kg); (II) 23 miles (37km) at 131mph (211km/h) with 23,212lb (10,528kg).

Armament: Normally, none.

History: First flight (YCH-47A) 21 September 1961; (CH-47C) 14 October 1967.

Users: Australia, Canada, Iran*, Israel, Italy*, Spain, Thailand, US Army. (*Italian-built).

Development: Development of the Vertol 114 began in 1956 to meet the need of the US Army for a turbine-engined all-weather cargo helicopter able to operate effectively in the most adverse conditions of altitude and temperature. Retaining the tandem-rotor configuration, the first YCH-47A flew on the power of two 2,200shp Lycoming T55 turboshaft engines and

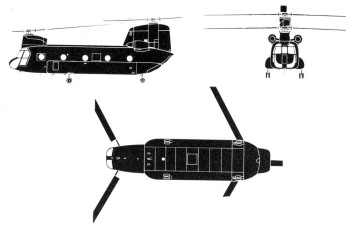

Above: Three-view of CH-47C (CH-47B similar)

led directly to the production CH-47A. With an unobstructed cabin 7½ft (2·29m) wide, 6½ft (1·98m) high and over 30ft (9·2m) long, the Chinook proved a valuable vehicle, soon standardised as US Army medium helicopter and deployed all over the world. By 1972 more then 550 had served in Vietnam, mainly in the battlefield airlift of troops and weapons but also rescuing civilians (on one occasion 147 refugees and their belongings were carried to safety in one Chinook) and lifting back for salvage or repair 11,500 disabled aircraft valued at more than $3,000 million. The A model gave way to the CH-47B, with 2,850hp engines and numerous improvements and, finally, to the much more powerful CH-47C. Over 800 Chinooks were built, all at Boeing Vertol at Philadelphia (successor to Piasecki). Small numbers of C models continue in production in Italy.

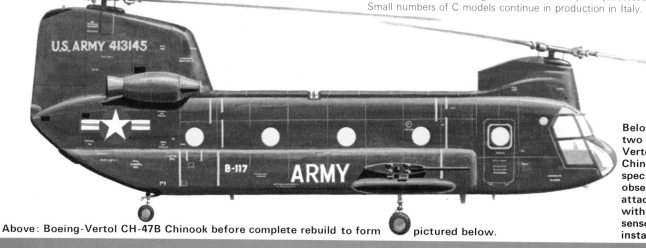

Above: Boeing-Vertol CH-47B Chinook before complete rebuild to form pictured below.

Below: These two Boeing-Vertol CH-47C Chinooks are special night observation attack transports with multi-sensor nose installations.

Hughes TH-55 Osage

Model 300 and 300C, TH-55A Osage, NH-300C

Origin: Hughes Helicopters, Culver City, USA; (NH-300C) BredaNardi, Ascoli, Italy; Kawasaki, Japan.
Type: Light helicopter.
Engine: One 180hp Lycoming HIO-360-A1A (TH-55A, HIO-360-B1A) flat-six; (300C, NH-300C) 190hp HIO-360-D1A.
Dimensions: Diameter of three-blade main rotor 25ft 3½in (7·71m), (300C) 26ft 10in (8·18m); length overall (rotors turning) 28ft 10¾in (8·80m), (300C) 30ft 11in (9·42m); height overall 8ft 2¾in (2·50m).
Weights: Empty (TH) 1,008lb (457kg), (300C) 1,050lb (476kg); maximum loaded (TH) 1,850lb (839kg), (300C) 2,050lb (930kg).
Performance: Max cruise (TH) 75mph (121km/h), (300C) 95mph (153km/h); range with no reserve (TH) 204 miles (328km), (300C) 230 miles (370km).
History: First flight (Model 269) October 1956, (300) 1961, (300C) August 1969.
Users: Brazil, Guyana, Italy, Japan, Nicaragua, Sierra Leone, US Army.

Development: The Hughes 269A seats two side-by-side and it was evaluated in 1958 as a US Army command/observation machine designated YHO-2HU. In 1964 it was adopted under the designation TH-55A Osage as the standard training helicopter, and 792 were delivered by 1969. Often as many as 100 could be seen airborne at once at Ft Wolters and Ft Rucker in the late 1960s. One Osage is flying with a Curtiss-Wright RC2-60 (Wankel) engine and another with a 317shp Allison 250-C18 turboshaft. Kawasaki made 48 for the JGSDF and many have been exported by Hughes. The 300 seats three on a wide bench, while the 300C carries 45 per cent greater payload. The BredaNardi NH-300C remains in low-rate production.

Above: Despite all the pupils can do, nearly 700 Osages are still training pilots to fly the 9,000 helicopters of the US Army.

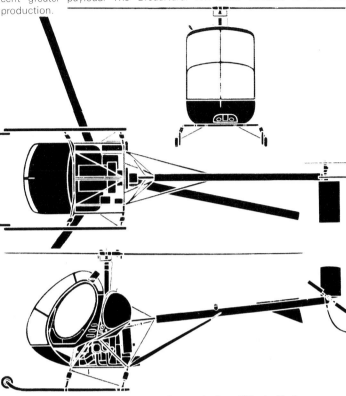

Above: Three-view of TH-55A Osage (other 300 similar).

Hughes OH-6 Cayuse and 500M

OH-6 Cayuse, 500M and NH-500M, 369HM, Defender and RACA-500

Origin: Hughes Helicopters, Culver City, USA; (NH) BredaNardi, Ascoli, Italy; (369HM) Kawasaki, Japan; (RACA) RACA, Buenos Aires, Argentina.
Type: Light multi-role helicopter.
Engine: One Allison turboshaft, (OH-6A) T63-5A flat-rated at 252·5shp, (500M) 250-C18A flat-rated at 278shp.
Dimensions: Diameter of four-blade main rotor 26ft 4in (8·03m); length overall (rotors turning) 30ft 3¾in (9·24m); height overall 8ft 1½in (2·48m).
Weights: Empty (OH) 1,229lb (557kg), (500M) 1,130lb (512kg); maximum loaded (OH) 2,700lb (1225kg), (500M) 3,000lb (1361kg).
Performance: Max cruise at S/L 150mph (241km/h); typical range on normal fuel 380 miles (611km).
Armament: See text.
History: First flight (OH-6A) 27 February 1963, (500M) early 1968.
Users: (Military) Argentina, Bolivia, Colombia, Congo, Denmark, Dominica, Italy, Japan, Pakistan, Philippines, Sierra Leone, Spain, Taiwan, United States.

Development: Original winner of the controversial LOH (Light Observation Helicopter) competition of the US Army in 1961, the OH-6A Cayuse is one of the most compact flying machines in history, relative to its capability. The standard machine carries two crew and four equipped troops, or up to 1,000lb (454kg) of electronics and weapons including the XM-27 gun or XM-75 grenade launcher plus a wide range of other infantry weapons. The US Army bought 1,434, and several hundred other military or para-military examples have been built by Hughes or its licensees. BredaNardi is helping Pakistan get into production. The Spanish Navy 500Ms carry MAD and two Mk 44 torpedoes. The 500D-M is a more powerful seven-seater. In 1977 an armed model was named Defender, carrying four TOW missiles and sight system; it is to go into production in South Korea.

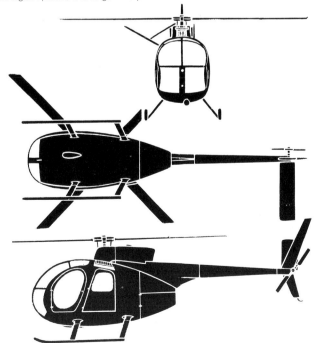

Above: Three-view of OH-6A (500M and Defender similar).

Left: The tadpole-like "Loach" (popular name for it in the US Army) is nimble and carries a wealth of weapons.

Hughes AH-64

Model 77, AH-64 (to be named)

Origin: Hughes Helicopters, Culver City, USA.
Type: Armed tactical helicopter.
Engines: Two 1,536shp General Electric T700 turboshafts.
Dimensions: Diameter of four-blade main rotor 48ft 0in (14·63m); length overall (rotors turning) 55ft 8½in (16·96m); height overall 12ft 1¼in (3·69m).
Weights: Empty 9,500lb (4309kg); maximum loaded 17,400lb (7892kg).
Performance: Maximum speed at 13,200lb (5987kg) 191mph (307 km/h); cruise 180mph (289km/h); max vertical climb 3,200ft (975m)/min; range on internal fuel 359 miles (578km).
Armament: Hughes XM-230 30mm "chain gun" in turret on underside, 76 FFAR rockets, 16 TOW missiles and sight system, forward-looking infra-red and other sensors and range of other options.
History: First flight 30 September 1975; Phase 2 go-ahead November 1976.
User: To be US Army.

Development: First helicopter in history to be adopted after having been planned from the start as a "gunship", the AH-64 was selected over the Bell YAH-63 at the end of 1976 after a tough but instructive competitive fly-off. Unlike the YAH-63 it seats the pilot behind the gunner/co-pilot, and it also has a small four-blade main rotor and tailwheel. Hughes developed the Chain Gun as a radically simpler and cheaper 30mm cannon with chain drive and rotary bolt action. Its turret is designed to fold under the armoured cockpit in a crash landing and the whole helicopter is designed to survive strikes at any point with shells up to 23mm calibre.

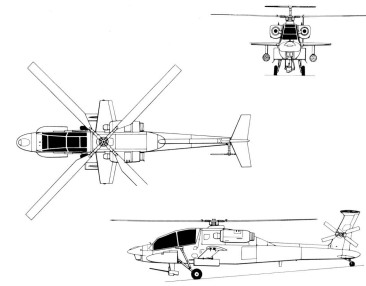

Above: Three-view of YAH-64 (note 60°/120° tail-rotor setting).

Below: Winner of the potentially enormous AAH competition, the first prototype YAH-64 blasts a ground target with folding-fin 2·75in rockets, 76 of which can be carried.

Kaman SH-2 Seasprite

UH-2, HH-2 and SH-2 in many versions (data for SH-2D)

Origin: Kaman Aerospace Corp, USA.
Type: Ship-based multi-role helicopter (ASW, anti-missile defence, observation, search/rescue and utility).
Engine(s): Original versions, one 1,050 or 1,250hp General Electric T58 free-turbine turboshaft; all current versions, two 1,350hp T58-8F.
Dimensions: Main rotor diameter 44ft (13·41m); overall length (blades turning) 52ft 7in (16m); fuselage length 40ft 6in (12·3m); height 13ft 7in (4·14m).
Weights: Empty 6,953lb (3153kg); maximum loaded 13,300lb (6033kg).
Performance: Maximum speed 168mph (270km/h); maximum rate of climb (not vertical) 2,440ft (744m)/min; service ceiling 22,500ft (6858m); range 422 miles (679m).
Armament: See text.
History: First flight (XHU2K-1) 2 July 1959; service delivery (HU2K-1, later called UH-2A) 18 December 1962; final delivery (new) 1972, (conversion) 1975.
User: USA (Navy).

Development: Originally designated HU2K-1 and named Seasprite, this exceptionally neat helicopter was at first powered by a single turbine engine mounted close under the rotor hub and was able to carry a wide range of loads, including nine passengers, in its unobstructed central cabin, with two crew in the nose. The main units of the tailwheel-type landing gear retracted fully. About 190 were delivered and all were later converted to have two T58 engines in nacelles on each side. Some are HH-2C rescue/utility with armour and various armament including chin Minigun turret and waist-mounted machine guns or cannon; others are unarmed HH-2D. One has been used in missile-firing (Sparrow III and Sidewinder)

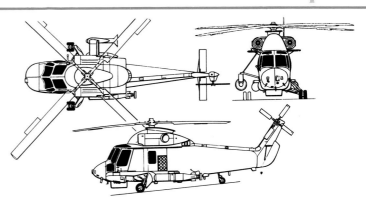

Above: Three-view of Kaman SH-2F Seasprite (gear extended).

trials in the missile-defence role. All Seasprites have since 1970 been drastically converted to serve in the LAMPS (light airborne multi-purpose system) for anti-submarine and anti-missile defence. The SH-2D has more than two tons of special equipment including powerful chin radar, sono-buoys, MAD gear, ECM, new navigation and communications systems and Mk 44 and/or Mk 46 torpedoes. All will eventually be brought up to SH-2F standard with improved rotor, higher gross weight and improved sensors and weapons. The same basic design is one of the contenders for the future competition for a purpose-designed LAMPS helicopter of greater size and power.

Below: One of the world's neatest helicopter platforms, the SH-2F is the only helicopter to meet the US Navy interim LAMPS need for ASW and anti-ship missile defence. Clearly visible are radar, sonobuoys, MAD "bird", homing torpedo and extensive avionics aerials.

Kamov Ka-25

Ka-25

(several versions, designations unknown)

Origin: Design bureau named for Nikolai I. Kamov, Soviet Union.
Type: Ship-based ASW, search/rescue and utility helicopter.
Engines: Two 900hp Glushenkov GTD-3 free-turbine turboshaft.
Dimensions: Main rotor diameter (both) 51ft 8in (15·75m); fuselage length, about 34ft (10·36m); height 17ft 8in (5·4m).
Weights: Empty, about 11,023lb (5000kg); maximum loaded 16,535lb (7500kg).
Performance: Maximum speed 120mph (193km/h); service ceiling, about 11,000ft (3350m); range, about 400 miles (650km).
Armament: One or two 400mm AS torpedoes, nuclear or conventional depth charges or other stores, carried in internal weapon bay.
History: First flight (Ka-20) probably 1960; service delivery of initial production version, probably 1965.
Users: Soviet Union (AV-MF), Syria.

Development: Nikolai Kamov, who died in 1973, was one of the leaders of rotorcraft in the Soviet Union, a characteristic of nearly all his designs being the use of superimposed co-axial rotors to give greater lift in a vehicle of smaller overall size. Large numbers of Ka-15 and -18 piston-engined machines were used by Soviet armed forces, but in 1961 the Aviation Day fly-past at Tushino included a completely new machine designated Ka-20 and carrying a guided missile on each side. It was allotted the NATO code-name of "Harp". Clearly powered by gas turbines, it looked formidable. Later in the 1960s it became clear that from this helicopter Kamov's bureau, under chief engineer Barshevsky, had developed the standard ship-based machine of the Soviet fleets, replacing the Mi-4. Designated the Ka-25 and allotted the new Western code name of "Hormone", it is in service in at least five major versions, with numerous sub-types. Whereas the "missiles" displayed in 1961 have never been seen since, and are thought to have been dummies, the Ka-25 is extremely fully equipped with all-weather anti-submarine sensing and attack equipment. The four landing wheels are each surrounded by a buoyancy bag ring which can be swiftly inflated by the gas bottles just above it. Ka-25s are used aboard the carriers (ASW) cruisers *Minsk*, *Kiev*, *Moskva* and *Leningrad*, *Kresta* and *Kara* class cruisers and from shore bases.

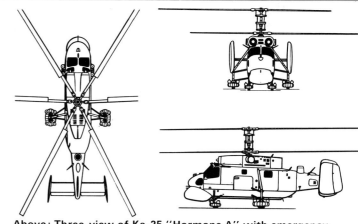

Above: Three-view of Ka-25 "Hormone A" with emergency flotation system.

Above and below: Two examples of the basic ASW version of the Ka-25, called "Hormone A" by NATO. The upper photograph was taken by the US Navy and the lower by the Royal Navy (note Buccaneer and Phantom aboard "Ark Royal").

MBB BO 105

105C and 105VBH

Origin: Messerschmitt-Bölkow-Blohm, Munich, West Germany; licence production by PADC, Philippines.

Type: Multi-role all-weather helicopter.

Engines: Two 400shp Allison 250-C20 turboshafts.

Dimensions: Diameter of four-blade main rotor 32ft 2¾in (9·82m); length overall (rotors turning) 38ft 10¾in (11·84m); height overall 9ft 9½in (2·98m).

Weights: Empty 2,469lb (1120kg) (with tactical armament about 2,645lb, 1200kg); maximum loaded 5,070lb (2300kg).

Performance: Maximum speed S/L 167mph (270km/h); max cruise 144mph (232km/h); max climb 1,378ft (420m)/min; range with standard fuel, no reserve (S/L) 363 miles (585km).

Armament: Various options including six Hot or TOW missiles and stabilised sight system.

History: First flight 16 February 1967; type certification October 1970.

Users: (Military) W Germany, Netherlands, Nigeria, Philippines.

Development: Using an advanced rotor developed with Aérospatiale, this small twin-turbine helicopter is expensive but extremely capable, and is fully aerobatic and cleared for IFR operation in the most adverse conditions. By 1977 some 350 had been sold, including a small number for military use. The German Army has evaluated the 105VBH liaison and observation version, and an anti-tank 105 with six Hots and all-weather sight system. An order for about 300 had long been expected for the German Army when this book went to press, and several other military sales were being negotiated. Boeing Vertol sell in the Americas and PADC assemble the basic 105C in the Philippines. The BO 106 is a wider version, seating seven instead of four.

Right: Launch of a HOT missile from the No 4 tube of a BO 105 equipped with only four tubes.

Below: The standard six-tube HOT installation, with the head of the stabilized sight projecting above the cabin.

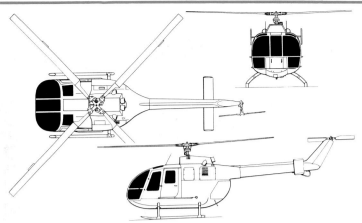

Above: Three-view of the wide-body BO 106.

Mil (WSK-Swidnik) Mi-2

Mil Mi-2 (V-2) and Mi-2M (NATO name "Hoplite")

Origin: WSK-PZL-Swidnik, near Lublin, Poland; original design by Mil bureau, Soviet Union.
Type: Multi-role utility.
Engines: Two WSK-Rzeszów (Isotov licence) GTD-350P turboshafts, each with contingency rating of 431shp.
Dimensions: Diameter of three-blade main rotor 47ft 6¾in (14·50m); length overall (rotors turning) 57ft 2in (17·42m); height overall 12ft 3½in (3·75m).
Weights: Empty (2) 5,213lb (2365kg); maximum loaded 8,157lb (3700kg).
Performance: Max cruise 124mph (200km/h); range with max payload of 1,763lb (800kg) and 5 per cent reserve 105 miles (170km).
History: First flight (Mil) 1961, (WSK) November 1963, (2M) 1 July 1974.
Users: (Military) include Bulgaria, Czechoslovakia, Hungary, Poland, Romania, Soviet Union.

Development: The first production helicopter in the Soviet Union was the Mi-1, modelled along the lines of the S-51 and Sycamore and flown by Mikhail Mil's bureau in September 1948. During the 1950s it became evident, and confirmed by American and French development, that helicopters could be greatly improved with turbine engines. S. P. Isotov

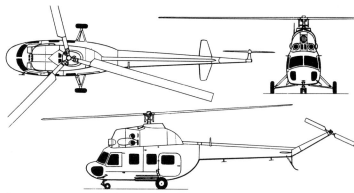

Three-view of WSK-Swidnik Mi-2 without special role equipment.

developed the GTD-350 engine and Mil used two of these in the far superior Mi-2. After initial development at the Mil bureau (Soviet designation V-2) this was transferred to Poland in 1964, after the first Swidnik-built example had flown. WSK-Swidnik has since delivered many hundreds, possibly one-third of them to military customers, and developed plastics rotor blades and the wide-body Mi-2M seating 10 passengers instead of eight. Role kits include two rocket or gun-pod pylons or four stretchers.

Above: A WSK-Swidnik Mi-2 of the Polish Air Force (skis often added round wheels).

Mil Mi-4

Mi-4 (sub-designations unknown) (NATO name "Hound")

Origin: The design bureau of Mikhail L. Mil, Soviet Union.
Type: Multi-role transport and ASW helicopter.
Engine: One 1,700hp Shvetsov ASh-82V 18-cylinder two-row radial.
Dimensions: Diameter of four-blade main rotor 68ft 11in (21·00m); length of fuselage (ignoring rotors) 55ft 1in (16·80m); height overall 17ft 0in (5·18m).
Weights: Empty (typical, not ASW) 11,650lb (5268kg); maximum loaded 17,200lb (7800kg).
Performance: Economical cruise 99mph (160km/h); range 250 miles (400km) with 8 passengers or equivalent, 155 miles (250km) with 11.
Armament: (Most) none; (army assault) fixed or movable machine gun or cannon in front of ventral gondola, optional weapon pylons for rocket or gun pods; (ASW) nose radar, towed MAD bird, sonobuoys, marker flares and other search gear, and torpedo or depth bombs.
History: First flight (prototype) 1951, (production) 1952; service delivery 1953; final delivery after 1961.
Users: (Military) Afghanistan, Albania, Algeria, Bulgaria, China, Cuba, Czechoslovakia, Egypt, Finland, E Germany, Hungary, India, Indonesia, Iraq, Jugoslavia, Khmer, N Korea, Mali, Mongolia, Poland, Romania, Somalia, Soviet Union, Syria, Vietnam, Yemen.

Development: Produced in a frantic hurry on Stalin's direct order, this helicopter looked very like a Sikorsky S-55 when it appeared, but was gradually recognised in the West as considerably bigger and more capable

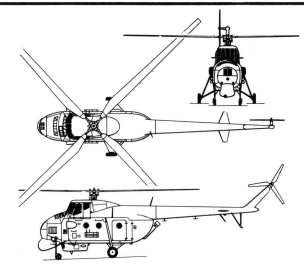

Three-view of Mi-4 ASW version (Soviet designation unknown).

even than the S-58. Among its many versions are assault, ambulance and naval ASW variants, the normal transports having large rear doors for artillery, missiles and small vehicles, and seats for 14 equipped troops. Several thousand were built, and nearly all remain in service, except that some of those exported (to Cuba and Egypt, especially) are no longer operational.

Right: Basic transport Mi-4, Czech Air Force.

Mil Mi-6 and Mi-10

Mi-6 ("Hook"), Mi-10 and -10K ("Harke")

Origin: The design bureau named for Mikhail Mil, Soviet Union.
Type: -6, heavy transport helicopter; -10, crane helicopter for bulky loads; -10K, crane helicopter.
Engines: (-6, -10) two 5,500shp Soloviev D-25V single-shaft free-turbine engines driving common R-7 gearbox; (-10K) two 6,500shp D-25VF.
Dimensions: Main rotor diameter 114ft 10in (35m); overall length (rotors turning) (-6) 136ft 11½in (41·74m); (-10, -10K) 137ft 5½in (41·89m); fuselage length (-6) 108ft 10½in (33·18m); (10, -10K) 107ft 9¾in (32·86m); height (-6) 32ft 4in (9·86m); (-10) 32ft 2in (9·8m); (-10K) 25ft 7in (7·8m).
Weights: Empty (-6, typical) 60,055lb (27,240kg); (-10) 60,185lb (27,300kg); (-10K) 54,410lb (24,680kg); maximum loaded (-6) 93,700lb (42,500kg); (-10) 96,340lb (43,700kg); (-10K) 83,776lb (38,000kg) with 5,500shp engines (90,390lb, 41,000kg expected with D-25VF engines).
Performance: Maximum speed (-6) 186mph (300km/h) (set 100km circuit record at 211·36mph, beyond flight manual limit); (-10) 124mph (200km/h); service ceiling (-6) 14,750ft (4500m); (-10, -10K, limited) 9,842ft (3000m); range (-6 with half payload) 404 miles (650km); (-10 with 12,000kg platform load) 155 miles (250km); (-10K with 11,000kg payload, 6,500shp engines) over 280 miles (450km).
Armament: Normally none, but Mi-6 often seen with manually aimed nose gun of about 12·7mm calibre.
History: First flight (-6) probably early 1957; (-10) 1960; (-10K) prior to 1965.
Users: (6) Bulgaria, Egypt, Indonesia (in storage), Iraq, Soviet Union, Syria, Vietnam, Zambia; (10) Soviet Union.

Development: Development by Mikhail L. Mil's design bureau at Zaporozhye of the dynamic system (rotors and shafting) of the Mi-6 was a task matched only by Soloviev's development of the huge R-7 gearbox, which

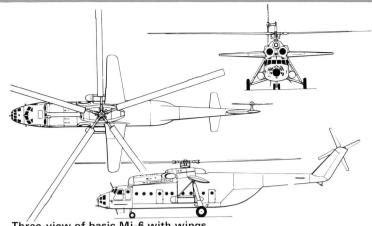
Three-view of basic Mi-6 with wings.

weighs 7,054lb (much more than the pair of engines). By far the biggest rotor system yet flown, this served to lift by far the biggest helicopter, the Mi-6 (NATO code name "Hook"), which quickly set world records for speed and payload, though the normal load is limited to 26,450lb (12,000kg) internally, loaded via huge clamshell rear doors, or 19,840lb (9000kg) externally slung. About 500 have been built, possibly half being in military use. Most have the rotor unloaded in cruising flight (typically 150mph) by a fixed wing of 50ft 2½in span. These huge helicopters have played an active role in field exercises carrying troops (typically 68) and tactical missiles or vehicles in the class of the BRDM. The Mi-10 (code name "Harke") has lofty landing gears which enable it to straddle a load, such as a bus or prefabricated building, 3·75m (12ft 3½in) high; heavy loads weighing 33,070lb (15,000kg) and up to over 65ft in length have been flown. It uses a TV viewing system for load control, but the short-legged Mi-10K has an under-nose gondola.

Mil Mi-8

Mi-8, Mi-8T (NATO names "Hip", Haze")

Origin: The design bureau named for Mikhail Mil, Soviet Union.
Type: General utility helicopter for internal loads and externally mounted weapons; "Haze", ASW.
Engines: Two 1,500shp Isotov TV2-117A single-shaft free-turbine engines driving common VR-8A gearbox.
Dimensions: Main rotor diameter 69ft 10½in (21·29m); overall length, rotors turning, 82ft 9¾in (25·24m); fuselage length 60ft 0¾in (18·31m); height 18ft 6½in (5·65m).
Weights: Empty (-8T) 15,026lb (6816kg); maximum loaded (all) 26,455lb (12,000kg) (heavier weights for non-VTO operation).
Performance: Maximum speed 161mph (260km/h); service ceiling 14,760ft (4500m); range (-8T, full payload, 5 per cent reserve at 3,280ft) 298 miles (480km).
Armament: Optional fitting for external pylons for up to eight stores carried outboard of fuel tanks (always fitted); typical loads eight pods of 57mm rockets, or mix of gun pods and anti-tank missiles (Mi-8 not normally used in anti-tank role).
History: First flight 1960 or earlier; service delivery of military versions, before 1967.
Users: Afghanistan, Bangladesh, Czechoslovakia, Egypt, Ethiopia, Finland, E Germany, Hungary, India, Iraq, N Korea, Libya, Pakistan, Peru, Poland, Romania, Somalia, Soviet Union, S Yemen, Sudan, Syria, Vietnam, Yugoslavia.

Development: Originally powered by a single 2,700shp Soloviev engine, the Mi-8 soon appeared with its present engines and in 1964 added a fifth blade to its main rotor. It has since been the chief general utility helicopter of the Warsaw Pact powers and many other nations. By mid-1974 it was announced that more than 1,000 had been built, the majority for military purposes and with about 300 having been exported. Since then the Mi-8 has continued in production. The basic version is a passenger and troop carrier normally furnished with quickly removable seats for 28 in the main cabin. The -8T is the utility version without furnishing and with circular windows, weapon pylons, cargo rings, a winch/pulley block system for

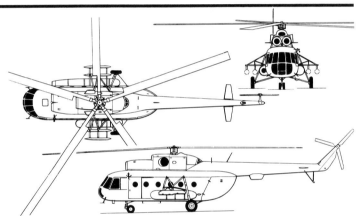
Three-view of assault Mi-8 with weapon pylons and tailboom radar.

loading and optional electric hoist by the front doorway. All versions have large rear clamshell doors (the passenger version having airstairs incorporated) through which a BRDM and other small vehicles can be loaded. "Haze" has AS radar, MAD bird and weapons.

Above: Ilmavoimat means the Finnish Air Force, which has four of the capable Mi-8 helicopters for general airlift missions.

An Mi-8 serving with the Egyptian Air Force (no radar or weapons).

Mil Mi-24

Mi-24 versions with NATO names "Hind A" to "Hind D"

Origin: The design bureau named for Mikhail Mil, Soviet Union.
Type: Tactical multi-role helicopter.
Engines: Almost certainly two 1,500shp Isotov TV2-117A free-turbine turboshaft.
Dimensions: (Estimated) diameter of five-blade main rotor 55ft 9in (17m); length overall (ignoring rotors) 55ft 9in (17m); height overall 14ft (4·25m).
Weights: (Estimated) empty 14,300lb (6500kg); maximum loaded 25,400lb (11,500kg).
Performance: Maximum speed 170mph (275km/h); general performance, higher than Mi-8.
Armament: (Hind-A) usually one 12·7mm gun aimed from nose; two stub wings providing rails for four wire-guided anti-tank missiles and four other stores (bombs, missiles, rocket or gun pods). (Hind-B) two stub wings of different type with four weapon pylons.
History: First flight, before 1972; service delivery, before 1974.
Users: Soviet Union (probably with other Warsaw Pact forces, but not reported by early 1977).

Development: Few details are yet known of this attractive-looking battle-field helicopter, though in 1974 many were seen in service in East Germany and two versions were disclosed to the West in photographs. It appears to be based on the Mi-8, though the engines look smaller and the main rotor has blades of considerably shorter length but increased chord. The nose-wheel-type landing gear is fully retractable, and the cabin is large enough for a crew of two and 12 to 14 troops. The exterior is well streamlined, broken only by avionic aerials and the prominent weapon stub-wings. The Mi-24 is much larger than the British Lynx, yet smaller than the Mi-8. One reason may be that it is the smallest machine capable of using the well-tried Mi-8 dynamic components, and in the anti-tank role the surplus payload could be used for spare missiles or infantry teams that could be dropped and then recovered later. Maximum slung load is estimated at 8,000lb (3630kg).

Above: Mi-24 of the "Hind A" sub-type, serving with the GSFG (Group of Soviet Forces in Germany).

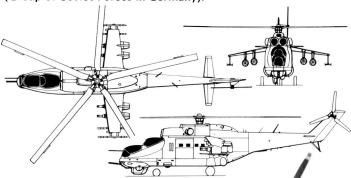

Above: "Hind D", the gunship first seen in May 1977 with new sensors and four-barrel cannon.

Above: Prepared for this book, provisional drawing of "Hind A" sub-type (landing gear extended).

Below: Rare Soviet colour picture of "Hind A" version showing four 32-round rocket pods and outboard anti-tank guided weapon pylons (empty).

Sikorsky S-58

H-34 Seabat, Seahorse, Choctaw

Origin: Sikorsky Aircraft, Division of United Aircraft (now United Technologies) Corporation, Stratford, USA; licence-built by Sud-Aviation (now Aérospatiale), France, and redesigned with turbine power by Westland (see Wessex).

Type: Utility transport, ASW, search/rescue and other roles.

Engine: One 1,525hp Wright Cyclone R-1820-84 nine-cylinder radial.

Dimensions: Diameter of four-blade main rotor 56ft 0in (17·07m); fuselage length (ignoring rotors) 46ft 9in (14·25m); height overall 14ft 3½in (4·36m).

Weights: Empty (typical) 7,750lb (3515kg), (ASW) 8,275lb (3745kg); maximum loaded 14,000lb (6350kg).

Performance: Typical cruise 98mph (158km/h); range with full payload, no reserve 280 miles (450km).

History: First flight 8 March 1954, (S-58T) 19 August 1970.

Users: (Military) include Argentina, Belgium, Brazil, Canada, Central African Republic, Chile, France, W Germany, Haiti, Indonesia, Israel, Italy, Japan, Laos, Netherlands, Nicaragua, Philippines, Thailand.

Development: This useful helicopter was designed to meet the need of the US Navy for an anti-submarine platform (but still not capable of independent search/strike operation), and it entered service in 1955 as the HSS-1. Restyled SH-34G, and with autostabilization designated SH-34J, this model was named Seabat, while the Marines' UH-34D and E and executive VH-34D are Seahorses. Large numbers were built as assault transports for the Army (CH-34A and C Choctaw), while Sud built 166 for the Algerian war. Sikorsky delivered 1,821, and is today busy converting and rebuilding many of these tough but outdated machines with the PT6T Twin Pac engine, giving them a new lease of life as the S-58T. New S-58T versions are planned.

Above: Three-view of basic S-58 (-58T has different front end).

Below: There is justification for describing the S-58 as the first helicopter in the world capable of doing a really worthwhile military job (the only rival, in the same time-scale, is the larger Mil Mi-4). This UH-34D Seahorse is trucking an M-274 Mechanical Mule (with 106mm recoilless rifle) from an assault carrier to beach landing.

Sikorsky S-61

SH-3A and -3D Sea King, HH-3A, RH-3A and many other variants

Origin: Sikorsky Aircraft, Division of United Technologies, USA; built under licence by Agusta (Italy), Mitsubishi (Japan) and Westland (UK).
Type: See text.
Engines: Two General Electric T58 free-turbine turboshaft; (SH-3A and derivatives) 1,250shp T58-8B; (SH-3D and derivatives) 1,400shp T58-10; (S-61R versions) 1,500hp T58-5.
Dimensions: Diameter of main rotor 62ft (18·9m); length overall 72ft 8in (22·15m); (61R) 73ft; height overall 16ft 10in (5·13m).
Weights: Empty (simple transport versions, typical) 9,763lb (4428kg); (ASW, typical) 11,865lb (5382kg); (armed CH-3E) 13,255lb (6010kg); maximum loaded (ASW) about 18,626lb (8449kg); (transport) usually 21,500lb (9750kg); (CH-3E) 22,050lb (10,000kg).
Performance: Maximum speed (typical, maximum weight) 166mph (267km/h); initial climb (not vertical but maximum) varies from 2,200 to 1,310ft (670–400m)/min, depending on weight; service ceiling, typically 14,700ft (4480m); range with maximum fuel, typically 625 miles (1005km).
Armament: Very variable.
History: First flight 11 March 1959.
Users: Argentina, Australia, Belgium, Brazil, Canada, Denmark, Egypt, W Germany, India, Indonesia, Iran, Israel, Italy (Agusta), Japan (Mitsubishi), Malaysia, Norway, Pakistan, Spain, USA (Air Force, Navy, Marine Corps, Army).

Development: Representing a quantum jump in helicopter capability, the S-61 family soon became a staple product of Sikorsky Aircraft, founded in March 1923 by Igor Sikorsky who left Russia after the Revolution and settled in the United States. He flew the first wholly practical helicopter in 1940, and his R-4 was the first helicopter in the world put into mass production (in 1942). A development, the S-51, was in 1947 licensed to the British firm Westland Aircraft, starting colloboration reviewed on later pages. The S-55 and S-58 were made in great numbers in the 1950s for many civil and military purposes, both now flying with various turbine engines. The S-61 featured an amphibious hull, twin turbine engines located above the hull close to the drive gearbox and an advanced flight-control system. First versions carried anti-submarine warfare (ASW) sensors and weapons, but later variants were equipped for various transport duties, minesweeping, drone or spacecraft recovery (eg lifting Astronauts from the sea), electronic surveillance and (S-61R series) transport/gunship and other combat duties.

Below: One of the 80-odd SH-3D Sea King ASW helicopters serving with ten helicopter ASW squadrons (in this case, HS-2). The only obvious mission equipment is the towed MAD "bird"; soot from the engines testifies to hard flying.

Above: S-61R (Air Force CH-3E) with sponsons, retractable tricycle landing gear and rear cargo ramp.

Above: Agusta-Sikorsky SH-3D of the Marinavia (Italian Navy) launches a Sea Killer Mk 2, the delivery weapon in the Marte air-to-ship system developed by the Italian Sistel company. Effective range is 15·5 miles (25km).

Above: Three-view of SH-3H showing radar, sonobuoys and MAD.

Sikorsky S-64

S-64, CH-54A and B Tarhe

Origin: Sikorsky Aircraft, Division of United Technologies, Stratford, USA.
Type: Crane helicopter.
Engines: (CH-54A) two 4,500shp Pratt & Whitney T73-1 turboshafts, (CH-54B) two 4,800shp T73-700.
Dimensions: Diameter of six-blade main rotor 72ft 0in (21·95m); length overall (rotors turning) 88ft 6in (26·97m); height overall 18ft 7in (5·67m).
Weights: Empty (A) 19,234lb (8724kg); maximum loaded (A) 42,000lb (19,050kg), (B) 47,000lb (21,318kg).
Performance: Maximum cruise 105mph (169km/h); hovering ceiling out of ground effect 6,900ft (2100m); range with max fuel and 10 per cent reserve (typical) 230 miles (370km).
History: First flight (S-64) 9 May 1962; service delivery (CH-54A) late 1964, (B) late 1969.
User: US Army.

Development: Developed from the first large US Army helicopter, the S-56, via the piston-engined S-60, the S-64 is an efficient weight-lifter which in Vietnam carried loads weighing up to 20,000lb (9072kg). The CH-54A Tarhes used in that campaign retrieved more than 380 shot-down aircraft, saving an estimated $210 million, and carried special vans housing up to 87 combat-equipped troops. The improved CH-54B, distinguished externally by twin main wheels, has lifted loads up to 40,780lb (18,497kg) and reached a height of 36,122ft (11,010m). There is no fuselage, just a structural beam joining the tail rotor to the cockpit in which seats are provided for three pilots, one facing to the rear for manoeuvring with loads. The dynamic components (rotor, gearboxes, shafting) were used as the basis for those of the S-65. With cancellation of the HLH (Heavy-Lift Helicopter) the S-64 remains the only large crane helicopter in the West.

Above: Three-view of S-64 (all versions similar).

Below: A 155mm howitzer of the M-114 family makes a reasonable load of almost six US tons for a CH-54A Tarhe of the US Army. Note main-rotor tip trails.

Sikorsky S-65

CH-53A Sea Stallion, HH-53, RH-53 and many other variants

Origin: Sikorsky Aircraft, Division of United Technologies, USA; licence-built by VFW-Fokker, Germany.

Type: See text.

Engines: (Early versions) two 2,850shp General Electric T64-6 free-turbine turboshaft; (CH-53D and G) 3,925shp T64 versions; (RH-53D) 4,380shp T64 versions; (CH-53E) three 4,380shp T64-415.

Dimensions: Diameter of main rotor (most) 72ft 3in (22·02m); (CH-53E) seven-blades, 79ft (24·08m); length overall (typical) 88ft 3in (26·9m); height overall 24ft 11in (7·6m).

Weights: Empty (CH-53D) 23,485lb (10,653kg); maximum loaded (most) 42,000lb (19,050kg); (RH-53D) 50,000lb; (CH-53E) over 60,000lb.

Performance: Maximum speed (most) 196mph (315km/h); (CH-53E) over 200mph; initial climb (maximum) typically 2,180ft (664m)/min; service ceiling, typically 20,400ft (6220m); range, typically 540 miles 869km).

Armament: most, none.

History: First flight 14 October 1964; service delivery (CH-53A) May 1966.

Users: Austria, W Germany, Iran, Israel, USA (Air Force, Navy, Marine Corps).

Development: Obviously developed from the S-61, the S-65 family includes the largest and most powerful helicopters in production outside the Soviet Union. The dynamic parts (rotors, gearboxes and control system) were originally similar to those of the S-64 Skycrane family, but using titanium and with folding main-rotor blades. Most versions served in Vietnam from January 1967, performing countless tasks including recovery of downed aircraft. In 1968 a standard CH-53A completed a prolonged series of loops and rolls, while others set records for speed and payload. Most of the 153 CH-53D for the German army were built in Germany, together with the engines. Latest versions are the RH-53D for mine countermeasures (MCM) with comprehensive tow/sweep systems and 0·5in guns for exploding surfaced mines, and the three-engined CH-53E for carrying slung loads up to 18 tons.

Above: CH-53D of the Heer (Federal German Army).

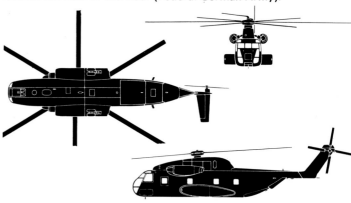

Above: Three-view of the CH-53D (other twin-engined versions similar).

Below: Sikorsky were fortunate in being able to put together the S-64 dynamic parts and the T64 engine to produce the CH-53A for the Marine Corps. This has served as the basis for the most capable family of Western helos.

Sikorsky UH-60A

S-70, YUH-60A

Origin: Sikorsky Aircraft, Division of United Technologies, Stratford, USA.
Type: Multi-role tactical transport.
Engines: Two 1,536shp General Electric T700-700 turboshafts.
Dimensions: Diameter of four-blade main rotor 53ft 8in (16·36m); length overall (rotors turning) 64ft 10in (19·76m); height overall 16ft 5in (5·00m).
Weights: Empty about 10,000lb (4536kg); maximum loaded 21,400lb (9707kg).
Performance: Maximum speed at 16,750lb (7597kg) mission weight 198mph (318km/h).
History: First flight 17 October 1974.
Users: See text.

Development: As this book was written Sikorsky was locked in competition with Boeing Vertol for two potentially very large production programmes: the UTTAS (Utility Tactical Transport Aircraft System) for the US Army and the Mk III LAMPS (Light Airborne Multi-Purpose System) for the US Navy. The S-70 has been planned to fulfil the requirements of both, though the three prototypes evaluated since 1974 have all been built for and flown chiefly by the Army for the UTTAS mission. This mission is primarily transport of an assault squad of 11 men plus crew of three, though other loads include four stretcher casualties or a slung load of 7,000lb (3175kg) (12,000lb, 5443kg, in the civil S-78 version). There is provision for a side-firing machine gun, and the whole machine is made squat so that when folded it fits a C-130; six can be carried in a C-5A. A LAMPS version would carry radar, MAD, sonobuoys and two Mk 46 torpedoes.

In December 1976 the UTTAS order went to Sikorsky; the LAMPS choice has yet to be made.

Above: Three-view of UH-60A (LAMPS III would look different).

Right and below: The YUH-60 could carry a squad of eleven troops and manoeuvre with bank angles greater than 90°.

Westland Scout and Wasp

Scout AH.1 and Wasp HAS.1

Origin: See text, production by Westland Helicopters, UK.

Type: (S) multi-role tactical helicopter; (W) general utility and ASW helicopter for use from small surface vessels.

Engine: (S) one 685shp Rolls-Royce Nimbus 102 free-turbine turboshaft; (WV) 710shp Nimbus 503 (both engines flat-rated from thermodynamic output of 968shp).

Dimensions: Diameter of four-blade main rotor 32ft 3in (9·83m); length overall (rotors turning) 40ft 4in (12·29m); length of fuselage 30ft 4in (9·24m); height (rotors turning) 11ft 8in (3·56m).

Weights: Empty (S) 3,232lb (1465kg); (W) 3,452lb (1566kg); maximum loaded (S) 5,300lb (2405kg); (W) 5,500lb (2495kg).

Performance: Maximum speed at sea level (S) 131mph (211km/h); (W) 120mph (193km/h); maximum (not vertical) rate of climb (S) 1,670ft (510m)/min; (W) 1,440ft (439m)/min; practical manoeuvre ceiling (S) 13,400ft (4085m); (W) 12,200ft (3720m); range with four passengers and reserves (S) 315 miles (510km); (W) 270 miles (435km).

Armament: (S) various options including manually aimed guns of up to 20mm calibre, fixed GPMG installations, rocket pods or guided missiles such as SS.11; (W) normally, two Mk 44 torpedoes.

History: First flight (P.531) 20 July 1958; (pre-production Scout) 4 August 1960; (production, powered-control AH.1) 6 March 1961; (Wasp HAS.1) 28 October 1962; final delivery (Wasp) 1974.

Users: Australia, Bahrein, Brazil, Jordan, New Zealand, Netherlands, S Africa, Uganda, UK (Royal Navy, Army).

Development: Designed and originally developed by Saunders-Roe at Eastleigh, these neat helicopters were transferred to Hayes (the former Fairey works) on the merger with Westland and finally all helicopter work was concentrated at Yeovil. Westland built over 100 Scouts for the Army Air Corps, which has used them for every tactical purpose except heavy transport; small numbers were exported to overseas air forces, police, and even the Royal Australian Navy. The more specialised Wasp is used for liaison, ice reconnaissance, search/rescue and many other duties, but its basic task is ASW strike, operating from small destroyer or frigate platforms. Again well over 100 Wasps were built, and about 40 were exported.

Above: A blue-headed AS.11 anti-tank missile blasts from its launcher on a British Army Scout AH.1 resting on its skids.

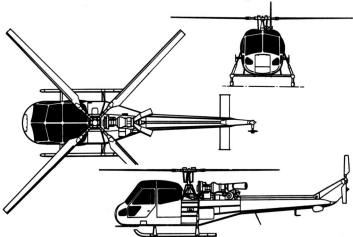

Above: Three-view of Scout (no weapon pylons or sight).

Below: Another blue warhead, this time on a bigger AS.12 fired in the anti-ship role by a Royal Navy Wasp HAS.1.

Westland Wessex

Wessex HAS.1, HC.2, HAS.3, CC.4, HU.5 and civil/export versions

Origin: Westland Helicopters, UK (licence from Sikorsky).
Type: Multi-role helicopter (see text).
Engine(s): (1) one 1,450shp Rolls-Royce (Napier) Gazelle 161 free-turbine turboshaft; (2) Rolls-Royce Coupled Gnome 101/111 with two 1,350shp power sections; (3) one 1,600shp flat-rated Gazelle 165; (others) as Mk 2 except HAS.31 has 1,540shp Gazelle 162.
Dimensions: Diameter of four-blade main rotor 56ft (17·07m); length overall (rotors turning) 65ft 9in (20·03m); length of fuselage (2) 48ft 4½in (14·74m); height overall 16ft 2in (4·93m).
Weights: Empty (1) 7,600lb (3447kg); (5) 8,657lb (3927kg); maximum loaded (1) 12,600lb (5715kg); (2, 5, 31) 13,500lb (6120kg).
Performance: Maximum speed 133mph (214km/h); cruising speed 121mph (195km/h); maximum (not vertical) rate of climb (2) 1,650ft (503m)/min; service ceiling 10,000–14,000ft (3048–4300m); range with standard fuel (1) 390 miles (630km).
Armament: See text.
History: First flight (rebuilt S-58) 17 May 1957; service delivery (HAS.1) April 1960; final delivery (civil) 1970.
Users: Australia, Brunei, Ghana, Iraq, UK (RAF, Royal Navy/Marines).

Development: In 1956 the Royal Navy dropped its plan to buy the twin-Gazelle Bristol 191 and opted for a cheaper and less risky solution with a Sikorsky S-58 (US Navy HSS-1) using a single Gazelle. Development was fast, and about 150 anti-submarine versions were used by the Fleet Air Arm, the HAS.1 being supplanted by the refined HAS.3 called "Camel" because of its hump-backed radome. The RAF bought a version with Coupled Gnome engines, over 100 HC.2 utility versions being followed by almost 100 HU.5 Commando assault machines. Two CC.4 VIP transport serve the Queen's Flight. HMAS *Melbourne* is main base afloat for 27 HAS.31 of the RAN which, like those in British service, have undergone progressive updating since 1965. Many weapon fits are in use, the HAS marks carrying one or two homing torpedoes and all having capability to mount guns or a wide range of missiles and rockets.

Above: A Wessex HU.5 used as a Commando assault transport by the Royal Navy puts down on the right numbered spot.

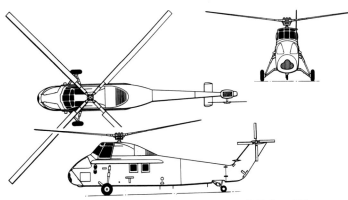

Above: Three-view of typical Gazelle-Wessex (Mk 3 or 31).

Below: Winter exercises in Norway look tough, but this RAF Wessex HC.2 finds it easier to hover at maximum weight.

Westland Sea King and Commando

Sea King HAS.1 and Mks 41-50; Commando 1 and 2

Origin: Westland Helicopters, Yeovil, UK (licence from Sikorsky).

Type: (Sea King) either anti-submarine or search/rescue transport helicopter; (Commando) tactical helicopter for land warfare.

Engines: Two Rolls-Royce Gnome (derived from GE T58) free-turbine turboshaft; past production, mostly 1,500shp Gnome H.1400; current, 1,590shp H.1400-1; future, 1,795shp H.1400-3.

Dimensions: Diameter of five-blade main rotor 62ft (18·9m); length overall (rotors turning) 72ft 8in (22·15m); length of fuselage 55ft 10in (17·02m); height (rotors turning) 16ft 10in (5·13m).

Weights: Empty (Sea King ASW) 15,474lb (7019kg); (Commando) 12,222lb (5543kg); maximum loaded (H.1400-1 engines) 21,000lb (9525kg).

continued on page 222▶

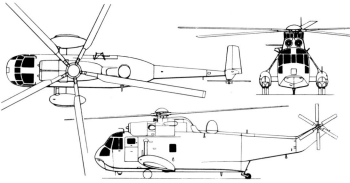

Above: Three-view of Sea King (Commando differs significantly).

Above: Though its airframe is generally similar to that of the Sea King, the Commando is a totally different helicopter for land warfare. Here the simple fixed landing gears are prominent. This design change, and removal of the comprehensive ASW or SAR equipment carried by the Sea King, enables the Commando to carry 28 equipped troops and a wide range of air/surface weapons.

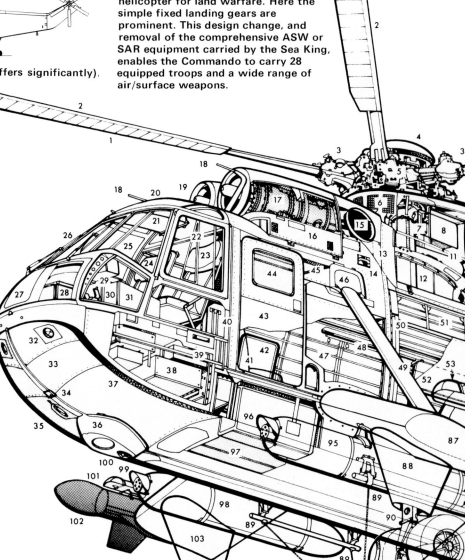

1 Main rotor blades, incorporating pressurized nitrogen BIM (blade inspection method)
2 Stainless-steel leading-edge strips
3 Blade root fittings
4 Rotor head cowling
5 Fully-articulated main rotor head
6 Cooling grilles
7 Main transmission
8 Access panels
9 Utility reservoir
10 Fire extinguishers
11 Generator
12 Accessories housing
13 Firewall
14 Handhold
15 Turbine exhaust
16 Hinged engine access panel/work platform
17 Rolls-Royce Gnome 1400-1 turboshaft engine 1,590 hp
18 Pitot heads
19 Turbine intakes
20 Cabin glazing
21 Overhead instrument console
22 Pilot's side window (jettisonable)
23 Co-pilot's (training) seat
24 Pilot's seat
25 Electrically de-iced windscreen
26 Screen washer/wipers
27 Nose access hatch
28 Battery compartment
29 Instrument panel shroud
30 Directional control pedals
31 Side console
32 Fixed landing lights
33 Forward electronics bay
34 Electronics bay handle
35 Adjustable landing light
36 Nose beacon
37 Underfloor avionics bay
38 Navigation systems (Dopper/ADF/VOR)
39 Automatic flight control system
40 Cockpit/cabin bulkhead
41 Commander's folding jump seat
42 Starboard cabin window/escape hatch
43 Port entry door (lower half with integral steps)
44 Port entry door (upper half)
45 Engine/cabin firewall bulkhead
46 Strut/fuselage attachment fairing
47 Foothold
48 Door rail (starboard)
49 Fixed strut (emergency energy-absorbing)
50 Fuselage frame
51 Fuselage structure
52 Starboard sliding cargo door
53 Port missile shoe (optional)
54 Port cabin window/escape hatch
55 Door-mounted machine-gun (starboard)
56 Inflatable rubberized nylon troop seats (26)
57 Auxiliary internal fuel tanks
58 Fuselage stringers
59 Aft fixed window
60 Aft cabin bulkhead
61 UHF aerial
62 Spine shaft housing
63 Transmission shaft
64 Tailboom L-section stringers
65 Intermediate gearbox
66 Fixed tailplane (starboard)
67 Tail-rotor transmission shaft
68 Anti-collision beacon
69 Six-blade aluminium-alloy rotor
70 Hub spider
71 Rail rotor stub
72 Fixed tail pylon
73 Glass-fibre access panels
74 Cable/push-rod transition quadrant
75 Tailboom skinning
76 Tailboom frames
77 Tailwheel mounting
78 Aft keel frame
79 Tailwheel shock-absorber
80 Fixed tailwheel
81 Fuel jettison pipe
82 Aerial
83 Fuel system aft bay
84 Underfloor bulkhead
85 Cargo floor (tie-down points)
86 Ventral skinning
87 Undercarriage fixed sponson
88 Mainwheel leg fairing
89 Cargo sling frame
90 Mainwheel shock-absorbers
91 Port twin mainwheels
92 Personnel rescue hoist (winch above starboard cargo door)
93 Cargo sling
94 Sling wires
95 Port Minigun pöd
96 Multi-barrel muzzle shroud
97 Fuel-system forward bay
98 Starboard gun pod
99 Muzzle shroud
100 Anti-collision beacon
101 Missile shoe
102 Starboard ASM (optional provision)
103 Starboard mainwheel leg fairing
104 Oleo shock absorbers
105 Starboard mainwheels

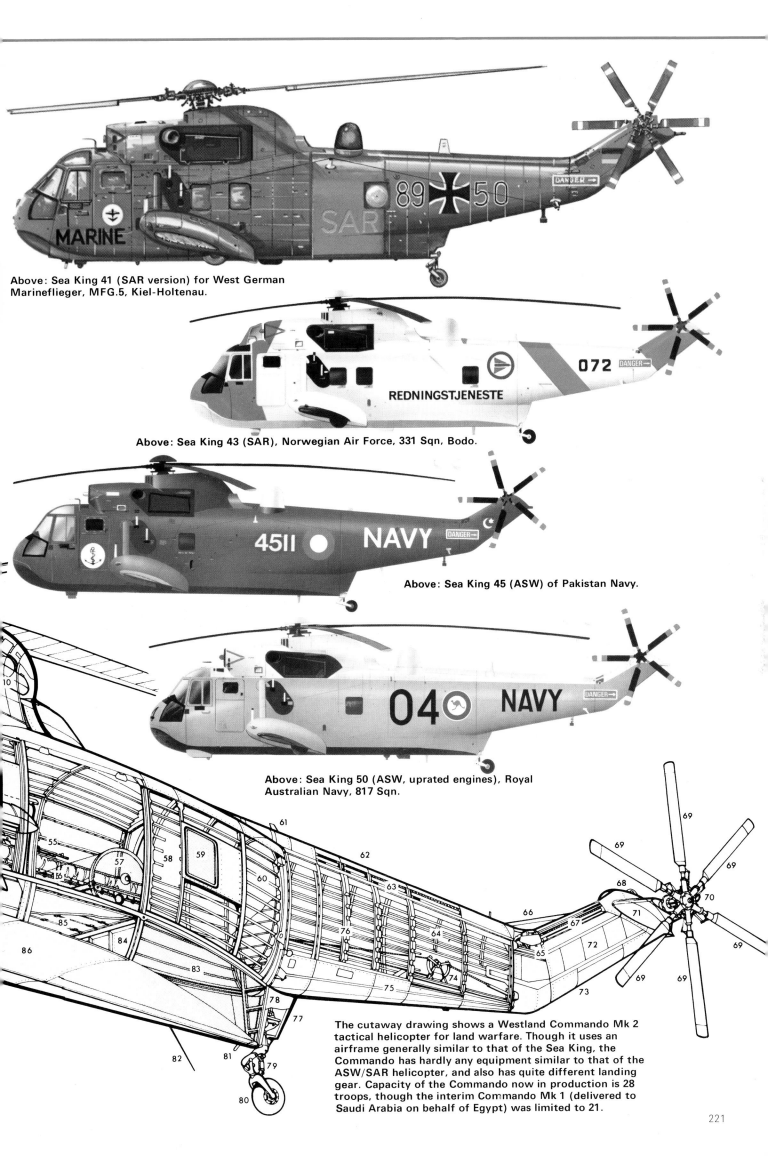

Above: Sea King 41 (SAR version) for West German Marineflieger, MFG.5, Kiel-Holtenau.

Above: Sea King 43 (SAR), Norwegian Air Force, 331 Sqn, Bodo.

Above: Sea King 45 (ASW) of Pakistan Navy.

Above: Sea King 50 (ASW, uprated engines), Royal Australian Navy, 817 Sqn.

The cutaway drawing shows a Westland Commando Mk 2 tactical helicopter for land warfare. Though it uses an airframe generally similar to that of the Sea King, the Commando has hardly any equipment similar to that of the ASW/SAR helicopter, and also has quite different landing gear. Capacity of the Commando now in production is 28 troops, though the interim Commando Mk 1 (delivered to Saudi Arabia on behalf of Egypt) was limited to 21.

▶**Performance:** Maximum speed 143mph (230km/h); typical cruising speed 131mph (211km/h); maximum (not vertical) rate of climb (ASW) 1,770ft (540m)/min; (Commando) 2,020ft (616m)/min; approved ceiling 10,000ft (3048m); range (maximum load) about 350 miles (563km), (maximum fuel) 937 miles (1507km).

Armament: See text.

History: Derived from Sikorsky S-61 of 1959; first flight of Sea King 7 May 1969; (Commando) September 1973.

Users: Belgium, Egypt, W Germany, India, Norway, Pakistan, Qatar, Saudi Arabia, UK (RAF, Royal Navy).

Development: Sikorsky's S-61 was almost inevitably the subject of a licence agreement between the company and Westland Aircraft, continuing an association begun in 1947 when a licence was purchased to make the S-51. In the case of the S-61 the most immediate significant customer was the Royal Navy, which was searching for an ASW (anti-submarine warfare) helicopter to supplement and eventually replace the Wessex in operation from surface ships. Unlike the US Navy, which chose to regard its ASW helicopters as mere extensions of the all-important ship, the Fleet Air Arm concluded it would be preferable to allow the helicopter to operate independently. The Sea King HAS.1 was thus designed to carry sensors, weapons and a complete tactical centre to hunt down and destroy submerged submarines. The normal equipment for Sea Kings in the ASW role includes dunking sonar, doppler navigator, search radar and an auto-pilot and weapon system providing for automatic hovering at given heights or for a range of other automatic manoeuvres in all weather. The RN bought 56, with 13 more ordered in 1975 and eight in 1976. Total Sea King sales are close to 150, many of them being for the much simpler SAR (search and rescue) version with seats for up to 22, apart from the crew, and special provision for casualties, cargo and slung loads. The future RAF rescue helicopter is the Sea King HAR. 3.

Likely to find as large a market during the coming decade, the Commando is a purely land-based aircraft with fixed landing gear devoid of floats. It has been optimised to the range/payload needs of tactical operations, and carries much special equipment for use in a wide range of roles. The basic Commando provides accommodation for up to 28 troops in the transport role, or equivalent cargo payload (or 8,000lb, 3630kg, slung externally). Other roles include logistic support, casualty evacuation, search/rescue or, with any of a wide range of armament fits, air/surface strike. So far no armed Commandos have been ordered (the first sale was a large batch for Egypt, bought by Saudi Arabia in 1973), but various turrets and launchers, manually aimed guns, guided missiles and rocket pods can be fitted. Internal load can include a 105mm gun or Shorland armoured car.

Westland/Aérospatiale Lynx

Lynx AH.1, HAS.2 and 2(FN) and HT.3.

Origin: Westland Helicopters, UK, in partnership with Aérospatiale, France.

Type: Multi-role helicopter (see text).

Engines: Two 900shp Rolls-Royce Gem 10001 three-shaft turbines; customer option, two 750shp P&WC PT6A-34.

Dimensions: Diameter of four-blade main rotor 42ft (12·80m); length overall (rotors turning) 49ft 9in (15·16m); height overall (rotors turning) 12ft (3·66m).

Weights: Empty weight (basic) 5,225lb (2370kg); empty (equipped for troop transport) 5,641lb (2558kg), (anti-tank) 6,313lb (2863kg), (dunking sonar search/strike) 7,218lb (3274kg); maximum loaded (army) 9,250lb (4196kg), (navy) 9,500lb (4309kg).

Performance: Maximum speed 207mph (333km/h); continuous cruise 176mph (284km/h); single-engine cruise 164mph (263km/h); maximum (not vertical) rate of climb 2,370ft (722m)/min; ceiling, well over 25,000ft (7600m); range (army) 473 miles (761km), (navy) 418 miles (673km); ferry range with cabin tank 861 miles (1386km).

Armament: See text.

History: First flight 21 March 1971; (HAS.2) 25 May 1972; service delivery (Royal Navy) May 1976.

Users: Argentina, Belgium, Brazil, France, Netherlands, Qatar, UK (RAF, Royal Navy, Army); Egypt discussing purchase of large batch plus manufacturing licence and facilities.

Development: Certain to be manufactured in very large numbers over a period greater than ten years, the Lynx is probably the outstanding example

Above: A Royal Navy Sea King HAS.1 dunks its Plessey Type 195 sonar to listen for submarines. Note the twin depressions caused by the split rotor downwash (not heard by the sonar).

today of a military multi-role helicopter. Its agility is unsurpassed and its avionics and flight system provide for easy one-man operation in bad weather with minimal workload. Designed by Westland but built in 70/30 partnership with Aérospatiale of France, with contributions from certain other nations, the Lynx is sized to carry ten men (13 in civil versions) and has outstanding performance and smoothness, and early in development was looped, rolled at 100°/sec and flown backwards at 80mph. The AH.1 is tailored to many battlefield duties, can carry almost all available helicopter sight systems, guns and missiles, and is proving a superior tank-killer. The HAS.2, with the Seaspray radar, performs virtually all shipboard roles including anti-submarine classification/strike, vertical replenishment, air/surface search/strike (using Sea Skua missiles), search/rescue, fire support and other duties. Contracts by 1977 included 50 for the French Aéronavale designated Lynx 2(FN); this has OMERA Herculès radar and other sensors differing from the RN fit. The HT.3 is an RAF trainer and liaison machine, and there are also many export variants plus a proposed civil model, the Westland 606.

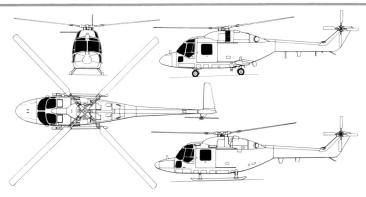

Above: Three-view of Lynx AH.1 with side view (top) of HAS.2.

Facing page, upper: A Lynx HAS.2 of the Royal Navy comes aboard HMS *Sheffield*, first of the Type 42 surface warships.
Facing page, lower: Lynx HAS multi-role variant of Royal Netherlands Navy, with Seaspray radar. The final ten Dutch Lynx are fitted with uprated Gem engines and weigh 10,500lb (4763kg).

Below: The Lynx is the world's most manoeuvrable combat helo, and it has rolled (like this Army AH.1) at over 100° per second and flown backwards at 80mph.

Above: Prototype Lynx HAS.2 with AS.12 (now replaced by Sea Skua).

Trainers and utility aircraft

In World War I a junior officer in the Royal Flying Corps, R. R. Smith-Barry, achieved the remarkable feat of working his way to the command of a front-line fighter squadron after having had both legs shattered and been told he had no hope of even returning to flying duty. But his name lives in history because he was so appalled at the quality of young replacement pilots that he said so in public. General Trenchard said, ''Go and do something about it'', and Smith-Barry laid down such basic principles (which seem obvious today, but were far from obvious then) as the use of specially designed training aircraft, with dual controls, and the employment of instructors trained for the job, instead of combat pilots ''resting'' from the Front and usually totally disinterested in what they achieved. He also drafted a complete syllabus of flying instruction, and this has remained the basis for all flying instruction ever

since. The methods have changed only in minor ways, though the aircraft have changed dramatically over the years.

Many air forces use aircraft for contrasting purposes, and it is difficult to be dogmatic. Modern jet trainers are quite capable of being used as attack aircraft and even as ''fighters'' provided the hostile aircraft are not beyond their capability. Such aircraft as the T-28 and Magister have been in the news far more often when engaged in warfare than when in the uncertain hands of pupils, while the Alpha Jet, Hawk, Saab 105 and several Aermacchi models are available equipped primarily as multi-role attack weapon platforms, with training a secondary role (in fact, some are single-seaters). Again, some Supporters are not used in the training role but as utility machines, while many aircraft we have categorised as ''utility'' spend their lives being

The Japanese are good at doing things that are different, smaller and more sophisticated than rival products. The Mitsubishi MU-2 flies like a Spitfire and can accommodate not only Japanese but also Texans, in whose state many are assembled.

utilised solely for the purpose of training crews.

The utility category is a valid one, though it is difficult to define. One could argue that many retired combat aircraft serve in the utility role; but the purpose-designed utilities, which are the ones in this chapter, are often derived from a civil lightplane, a civil transport or other categories, but almost without exception the result today is a vehicle that can go almost anywhere, be maintained and refuelled at any airfield, and can fly simple transport duties or carry almost any kind of equipment or special installation provided it is not large or heavy enough to warrant a true Transport category aircraft. Most of the utility missions are simply taking a handful of people to look at something or meet someone, but there is far more to it than this.

Subdivisions include: the Forward Air Control (FAC) aircraft, which played a central role in directing attacks of other aircraft on invisible ground targets in South-East Asia; the observation aircraft, which was an earlier form of the same species and borders on the edges of the category labelled Reconnaissance; the psy-war (psychological warfare) aircraft, equipped with loudspeakers, leaflet dispensers and other devices to persuade or intimidate those on the ground below; lightplanes, too small to be termed transports, engaged in local supply transport (often by parachuting supply containers or bundles); a very wide range of electronic and radio duties, many of which grossly modify the appearance of the aircraft; executive-type duties, notably by air attachés; ambulance duties; missile-site inspection and communications; and a diverse spectrum of para-military duties concerned with civil law and order, forestry patrol, coastal patrol, survey and similar tasks.

Aermacchi M.B. 326 and 339

M.B.326 and 326 GB and GC (AT-26 Xavante), 326K (Atlas Impala), 326L and M.B.339

Origin: Aeronautica Macchi SpA (Aermacchi); licence-production in Australia, Brazil and S Africa.

Type: Two-seat basic trainer and light attack aircraft; (326K) single-seat trainer/attack; (339) two-seat all-through trainer.

Engine: One Rolls-Royce Viper single-shaft turbojet; (original production versions) 2,500lb (1134kg) thrust Viper 11; (GB, GC, H and M) 3,410lb (1547kg) Viper 20 Mk 540; (K, L and 339) 4,000lb (1814kg) R-R/Fiat Viper 632-43.

Dimensions: Span (over tip tanks) 35ft 7in (10·85m); length 34ft 11in (10·64m); height 12ft 2½in (3·72m).

Weights: Empty (G trainer) 5,920lb (2685kg); (G attack) 5,640lb (2558kg); (K) 6,240lb (2830kg); maximum loaded (G trainer) 10,090lb (4577kg); (G attack) 11,500lb (5217kg); (K and 339) 12,500lb (5670kg).

Performance: Maximum speed (G clean) 539mph (867km/h); (K clean) 553mph (890km/h); (339) 560mph (901km/h); initial climb (G clean) 6,050ft (1844m)/min; (G attack at max wt) 3,100ft (945m)/min; (K clean and 339) 6,500ft (1980m)/min; service ceiling (G trainer clean) 47,000ft (14,325m); (G attack, max wt) 35,000ft (10,700m); range on internal fuel (G trainer) 1,150 miles (1850km); (K with max weapons) about 160 miles (260km).

Armament: Six underwing pylons for load of up to 4,000lb (1814kg) including bombs, rockets, tanks, missiles, reconnaissance pods or gun pods; some versions have single 7·62mm or similar gun (or Minigun) in fuselage; 326K (Impala) has two 30mm DEFA 553 cannon in fuselage, each with 125 rounds. (339) two 30mm DEFA cannon can be carried in wing-mounted slipper pods; other options as 326.

History: First flight 10 December 1957; (production 326) 5 October 1960; (K prototype) 22 August 1970; (339) 12 August 1976.

Users: Argentina, Australia, Bolivia, Brazil, Dubai, Ghana, Italy, S Africa, Togo (Xavante), Tunisia, Zaïre, Zambia.

Development: The most successful Italian military aircraft programme in history, the 326 was designed by a team led by Ermanno Bazzocchi and was put into production as a trainer for the Regia Aeronautica, which received 90. In addition the South African AF has over 150 K models, built by Atlas Aircraft with locally built engines, and expects to build over 200, while other big customers include Australia (114, 85 built by CAC in Melbourne), Brazil (122 locally built Xavantes) and many emergent nations. The latest sub-types are the 326K with the most powerful Viper, the 326L with two seats but K attack capability, the M uncompromised dual trainer and the M.B. 339 with redesigned airframe for all-through training, with raised instructor seat under a sloping canopy. Despite having a largely redesigned structure the 339 is hoped (optimistically) to be priced at only £850,000.

Above: First prototype M.B.339, a completely redesigned aircraft with modern stepped cockpits. Aermacchi hope to sell to many air forces by being cheaper than the opposition.

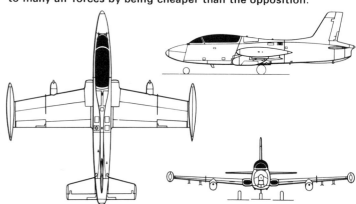

Above: Three-view of typical M.B.326G with wing gun pods.

Below: The EMBRAER AT-26 Xavante of the Brazilian Air Force is the M.B.326GB built under licence. By spring 1977 over 120 had been delivered to attack, recce and training units.

Aero L-29 Delfin

L-29 Delfin (NATO name "Maya")

Origin: Aero Vodochody national corporation, Czechoslovakia.
Type: Basic trainer.
Engine: One 1,960lb (890kg) thrust M-701 single-shaft turbojet.
Dimensions: Span 33ft 9in (10·29m); length 35ft 5½in (10·81m); height 10ft 3in (3·13m).
Weights: Empty 5,027lb (2280kg); maximum loaded 7,804lb (3540kg).
Performance: Maximum speed at 16,400ft (5000m) 407mph (655km/h); initial climb 2,755ft (840m)/min; service ceiling 36,090ft (11,000m); maximum range on internal fuel 397 miles (640km).
Armament: Two wing hardpoints on which can be attached two 7·62mm guns, small tanks, or various other loads including bombs of up to 220lb (100kg).
History: First flight 5 April 1959; service delivery 1963; final delivery 1974.
Users: Bulgaria, Czechoslovakia, Egypt, E Germany, Guinea, Hungary, Indonesia, Iraq, Nigeria, Romania, Soviet Union, Syria, Uganda.

Development: Designed by a team led by K. Tomas and the late Z. Rublic, the L-29 was Czecholsovakia's submission in 1960 as the standard Warsaw

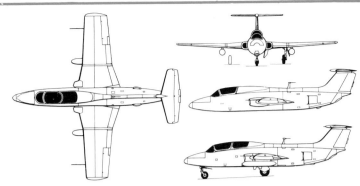

Above: Three-view of L-29 (plus side view of L-29A Akrobat single-seat version for aerobatic demonstration).

Pact trainer. It won, and though disgruntled Poland went ahead with the TS-11 Iskra, other Communist countries and several other air forces adopted this trainer and more than 3,000 were delivered. Two variants, not built in quantity, were the L-29A single-seat aerobatic version and the L-29R for counter-insurgency operations with nose cameras and under-wing stores.

Aero L-39 Albatros

L-39, L-39Z

Origin: Aero Vodochody national corporation, Czechoslovakia.
Type: Basic and advanced trainer.
Engine: One 3,792 (1720kg) thrust Walter Titan two-shaft turbofan (licence-built Ivchenko AI-25-TL).
Dimensions: Span 31ft 0½in (9·46m); length 40ft 5in (12·32m); height 15ft 5½in (4·72m).
Weights: Empty 7,341lb (3330kg); maximum loaded 10,141lb (4600kg).
Performance: Maximum speed at 16,400ft (5000m) 466mph (750km/h); Mach limit in dive 0·80; cruising speed at 5000m, up to 423mph (700km/h); initial climb 4,330ft (1320m)/min; service ceiling 37,075ft (11,300m); max range at 5000m on internal fuel 565 miles (910km).
Armament: Provision for light external load of tanks, bombs, rockets or 7·62mm gun pods (weight unstated) on two hardpoints under wings; internal fittings confined to gun-camera and sight.
History: First flight 4 November 1968; service delivery late 1973.
Users: Czechoslovakia, Iraq, Soviet Union (other Warsaw Pact countries in due course).

Development: Designed by a team led by Jan Vlcek, the L-39 is succeeding well in its task of replacing the L-29, and in 1972 it was accepted in principle as the future trainer of all Warsaw Pact countries except Poland. It forms

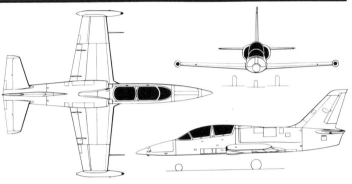

Above: Three-view of L-39 Albatros.

part of an integrated pilot-training system which includes a flight simulator, ejection-seat trainer and mobile automatic test equipment. The L-39Z was under development in 1973 as a light attack version which, like all L-39s, can be operated from unpaved surfaces. Iraq is believed to have ordered both models.

Below: The shapely turbofan-powered Albatros marks a great advance over the mass-produced Delfin. It will be interesting to see how well it does in the world trainer market.

Alpha Jet (Dassault Breguet/ Dornier)

Alpha Jet

Origin: Jointly Dassault/Breguet, France, and Dornier GmbH, W Germany, with assembly at each company.

Type: Two-seat trainer and light strike/reconnaissance aircraft.

Engines: Two 2,976lb (1350kg) thrust SNECMA/Turboméca Larzac 04 two-shaft turbofans.

Dimensions: Span 29ft 11in (9·12m); length (excluding any probe) 40ft 3¾in (12·29m); height 13ft 9in (4·2m).

Weights: Empty 6,944lb (3150kg); loaded (clean) 9,920lb (4500kg), (maximum) 15,432lb (7000kg).

Performance: (clean) maximum speed 576mph (927km/h) at sea level, 560mph (900km/h) (Mach 0·85) at altitude; climb to 39,370ft (12,000m), less than 10 minutes; service ceiling 45,930ft (14,000m); typical mission endurance 2hr 30min; ferry range with two external tanks 1,510 miles (2430km).

Armament: Optional for weapon training or combat missions, detachable belly fairing housing one 30mm DEFA or 27mm Mauser cannon, with 125 rounds, or two 0·50in Brownings, each with 250 rounds; same centreline hardpoint and either one or two under each wing (to maximum of five) can be provided with pylons for maximum external load of 4,850lb (2200kg), made up of tanks, weapons, reconnaissance pod, ECM or other devices.

History: First flight 26 October 1973; first production delivery originally to be early 1976, now to be in 1978.

Users: Belgium, France, W Germany.

Development: Realisation that the Jaguar was too capable and costly to be a standard basic trainer led to the Armée de l'Air issuing a requirement for a new trainer in 1967. The chosen design was to be capable of use in the light ground attack role, in which the Luftwaffe had a parallel need for an aircraft. On 22 July 1969 the two governments agreed to a common specification and to adopt a common type of aircraft produced jointly by the two national industries. After evaluation against the Aérospatiale (Nord)/MBB E650 Eurotrainer, the Alpha Jet was selected on 24 July 1970. Aircraft for the two partners are nearly identical. France makes the fuselage and centre section and Germany the rear fuselage, tail and outer wings. SABCA of Belgium makes minor portions. Engines, originally shared by two French companies (see above), are being produced in partnership with MTU and KHD of Germany, plus a small share by FN of Belgium. Trainer aircraft are assembled at Toulouse (France) and attack versions at Oberpfaffenhofen (Germany). Decision to go ahead with production was reached on 26 March 1975. It was expected at that time that France and Germany would each buy 200, and that Belgium would buy 33, but the programme has slipped by approximately two years (so that deliveries will not begin until "the first half of 1978") and costs have escalated.

Above: Unfortunately the most colourful Alpha Jet, the 04 prototype, was lost in a crash in 1976, but this was not due to a fault in the aircraft.

Above: Three-view of Alpha Jet prototype with armament.

Below: The Luftwaffe Alpha Jets will be equipped for battlefield reconnaissance and close support. The first production delivery is due on 1 October 1978.

Aerospace Airtrainer CT-4

CT4 and CT4B

Origin: NZ Aerospace Industries, Hamilton, New Zealand.
Type: Primary and aerobatic trainer.
Engine: One 210hp Rolls-Royce Continental IO-360-H flat-six.
Dimensions: Span 26ft 0in (7·92m); length 23ft 2in (7·06m); height 8ft 6in (2·59m).
Weights: Empty 1,460lb (662kg); maximum loaded 2,400lb (1088kg).
Performance: Maximum speed 178mph (286km/h); initial climb 1,350ft (411m)/min; take-off or landing over 50ft (15m) about 1,200ft (366m); service ceiling 17,900ft (5455m); max range with reserves (no tip tanks) 815 miles (1311km, 5hr 47min).
History: First flight (Victa Airtourer) 31 March 1959, (CT4) 23 February 1972; service delivery (Thai) 23 October 1973.
Users: Australia, Hong Kong, Indonesia, New Zealand, Singapore, Thailand.

One of the 37 CT4 Airtrainers of the Royal Australian Air Force. An aggressive development and market research policy should keep this attractive machine selling.

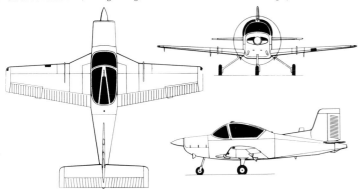

Above: Three-view of standard Airtrainer CT4.

Development: In 1953 Australian Henry Millicer won a lightplane design contest held by the Royal Aero Club. The eventual result was the four-seat Airtourer, made by Victa in Australia, which in turn led to one of the world's better lightplane trainers, produced by the amalgamated NZ industry. The Airtrainer is all-metal, has electric flaps, a constant-speed propeller and optional third seat. Armed versions remained paper studies as this book went to press, as did a FAC (forward air control) version and more powerful models, one having a turboprop. In 1976 several air forces were negotiating orders, but Aerospace terminated a NZ$1·5 million deal "for a Swiss flying club" because, according to unofficial reports, the destination was Rhodesia.

Boeing T-43A and 737

T-43A

Origin: The Boeing Company, USA.
Type: Navigational trainer.
Engines: Two 14,500lb (6575kg) thrust Pratt & Whitney JT8D-9 two-shaft turbofans.
Dimensions: Span 93ft (38·35m); length 100ft (30·48m); height 37ft (11·28m).
Weights: Empty, about 62,000lb (28,123kg); maximum 115,500lb (52,390kg).
Performance: Maximum speed 586mph (943km/h); maximum cruising speed 576mph (927km/h) at 22,600ft (6890m); economical cruise, Mach 0·7 at 35,000ft (10,670m); initial rate of climb at gross weight 3,750ft (1143m)/min; range with military reserves 2,995 miles (4820km); endurance 6hr.
Armament: None.
History: First flight (737-100) 9 April 1967; (T-43A) 10 April 1973.
User: US Air Force (Air Training Command, though the Navigator Training Wing at Mather AFB is a joint AF/Navy/Marines/Coast Guard unit); basic 737 is used by Brazilian and Venezuelan AF.

Development: Derived from the commercial 737-200, the T-43A is the world's most advanced navigational trainer. Though the "baby" of current Boeing production aircraft, it is nevertheless much more capacious and powerful than any Superfortress, and the fleet of 19 used at Mather Air Force Base, California, have replaced 77 Convair T-29 crew trainers previously used. This has been possible because of the T-43's much higher utilisation and ability to carry 12 trainee navigators (each with a complete aircraft instrument and systems station), four proficiency students and three instructors, apart from the T-43A crew. In addition the T-43A is used in conjunction with a comprehensive computer-based mission simulation

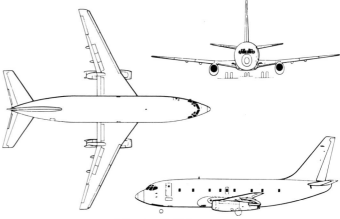

Above: Three-view of Boeing T-43A

system which enables every kind of combat mission up to Mach 2 at 70,000ft (21,340m) altitude to be "flown" on the ground. Each T-43A carries complete inertial navigational systems, Loran and other radio systems, and provision for celestial and even dead-reckoning navigation techniques. Mission endurance is increased by a 667 gal (3027 litre) tank in the rear cargo compartment.

Below, left: A Boeing T-43A could be voted the aircraft least likely to fly into a mountain through a navigation error.

Below: The Brazilian Air Force is one of the customers for the VIP executive 737-200, which can fly 3,857 miles (6207km) and operate from unpaved airstrips.

Beech trainers

T-34C Turbo Mentor

Origin: Beech Aircraft Corporation, Wichita, USA.
Type: Primary Trainer.
Engine: One 715shp Pratt & Whitney Canada PT6A-25 turboprop, derated to 400shp.
Dimensions: Span 33ft 4in (10·2m); length 28ft 8½in (8·75m); height 9ft 11in (3·03m).
Weights: Empty 2,630lb (1193kg); maximum loaded 4,274lb (1938kg).
Performance: Maximum speed at 17,500ft (5335m) 257mph (414km/h); initial climb 1,275ft (338m)/min; service ceiling 30,000ft (9144m); range at 20,000ft (6096m) 749 miles (1205km).
Armament: Normally none, but Pave Coin (Bonanza) armament of 16 possible external loads up to 1,180lb (535kg) including Minigun pods, Snakeye bombs and FFAR rockets, can be fitted with limits of +6/−3g.
History: First flight 21 September 1973 (conversion); service delivery September 1976.
Users: Morocco, US Navy.

Development: In 1973 Beech was awarded a US Navy contract to rebuild a T-34B (see below) as a turboprop trainer with upgraded equipment. After exhaustive trials with the resulting YT-34C rebuilds the Navy placed orders for 256 by late 1976, with further batches likely to bring the total to the requirement of 400. The third batch of 98 were priced at $36·5 million. The airframe has been modified in many details compared with the T-34B to give a fatigue life of 16,000hr at greatly increased weights.

T-24A and T-34B Mentor

Constructor's designation, Model 45.
In March 1953 the US Air Force selected the trim T-34 as its standard primary trainer. Powered by the 225hp Continental O-470-13 flat-six, 450 were delivered to the Air Force and 423 basically similar T-43B Mentors to the US Navy. Beech supplied further batches to Argentina, Chile, Colombia, Indonesia, Japan, Mexico, Morocco, Peru, Salvador, Turkey, Venezuela and Uruguay. CanCar built 100 for the RCAF and USAF, Fuji built 140 for the Japan Air SDF and 36 for the Philippine AF, and 75 were built at Cordoba for the Argentine AF. Subsequently aircraft were built for, or transferred to, Greece, Saudi Arabia, Spain (designation E-17) and Turkey. Last delivery 1962. The Fuji LM-1 and -2 Nikko of the Ground SDF and KM-2 and -2B of the Japan Maritime SDF are trainers or 4/5 seat liaison aircraft based on the T-34A.

Beech 18

This twin-engined aircraft began life as a civil transport in 1937, but when it passed out of production 32 years later (an all-time record) 5,204 out of a total of 7,091 had been military. There were more than 22 military variants, the most numerous class at present being communications and training sub-types of the Japanese armed forces; more than 400 are used by other air forces as navigation trainers, photographic and mapping aircraft and as utility transports.

Beech Bonanza

Produced as a lightplane since 1947, the Bonanza has been built in large numbers in military versions, all with conventional tail and mostly in the A36 family with 285hp IO-520 engine. The US Air Force bought armed Pave Coin versions, as well as various QU-22 Pave Eagle electronic-reconnaissance platforms. Users of the F33 series of trainers include Iran, Mexico and Spain (designation E-24).

Beech Musketeer/Sundowner

Military variants of this popular family, with fixed landing gear, are in service with Canada (designation CT-134) and Mexico.

Beech Baron

This mass-produced twin is the US Army's standard instrument trainer (designation T-42A Cochise); other military customers include Spain and Turkey.

Beech B99 Airliner

This twin-turboprop transport is used by the Chilean AF for search and rescue, and by the Royal Thai Army.

Beech Queen Air

Powered by two Lycoming GO-480, GSO-480 or IGSO-480 flat-sixes, this attractive machine is used by the US Army (six U-8 Seminole versions) and the air forces of Uruguay and Venezuela and the Japan Maritime SDF.

Beech King Air

Powered by two 550 or 620hp PT6A turboprops, the first military King Air versions were the US Army's U-21 Ute (nine sub-types for transport, VIP use by attachés and electronic reconnaissance) and US Air Force U-21G. The VC-6B is a VIP Presidential model, and the T-44A is in quantity production as the US Navy multi-engine pilot trainer replacing the Grumman TS-2A and -2B. The U-21F is the US Army version of the pressurised King Air 100 (680hp PT6 engines).

Beech Super King Air

Much larger, powered by 750hp PT6 engines and distinguished by a T-tail, this fine pressurized transport is widely used by the US forces. Off-the-shelf purchases were made of the C-12A, with pax/convertible interiors and two-pilot flight decks, to the Air Force and Army, the latter bestowing the name Huron. The RU-21J is a grossly modified electronic platform, most examples of which have grotesque vertical dipole aerials along the wings and behind the tail for use in the Army Cefly Lancer programme.

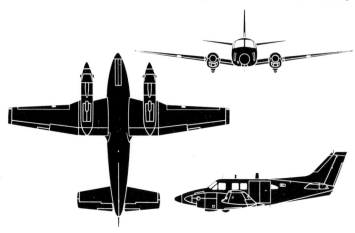

Above: Three-view of U-21 Ute family (Queen Air/King Air mix).

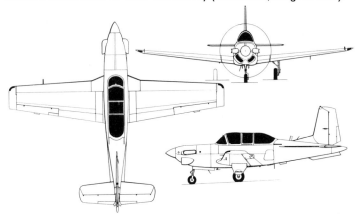

Above: Three-view of the T-34C Turbo Mentor.

Above: The US Navy plans eventually to buy or convert 278 T-34C Turbo Mentors. They are extremely fully equipped.

Above: Two variants of the big pressurized Super King Air, the C-12A Huron of the Army and the VIP C-12A of the Air Force.

Canadair CL-41 Tutor

CL-41A (CT-114 Tutor), CL-41G and CL-41R

Origin: Canadair Ltd., Montreal, Canada.
Type: basic trainer; (G) light attack aircraft.
Engine: one General Electric J85 single-shaft turbojet; (A) J85-CAN-40 of 2,633lb (1195kg) thrust, (G) J85-J4 of 2,950lb (1340kg) thrust.
Dimensions: Span 36ft 6in (11·13m); length 32ft 0in (9·75m); height 9ft 9¾in (2·84m).
Weights: Empty (A) 4,895lb (2220kg), (G) 5,296lb (2400kg); maximum loaded (A) 7,397lb (3355kg), (G) 11,288lb (5131kg).
Performance: Maximum speed at 28,500ft (8700m) (A) 498mph (801 km/h), (G) 480mph (774km/h); initial climb (A) 4,220ft (1286m)/min; service ceiling (both) 43,000ft (13,100m); maximum range (A) 944 miles (1520m), (G, six drop tanks) 1,340 miles (2157km).
Armament: (G) six wing hardpoints for up to 4,000lb (1815kg) of assorted ordnance.
History: First flight 13 January 1960; service delivery (A) 29 October 1963, (G) 1967; final delivery 1968.
Users: Canada, Malaysia, Netherlands.

Development: The RCAF, now Canadian Armed Forces, bought 190 of these neat side-by-side trainers, and uses them as standard pilot trainers

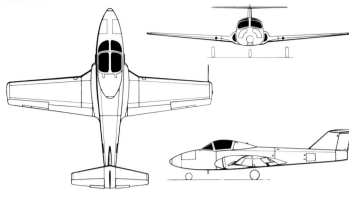

Three-view of Canadair CL-41A Tutor.

designated CT-114 Tutor. They equip the Snowbirds aerobatic team. The CL-41R was a one-off systems trainer with Nasarr (CF-104) radar in a long conical nose. Malaysia has two squadrons of the more powerful G model, calling it Tebuan (Wasp). RNethAF pilot training is done on Tutors in Canada.

Above: CL-41G Tebuan of Royal Malaysian Air Force Nos 6 and 9 Sqns.

Below: The 85 CT-114 Tutors of the Canadian Armed Forces are assigned mainly to No 2 Flying School at Moose Jaw, Saskatchewan, where pupils are trained to wings standard. The environment—which looks rather like this for as far as the eye can see—is familiar to thousands of former WW2 aircrew.

CASA C-101

C-101 (to receive EdA designation and name later)

Origin: Construcciones Aeronauticas SA, Getafe, Spain.
Type: Basic and advanced trainer, attack and reconnaissance aircraft.
Engine: One Garrett-AiResearch TFE 731-3 two-shaft turbofan rated at 3,700lb (1678kg).
Dimensions: Span 34ft 9½in (10·60m); length 40ft 2¼in (12·25m); height 14ft 1¼in (4·30m).
Weights: Empty (fully equipped) 6,570lb (2980kg); maximum loaded 10,360lb (4700kg).
Performance: (Estimated at 4700kg) maximum speed at 25,000ft (7620m) 494mph (795km/h); limiting Mach number 0·80; initial climb 3,660ft (1116m)/min; service ceiling 43,000ft (13,100m); take-off over 50ft (15m) 2,950ft (900m) (landing distance 2,165ft, 660m); maximum range (presumably with external fuel) 1,883 miles (3030km).
Armament: Seven hardpoints for total external load of 4,740lb (2150kg), including multisensor reconnaissance pods, gunpacks or ECM payloads.
History: Development contract September 1975; first flight scheduled for 1977.
User: Spain.

Development: The EdA (Ejercito del Aire, Spanish AF) is funding at a

cost of 1,297 million pesetas the development of this completely new multi-role trainer and tactical aircraft to replace the E-14 and C-10 versions of the Saeta. Unlike other aircraft in this category the C-101 uses an off-the-shelf civil turbofan of high by-pass ratio, which will reduce noise and smoke, and give good fuel economy at all heights, at the cost of reduced speeds and poor high-altitude performance. Northrop and MBB are participating in the programme, mainly through provision of design and development skills and facilities. Six prototypes are being built, two for static/fatigue testing.

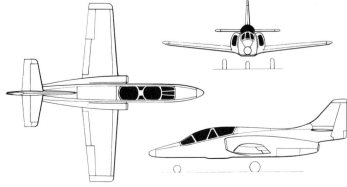

Three-view of CASA C-101 (provisional).

Cessna 172

T-41 Mescalero, Reims FR 172 Rocket

Origin: Cessna Aircraft, Wichita, USA; licence production by Reims Aviation, France.
Type: basic pilot trainer and utility.
Engine: One flat-six piston engine; (T-41A, F172) 150hp Lycoming O-320-E2D; (T-41B, C, D) 210hp Continental IO-360-D; (FR 172) Rolls-Royce IO-360-H.
Dimensions: Span 35ft 10in (10·92m); length 26ft 11in (8·20m); height 8ft 9½in (2·68m).
Weights: (T-41A) empty 1,363lb (618kg); maximum loaded 2,300lb (1043kg) (T-41B/C/D 2,550lb, 1157kg).
Performance: Maximum speed (A) 144mph (232km/h), (others) 156mph (251km/h); initial climb (A) 645ft (196m)/min, (others) 880ft (268m)/min; service ceiling (A) 13,100ft (3995m), (others) 17,000ft (5180m); range with max fuel at 10,000ft (3048m) (A) 737 miles (1186km), (others) 1,010 miles (1625km).
History: First flight (civil 172) 1955; (T-41A) August 1964.
Users: Argentina, Colombia, Ecuador, Honduras, Peru, Philippines, Saudi Arabia, Singapore, Thailand, Turkey, US Air Force and Army; Pakistan to build under licence.

Development: When in 1964 the US Air Force decided to abandon ab initio jet training, and give pilot candidates an initial 30hr on piston-engined lightplanes, it selected the best-selling Cessna 172/Cardinal basic design, of which more than 25,000 have been delivered. Some 240 T-41A Mescaleros serve at USAF civilian schools, with civil registration duplicating the USAF serial numbers. The US Army's 255 T-41B Mescaleros fly training and installation-support missions, while 52 T-41C cadet trainers serve at the USAF Academy at Colorado Springs. Colombia was first customer for the equally powerful T-41D with constant-speed propeller. Pakistan plans to build 60 T-41Ds a year at a new factory near Cambellpur.

Above: That is not a pylon on this T-41A but the reflection of the civil/military serial number in the polished wing.

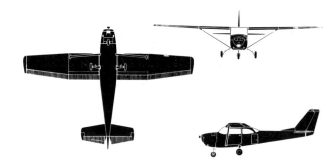
Above: Three-view of Cessna T-41 (FR 172 similar).

Fuji T1

T1A, T1B and T1C

Origin: Fuji Heavy Industries, Utsonomiya, Japan.
Type: Basic and intermediate trainer.
Engine: (A) one 4,000lb (1814kg) thrust Rolls-Royce (Bristol) Orpheus 805 single-shaft turbojet; (B) one 2,645lb (1200kg) IHI J3-3 single-shaft turbojet; (C) one 3,087lb (1400kg) J3-7.
Dimensions: Span 34ft 5in (10·50m); length 39ft 9in (12·12m); height 11ft (3·35m).
Weights: Empty (A) 6,078lb (2755kg), (B) 6,261lb (2840kg); maximum loaded (A) 11,025lb (5000kg), (B) 9,678lb (4390kg).
Performance: Maximum speed (A) 575mph (925km/h), (B) 518mph (834km/h); initial climb (A) 6,500ft (1981m)/min, (B) 4,724ft (1440m)/min; service ceiling (A) 47,244ft (14,400m), (B) 39,370ft (12,000m); max range (both, clean) about 800 miles (1290km).
Armament: Provision for one 0·5in Browning machine gun in nose; two wing hardpoints for tanks, Sidewinder air-to-air missiles or other loads to total of 1,500lb (680kg).
History: First flight 19 January 1958; (B) 17 May 1960; service delivery (A) 1960; final delivery 1963.
User: Japan.

Development: The first jet aircraft designed in Japan after World War II, the T1 was ordered in 1956 as a replacement for the T-6 as standard basic trainer of the Air Self-Defence Force. The tandem cockpit was made similar to that of the Lockheed T-33, but the airframe was based on that of

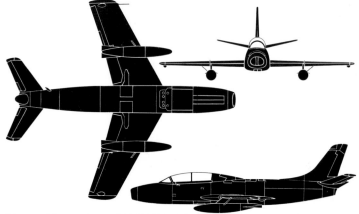
Above: Three-view of Fuji T1 (all basically similar).

the F-86 Sabre. The home-grown J3 engine was not ready so production began with the imported Orpheus engine, giving considerably higher performance. Styled T1F2 by Fuji and T1A by the JASDF, 40 were delivered in 1960–61. The T1F1, the original planned version with the J3 turbojet, eventually became available and 20 were delivered as the T1B in 1962–3. Only one example was flown of the T1F3 (T1C).

Below: Short Japanese heads barely show in this T1A of the 13th Training Wing, JASDF, at Hyakuri AB.

Hawker Siddeley 125

HS 125 and Dominie

Origin: Hawker Siddeley Aviation, UK.
Type: Navigation/pilot/radio trainer, communications and utility.
Engines: Two Rolls-Royce Viper single-shaft turbojets; (Series 3 and 400 Dominie) 3,000lb (1360kg) Viper 301; (Series 600) 3,750lb (1701kg) Viper 601-22.
Dimensions: Span 47ft 0in (14·33m); length (600) 50ft 6in (15·39m), (others) 47ft 5in (14·45m); height (600) 17ft 3in (5·26m), (others) 16ft 6in (5·03m).
Weights: Empty (600) 12,530lb (5683kg), (others, typical) 10,100lb (4581kg); maximum loaded (600) 25,000lb (11,340kg), (others, typical) 21,200lb (9615kg).
Performance: Maximum speed (600) 368mph indicated, equivalent to about 570mph (917km/h) or Mach 0·78; cruising speed (600 at 28,000ft, 8534m) 522mph (840km/h); initial climb (600) 4,900ft (1493m)/min, (others) 4,000ft (1219m)/min; service ceiling (typical) 41,000ft (12,500m); range with max payload of 2,000lb (907kg) and max fuel (600) with reserves 1,796 miles (2891km).
History: First flight (125 prototype) 13 August 1962; first deliveries September 1964; first flight (600) 21 January 1971.
Users: (Military) Argentina, Australia, Brazil, Ghana, Malaysia, S Africa (name Mercurius) and UK (RAF).

Development: Sold widely as a civil business transport, the HS 125's blend of interior space, high performance, good field length and low costs have suited it to many military duties. The Dominie T.1 is the navigation trainer derived from the Series 2, with lengthened belly fairing to accommodate Decca doppler. The RAF uses two communications sub-types, the Dominie CC.1 derived from the Series 400 and CC.2 based on the more capable 600. Most export military models are early-series communications aircraft. The fan-engined 125-700 has not yet been bought for military duties.

Above: Not a Dominie but a Royal Air Force HS 125 CC.2, a long-body (600 series) communications aircraft of 32 Sqn.

Above: Three-view of Dominie T.1 (125-400 similar).

Hindustan HJT-16 Kiran

HJT-16 Kiran I and II

Origin: Hindustan Aerospace, Bangalore, India.
Type: (I) basic trainer, (II) weapon trainer and light attack.
Engine: (Mk I) one 2,500lb (1134kg) thrust Rolls-Royce Viper 11 single-shaft turbojet made under licence by HAL; (Mk II) one Rolls-Royce (Bristol) Orpheus 701 single-shaft turbojet made under licence by HAL and de-rated to 3,400lb (1542kg).
Dimensions: Span 35ft 1¼in (10·70m); length 34ft 9in (10·60m); height 11ft 11in (3·63m).
Weights: Empty (I) 5,644lb (2560kg), (II) 5,909lb (2680kg); maximum loaded (I) 9,039lb (4100kg).
Performance: (I): maximum speed at low level (speed at 30,000ft, 9144m similar) 432mph (695km/h); max cruise 201mph (324km/h); time to reach ceiling of 30,000ft (9144m) 20min; range at 30,000ft (9144m) 464 miles (747km).
Armament: (I) none to 68th aircraft, subsequently one hardpoint under each wing for tank, gun pod, bomb or other store to total external load of 1,000lb (454kg); (II) two 7·62mm machine guns in nose, and two hardpoints beneath each wing (inners only equipped for tanks) to total external load of 2,000lb (907kg).
History: First flight 4 September 1964; service delivery March 1968; first flight (II) 6 January 1977.
User: Indian AF and Navy.

Development: Development of this side-by-side trainer was authorised in 1959, but the programme was delayed by priority accorded the HF-24 fighter. It is a very simple aircraft, but has ejection seats (Martin-Baker H4),

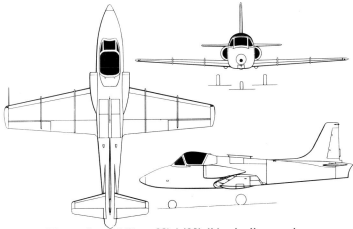

Above: Three-view of Kiran Mk I (Mk II basically same).

a hydraulic system and slight pressurization. The Mk II was planned to be powered by HAL's own HJE-2500 turbojet, but as this is developing slowly the decision was taken in 1975 to fit the Orpheus as already in production for the HAL-built Gnat and Ajeet. The first flight of a Mk II, scheduled for October 1976, took place as this book went to press. Meanwhile, production of the Mk I was continuing, with 119 delivered of a total requirement for 180.

Below: Another HJT-16 Kiran Mk I comes off the line at the Bangalore factory. By mid-1977 about 140 had been delivered.

Hawker Siddeley Hawk

P.1182 Hawk T.1

Origin: British Aerospace, UK.
Type: Two-seat trainer and tactical multi-role.
Engine: One 5,340lb (2422kg) Rolls-Royce/Turboméca Adour 151 two-shaft turbofan.
Dimensions: Span 30ft 10in (9·4m); length (over probe) 39ft 2½in (11·95m); height 13ft 5in (4·09m).
Weights: Empty 7,450lb (3379kg); loaded (trainer, clean) 12,000lb (5443kg), (attack mission) 16,260lb (7375kg).
Performance: Maximum speed 630mph (1014km/h) at low level; Mach number in shallow dive, 1·1; initial climb 6,000ft (1830m)/min; service ceiling 50,000ft (15,240m); range on internal fuel 750 miles (1207km); endurance with external fuel 3 hr.
Armament: Three or five hard-points (two outboard being optional) each rated at 1,000lb (454kg); centreline point normally equipped with 30mm gun pod and ammunition.
History: First flight 21 August 1974; service delivery 1976.
User: Finland, UK (RAF), with many others probable.

Development: The only new all-British military aircraft for 15 years, the Hawk serves as a model of the speed and success that can be achieved when an experienced team is allowed to get on with the job. To some degree it owes its existence to the escalation of the Jaguar to a power and weight category well above that economic for use as a pure trainer. Britain never participated in the Franco-German Alpha Jet programme and instead played off the two British airframe builders, finally making a choice between the Adour without afterburner and the less powerful Viper 632. With the Adour, the Hawk had a chance to be a world-beater, and backed by an immediate RAF order for 175 the Hawker Siddeley plants rapidly completed design, tooled for fast manufacture with assembly at Dunsfold and completed development of the RAF T.1 version all within the first two years of the programme. By October 1976 a dozen aircraft had flown and deliveries had begun to the RAF to replace the Gnat, Hunter and, eventually, Jet Provost, in roles ranging from basic flying to advanced weapon training. Partly as a result of the 21-month time-lead over the rival Alpha Jet, and partly because of its much lower price (equivalent to about $2 million) the Hawk is likely to be a worldwide best-seller, a proportion being single-seat tactical multi-role machines. It is significant that the aircraft now in service have all-round performance superior to the original brochure figures.

Above: Most of the 175 Hawks for RAF Training Command are finished in this colour scheme, for pilot training.

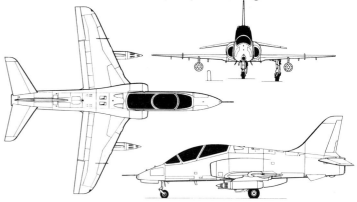

Above: Three-view of Hawk with centreline gun and rockets.

Below: Several air forces are negotiating for multi-role tactical Hawks with two extra outboard pylons and total external weapon load of 5,600lb (2540kg).

Ilyushin Il-28

Il-28, 28R, 28T and 28U

Origin: Design bureau of Sergei V. Ilyushin, Soviet Union; also built in Czechoslovakia (as B-228) and China.

Type: Three-seat bomber and ground attack; (28R) reconnaissance; (28T) torpedo carrier; (28U) dual trainer.

Engines: (Pre-1950) two 5,005lb (2270kg) thrust Klimov RD-45F; (post-1950) two 5,952lb (2700kg) thrust Klimov VK-1 single-shaft centrifugal turbojets.

Dimensions: Span (without tip tanks) 70ft 4¾in (21·45m); length 57ft 10¾in (17·65m); height 22ft (6·7m).

Weights: Empty 28,417lb (12,890kg); maximum loaded 46,297lb (21,000kg).

Performance: Maximum speed 559mph (900km/h); initial climb 2,953ft (900m)/min; service ceiling 40,355ft (12,300m); range with bomb load 684 miles (1100km).

Armament: (Il-28, typical) two 23mm NR-23 cannon fixed in nose and two NR-23 in powered tail turret; internal bomb capacity of 2,205lb (1000kg), with option of carrying double this load or external load (such as two 400mm light torpedoes).

History: First flight (prototype) 8 August 1948; (production Il-28) early 1950; service-delivery 1950; final delivery (USSR) about 1960, (China) after 1968.

Users: Afghanistan, Algeria, Bulgaria, China, Cuba (not operational), Czechoslovakia (-28U), Egypt, Finland (target tugs), E Germany (U), Indonesia, Iraq, N Korea, Nigeria, Poland (U), Romania (U), Somalia, Soviet Union, S Yemen, Syria, Vietnam, Yemen Arab.

Development: After World War II the popular media in the West published a succession of indistinct photographs, drawings and other pictures purporting to show Soviet jet aircraft. Apart from the MiG-9 and Yak-15 (and, after 1951, MiG-15) all were fictitious and by chance none happened to bear much resemblance to aircraft that actually existed. Thus, whereas the 1950 *Jane's* published a drawing and "details" of an Ilyushin four-jet bomber, it knew nothing of the extremely important Il-28 programme then coming to the production stage. Roughly in the class of the Canberra, the Il-28 prototype flew on two RD-10 (Jumo 004 development) turbojets, but the much superior British Nene was quickly substituted and, in VK-1 form, remained standard in the 10,000 or more subsequent examples. Unusual features are the sharply swept tail surfaces, the single-wheel main gears retracting in bulges under the jetpipes, the fixed nose cannon and the rear turret manned by the radio operator. Known to NATO as "Beagle", it equipped all the Warsaw Pact light bomber units in 1955-70 and was also adopted by the AV-MF as the Il-28T torpedo bomber (that service having originally chosen the rival Tu-14T). The Il-28U dual trainer has distinctive stepped cockpits, and the 28R reconnaissance version (many probably converted bombers) carry a wide range of electronics and sensors. No longer a front-line type in the Soviet Union, the Il-28 remains in service with some 12 air forces outside Europe, the most important being that of China where some hundreds were built under a licence granted before 1960.

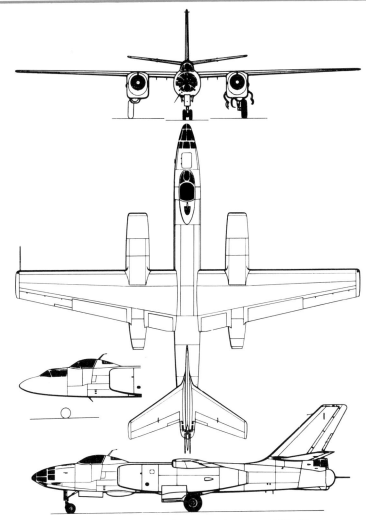

Above: Three-view of Il-28 with inset showing -28U. Many examples in second-line service with Warsaw Pact air forces now carry additional electronics aerials.

Below: The Il-28U conversion trainer is still standard equipment with the Air Force of the People's Liberation Army of

China. The bomber version is used by the Navy.

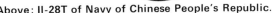

Above: Il-28T of Navy of Chinese People's Republic.

Lockheed T-33

T-33A, T-1A SeaStar, CL-30 Silver Star

Origin: Lockheed Aircraft Corporation, Burbank, USA; licence-built by Canadair, Montreal, and Kawasaki, Japan.

Type: Dual-control trainer.

Engine: (T-33A) one 5,200lb (2360kg) Allison J33-35; (T-1A) 6,100lb (2767kg) J33-24; (Silver Star) 5,100lb (2313kg) R-R Canada Nene 10; all are single-shaft turbojets.

Dimensions: Span (without tip tanks) 38ft 10½in (11.85m); length 37ft 9in (11·48m); height 11ft 8in (3·55m).

Weights: Empty (T-33A) 8,084lb (3667kg), (T-1A) 11,965lb (5428kg); maximum loaded (T-33A) 14,442lb (6551kg), (T-1A) 15,800lb (7167kg).

Performance: Maximum speed (all) about 590mph (950km/h); service ceiling (all) about 47,500ft (14,480m); maximum range (all) about 1,345 miles (2165km).

Armament: If fitted, usually two 0·5in (12·7mm) M-3 machine guns; often provision for underwing ordnance, normally 1,000lb (454kg) on each side.

History: First flight (TF-80C) 22 March 1948; last delivery (Japan) 1959.

Users: Belgium, Bolivia, Brazil, Burma, Canada, Chile, Colombia, Denmark, Ecuador, Ethiopia, France, Greece, Guatemala, Honduras, Indonesia, Iran, Japan, Jugoslavia, S. Korea, Libya, Mexico, Netherlands, Nicaragua, Pakistan, Peru, Philippines, Portugal, Spain, Taiwan, Thailand, Turkey, Uruguay.

Development: The world's first jet trainer was produced by adding almost three feet to an F-80 Shooting Star fuselage to accommodate a second cockpit, with a clamshell canopy covering both. Lockheed built 5,691, Kawasaki 210 and Canadair 656 with Nene engines. About 800 are still in use, many of the countries listed using the AT-33 close-support attack trainer or RT-33 photographic-reconnaissance trainer.

Above: Lockheed T-33A of Japan Air Self-Defence Force.

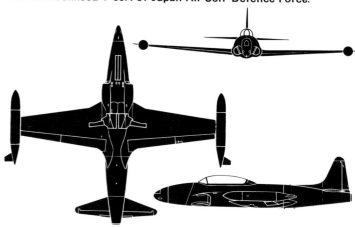

Above: Three-view of Lockheed T-33A (RT has blunt nose).

Mikoyan/Gurevich MiG-15UTI

MiG-15 and -15bis (Lim-2, S-103), MiG-15UTI (SBLim-1, CS-102, F-2)

Origin: Design, the Mikoyan/Gurevich bureau, Soviet Union; licence production as described in text.

Type: (-15) single-seat fighter; (-15UTI) dual-control trainer.

Engine: (-15) one 5,005lb (2270kg) thrust RD-45F single-shaft centrifugal turbojet; (-15bis and most -15UTI) one 5,952lb (2700kg) VK-1 of same layout; (later -15bis) 6,990lb (wet rating) VK-1A.

Dimensions: Span 33ft 0¾in (10·08m); length (-15, -15bis) 36ft 3¼in (11·05m); (-15UTI) 32ft 11¼in (10·04m); height (-15, -15bis) 11ft 1¾in (3·4m); (-15UTI) 12ft 1½in (3·7m).

Weights: Empty (all) close to 8,820lb (4000kg); maximum loaded (-15) 12,566lb (5700kg), (11,270lb clean); (-15UTI) 11,905lb (5400kg), (10,692lb clean).

Performance: Maximum speed (-15) 668mph (1075km/h); (-15bis) 684mph (1100km/h); (-15UTI) 630mph (1015km/h); initial climb (-15, -15UTI) 10,500ft (3200m)/min; (-15bis) 11,480ft (3500m)/min; service ceiling (-15, -15bis) 51,000ft (15,545m); (-15UTI) 47,980ft (14,625m); range (at height, with slipper tanks) 885 miles (1424km).

Armament: (-15, as first issued) one 37mm N cannon under right side of nose and one 23mm NS under left side; (-15, -15bis and variants) one 37mm with 40 rounds under right and two 23mm each with 80 rounds under left, with two underwing hard-points for slipper tanks or stores of up to 1,102lb (500kg); (-15UTI) single 23mm with 80 rounds or 12·7mm UBK-E with 150 rounds under left side, plus same underwing options.

History: First flight 30 December 1947; (MiG-15UTI) 1948; service delivery August 1948; final delivery, probably 1953 (USSR) and about 1954 in Poland and Czechoslovakia.

Users: Afghanistan, Albania, Algeria, Angola, Bulgaria, China, Cuba, Czecholsovakia, Egypt, Finland, E Germany, Guinea, Hungary, Indonesia (in storage), Iraq, N Korea, Mali, Mongolia, Morocco (in storage), Nigeria, Poland (?), Romania, Somalia, Soviet Union, S Yemen, Sri Lanka, Syria, Tanzania, Uganda, Vietnam.

Development: No combat aircraft in history has had a bigger impact on the world scene than the MiG-15. Its existence was unsuspected in the West until American fighter pilots suddenly found themselves confronted by all-swept silver fighters which could fly faster, climb and dive faster and turn more tightly. Gradually the whole story, and the start of the world pre-eminence of the Mikoyan-Gurevich bureau, could be traced back to the decision of the British government to send to the Soviet Union the latest British turbojet, the Rolls-Royce Nene (long before the Nene was used in any British service aircraft). At one stroke this removed the very serious lack of a suitable engine for the advanced fighter the bureau were planning, and within eight months the prototype MiG-15 had flown and the Nene was frantically being put into production (without a licence) in slightly modified form as the RD-45. The original MiG-15 owed a lot to the Ta-183 and other German designs, but the production machine had a lower tailplane, anhedral, wing fences, and other changes. Notable features were the extensive use of high-quality welding and the quick-detach package housing the two (later three) heavy cannon. Production rapidly outstripped that of any other aircraft at that time, at least 8,000 being built in the Soviet Union in about five years, plus a further substantial number at Mielec, Poland, as the Lim-2, and at the newly established Vodochody works near Prague as the S-103 (S = stihac, fighter). The two satellite countries also made the UTI trainer under an extension of their original licences, finally producing several thousand trainers by rebuilding MiG-15 fighters phased out of front-line service after 1954. In 1958 the Chinese plant at Shenyang began licence-production of the MiG-15UTI as the F-2. Most MiG-15 fighters were of the more powerful 15bis type with perforated flaps and redesigned rear-fuselage airbrakes; small numbers were made of a night fighter version with simple AI radar and of a ground-attack version with large ordnance carriers inboard of the drop tanks (the latter being originally of the slipper type but after 1952 often being carried below the wing on braced pylons). Known to NATO as "Fagot" (the trainer being "Mongol"), the MiG-15 saw considerable combat in Korea but suffered from the inexperience of its hastily trained Chinese and Korean pilots. As late as 1960 it was still used as a fighter by 15 countries and in 1977 the UTI trainer was still a standard type in the Soviet Union, and in all the countries listed earlier. Very few air forces today use the single-seater.

Above: A MiG-15UTI of the Ilmavoimat (Finnish Air Force) No 31 Sqn gets rolling on hard-packed snow.

Above: Three-view of MiG-15UTI (without tanks).

North American (Rockwell) T-28 Trojan/Fennec

T-28A Trojan and 16 developments (see text)

Origin: North American Aviation, Inglewood, USA; see text for subsequent developments.
Type: (T-28A) basic trainer; see text.
Engine: (T-28A) one 800hp Wright R-1300-1A; see text for later.
Dimensions: span 40ft 0in (12·19m) to 40ft 7½in (12·35m); length 32ft 10in (10·00m) to 33ft 8in (10·26m); height 12ft 8in (3·86m) (YAT-28E 14ft 9in, T-CH-1 12ft 0in).
Weights: Empty (A) 5,700lb, (D) 6,521lb (2958kg), (T-CH-1) 5,750lb (2608kg); maximum loaded (A) 8,000lb (3629kg), (D) 8,495lb (3853kg), (E) 12,000lb (5443kg), (T-CH-1) 9,200lb (4173kg).
Performance: Maximum speed (A) 283mph, (D) 380mph (611km/h), (T-CH-1) 368mph (592km/h); typical range (D) 500 miles (805km) with full weapon load, 1,000 miles (1610km) with max fuel.
Armament: See text.
History: First flight (A) 26 September 1949; see text.
Users: Argentina, Bolivia, Brazil, Dominica, Ecuador, Ethiopia, Haiti, S Korea, Laos, Mexico, Morocco, Nicaragua, Philippines, Taiwan, Thailand, Vietnam, Zaïre.

Development: The NA-159 won the contest to replace the T-6 as the standard USAF basic trainer, and as the T-28A Trojan was delivered from January 1950. By 1953 1,194 of these tandem nosewheel aircraft had been delivered, and in 1955–7 the Columbus factory delivered 489 T-28Bs to the US Navy with 1,425hp R-1820-86 Cyclone, followed by 299 T-28Cs with arrester hooks. Hamilton made T-28R Nomairs, while Pacair built Nomads for desert warfare and reconnaissance, leading to the Sud-Aviation Fennec (desert rat) used in Algeria with two twin 0·5in gun pods and two 1,000lb (454kg) bombs. In 1961–69 the original maker received 13 USAF contracts to convert As to T-28D Mutual Aid Program attack configuration, with R-1300 engine but six pylons for a 4,000lb (1814kg) weapon load; Fairchild Republic converted 72 more. In 1963–68 YAT-28E attack prototypes powered by the 2,450hp Lycoming T55 turboprop carried up to 7,000lb (3175kg) on 12 pylons. In Taiwan the Aircraft Industry Development Centre used the T-28 as the basis for the T-CH-1 trainer and light attack aircraft with a 1,450ehp Lycoming T53-L-701 turboprop, derived from a prototype flown on 23 November 1973.

Above: Many of the B and low-powered A trainers were rebuilt into the T-28D attack version with gun pods and weapon pylons.

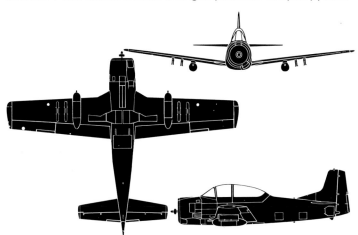

Above: Three-view of typical T-28D (Fennec similar).

Northrop T-38 Talon

T-38A

Origin: Northrop Corporation, Hawthorne, USA.
Type: All-through (basic and advanced) trainer.
Engines: Two General Electric J85-5 single-shaft turbojets each rated at 2,680lb (1216kg) thrust dry and 3,850lb (1748kg) with maximum afterburner.
Dimensions: Span 25ft 3in (7·70m); length 46ft 4½in (14·13m); height 12ft 10½in (3·92m).
Weights: Empty, not stated; maximum loaded 12,093lb (5485kg).
Performance: Maximum speed at 36,000ft (11,000m) 812mph (1305 km/h, Mach 1·23); initial climb 30,000ft (9144m)/min; service ceiling 53,600ft (16,335m); range with max fuel (all internal) 1,093 miles (1760km).
Armament: No provision.
History: First flight 10 April 1959; first operational duty 17 March 1961; final delivery January 1972.
Users: W Germany (Luftwaffe, in USA), US (Air Force, Navy and NASA).

Development: Northrop's study for a light fighter, which led to the F-5, also generated a tandem-seat trainer, the N-156T. After two years of company funding six prototypes were ordered in May 1956, and when production finished 1,187 had been delivered. This was an exceptional number of supersonic aircraft of one design for one customer, but today — despite a good record of safety and reliability — the T-38 is judged to have been a mistake, and no air force has plans to buy supersonic trainers of this kind. Control surfaces are fully powered, but the only external load carried is a travel pod for spares and crew baggage. The Luftwaffe bought 46 retaining US markings, the Navy five and NASA 24 for Astronaut practice.

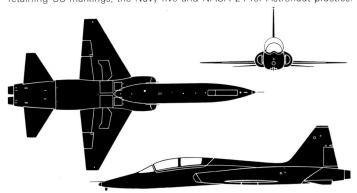

Above: Three-view of T-38A without centreline pod.

Below: Though it was probably a procurement error, the T-38A Talon is a pleasant aircraft with a fine safety record. Here is No 6 from the USAF Thunderbirds display team.

Potez (Aérospatiale) Magister

CM 170, CM 170-2, CM 175

Origin: Fouga et Cie, France; subsequently, see text.
Type: Basic trainer and light attack.
Engines: (CM 170, 175) two 880lb (400kg) thrust Turboméca Marboré IIA centrifugal turbojets; (CM 170-2) two 1,058lb (480kg) Marboré VIC.
Dimensions: Span 37ft 5in (11·4m) (39ft 10in, 12·15m, over tip tanks invariably fitted); length 33ft (10·06m); height 9ft 2in (2·80m).
Weights: Empty (170, 175) about 4,740lb (2150kg); (170-2) 5,093lb (2310kg); maximum loaded (all) 7,055lb (3200kg).
Performance: Maximum speed 403mph (650km/h); (170-2) 440mph (710km/h); initial climb 2,950ft (900m)/min; (170-2) 3,540ft/min; service ceiling 36,090ft (11,000m); (170-2) 44,300ft: range (all) about 735 miles (1250km).
Armament: Normally two rifle-calibre (usually 7·5mm or 7·62mm) machine guns in nose and two underwing pylons for 110lb (50kg) bombs, AS.11 missiles, rocket pods or other stores.
History: First flight 23 July 1952; (production CM 170) 29 February 1956; final delivery, 1967.
Users: Algeria, Belgium, Brazil, Cameroun, Finland, France, Ireland, Israel, Kampuchea, Lebanon, Morocco, Rwanda, Salvador, Togo, Uganda.

Development: The first jet basic trainer in history, the Magister has remained an active programme through a succession of upheavals in its manufacturer. The initials in its designation signify Castello and Mauboussin, who designed it at the Fouga company in 1950. Despite its novel butterfly tail, with just two surfaces inclined diagonally serving as rudders and elevators, it was a delight to fly and gave a much-needed boost to French morale as the first really useful post-war aircraft from the French industry that did not tag along behind other nations. After prolonged testing the Magister was put into production for the Armée de l'Air, while a hooked version for the Aéronavale was produced as the CM 175 Zéphyr. Total production of these, plus five for the CEV test centre, amounted to 437. Total output was brought up to 916 by the many versions built for foreign customers, the last 130 of which were of the more powerful 170-2 type. Fouga was absorbed into Potez in 1958 and in turn Potez was absorbed into Aérospatiale in 1967.

Potez built 40 for the German Luftwaffe, for which 210 more were built by Heinkel/Messerschmitt (Union-Süd); of 82 for Finland, 62 were built by Valmet Oy; of 52 for Israel, 36 were built by IAI. Israeli Magisters set the trend in the Six-Day War in June 1967 of using this nimble machine in combat roles. Subsequently Magisters were popular in local wars, especially in Africa.

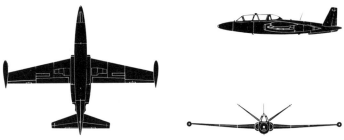

Above: Three-view of basic CM 170 Magister.

Above: Many years ago Potez-Air Fouga supplied 28 Magisters to the Force Aérienne Algérienne (Algerian AF), where they are used in the armed trainer role. This is one of a dozen countries where the trim little French trainer is in fact serving in a tactical combat role, though it would be of value only in a minor dispute or in counter-insurgency operations.

Above: Magister built by Flugzeugunion Süd for Luftwaffe.

Rockwell International

T-39 Sabreliner

T-39A, B, D and F, CT-39E and G

Origin: Rockwell International Sabreliner Division, El Segundo, USA.
Type: See text.
Engines: (A to D and F) two 3,000lb (1360kg) Pratt & Whitney J60-3 single-shaft turbojets; (E and G) two 3,300lb (1497kg) JT12A-8 (commercial version, uprated); (Sea Sabre 75) two 6,500lb (2948kg) Avco Lycoming ALF 502 geared turbofans.
Dimensions: Span 44ft 5in (13·53m); length (A-F) 43ft 9in (13·33m), (G) 48ft 4in (14·73m), (Sea) suggested 56ft; height 16ft 0in (4·88m).
Weights: Empty, equipped (A-F) 9,257lb (4200kg), (G) 11,250lb (5103kg); maximum loaded (A-D, F) 17,760lb (8055kg), (E, G) 20,172lb (9150kg), (Sea) about 30,000lb.
Performance: Maximum speed at 21,500ft (6550m) (all, typical) 563mph (906km/h, Mach 0·8); economical cruise at high altitude Mach 0·75; service ceiling or max certificated altitude 45,000ft (13,715m); max range with typical load and reserves (all) 2,000 miles (3219km).
History: First flight (NA-246 prototype) 16 September 1958; (T-39A) 30 June 1960.
Users: Argentina (LADE), US (Air Force, Navy).

Development: North American Aviation built the NA-246 as a private venture to meet the Air Force's UTX requirement for a "utility and combat-readiness trainer", and in 1961–64 delivered 143 T-39As now classed as pilot proficiency and administrative support aircraft (and called "the most efficient non-combatant aircraft in the inventory"). They include among their duties training of multi-engine pilots, navigators and instrument-rating instructors. The T-39B is a doppler/Nasarr trainer for F-105 pilots, the D has a twin-pronged nose for Navy avionics training, the CT-39E is a rapid-response airlift transport for the Navy, the F trains ECM operators for Wild Weasel F-105G and EF-4G platforms, and the CT-39G is a stretched Fleet tactical support aircraft. The G corresponds to the civil Sabreliner 60, others being members of the Sabreliner 40 family. The Sea Sabre 75, much larger and more powerful, was developed for the US Coast Guard competition for an offshore patrol aircraft.

Above: One of the 143 original T-39A Sabreliners of the US Air Force. Some have now been converted in various ways.

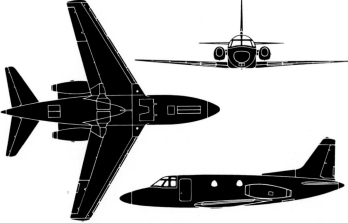

Above: Three-view of T-39A (most variants have more windows).

Rockwell International
T-2 Buckeye

T-2A (T2J-1), B, C, D and E

Origin: Rockwell International, Columbus Aircraft Division, USA.
Type: Basic trainer and light attack aircraft.
Engine: (A) one 3,400lb (1542kg) thrust Westinghouse J34-48 single-shaft turbojet; (B) two 3,000lb (1360kg) Pratt & Whitney J60-6 single-shaft turbojets; (C/D/E) two 2,950lb (1339kg) General Electric J85-4 single-shaft turbojets.
Dimensions: Span (over tip tanks) 38ft 1½in (11·62m); length 38ft 3½in (11·67m); height 14ft 9½in (4·51m).
Weights: Empty (C) 8,115lb (3680kg); maximum loaded (C) 13,179lb (5977kg).
Performance: Maximum speed (B) 540mph (869km/h), (C) 522mph (840km/h); initial climb (C) 6,200ft (1890m)/min; service ceiling (B) 42,000ft (12,800m), (C) 40,400ft (12,315m); max range (C) 1,047 miles (1685km).
Armament: (See text for E) total external load up to 640lb (290kg) may be carried on two underwing hardpoints, with provision for gun or other pods.
History: First flight 31 January 1958, (B) 30 August 1962, (C) 17 April 1968.
Users: Greece, Morocco, US Navy, Venezuela.

Development: North American Aviation's Columbus Division won a 1956 competition for the standard US Navy jet trainer, and delivered 217 T2J-1 Buckeyes, later redesignated T-2A. The T-2B, of which 97 were delivered in 1965–69, almost doubled the installed thrust, and the final Naval Air Training Command model was the T-2C of which 231 were built from new in 1968–75. Venezuela uses the D, without carrier equipment and with the second batch of 12 having the attack kit of the E. The latter, of which 40 were built for the Royal Hellenic AF in 1976–7, has six stores pylons for a total external load of 3,500lb (1587kg), and tanks protected against small-arms fire.

Above: Rockwell International T-2D Buckeye of Venezuelan AF.

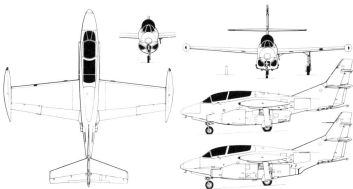

Above: Three-view of T-2C (upper side and scrap front views depict single-engined T-2A).

Below: This pair from VT-4 represent 231 US Navy T-2C Buckeyes, which are the standard carrier-indoctrination trainers.

Saab 105

SK 60A, B and C, Saab 105O and 105G

Origin: Saab-Scania, Linköping, Sweden.
Type: Trainer and multi-role tactical aircraft.
Engines: (SK 60) two 1,640lb (743kg) thrust Turboméca Aubisque geared turbofans; (others) two 2,850lb (1293kg) General Electric J85-17B single-shaft turbojets.
Dimensions: Span 31ft 2in (9·50m); length (SK 60) 34ft 5in, (others) 35ft 5¼in (10·80m); height 8ft 10in (2·70m).
Weights: Empty (SK 60) 5,534lb (2510kg), (G) 6,757lb (3065kg); maximum loaded (SK 60) 8,380lb (3800kg) aerobatic or 8,930lb (4050kg) other, (G) 14,330lb (6500kg).
Performance: Maximum speed (clean, low level) (SK 60 at 8,820lb) 447mph (720km/h), (G) 603mph (970km/h); initial climb (SK 60) 3,440ft (1050m)/min, (G) 11,155ft (3400m)/min; service ceiling (SK 60) 39,370ft (12,000m), (G) 42,650ft (13,000m); max range, high altitude on internal fuel (SK 60) 1,106 miles (1780km), (G) 1,230 miles (1980km).
Armament: Wing stressed for six hardpoints to carry total external load of (SK 60) 1,543lb (700kg), (G) 5,180lb (2350kg) including gun pods to 30mm calibre, 1,000lb bombs, missiles, tanks and target gear.
History: First flight 29 June 1963, (production SK 60A) 27 August 1965, (G) 26 May 1972.
Users: Austria, Sweden.

Above: It has long been Flygvapen policy to disperse combat units to straight public highways. These four SK 60Cs from F20 at Uppsala have recce noses and full weapons capability.

Development: Developed as a private venture, a rare thing for Saab, this neat side-by-side trainer and multi-role aircraft has hydraulically boosted elevators and ailerons, ejection seats replaceable by four fixed seats for liaison duties, and a wide range of avionics and weapon options. The 150 SK 60s of the Royal Swedish AF comprise A (basic trainers), B (weapon training and strike) and C (reconnaissance) sub-types. Austria uses the 105O. The G has airframe modifications, heavier and more varied weapon loads and a precision nav/attack system.

Below: Another multi-role Saab 105 wing is F21 at Lulea. Many of their aircraft are SK 60C models, but this formation is of the basic series without reconnaissance cameras in the nose.

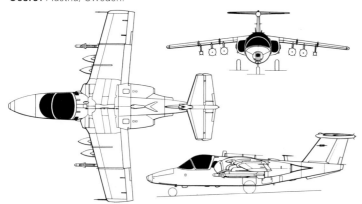

Above: Three-view of basic SK 60A, with Sidewinders.

Saab Supporter

Supporter (formerly MFI-17)

Origin: Saab-Scania, Linköping, Sweden.
Type: Light trainer and multi-role tactical aircraft.
Engine: One 200hp Avco Lycoming IO-360-A1B6 flat-six.
Dimensions: Span 29ft 0½in (8·85m); length 22ft 11½in (7·00m); height 8ft 6½in (2·60m).
Weights: Empty, equipped 1,424lb (646kg); maximum loaded 2,645lb (1200kg).
Performance: (at 2,480lb): maximum speed 146mph (236km/h); initial climb 807ft (246m); service ceiling 13,450ft (4100m); typical take-off or landing over 50ft (15m) 1,280ft (390m); maximum range with reserves 672 miles (1080km).
Armament: Six underwing hardpoints, inners stressed to 330lb (150kg) each, and remainder to 220lb (100kg) for bombs, gun packs, guided missiles, supply packs or other stores.
History: First flight 6 July 1972; service delivery 1974.

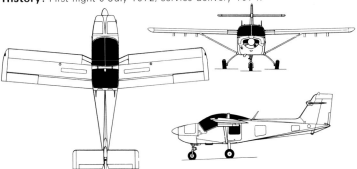

Above: Three-view of Saab Supporter.

Users: Denmark, Pakistan.

Development: Developed from the civil Safari (formerly MFI-15), which in turn was an enlarged version of the 1958 MFI-9B Mili-Trainer/BA-7 made by Malmö Flygindustri, the Supporter is possibly the cheapest military aircraft in the world today. Yet it is extremely capable and versatile and can serve for training, supply dropping, FAC, reconnaissance, light attack, liaison, anti-tank or target towing. Pakistan has 45 and the Royal Danish AF will have 32, designated T-17, when this book is published.

Above: One of the 32 T-17 Supporters delivered to the Flyvevaabnet (Royal Danish Air Force) to replace Chipmunks as trainers and KZ.VIIs and Super Cubs in the observation role.

Scottish Aviation SA-3 Bulldog

Bulldog Series 100 and Series 120

Origin: Scottish Aviation, Prestwick, UK
Type: Primary trainer.
Engine: One 200hp Avco Lycoming IO-360-A1B6 flat-six.
Dimensions: Span 33ft 0in (10·06m); length 23ft 3in (7·09m); height 7ft 5¾in (2·28m).
Weights: Empty 1,475lb (669kg); maximum loaded 2,350lb (1066kg).
Performance: Maximum speed 150mph (241km/h); initial climb 1,034ft (315m)/min; service ceiling 16,000ft (4875m); take-off or landing over 50ft (15m) within 1,400ft (425m); max range without reserves 621 miles (1000km).
Armament: Optional four underwing hardpoints for total external load of 640lb (290kg).
History: First flight 19 May 1969, (production Series 100) 22 July 1971, (Series 120) 30 January 1973.
Users: Ghana (Series 122), Jordan (125), Kenya (103), Lebanon (126), Malaysia (102), Nigeria (123), Sweden (101, designation SK 61) and UK (RAF, 121).

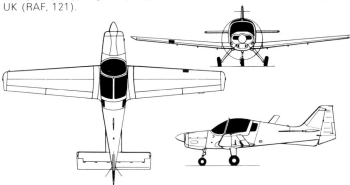

Above: Three-view of Scottish Aviation Bulldog.

Development: Produced by defunct Beagle Aircraft in 1968 as a military trainer version of the Pup, the Bulldog is widely considered to be the best light piston-engined trainer in the world today — a view reinforced by its early selection by Sweden instead of a competing Swedish machine. A third seat or 120lb (54kg) baggage can be accommodated, as can a glider towing hook and a wide range of avionics and special fittings. The first 98 were Series 100, and since 1973 a further 183 have been ordered of the 120 series restressed for semi-aerobatic manoeuvres at maximum weight. In August 1976 the first flight took place of the lengthened and cleaned-up Series 200 (civil name Bullfinch) with retractable landing gear and optional fourth seat.

Above: This pretty picture was taken near Little Rissington, Gloucestershire, soon after the first Bulldog T.1 trainers had been delivered to the Central Flying School. CFS has now closed and most RAF Bulldogs are at 2 FTS, Leeming, Yorks. Many others are serving with the University Air Squadrons throughout the United Kingdom. British Bulldogs are unarmed, but the aircraft has been cleared for SNEB 68mm rockets and dropping of free-fall stores, while Swedish Bulldogs (left) are operational with Bofors Bantam wire-guided missiles.

Above: SK 61 Bulldog of F5 at Ljungbyhed, Sweden.

SIAI/Marchetti SF.260

SF.260M, W and SW

Origin: SIAI-Marchetti SpA, Varese, Italy.
Type: (M) trainer, (W) tactical multi-role, (SW) surveillance.
Engine: One 260hp Avco Lycoming O-540-E4A5 flat-six.
Dimensions: Span 27ft 0¾in (8·25m) (8·35m over tip tanks); length 23ft 3½in (7·10m); height 7ft 11in (2·41m).
Weights: Empty (M, equipped) 1,664lb (755kg); maximum loaded 2,645lb (1200kg).
Performance: (M at max wt) maximum speed 211mph (340km/h); initial climb 1,496ft (456m)/min; service ceiling 16,400ft (5000m); take-off or landing over 50ft (15m) within 2,543ft (775m); range with max fuel 925 miles (1490km) (SW, about 1,400 miles, 2250km).
Armament: (W) one underwing hardpoint on each side rated at 330lb (150kg) for Matra 7·62mm gun pods, 120kg bombs or wide range of other stores.
History: First flight (MX) 10 October 1970, (W) May 1972.
Users: Belgium (M), Burma (M), Dubai (W), Ireland (W), Italy (M), Morocco (M), Philippines (M, W), Singapore (M), Thailand (M), Tunisia (W), Zaire (M), Zambia (M).

Development: The original SF.260 was a civil three-seat fully aerobatic machine designed by Stelio Frati and flown in 1964. The military M (or MX) series found an immediate market, despite being unnecessarily costly and powerful for a primary trainer and very limited as a combat machine. The three seats, good payload/range at high speed and fully aerobatic capability have made the M series popular, with 138 sold by 1975. Since then the fully armed W (formerly called Warrior) has also found customers, though no sales have been reported of the SW, with increased fuel for 10hr 55min endurance and tip pods housing a camera installation on the right and a Bendix digital radar on the left.

Above: SIAI-Marchetti SF.260WP light attack aircraft of the Philippine Air Force with gun pods replaced by rockets.

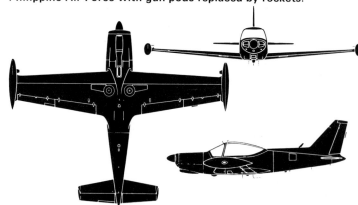

Above: Three-view of SIAI-Marchetti 260M without pylons.

Soko Galeb and Jastreb

G2-A, Galeb, J-1 Jastreb

Origin: "Soko" Metalopreradivacka Industrija, Yugoslavia.
Type: (Galeb) dual armed trainer; Jastreb, single-seat attack.
Engine: One Rolls-Royce Viper single-shaft turbojet; (G) 2,500lb (1134kg) thrust Mk 22-6; (J) 3,000lb (1360kg) Mk 531.
Dimensions: Span (excluding tip tanks) 34ft 4½in (10·47m); (J) 34ft 8in; length 33ft 11in (10·34m); (J) 35ft 1½in; height 10ft 9in (3·28m); (J) 11ft 11½in.
Weights: Empty 5,775lb (2620kg); (J) 6,217lb maximum loaded 9,210lb (4178kg); (G, clean, fully aerobatic) 7,438lb; (J) 10,287lb.
Performance: Maximum speed 505mph (812km/h); (J) 510mph; initial climb 4,500ft (1370m)/min; service ceiling 39,375ft (12,000m); range (hi, max fuel) 770 miles (1240km); (J) 945 miles.
Armament: (G) 12·7mm guns in nose, each with 80 rounds; underwing pylons for two 220lb (100kg) bombs, or light loads of rockets. (J) three 12·7mm in nose, each with 135 rounds; eight underwing hardpoints, two furthest inboard carrying stores of 551lb (250kg), the rest single 127mm rockets.
History: First flight (G) May 1961; service delivery (G) 1965.
Users: Libya, Yugoslavia, Zambia.

Development: The first Yugoslav jet to go into production, the tandem-seat Galeb (Seagull) has been fully developed and built in modest numbers for the Yugoslav Air Force and Zambia. Pupil and instructor sit in Folland lightweight seats, and an air-conditioning system is an option. The Jastreb (Hawk) uses a similar airframe, with local strengthening for the more powerful engine and heavier external stores. Again Zambia has received an export version, but without the optional cabin pressurization and self-contained engine-start system. Jastrebs can carry cameras in the fuselage and in the nose of the tip tanks, and also tow an aerial target.

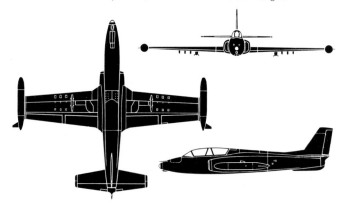

Above: Three-view of Soko G2-A Galeb (TJ-1 similar).

Below: The Yugoslav Air Force has about 60 G2-A Galebs, and is receiving a dual trainer/attack model designated TJ-1. About 150 single-seat Jastrebs include the RJ-1 reconnaissance version.

WSK-Mielec TS-11 Iskra

TS-11 Iskra (Spark) Series 100, 200 and single-seater.

Origin: WSK-PZL-Mielec, Mielec, Poland.
Type: Basic trainer and light attack aircraft.
Engine: One 2,205lb (1000kg) thrust IL SO-1 or SO-3 single-shaft turbojet.
Dimensions: Span 33ft 0in (10·06m); length 36ft 7in (11·15m); height 11ft 5½in (3·50m).
Weights: Empty (trainer) 5,644 (2560kg); maximum loaded 8,465lb (3840kg).

Above: TS-11 in original form but with nose cannon.

Performance: maximum speed (trainer at 3800kg at 16,400ft, 5000m) 447mph (720km/h); initial climb 2,913ft (888m)/min; service ceiling 36,100ft (11,000m); take-off or landing over 50ft (15m) within 3,900ft (1190m); range with max fuel 776 miles (1250km).
Armament: (Series 100, 200 and single-seater) 23mm gun in starboard side of nose, with gun camera, plus four underwing hardpoints for gun pods, rockets or bombs up to 220lb (100kg).
History: First flight 5 February 1960; service delivery March 1963.
Users: India, Poland.
Development: Rejected in ·favour of the Czech L-29 as standard trainer for the Warsaw Pact, the sleek TS-11 was nevertheless put into production as standard trainer of its home air force. Most are tandem-seat dual trainers in natural metal finish, but limited numbers have been made for the Polish AF of a camouflaged single-seat attack version. The Iskra 100 carries the same armament provisions, and in 1975 production switched to the 200 with long-life SO-3 engine and other changes. India bought 50 in 1975, and by 1977 about 400 Iskras had been built.

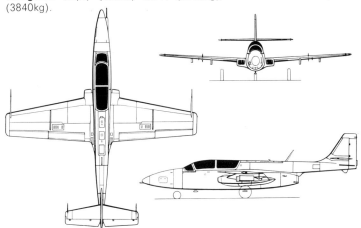

Above: Three-view of WSK-Mielec TS-11 Iskra 200.

Yakovlev Yak-18

Yak-18, 18U, 18A, 18P, 18PM and 18T

Origin: The design bureau of Alexander Yakovlev, Soviet Union.
Type: Primary trainer; see text for other roles.
Engine: (18, 18U) one 160hp Shvetsov M-11FR five-cylinder radial; (18A, P, PM) one 300hp Ivchenko AI-14RF nine-cylinder radial; (T) one 360hp Vedeneev M-14P nine-cylinder radial.
Dimensions: Span (18) 33ft 9½in, (18U, A and P) 34ft 9¼in (10·60m), (T) 36ft 7¼in (11·16m); length (18, 18U) 26ft 5½in (8·07m), (18A, P and T) 27ft 4¾in (8·35m); height (18, PM) about 7ft (2·13m), (U, A, P, T) 11ft 0in (3·35m).
Weight: Empty (18) about 1,800lb, (U, A, P) typically 2,259lb (1025kg), (T) 2,450lb; maximum loaded (18) 2,469lb (1120kg), (U, A,·P) 2,910lb (1320kg), (T) 3,637lb (1650kg).
Performance: Maximum speed (18) 133mph (215km/h), (U) 143mph (230km/h), (U, A, P, T) 186mph (300km/h); range with max fuel (A) 435 miles (700km), (T) 560 miles (900km).
History: First flight 1946, (U) 1955, (A) 1956, (P) probably 1959, (PM) probably 1965, (T) 1967.
Users: China, E Germany, N Korea, Mongolia, Romania, S Yemen, Soviet Union, Syria, probably others.

Development: Most of the primary training of the Warsaw Pact air forces (apart from Poland, which uses the TS-8 Bies) is done in civil or para-military schools, and it is to these that the bulk of some 8,000 of these popular and robust aircraft have been supplied. The original Yak-18 had an M-11 with helmeted cowling and tailwheel-type landing gear with the main legs retracted to the rear. The 18U introduced a long nosewheel gear with forward-retracting main legs, while the much more powerful A was cleaned up and had a variable-pitch propeller. The P and PM were refined single-seat aerobatic versions, the PS being a tailwheel derivative leading to today's Yak-50. The T has a wider centre section and a new stressed-skin fuselage with four-seat cabin, suitable for training, ambulance, patrol and similar duties, with wheel, ski or float landing gear.

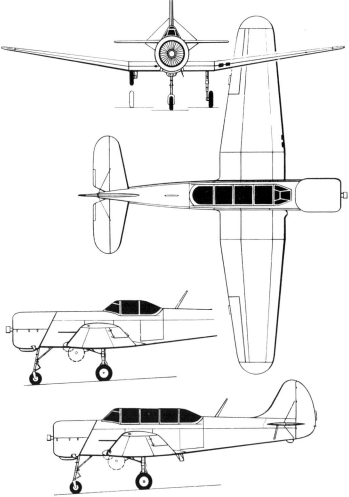

Above: Three-view of Yak-18A with extra side view of the Yak-18P single-seater. Today there are many models with nosewheel or tailwheel and one to four seats.

Above: Standard basic trainer of the Air Force of the Chinese People's Liberation Army, this version of Yak-18 has a tail unlike that of standard Soviet sub-types.

Aeritalia AM.3C

AM.3C, Bosbok

Origin: Developed jointly by Aerfer (now part of Aeritalia) and Aermacchi, Italy.
Type: Utility multi-role.
Engine: One 340hp Piaggio (Lycoming licence) GSO-480-B1B6 flat-six.
Dimensions: Span 41ft 5½in (12·64m); length 29ft 3¾in (8·93m); height 8ft 11in (2·72m).
Weights: Empty 2,380lb (1080kg); maximum loaded 3,750lb (1700kg).
Performance: Maximum speed (clean at 8,000ft, 2440m) 173mph (278km/h); service ceiling 27,550ft (8400m); takeoff or landing over 50ft (15m) 560ft (170m); max range with 30min reserve 615 miles (990km).
Armament: Two underwing hardpoints each rated at 375lb (170kg) for wide range of ordnance and other loads including Matra twin-gun pods, GE Miniguns, retarded or cluster bombs and missiles.
History: First flight 12 May 1967; service delivery July 1973.
Users: Italy, Rwanda, S Africa.

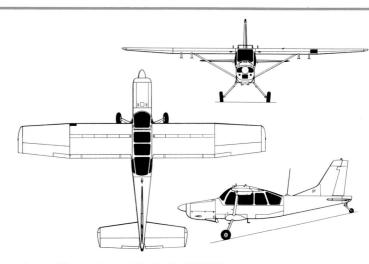

Above: Three-view of Aeritalia AM.3C.

Development: The first modern Italian utility aircraft was the stressed-skin LASA-60 transport designed by Lockheed-Georgia in 1959 and produced by Aermacchi as the AL.60 and by LASA in Mexico. The LASA-60 serves with the Mexican AF, while the more powerful (400hp) tailwheel AL.60 made in Italy serves in Rhodesia (named Trojan) and the Central African Republic. The high-lift wing of this aircraft was used in the small-bodied AM.3C, built to meet an Italian AF requirement and to replace the O-19 in the Italian Army. The largest customer was the S African AF, whose 50 Bosboks equip 41 Sqn at Johannesburg and 42 at Potchefstroom. From the Bosbok Atlas Aircraft has developed the eight-seat C4M Kudu, being evaluated by the S African AF.

Above: Bosbok of the SAAF (without underwing stores).

Below: A South African Bosbok on test in Italy before delivery. These powerful aircraft have proved extremely versatile, and are used for FAC, observation, casualty evacuation, supply dropping, tactical transport and armed close support. The high-capacity Kudu is now reported to be in production.

Antonov (WSK) An-2

An-2 (many variants) and WSK-Mielec An-2 (NATO name "Colt")

Origin: The bureau of Oleg K. Antonov, Soviet Union; today made only by WSK-Mielec, Poland, and State Industry of China.
Type: STOL transport.
Engine: One 1,000hp Shvetsov ASh-62IR nine-cylinder radial; (since 1960) one 1,000hp WSK-Kalisz ASz-62IR.
Dimensions: Span 59ft 8½in (18·18m) (lower wing 46ft 8½in, 14·24m); length 41ft 9½in (12·74m); height 13ft 1½in (4·00m).
Weights: (2P): Empty 7,605lb (3450kg); maximum loaded 12,125lb (5500kg).
Performance: Maximum speed (P, 11,574lb, 5250kg) 160mph (258 km/h); typical cruise 115mph (185km/h), min safe speed 56mph (90km/h); service ceiling 14,425ft (4400m); typical takeoff or landing over 35ft (10·7m) on grass 1,050ft (320m); range with 1,102lb (500kg) payload 560 miles (900km).
History: First flight 31 August 1947; service delivery (An-2) July 1948, (Fong Chou) December 1957, (WSK) 1960.
Users: 44 countries including the following air forces or other military operators: Afghanistan, Algeria, Bulgaria, China, Cuba, Egypt, Ethiopia, E Germany, Hungary, Iraq, N Korea, Mali, Mongolia, Poland, Romania, Somalia, Soviet Union, Sudan, Syria, Tanzania, Tunisia, Vietnam.

Development: When this bulky biplane appeared in 1947 it appeared to be an obsolete mistake. So unmistaken was it that it has been manufactured in larger quantities than any other single type of aircraft since World War II:

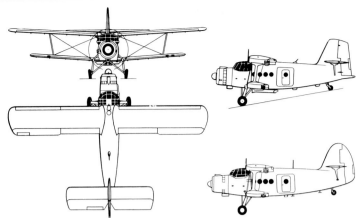

Above: Three-view of An-2M, with side view of standard An-2.

Soviet production had topped 5,000 when responsibility was passed to Poland in 1960, and a few hundred additional aircraft with angular tails were made in the Soviet Union in 1964–70; Polish output was continuing in 1977 with the nation's total well over 7,500, and the Chinese Fong Chou output is thought to exceed 5,000, making a combined figure of something over 18,000. Of these perhaps one-quarter are military, and many serve in para-military roles. Versions are numerous, and have different designations in the Soviet Union and Poland, but the chief military roles are paratroop and aircrew training, supply of frontier posts and general transport/casevac duties.

Britten-Norman Defender

BN-2A Defender

Origin: Britten-Norman (Bembridge) Ltd, UK (member of Fairey Group, which has production line at Gosselies, Belgium; third production line at IRMA, Romania).
Type: Multi-role light military aircraft.
Engines: Two 300hp Lycoming IO-540-K1B5 six-cylinder direct-injection horizontally-opposed.
Dimensions: Span (extended raked tips) 53ft (16·15m); length 35ft 8in (10·86m); height 13ft 8¾in (4·18m).
Weights: Empty 3,708lb (1682kg); loaded 6,600lb (2993kg).
Performance: Maximum speed (clean) 176mph (283km/h), (pylons loaded) 168mph (270km/h); initial climb (clean) 1,300ft (396m)/min; service ceiling 17,000ft (5180m); range (maximum combat load) 375 miles (603km), (maximum fuel) 1,723 miles (2772km).
Armament: Weapons normally all carried on four underwing hardpoints, inner pair stressed to 700lb (318kg) and outers to 450lb (204kg). Typical loads include 7·62mm Minigun pods, twin 7·62mm machine guns, bombs up to 500lb (227kg), Matra or SURA rocket dispensers, wide variety of grenades and markers, loud hailers, guided missiles or 50gal (227 litre) drop tanks.
History: First flight (civil Islander) 13 June 1965; (Defender) March 1971.
Users: Abu Dhabi, Belgium, Brazil, Egypt, Ghana, Guyana, Hong Kong, India (Navy), Iraq, Israel, Jamaica, Lesotho, Liberia, Malagasy, Mauritania, Mauritius, Mexico, Nigeria, Oman, Panama, Philippines, Qatar, Rhodesia, Rwanda, Thailand, Turkey Zaïre, Zambia.

Development: The Britten-Norman Islander has become one of the dominant light utility transports all over the world and it was natural that the enterprising company should have produced a military version. Roles for which the Defender has been planned include internal security, long-range patrol, search/rescue, forward air control, battlefield supply and casualty evacuation, reconnaissance and mapping, and indeed all forms of light limited-war combat, including ground attack, anti-ship and psy-war

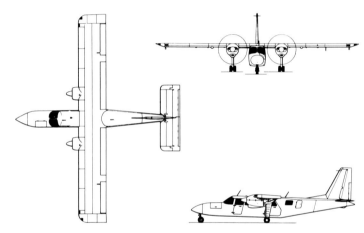

Above: Three-view of basic BN-2A Islander.

(psychological) operations. One of the major options is nose-mounted weather radar, providing a marine search capability. Within a year of first flight the Defender had been cleared for most kinds of ordnance dropping, rocket launching and gun firing, including firing of beam guns in the fuselage. Among the options already available are nose radar, various reconnaissance sensors, skis or amphibious floats; by 1978 a turboprop version powered by the 650hp Avco Lycoming LTP101 is expected to be in production. In 1976 marketing began on a proposed military Trislander (the larger three-engined model), with 9-hr endurance and ability to carry 17 troops or 3,745lb loads.

Below: As there are Defenders already flying with air forces all over the world, Hughes Helicopters has caused confusion by giving the same name to its armed 500M helicopter.

Cessna U-17

Model 185 and U-17

Origin: Cessna Aircraft Company, Wichita, USA.
Type: Utility transport.
Engine: One 300hp Continental IO-520D flat-six; (U-17C) 230hp O-470L.
Dimensions: Span 35ft 10in (10·92m); length overall 25ft 7½in (7·81m); height overall 7ft 9in (2·36m).
Weights: Empty 1,600lb (725kg); maximum loaded 3,350lb (1519kg).
Performance: Maximum cruise 169mph (272km/h); range on standard tankage, no reserve 660 miles (1062km).
History: First flight (civil 185) July 1960; service delivery (U-17A) 1963.
Users: (185 Skywagon bought from Cessna) Honduras, Indonesia (army), Iran (army), Jamaica, Paraguay, Peru, S Africa; (U-17) Bolivia, Costa Rica, Greece, S. Korea, Laos, Panama, Turkey, Vietnam; (206) Guatemala, Israel; (207) Argentina (army), Indonesia.

Development: Cessna's Model 185 Skywagon is a capable and powerful utility machine carrying up to six people with an optional glassfibre cargo pack under the fuselage. In 1963 the USAF bought 169 U-17A versions for MAP issue to friendly air forces, followed by 136 U-17B and a few U-17C

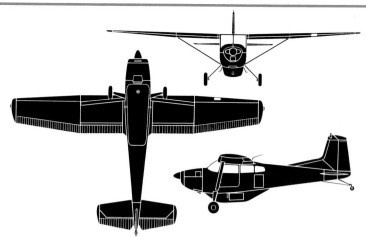

Above: Three-view of Cessna U-17A/Model 185.

with less power. The 206 Stationair has tricycle gear, swept fin and large side cargo doors. The 207 Turbo-Skywagon is similar but longer, with seventh seat.

Cessna O-2

O-2, Reims FTB 337G

Origin: Cessna Aircraft, Wichita, USA; licence-built by Reims-Aviation, France.
Type: (O-2A) FAC, (O-2B) psy-war, (FTB 337G) multi-role.
Engines: Two (front and rear) 210hp Continental IO-360C flat-sixes, (Reims) two 225hp Rolls-Royce Continental TSIO-360D.
Dimensions: Span 38ft 2in (11·63m) (Reims 39ft 8½in, 12·1m); length 29ft 9in (9·07m); height 9ft 2in (2·79m).
Weights: Empty (A) 2,848lb (1291kg), (Reims) 3,206lb (1454kg); maximum loaded 4,630lb (2100kg) (USAF overload 5,400lb, 2450kg).
Performance: Maximum cruise (O-2) 195mph (314km/h), (Reims) 230mph (370km/h); takeoff or landing over 50ft (15m) 1,675ft (510m) (Reims 1,200ft, 366m); max range with max fuel (typical) 1,325 miles (2132km).
History: First flight (civil Skymaster) February 1961, (O-2A) 1967.
User: Benin, Ecuador, Gabon, Haute-Volta, Iran, Ivory Coast, Malagasy,
Mauritania, Niger, Senegal, US (AF), Venezuela.

Development: Produced to meet a market for a twin-engined aircraft that could be flown by private pilots not possessing a twin rating, the push/pull Skymaster is a popular and safe aircraft seating up to six. The USAF selected it in 1966 to provide a superior Forward Air Control aircraft to replace the O-1A Bird Dog. By early 1969 346 had been delivered, and 12 were sold to the Imperial Iranian AF. The USAF also bought 164 O-2B psychological-warfare O-2Bs. Most O-2s have side-by-side dual controls and the O-2A has special electronics and four wing pylons for rockets, Minigun packs, flares and other loads. Cessna dropped the larger turboprop O-2TT. Reims has built over 100 of the more powerful FTB 337G (previously called Milirole), some with radar and/or infra-red pods.

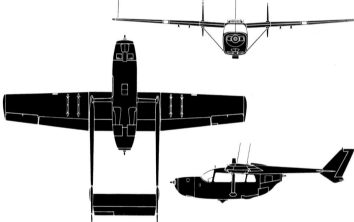

Above: Three-view of O-2A (337G similar).

Left: Cessna O-2A of the US Air Force, with supply containers.

Cessna U-3

U-3A (formerly L-27A) and U-3B

Origin: Cessna Aircraft Company, Wichita, USA.
Type: Administrative liaison and cargo transport.
Engines: Two 240hp Continental O-470M flat-sixes; (U-3B) two 285hp Continental IO-520M.
Dimensions: Span (over tanks) 36ft 11in (11·25m); length overall (U-3A) 27ft 1in (8·25m), (U-3B and modern 310) 31ft 11½in (9·73m); height overall 10ft 8in (3·25m).
Weights: Empty (U-3B, modern 310) 3,337lb (1514kg); maximum loaded (U-3A) 4,700lb (2132kg), (U-3B and modern 310) 5,500lb (2494kg).
Performance: Maximum cruise 223mph (359km/h); range, depending on sub-type and fuel, up to 1,740 miles (2800km).
History: First flight (310) 3 January 1953; (L-27A) 1957; (U-3B) 1960.
Users: Tanzania, Thailand, USA (AF), Zaïre.

Development: The Cessna 310 was one of the first of the modern light twins, with usual seating for five. In 1957 the USAF bought 80 off the shelf as L-27A utility (liaison/cargo) aircraft, subsequently doubling this order. In 1962 these were redesignated U-3A, and 36 U-3Bs were added similar to the later and more powerful 310E with swept fin and "all-weather" avionics. Zaïre bought 15 new 310s in 1975. Armée de l'Air communications between the Bretigny and Istres test bases is provided by 12 Cessna 411, with 340hp GTSIO-520 engines. Malaysia uses 10 Model 402s (300hp TSIO-520E) for multi-engine pilot training, and two for photo/liaison; other users of the 402 include Finland.

Above: In service since 1957, the U-3A is known throughout the US Air Force as the "Blue Canoe". Most military Cessna twins are later, larger and more powerful.

DH Canada Twin Otter

DHC-6, CC-138, UV-18A

Origin: The de Havilland Aircraft of Canada, Downsview, Canada.
Type: Multi-role transport.
Engines: Two Pratt & Whitney Canada turboprops: (Series 100, 200) 579ehp PT6A-20; (300) 652ehp PT6A-27.
Dimensions: Span 65ft (19·81m); length 51ft 9in (15·77m) (shortnose and seaplane 48ft, 14·7m); height 19ft 6in (5·94m) (seaplane higher).
Weights: Empty (typical military 100, 200) 6,500lb (2950kg), (300) 7,000lb (3175kg); maximum loaded (100, 200, seaplane) 11,600lb (5261kg), (300) 12,500lb (5670kg).
Performance: Maximum cruise (300) 210mph (338km/h); range (300) 1,103 miles (1775km) with 2,131lb (966kg) payload and wing tanks, 115 miles (185km) with 4,420lb (2004kg) payload.
History: First flight 20 May 1965; customer delivery (100) July 1966, (300) spring 1969.
Users: (Military) Argentina, Canada (CC-138), Chile, Ecuador, Jamaica, Norway, Panama, Paraguay, Peru, United States (UV-18A).

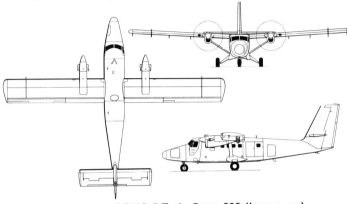

Above: Three-view of DHC-6 Twin Otter 300 (long nose).

Above: Ten of the 12 Twin Otters supplied to the Fuerza Aerea del Peru (Peruvian Air Force) are seaplanes. They are used by Grupo Aéreo 42, based at Iquitos.

Development: Funded entirely by the company when it was a member of the British Hawker Siddeley Group, the Twin Otter is a twin-turboprop outgrowth of the DHC-3 Otter (with single R-1340 Wasp, the Otter still serves as the US U-1 and in many other air forces). Unpressurized and simple, the Twin Otter has good STOL performance which is further improved in the current 300S model announced in 1973. Seating can be provided for 20 passengers, and options include wheels, skis or floats, and several special-role kits.

Dornier Do 28D Skyservant

Do 28D-1 and D-2

Origin: Dornier GmbH, Friedrichshafen, West Germany.
Type: Multi-role transport
Engines: Two 380hp Lycoming IGSO-540-A1E flat-sixes.
Dimensions: Span 51ft 0¼in (15·55m); length 37ft 5¼in (11·41m); height 12ft 9½in (3·90m).
Weights: Empty 5,080lb (2304kg); maximum loaded 8,853lb (4015kg).
Performance: Typical cruising speed at 10,000ft (3050m) 170mph (273km/h); min-control speed, full flap and power 40mph (65km/h); range with max fuel 1,831 miles (2950km).
History: First flight 23 February 1966; service delivery summer 1967 (military type approval January 1970).
Users: W Germany, Israel, Morocco, Nigeria, Somalia, Turkey, Zambia.

Development: Dornier's first post-war aircraft was the Do 27 built in Spain, a very attractive STOL machine built in large numbers for many air forces, Spanish production being designated CASA 127. The twin-engined Do 28 also sold well (120) in military forms, but despite its type-number the Do 28D is an entirely new design, considerably larger and more powerful. Most Skyservants are of the Do 28D-2 model with many refinements and greater weight. Up to 13 passengers can be carried, and there are

various role kits, but the wing pylons have been used only for auxiliary tanks. By 1977 sales exceeded 200, including 101 for the Luftwaffe and 20 for the Marineflieger.

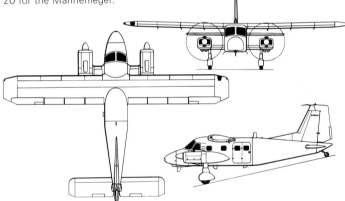

Above: Three-view of Do 28D-2 Skyservant.

Below: The West German Marineflieger (Naval AF) has 20 Skyservants (left), while every Luftwaffe Geschwader has four (right).

Douglas DC-3/C-47

C-47 and AC-47, R4D, C-53, Dakota, C-117, L2D and Li-2

Origin: Douglas Aircraft Company, Santa Monica, USA; later built by many other US plants, and licence-built in Japan and Soviet Union (see text).
Type: Utility transport (formerly also paratroop/glider tug); AC-47 air/ground weapon platform.
Engines: Usually two 1,200hp Pratt & Whitney R-1830-90D or -92 Twin Wasp 14-cylinder two-row radials; (C-117D) two 1,535hp Wright R-1820-80 Cyclone nine-cylinder radials; (Li-2) two 1,000hp M-62IR (Cyclone-derived) nine-cylinder radials.
Dimensions: Span 95ft (28·96m); length 64ft 5½in (19·64m); height 16ft 11in (5·16m).
Weights: empty, about 16,970lb (7700kg); loaded, about 25,200lb (11,432kg); overload limit 33,000lb (14,969kg).
Performance: Maximum speed, about 230mph (370km/h); initial climb, about 1,200ft (366m)/min; service ceiling 23,000ft (7000m); maximum range 2,125 miles (3420km)..
Armament: (AC-47) usually three 7·62mm Miniguns; many other types of armament in other versions, but none usually fitted.
History: First flight (DST) 17 December 1935; first service delivery (C-47) October 1938.
Users: Argentina, Australia, Bolivia, Brazil, Bulgaria (Li-2), Burma, Canada Central African Rep., Chad, Chile, Colombia, Congo, Dahomey, Denmark, Dominica, Ecuador, Ethiopia, Finland, France, Gabon, Germany (E, Li-2; W, C-47), Greece, Guatemala, Haiti, Haute-Volta, Honduras, India, Indonesia, Israel, Italy, Ivory Coast, Khmer, Laos, Libya, Malagasy, Malawi, Mali, Mauretania, Mexico, Morocco, New Zealand, Nicaragua, Niger, Nigeria, Norway, Oman, Pakistan, Panama, Papua/NG, Paraguay, Peru, Philippines, Poland (Li-2), Portugal, Rhodesia, Rwanda, Salvador, Senegal, Somalia, S Africa, Soviet Union (Li-2), Spain, Sri Lanka, Sweden, Syria, Taiwan, Thailand, Togo, Turkey, Uganda, Uruguay, Venezuela, Vietnam (Li-2, C-47), Yemen Arab AF, Yugoslavia, Zaïre, Zambia.

Development: When, in 1935, Douglas designer Arthur E. Raymond planned the Douglas Sleeper Transport (DST) as an enlarged and improved

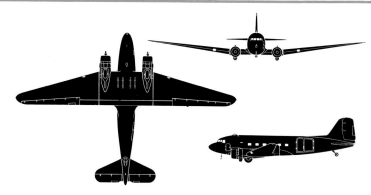

Above: Three-view of typical C-47 with wing supply racks.

DC-2, he little thought that, as well as becoming the worldwide standard airliner of its day, it would be by far the most widely used military transport in history. During World War II there were numerous versions, some civil aircraft impressed into military use, some paratroopers and tugs and the vast majority utility C-47 versions with a strong cargo floor and large double doors. Oddities included a glider and a twin-float amphibian. US military production totalled 10,048 by June 1945, followed by small batches of redesigned Super DC-3 versions including the R4D-8 and C-117. Showa and Nakajima in Japan built about 571 of the L2D family and in the Soviet Union production of the Li-2 (with door on the right) is estimated to have exceeded 2,700. Many hundreds of these aircraft, most of them C-47s, remain in daily use in almost every air force (the RAF retired its last in 1970). Many serve as platforms for research projects and counter-measures and in Vietnam the AC-47 — called "Puff the Magic Dragon" — was developed in several versions to deliver suppressive fire against ground targets. Other important variants are the EC-47 series used for multi-spectral sensing and electronic reconnaissance.

Above: This C-47 of Flyvevaabnet (Royal Danish AF) 721 Sqn is being replaced by a C-130.

In 1977 the DC-3 military versions—most of them rebuilt or otherwise updated C-47s built during World War II—were still among the most widely used military aircraft, though their numbers are gradually being thinned. There are too many different designations to list above; for example, C-47 and C-53 names were Skytrain and Skytrooper, the AC-47 name was Dragon Ship (also "Spooky") and Canadian examples are now known as CC-129.

Embraer Bandeirante and variants

EMB-110 (versions, see text) and EMB-111

Origin: EMBRAER, São José dos Campos, Brazil.
Type: Multi-role transport; (111) maritime patrol.
Engines: Two Pratt & Whitney Canada turboprops, (110) 680shp PT6A-27, (111) 750shp PT6A-34.
Dimensions: Span 50ft 3in (15·32m), (111, over tip tanks) 51ft 5¾in (15·69m); length 46ft 8¼in (14·23m), (111) 48ft 3¼in (14·71m); height 13ft 6½in (4·13m), (111) 15ft 6¼in (4·73m).
Weights: Empty, equipped 7,451lb (3380kg), (111, basic operating with crew of six) 9,259lb (4200kg); maximum loaded 12,345lb (5600kg), (111) 13,558lb (6150kg).
Performance: (Max wt) maximum speed at 15,000ft (4575m) 270mph (434km/h); cruise at 15,000ft 262mph (422km/h), (111 cruise at 9,845ft, 3000m, estimated) 288mph (464km/h); takeoff over 50ft (15m) 1,770ft

(540m), (111) 2,740ft (835m); range 1,379 miles (2220km) with max fuel, 153 miles (246km) with max payload, (111) over 2,000 miles (3220 km) with 8hr endurance.
Armament: (111 only) see text.
History: First flight 26 October 1968, (111) scheduled for July 1977; service delivery 9 February 1973.
Users: Brazil, Chile, Uruguay (and 17 non-military customers).

Development: Designed under the direction of former French constructor Max Holste, this excellent unpressurized twin-turboprop is one of the first latin-American aircraft owing nothing to any foreign design to have sustained a successful programme. By 1977 sales had reached nearly 200, the main military versions being the EMB.110 12-seat transport, (Brazilian AF C-95), 110A navaid/ILS calibration (EC-95), 110B mapping and photogrammetry (RC-95), 110K cargo and 111. The EMB-111 is a redesigned model for the Comando Costeiro (Coastal Command) with extra fuel, more power, APS-128 nose radar, LN-33 inertial system, and extensive equipment including provision for all-weather marking and surface attack with eight 5in (127mm) rockets or other weapons.

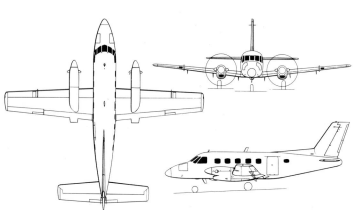

Above: Three-view of EMB-110.

Above: A FAB C-95 of the kind which formed the foundation of the production programme, which in turn has turned EMBRAER into one of the world's most capable planemakers.

GAF Mission Master

N22B and N24 (basic civil name, Nomad)

Origin: Government Aircraft Factories, Fishermen's Bend, Australia.
Type: Multi-role transport.
Engines: Two 400shp Allison 250-B17B single-shaft turboprops.
Dimensions: Span 54ft 0in (16·46m); length 41ft 2½in (12·56m) (N24, 47ft 1¼in, 14·36m); height 18ft 1½in (5·52m).
Weights: Empty 4,451lb (2019kg) (N24, 4,549lb, 2063kg); maximum loaded 8,500lb (3855kg).
Performance: (Both, max wt, sea level) normal cruise 193mph (311km/h); STOL takeoff over 50ft (15m) 1,260ft (384m); STOL landing over 50ft (15m) 635ft (194m); max range with 45min reserves 668 miles (1074km), (at 10,000ft, 3050m) 840 miles (1352km).
Armament: Four wing hardpoints each rated at 500lb (227kg) for gun pods, bombs, rockets or other stores.
History: First flight (Nomad) 23 July 1971; Mission Master service delivery April 1975.
Users: Australia, Indonesia, Philippines.

Development: One of the world's newest utility aircraft, the GAF Nomad was designed to appeal equally to civil and military customers, with emphasis on the ability to operate reliably in austere environments away

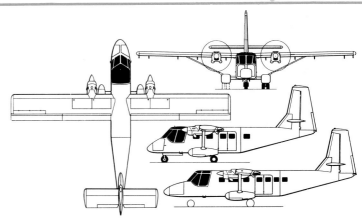

Above: Three-view of N22B, with side view (bottom) of N24.

from proper airfields. The Nomad is built in two forms, the main production model being the N22B called Mission Master in military guise. Unpressurized, it seats up to 12 plus two pilots, and can carry seat armour, self-sealing tanks and various night-vision and other sensors. The stretched N24 seats 15 passengers but had not achieved military sales by mid-1977.

Mitsubishi MU-2

MU-2 sub-types, see text.

Origin: Mitsubishi Heavy Industries, Nagoya, Japan.
Type: Multi-role transport.
Engines: Two Garrett-AiResearch TPE331 single-shaft turboprops, (A to E) 605shp TPE331-25, (F, G) 665shp TPE331-1, (J, K, M) 724shp TPE331-251, (L) -251 engines re-rated at 776shp.
Dimensions: Span (over tip tanks) 39ft 2in (11·94m); length (A to E) 33ft 3in (10·13m), (with nose radar) about 36ft, (J, L) 39ft 5in (12·01m); height 12ft 11in (3·94m), (J, L) 13ft 8in (4·17m).
Weights: Empty (early models) 5,700lb (2586kg), (K) 5,920lb (2685kg), (J) 6,800lb (3084kg); maximum loaded (early) 9,350lb (4240kg), (K) 9,920lb (4500kg), (J) 10,800lb (4900kg).
Performance: Max cruising speed (typical, 15,000ft, 4575m) 363mph (584km/h); service ceiling (typical) 33,200ft (10,120m); takeoff or landing over 50ft (15m) (typical) 1,700ft (518m); max range at 25,000ft (7620m) with max fuel and 30min reserve (typical) 1,680 miles (2705km).
History: First flight 14 September 1963; service delivery (C) 30 June 1967.
User: Japan.

Development: This compact high-wing machine is technically clever, with full pressurization, anti-icing, chem-milled skins, spoilers and double-slotted Fowler flaps. Though small, and not suited to bulky loads, it has exceptional performance. By 1977 about 500 had been sold, mostly to civil customers outside Japan. Main military variants are the MU-2C with

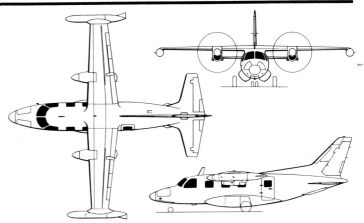

Above: Three-view of MU-2L, cleared to 11,575lb (5250kg).

cameras, guns, rockets and bombs, designated LR-1 by the JGSDF; the radar-equipped E used by the JASDF for search and rescue, and the derived K still in production; the J used by the JASDF for flight calibration; and the similar L cleared for use at 11,575lb (5250kg) but not yet in military operation.

Below: The radar-equipped MU-2K, used by the JASDF as a tactical rescue and liaison aircraft.

Pilatus/Fairchild Porter and Peacemaker

PC-6/A and B Turbo-Porter and Fairchild AU-23 Peacemaker

Origin: Pilatus Flugzeugwerke, Stans, Switzerland; (Peacemaker) Fairchild Industries, Germantown, USA

Type: Multi-role utility.

Engine: (PC-6/A, A1, A2) one Turboméca Astazou turboprop rated from 523 to 573shp; (B, B1, B2) Pratt & Whitney Canada PT6A turboprop rated at 550shp; (C, C1 and AU-23 Peacemaker) AiResearch TPE331-25D or 101F rated at 575 or 650shp.

Dimensions: Span 49ft 8in (15·14m); length (AU) 36ft 10in (11·23m) (others up to 1ft shorter); height 12ft 3in (3·73m).

Weights: Empty (typical) 2,612lb (1185kg); maximum loaded 6,100lb (2767kg).

Performance: (Typical, max weight) cruising speed 163mph (262km/h); slow-flight 65mph (105km/h); service ceiling 22,800ft (6950m); ground run (T-O/landing) 500ft (150m); max range on internal fuel 558 miles (898km).

Armament: (AU-23) side-firing XM-197 20mm cannon or 7·62mm Miniguns with various sensors; external load up to 2,000lb (907kg) on belly and four wing pylons.

History: First flight (turboprop) 2 May 1961; (PC-6/B) 1 May 1964; (Fairchild) October 1965.

Users: (Military) Australia, Austria, Bolivia, Chad, Colombia, Ecuador, Israel, Peru, Sudan, Thailand, US Air Force.

Development: In 1959 the Swiss Pilatus company flew a large STOL transport, the Porter, with Lycoming piston engine and an appearance reminiscent of 30 years earlier. In fact it had outstanding capability, and with turboprop engines the Turbo-Porter is doing a great job in some of the most inaccessible and challenging places. Most are ten-seat utility transports, often carrying much special role equipment, but the AU-23 armed reconnaissance (Credible Chase) version is a more sophisticated Co-In machine with extensive sensors, psychological-warfare broadcast and leaflet installations and comprehensive nav/com equipment.

Above: Fourth of 12 PC-6/B2 Turbo-Porters delivered in 1976 from Stans to the OL (Austrian Air Force).

Above: Three-view of Fairchild AU-23A Peacemaker.

Below: Powered by a different engine from the Swiss-built aircraft, a Peacemaker makes one of its amazing STOL takeoffs.

Rockwell International
OV-10 Bronco

OV-10A to -10E

Origin: Rockwell International Corp, USA.
Type: (Except B) two-seat multi-role counter-insurgency; (B) target tug.
Engines: (Except B(Z)) two 715ehp AiResearch T76-410/411 single-shaft centrifugal turboprops; (B(Z)) as other versions plus General Electric J85-4 turbojet of 2,950lb (1338kg) thrust above fuselage.
Dimensions: Span 40ft (12·19m); length (except D) 41ft 7in (12·67m); (D) 44ft (13·4m); height 15ft 2in (4·62m).
Weights: Empty (A) 6,969lb (3161kg); maximum loaded (A) 14,466lb (6563kg).
Performance: Maximum speed (A, sea level, clean) 281mph (452km/h); initial climb 2,300ft (700m)/min; (B(Z)) 6,800ft/min; service ceiling 30,000ft (9150m); range with maximum weapon load, about 600 miles (960km); ferry range at 12,000lb gross, 1,428 miles (2300km).
Armament: Four 7·62mm M60C machine guns in sponsons; 1,200lb (544kg) hardpoint on centreline and four 600lb (272kg) points under sponsons; one Sidewinder missile rail under each wing; (OV-10D) as other versions plus three-barrel 20mm cannon in remotely aimed ventral power turret.
History: First flight 16 July 1965; (production OV-10A) 6 August 1967; (YOV-10D) 9 June 1970.
Users: W Germany, Indonesia, S Korea, Thailand, USA (Air Force, Marine Corps), Venezuela.

Development: Recognising that no US aircraft was tailored to the urgent task of fighting Co-In (counter-insurgency) operations, or "brush-fire wars", the US Department of Defense in 1960 began study of the problem and in 1962 issued a joint USAF/Navy/Marine Corps specification for a Light Armed Reconnaissance Aircraft (LARA). The winner, in 1964, was the Bronco. Designed to operate from short rough strips (or on floats or skis) it can carry a wide range of tactical equipment and weapons, including doppler radar, TV reconnaissance, five paratroops or two casualties. The OV-10A was ordered in October 1966 and by 1969 the Marine Corps had 114, while the USAF were using 157 for Forward Air Control (FAC) duties in Vietnam. In 1969 Pave Nail Conversion of 15 aircraft fitted them with laser rangers, stabilized night sighting system, Loran and other devices for night FAC, attack or target illumination for other aircraft. The B and jet-boosted B(Z) are used by the Luftwaffe. The OV-10D has Night Observation Gunship (NOGS) equipment, with long-nosed IR sensor, cannon turret and, as a conversion, 1,000ehp T76 engines.

Above: Most sophisticated Bronco is the NOGS (Night Observation/Gunship System), the Marine Corps YOV-10D.

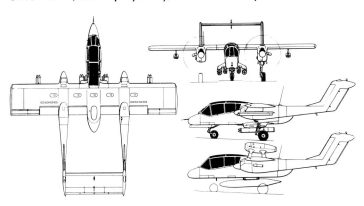

Above: Three-view of OV-10A with side view (bottom) of OV-10B(Z).

Above: Rockets ripple away from launchers on the body pylons of an OV-10D Bronco of the US Air Force.

Below: Fastest of the Bronco family, the jet-boosted OV-10B(Z) is used by West Germany as a target tug.

Short Skyvan 3M

Skyvan Series 3M

Origin: Short Brothers & Harland (Shorts), Belfast, UK.
Type: Multi-role transport.
Engines: Two 715shp Garrett-AiResearch TPE331-201 single-shaft turboprops.
Dimensions: Span 64ft 11in (19·79m); length (with radome) 41ft 4in (12·60m); height 15ft 1in (4·60m).
Weights: Empty 7,400lb (3356kg); max payload (overload) 6,000lb (2721kg); overload weight 14,500lb (6577kg) (normal weight with 5,200lb load, 13,700lb, 6214kg).
Performance: (Max wt) max cruise at 10,000ft (3050m) 203mph (327km/h); economical cruise 173mph (278km/h); service ceiling 22,000ft (6705m); typical STOL takeoff or landing over 50ft (15m) 1,395ft (425m); range with 45 min reserve 240–670 miles (386–1075km) depending on payload.
History: First flight (SC.7) 17 January 1963, (3M) early 1970.
Users: (Military) Argentina, Austria, Ecuador, Ghana, Indonesia, Mauretania, Mexico. Nepal, Oman, Singapore, Thailand, S Yemen.

Above: A Skyvan 3M of the Sultan of Oman's Air Force No 2 Sqn, based at Seeb. This unit has 15 such aircraft, which do not have radar (in such a climate it is hardly needed).

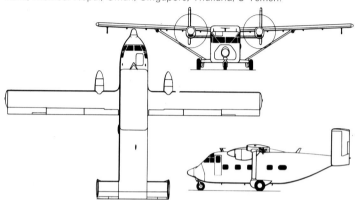

Above: Three-view of Short Skyvan 3M with radar.

Development: First flown as a piston-engined civil aircraft, the Skyvan has been developed in several versions of which one of the most successful is the military Srs 3M. This is a robust all-metal, unpressurized airlifter with outstanding STOL performance, even in hot/high conditions. It has a full-section rear door openable in flight for heavy dropping; loads can include 22 troops or 12 stretcher cases and two medical attendants, and options are available for various armaments, multi-sensor reconnaissance, search/rescue and other duties.

SIAI/Marchetti SM.1019

SM.1019EI

Origin: SIAI-Marchetti SpA, Sesto Calende, Italy.
Type: Two-seat STOL utility (see text).
Engine: One 400shp Allison 250-B17 turboprop.
Dimensions: Span 36ft 0in (10·972m); length overall 27ft 11½in (8·52m); height overall 9ft 4½in (2·86m).
Weights: Empty 1,521lb (690kg); maximum loaded 3,196lb (1450kg).
Performance: Maximum cruise 186mph (300km/h); takeoff or landing over 50ft (15m) 722ft (220m); tactical radius in attack mission 69 miles (111km); maximum range in reconnaissance mission, cruise at 9,845ft (3000m) 832 miles (1340km).
Armament: One hardpoint under each wing for light attack loads such as Minigun pod, rocket pod or reconnaissance pod.
History: First flight 24 May 1969; service delivery 1975.
User: Italy (army).

Development: One of the latest light tactical aircraft, the SM.1019E differs from most in having a gas-turbine engine, giving improved performance and better military fuel compatibility. Seating two in tandem cockpits with full dual control, the 1019EI, as delivered in a series of 100 to the Italian

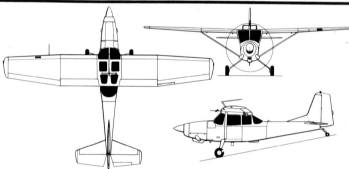

Above: Three-view of SIAI-Marchetti SM.1019E.

Aviazione Leggera dell'Esercito, has electronic, photo and navigation equipment for day or night reconnaissance and also flies FAC, helicopter escort, cargo or training missions. The avionics are comprehensive and include ADF, IFF, Omega VLF, Tacan and ILS, as well as several communications radios.

Below: New SIAI-Marchetti SM.1019EI turboprop STOL tactical aircraft awaiting collection by the Italian Army (ALE).

Glossary of Terms

The following are some of the terms used in this book which are not part of common language.

AAM Air/air missile, fired from one aircraft against another.
AB Airbase, airfield forming permanent home of military unit(s).
Active Describes device emitting radiation, sound waves or other phenomena.
ADC US Air Force Aerospace Defense Command.
ADD Soviet Union Aviatsiya Dal'Nevo Deistviya, long-range bombers.
Aéronavale French naval aviation.
AFB US Air Force base.
Afterburner Device added to rear of jet engine (turbofan or turbo-jet) in which extra fuel is burned to give extra thrust; in UK often called reheat jetpipe.
AGM Air/ground missile (US designation system).
AIL US electronics, piloted aircraft, countermeasures.
AIM Air intercept missile (ie, AAM, US designation system).
ALQ US electronics, piloted aircraft, countermeasures, special or combination of purposes.
ALR US electronics, piloted aircraft, countermeasures, passive detecting.
AMI Aeronautica Militare Italiano (Italian air force).
AMST Advanced Medium STOL Transport.
ANG US Air National Guard.
APG US electronics, piloted aircraft, radar, fire control.
APQ US electronics, piloted aircraft, radar, combination of purposes.
APS US electronics, piloted aircraft, radar, search/range/bearing.
APY Special designation for AWACS radar.
Armée de l'Air French air force.
ASM Air/surface missile.
ASW Anti-submarine warfare.
ATO Assisted takeoff.
Attack Combat mission flown against tactical surface targets on land or sea.
Avionics Aviation electronics, ie electronic systems carried in aircraft.
AV-MF Soviet Union Aviatsiya Voenno-morskovo Flota, naval air force.
AWACS Airborne Warning And Control System.
AWG US electronics, piloted aircraft, armament, fire control.
BLC Boundary-layer control, method of increasing lift, reducing drag or improving control by blowing air under pressure from thin slits in aircraft skin.
Bomber Term virtually defunct; originally meant large aircraft that dropped bombs, but today this is done by virtually all combat aircraft, while role of modern bomber is to carry stand-off missiles within range of enemy strategic targets.
CAF Canadian Armed Forces.
CAP Combat Air Patrol (in defence of fleet at sea).
CAS Close air support.
Casevac Casualty evacuation (assumed from land battle).
CFS Central Flying School (UK).
Close support Combat mission flown against surface targets hindering friendly ground forces.
Code name NATO compiles a list of invented names, easily remembered and unambiguously transmitted quickly by radio, for Soviet and Chinese aircraft, missiles and radars. This is because the true designations are either not known or complex. Also called "reporting name".
Coin Counter-insurgent, designed for use against unsophisticated enemy in "limited" or "brushfire" conflict.
Countermeasures Equipment and operations intended to nullify or confuse hostile sensors, such as chaff, jammers, decoys; could even include a smokescreen.
Chaff Small metal slivers, such as strips cut from roll of aluminium foil, scattered by million by aircraft in hostile airspace to blanket enemy radars.
Cruise missile Missile that flies to its target like aircraft, with sustained propulsion and lifted by wing.
CW Continuous-wave e.m. radiation (as distinct from pulse).
Decoy Small aircraft or other object arranged to look like attack or bomber aircraft on hostile radars or other sensors, to confuse or dilute enemy defences.
Delta wing Shaped like triangle in plan, with sharply swept leading edge and almost straight trailing edge.
Development aircraft Aircraft built for flight testing to eliminate faults or deficiencies; may later be brought up to production standard.
Drogue Device trailed on cable, hose or other filament from aircraft (especially on FR hose, to keep latter steady, pull it out from hose-reel and provide receptacle for receiver's probe).
ECM Electronic countermeasures, equipment or techniques intended to nullify or confuse enemy electronic sensors such as radars.
EdA Ejercito del Aire, Spanish air force.
Elint Electronic intelligence, mission flown to find out maximum about enemy (or potential enemy) e.m. emissions such as radars, communications, IR, lasers and ECM.
E.m. radiation Electromagnetic radiation, which includes visible light, radio waves (including radar microwaves) and IR (heat).
ESM Electronic support measures (sometimes, electronic surveillance measures), including ECM, Elint and related activities.
EVS Electro-optical viewing system.
EW Electronic warfare, all use of e.m. radiation in war.
FA Soviet Union Frontovaya Aviatsiya, frontal aviation, ie tactical air force.
FAC Forward Air Controller, experienced airborne manager of tactical air strike on surface target.
FFAR Folding-fin (or free-flight) aircraft (or air-to-air) rocket.
Fighter Combat aircraft intended primarily for destruction of enemy aircraft in the air.
FIS Fighter Interceptor Squadron (USAF).
FIW Fighter Interceptor Wing (USAF).
FLIR Forward-looking infra-red.
Flying Boom Boeing-patented method of FR using rigid telescopic boom (pipe) steered into receiver's receptacle by operator in tanker.
FR Flight refuelling.
FTS Flying training school.
g Acceleration due to Earth gravity; on Earth's surface bodies experience 1g and appear to weigh their normal amount, but in free fall they experience 0g while in air combat they may be accelerated in tight turns and dive pull-outs to 6g or more, modern fighters being designed to withstand up to 12g.
GAU Gun, aircraft unit (US designation system).
Hardpoint Part of aircraft strengthened to carry pylon.
Head-up-display Optical device which projects information and/or pictures on pilot's windscreen, focussed at infinity so that he can simultaneously search sky/ground ahead.
Homing Able to steer automatically towards target or other objective.
HUD Head-up display.
IA-PVO Soviet Union Istrebitel'naya Aviatsiya Protivo-vozdushnaya Oborona, interceptor force of air defence force.
Inertial Deriving information from gyros and accelerometers of extreme accuracy, able to calculate exact position of aircraft or other vehicle without external information.
Interceptor Fighter designed for finding and destroying hostile aircraft even in bad weather or at night.
IR Infra-red (ie, heat).
Jammer EW device emitting such powerful e.m. radiation as to blot out hostile reception on same wavelength(s).
JASDF Japan Air Self-Defence Force.
Jato, JATO Jet-assisted takeoff (a misnomer, because it invariably means rocket-assisted).
JMSDF Japan Maritime Self-Defence Force (includes naval air arm).
LABS Low-altitude bombing system, method of delivering nuclear bombs at low level by "tossing" them much higher than the aircraft to increase time available for latter to get clear.
Laser Device for emitting beam of coherent (waves in phase) light, which can be made intense, focussed precisely and used with receiver at same wavelength.
LLTV, LLLTV Low-light TV, low-light-level TV, TV able to be used in poor visibility (but not on pitch-black night).
Loiter To cruise at economical low airspeed.
LRMTS Laser ranger and marked-target seeker.
MAC US Air Force Military Airlift Command.
Mach Scale used for speed of fast aircraft; Mach 1·0 is speed of sound, about 760mph (1223km/h) at sea level (more on hot day, less in winter) and 660mph (1062km/h) at high altitude, thus Mach 1·6 is 60 per cent faster and Mach 2·0 twice as fast.
MAD Magnetic-anomaly detector, sensitive device able to detect local irregularity in Earth's magnetic field due to presence of submerged submarine.
Marked target Target illuminated by e.m. radiation (usually laser) so that attacking aircraft can spot it and missile home on to it.
Multi-sensor Equipped with radar, optical cameras and IR to give fullest picture of hostile target, eg to defeat camouflage.
NAS Naval Air Station.
NATO North Atlantic Treaty Organization.
Passive Receiving but not emitting (human ear is example, but in aircraft usually concerned with e.m. radiation).
PD Pulse-doppler, kind of radar.
Pod Streamlined container carrying equipment outside aircraft.
Pre-production aircraft Batch of aircraft built in production tooling but still subject to progressive modifications as result of flight testing and engineering development.
Pressurized Aircraft interior inflated to pressure which, though lower than at sea level, is higher than surrounding air at high altitude, for comfort of crew.
PRF Pulse-recurrence frequency (radar).
Probe Long boom (rod) projecting ahead of aircraft, especially pipe for taking fuel from FR drogue
Profile Combat mission drawn with distance horizontally and height vertically; attack mission may be hi-lo-hi, as much as possible being flown at high altitude to save fuel but attack being at treetop height to escape radar detection.
Prototype First aircraft built of new type; strictly does not apply to "one-off" experimental aircraft but only to type intended later to be mass-produced, after development is completed.
Pulse radiation E.m. emission in form of succession of bursts, as distinct from CW.
PVO See IA-PVO.
Pylon Attachment for external store, usually embodying means for release and positive ejection to throw clear of aircraft.
Radar System using e.m. radiation to detect, locate and track targets.
RAF Royal Air Force (UK air force).
RB Robot, Swedish designation for guided missiles.
Receiver In FR, the aircraft accepting fuel.
Reporting name See code name.
Retarded bomb Bomb fitted with airbrakes and/or parachute to allow low-flying attack aircraft to get clear of burst.
RNAS Royal Naval Air Station.
RPV Remotely piloted vehicle, aircraft (usually small) flown by human pilot not carried on board.
SAC US Air Force Strategic Air Command.
SAM Surface/air missile, fired from ground or ship to destroy aircraft
Semi-active Guidance system using passive e.m. receiver to home on to target illuminated by external radiation source.
Sensor Device for detecting, and often recording, e.m. and other radiation (optical, radar, IR, magnetic, sound).
Signature Precise characteristics of e.m. or other signal, such as radar echo from particular type of aircraft, which when analysed acts as kind of fingerprint.
Slab tailplane Made in one piece, without separate elevators (US = stabilizer).
SLAR Side-looking aircraft (or airborne) radar.
Sonobuoy Acoustic device for detecting submerged submarines by sound; active sonobuoy sends out intense pulses of sound and listens for reflection; passive sonobuoy listens for sound generated by submarine itself.
Sqn Squadron.
SRS Strategic Reconnaissance Squadron.
SRW Strategic Reconnaissance Wing.
Stand-off missile ASM designed to hit target when launched from bomber outside range of enemy defences.
STOL Short takeoff and landing, fixed-wing aircraft able to use small rough fields or clearings.
Store Any object carried on external pylon.
Strategic Concerned with attacks on enemy heartlands (cities, industries &c) as distinct from targets associated with surface battles.
Subsonic Below the local speed of sound.
Supersonic Above the local speed of sound.
Sweep Angle at which wings are raked back (often measured at ¼-chord, ie one-quarter of way back from leading edge).
TAC US Air Force Tactical Air Command.
Tactical Concerned with local surface warfare on land or sea.
Terrain-following radar Equipment able to guide attack aircraft safely at lowest possible height across enemy territory, missing hills or telephone poles even at night or in fog.
TFS Tactical Fighter Squadron.
TFW Tactical Fighter Wing.
Turbofan Gas-turbine jet engine with large fan (similar to multi-blade ducted propeller) generating half or more of total thrust, rest coming from hot core jet that drives fan.
Turbojet Gas-turbine jet engine of simplest kind, generating single jet of hot gas.
Turboshaft Gas-turbine engine delivering all power through shaft, for driving helicopter or other shaft-drive vehicle.
TV Television, which in combat aircraft is usually not just passive as in household receiver but active system taking own pictures.
UHF Ultra-high frequency e.m. radiation.
USAF United States Air Force.
USMC United States Marine Corps.
USN United States Navy.
VAQ US Navy tactical EW (jammer) squadron.
Variable-geometry Aircraft able to change shape, especially by varying sweep angle of wings.
VAW US Navy tactical electronic surveillance squadron.
VF US Navy fighter squadron.
VHF Very high frequency e.m. radiation (lower frequencies than UHF).
VMA US Marine Corps tactical attack squadron.
VMF US Marine Corps fighter squadron.
VTOL Vertical takeoff and landing.
V-TA Soviet Union Voenno-transportnaya Aviatsiya, transport aviation.
VVS Soviet Union Voenno-vozdushniye Sily, combined air forces.
Wire guidance Guidance by electrical signals transmitted from operator through fine wires unreeled from missile in flight.

Aircraft Designations

The following are some of the designations used for modern military aircraft:

A (US, France, Sweden) attack
AC (US) attack aircraft based on transport
AEW (UK) airborne early-warning
AH (US) attack helicopter
AH (UK) Army helicopter
AJ (Sweden) attack, secondary role fighter
AT (US) attack aircraft based on trainer
AV (US) attack, V/STOL
B (US, UK, Soviet Union) bomber
C (US, Japan) transport
C (Spain) fighter
CC (UK) communications and VIP transport
CC (Canada) transport
CF (Canada) fighter
CH (US) transport helicopter
CH (Canada) helicopter
CP (Canada) patrol
CT (Canada) trainer
D (Soviet Union) long-range
DC (US) director aircraft (of drones or RPVs) based on transport
DF (US) director aircraft based on fighter
E (US) electronic missions
E (France, Spain) trainer
EA (US) electronic aircraft based on attack aircraft
EB (US) electronic aircraft based on bomber
EC (US) electronic aircraft based on transport
EF (US) electronic aircraft based on fighter
EKA (US) electronic and tanker aircraft based on attack aircraft
EP (US) electronic aircraft based on patrol aircraft
F (US, UK) fighter
F (Soviet Union) boosted, augmented thrust
FB (US) literally "fighter bomber", actually applied to a strategic bomber based on a tactical bomber
FG (UK) fighter, ground attack
FGA (UK) fighter, ground attack (superseded)
FGR (UK) fighter, ground attack, reconnaissance
FRS (UK) fighter, reconnaissance, strike
FST (Mitsubishi) fighter, supersonic trainer
G (Aeritalia) designed by Giuseppe Gabrielli
GA (UK) ground attack
GR (UK) ground attack, reconnaissance
H (US) helicopter
HAR (UK) helicopter, rescue
HAS (UK) helicopter, anti-submarine
HC (UK) helicopter, transport
HC (US) rescue or recovery aircraft based on transport (fixed-wing)
HCC (UK) helicopter, communications
HF (HAL, India) Hindustan, Fighter
HH (US) rescue or recovery helicopter
HJT (Hindustan, India) Hindustan Jet Trainer
HT (UK) helicopter, trainer
HU (UK) helicopter, Commando assault
J (Sweden) fighter
JA (Sweden) fighter, secondary role attack
K (UK) tanker
KA (US) tanker based on attack aircraft
KB (US) tanker based on bomber
KC (US) tanker based on transport
L (Soviet Union) fitted with search radar
LC (US) transport with wheel/ski landing gear
LP (US) patrol aircraft with wheel/ski landing gear
LR (Japan) liaison, reconnaissance
M (Soviet Union) modified
M.B. (Aermacchi) designed by Ermanno Bazzocchi
MR (UK) maritime reconnaissance
NB (US) bomber converted for special testing
NF In F-5 programme, Netherlands (built by Netherlands/Canada)
NKC (US) transport converted for special testing
O (US) observation (ie battlefield reconnaissance, FAC)
OH (US, Japan) observation helicopter
OV (US) observation, V/STOL
P (US, Japan) patrol, meaning ocean surveillance
P (Soviet Union) interceptor
PM (Soviet Union) special aerobatic version
PQM (US) pilotless RPV developed from fighter
PS (Japan) patrol, anti-submarine
QB (US) remotely piloted bomber (possibly with safety pilot)
QF (US) remotely piloted fighter (possibly with safety pilot)
R (US, UK, Soviet Union) reconnaissance
RA (US) reconnaissance aircraft based on attack aircraft
RB (US) reconnaissance aircraft based on bomber
RC (US) reconnaissance or special-mission aircraft based on transport
RF (US) reconnaissance aircraft based on fighter
RTF (US) reconnaissance aircraft based on dual fighter trainer
RP (US) mapping/survey aircraft based on patrol aircraft
RU (US) special-mission aircraft based on utility aircraft
S (UK) strike
S (US) anti-submarine
SF (Sweden) unarmed reconnaissance
SF In F-5 programme, Spain
S.F. (Savoia-Marchetti) designed by Stelio Frati
SH (US) anti-submarine helicopter
SH (Sweden) armed ocean surveillance
Sk (Sweden) trainer
SP (US) anti-submarine aircraft based on patrol aircraft
SPS (Soviet Union) fitted with blown flaps
SR (US) strategic reconnaissance
T (US, UK) trainer
T (Soviet Union) torpedo-equipped
T (Spain) transport
TA (US) trainer based on attack aircraft
TE (US) trainer version of electronic aircraft
TF (US, Sweden) trainer version of fighter
TH (US) trainer helicopter
U (US) utility
U (Soviet Union, strictly the sound "oo" represented by a character resembling a capital Y) trainer
UH (US) utility helicopter
US (US) utility (ie transport) aircraft based on anti-submarine aircraft
UTI (Soviet Union) fighter trainer
VC (US) executive VIP transport
VH (US) executive VIP helicopter
WB (US) weather aircraft based on bomber
WC (US) weather aircraft based on transport
WP (US) weather aircraft based on patrol aircraft
WU (US) weather aircraft based on utility (hardly utility, the U-2)
X (US) experimental research aircraft
XFV (US) experimental fighter V/STOL
YAH (US) service-test attack helicopter
YC (US) service-test transport
YF (US) service-test fighter
YO (US) service-test observation aircraft
YUH (US) service-test utility helicopter

Picture credits

Photographic research: J. C. Scutts

The publishers wish to thank the following organisations and individuals who have supplied photographs for this book. Photographs have been credited by page number. Some references have, for reasons of space, been abbreviated as follows:

Ministry of Defence, London: MOD
Royal Canadian Air Force: RCAF
United States Marine Corps: USMC
British Aerospace Corporation: BAC
All photographs credited USAF are "official United States Air Force photography".

Jacket front: General Dynamics. **End papers:** MOD. **Half-title** (page 1): Saab-Scania. **Full-title** (pages 2-3): Lockheed. **Credits** (pages 4-5): Mitsubishi. **Page 6-7:** Saab-Scania. **8:** MOD. **9-13:** Dassault-Breguet. **14-16:** General Dynamics. **17:** USAF. **18:** top, via H. R. Muir; bottom, Jay Miller, via Roger Wright collection. **18-21:** Grumman. **22:** top, Brian M. Service, via *Flight International* library; bottom, William Green collection. **23:** William Green collection. **24:** Israeli Aircraft Industries. **25:** RCAF. **26-27:** USAF. **28:** Top, Roger Wright; bottom, Picciani Aircraft Slides, 434 Arbutus Avenue, Horsham, P.A., 19044, USA. **29-30:** McDonnell Douglas. **31:** left, Popperfoto; right, McDonnell Douglas. **32:** McDonnell Douglas. **33:** left, Novosti; right, Bill Gunston collection. **34-35:** Pakistan AF. **36-37:** *Flight International* library. **39:** William Green collection. **40:** top, E. and TV Films; bottom, William Green collection. **41:** *Flight International* library. **42:** Japanese ASDF. **43:** USAF. **44:** US Navy. **45:** USAF. **46:** Saab-Scania. **47:** top, E. and TV Films; bottom, William Green collection. **48:** top and centre, Novosti; bottom, Tass. **49:** E. and TV Films. **50:** LVT Aerospace. **51:** William Green collection. **52-53:** McDonnell Douglas. **54:** *Flight International* library. **55:** BAC. **56:** MOD. **57:** Martin/General Dynamics. **58:** Cessna. **60:** Champlong-Arepi Agency. **61:** Dassault-Breguet. **62:** USAF. **63:** top, William Green collection; bottom, J. W. R. Taylor collection. **64:** USAF. **65:** left, USAF; right, Fairchild. **66:** Fairchild. **67:** General Dynamics. **68:** top, Grumman, via Bill Gunston collection; centre and bottom, General Dynamics. **70-71:** US Navy. **72:** top, H. Levy, via *Flight International* library; others, US Navy. **73:** top and centre, MOD; bottom, Hawker Siddeley Aviation. **75:** MOD. **76:** Hawker Siddeley Aviation. **77:** USMC. **78:** MOD. **79:** centre, left and right, Hawker Siddeley Aviation; bottom, William Green collection. **80-81:** top, Lockheed; bottom left, *Flight International* library; bottom right, MOD. **82:** J. W. R. Taylor collection. **83:** Bill Gunston collection. **84-85:** McDonnell Douglas. **86:** Tass; bottom, *Flight International* library. **87:** Mitsubishi. **88-89:** Roger Wright. **90:** top, USAF; bottom, Turkish AF. **91:** Panavia. **92-93:** BAC. **94:** top, via H.R. Muir; bottom, Photri. **95:** Rockwell. **97-98:** Saab-Scania. **99-101:** BAC. **102:** E. and TV Films. **104:** top, *Flugrevue & flugwelt*; bottom, left, Interinfo; bottom right, E. and TV Films. **104:** Interinfo. **105:** USAF. **106:** LVT Aerospace. **107:** MOD. **108-109:** Boeing. **110:** top,

Boeing; centre, USAF; bottom, Bill Gunston collection. **111:** top, USAF; bottom, Photri. **112:** Dassault-Breguet. **113:** Hawker Siddeley Aviation. **114:** J.W.R. Taylor collection. **115-117:** Rockwell. **118-119:** Lockheed. **120:** top, Grumman; bottom, William Green collection. **121:** top, USAF; centre and bottom, via H.R. Muir. **122:** top, D. Jenkins, via H.R. Muir; bottom, USAF. **123:** top, MOD; bottom, E. and TV Films. **124:** US Navy. **125:** Saab-Scania. **126:** MOD. **127:** top, E. and TV Films; bottom, MOD. **128:** E. and TV Films. **129:** top, William Green collection; bottom, E. and TV Films. **130-131:** Lockheed. **132:** top, J.W.R. Taylor collection; bottom, Tass. **133:** top, McDonnell Douglas; bottom, US Navy. **134:** Champlong-Arepi Agency. **135:** Breguet. **136:** RCAF. **137:** Canadian Armed Forces. **138:** Hawker Siddeley Aviation. **139-141:** MOD. **143-144:** Roger Wright. **145-148:** Lockheed. **149:** top, Mitsuo Shibata; bottom, Roger Wright. **150:** MOD. **152:** Aeritalia. **153:** E. and TV Films. **154:** J.W.R. Taylor collection. **155:** William Green collection. **156:** top and below, Boeing; centre, RCAF; bottom, USAF. **157:** top, Boeing; bottom, Roger Wright. **158:** Roger Wright. **159:** Boeing. **160:** left, CASA; right above and below, de Havilland Aircraft Co. **161-162:** de Havilland Aircraft Co. **163-164:** USAF. **165:** Fokker VFW. **166:** MOD. **167:** Hawker Siddeley Aviation. **168:** Israel Aircraft Industries. **169:** top, US Navy; bottom, Novosti. **171:** via H. R. Muir. **172:** top, USAF; bottom, MOD. **173:** top, USAF; bottom, Rolls-Royce. **174:** top, USAF; bottom, Roger Wright. **175:** top, Kawasaki; bottom, Roger Wright. **176-178:** McDonnell Douglas. **179:** top, Rolls-Royce; bottom, Transall. **180-181:** Grumman. **182-185:** Boeing. **187:** Grumman. **188:** top, Brian Mackenzie Service, via *Aeroplane Monthly*; bottom, Grumman. **189:** Aviation Photo News. **190:** top, USAF; bottom, Roger Wright. **191:** E. and TV Films. **192-193:** MOD. **194:** top, Aerospatiale; bottom, Rolls-Royce. **195:** Aerospatiale. **196-197:** Rolls-Royce. **198:** Agusta. **199:** Bell. **200:** left, Agusta; right Swedish Army. **201:** top, US Army; bottom left, Sistel; right centre, US Navy; bottom, US Army. **202:** top, Canadian Armed Forces; bottom, Bell. **203:** left top and bottom, Boeing Vertol; top right, Kawasaki; bottom right, Rolls-Royce. **204:** Boeing Vertol. **205-207:** Hughes. **208:** top, William Green collection; bottom, MOD. **209:** MBB. **211:** Finland Defence Department. **213:** Sikorsky. **214:** top, USAF; centre, Sistel; bottom, US Navy. **215:** US Army. **215:** top, David Windsor; bottom, USMC. **215:** Sikorsky. **218-219:** MOD. **220:** Westland. **222:** left and top, Westland; bottom right, Bill Gunston collection. **223:** MOD. **224-225:** Japanese ASDF. **226:** top, Rolls-Royce; bottom, Brazilian AF. **227:** top, Dassault-Breguet; bottom, Dornier. **229:** top, NZ Aerospace Industries; bottom, Boeing. **230:** Beech. **231:** RCAF. **232:** top, Cessna; bottom, Roger Wright. **233:** top, Hawker Siddeley Aviation; bottom, Hindustan Aerospace. **234:** top, Hawker Siddeley Aviation; bottom, Industrial Photo Laboratories. **235:** China News Agency. **236:** top, Roger Wright; bottom, Finland Defence Department. **237:** top, USAF; bottom, via H.R. Muir. **238:** top, Fouga et cie; bottom, USAF. **239:** Rockwell. **240:** Saab-Scania. **241:** top, Saab-Scania; bottom, MOD. **242:** top, *Flight International* library; bottom, "Soko" Metalopreradivacha Industrija. **243:** top, *Flight International* library; bottom, Camera Press. **245:** Aeritalia. **245:** Britten-Norman. **246:** top, USAF; bottom, Cessna. **247:** top, de Havilland Aircraft Co; bottom, Dornier. **248:** Brazilian AF. **249:** Mitsubishi. **250:** top, Pilatus; bottom, Fairchild. **251:** top, Rockwell; bottom and centre, USAF. **252:** top, Short Bros and Harland; bottom, SIAI-Marchetti.